Perspectives on People at Work

We work with leading authors to develop the strongest educational materials bringing cutting-edge thinking and best learning practice to a global market.

Under a range of well-known imprints, including Financial Times/Prentice Hall, Addison Wesley and Longman, we craft high quality print and electronic publications which help readers to understand and apply their content, whether studying or at work.

Pearson Custom Publishing enables our customers to access a wide and expanding range of market-leading content from world-renowned authors and develop their own tailor-made book. You choose the content that meets your needs and Pearson Custom Publishing produces a high-quality printed book.

To find out more about custom publishing, visit www.pearsoncustom.co.uk

A Pearson Custom Publication

Perspectives on People at Work

Compiled from:

*Organising and Managing Work:
Organisational, Managerial and Strategic Behaviour
in Theory and Practice*
by Tony J. Watson

*Management and Organisational Behaviour
7th Edition*
by Laurie J. Mullins

Human Resource Management 6th Edition
by Derek Torrrington, Laura Hall and Stephen Taylor

*Contemporary Human Resource Management:
Text and Cases*
Edited by Tom Redman and Adrian Wilkinson

PEARSON
Custom
Publishing

Pearson Education Limited
Edinburgh Gate
Harlow
Essex CM20 2JE

And associated companies throughout the world

Visit us on the World Wide Web at:
www.pearsoned.co.uk

First published 2006
This Custom Book Edition © 2006 Published by Pearson Education Limited

Taken from:

Organising and Managing Work: Organisational, Managerial and Strategic Behaviour in Theory and Practice
by Tony J. Watson
ISBN 0 273 63005 9
Copyright © Pearson Education Limited 2002

Management and Organisational Behaviour 7th Edition
by Laurie J. Mullins
ISBN 0 273 68876 6
Copyright © Laurie J. Mullins 1985, 1989, 1993, 1996, 1999, 2002, 2005
Chapter 9 Copyright © Linda Hicks 1999, 2002, 2005

Human Resource Management 6th Edition
by Derek Torrington, Laura Hall and Stephen Taylor
ISBN 0 273 68713 1
Copyright © Prentice Hall Europe 1987, 1991, 1995, 1998
Copyright © Pearson Education Limited 2002, 2005

Contemporary Human Resource Management: Text and Cases
Edited by Tom Redman and Adrian Wilkinson
ISBN 0 201 59613X
Copyright © Tom Redman, Adrian Wilkinson and Pearson Education Limited 2001

ISBN-13   978 1 84479 593 2
ISBN-10   1 84479 593 4

Printed in Great Britain by Antony Rowe

Contents

KEY TO SYMBOLS

This symbol indicates a topic summary. Here you will be able to read a short description of the chapter contents.

Blackboard

When you see this symbol, go to the Blackboard site and complete the E-tivity indicated. You will achieve the greatest benefit if you attempt these after you are familiar with the topic.

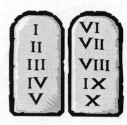

This is a module milestone – look out for these as they alert you to important events.

TOPIC 1: INTRODUCTION – THE NATURE OF WORK

Why study this topic?

This chapter will help you to gain a better understanding of how organisations function and how work is organised. Managing people effectively while trying to achieve organisational goals is a difficult process and one which will be/is central to our own working lives. This is certainly true regardless if we are the 'manager' or the 'managed'.

Take the time to read this chapter – it provides you with a comprehensive overview and will prepare you for the topics you will encounter during this module.

E-tivity 1: Introduction

CHAPTER 1

Organising and managing work: study and practice

Objectives

Having read this chapter and completed its associated activites, readers should be able to:

● Appreciate the value of a focus on the management of work as a starting point for thinking about work organisations and their management.

● Recognise the advantage of a *management of work* focus over both a 'people management' or a 'structures and procedures' way of talking and thinking about management and work organisation.

● See how the style of *Work Organisation and Management Studies* adopted in the present book builds upon and goes beyond the traditional business school subject of *Organisational Behaviour*.

● Note the contribution which various social science disciplines make to Work Organisation and Management Studies.

● Recognise a continuity between social-science thinking and a critical form of common sense.

● Understand the importance and value of developing Work Organisation and Management Studies as a critical study.

● Discriminate between perspectives, theories and research findings in terms of how useful (or 'true') they are when it comes to relating theory and practice.

Managing work

To create the goods, services and quality of life people look for in the modern world some rather complex patterns of cooperative human behaviour have to be orchestrated or 'managed'. The academic study of the organising and managing of work involves taking a step back from our day-to-day involvement in these patterns of behaviour and trying systematically to understand how they come about. Such a study also has the potential to help us achieve a better quality of productive cooperation than we typically manage in contemporary work organisations.

We study work organisation and its management because we are interested in the various individual human motivations, interests, values and meanings which play a part in bringing about the patterns of behaviour we see in workplaces ranging from shops, offices and factories to schools, hospitals and universities. But the study also has to concern itself with the ways in which these patterns of human activity and meaning themselves come to be an influence on what occurs in the world. Once human beings create groups, societies, cultures, classes, governing institutions and organisations, what they do in their lives becomes significantly shaped by them. One of the things which makes the study of the organising and managing of work so challenging is that it has to understand how individual choices and initiatives, on the one hand, and already existing and *emerging* structures and patterns on the other hand, both play their parts in social life. And these two influences – of human initiative and structural context – do not work separately. They are inextricably intertwined.

To understand these complexities is not simply an exciting intellectual challenge. It is not just something one might do as an alternative to getting practically involved in work organisation and management. The complexities are ones with which we have to come to terms if we are to be more than direction-less and muddled practitioners in the world of work organisation. In this first chapter of *Organising and Managing Work* we will be looking carefully at ways in which we can take up these challenges. A further key aim of the chapter, however, is to establish, from the start, a critical frame of mind and to challenge some of the over simplifications which we tend to make in our ordinary or 'everyday' thinking about work and its management. Let us consider one of these tendencies now – and look at how we can usefully challenge such apparently reasonable ways of looking at work management.

Activity 1.1

Look carefully at what Mark Merryton has to say about the most difficult aspects of his job, in Cases and Conversations 1.1. Ask yourself what you think his notion of being a manager is – beyond the obvious role of applying the market research skills that he has 'at his fingertips' and being 'creative' about customers.

Managing people and herding cats   Cases and Conversations 1.1

What would you say is the most difficult aspect of your job as marketing director for the company, then?

Oh, without doubt it's the people side, if you know what I mean.

Trying to work out what the customers are going to want next – that sort of thing?

Good heavens, no. That's the straightforward side. I think I know what I'm doing on that one. I've got the market research techniques at my fingertips and I'm sharp enough to keep on top of things customer-wise and product-wise. But since my last promotion I find that managing the department has almost wholly become a matter of managing the people in it.

So the problem is . . . ?

It's the people management thing. It's handling the people who work for me. They are a constant headache. I've tried to read the books and I've been on people management courses. I didn't miss one of the OB classes on my MBA course. But I still despair at the difficulty I have with managing the people in my function: sorting out who is going to do what, getting them to do the things I want, getting them to finish things on time, even getting them to be where I want them. And that's before I get into all the recruiting, training, appraising and all that stuff.

Why is this do you think?

Perhaps it's because they are marketing people. We often say that managing marketing people is like herding cats. Can you imagine trying to herd cats? It's a powerful image, isn't it?

Indeed it is. And I've heard it numerous times. Only the other day I heard it applied to university lecturers by a faculty dean. And I've heard it applied to engineers, shop workers, hospital staff, secretaries . . .

Yes, I'm sure. And just look at my secretary. I'm meant to be her boss. She can be quite good but I often feel that she is managing me more than I am managing her.

So it's not just marketing people then?

No, I suppose it's not.

And what about your fellow managers, how do you get on with them?

Some good and some bad. But there are some really difficult people in the business I have to deal with. And this includes several people that I don't myself manage – you know, people in other functions. They can make life difficult. I think it's down to their not being properly managed. The managing director himself is not very good at managing his top team. And my finance director friend is utterly hopeless at managing the people who work for him.

This conversation will surprise no one who has been involved in managerial work. As you read this you may be puzzled at why your attention is being drawn to language that is utterly normal in many workplaces – to wording that you hear every day and take for granted. But, as has already been implied, a key purpose of this book is to encourage you to stop short from time to time and think about just what is going on beneath the 'taken-for-granted' surface of everyday organisational life. To pause and reflect critically from time to time on what one is saying, how one is framing reality, and what is happening as a consequence of this, is a valuable habit for any organisational practitioner. Mark Merryton appears to subscribe to a popular notion of what 'management' is about. Let us examine his arguments carefully.

One of the key themes to be developed and applied throughout the book is the idea that the way we talk and think about the world is closely implicated in how we act in the world. We will be considering the idea that the language and concepts we apply to the world around us can be seen as a *framing of reality* that, to a certain extent, brings about that reality. This is similar to an insight which people often draw upon when explaining how a particular 'mindset' shaped the way someone behaved in a certain situation. Without going into a detailed explanation of this idea at this stage, we can helpfully apply the 'framing' idea to the above conversation. Mark Merryton is in effect telling the interviewer about how difficult people are to relate to or 'deal with' at work. This is a fairly straightforward point to make. We all know that our fellow human beings are quirky, unpredictable and not readily amenable to doing what anyone else tells them to do. But Mark is more specific in the way he frames this general argument. He adopts as a key framing idea the notion of *managing people*. He sees part of his job as one of 'managing the people in my department' and he mentions the courses on 'people management' that he has attended. He tells us that he believes he should be 'managing' his secretary and that the managing director should be 'managing' the directors in his 'top team'. Not only does he refer to the finance director as being bad at 'managing the people' in the finance function, he speaks of the people in that department *working for* the finance director as opposed to working for the organisation which is their actual employer.

The idea of people management and the concept of employees working for a particular 'boss', as opposed to working for the employing organisation is probably a widely accepted notion in modern culture. One of the leading British management magazines, for example, is called *People Management*. But is this title one that can easily be accepted as a realistic and helpful way of thinking about or 'framing' managerial work? Let us think hard about this often taken-for-granted notion.

Activity 1.2

-It is common to hear talk about managers *managing people* or to come across books and courses on *people management*. Given that the word 'manage' generally implies controlling and directing (and, in Mark Merryton's case at least, 'herding'), consider the extent to which this way of talking and thinking about managerial activity is:

- Morally acceptable – is it at all ethical to ask some people to 'manage' other people?
- Realistic – is it at all feasible or practicable for some human beings to be given the job of 'managing' other human beings?

Each reader will have answered the first question according to his or her own personal feelings about work and authority. It is not the place of an academic text to lay down or prescribe one particular moral position rather than another. However, it is one of the key arguments of this book that moral issues and choices run through every aspect of organisational and managerial work. It is therefore important to note that Mark Merryton was taking a particular ethical position about work and employment generally and his managerial role specifically when he spoke in the way he did. He may or may not have fully thought out his personal ethical view of the relationship between managers and the people working in the area for which they have responsibility. But such a position is implicit in the words he uses. To help us reflect on what this might be, let us set out a contrary view to the one Mark expresses.

It can be argued that a manager does not have the moral right to direct, manage or 'boss' any individual in their area of responsibility *as a whole person* or in *the totality of their workplace behaviour*. Instead, they have a limited authority to give instructions to employees in tightly prescribed and limited areas of activity. The moral basis of that authority lies in its purpose – to fulfil those work tasks in which the employees have contractually agreed to participate. Employees in modern democratic societies do not sign a contract of employment on the assumption that managers appointed by their employer will have the right to manage them as a person. The manager is appointed to manage the work tasks – and as part of this has limited rights to instruct people. But these rights only exist as means to specific organisational ends and not because of any 'right to command' over the person as a whole. It is thus morally improper to encourage a view of managerial and organisational work based on a principle of 'managing people'.

Is this ethical view simply an alternative to the one implicit in Mark Merryton's words, one that we can adopt or reject solely in terms of our personal ethical position? It is not. It is much more than this. While accepting that it has been expressed in words that might not be fully acceptable to everyone, this ethical position is one implicit in the cultures of modern democratic societies. Moving out of an ethical mode of discussion, then, back into a social-science analytical mode, one can argue that there is a conflict between the 'managing people' view of managerial authority that some managers take and the values or the morality of the wider society of which they are a part. And this suggests that to adopt a focus on people management when one is looking at the 'human aspects' of work organisation is unrealistic – as well as morally dubious.

To recognise a clash between a 'people management' ethic and the ethical assumptions of the wider society, then, is already to accept one significant way in which such a framing of managerial activity is unrealistic. And further grounds readily suggest themselves if we go on to think generally about the people who are allegedly to 'be managed'. While there may be people in the labour markets of modern societies who are happy to subjugate themselves to the wills of 'bosses' at work, such individuals are surely very rare. We will be looking more closely at the complex issue of just what a human being is in Chapter 4. For present purposes, however, it is sufficient to note that one of the key ways that members of the human species differ from other animals is that they are active agents in the shaping of their lives. However meek or submissive particular individuals might be, each human being is nevertheless always the owner and shaper of their own identity, to some degree. As far as the historical record can tell us, no human group in the history of the human species has yet found another group over which it could exert complete control. And this applies even in the extreme conditions of slave societies or extermination camps, where human beings have still demonstrated what looks like an inherent tendency of the species – to resist being managed. We might say that it is not just that cats are inherently 'un-herdable' but that human beings are inherently 'unmanageable'. Which, of course, is not to say that work tasks, involving human beings, cannot be managed.

What is to be concluded from all this reflection? It is to suggest that the widespread tendency to frame – to think about and understand – managerial and organisational work in terms of the management of people is unwise and misleading. It is unrealistic and impracticable, therefore, to focus on the 'management of people' when studying organisational and managerial behaviour. The focus, instead, needs to be on the management of work. The starting point for any consideration of organisational and managerial behaviour is more usefully taken to be the work tasks that are to be carried out. It is these which are organised and 'managed', not the people who carry out the tasks. To understand the behaviours that arise when work tasks are to be done, it is necessary to recognise that work tasks are always *to an extent managed by everyone involved in those tasks*. Work management is not simply what people formally designated as 'managers' do. The nature of the work done by people holding managerial posts will be a concern of Chapter 3. However, there is another common and over simplified idea about management that we need to address at this stage of our thinking – one that perhaps needs even more critical attention than the 'people management' conception that we have looked at.

Activity 1.3

The manager we are about to meet in Cases and Conversations 1.2, 'The madness of Hands-off Harry', has a conception of his job which seems to have little of the 'people management' con- cerns which were expressed by Mark Merryton. Compare Harry's way of 'framing' managerial work with that of Mark. How would you characterise his view of how work should be managed?

The madness of Hands-off Harry

You've heard what the team leaders call me, haven't you?

What is that, Harry?

Come on, I'm sure they've told you that they call me Hands-off Harry.

Well yes, now that you mention it. Do you mind?

Not at all. Well, I did at first because I thought they weren't taking me seriously. I thought they might be laughing at the way I talk about running the department in a 'hands-off' manner. I think they understand my philosophy though, really.

And that philosophy is?

That the manager's job is to lay down all the procedures, the schedules, the targets and the monitoring systems and to keep an eye on all the reports that come up from the shopfloor and all that. You ensure that everyone's been trained in the training school in exactly how to do the job and that they value the job they've got in such a modern facility. They know they will get the pay they want if they meet the targets. Nothing should go wrong if I, as the manager, have got all these systems running properly.

And have you?

More or less – I recognise that things have to be tweaked as you go along. But the team leaders can do that. You just don't need the manager to go out there and, well, sort of get in the way.

But surely people don't simply go along with all the rules and procedures coming from an invisible figure in this office at the end of this long corridor.

Oh, so you've heard the 'invisible man' quip from Joe, have you? He's never been happy with the team leader role but, as I have said to him, modern factories should not need overseer types watching over them. But I do respect what you are saying. And you are right, that all my brilliant paperwork procedures are not enough. There is also the set of values that everyone has absorbed – they've all been through the total quality scheme. All those cultural things are in place. Maybe it doesn't all work like clockwork. But it does work, as long as I do my bit here with my charts and things – and do all the business at the management meetings – I can be Hands-off Harry in the department.

What it appeared that Harry Carse did not know was that the machine operators in his department treated their invisible manager with contempt. They would joke that he stayed in his office (which was indeed at the end of a long corridor off the shopfloor) because he was a madman. They did, however, more or less meet all the targets that Harry set – albeit working in a generally sullen manner. So perhaps it did not 'matter' that Harry remained remote. The three team leaders in the department argued, however, that if Harry 'managed in a more hands-on manner' and 'got to know' the machinists, that there was a strong possibility that much higher output and quality targets could be set.

It is impossible for us to know whether these team leaders are right about whether the department might increase its output if Harry managed it in a different way. However, his case is useful because he talks about managing in a way which helpfully contrasts with Mark Merryton's. He frames managerial work very much as a matter of setting up formal arrangements, procedures, structures and so on. These are not entirely mechanistic notions. His concept of formal arrangements includes cultural matters like 'values' and the idea of people being influenced by principles such as those of total quality management. This means that we cannot argue that he necessarily rejects the idea of 'managing people' – he might argue that he does this but does it remotely – as his nickname of Hands-off Harry implies. However, in the terms preferred here, we can say that his conception of managing work is one that prioritises the structural arrangements side of things rather than the human initiatives side of things.

As we implied earlier we must not go too far in separating out the two aspects of work organisation and management – the direct human initiative aspect, and the structural arrangements aspect. The two are intertwined. Harry Carse may appear simply to run his department through systems, rules and values rather than through direct 'human' interventions. But those procedures and principles were devised by human initiatives taken by Harry and by other managers. Rules, structures and procedures – as much as they sometimes seem to take on a life of their own – do not exist separately from either the human initiatives that are behind them or from the human interpretations of those whose actions at first sight are shaped by them. And it is important to remember that part of the justification for focusing on the 'management of work' in a broad sense was to recognise that the formal managerial work done by 'the manager' – whether it takes the form of setting up procedures or directly attempting to influence people – is only one part of the overall way in which the organisation and management of work is achieved. This is something which appears to be recognised in what Sadie Rait has to say about the case of hospital Ward 17.

Activity 1.4

Read what Sadie Rait has to say in Cases and Conversations 1.3 about her job as a hospital ward manager. Ask yourself:

■ What is Sadie's idea of being a manager?

■ How does her concept of managerial work differ from that of Mark Merryton or Harry

Managing Ward 17

Cases and Conversations 1.3

Although I am called the Ward Manager, the job is not very different from when my predecessor did it. She was called the Ward Sister though.

Does the new title mean you are a 'manager' in any sense that she was not, would you say?

No, I wouldn't – except strangely that she was much more a manager type than I am. Strange perhaps, but she managed things much more than I do. It was much more, 'You do this, you do that'. She was the one you might want to call a manager rather than me.

In what sense are you less a manager than she was, then?

Thinking about it, I wouldn't actually. We are both managers, but I see management in a different way. You would see Mary Ann obviously 'managing', if you know what I mean. But I work differently. The way I see it is that there is a great deal on the ward that has to be managed – and that I cannot take all of that on. So every nurse, porter, ancillary and clerk is managing the place.

And the doctors?

Whoops, sorry. I suppose them too. Well what I was going to say – and perhaps it's why I forgot the doctors – but perhaps not [laughing], was that the nurses as a team manage this ward. I don't manage the nurses. I wouldn't even try. What I say to them is that I am just the first among equals. I say we manage it together and that I just have watch how it all adds up – and, of course, be accountable to Hospital Trust management.

So you don't find yourself giving people instructions or even disciplining nurses who fall short?

Oh yes I do. I draw up work rosters for example and I've had to do formal disciplines on several occasions. I frequently have to chase people up. But, you see, that is all within the whole set of rules that the Trust sets. The hospital is managed by people but also through rules, systems, procedures, protocols, professional knowledge we all bring with us – all that.

By The Trust, you mean . . .?

Well, the management board have done a lot to change how the hospital's work is managed – through the mission and key values statements they've developed and the new culture that everybody has had a say in.

From this account of her approach to hospital ward management we can identify something of Sadie Rait's style of relating to the people who work on the ward. But what is most interesting to us at this stage is not so much how she manages relationships in her job. It is that she appears to 'frame' the managerial task in the hospital as one that many people contribute to, in addition to the not insignificant directing role undertaken by herself as the official 'manager' – including 'chasing people up'. And without taking on a Hands-off Harry type of faith in the power of structures and procedures, she clearly frames the management of work as something going well beyond managerial *behaviours* as such. Work is managed through structures, procedures and meanings (the hospital is 'managed through rules, systems, procedures, protocols, professional knowledge . . . mission and key value statements . . . the new culture') as well as by specific actions of human actors – managerial and non-managerial. The work of Ward 17 is managed by the day-to-day actions and initiatives of Sadie and her staff but it is also in part managed by the structures and procedures of the hospital. Not only this but the factors which might impede or undermine the effective managing of the ward include both these types of factor. Members of staff choosing for personal reasons not to work cooperatively with others would be an example of the human choice and initiative type of factor. And a set of financial circumstances which meant that the ward was always short of the necessary number of nurses would be an example of the more structural type of factor.

We have then identified three ways of talking about management or 'framing' it, as we see in Figure 1.1. The preference here is clearly for Sadie Rait's notion of what management is – her way of 'framing' her managerial role. It is preferred because it is a much more realistic way of talking about the activity, not least in its recognition that the management of work is only partly done by 'managers'. It also implies that what occurs in workplaces is not just an outcome – or sum – of direct human actions. It also involves structures or arrangements which stand in some sense outside specific actions as such. This

Managing people

Managing structures
and procedures

Managing work
through relationships
and procedures

FIGURE 1.1   Three ways of talking about organising and managing

latter facet of work organisation is given primacy of attention by Harry Carse
while, it would seem, Mark Merryton lays emphasis on the direct action side of
things. The relationship between these two facets of work management and
organisations – the direct action and the structural – is an important matter for
understanding the organising and managing of work. However, the importance
of looking at how relatively direct and individualistic actions like 'leading' or
'motivating' are related to more structural phenomena like bureaucratic
structures or cultural patterns is rarely acknowledged in the 'subject' of
Organisational Behaviour (OB) as it is taught in business and management
courses. It is in giving a fuller consideration to such matters that we go beyond
orthodox organisational behaviour thinking.

Building on the Organisational Behaviour tradition

The latter part of the twentieth century has seen enormous growth in institutions engaged in educating people for careers in business and management.
Increasingly these activities have been concentrated in the departments of management or the 'business schools' of universities and colleges. A fairly standard
type of curriculum has developed in the business schools of the USA and other
English speaking countries that have followed the American lead in this style of
education. This has involved dividing up the knowledge and teaching relevant to
the directing of complex work enterprises into different 'subjects'. Some of that
packaging follows an immediately obvious logic. Knowledge related to dealing
with customers, for example, has been gathered into the subject area of *marketing*
while issues of finance and accounting control form another subject and techniques of planning and coordinating production and service activities a further
one of *operations management*. Other parts of the curriculum deal with areas
which similarly reflect the way businesses tend to be functionally divided – purchasing, personnel or human resource management for example. But how much
attention is given to the issue of how the enterprise as a whole is to be managed?

Activity 1.5

Look at the basic curriculum of a business school you know about or a general management programme within the school and ask yourself (or even a tutor!):

■ Is there a section of the programme or a 'subject' called 'management' available for study?

■ If there is not, where in the curriculum are all the specialist or functional elements brought together into an overview of how the enterprise or *the organisation as whole* is managed or directed?

Quite often there is no such subject as 'management', even within those university or college departments which name themselves 'school of management' or where there are individuals with the title, 'Professor of Management'. This might seem strange. This does not mean, however, that there is no attempt to provide an integrative subject. And the area where one will typically be told the curriculum provides the kind of integrative study we have in mind is in a subject called 'Strategy' or, sometimes, 'Strategic Management'. This gets students to study the way organisations – and predominately commercial business organisations – behave or 'perform' as entities in their economic and societal environment. It is here one might therefore expect to see the social sciences used to analyse how such complex patterns of human activity and structural dynamics come about and are *managed*. But generally, and with the exception of the use of a limited amount of material from economics, there is only a marginal use of theoretical or research insights in strategy teaching into how human behaviours and meanings are shaped into the complex patterns of activity which enable them to relate to their customers, clients, markets or environments. A large part of the time spent studying 'strategy' involves students reading, talking and writing about descriptive case studies of relationships between corporations and their efforts to compete with other corporations. Strangely perhaps, issues of human patterning of behaviour and cooperation and the task of demonstrating the potential of social science analysis are handed over to another subject: organisational behaviour or 'OB' as generations of business students have come to know it.

One might expect a subject with the title of 'Organisational Behaviour' to study the managing and organising of cooperative activities in the context of how the organisation relates to all those external bodies upon which its future is dependent. OB only does part of this job however. It intends to look 'inward', leaving much of the 'outward' focus of the study of organisational performance to the subject of strategy. Its emphasis tends to be on the 'means' through which organising is brought about, with little reference to the 'ends' that it serves. And in doing this, it seriously risks its analytical integrity since these 'ends' – in practice if not in the classroom – fundamentally influence the organisational 'means'. Issues of profitability, market share or government policy, for example, lie in the realm of the strategists while the OB people look at the individual human behaviours, the group formations, the job designs and the organisation structures *in their own terms*, isolating them from their vital strategic context. But even attention to these internal processes is limited in the typical OB curriculum – restricted in large part to the more formal or official aspects of management. It gives only limited attention to the ambiguities, confusions and conflicts which are as much a part of work management activities as all the motivational and leadership efforts, the job and organisation designing, the culture and organisational change initiatives which form the bulk of the curriculum. Even at the level of formal managerial processes, a proportion of these is left to another area of the curriculum. Where are the processes of selecting, recruiting and dispensing with organisational members or the relationships with organised labour dealt with? By and large, these are left to the subject of 'human resource management'.

Organisational Behaviour is a thriving area of teaching and study activity and, indeed, of book publishing. It is developing in sophistication. There are attempts to develop the curriculum in places by bringing into the story the politics of managerial relationships or devoting chapters to conflict more generally. And some attention is given to contextual influences on certain aspects of organisational choice in the guise of 'contingencies' (covered below in Chapter 8). But the tendency for books and courses to run through unlinked accounts of matters of individual behaviour in one section, group behaviours in another and structural and change issues in others is dominant. At a theoretical level, this means that a fault line runs beneath the whole OB landscape. There is a deep hole beneath the surface created by the neglect of what is perhaps the most fundamental challenge which social science has grappled with over the years. This is the issue, referred to earlier, of understanding how the aspects of human choice and initiative in social life, on the one hand, relate to structural and cultural aspects on the other. Leadership, for example, has to be seen as related to wider cultural patterns and not just to the characteristics and actions of particular individuals. What happens at the level of group behaviour must be seen in the context of the overall structural pattern of the organisation, if not of the whole society, in which the group is located. We need to have some understanding of these matters if, for example, we are going to recognise where as human actors in organisational contexts we have choices and where we are structurally constrained. It has to be understood if we want to recognise where we can influence matters by direct actions and where we have to influence them by devising structures and procedures and encouraging shared understandings. These are surely vital things for us to understand if we are interested in how work is managed or might be managed differently. To do this we have both to build upon and 'go beyond' OB.

One of the first things that has to be done to go beyond OB is to abandon the popular device used in many texts or presenting a whole series of different theoretical approaches (the classical approach, the human relations approach, the systems approach and so on) and, after some limited indication of the strengths and weaknesses of each of these, leaving the reader to make up his or her own mind. This might sound fair-minded and liberal, but it is an opting out of the social science writer's responsibility to provide the reader or student with some general criteria by which they might judge what is a useful or a misleading model, a good theory or a bad theory. The failure to develop an integrative theoretical framework makes it very difficult for any connections to be drawn between, say, the 'motivations' of individual organisational members and the prevailing culture of the organisation or, say, between the principles of job design adopted in an organisation and the values and beliefs of the senior managers. OB books fail badly in this respect by, for example, discussing individual 'motivation' in one section of the book and 'organisational culture' in another, without seriously examining how these relate to each other.

Organising and Managing Work, while trying to overcome this problem, is not turning its back on the organisational behaviour tradition. While dealing with many of the issues traditionally tackled in OB and looking at much of the work normally covered in the subject, it attempts both to overcome some of the existing weaknesses and to build upon the firmer base thus laid down. It will do this by:

- organising and integrating the various areas and levels of analysis within a single unifying theoretical perspective – one which has at its heart a recognition of the constant interplay between individual initiatives and structural circumstances;

- explaining and then applying a commitment to a particular style of critical management studies;

- providing the reader with a criterion for judging how some perspectives and theories are 'better' than others;

- connecting the concerns normally associated with the 'subject' of Organisational Behaviour with some of those generally tackled in the separate subjects of Strategic Management and Human Resource Management, as represented in Figure 1.2.

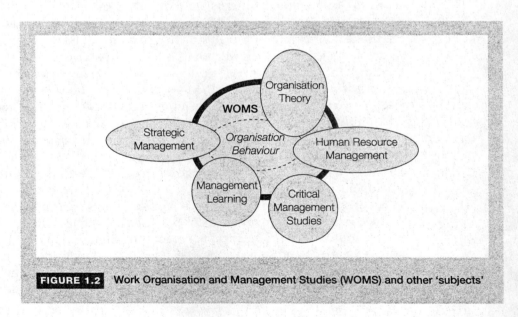

FIGURE 1.2   Work Organisation and Management Studies (WOMS) and other 'subjects'

Figure 1.2 includes three further 'subjects' alongside the fairly standard business school subjects of Strategic Management and HRM. These are Organisation Theory/Organisation Studies, Management Learning, and Critical Management Studies. The first of these looks at many of the same issues as OB but does it with a primarily academic focus – concerning itself first and foremost with scholarly understanding rather than with the implications of such understandings for practice. The materials to be found in journals such as *Organisation Studies* or many of the books listed in Reading Guide 1 are nevertheless invaluable for the more practice-oriented *Work Organisation and Management Studies*. This is especially so because the subject has been much more attentive to the question of relating individual level activities to bigger 'structural' patterns. It has also been more concerned with taking a critical stance than OB, something which has also informed the emergence of Critical Management Studies (Reading Guide 13) – in effect an application of the more critical ideas of Organisation Theory directly to issues of managerial activity. Management Learning is another emergent field of specialist study with its own academic journal, *Management Learning*, and a concern to bring together theoretical developments in the understanding of human learning processes with issues of both educating and 'developing' managerial practitioners (see Reading Guide 11). *Organising and Managing Work* is informed by this development in its recognition of the central importance of issues of learning to all aspects of the organisation and management of work.

All of these developments in the study of the organisation and management of work in modern societies can be understood, perhaps ironically, as aspects of work organisation themselves. This is to say that these different 'subjects' have not 'come about' straightforwardly to reflect different aspects of human activity which exist 'out there' in the world of work and its management. There is no chunk of work activity going on in the world which is 'strategic management' and which can be separated from another chunk of reality which is 'management learning'. In part, the academic subjects reflect a division of labour among managerial practitioners. Some managers, for instance, are paid to operate more 'strategically' than others are. However, the pattern of academic subjects we tend to see in business schools are probably more an outcome of the ways in which teachers, researchers, writers and publishers have chosen to carve up their territories than a straightforward reflection of the 'realities' of organisational practice. This carving up involves all the career building interests, interpersonal conflicts, market pressures, confusions and ambiguities which characterise all work organisations and the people who work in them. We cannot expect those working in academic organisations to be immune to any of this.

These comments inevitably apply to the writing of *Organising and Managing Work* itself, of course. We will shortly consider the justification that can be offered for such a departure and what it involves. First, however, it is time to clarify formally where we have got to with our notion of Work Organisation and Management Studies.

Work Organisation and Management Studies

Work Organisation and Management Studies, as a subject which both incorporates and goes beyond existing ways of looking at work organisation and
management, can be formally defined.

Work Organisation and Management Studies   *Concept*

The analysis of the human aspects of work organisation and its management which draws on the
social sciences to develop insights, theories and research findings with a view to informing the
choices, decisions and actions of people who have a practical involvement with organisations.

We need to note several things about this concept of Work Organisation and
Management Studies.

- What is studied is the 'human aspects of work organisation and its management'. This language is not meant to imply that attention is only paid to
  'human aspects' at the level of the human individual. The focus is on work
  organisation and management, which means that patterns of human activity
  and thinking going beyond the level of the individual are as important as
  thinking about the human individual. As has already been explained, the concern is with the interplay of factors at the level of human initiative and choice
  and factors at the level of social, political and economic context, or structure.

- The subject *informs* the choices, decisions and actions of people involved in
  practices in organisations. There is no question of developing an academic subject which can tell people what they should do in the complex area of work
  management. The area is far too complex for there to be any basic rules or even
  sets of guidelines about 'how to do management'. Not only this but, given the
  moral factors which must come into every human situation where power and
  authority are involved, it would be quite wrong for a textbook to attempt to
  provide guidance in this way. What it can do, however, is to provide insights
  into the range of factors and issues which are relevant to any particular choice
  (of, say, job design or planning an organisational change programme). The
  actual choice or decision that is made is a matter for those involved in the particular organisational situation – with all the political, moral and specific local
  considerations coming into play alongside the insights which can be derived
  from academic study of the managing and organisation of work.

- Reference is made to 'organisational practitioners' rather than 'managers' as
  the potential 'users' of the subject. This is done in recognition of the fact that
  people other than those formally designated as managers are closely involved
  in the way work tasks are managed. If there are ideas in Work Organisation
  and Management Studies which would be helpful to a manager in an organisational situation wishing to have his or her understanding enhanced by
  academic thinking then surely those ideas are going to be equally relevant to

anyone else concerned with that situation. This would be the case regardless of the person's formal authority in the organisation or, for that matter, their degree of commitment to official organisational policies.

- The social sciences are 'drawn on' by Work Organisation and Management Studies. The subject is not seen as a social science in its own right. A variety of social science disciplines can be turned to provide research findings, theoretical resources or insights that might be helpful in understanding organisational issues. This does not mean, however, that we simply turn in a random or *promiscuous* manner to the vast bank of social science materials every time they wish to analyse a particular situation. Each individual is likely to build up their set of preferred social science concepts as their learning proceeds. They then turn to the books and journals for further insight, as the need arises, and incorporate the new learning into their ever-developing personal framework of understanding.

Organisational behaviour has tended to draw primarily on the social science disciplines of sociology, psychology and social psychology. Work Organisation and Management Studies, as conceived of here, follows this and similarly supports the contributions of the main disciplines with insights from economics, political science and anthropology. The key concerns of each of these are outlined in Table 1.1.

All of these disciplines can be seen as providing resources which can be drawn upon when wishing to understand the organising and managing of work in general or any particular organisational situation or problem in particular. Many of the human issues that can arise in the organisational context do not fall into any one obvious disciplinary territory and many of them might use ideas from more than one discipline. Bearing this in mind, see how you get on with Activity 1.6.

TABLE 1.1 Focal and supporting social science disciplines for Work Organisation and Management Studies	
Focal social science disciplines	**Supporting social science disciplines**
Psychology focuses on individual characteristics and behaviour and on such matters as learning, motivation and individual ('personality') differences	**Economics** supports the sociological concern with the economic context and, also, the psychological concern with decision-making (through its attention to 'rational' decisions made by economic actors)
Social psychology focuses on group characteristics and behaviour, on roles, attitudes, values, communication, decision-making and so on	**Political science** supports the sociological concern with power and conflict and the social–psychological concern with decision-making (through its concern with the state and other institutions handling matters of power and difference of interest)
Sociology focuses on structures, arrangements or patterns and how these both influence and are influenced by individual and group behaviour. It is concerned with the structure of the social and economic system as well as with the organisational structure and issues of technology, conflict, power and culture	**Anthropology** supports the social-psychological concern with norms, values and attitudes and the sociological concern with cultures (both organisational and societal) with insights taken from the study of non-industrial or 'less advanced' societies about such things as rites, rituals, customs and symbols

Activity 1.6

Read the story about Rose Markey taking over as the manager of The Canalazzo restaurant (Cases and Conversations 1.4), thinking about the issues which Rose is going to have to deal with to satisfy her employers. Following the characterisations of the six social sciences set out in Table 1.1, note the factors or issues that you think might be identified as, respectively, psychological, social–psychological, sociological, economic, political and anthropological.

Rose takes over The Canalazzo

Cases and Conversations 1.4

Rose Markey had been working for a national chain of restaurants for only a couple of years when they asked her to take over a restaurant which they had recently acquired. They had bought The Canalazzo restaurant from the Italian family which had established the business some twenty or so years previously. The family had decided to return to Italy and to warmer summers. The company had originally put in one of their older managers to run the newly acquired restaurant. However, they were very disappointed with what was being achieved. Their director of finance argued that the turnover of the business simply did not justify the investment that had been made in the purchase of the business and in the redecoration of the premises. When they challenged the first manager they had put in, he talked of his resentment at being asked to move to a new part of the country at the age of 55. He persuaded the company to give him an early retirement settlement so that he could return to the part of the country he had lived in for most of his life. They were pleased to do this because it was clear, the human resources manager told Rose, that this man's poor motivation and attitude to customers was increasingly being reflected in the way the staff of the restaurant went about their work.

When Rose arrived at the restaurant she soon learned that her predecessor had clashed on several occasions with local police officers about serving late drinks. This was likely to get back to the magistrates and the

restaurant would be in danger of failing to have its drinks licence renewed when it was next due for review. The manager's defence was that he was simply following local customs in the town whereby customers would have a night out that would bring them into the restaurant only after spending most of the evening in a public house. It was not his fault, he said, that the police officers and the magistrates all lived outside of the town and didn't know about this.

When it came to the problems with the staff, Rose found that her predecessor had set up a strongly hierarchical set of relationships among them. This seemed to be accepted, albeit grudgingly, by the people who worked in the kitchen. But it was resented by the waiting staff who were largely part-time workers studying at the local university. Not only this, but the group of waiters – who all knew each other from the university – and the kitchen workers, all of whom had left school at 16, tended only to speak to members of their own group. The chef, who was a middle-aged Italian, regularly fell out with the headwaiter – a woman a dozen years younger than him. Their respective ideas about how young female staff should be treated were poles apart and these differences led to frequent arguments. Overall there was very little coordination between the kitchen and the restaurant. All of this, Rose decided, seriously affected the quality of service the customers received.

Perhaps psychological factors are the first to suggest themselves here, ranging from issues of differences of personality and temperament among different employees of the restaurant to ones of motivation and personal commitment. The varying sets of attitude in the restaurant are clearly a matter of social–psychological interest as are the problematic patterns of communication and the way the two groups of kitchen and restaurant staff have developed to create a division among the junior staff as a whole. All of this feeds into the sociological factors and issues. There is a power structure within the restaurant and this has elements which relate to sociological variables such as age, gender and ethnicity – all of which relate to the way society as a whole is organised. But there are also sociological factors about the way the restaurant fits into the local economy and community, both as a provider of services and a source of labour. Here there is a clear overlap with economic issues of market organisation and this, in turn, relates to the most obvious economic issues of financial performance, turnover (and, by implication, profitability) and investment. Issues of a formal political nature (i.e. relating to issues of the role of the state) are present with regard to the police and magistrates, and there are obvious informal 'political' issues running right through the whole set of relationships in the restaurant. This is in addition to whatever the 'informal' politics of the relationship between local police officers and restaurant managers might be. Anthropological issues of informal customs might also be involved but, more obviously, the anthropological notions of custom and ritual are highly relevant to the patterns of restaurant use which influence the pattern of work which has to be managed by Rose Markey and the rest of the staff of The Canalazzo.

Common sense and social science

One of the first thoughts occurring to anyone trying to make sense of the problems of The Canalazzo restaurant might be that 'common sense' is likely to be just as helpful as ideas from psychology, sociology or anthropology. It has, nevertheless, been a tradition of social science teachers to contrast social science thinking with common-sense thinking and, not surprisingly, to argue that social science analysis is to be preferred to common sense. But an alternative response might be to say, 'It all depends on what you mean by common sense'. This is necessary, in fact, because there are two quite different usages of the term 'common sense' that often get muddled up. It is useful to distinguish between *everyday common sense* and *critical common sense*.

Everyday common sense   *Concept*

Analysis based on unthought-out, taken-for-granted, immediately 'obvious', everyday assumptions about the world and human activity within it.

Everyday common sense is necessary for 'getting by' in our daily lives. We all make quick assumptions about what is going on around us, drawing on all kinds of stereotypes, half-remembered experiences and simplistic cause–effect connections. This is necessary to cope with our daily lives. We would not cope with life if we stopped, sat back and deeply pondered on every eventuality that faced us between getting up in the morning and going to bed at night. But perhaps we can see why social scientists claim that their more analytical style of thinking has advantages over this. In the work context, for example, individuals frequently offer woefully simplistic generalisations such as 'People only go to work for the money' – typically adding, 'It stands to reason' or, 'It's obvious' or, 'It's common sense isn't it?' This is a good example of everyday common sense, based as it is on easy, unthought-out, taken-for-granted assumptions. Assumptions like these make life simpler – at first sight, anyway. But such assumptions are often dangerous guides to action on matters of any importance or complexity such as designing a pay system or 'reward structure', for example.

We therefore turn to critical common sense as a style of thinking which involves being essentially logical or rational about things in the way which is common to all human beings when they are alertly and critically putting their mind to whatever matter is in hand.

Critical common sense   *Concept*

Analysis based on the basic logic, rationality, hard-headedness to be found in human beings whenever they step back from the immediate situation and critically put their minds to an issue or problem.

This is the kind of common sense that we can more reliably use as a guide to action when more complex matters of work organisation and management arise. It is an activity of the same order as that in which the scientist engages. Science,

TABLE 1.2 Two types of common sense in practice	
Everyday common sense and pay	**Critical common sense and pay**
If you pay employees in proportion to their output they will produce more than if they get the same wage whatever they turn out	Pay for output might work. But employees might prefer the comfort of a steady work rate and the security of a steady wage. They might resent the pressures of a bonus system on group relations
They will clearly work better under a performance-related pay system	It would be wise to find out what the particular employees' requirements are before deciding for or against a performance-related pay system

in this view, is essentially a formalised version of critical common sense. Scientific thinking – in principle if not always in practice – is the more formal, systematic and painstakingly analytical application of critical common sense.

Critical common sense analysis tends to start from a consideration of the most obvious or likely explanation of what is going on; the everyday common sense explanation in fact. But it then goes on to ask whether things are really as they seem at first. Alternative explanations are considered and attention is paid to available evidence in judging the various rival explanations. We can see the two types of common sense compared in Table 1.2 and the managerial implications of applying each of them, in this case in deciding for or against a performance-related pay system.

The considerations about performance related pay connected in Table 1.2 to a critical common sense way of thinking about work behaviour are indeed similar to ones which have emerged from social science research and theorising about the relationship between pay and behaviour.

 **Link**   See, in particular, the 'expectancy' theory of work motivation explained in Chapter 9, p. 300. Similar arguments to these critical common sense ones were developed in the light of one of the famous Hawthorne experiments – The Bank Wiring Observation Room experiment – by Roethlisberger and Dickson (1939, Reading Guide 1).

The critical study of organising and managing

A critical common sense frame of mind is obviously relevant to any kind of practical human endeavour. But it has particular relevance to academic work – and especially to studies that claim to be scientific. Scientific analysis, as has already been suggested, can be understood as an especially rigorous or systematic application of critical common sense. And this would suggest that we could not do social science at all without being critical in the sense of constantly questioning taken-for-granted ideas and practices. However, there has been a growing trend of questioning the extent to which social-science study of work behaviour and managerial practice has been sufficiently critical.

The crux of the problem that all writers and researchers interested in managerial issues have to face up to is the fact that managerial activities are always and inevitably implicated in issues of power and relative advantage and disadvantage between human groups and human individuals. Everyone engaged in management research and management education is therefore faced with a dilemma. How do they reconcile providing knowledge that might help improve the effectiveness of work activities with the fact that in doing so might help some people ('managers' and the employers of managers, say) more than others ('the managed', for example)? Helping make work organisations more efficient or more effective is not a politically neutral matter.

In a world where valued resources tend to be scarce and there is continuous competition for the goods, services and rewards provided by work organisations, any intervention can involve one in taking sides between the relatively advantaged and the relatively disadvantaged. The social scientist is in danger of becoming a 'servant of power', as an early polemic on such matters put it (Baritz, 1960, p. 39, Reading Guide 13). One way of handling this dilemma is suggested by some members of the emergent 'critical management studies' movement. Their strategy amounts, in effect, to 'going on the attack' against managerial ideologies and activities that are felt by the critical scholar to be 'wrong' or 'harmful'. Critical research and writing would, for example, offer its students 'an appreciation of the pressures that lead managerial work to become so deeply implicated in the unremitting exploitation of nature and human beings, national and international extremes of wealth and poverty, the creation of global pollution, the promotion of "needs" for consumer products etc.' (Alvesson and Willmott, 1996, p. 39, Reading Guide 13). Such a critical management study is committed to exposing the political implications of managerial work with an ambition of helping achieve 'emancipatory transformation' – the transformation of both people and society. And, in the workplace itself, a 'critical' version of the concept of empowerment is called for, 'empowering employees to make more choices and to act more effectively to transform workplace relations' (Thompson and McHugh, 1995, p. 22, Reading Guide 13).

These advocates of critical management studies, critical management education and critical organisation studies want their work to help change the balance of power in the worlds of work and employment. But they are not just critical of the existing patterns of power prevailing in organisations and society at large. They also aim their critical fire at the type of writing and teaching which constitutes the orthodoxy in contemporary business and management schools. And the main thrust of this critique is against the assumption behind much of this orthodoxy that success in managerial and organisational work comes from acquiring, developing and applying *skills* and *techniques* – skills and techniques which are neutral and 'innocent' in a political sense. Issues of power, inequality, conflict (at interpersonal, group and class levels), gender and ethnicity are either ignored or treated as peripheral matters which, from time to time, get in the way of smooth organisational functioning. Sympathy with this latter criticism has been an important inspiration for the writing of the present text and it informs the critique of what is called the *systems-control* orthodoxy and its displacement

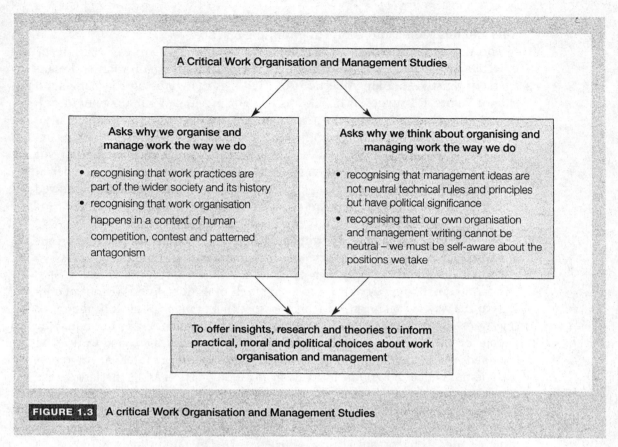

FIGURE 1.3 A critical Work Organisation and Management Studies

by a more realistic and politically sensitive *process-relational* perspective. But the whole text is underpinned by a particular notion of a critical organisation and management study, which is summarised in Figure 1.3. It is a notion that shares much ground with the work being produced under the flag of 'critical management studies' but its overlap is only partial, as the earlier Figure 1.2 suggested.

The conception of a critical organisation and management study adopted in *Organising and Managing Work* differs from that taken by some of the critical thinkers whose ideas were looked at above. This is primarily with regard to the issue of arguing for 'transformation', at both the personal and the social levels. It is felt that the choices that these transformations would entail are a matter for political and moral debate in society generally and for contestation within organisations themselves. They are not transformations which social science can or should push people towards. What the social sciences can do is to illuminate or inform those debates with information and insights derived from both research investigations and theoretical reflections. And if these insights, research contributions and theories are going to have any real potential to *make a difference* to practices in the world outside the classroom and library, there has to be an openness about the fact that all social science analysis is itself value-laden. To contribute to either societal or organisational debates about how work tasks are to be organised and managed as if this were simply a matter of deciding which power-neutral technique or procedure to adopt would be dishonest at the moral level and misleading at the level of informing practice.

This means that no study of organisations and management can claim to be objective or in some sense 'value-free'. A critical study of organisation and management must keep asking questions of itself – as the words on the right-hand side of Figure 1.3 suggest. This entails recognising that the management and organisational ideas that are dealt with are not matters of technique or neutral principles, devoid of political significance. It also requires a degree of self-awareness in writing and teaching and a commitment to judiciously revealing our own biases and moral inclinations where this is necessary to help the reader or student take one's inevitable partiality into account. This principle was followed early in the present chapter where the notion of 'people management' was *engaged with* as a matter of morality as well as pragmatic realism.

The writing of the early part of this chapter was also relevant to the words on the left-hand side of Figure 1.3. The essence of critique is *questioning* and a critical study has to ask questions about the organisational activities that it is studying as well as constantly questioning what it is producing itself in its 'literature'. We looked critically at the way several practising managers speak about managerial work and raised questions about the practice of speaking of management in terms of 'managing people' or 'managing structures and procedures' rather than 'managing work'. This argument will be built upon as *Organising and Managing Work* develops. And as we ask questions about how and why work organisation practices are as they are we will constantly bear in mind that work organisations are only in an extremely limited way a separate phenomenon from the economy and society of which they are part. They did not historically 'evolve' in the working out of some divine or abstract principle of increasing organisational efficiency. The hierarchy of jobs in today's organisations, for example, is both an outcome of and a contributor to the hierarchy of class and status which has developed in society as individuals and groups have competed with each other for advantage over the years. By the same token, markets do not exist 'out there' as part of the 'economic context' of business organisations. They are *made* by organisational initiatives as much as they are served by organisations. A critical perspective also requires us constantly to observe that differences of interest – and the frequent alignment and re-alignment of interests – are inherent in organisations. They permeate the managerial strata of organisations as well as underlying the basic tensions between employees and employers.

Activity 1.7

Quickly re-read Cases and Conversations 1.4 and how Rose Markey 'took over' at The Canalazzo restaurant. Then read the sequel to that story (Cases and Conversations 1.5), 'Rose and The Canalazzo under threat'. Make a note of all the ways in which an understanding of both parts of The Canalazzo story would require attention to factors to which, it is argued above, a critical study of organisation and management draws attention. The wording on the left-hand side of Figure 1.3 is a starting point for your analysis.

After six months' managing The Canalazzo restaurant, Rose Markey prepared for her annual performance appraisal at the headquarters of the company which owned the restaurant. She was still finding her job quite a struggle. She had begun to adjust to living in the north of the country, having only ever lived in the south previously. She had established good relationships with the local police and the worry about losing the drinks licence had disappeared. However, she was having difficulties with the chef, who resented a woman being in charge of the restaurant. The problems with the chef were exacerbated by the fact that the kitchen staff seemed pleased to see her discomforted whenever she got into an argument with him. And the kitchen staff's uncooperative attitude towards the waiters had got worse. They knew that Rose was a university graduate and frequently mocked her southern middle-class accent in the same way they regularly mimicked what they called the 'posh' accents of the largely-student waiting staff. They saw Rose and the waiters as people who were only in their present jobs as a means towards something better later on.

In spite of these difficulties, Rose felt sure she could succeed in improving the restaurant's popularity. She believed she could win over the chef in the long run, by encouraging him to develop some more adventurous menus and attracting a new clientele. This, she thought, would encourage him to discipline his kitchen staff more effectively – especially with regard to their relationships with the waiters.

Rose was excited about explaining all of this to the manager who was to do her appraisal. However, before she could even begin to talk about what she was doing, he told her that the company was considering closing the restaurant. A rival had ousted the chief executive of the company. The new managing director wanted, she said, to take the whole business 'up-market'. A restaurant in a northern town with a declining local economy did not 'fit into the new scheme of things'. Rose was to be offered redundancy – the terms of which she was invited to go and discuss with the Human Resources manager.

When Rose found the HR manager, he immediately invited her to go to a nearby wine bar for a drink. He explained that as an old friend of the former managing director he had felt it wise to seek a job with another business. He had been successful in this and therefore felt able, he said, to let Rose know that he believed she had been badly treated. He said that the possibility of closing the restaurant had arisen before Rose had been moved there. Rose had been chosen to take the Canalazzo job because one or two of the headquarter's managers felt that her 'face did not fit'. She was not only the one graduate trainee manager they employed. She was the only one with a black face.

The story of Rose and The Canalazzo involves many of the normal problems that someone is likely to face when trying to manage work – in a struggling restaurant or anywhere else. Alongside the obvious problems about the nature of the market for the particular services offered, and the need to achieve better coordination of the restaurant's division of labour, are a whole series of interpersonal and intergroup relationship problems. But most of these relate in some way to the patterns of conflict, inequality and discrimination existing in the wider culture and society. A critical organisation and management study would take all of this into account in an analysis of what was occurring. This would take it well beyond attention to orthodox issues of motivation, leadership and group relations. But it would also recognise the wider pattern of economic ownership which was relevant to issues in The Canalazzo and observe the way in which boardroom politics can affect what happens at a local workplace level in an organisation. There are politics at every level – workplace, organisation and society. A critical Work Organisation and Management Studies would see these as centrally important matters, not merely as ones providing the 'context' in which the basic day-to-day application of managerial techniques and motivational skills have to be applied.

By now, after two visits to The Canalazzo restaurant, two things should be apparent about analysing all the complexities of organisational and managerial behaviour as it occurs in 'real life' (as opposed to how it appears in the idealised world of standard management texts). First, as we saw in Activity 1.7, we have to look critically at facets of social, cultural, political and economic life that go way beyond a simple search for efficient management techniques. A whole series of moral issues arise in the Canalazzo story. Second, as we saw in Activity 1.6, we have to turn to a range of social-science sources for help in analysing these matters. But each of these social sciences itself has a range of perspectives, models, concepts, theories and research studies on which we might draw when analysing whatever organisational or managerial issues interest or concern us. How do we choose between these?

Knowledge and the informing of practice

One of the ways in which we said that we needed to 'go beyond' Organisational Behaviour was to avoid the very popular OB textbook device of organising material according to a variety of different 'schools' or theoretical approaches or perspectives (the 'classical', 'human relations' or 'systems', for example). Although some texts point out the merits and demerits of each of these, readers are more or less left to decide for themselves which way of looking at organisations they prefer. However fair and reasonable this may seem at first, it avoids the issue of advising students of work organisation and management about what broad criteria they might apply to any piece of research or theorising they come across when trying to understand organisational or managerial practices. And this militates against taking a critical stance with regard to the study of work organisation and management itself. How do we make judgements about the relative value of one piece of analysis or knowledge compared with another?

To deal with this question we have to get involved with issues of *epistemology*. This is the branch of philosophy that deals with the relationship between the way the world is and the knowledge we have of that world. And it has a specific concern with the sort of truth claims that can be made for particular propositions or pieces of knowledge. This might seem a rather complex issue for us to get involved in here, something we can leave to philosophers while we get on with looking directly at organisations and their management. However, we really cannot duck the matter. It is vital to any understanding of how we relate 'theory and practice'.

Whether we like it or not, we all make epistemological judgements every day of our lives. We may have to decide, for example, 'how much truth there is' in the story we just read in our newspaper about an imminent business takeover. We might be concerned with 'how much truth there is' in the picture of society painted by the politician whose speech we have just listened to. Or we might be anxious about 'how much truth there is' in stories we have heard about a local school 'failing' and being closed down. Broadly speaking there are three approaches or 'theories' we can apply to such matters – approaches we can also take to the sort of accounts and analyses we come across when studying organisations and management. These are shown in Table 1.3.

TABLE 1.3 Three ways of deciding the 'truth' of knowledge	
Three ways of deciding the 'truth' of an item of knowledge	**For example . . .**
Correspondence theories of truth judge an item of knowledge in terms of how accurately it paints a picture or gives a report of what actually happened or 'is the case'	A jury is asked to apply this principle (qualified by the notion of 'beyond reasonable doubt') when deciding between the accounts given by the prosecution and the defence. A judgement has to be made as to whether 'x' actually did or did not kill 'y'
Coherence/plausibility theories of truth judge an item of knowledge in terms of how well it 'fits in with' everything else we have learned about this matter previously	We might apply this principle when deciding whether a piece of gossip about somebody we know is true or false. We ask whether or not it fits with everything else we have seen of them and heard about them
Pragmatist theories of truth judge knowledge in terms of how effectively one would fulfil whatever projects one was pursuing in the area of activity covered by the knowledge, if we based our actions on the understanding of those activities which it offers	We might apply this principle when comparing what a promotional tourist brochure says about a foreign city we are going to visit and what is said in a book by an independent author drawing on their first-hand experiences. We have to decide which account of that city we are going to heed when deciding what to wear, how to address local people, how to find food that we like, or avoid being robbed

In everyday life we apply all three ways of deciding the validity of a piece of knowledge. We do this in organisational contexts as much as we do in the other areas of life used in the examples in Table 1.3. But the pragmatist approach to making judgements is obviously the most relevant to deciding what practices we are going to follow in any situation, in the light of the knowledge about that situation which is available to us. In the case of deciding which of the two tourist guides to trust, we would clearly be wise to apply the pragmatist 'theory of truth'. We would similarly be wise to apply this principle if we were considering taking a job with a particular organisation and had available to us, say, both the organisation's recruitment brochure and an article written by a researcher who had carried out participant observation research in that organisation. Which of these two 'pieces of knowledge' is the 'truer' one, we would tend to ask. And we would ask ourselves this question because we would be concerned to decide the most appropriate way to behave when entering the organisation. We would, in this respect, be applying a pragmatist theory of truth claims in the same way that we do when we compare the account of a product given in the manufacturer's advertisement and a report on the product published by an independent consumer association.

In the light of these examples, it is clear that a pragmatist approach to judging the sorts of material one comes across in studying organisations and management is invaluable. The wisdom of such an approach derives from its pragmatically realistic acceptance to two things:

- It is impossible when looking at organisational issues to have enough information – free of interpretation, free of biased reporting, free of the tricks of human memory and free of ambiguity – to apply the correspondence theory of truth. This applies to social life in general as well as to organisations specifically. Because everything we are told about the world is mediated by language and interpretation, we can never receive an account which accurately reports or 'mirrors' that world.

- There are no absolute truths or 'final laws' which social scientific analysis can offer with regard to organisations or any other aspect of social life. One proposition, theory or research study can be judged to be truer than another, however. But this is only to the extent that it will tend to be a *more trustworthy, broad guide to practice* in the aspect of life it covers than the other. It cannot be wholly correct, totally true, or completely objective. One piece of knowledge is simply more useful than the other as an account of 'how things work' which we can use to inform our practices.

This pragmatist approach to judging the validity of the sorts of material we are going to study derives from a particular school of philosophy, the pragmatist philosophy of Charles Pierce, William James and James Dewey as well as, in part, the neo-pragmatist thinking of Richard Rorty (see Reading Guide 4). But it also fully accords with the relatively straightforward notion of *critical common sense* looked at earlier. It leads us to the eminently sensible critical common sense practice of reading management and social science books (or considering any other kind of knowledge for that matter) and asking ourselves, 'To what extent should I take into account this knowledge when deciding what to do in practice?'. If one theory, one research study, or even one piece of fictional writing, is thought to be more helpful in informing our practical projects than another, then it is a *better* theory, article or book. It is 'truer' in the pragmatist sense of 'true'.

To emphasise the relevance of pragmatist criteria for evaluating pieces of organisational and management knowledge is not to argue for completely turning our backs on the other criteria for judging truth. The concept of justice applied in many societies requires us to work with the correspondence theory of truth, for example, in courts of law or other types of judicial or bureaucratic enquiry. Yet, even here, as we noted earlier, the ultimate impossibility of this is recognised in the acceptance that a judgement can only achieve a reliability which is 'beyond *reasonable* doubt'. We are therefore much safer, for most purposes, applying the more modest pragmatist criterion for judging truth claims. And we are certainly much safer applying this approach than making too much use of coherence or plausibility theories of truth. We apply these all the time – when, for example, we ask how one statement on some issue 'stacks up against' everything else we have heard on that matter. At the level of ordinary or everyday common sense we have to do this. But it is not good enough when we are engaged in the more rigorous and critical common sense type of thinking which we frequently have to do in the complex area of organising and managing work. Too many poor theories in the organisational and management sphere have an immediate plausibility, one that soon disappears when rigorous and critical common sense is applied to them.

Link   The endlessly taught and cited 'hierarchy of needs' theory of work motivation is subjected to this kind of analysis in Chapter 9, pp. 291–7, and shown to fall down badly in pragmatist terms.

The reader of *Organising and Managing Work* is invited to apply the pragmatist criterion of validity to everything that is offered in the forthcoming chapters. It is the criterion that has been applied to the arguments developed throughout the book. It informs the recommendation of a *process-relational* perspective for looking at organising and managing work, instead of the orthodox *systems-control* perspective which is critically examined in Chapter 2, for example. Also, it can be applied to the different ways of talking about managerial work that we have considered in the present chapter. Activity 1.8 can help demonstrate this.

Activity 1.8

Apply the 'pragmatist theory of truth' to the view of managerial work expressed in Cases and Conversations 1.1, 1.2 and 1.3, respectively, by Mark Merryton, Harry Carse and Sadie Rait (summarised in Figure 1.1). You can do this by assuming that you are planning to take up a managerial career and are wondering which of these informal 'theories of management' is likely to be most useful to you when deciding how you will act once in a managerial post.

This activity should help you see why Sadie Rait's account of 'what management is all about' was identified earlier as a 'more realistic way' of talking about that activity than the way Mark and Harry 'framed' managerial work. Pragmatist thinking suggests that anyone doing managerial work is likely to be more effective at whatever they are trying to do in that job if they recognise that:

● 'management' is done by non-managers as well as managers;
● that managerial work involves *both* dealing directly with 'people' and setting up structures and procedures.

Mark and Harry's 'theories of management' were much more simplistic than this and would tend to be less helpful when it came to informing practice. They are less 'true' than Sadie's account in the sense that they would be less useful as indicators of 'how things work' in managerial activities and would thus be less useful when it comes to informing practice.

One way in which this broad principle of utility applies to all scientific thinking is in science's use of concepts.

Concepts   *Concept*

Concepts are the working definitions that are chosen or devised to make possible a particular piece of scientific analysis. They are the way scientists define their terms for the purpose of a specific investigation. They therefore differ from dictionary definitions which tend to have a much more general applicability.

In our everyday lives, we are used to looking for *correct definitions* of phenomena, ones that will be generally helpful to us when communicating within a broad public language. If we wish to analyse phenomena with the greater degree of rigour and focus that distinguishes scientific analysis, however, we find ourselves having more carefully to *conceptualise* phenomena. This means devising working definitions which are helpful to us in trying to analyse and understand some aspect of the world. Thus an economist will conceptualise money more rigorously than the person in the street will 'define' it. Psychologists will do similarly with regard to 'intelligence' – working with different concepts of intelligence at different times. What this means is that in engaging in an enterprise like writing *Organising and Managing Work*, one develops concepts that are useful to one's purposes. One does not turn to a dictionary for the universally 'correct' definition. Thus, every time there is a 'defining of terms' in this book (usually using the device of a 'concept box'), it is done to be *helpful* to the purposes of the book – and *useful* to the readers who are interested in improving their understanding of how work is organised and managed. The whole enterprise of the book is based on the notion that some ways of conceptualising, 'management' or 'organisation', say, are more useful than others. The intent is not to find a 'correct' definition of what 'management' or 'organisation' is but to use concepts that help us critically engage with the world.

The pragmatist style of thinking is also relevant, in a very basic way, to the arguments set out earlier for the *critical analysis* of *Work Organisation and Management Studies*. Doing this, it was argued, involved appreciating that work organisation happens in a context of contest, inequality and conflict and that management ideas are more than neutral rules, principles or guides to action; they always have political significance. Knowledge of organisations and management which gives full recognition to these matters, according to the pragmatist principles, would be better – as a set of resources for informing practice – than knowledge which ignored them. This is because an organisational practitioner, managerial or non-managerial, would be better placed to succeed in whatever their purposes might be if they were informed in this way. We might go as far as to say that an individual who tried to undertake any kind of organisational task without a strong awareness of the political dimension of organisational life would be a fool! It follows from this that critical thinking is equally relevant to a manager, a non-managerial worker or someone wishing to challenge and undermine the whole enterprise. To put this another way, there cannot be 'managerially biased' knowledge – other than inadequate or misleading knowledge. If there is work organisation knowledge which helpfully informs the practices, projects and purposes of managers, then it is likely to be equally helpful to anyone else operating in that context – including someone wishing to oppose 'managerial' initiatives. The same principle applies to other spheres of human activity: knowledge which helps a government rule can also help an opposition to bring it down; knowledge which helps a police force fight crime can equally help criminals carry out crimes more successfully, for example.

As far as *Organising and Managing Work* is concerned, everything in the book is intended to inform people involved in the management of work – whatever the nature of that involvement might be. The book should be helpful to those designated as 'managers'. But it should be equally relevant to someone whose 'project' is to have a quiet life at work, make an investment or customer decision about a work organisation or set out in some way to oppose the managers of an organisation. In this spirit, we now move forward in Chapters 2 and 3 to look at some of the major ways in which our understanding of organisations and managerial work is changing – and changing in a direction which can make it more effective than previously as a resource for informing our practices in the management of work.

Summary

In this chapter, the following key points have been made:

- The most helpful way to think about issues of work organisation and management is to focus on all those activities which contribute to the management of work tasks, only then considering how such activities are divided up between people who have the title of 'manager' and those which do not.

- There are both moral and practical problems with the notion of 'managing people'.

- Approaches to managerial work that focus on the 'management of structures and procedures' are equally inadequate.

- There are both 'people' elements and 'structure-procedure' aspects to managerial work, and both have to be taken into account both in thinking about management and engaging in it. Managerial work needs to be recognised as something which entails both directly relating to people and establishing working structures or procedures. The inter-play between these two aspects of management – and between the choices that are possible and the factors which influence those choices – is complex and will be a theme of much of what is to follow in later chapters.

- Although the academic subject of Organisational Behaviour has been the main vehicle for bringing social science thinking into the study of management and organisation, it has a number of inadequacies. The present book attempts to overcome many of these.

- Work Organisation and Management Studies, as a subject attempting to build upon and go beyond Organisational Behaviour, is linked with several other established and developing academic subjects, including management learning, critical management studies, strategic management and human resource management.

- Work Organisation and Management Studies is the study of the human aspects of work organisation and its management which draws on the social sciences to develop insights, theories and research findings with a view to informing the choices, decisions and actions of organisational practitioners.

- The social science disciplines drawn upon by *Organising and Managing Work*, and their analytical styles, are not essentially different from 'common sense' thinking. In fact, they have a close continuity with what can be called 'critical common sense'.

- In the spirit of 'critical common sense', the style of *Work Organisation and Management Studies* adopted here can be identified with certain aspects of the emergent tradition of 'critical management studies'. This entails continually asking, first, why work is organised and managed in the way it is and, second, why we think about and study work and its management in the ways we do. It also involves continuous recognition of the extent to which work organisation happens in a context of human competition, context and patterned antagonism as well as recognising that management ideas are not neutral technical rules and principles but always have political significance.

- To be able to relate what we study to issues of practice in the organisational and managerial world we need some criteria for judging the relative merits of the theories, research studies and other materials that are available to us. The most useful criterion we can apply to judging theories, and the rest, is one derived from pragmatist philosophy. There is no way of judging absolute truth or validity. But some accounts can be seen as 'truer' than others. It is suggested that one piece of material may be judged to be 'truer' than another to the extent to which it better informs human practices or 'projects' in the aspect of human activity with which it deals.

Reading

Reading Guides 1, 2, 4 and 13 contain material that supports and takes further much of what is covered in Chapter 1.

TOPIC SUMMARY SHEET

What are the key learning points from this topic?

TOPIC 2 – INDIVIDUAL DIFFERENCES AND PERCEPTION

E-tivity 1: Introduction

Why study this topic?

Throughout our working life most of us will meet many different people. They may be very different to us physically, socially, emotionally, or culturally. The challenge for today's organisation is to achieve an effective blend of people so that organisational goals can be met.

This chapter provides us with an insight as to how personality forms and develops. This enables us to begin to understand and appreciate how our own personality has been shaped and its impact on our own workplace activities. By gaining a knowledge of the main theories underpinning perception we can attempt to decipher the reasons behind the actions of ourselves and those around us. This makes it easier for us to attempt to modify behaviour patterns and improve our relationships with others.

Blackboard

E-tivity 2: Individual differences and perception

9 INDIVIDUAL DIFFERENCES
Linda Hicks

Individuals have different abilities, personalities, learning experiences and attitudes. It is not surprising that they perceive work in different ways. Differences between individuals can be a source of developing creativity or the root of conflict and frustration. The skill of management is to be able to match the needs of the individual with the needs of the organisation so goals can be met and satisfaction achieved. Emphasising individual differences and valuing diversity is a key driver in the search for equality at work.

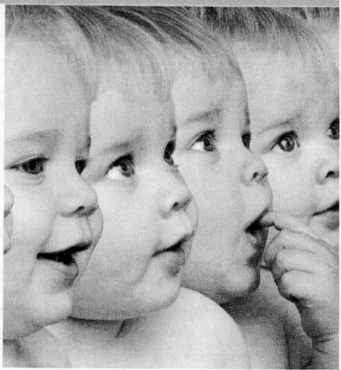

Photo: Bluestone/Science Photo Library

LEARNING OUTCOMES

After completing this chapter you should be able to:

► focus on the changing relationships at work and the significance of valuing difference and diversity;

► outline the importance of the individual's contribution to the organisation and factors affecting behaviour and performance;

► examine the major difficulties of studying personality and apply the key issues of personality studies to the work organisation;

► explain how differences in ability are identified and measured, and how psychological tests are used in the workplace;

► detail the significance of attitudes, their functions, change and measurement;

► apply the principles of attitude change to the workplace;

► examine the importance of gender research and organisational behaviour, and women's position and status.

Your own perspectives on problems are important when thinking about the many perspectives and views understood by all of the other people in the organization. Indeed, they are often your only and best guides. With personally different backgrounds, ethnicity, gender and socialization, no one can expect all individuals to view one event in the same way.

Bob Hamlin, Jane Keep and Ken Ash

Organization Change and Development: A Reflective Guide for Managers, Trainers and Developers, Financial Times Prentice Hall, (2001)

THE CHANGING NATURE AND SCOPE OF MANAGING INDIVIDUALS AT WORK

Managing relationships in the twenty-first century

Are organisations moving into a mature multi-cultural phase? Is there sensitivity within organisations to tackle issues of racism, sexism, and ageism? Are managers able to cope with the changes in structure, culture, work attitudes and expectations? Managing relationships at work has always been a key skill, but in the twenty-first century there are new demands for an unpredictable future. The speed at which organisations are undergoing change places continuous pressure on individuals at work. The paradox that 'change is now a constant feature' in organisational life has become a key feature in academic journals. Being able to manage the process of change is a necessity for all managers regardless of the size, type and nature of the organisation.

Although hierarchy and bureaucracy still exist in many organisations, the trend towards flatter, matrix-based structures has grown. It is commonplace for employees to work in project teams, to work at home, to communicate informally to colleagues and to cope with the juggling of family demands and work. Managers require skills that facilitate achievement through working with colleagues rather than dictating to subordinates. They need sensitivity to the work climate and they require skills, which will enable them to effect changes that foster well-being and satisfaction.

Equal opportunities to managing diversity

Future demographic patterns may also present new challenges for managers. Equality Direct[1] predicts that by the year 2010, 40 per cent of the labour force will be over 45 years of age. Alterations to the identity that individuals hold have also been apparent over the last decade. Devolution and regionalisation have increased and paradoxically so too has the trend towards greater integration into multinational groupings (in terms of both company mergers and political agendas). A complex range of possible identities and affiliations results. Consider a Scottish national living in the United States, working for a Japanese company and directing European markets: such a manager will have a diverse set of allegiances which may in turn affect motivation and morale. The growth of the portfolio worker and contract worker results in an employment relationship which is short term, instrumental and driven by outcomes and performance. Loyalty to the organisation and commitment to mission statements does not enter into such a partnership. The rise of consumerism in and out of the workplace has led to greater understanding and expectations of 'rights' and redress of perceived injustice. It is not only morally and socially acceptable to treat all people fairly in the workplace; legislation insists that managers do so.

The government is committed to protect individuals at work against discrimination in employment on the basis of sex, disability or race. Under the Race Relations Amendment Act 2000 there is a positive duty on public authorities to promote racial equality in the provision of services and to improve equal opportunities in employment. One of the specific duties required by public authorities is to prepare and publish a race equality scheme and assess, monitor and control functions and policies that have a bearing on race equality. Encouraging a diverse workforce is high on the government's agenda and the reluctant employer is having its hand forced by statutory obligations.

The business case

All these changes amount to a picture in which the white males will no longer dominate. Instead, we can anticipate a complex pattern where, ideally, individual differences will be valued and celebrated and, at the very least, equal opportunities practice will be observed. Personal qualities and characteristics that may have been downgraded, ignored or regarded as nuisance factors will be perceived as adding value. Organisations which embrace difference and **diversity** as opposed to those which are merely compliant will, it is claimed, succeed in a fiercely competitive climate. As J. M. Barry Gibson, Chief Executive of Littlewoods, has stated:

The fact is that if we effectively exclude women, ethnic minorities and disabled people we are fishing in a smaller pool for the best possible talent. As a service organisation, we ought to reflect the style, taste and opinions of our consumers, who of course represent sexes, all colours and creeds, all ages and disabilities. The main point is that cultural diversity will strengthen the quality of the company and will make us much more outward-looking.[2]

However, *Kirton and Greene*[3] believe that the 'business case' should be broadened to include wider issues of social justice and social responsibility. *Liff and Cameron*[4] argue that organisational culture needs to radically shift to win the 'hearts and minds rather than just achieve reluctant compliance'. In their article, which uses women as their illustration, they assert that there are real dangers in conventional equality measures. Focusing on women as having special problems requiring special treatment results in resentment and defensive attitudes from managers. They believe that one of the first essential stages to enact change is to consider the organisational culture and the way in which it could move to an equality culture. Further examination of equality practices will be discussed at the end of this chapter.

Defining diversity

Valuing differences is easier said than done. It means relating and working with people who hold different perspectives and views; bringing different qualities to the workplace; having different aspirations and having different customs and traditions. Differences are challenging; they challenge people's views, perceptions and attitudes and require individuals to see things from a different frame of reference. Managing diversity does not mean that managers champion their own values and try and shift other people's values to conform and match their own! For *Kandola and Fullerton* diversity is defined as:

The basic concept of managing diversity accepts that the workforce consists of a diverse population of people. The diversity consists of visible and non-visible differences which will include sex, age, background, race, disability, personality and workstyle. It is founded on the premise that harnessing these differences will create a productive environment in which everybody feels valued, where their talents are being fully utilised, and in which organisational goals are met.[5]

Encouraging individuality and at the same time expecting group co-operation and teamwork are potential triggers for tension. It requires managers to have greater reserves of emotional intelligence if they are to be successful managers of diversity. In turn this suggests that managers need to have an awareness of, and be able to get in touch with, their own attitudes, values and beliefs – what they are and where they come from. *Clements and Jones* recognise that the process can be uncomfortable:

A model of good diversity training will recognize that when people engage in an exploration of their attitudes, values, beliefs and prejudices, this may be an uncomfortable process. Some will find out things about themselves that will cause them emotional pain, and often the tension in learners will relate to how they should respond.[6]

Significance of emotional intelligence

Recognising and understanding the implications of emotions and being able to accurately self-assess one's inner resources, abilities and limits are key to becoming an emotionally intelligent leader. Being able to read the emotional currents are important skills for managers to develop and employ. It requires them to know and understand the individuals within their teams and the way in which the individuals relate and interact.

At no time is this more important that when selecting a new member to join the team. Recruiting and selecting committed company staff who offer valuable individuality is a key to an organisation's health and effectiveness. The criteria used to reject or accept applicants are a major indicator of an organisation's values and beliefs. The selection process has been described as a 'cultural sieve'[7] and as an important method of control.[8] Indeed *Tom Peters*[9] has suggested that organisations need to review their selection requirements and, instead of checking that every minute of every day is accounted for when appointing applicants, they should consider applicants who have 'broken out' from the mould, rebelled from the system and thus demonstrated original thought. Peters regards such personal qualities as key attributes for leading-edge organisations.

However, this individualistic approach contrasts with the notion that organisations need team players who will be co-operative. As soon as the new recruits begin their employment a 'psychological contract' is struck which forms the basis for obedience and conformity expected of the employees by the company. The manager's responsibility is to ensure that the socialisation process enables the new recruits to quickly learn the rules of the system. Rewards, if given at this stage, for correct behaviour and attitudes, will promote conformity and provide further incentives for the individuals to match the organisation's needs. (The recruitment and selection of staff is discussed in Chapter 20.)

Recognition of individuality

Recognition of good performers and performance is an essential part of the process of management. Managing people in organisations requires not only an understanding of the employees, but also a recognition of the culture of the organisation; for some organisations, creativity and individuality may be the last thing they would want to see between 9 and 5, but for others these characteristics are essential.

A discussion of individual behaviour in organisations is therefore riddled with complexity and contradictions! Managers are required to be competent at selecting the individuals who will be valuable to the organisation. They need to be observant about the individuals who are performing well and have the potential to develop within the organisation. They also need to be able to value difference and be sensitive to contrasting needs. Finally managers need to know themselves and understand their own uniqueness and the impact their personality has on others.

Organisation change and individual differences

Sensitivity to individual needs and differences especially in terms of their resilience becomes significant when organisations embark on change initiatives. Even when the change appears to be relatively straightforward (e.g. introduction of a new computer system) the reality is more likely to be messy and complex. When organisations are working through change and when change appears to be externally imposed, the management of people takes on a different dimension in terms of the sensitivity required. In this situation there is an implicit requirement of changes in attitudes and beliefs. Such changes may lead to new mind-sets, new attitudes and new perceptions which enable people to cope and adjust to the different world. At these times effective management is vital; managers will be expected to understand the strains that their employees feel during times of change, but at the same time be able to deal with their own stress levels.

This part of the book addresses the ways in which it is possible to differentiate between individuals. Personality, the heart of individual differences, is explored first in this chapter. The emotional demands required by organisations of their employees are identified and discussed. There then follows an examination of the importance and functions of attitudes. This leads to a discussion where we focus on the gender dimension in organisations. In addition to analysing the historical, psychological and societal context we will also consider issues related to the implementation of equality practices. An understanding of the ways in which people learn is fundamental to an appreciation of individual differences and is considered in Chapter 10. The process of perception and the impact of gender differences are examined in Chapter 11.

PERSONALITY

Our sense of self is shaped by our inherited characteristics and by influences in our social environment. The process of growing up – such as the impact of our early family life, the country in which we live – has a significant part to play in our identity. Most social scientists would agree that both inherited and environmental factors are important in our development, and it is the way in which these factors interact which is the key to our adult personality. However, scientists differ with regard to the weight they place on these factors – some believing that our personality is heavily influenced by our inherited characteristics and will never change, with others believing the reverse.

This section of the chapter will unpack the major theories of personality and will look at the implications for organisations and managing people. Using psychometric instruments to measure personality will be reviewed towards the end of the section.

But first, how do individuals differ?

- Ethnic origin
- Physique
- Gender

- Early family experiences
- Social and cultural factors
- National culture

- Motivation
- Attitudes

- Personality traits and types
- Intelligence and abilities
- Perception

Some of these characteristics are shared with others, for example individuals who are from the same ethnic group, or who have the same ability levels or who share similar physical attributes such as short-sightedness. But our uniqueness stems from the dynamic ways in which these inherited and environmental factors combine and interact with each other.

What is meant by the term personality?

Psychologists have defined it as consisting of stable characteristics which explain why a person behaves in a particular way. So for instance, independence, conscientiousness, agreeableness, self-control would be examples of these personality characteristics. However, it is only when we see/hear a person that we can gain an understanding of their personality. So for instance a person who is independent may show that characteristic by showing a strong sense of self-sufficiency. We would expect him or her to take initiative and not to depend on other people. Furthermore, if the characteristic is 'stable' we can rely on this being a consistent part of the person's behaviour. We would be surprised if the person on one day demonstrated autonomy and initiative and on the next withdrew and delayed any decisions. We anticipate that individuals are generally consistent in the way in which they respond to situations.

There are times when we might be surprised by somebody's behaviour and we may feel they are 'acting out of character'. Of course this would only be known if we had an understanding of their 'typical behaviour' in the first place. Individuals may exaggerate or suppress certain personality traits if they are under stress or influenced by drink/drugs. It is self-evident that managers should have a keen interest in the characteristics and behaviour of their team and should be able to discern when a team member is behaving inconsistently.

Dynamics – the key to understanding personality

Psychological research into personality can develop the manager's skills in observing and assessing personality and behaviour. Psychologists tend to specialise and focus their research on one of the features listed above. Clearly, this is essential for scientific enquiry but, when applying theories to people at work, it is important to remember that a holistic view should be taken which takes into account the dynamic processes. If we consider the interaction of a person with a high intelligence score and a strong sense of honesty, the dynamics will result in a completely different set of behaviour patterns to someone with high intelligence and a tendency towards dishonesty. We could predict a very different set of attitudes too. To have a 'whole' understanding of the individual at work, we must take into account the ways in which an individual's traits interact. We must go beyond the study of pure psychology and evaluate the extent to which their studies can be applied in practice.

The application of theory to the world of work is not always easy and some students find the process confusing when the theory does not match with their own experiences. Psychological investigations emphasise the complexity and variety of individual behaviour and insist that simple answers and explanations are generally inadequate. Students may therefore have to adjust their attitudes and perceptions about the world and for some this experience may be uncomfortable. The study of personality provides an excellent example of some of the complexities involved in applying psychological theory in practice.

Let us consider two individuals who share similar characteristics. They are both 24 years old, and have lived in the same area; both have a first class honours degree in engineering and they have identical personality assessment profiles. However, we would still predict differences with regard to their attitude and performance in the workplace. In addition, differences would be predicted in the ways that they interacted with others and in the ways that others interacted with them. If one of the engineers was female and/or Asian, a further set of assumptions might start to appear. It is not only the features themselves which identify individuals as being different but it is also their interaction which leads to a unique pattern of behaviour. The complexities of the process pose a number of interesting questions which psychologists have tried to solve and in this context it is not surprising perhaps that differing theories and ideas have evolved. (See Tables 9.1 and 9.2.)

Table 9.1 Dilemma 1 – The role of early experiences

To what extent is our personality constant throughout life?	
Solution (a) – Adaptable	*Solution (b) – Constant*
If we consider the two young engineers described above, it could be argued that the personality of each is a culmination of experiences. Their personalities have been shaped by the people around them from their very earliest years. Early family life – the relationship between family members, the size of the family, the rewards and punishments exercised by parents – would have had an influence on the type of person each is now. In other words, the environment and early learning experiences have contributed to their personality development.	Perhaps the young engineers have a core-inherited part of their personality which has remained resistant to change. The way in which they have responded to the world has remained consistent with their true 'self'.

Table 9.2 Dilemma 2 – Assessment of personality

Is it possible to 'measure' an individual's personality?

Solution (a) Yes, there are identifiable traits.
Identifying an individual's personality typically refers to distinguishing traits or types. For instance, Joe is an introvert (type); he is placid, quiet and reflective. John, however, is an extrovert (type); he is excitable, sociable and loud. Personality traits are usually identified by what people do, the behaviour they exhibit. This is the way that all of us would normally describe another's personality. Some psychologists, instead of watching behaviour, ask questions about behaviour which the individual answers on a paper questionnaire. They would assert that asking a person to report on the way they feel or behave is a legitimate way of assessing personality. These self-reporting questionnaires would then be subject to quantitative methods. Thus, psychologists have made it possible to quantify the strength of a person's trait and to enable comparisons to be made with others. Such information then becomes a basis for prediction. For example, if a person has a high score on extroversion, it would be possible to predict the way in which the individual might behave in a given situation. These measuring techniques are subject to some controversy.

Solution (b) No, personality is unique.
Do people always reveal their true 'self'? Is it possible that circumstances may force them to behave in a way that is unlike their 'typical' behaviour? Or do people choose to act in a certain way because they think it is appropriate? Is it possible to measure the 'strength' of a trait? Can people reliably report on their own behaviour or is there a real difference between what people say and what people do? Instead of requiring individuals to respond to set questions, it may be more appropriate to use open-ended techniques. This ensures that individuals use their own definitions, and allows for greater understanding about their motivations and causes of behaviour.

Figure 9.1 identifies the links between the dynamics of **personality** and life's experiences.

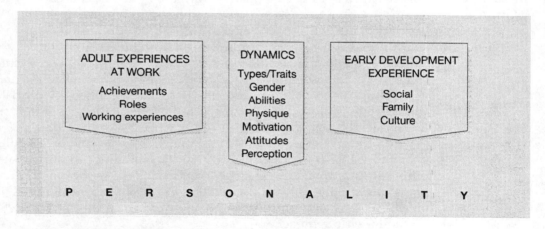

Figure 9.1 To what extent does our personality remain constant?

Uniqueness and similarities

The dilemmas described in Tables 9.1 and 9.2 focus on two major issues of prime importance in the study of personality. First, is personality a constant throughout our lifetime, which remains resistant to change and circumstances? Second, to what extent can we measure and compare individuals on the basis of their personality? This second question assumes that it is possible to distinguish personality characteristics in the first place. Psychologists have produced various theories to solve both these dilemmas and one of the ways of making sense of these theories is to see them working at different levels. (*See* Table 9.3.)

In a work context we tend to be more interested in understanding 'what' the personality is like, rather than why it is as it is. Furthermore it is important to understand how various personality characteristics relate to performance at work. The nomothetic approach described next explores the 'what' of personality and the idiographic approach enriches our understanding of 'why'.

Table 9.3 Different levels of personality research

Level	Psychologists' research interests
Level 3 ☺ ☺ ☺ ☺ ☺ ☺ ☺ ☺ ☺ ☺ ☺ ☺ Universal human features	Common human aspirations
LEVEL 2 ☺ ☺ ☺ ☺ ☺ ☺ ☺ ☺ Some shared features – gender; ability	Identification, measurements, comparison (nomothetic)
LEVEL 1 ☺ Unique combination of features	'Self' – Unique interaction with the world (idiographic)

NOMOTHETIC AND IDIOGRAPHIC APPROACHES

Broadly speaking, personality studies can be divided into two main approaches which have been labelled nomothetic and idiographic.

Nomothetic approaches

Nomothetic approaches are primarily concerned with the collection of group data. This means that such theorists accumulate evidence with regard to the identification of personality traits and produce effective measurements of the traits in order to draw comparisons between individuals. Being able to predict behaviour is a major aim and outcome of this approach. Researchers closely align themselves to studies which are 'scientific' in a positivistic sense. (The term positivism refers to the branch of science which is exclusively based on the objective collection of observable data – data which are beyond question.) Such an approach transfers methods used in natural sciences to the social world.

Nomothetic approaches tend to view environmental and social influences as minimal and view personality as consistent, largely inherited and resistant to change. Although they would not diminish the difficulties that measuring personality brings, nomothetic approaches would claim that it is possible to measure and predict the ways in which personality types would behave given certain circumstances.[10]

Nomothetic approaches would:

- solve dilemma 1 with solution (b) in Table 9.1;
- solve dilemma 2 with solution (a) in Table 9.2; and
- focus on level 2 as described in Table 9.3.

Idiographic approaches

Idiographic approaches are concerned with understanding the uniqueness of individuals and the development of the self concept. They regard personality development as a process which is open to change. They regard individuals as responding to the environment and people around them, and see the dynamics of the interactions as playing a critical part in shaping personality. The measurement of traits is seen as largely inappropriate in that one person's responses may not be comparable to another's. They suggest that personality assessment is not a valid method of understanding the unique ways in which a person understands and responds to the world. The depth and richness of a person's personality cannot be revealed in superficial paper-and-pencil questionnaires. Furthermore, the categories defined by psychologists are too narrow in scope and depth.

Idiographic approaches would:

- solve dilemma 1 with solution (a) in Table 9.1;
- solve dilemma 2 with solution (b) in Table 9.2; and
- focus on level 1 as described in Table 9.3.

Complementary approaches Some researchers do not fit easily into either of these two broad approaches. *Freud*, for instance, is idiographic in the sense that he is interested in the self and its development, but his theory does not allow for personality growth and change after childhood.[11] *Kelly's* Personal Construct Theory also bridges the two approaches.[12] His theory will be explored later in this chapter.

The approaches can be seen as complementary; indeed, it could be argued that different foci are important in understanding the many complicated facets of personality.

THEORETICAL APPROACHES: NOMOTHETIC

The two main theories discussed under this approach are:

- Eysenck's theory of main personality types; and
- Cattell's identification of personality traits.

Eysenck

Hans Eysenck followed a tradition of writers by applying the four basic types introduced by Hippocrates: melancholic; sanguine; phlegmatic; and choleric. Eysenck's approach was influenced by the positivistic tradition; his aim was to produce objective evidence of personality differences using large samples of the population. By investigating 700 servicemen, he was able to use rigorous statistical data to test his hypotheses.[13] His findings supported the notion that there were two major differences which could be measured: extroversion and stability (*see* Figure 9.2).

Individuals in Eysenck's theory could, therefore, be one of four main personality types. The type would lead to a predisposition of traits which would, itself, lead to the likelihood of certain behaviours. For instance, a person typed as an extrovert would be responsive and outgoing and in a new social situation s/he would predictably initiate conversation among a group of strangers. Eysenck's theory and his subsequent Personality Inventory allowed identification of a personality type. From this description,

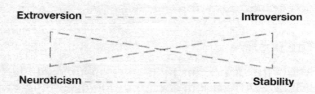

Figure 9.2 Eysenck's personality types

it was possible to predict likely behaviours. Eysenck had a clear view about the constancy of personality. He believed that personality was largely inherited and that introverts and extroverts are born with differing physiological tendencies. Furthermore, he argued that the personality we are born with is largely unalterable by environmental influences.

Supporting research evidence

Although it could be argued that Eysenck's theory is too simplistic in terms of the number and range of types proposed, his theory has an impressive amount of supporting research evidence. His approach has immediate appeal to managers in organisations who are concerned with predicting the future behaviour of their employees, either for selection or promotion.

Furnham surmises whether personality changes if an individual is in a job that is ill-suited to his/her personality. He cites research, which indicates that personality scores change as a result of being exposed to a different and challenging environment.[14] Given the evidence that personality is a useful predictor of behaviour it is not surprising that the use of psychometric tests has grown substantially over the past decade and that the majority of large companies use occupational tests.[15] (Further information about testing is given later in this chapter.)

Cattell

Cattell's work resembles Eysenck's in the methods used to study personality. He used quantitative, objective techniques in order to analyse his data (although he used a different factor analytic measure), and followed traditional scientific procedures in order to understand the basic dimensions of personality.[16] Cattell used three main sources for the collection of personality data.

1 **L-data** (life record data) – ratings by trained observers.
2 **Q-data** (self-rating questionnaire) – responses to a questionnaire which measured personality traits (Cattell 16PF Questionnaire).
3 **T-data** (test data) – observations collected in specific situation tests.

Personality factors

The data collected were factor-analysed by Cattell resulting in the identification of two main types of personality traits:

- **surface traits** – which seem to cluster together consistently; and
- **source traits** – which seem to underlie and determine the traits which are likely to 'surface' into behaviour.

Cattell identified 16 personality factors (or source traits). (*See* Table 9.4.)[17]

Unlike Eysenck, he did not 'type' individuals but used 'traits' as his main personality descriptor (although there is much similarity between Cattell's second-order factors and Eysenck's 'types'). They also differed with regard to the determinants of personality: Eysenck viewed the inherited physiological basis as the main determinant, whereas Cattell was more interested in taking social factors into account when understanding an individual's personality. Both theorists have contributed to a lively debate about personality structure and its measurement, and in doing so have advanced the selection techniques available to managers.[18]

The Big Five

Identifying the personality traits, which seem to be particularly dominant in distinguishing individuals, has been the dominant subject of personality research in UK and

Table 9.4 Cattell's personality factors

Factor	High score	Low score
A	Outgoing	Reserved
B	More intelligent (abstract thinker)	Less intelligent (concrete thinker)
C	Higher ego strength (Emotionally stable)	Lower ego strength (Emotionally unstable)
E	Dominant	Submissive
F	Surgency (optimistic)	Desurgency (pessimistic)
G	Stronger superego strength (conscientious)	Weaker superego strength (expedient)
H	Parmia (adventurous)	Threctia (timid)
I	Presmia (tender-minded)	Harria (tough-minded)
L	Protension (suspicious)	Alaxia (trusting)
M	Autia (imaginative)	Praxernia (practical)
N	Shrewdness	Artlessness (unpretentious)
O	Insecure – guilt-proneness	Self-assured
Q1	Radicalism	Conservatism
Q2	Self-sufficiency	Group dependence
Q3	High self-concept control (controlled)	Low self-concept control (casual)
Q4	High ergic tension (tense, frustrated)	Low ergic tension (relaxed, tranquil)

(Adapted and reproduced with permission from Cattell, R. B. and Kline, P., *The Scientific Analysis of Personality and Motivation*, Academic Press (1977) Table 4.1, pp. 44–5.)

USA. There is now a body of evidence, which suggests that five dimensions capture distinct differences between people. These traits, known as the Big Five,[19] are:

- extroversion/introversion
- agreeableness/hostility
- conscientiousness/heedlessness
- emotional stability/instability
- openness or intellect/closed-mindedness

Results from a wide number of studies have shown that these factors can be identified as being significant in measuring the variation between people.[20] Of these, conscientiousness is linked to high levels of job knowledge and performance across a range of different occupations. The strength and value of the Big Five model has been extolled in a review by *Lord and Rust*. They conclude that:

> *Indeed, the five factor model has become the linchpin that holds personality assessment together, at least within the work context. Without it, how would we generalize with confidence from the validity of one work-based instrument to that of another? Furthermore, the model links the study of assessment instruments within the HR field to research in personality and related areas carried out within clinical and mainstream psychology fields in which the Big Five have also become dominant.[21]*

However, some researchers are critical of the descriptors used.[22] *Bentall*[23] suggests they are 'tainted by the investigators' values' and continues: 'I suspect that most people will have a pretty clear idea of where they would like to find themselves on the dimensions of neuroticism, extraversion, openness, agreeableness and conscientiousness.' He questions the ethical and political nature of the scales.

THEORETICAL APPROACHES: IDIOGRAPHIC

Idiographic approaches emphasise the development of the individual and of individuals' views of themselves – their self concept. Supporters of idiographic approaches are critical of the nomothetic approach which attempts to categorise individuals on the basis of group data. They argue that the techniques used to collate the group data are questionable and the outcome inappropriate to an understanding of personality. For the idiographic researchers, personality is expressed through the experiences and development of the individual. It cannot be understood outside a social context and has to be studied in the light of individuals' own perceptions of their world. Idiographic researchers would always take into account the social circumstances of the person and in particular the relationships with others, family life and social conditions. The following theories are typical examples of the idiographic approach.

- *Carl Rogers*'s theory claims that personality is embedded within personal relationships. He emphasised the importance of fulfilment and psychological growth, placing at the centre people's knowledge of their own feelings. For Rogers, the expression of emotion was critical in freeing up people's autonomy and creativity in the quest for self-actualisation. The process of becoming a person requires the ability to give and receive unconditional regard – the warmth and respect for the *person*, who they *are*, regardless of how they behave.[24]
- *G. H. Mead* was unable to separate the notion of an individual's personality from the concept of society. He claimed that:

   A person is a personality because he belongs to a community, because he takes over the institutions of that community into his own conduct.[25]

As individuals we can only have a sense of self in relation to others. He proposed the idea that the self has two components: one which is spontaneous and unique (I), and the other which is learnt through exposure to society (me).

- *C. Cooley*, like Mead, emphasised the importance of early development and socialisation. He believed the emotion and sensation that we hold of 'self' was instinctive but was developed by experience. His phrase 'the looking-glass self' suggests that we come to know ourselves through our relationship with others and their reactions to us.[26]

Erikson

Erik Erikson's theory is a good example of the idiographic approach. He viewed personality development as continuing throughout life. He was interested in the effect of experiences on the development of the self concept and how different individuals resolved personal conflicts.[27]

Although he recognised the importance of early childhood in establishing certain basic concepts of trust, autonomy and initiative, he disagreed with *Freud's* emphasis on the effects of early development. (*See* section below.)

Tensions and conflicts

For Erikson, all eight stages of life produce different tensions and conflicts which have to be resolved. (*See* Table 9.5.)

Successful resolution produces a healthy personality, whereas difficulties in earlier stages may produce problems later on. Erikson's theory not only makes considerable sense in terms of face validity (i.e., 'it feels right' factor) but also links with other research indicating that managers' motivations and goals change with age. *Hunt*, for instance, identified nine different career/life stages.[28]

Table 9.5 Erikson's eight stages of personality development

Stage 1	Trust	v	Mistrust	1st year
Stage 2	Autonomy	v	Doubt	2–3 years
Stage 3	Initiative	v	Guilt	4–5 years
Stage 4	Industry	v	Inferiority	6–11 years
Stage 5	Identity	v	Role confusion	12–18 years
Stage 6	Intimacy	v	Isolation	Young adult
Stage 7	Generativity	v	Self-absorption	Middle age
Stage 8	Integrity	v	Despair	Old age

(*Source*: Adapted from Erikson, E. H. *Identity and The Life Cycle*, Norton (1980) Worksheet Table Appendix. © 1980 by W.W. Norton & Company, Inc. © 1959 by International Universities Press, Inc. Used by permission of W.W. Norton & Company Inc.)

OTHER THEORETICAL APPROACHES

Other significant theoretical approaches include:

- **Psychoanalytic approaches** – *Sigmund Freud* and neo-Freudians; and
- **Cognitive approaches** – *George Kelly*.

Freud

A discussion on personality would not be complete without a mention of *Sigmund Freud* (1856–1939). His psychoanalytic approach emphasised the importance of:

- early childhood experiences, particularly parental relationships and dealing with trauma;
- different levels of consciousness and the influence of the unconscious mind on behaviour;
- understanding the 'whole' person in relation to their past.[29]

Early childhood experiences were seen by Freud as paramount in understanding the adult personality. He described the development of all individuals as one which progressed through a number of stages: (i) oral; (ii) anal; and (iii) phallic (*see* Figure 9.3).

These changes are, for Freud, significant in that if the child finds the stage too difficult and the conflicts too hard and traumatic, an arrested development or 'fixation' could result. This means that the problems associated with the stage may be relived at a later time in adult life.

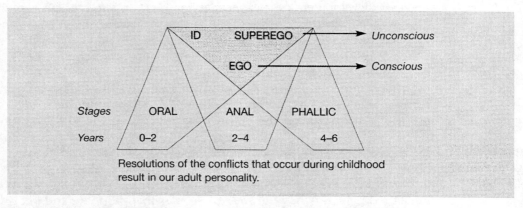

Figure 9.3 Representation of Freud's personality theory, development and structure

Freud's stages highlight the importance of the parent–child relationship. If the child finds the stage too problematic and the change results in a 'battle' between parent and child, the likelihood of the stage becoming fixated is higher. A fixation at the oral stage of development may result in the adult gratifying his/her oral needs in stressful situations as an adult. They may resort to cigarettes, chocolate, drink or they may be verbally aggressive or sarcastic to others.

An inner force (or libido) was also identified by Freud. The libido was seen as a universal human characteristic which provides the necessary life energy for progression through the developmental stages.

The personality structure of the individual develops as the child comes to terms with the new changes at each stage of life. Each stage was characterised by an internal struggle of domination by three personality structures – the **id**, **ego** and **superego** – as well as external conflict with outside relationships (*see* Figure 9.3).

- **Id** consists of the instinctive, hedonistic part of self. *Gross* described the baby at birth as:

  > bundles of id ... whenever we act on impulse, selfishly, or demand something here and now, it is our id controlling our behaviour at those times.[30]

  It is governed by the pleasure principle.
- **Superego** is the conscience of the self, the part of our personality which is influenced by significant others in our life.

  The id and superego are in conflict with each other, with the id desiring certain behaviours and the superego attempting to discipline and control behaviour.
- **Ego** has to make sense of the internal conflict in our mind between the id and superego and the external world. The ego is the decision-making part of our personality and is engaged in rational and logical thinking. It is governed by the reality principle.

These conflicts and tensions, rooted in the past and repressed within the unconscious, were seen by Freud as the key to an understanding of adult personality.

Freud's theory has been heavily criticised on the grounds that:

- it is not replicable and his arguments were circular;
- samples used were atypical;
- it is subjective and unscientific;
- a heavy emphasis on early childhood makes it highly deterministic; and
- it disregards later development and changes.

His theory should, however, be seen in its historical context and in terms of its impact upon the development of later theories and ideas. In a recent review of Freudian theory *Andrews and Brewin*[31] cite research supporting oral and anal tendencies and offer support for some of his ideas on depression and paranoia. Freud was also given positive review concerning 'slips of the tongue'. These incidents occur when what was actually said was not intended. For Freud 'slips of the tongue' illustrate the conflict that can exist between our mental forces and the struggle we have in suppressing our desires. In this review, *Reason* suggests that slips do indeed represent 'minor eruptions of unconscious processing' but would caution the idea that all slips were in some way intentional.[32]

Applications to organisational behaviour

With regard to organisational behaviour, Freud's theory still has much to offer with respect to understanding stress at work. When the going gets tough it is easy to slip into habitual ways of responding that have been learned as children. Within the working context, such behaviour may be seen as inappropriate and yet bring immediate relief or comfort to the individual. Instances include regressing into temper tantrums or gaining relief by excessive eating or drinking and can be seen to protect the ego from a painful memory or unwanted impulse. Freud labelled these **defence mechanisms**. The most readily observable ones in the workplace include:

- **Regression** – adopting childhood patterns of behaviour;
- **Fixation** – inflexible and rigid behaviour or attitudes;
- **Rationalisation** – elaborate 'covering-up' of ideas/motives;
- **Projection** – attributing feelings and motives to others.

(*See* also the discussion on frustrated behaviour in Chapter 12.)

Interest in the power of the unconscious has led some writers to consider the impact of repressed desires and wishes on organisational behaviour. These have been succinctly reviewed by *Gareth Morgan*[33] who uses the metaphor of a 'Psychic Prison' to visualise and emphasise its power. Such an image suggests that people are trapped by their unconscious. As prisoners of their personal history, they are constantly struggling to control their unwanted impulses which leads to repression and dysfunctional activities at work. *Kets de Vries*[34] explores some of this 'underworld' within leaders of organisations and examines some of the crises points in his book *Organizational Paradoxes*. His case studies illustrate the tensions that occur at different life stages; for instance at mid-career there can be a crisis if an executive has not reached his or her work goal.

> *They will be angry at their present situation and blame others for their misfortunes. Unable to reconcile themselves to their lack of appreciable gains, they may fall back into paranoiac hostility or adult delinquency, or take flight in illness.*

In summary, Freud saw adult personality as being largely determined by the strength of inner drives and impulses and the resolutions of these tensions within early childhood experiences. Freud's overwhelming interest lay in understanding the conflicts that exist for the person and how people come to terms with their anxieties and tensions. His interest therefore lay in understanding the whole person and not in identifying traits or types.

Neo-Freudians   Freud produced a generation of scholars who developed his ideas to produce their own theories and models of personality development. Although of course rooted in Freudian thinking, the neo-Freudians have deviated from Freud in important respects. Two of the most significant are *Karen Horney* and *Melanie Klein*.

- Although *Karen Horney* accepted certain principles of Freud's theory with regard to unconscious motivation, she disagreed with the predominance of sexual forces and her theory suggests far more optimism than Freud's.[35]
- *Melanie Klein* encouraged the study of the sources of anxiety. She suggested that the principal source of anxiety was the fear of the death instinct. She posited that early childhood is a critical time for the formulation and development of lifelong mental attitudes.

Jung

Carl Jung's theory is of particular significance in that it bridges Freudian ideas with modern approaches of personality test design. His theory identifies life energy as concerned with hopes and goals of the future and not just of the past. Unlike Freud, Jung describes three levels of personality:

- a conscious level (daily reality);
- an unconscious level (contains our own unique complexes); and
- a collective unconscious level (store of universal and evolutionary experiences).

Jung identified four universal aspects of our personality which he referred to as archetypes which we all share. For instance, according to Jung, we all strive for self-actualisation; have a darker self; have both masculine and feminine qualities; and have a persona – a role we can play.[36]

Personality functions and attitudes

However, it was Jung's identification of personality functions and attitudes which was applied to the rigours of systematic testing by *Isabel Briggs-Myers* and *Katherine Briggs*.[37] Jung identified differences between individuals in terms of their libidinal energy which could flow outwards to the external world (extrovert) or inwards to their inner world (introvert). Personality differences would also be manifest through differing cognitive functions of thinking, feeling, sensation and intuition. The **Myers–Briggs Type Indicator (MBTI)** is based on these theoretical constructs with the additional dimension of style of living. The personality types are shown in Figure 9.4.

The MBTI has promoted considerable research interest, particularly with regard to the correlation between personality type, occupations and management style. Myers-Briggs assert that people tend to be attracted to and have the most satisfaction in work that allows them to express and use their psychological type preferences. Such a match enables them to handle their tasks more effectively and generates more energy. Confidence is a likely outcome of this process. The Myers-Briggs instrument is an affirmatory tool and knowledge gained through using the MBTI can lead to recognition and respect for differences between people and appreciation and regard for the value such differences bring.

COGNITIVE THEORY: KELLY'S PERSONAL CONSTRUCT THEORY

Kelly's theory of personal constructs does not just consider personality development; it considers the whole person in terms of their perceptions, attitudes and goals. For Kelly, personality is the individual's way of construing and experimenting with their world. Kelly was critical of separating the study of personality apart from the 'whole' person:

> *The castrating effect of separating personality off as a mini-psychology in its own right is perhaps best seen in the curiously named study of 'individual differences', which in fact turns out to be the study of group sameness. As a result we have focused on the establishment of general dimensions, at some point along which all individuals can be placed, rather than on a study of the dimensions which each individual develops in order to organise his own world.*[38]

For Kelly it was critical to take data from one individual person (idiography) and to employ a technique which could cope with the qualitative nature of the data to be collected. He developed the Repertory Grid which was able to measure an individual's construct of the world. Kelly was thus able to employ a clear and valid measure within an idiographic approach. This was an important advance in idiographic techniques and the repertory technique has become increasingly important as a research tool. It enables the person to use his/her own constructions of the world but in such a way that they are comparable and measurable.

Illustration of Kelly's repertory grid technique

An example of the repertory grid technique is provided from a case study by *Fiona Wilson*. The research examined the impact of computer numerical control (CNC) technology in the engineering industry. Its main objective was to explore the effect of new technology on the responses of both craftsmen and managers in two differing companies. One of the research measures used to explore the subjective experiences of the workers was Kelly's Repertory Grid. Wilson describes it as a 'formalised conversation' and says that 'It is an attempt to stand in others' shoes, to see their world as they see it, to understand their situation, their concerns'.[39]

	Sensing types		Intuitive types	
Introverts	**ISTJ** Quiet, serious, earn success by thoroughness and dependability. Practical, matter-of-fact, realistic and responsible. Decide logically what should be done and work towards it steadily, regardless of distractions. Take pleasure in making everything orderly and organised – their work, their home, their life. Value traditions and loyalty.	**ISFJ** Quiet, friendly, responsible, and conscientious. Committed and steady in meeting their obligations. Thorough, painstaking and accurate. Loyal, considerate, notice and remember specifics about people who are important to them, concerned with how others feel. Strive to create an orderly and harmonious environment at work and at home.	**INFJ** Seek meaning and connection in ideas, relationships and material possessions. Want to understand what motivates people and are insightful about others. Conscientious and committed to their firm values. Develop a clear vision about how best to serve the common good. Organised and decisive in implementing their vision.	**INTJ** Have original minds and great drive for implementing their ideas and achieving their goals. Quickly see patterns in external events and develop long-range explanatory perspectives. When committed, organise a job and carry it through. Sceptical and independent, have high standards of competence and performance – for themselves and others.
	ISTP Tolerant and flexible, quiet observers until a problem appears, then act quickly to find workable solutions. Analyse what makes things work and readily get through large amounts of data to isolate the core of practical problems. Interested in cause and effect, organise facts using logical principles, value efficiency.	**ISFP** Quiet, friendly, sensitive and kind. Enjoy the present moment, what's going on around them. Like to have their own space and to work within their own time frame. Loyal and committed to their values and to people who are important to them. Dislike disagreements and conflicts, do not force their opinions or values on others.	**INFP** Idealistic, loyal to their values and to people who are important to them. Want an external life that is congruent with their values. Curious, quick to see possibilities, can be catalysts for implementing ideas. Seek to understand people and to help them fulfil their potential. Adaptable, flexible and accepting unless a value is threatened.	**INTP** Seek to develop logical explanations for everything that interests them. Theoretical and abstract, interested more in ideas than in social interaction. Quiet, contained, flexible and adaptable. Have unusual ability to focus in depth to solve problems in their area of interest. Sceptical, sometimes critical, always analytical.
Extroverts	**ESTP** Flexible and tolerant, they take a pragmatic approach focused on immediate results. Theories and conceptual explanations bore them – they want to act energetically to solve the problem. Focus on the here-and-now, spontaneous, enjoy each moment that they can be active with others. Enjoy material comforts and style. Learn best through doing.	**ESFP** Outgoing, friendly and accepting. Exuberant lovers of life, people and material comforts. Enjoy working with others to make things happen. Bring common sense and a realistic approach to their work, and make work fun. Flexible and spontaneous, adapt readily to new people and environments. Learn best by trying a new skill with other people.	**ENFP** Warmly enthusiastic and imaginative. See life as full of possibilities. Make connections between events and information very quickly, and confidently proceed based on the patterns they see. Want a lot of affirmation from others, and readily give appreciation and support. Spontaneous and flexible, often rely on their ability to improvise and their verbal fluency.	**ENTP** Quick, ingenious, stimulating, alert and outspoken. Resourceful in solving new and challenging problems. Adept at generating conceptual possibilities and then analysing them strategically. Good at reading other people. Bored by routine, will seldom do the same thing the same way, apt to turn to one new interest after another.
	ESTJ Practical, realistic, matter-of-fact. Decisive, quickly move to implement decisions. Organise projects and people to get things done, focus on getting results in the most efficient way possible. Take care of routine details. Have a clear set of logical standards, systematically follow them and want others to also. Forceful in implementing their plans.	**ESFJ** Warm-hearted, conscientious and cooperative. Want harmony in their environment, work with determination to establish it. Like to work with others to complete tasks accurately and on time. Loyal, follow through even in small matters. Notice what others need in their day-to-day lives and try to provide it. Want to be appreciated for who they are and for what they contribute.	**ENFJ** Warm, empathetic, responsive and responsible. Highly attuned to the emotions, needs and motivations of others. Find potential in everyone, want to help others fulfil their potential. May act as catalysts for individual and group growth. Loyal, responsive to praise and criticism. Sociable, facilitate others in a group, and provide inspiring leadership.	**ENTJ** Frank, decisive, assume leadership readily. Quickly see illogical and inefficient procedures and policies, develop and implement comprehensive systems to solve organisational problems. Enjoy long-term planning and goal setting. Usually well informed, well read, enjoy expanding their knowledge and passing it on to others. Forceful in presenting their ideas.

Figure 9.4 The Myers–Briggs Type Indicator showing characteristics frequently associated with particular personality types

(Modified and reproduced by special permission of the Publisher, CPP, Inc., Palo Alto, CA 94303 from *Introduction to Type*, *Sixth Edition* by Isabel Briggs Myers. Copyright 1998 by Peter B. Myers and Katharine D. Myers, Inc. All rights reserved. Further reproduction is prohibited without the Publisher's written consent.)

Table 9.6 An example of a first repertory grid

1	CNC job	Skilled turner's job	Ideal job (professional footballer)	Job I would enjoy (electrician, own business)	Job I would not enjoy (a job on an oil rig)	Job I would hate (miner)	7
Boring	3	4	7	7	2	1	Interesting
Unskilled	2	5	7	6	2	2	Skilled
Not physically demanding	4	5	7	2	7	7	Physically demanding
Gives no job satisfaction	2	5	7	6	2	2	Gives job satisfaction
Unsafe working conditions	5	3	5	6	2	1	Safe working conditions
Dirty work conditions	4	2	6	7	2	1	Clean work conditions
A job in which I am not respected	2	5	7	7	2	2	A job in which I am respected
A job with no challenge	3	6	7	7	3	3	A challenging job
A job in which I do not reap the gains	2	2	7	7	2	2	A job in which I reap the gains
A job where I am tied to one place	2	3	7	7	1	2	A job where I am free to move about

(Reprinted with permission of Fiona Wilson from Case 4, 'Deskilling of work?' The Case of Computer Numerical Control in the Engineering Industry', first published in Jim McGoldrick (ed.) *Business Case File in Behavioural Science*, Van Nostrand Reinhold (1987).)

Using this technique, Wilson was able to measure the workers' own feelings and motivations, and to understand the impact that technology had on their job, their skills and sense of self-worth. She noted in her conclusion that the strategic decisions made by the two companies in their utilisation of the new technology made a direct and measurable impact on the perception and attitudes of the craftsmen. An example of the repertory grid is given in Table 9.6.

APPLICATIONS WITHIN THE WORK ORGANISATION

Organisations regard personality as being of key significance in their decision-making and it would be rare for organisations not to take the personality of a candidate into consideration at a selection interview. For some organisations, personality is the major criterion for selection or rejection. The hospitality industry, for example, is replete with research studies demonstrating the potency of personality.[40] So, how do organisations assess a candidate's personality?

The interview remains the most usual method of selection, but there is an increasing use of objective psychometric measures. Such growth in psychometric testing is significant and a number of studies have demonstrated its growing popularity.[41] Concern has been expressed about the use and misuse of psychological instruments and there is a continuing debate within psychological circles with regard to the validity of these measures.[42] Psychological measures can be distinguished between tests of:

- typical performance (of which personality assessment is one example); and
- maximum performance (including ability and intelligence tests).

These differences are discussed in detail in the next section. There are controversies and sensitivities surrounding the use of any psychological test, but tests of typical performance are especially problematic in certain circumstances. As *Anastasi* has stated:

> *The construction and use of personality inventories are beset with special difficulties over and above common problems encountered in all psychological testing. The question of faking and malingering is far more acute in personality measurement than in aptitude testing.*[43]

Critics have accused consultants and practitioners of inappropriate use of personality assessments and claim low validity between non-work-related personality assessments and work performance.[44] *Goss* suggests that the use of personality assessments not only is an infringement of the individual's privacy but also leads to unfortunate organisational consequences with 'cloning' as an outcome. Such techniques can be perceived as a form of social engineering and an insidious form of organisational control.[45] Aware of these problems, the British Psychological Society has produced guidelines and codes of practice for users of psychometric tests. Furthermore, evidence is emerging to show that where personality questionnaires have been specifically designed and related to work characteristics, prediction and validity scores are much higher.[46]

Despite reservations concerning personality questionnaires, they can be particularly valuable if individuals complete them for their own benefit and development. As an introduction in a self-awareness programme, personality questionnaires can initiate discussion about individual differences. In these situations there is no judgement about better or worse characteristics or matching of individuals to personnel specifications; rather, the discussion centres on the value of individual differences and the strengths which each personality type can bring to the working situation. Producing a balanced team with complementary personalities, skills and abilities is ideal. Personality questionnaires can therefore be the first part of this process – an audit of strengths and weaknesses. This could be followed by group training exercises designed to develop strengths and balance the weaknesses of the team. An effective team at work should be aware of the division of their strengths and weaknesses.

> *None of us is perfect; but a group of people, whose strengths and talents complement each other, can be.*[47]

Although personality is a powerful determinant of a manager's effectiveness, account must also be taken of the social rules and expectations within the workplace. There is no doubt that in some organisations these expectations are very forceful and insist upon behaviour which conforms to cultural demands. In some roles the individual's personality is in danger of being undermined. For instance, it would be a surprise to meet an introverted, quiet and reflective Head Chef in a major hotel or a paramedic who was frantic, nervy and hysterical.

Furthermore organisations may require different temperaments depending on whether they are going through a period of growth or retrenchment. Whereas a manager may be rewarded for exciting promotional activity and product development in one situation, other personality characteristics may be needed if there is a period of slow-down and attention to detail and costs. *Gray* contends that researchers will never to able to solve and develop accurate, valid and reliable performance measures. 'Many jobs or critical aspects of them, cannot be quantified. Performance measures are often justifiably subjective, vague and contradictory.'[48]

STRESS AND THE INDIVIDUAL

Personality is a contributing factor in the understanding of stress. Individuals who have a personality classified as Type A are more likely to suffer from heart disease under severe stress than individuals with a Type B personality.[49] Stress is a complex topic. It is individually

defined and is intrinsically tied into an individual's perceptual system. Everyone has a range of comfort within which they can feel steady and safe. Stress occurs when the individual feels that they are working outside of that comfort zone. Individuals will differ when they feel discomfort. The effects of stress will differ too; for some, the incidence of stress may energise and activate but for others it may immobilise.

The costs of stress at individual, organisational and national levels are well known. *Cooper* has indicated the high incidence of stress throughout organisations irrespective of job senior-

Stock exchange traders show particularly high levels of stress

ity. He suggests that every job has its own stress fingerprint.[50] Stress is a term which is commonly used and misused; being 'stressed out' may be said by some individuals at the slightest amount of pressure and tension. It also contains a perverse sense of status; for instance a librarian complained bitterly that her role was regarded as having low stress, implying that jobs given a 'high stress' position also ranked high in prestige.

What causes stress?

Cooper and others[51] have identified six major sources of stress at work:

- intrinsic to the job – working conditions, shift work, etc.;
- role in the organisation – overload; underload;
- relationships at work – particularly with the boss;
- career development – mid-life being a critical stage;
- organisational structure and climate – the extent of rules and regulations;
- home–work interface – particularly the growth of dual-career families.

Conflicts at work are another undeniable cause of stress and a sub-category of Cooper's model.

Harassment not only puts strains on working life but can impact upon relationships at home. Victims may lose their commitment to work and, depending on how the incident(s) is dealt with, may lose their motivation to work, their respect of their line manager and work colleagues. Harassment is a type of direct discrimination if the victim can show that the behaviour caused injury to feelings. It is a serious offence.

It is defined as: conduct which is unreasonable, unwelcome and offensive, and which creates an intimidating, hostile or humiliating working environment.

Sexual harassment may take many forms and can include:

- *sexual innuendoes, lewd comments, sexually suggestive remarks or gestures, requests for sexual favours, insensitive jokes, fondling or touching, pestering for attention, displays of sexually oriented material such as pin-up calendars or graffiti, forwarding inappropriate emails or accessing pornographic websites, unwelcome sexual advances, and threats of, or actual, sexual violence.*

Racial harassment may also take many forms and can include:

- *racial innuendoes or offensive language, racist jokes and banter, practical jokes, the open display of racist publications, notes containing racial insults, physical assault, racist terminology, abusive email messages, and isolation or lack of co-operation at work.*

Whether the action was intended to cause offence or not does not matter – if the employee being subjected to the behaviour finds it unacceptable and he or she feels damaged or harmed by it, this constitutes potential harassment.

Harassment is normally characterised by more than one incident of unacceptable behaviour, but in some circumstances just one instance may constitute harassment if it is sufficiently serious.[52]

Because the nature of human stress is complex and socially and culturally bound, it is interesting to reflect on its possible developments. Is it the case that stress predominates nowadays because our expectations are still bound within the bureaucratic organisations of earlier decades of work? Personal life commitments are significantly tied into full employment and a career for life (with a 25-year mortgage and easier credit arrangements) and yet evidence is growing of organisations' requirements for shorter and more flexible working patterns. Perhaps, with an increasing awareness of the changing nature of work patterns and a reorganisation of the interface between work and home, stress may be reduced or at the very least may be perceived in new ways. Are we currently at the cusp of new changes where a new generation may have differing expectations and may adapt their lives to suit a new order and style? (Stress at work is also discussed in Chapter 18.)

ABILITY

It is self-evident that different occupations require different skills, competencies and abilities. It is also the case that individuals vary with regard to their mental abilities and the extent to which they apply them at work. The 'happy' scenario is one where a match occurs between the individual's abilities and their occupation, but reality suggests that this is not always the case. The extremes include employees bored rigid with a simple task who become careless and make a succession of mistakes, and the employees who have been promoted beyond their capability. The result could be stress either for the individuals unable to cope, or their work colleagues who are picking up the debris left behind. It can be assumed that a person's ability is dependent upon his or her intelligence, but the study of intelligence has revealed a number of controversies and sensitivities.

In a similar vein to the studies of personality, different schools of thought have emerged with regard to the study of abilities. Similar debates to the ones that surround the study of personality have also swirled around the research on intelligence.

- Is intelligence inherited? Is it constant throughout life? Is it dependent upon our life's experiences, our culture, our education, etc.?
- What is the nature of intelligence? Can it be measured and how?

Is intelligence inherited?

The **nativists** believe that intelligence is mostly inherited (nature), while the **empiricists** believe that our environment shapes our behaviour and mental abilities (nurture). *Galton's*[53] thesis suggested that genius seemed to run in families and proposed that intelligence must be inherited. He studied eminent families and noted that sons of famous fathers also showed special talents and abilities. The notion that such sons may have 'rich' and stimulating environments with the opportunity to learn and develop talents did not enter into Galton's argument.

Cyril Burt's influential work in the 1930s not only lent support to the genetic argument but also influenced educational policy. However, in the 1980s, his work was discounted when fraudulent practice was uncovered. Data and the research assistants had been invented by Burt.[54]

Studies completed on twins also supported the genetic argument. Researchers used the opportunity to study identical twins who, for whatever reasons, were separated at birth and reared in different homes, an ideal research situation to explore the impact of nature or nurture on adult intelligence. The twins' intelligence was measured in adulthood and the similarity in scores that emerged was strong evidence to support the genetics argument. It would appear that the different family environments did not have an impact on the intelligence measured. However, many critics argued that although the families were different there was great similarity in terms of the social class background. Rather than comparing twins who experienced substantial differences in their upbringing the twins had often been placed in homes which came from a similar community – thus the genetic argument was diluted.

Howe[55] summarises recent convincing evidence to show that intervention can have an impact on IQ. He cites evidence from early intervention programmes such as Head Start initiatives and other schooling effects, from studies of child adoption and from nutritional studies. Howe concludes that: 'The empirical findings provide no support for the pessimistic conclusion that low intelligence and the problems associated with it are inevitable and unalterable.'

The political implications of research into the nature of intelligence are striking. Some of the earliest theories influenced the educational philosophy of England and Wales, including how children were selected for different types of secondary education and the kind of help that should be given to children with special needs.

Can intelligence be measured and how?

Binet and Simon,[56] working in France, were the first psychologists to measure ability in a systematic and structured way. They were responsible for identifying children with special educational needs and they developed a battery of exercises for children to perform at specific ages. They established a mental age for each task based on the 'normal' ability of children and were therefore able to identify those children whose mental age was not the same as their chronological (actual) age.

Terman[57] working at Stanford University in the United States advanced the ideas of Binet and developed an intelligence test known as the Stanford–Binet Test which was designed to measure intelligence across a wide scale. The tests were able to provide a 'score' of the child's intelligence. The Intelligence Quotient (or IQ) was the calculation of the:

$$\frac{\text{Mental age}}{\text{Chronological (Actual) age}} \times 100 = \text{Intelligence Quotient}$$

Hence a child who is 10 years and has a mental age of 10 will have an IQ score of 100; a child of 10 years with a mental age of 12 will have an IQ score of 120; and a child of 10 years with a mental age of 8 will have an IQ score of 80.

Arguments have raged within psychologists' circles as to the nature of intelligence. Is it dependent on a general overall factor which will have an overarching effect on specific activities? Or are specific activities independent of each other? In other words, if a child shows a high level of ability at mathematics is this dependent on an overall high general ability? General ability can be seen as a kind of powerhouse which releases some of its energy into the child's ability at mathematics. (For other children it may act as a limiting factor.) *Spearman*[58] proposed a two-factor theory of intelligence and suggested that every intellectual task involves a level of mental agility – a general factor (g) – plus

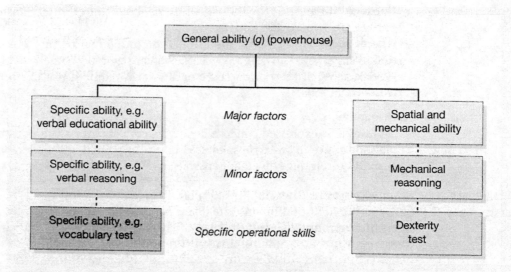

Figure 9.5 A hierarchy of abilities

(*Source*: Adapted from P. E. Vernon, 'The hierarchy of abilities', in Wiseman, S. (ed.) *Intelligence and Ability* (first published 1967, reprinted 1968, 2nd edition 1973). This selection copyright © the Estate of Stephen Wiseman 1967,1973. Reproduced by permission of Penguin Books Ltd.)

specific abilities (*s*). This idea, developed by *Vernon*,[59] resulted in a model which placed abilities in a hierarchy (*see* Figure 9.5). Abilities at the lower end of the hierarchy in Figure 9.5 are more likely to correlate, so hence if a child has a good vocabulary, he or she is more likely to have abilities in reading and comprehension too.

Crystallised and fluid intelligence

Cattell suggests that the *g* factor could be constructed as having one dimension which is independent of any direct learning or experience. He called this **fluid intelligence** which he suggested was the type of abstract reasoning ability which is free of any cultural influences. The second dimension, called the **crystallised intelligence**, is dependent upon learning, cultural experiences and is part of our general understanding of the world around us. *Bartram and Lindley*[60] suggested that the two abilities should not be seen as distinct but that:

> ... *in effect, there is a continuum from fluid ability at one end to crystallised ability at the other. In practice we do not have tests of 'pure ability' as there will always be some impact, however slight, of our culture and background. But the distinction is a useful one.*

Other psychologists have argued that the presence of '*g*' – this powerhouse – is an unnecessary artefact. What is important in understanding abilities is the way in which the different abilities can be identified and measured. *Thurstone*[61] claimed seven primary mental abilities which can be separately measured resulting in a profile of scores:

- spatial ability
- perceptual speed
- numerical reasoning
- verbal reasoning
- memory
- verbal fluency
- inductive reasoning.

Other models of intelligence

Guilford[62] criticised theories which aimed to simplify intelligence into a small number of factors. He devised a model which identified 120 different abilities and suggested that intellectual ability requires individuals to think in one of three dimensions.

▦ **Content**. What must the individual think about (for example, meaning of words or numbers)?

▦ **Operations**. What kind of thinking is the individual required to do (for example, recognising items, solving a problem, evaluating an outcome)?

▦ **Products**. What kind of outcome or answer is required (for example, classifying or reordering items)?

(*See* Figure 9.6.)

Guilford also expressed concern about the convergent nature of tests that required a single solution or answer. He suggested that tests should also be looking at an individual's ability to produce divergent answers.

Intelligence – one or many?

Gardner[63] regarded the simplification of intelligence in terms of an IQ measure as unrealistic in the light of different intelligent behaviour that could be observed in everyday life. Although intelligence tests may offer one explanation of why an individual performs better in an academic institution, and may be a legitimate measure of such behaviour, it failed to take into account the full range of intelligent activity. He suggested that there was a multiple of intelligences and categorised them into six varieties (all of which could be further divided):

Verbal	Akin to the factors described in earlier theories
Mathematical	
Spatial capacity	Ability shown by artists and architects
Kinaesthetic	Abilities of a physical nature
Musical	Abilities of musicianship
Personal intelligences	Interpersonal – skills with other people Intrapersonal – knowing oneself

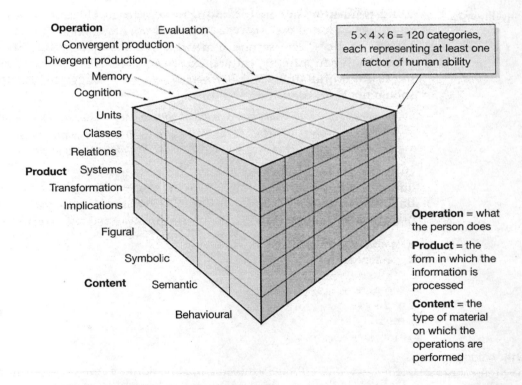

Figure 9.6 Guilford's structure of the intellect model

(*Source*: J. P. Guilford, 'Three faces of intellect', in Wiseman, S. (ed.) *Intelligence and Ability* (first published 1967, reprinted 1968, 2nd edition 1973). This selection copyright © the Estate of Stephen Wiseman 1967,1973. Reproduced by permission of Penguin Books Ltd.)

Emotional intelligence

An elaboration of some of Gardner's ideas was made by *Goleman*[64] who agreed that the classic view of intelligence was too narrow. He felt that the emotional qualities of individuals should be considered. These, he felt, played a vital role in the application of intelligence in everyday life. He identified the key characteristics as:

> *abilities such as being able to motivate oneself and persist in the face of frustrations; to control impulse and delay gratification; to regulate one's moods and keep distress from swamping the ability to think; to emphasise and to hope.*

Emotional intelligence has received considerable attention over the last few years as the concept has been identified as a key aspect of managing people effectively. Goleman suggests that emotional intelligence or EI predicts top performance and accounts for more than 85 per cent of outstanding performance in top leaders.[65] The Hay Group working with Goleman have identified 18 specific competencies that make up the four components of emotional intelligence and have produced an inventory designed to measure Emotional Competence (*see* Figure 9.7). The Emotional Competence Inventory defines EI as: 'The capacity for recognising our own feelings and those of others, for motivating ourselves and for managing emotions within ourselves and with others.'[66]

Research work into the effects of an emotional literacy policy at school demonstrates that children who feel safe, understood and appreciated for the things they do well are also more focused, more open to ideas and more willing to work at school. The schools that perform better are those that place emotional literacy first. Simple methods are used: 'Quality Circle time', 'Talk time', 'Friendship Stop', 'Quiet Rooms' – learning environments which encourage the students to discuss non-curriculum problems and help them resolve problems. The aim is to develop qualities that enable the students to become effective learners by developing their sense of self and sense of self-worth, qualities which are transferable into the work situation.[67]

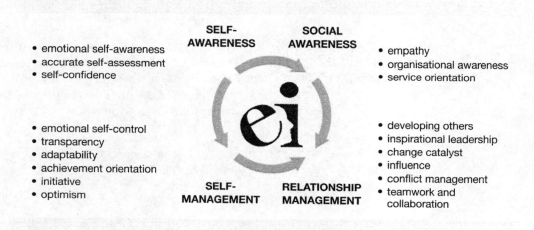

Figure 9.7 Emotional Intelligence Competence Model

TESTING

The early tests of intelligence have evolved into a large psychological business. Most people will have taken a **psychological test** of one kind or another by the time they are an adult in employment. Tests may be administered at school, college or as part of the selection assessment process at work. The use of tests is widespread and growing. They are perceived to be useful as an objective discriminating tool, but they are not without controversies and sensitivities.

Tests are broadly divided by the British Psychological Society into:

1 *Tests of typical performance*. These assess an individual's typical responses to given situations. Answers are not right or wrong but identify choices, preferences and strength of feelings. Personality assessments and interest inventories are examples of such tests.
2 *Tests of maximum performance*. These assess an individual's ability to perform effectively under standard conditions. Performance on these tests, which include ability and aptitude tests, can be judged as right or wrong. Ability tests come in many different forms and may test a **general intellectual functioning** or a **specific ability** (such as verbal reasoning, numerical reasoning, etc.).

Alice Heim (cited in *Anastasia*) developed a series of general ability tests – AH series – which are widely used to assess general ability. They test three key areas: verbal, numerical and diagrammatical reasoning. For example, an individual would be asked questions similar to the following:

Which one of the five words on the right bears a similar relation to each of the two words on the left?

		A	**B**	**C**	**D**	**E**
sensible	noise	sound	judgement	tone	silly	sensitive

Modern Occupational Skills Tests are an example of specific ability tests and measure a range of clerical and administrative skills: verbal checking; technical checking; numerical estimation, etc. They claim to be an aid in the selection of administrative staff. Their tests are short and can be used singly or together as a battery of tests. The individual would be asked questions similar to the following:

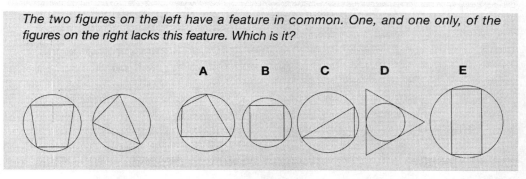

The two figures on the left have a feature in common. One, and one only, of the figures on the right lacks this feature. Which is it?

Some tests are designed to be given individually whereas others are suitable for administering within a group situation. However, there are certain minimum features and standards of conditions which distinguish psychological tests from other forms of informal assessments; tests are essentially 'an objective and standardised measure of a sample of behaviour'.[68]

Features of psychological tests

Psychological tests have certain standard features:

1 Tests will comprise a standard task, or a set of questions with a standard means of obtaining the score.
2 A technical manual will explain what the test is measuring, how it was constructed, the procedures for administering, scoring and interpreting the test.
3 Details of the test's validity (what the test claims to be measuring – and what it is not measuring) and reliability (the test's ability to measure consistently) will also be shown in the manual along with the inferences that can be drawn from the data.

For a test to be considered as a psychological instrument it must be **objective**, **standardised**, **reliable**, **valid** and **discriminating** (*but not discriminatory*). The selection and choice of the test should be based on a number of other key features such as its acceptability, practicality, time, costs and perceived and actual added value.

Limitations of tests

All tests have limitations. Tests can only sample behaviour at one particular moment in time. The information they provide is dependent upon good testing practice and will only add further evidence to the decision-making process. Tests will not provide the answer. Some individuals are very nervous and may not perform at their best and indeed some may feel indignant that they are obliged to take a test at all.

Jackson[69] identifies a central area of concern in his discussion of fairness in testing. He distinguishes between fairness of outcome and fairness of process. In the selection process **fairness of outcome** implies 'choosing the best person for the job'. This is dependent upon measures of later performance to confirm the predictive validity of the test. Such processes are essential if organisations are to be certain of the value of tests and are not merely using tests as an administrative convenience to keep the shortlist shorter! By **fairness of process**, Jackson refers to errors and bias that can occur during the testing process. Some problems can be limited by good testing practice, but other sources of bias are more complex. Certain tests have been found to show differences in average performance levels between men and women or between different racial or ethnic groups. *Feltham et al.* suggests that the test may not in itself be unfair but using the test will lead to different outcomes and different proportions of people being selected.[70] Some tests have been found to have an adverse impact. Psychologists need to work with personnel professionals to be certain that all parts of the testing process are fair and objective.

Tests should be kept under review. Were they useful? Did they enable a confident prediction of future work behaviour and performance? Unfortunately, many organisations may spend considerable time and money on training and in choosing a test, but then do not perform adequate research and set up suitable evaluation procedures for testing the test. If organisations do not treat the candidate fairly – that is, provide them with feedback of results – a damaging impact on the reputation of the organisation can result. The testing process means that candidates spend a considerable amount of their own personal time on a process which is demanding and potentially intimidating. If they feel they have been treated with respect they maintain a positive image of the organisation even if it has rejected them.[71] The personal, intrusive and threatening nature of the psychological tests should not be forgotten.

Exhibit 9.1 illustrates the main arguments for and against the use of psychological tests.

Why use psychological tests?

1 They make decisions about people
  – more systematic
  – more precise.
2 They predict future performance and reduce uncertainty.
3 They provide more accurate descriptions of people and their behaviour. Precise definitions and measured variables lead to further studies and improve understanding of the relationship between tests and performance.

But
- Tests should be seen as an additional source of information only.
- Tests may be expensive and time-consuming.
- Without proper professional practice, they can be misused and results abused.
- They may be seen as an intrusion.
- They may be regarded as inappropriate.
- Practice may have an effect on test results.

ATTITUDES

There are no limits to the attitudes people hold. Attitudes are learned throughout life and are embodied within our socialisation process. Some attitudes (such as religious beliefs) may be central to us – a core construct – and may be highly resistant to any change, whereas other, more peripheral attitudes may change with new information or personal experiences. Specific events, particularly traumatic ones such as redundancy, may have a dramatic effect on our attitudes.

So what are **attitudes** and how can they be distinguished from beliefs and values?

- **Attitudes** can be defined as providing a state of 'readiness' or tendency to respond in a particular way.[72]
- **Beliefs** are concerned with what is known about the world; they centre on what 'is', on reality as it is understood.
- **Values** are concerned with what 'should' be and what is desirable.

Gross suggests that

to convert a belief into an attitude, a 'value' ingredient is needed which, by definition, is to do with an individual's sense of what is desirable, good, valuable, worthwhile and so on.

It has been suggested by Gross that whereas 'adults may have thousands of beliefs, they may have only hundreds of attitudes and a few dozen values'.[73] *Hofstede* defines values as a 'broad tendency to prefer certain states of affairs over others'.[74]

The functions of attitudes

Katz has suggested that attitudes and motives are interlinked and, depending on an individual's motives, attitudes can serve four main functions.

- **Knowledge**. One of the major functions is to provide a basis for the interpretation and classification of new information. Attitudes provide a knowledge base and framework within which new information can be placed.
- **Expressive**. Attitudes become a means of expression. They enable individuals to indicate to others the values that they hold and thus to express their self-concept and adopt or internalise the values of a group.
- **Instrumental**. Held attitudes maximise rewards and minimise sanctions. Hence, attitudes towards other people (or objects) might be held because of past positive (or negative) experiences. Behaviour or knowledge which has resulted in the satisfaction of needs is thus more likely to result in a favourable attitude.
- **Ego-defensive**. Attitudes may be held in order to protect the ego from an undesirable truth or reality.[75]

Prediction of behaviour

Is it possible to predict behaviour, if we know an individual's attitude?

Research suggests the answer is 'No'. It seems that we do not always behave in a way that is true to our beliefs; what we say and what we do may be very different. Such evidence indicates that attitudes can be revealed not only in behaviour but also by the individual's thoughts (although these may not be revealed in public) and by feelings, the strength of which demonstrates the extent to which the attitude is a core or peripheral construct.

A classic study by *La Piere* illustrates this point. Visiting American hotels and restaurants with a Chinese couple, *La Piere* found no sign of prejudiced attitudes in the face-to-face situation, but there were marked racist attitudes in the follow-up attitude survey. He found complete contradictions between public and private attitudes.[76]

These findings have important implications for the study of attitudes and reveal two important issues for the psychologist and manager.

1 Attitudes cannot be seen; they can only be inferred.

Given that the attitudes employees hold are important for morale and the effectiveness of organisations, it is important that there is confidence in the measurement techniques used to assess the strength of attitudes. As attitudes are inferred, heavy reliance is placed therefore on the accuracy of assessment. Although there are a number of different techniques which could be used to measure attitudes, the two most common techniques are **direct observation** and **self-reporting techniques**.

All of us observe others and assess attitudes on the basis of communication style (both verbal and non-verbal) and behaviour. This is an example of an informal approach – unsystematic, spontaneous and based on our understanding of social cues. We may be wrong in our judgement. Students who turn up late for classes, slouch on their seat and do not ask questions may still hold very positive attitudes towards the subject. Managers may also be erroneous in their assumptions and beliefs about their colleagues (both subordinates and superiors). Their beliefs may never have been tested out – merely assumed to be correct.

Serious mistakes can be made when dealing with people across different cultures. For instance eye contact in Western countries is normally associated with confidence, politeness and attentiveness but in some African countries may be seen as rude and disrespectful. Bulgarians nod when they mean 'no' and shake their heads when they mean 'yes' while the Greeks nod upwards or raise their eyebrows for 'no' and shake the head side to side or tilt it to say 'yes'. A lack of 'cultural literacy' can lead to incorrect assumptions, poor relationships and a failure to make useful business connections.[77]

Organisations which assess their employees' attitudes by using attitude questionnaires (self-reporting techniques) are attempting to systematically gauge and measure these assumptions. Attitude questionnaires are time-consuming to design and administer. The questions asked, their relevance, style and length are all important variables in the validity of the questionnaire. So, too, is the honest completion of questionnaires. Making public people's private attitudes may also have its dangers as expectations of change may be envisaged. If these do not occur, disappointment and low morale may be the result.[78] (*See also* the discussion on the Johari window in Chapter 14.) Attitude questionnaires are used by many companies as a barometer for the attitudinal climate of organisations and as such enable managers to be in touch with employees' views and feelings. (*See* Table 9.7.)

Table 9.7 An example of an attitude questionnaire

Please tick one box that most closely represents how you feel about each statement	Strongly disagree				Strongly agree
I believe in what OrgCo is trying to achieve	1	2	3	4	5
I enjoy discussing OrgCo with people who do not work here					
I know how my job contributes to OrgCo's aims and objectives					
Good and bad news about what is happening at OrgCo is communicated regularly					
My values and those of the organisation are very similar					
Right now, staying with OrgCo is a matter of necessity as much as desire					
I am constantly interrupted in my work					
I enjoy my job					
I am encouraged to seek out new training opportunities					
My manager discusses with me ways in which I can improve my work performance					
OrgCo is serious about removing barriers to ensure equality of opportunity					
Staff at OrgCo regularly help and support each other at work					
I lack direction from my manager					
When things do not go well in our team/department we learn from the experience					
Communication within my team is positive and effective					
Taking everything into account I have a high level of job satisfaction with my team					

2 Attitudes are often shared within organisations and as such are embodied in the culture of organisations.

Classic research has shown the influence of the wider community in the formation of orientations towards work. Differences in class/orientation may elicit a range of loyalties and possibly produce opposing perceptions of commitment, loyalty and co-operation. Attitudes are not just individually formed but arise out of interaction with others. They are often 'locked-in', often regarded as obvious, mere common sense, and are so much taken for granted that they may be overlooked. Sharing the belief system of others also has affective outcomes. If people feel that they belong and are included, it enables them to feel good about working in an organisation. If, on the other hand, people do not feel part of the organisation – if they feel that they do not share the dominant attitudes and beliefs – negative emotional consequences are likely to result.

Researchers of organisational culture suggest that it is the shared perceptions of daily practices that are at the core of organisational cultures.[79] 'The reality of everyday life is taken for granted *as* reality.'[80] (Organisational culture is explored in more detail in Chapter 22.) Implications of the unquestioning nature of 'reality' of what can or cannot be done can lead to individuals becoming 'culturally blinkered'. Insitutionalised attitudes result. Major problems arise when these attitudes are formed on the basis of stereotypes and prejudice as was evidenced in the Stephen Lawrence Inquiry:

> *Unwitting racism can arise because of lack of understanding, ignorance or mistaken beliefs. It can arise from well intentioned but patronising words or actions. It can arise from unfamiliarity with the behaviour or cultural traditions of people or families from minority ethnic communities. It can arise from racist stereotyping of black people as potential criminals or troublemakers.*

Often this arises out of uncritical self-understanding born out of an inflexible police ethos of the 'traditional' way of doing things. Furthermore such attitudes can thrive in a tightly knit community, so that there can be a collective failure to detect and to outlaw this breed of racism. The police canteen can too easily be its breeding ground. (Section 6.17)[81]

Attitudes are not just created within organisations. Attitudes inherent within wider society are reinforced or reshaped by the organisation.

A shared understanding

Research by *Hicks* in the hotel industry revealed that irrespective of personal circumstances (age, gender, education, social class) managers had been exposed to a process which had 'encultured' them to a shared understanding of the industry, resulting in common attitudes on a range of topics. Attitudes towards their management trainees were found to be significant with regard to the trainees' development; high expectation of their trainees ensured broad training opportunities and the use of their own personal network of contacts to ensure their protégés' success. The significance of positive attitudes of managers towards their trainees cannot therefore be over-emphasised.[82]

Attitude change

The permanency of attitudes clearly has implications for attitudinal change. At the beginning of this section it was pointed out that whereas peripheral attitudes may easily change with new information or experiences, central attitudes tied into other cognitive systems may be much more difficult to shift.

Theories on attitude change stress the importance of **balance** and **consistency** in our psyche.

- *Heider*, for example, suggests that not only would we find it uncomfortable to hold two conflicting attitudes, but to do so would motivate us to change one of the attitudes in order to reach a balanced state.[83]
- Cognitive dissonance is the term given to the discomfort felt when we act in a way that is inconsistent with our true beliefs. Like balance theory, it suggests that we are motivated to reduce its impact.[84]

The process of attitude change is dependent on a number of key factors, the most important being:

- why an attitude is held in the first place;
- why it should change;
- what the benefits are and to whom;
- what the outcomes are if it does not change.

Considerable research has demonstrated the importance of the following variables in a programme of attitude change:

- the persuader's characteristics;
- presentation of issues;
- audience characteristics;
- group influences;
- outcome of attitude change (reward or punishment).

The last decade has produced tumultuous change for employees and their managers. It would be rare indeed to find an organisation which has not experienced some degree of change in structure, product, processes, philosophy, culture or ownership. The way in which these changes are implemented can have a dramatic impact on the attitudes of staff. The ways that organisations can promote a positive climate to change will be examined in Chapter 10.

GENDER AND ORGANISATIONS

This section examines the participation of men and women in the workforce, and in particular reviews the position and status of women.

One of our initial perceptions and classifications of another individual is the identification of his or her gender.

- How does this perception affect our behaviour?
- What difference does it make if our work group is predominantly male or female?
- Do women and men have different experiences at work?
- Are organisations rational and neutral institutions – if so, why should gender make a difference?
- Does it matter that many classic theories have been carried out on men, by male researchers?
- What has been the influence of equal opportunity policies on work behaviour and on the position of women in organisations?

This section will explore the ways in which organisational behaviour can be more clearly understood by looking at the gender dimension. Traditionally, this area has been ignored and the result of this neglect has only recently been raised as an issue for concern. *Alvesson and Due Billing* suggest that:

> *A gender perspective implies analysing the importance, meaning and consequences of what is culturally defined as male or masculine as well as female or feminine ways of thinking (knowing), feeling, valuing and acting. A gender perspective also implies an analysis of the organisational practices that maintain the division of labour between the sexes.*[85]

They claim that knowing and understanding these perspectives is important in a full analysis of organisational behaviour. Organisations may reinforce thinking patterns and behaviour, and individuals may in their turn maintain and encourage such patterns. The relationships between individuals and organisations are dynamic and may be reaffirmed in a number of subtle as well as explicit and overt ways. For example, a waitress attending tables may earn tips by being effective *and* feminine. The service and caring aspects of the role are reinforced and she may learn to focus on certain behaviours that attract more tips. For example, she may be particularly attentive to men.

However, gender research is replete with contradictions and confusions. Although there is a body of evidence to confirm the position, status and (lack of) power of women in organisations – aspects that can be measured and quantified – such clarity is blurred when it comes to understanding the subjective and qualitative aspects of working life. It is not helpful to view all men and all women as homogeneous. There may be as many differences within each gender as between the two genders. Social class, race and age will affect attitudes, beliefs and values and may impinge upon different understandings of gender. Although earlier organisational research could be criticised as having been conducted by men largely investigating male behaviour, so too much of the research on women has been dominated by white middle-class women assuming their values are those ones which should be upheld.

Emotions, politics and gender

Emotions and politics surround the issue of gender. *Alvesson and Due Billing*[86] suggest that some people may be over-sensitive to gender and interpret any negative comment as if it is symbolic of an act of discrimination. Likewise under-sensitivity may also occur and organisations may remain gender blind to everyday instances of bias and distortion. Although not easy, achieving the right balance (neither overwhelming nor rejecting the pervasiveness of gender) is an important skill in managing men and women at work.

Gender research illustrates the often contradictory nature of thinking and behaviour. Although stereotyped views attempt to bring some simple consistency and predictabilities into our worlds, the reality of behaviour confounds the issues. For instance, is the stereotype valid that women are more emotional and caring than men?

- Are men and women really so different in the expression of their emotions? Emotions of pleasure, stress and aggression are not just dominated by the one gender; observation of men and women at work reveals the spread of emotional responses.
- Are women really more caring than men? Aren't some men as empathetic as some women, but is such behaviour similarly interpreted?

Women and men can be seen as both weak and strong, rational and emotional; but the interpretation and judgement may be different depending on the gender of the individual. An aggressive response by a man may be seen to be powerful, but by a woman may be seen as unfeminine and bossy.[87]

Glass ceiling and other practices

A view of the position and status of women at work does produce consistency of evidence in respect of where women work. Male domination of privilege and power within organisations is still an identifiable feature in organisations.

A review of statistical evidence reveals that the places where women work have not changed substantially and remain different in kind from male occupations. In essence, women are working in occupations which reflect their perceived role in society, and they are generally found servicing and caring for others. It is recognised that many organisations have adopted equal opportunity policies and are seriously examining whether they are fulfilling the potential of all their staff. However, statistics reveal that progress is slow and the number of women holding senior managerial positions is still insignificant (from 2 per cent in 1974 to 22 per cent in 2000).[88]

A '**glass ceiling**' still exists in many organisations, preventing women from rising to the top. Other reports also reveal slow progress and conclude that the glass ceiling is being penetrated, but at a very slow pace. Women executives are still a rare sight in the city and in business generally.[89] This slow pace is mirrored in a diverse range of occupational settings including institutions of Higher Education. In 2000/2001 statistics revealed that only 12 per cent of professors in UK universities are women and that women tend to be located within the lower points of the lecturer grades.[90]

Equal Opportunities Policy – progress and best practice

A recent study by *Kate Purcell* demonstrated that there were persistent inequalities among graduate employees. Women had lower expectations than men in terms of their predicted salaries in their first post and five years later. Purcell showed they were right to think this. She concludes: '... the evidence suggests that even among graduates, women's work tends to be undervalued in relation to that of men, wherever they work and whatever they are qualified to do' (p. 30). Even in the youngest age group (20–24) average male graduate earnings were 15 per cent higher than those of a female graduate and in older age groups the differential was wider still.[91]

Opportunity Now (the renamed Opportunity 2000 organisation) maintains an encouraging and positive campaign to keep 'gender on the agenda'. Some 216 of their 355 members participated in a benchmarking scheme and they report evidence of real progress on gender equality in the work place. Best practice awards are presented to organisations that show progress in three key elements which relate to their Diversity Change Model:

- motivate the organisation and its people to undertake diversity action;
- take action in order to develop and value diversity;
- assess the impact of diversity action and learn from this assessment in order to re-motivate the organisation and establish future goals.

Organisations must impress the judges on their innovative and sustainable initiative with clear goals and evidence of measurable and monitored impact.[92]

Liff and Cameron[93] argue that such policies have two elements:

- measures to ensure that women are treated in the same way as men;
- measures to address the distinctive characteristics of women which seem to disadvantage them in the workplace.

For Liff and Cameron measures which fall in the second category expose women to be perceived as different/deficient and requiring 'help'. But benefiting from such special treatment leads to potential hostility and resentment from men; a backlash could result. *Blakemore and Drake*[94] also point out the controversies that surround equal opportunities policies. They suggest that one of two images are portrayed: one which suggests that policies are concerned too much with power, influence and political correctness; the other image suggests that they are trying to mask real and continuing discrimination behaviour.

In their conclusion, Blakemore and Drake believe there is some room for optimism and quote examples from legislation which identify some progress and achievement. In particular, they note that best practice has occurred where attention has been focused on practical steps and actions rather than trying to change hearts and minds. Although they suggest changes have been rather of a 'ratchet' variety than an engine of change, change has occurred nonetheless. Such positive steps should be tempered by the prevalence of sexual harassment in the workplace and the unchanging roles of men and women. Men are unwilling to take on more domestic work or child care which leads Blakemore and Drake to propose that:

> a 'role' related model of equality policy in the future will perhaps have to address the question of how to resocialise men for domestic work rather than women for paid work.

The message that these writers are advocating is one of partnership. It is of little value to focus on just 'women's issues' without taking a view on the changing role of men. The part that organisations can play is to look at the encouragement they are giving to men as well as women in balancing their lives. We will consider some of these work/life balance initiatives at the end of this section, but first a consideration of the changing nature of men's and women's contribution to work.

UNDERSTANDING WOMEN'S POSITION AND STATUS

Why should men's and women's working experiences be so different? Five explanations are presented. These should not be seen as competitive but as all contributing to the understanding of women's position and status in the organisational world. The explanations are:

- economic theories;
- psychological sex differences;
- the socialisation process;
- orientations and motivations towards work; and
- working practices.

ECONOMIC THEORIES

Two major economic theories seek to explain and predict labour patterns of women's employment:

- human capital theory; and
- dual labour market theory.

Human capital theory

The main tenet of human capital theory is that to have the benefit of choices in the workplace, individuals are required to make a substantial investment – for example, in education and training.[95] Human capital theory predicts that women will acquire less schooling and training than men, and will have less time to reap rewards of investment. Whatever skills they had learned will be outdated during their period at home.

The interrupted pattern of women's employment therefore decreases the incentives for both women and employers to engage in their training. Although this may explain the position for some it does not explain the position of women who *do* invest their time in education and training. Neither does it explain the disparities in earnings which exist between men and women where *neither* have committed themselves to education and training.

Dual labour market theory

Dual labour market theory argues that the labour market is divided into two separate markets: the primary market consisting of jobs with career prospects, high wages and stable employment; and the secondary market whose jobs are dead-end, low paid and with poor prospects. Research evidence shows that women, and ethnic groups, are over-represented in the secondary market.[96] *Loveridge and Mok* suggest that women comprise an 'outgroup' and are treated as such, and form the basis of an industrial reserve providing the source of additional labour when society requires it.[97]

Although these explanations are rich in detail they leave unexplored the origin of women's roles as looked at by psychologists and sociologists.

PSYCHOLOGICAL SEX DIFFERENCES

Is it the case that men and women follow different occupational routes because these match their particular sex type? Significantly, it has been found that the male species are far more vulnerable physically. For example, *Gross* comments that 'there is no doubt that males are, biologically, the weaker sex!'[98] In their classic review of this subject, *Maccoby and Jacklin* claimed support for differences between males and females in terms of visuo-spatial ability, mathematical ability and aggressiveness (male scores higher); and verbal ability (female scores higher). But they also explored a number of myths which surround sex differences and concluded there were more similarities than differences between the sexes.[99]

Biological differences

Studies focusing on biological differences remain unsupported without the inclusion of interrelational factors. The reciprocal effect that babies and parents have on each other provides fascinating data on the preferential treatment that parents give their babies depending on their sex. It has been found that mothers are less responsive to boys crying than girls, even at the age of three weeks.[100] Studies have also shown the different interpretative connotations placed on behaviour which fits the stereotype of active, energetic boy, and passive, nurturing girl.[101] One conclusion to draw is that biology alone cannot explain differences in women's position. Attention must be focused on social issues, and the influence and impact of the socialisation process.

THE SOCIALISATION PROCESS

The family consists of a number of psychologically intense and powerful social relationships in which it is possible to see how little girls and little boys learn their gender, identity and role. The definition of gender, what it is and what it means to family members, is reinforced from external agencies (for example, the media and school) so that messages concerning gender are continuously being processed and reaffirmed. As *Barrett* has said:

> gender identity is not created once and for all at a certain point in the child's life but is continually recreated and endorsed, modified or even altered, substantially through a process of ideological representation.[102]

One study demonstrated the overriding effect of societal influences on a child's gender role learning. The trivia, tiny events and language all created a particular picture and image which established a gender consciousness. Many studies support the notion that everyday language and events identify, acknowledge and maintain the dependent, subordinate position of women.[103]

Gender shaping

Gender shaping occurs in education in overt forms of schooling, for example curriculum; and in the 'hidden' patterns of behaviour such as teachers' values and expectations. Examination entries for A level grades in 2000/01 indicated that there were still some traditional gender differences in terms of subjects chosen with more girls electing to do English and Humanities subjects and more boys choosing to study maths and physics. However, females had higher average point scores than males across all educational institutions and had greater success rates than boys in all subjects at grade C or above. At GCSE the girls also passed more subjects than the boys with a grade C or above (females 81 per cent and males 72 per cent).

Schools are becoming female environments with the latest figures from the DfES showing that in March 2001 women made up 70 per cent of classroom teachers, 63 per cent of deputy head teachers and 55 per cent of head teachers.[104] Given the achievements and success of female students and teachers it is surprising that studies have shown differences between boys and girls in their self-evaluation of intelligence and ability.

Furnham[105] cites work by Beloff in which she found a six-point difference by males who estimated their intelligence significantly higher than females. She suggests that 'women see themselves as intellectually inferior compared to the young men'.[106] Furnham also reports on studies, which show consistent sex differences in self-estimates of mathematical and spatial intelligence, but not for verbal intelligence. Three explanations are suggested for these self-estimates: sociological variables, biological reasons and data interpretation, and he concludes:

> For some researchers this remains a shocking finding explicable only by sociological processes; for others it represents a reasonable grasp of reality. (p. 15)

ORIENTATIONS AND MOTIVATIONS TOWARDS WORK

It is perhaps salutary to recognise that women workers have tended to be overlooked within many of the classical studies on orientation and motivation. Early studies tended to focus entirely on men (for example, the work of *F. W. Taylor*); or avoid an interpretation of gender divisions (recall, for example, the discussion in Chapter 3 on sex power differential in the Hawthorne experiments).

There is also a common, underlying suggestion that for 'he' one may also assume 'she'. For example, *Alban-Metcalfe* commented that anyone reading the management literature may well:

gain the impression that the managerial population is hermaphrodite since the vast majority of studies (which transpire when examined) have been based upon exclusively male samples which are interpreted as if the findings apply equally to females and males.[107]

Early studies by *Hunt* revealed that decisions about working revolved around women's primary responsibility for home care. Differences in motivations among the sampled women depended on the life stage which they had reached. Hunt claimed it was not possible to discuss motivation without taking into account the social context of work and home.[108]

Of course, there are dangers inherent in gender research, which studies of motivation highlight. It is self-evident that not all women (or all men) share similar motives. There will be differences within each gender as well as between the genders. A study carried out in Australia illustrate this. They focused attention on the grouping traditionally considered to be the most homogeneous, that of the female part-time worker. Although the majority were content with their working hours and the freedom it gave them to look after dependent children, not all the sample had family responsibilities and some (20 per cent of the sample) would have preferred to work full-time. The study drew attention to the diverse range of motivations and reasons for part-time working.[109]

WORKING PRACTICES

Is it the case that men and women experience different working practices? This idea contradicts the view that organisations are neutral and objective entities but suggests that work itself has a masculine blue print. Recent research has suggested that the following practices seem to have gendered bias:

- recruitment and selection;
- informal communication;
- attitudes; and
- career development.

Recruitment and selection

Investigations into (supposedly) neutral personnel procedures have found that informal criteria based on gendered stereotypes are maintained in selection decisions.[110] It has been suggested that there is a gap between the rational procedures of specifying scientifically the job, and the informal evaluation of recruiting candidates and evaluating their suitability.[111]

Informal communication

Informal communication within organisations has also been studied and it has been shown that advice from 'gatekeepers' affect women's opportunities and their perceptions of themselves. For example, one study reported that males and females received different career advice.[112] In another study, young female lawyers were subjected to greater scrutiny than male applicants in terms of their motivation and attitude.[113]

Attitudes

Paternalistic attitudes also reveal that male managers frequently think it 'best' not to send a woman on an assignment or ask her to attend late meetings. Although intentions might be well-meaning, the lack of opportunities for women to be placed in challenging or risky situations places them at a disadvantage *vis-à-vis* men.

The term 'homosociability', coined by *Kanter*,[114] labels the process whereby members of the same sex are preferred, promoted and developed. Inevitably in most organisations this equates with male development. It is often a pleasure for senior managers to mentor and develop a younger person with whom they can identify. Given that informal relations and networks within organisations play a powerful part in determining career opportunities, then young men are placed in an advantaged position.

CAREER DEVELOPMENT

The socialisation period has been found to have a marked effect on subsequent performance and work-related values. The formation of appropriate bonds between individuals and the group are crucial in order that the new member feels involved and accepted by the organisation. Exclusion from a group has far-reaching effects for information transmission, decision-making and eventual career progression.[115]

Training opportunities are vital for personal development and career success. The under-representation of women in one study was blamed on the male bias in professional development. They urged a rethink of the content of senior management courses and a move towards more mentoring.[116] Training and development programmes at the start of the employment career have also been examined for gender bias. Barriers and problems in choice and selection of training were examined in a study conducted by the (then) DfEE and the Local Government National Training Organisation. They were concerned at the gender imbalance of the Modern Apprenticeship scheme. (The work-based training scheme was introduced in the UK in the early 1990s.) Barriers included peer group and parental pressure as well as poor careers advice.[117]

Constraints still prevail

Crompton and Harris conducted research on 150 women employed in banking and medicine across five countries. They noted the choices and constraints made by women and the weight that they place on domestic and employment careers. They observed that demands of employment and family are often in conflict and that many women (and some men) will consciously make sacrifices in one sphere or both. The differences that women made in the way they managed the employment family interface were linked to the variations in the kinds of constraints and opportunities offered by their organisation – banking and medicine. Crompton and Harris suggested there were clear occupational effects. They concluded 'certainly women can and do make choices – although in aggregate their relative lack of power and resources relative to men means that both today and in the past they have been less able to do so than the opposite sex.'[118]

International career moves

Many female managers encounter more barriers in their career progression than their male counterparts especially in pursuing an international career, according to *Lineham and Walsh*. These barriers included:

- practical relocation issues;
- resolving the male partner's career on hold – perceived to be considerably more difficult;
- the balancing of domestic/work issues as they established that women take primary responsibility for domestic tasks and child rearing;
- organisations too inflexible in their demands;
- mentor support often not available;
- isolation in host countries compounded by language, culture and gender barriers and exclusion from the old boy network in Europe (evidently still strong).[119]

When organisations get it wrong

The reasons why women move from organisations to self-employed status was the focus of research by *Mallon and Cohen*.[120] They explored the push and pull factors and noted that women admitted that the 'organisational world continues to erect barriers against their progress to the assumed fruits of the traditional career' (p. 228). Women judged their actions against the still-dominant script of the traditional progressive career. For all but 14 per cent of the sample they felt that organisational life had let them down and perceived that self-employment would lead to the autonomous, independent life they craved.

Moving away from a traditional linear path

Evetts suggested that the uni-dimensional, hierarchical, linear career has gendered overtones and that careers which are different (for example, mainly women's careers) are considered to be deficient or lacking. She therefore asserts that the language of careers needs to be de-gendered; by this she means that:

- the necessity for regarding work/family issues as universal and not just women's concern;
- there needs to be a shift away from the mono-dimensional interpretation of career as promotion into management alongside the perceptions of management as aggressive, independent, competititve, ambitious etc.;
- a new language for careers needs to be developed which is gender neutral. Career success needs to be redefined to embrace different kinds of career patterns which include social, domestic and community goals. There is a need to recognise the wide diversity of careers and of combining paid and unpaid work: the 'multi-dimensional career'.

Evetts proposes that the 'successful career is ready for redefinition' and suggests that it should have a multi-dimensional nature. Three major dimensions are identified as being critical: cultural (family and feminine ideologies); structural issues (organisational processes) and action (women's strategies and preferences). Such a view is also in keeping with other research on careers which promotes a portfolio approach.[121]

Casting the ladders aside and moving to portfolios – redefinition of careers

So, traditionally the concept of career has been one of upward movement ... the metaphor of the 'career ladder' used to describe the planned structure and promotional steps. Measurement of career success was possible using objective measures of salary and position. Career achievements were within the boundaries of hierarchy and linear progression.

Downsizing, delayering and generally flattening the hierarchy has reinforced the fact that organisations are not longer able to guarantee a job for life or with regular promotion. There has been general agreement in the literature that the notion of careers has become destabilised, but the extent to which careers have completely departed from traditional patterns is the subject of debate. However, there does seem to be acknowledgement that traditional career pathways are shifting and becoming less linear and less organisationally confined. Careers seem to be more individual centred than organisation centred. Organisations rely 'on the individual's ability to learn and adapt rather than perform as required'.[122]

New terms have been coined to address these changes, such as:

- Boundary-less career
- Portfolio careers
- Explicit contracting

The emergence of these changes to a flexible, boundary-less portfolio world should bode well for women who are also looking for independence and autonomy. Women arguably should be well placed to take advantage of these changes ... but are they? And yet the recent research suggests that the values of the traditional career paths still dominate.

So, what should organisations do?

The trick appears to be to use the need for flexibility and constant change for the mutual benefits of the individual and the organisation. But how?

Focus must be on the psychological contract and its negotiation and renegotiation. To achieve mutuality requires negotiation at clear career transition points in order to reflect, to evaluate and to plan next steps. According to *Harrison*:

> *if the basis of the psychological contract changes during the individual's career with the organisation then that too should be acknowledged as cause for the parties jointly to identify the key issues raised by the changed situation, what each party wants in that new situation, and a renegotiation of what each will offer to the other.*[123]

Without this mutuality Harrison predicts a crisis of credibility and a negative impact on organisational as well as individual learning and growth. This suggests that management for growth requires qualitatively different employment relations.

People need help in managing their careers and in the building of new contracts:

- Research conducted in 1995 by the *Institute of Employment Studies* noted that people needed support and a purposive approach.
- *Roffey Park* claimed that few organisations were taking into account the strains that new structures were having on people and their sense of isolation. They developed new Peer Centres to help people maximise their potential.[124]
- *Nicholson and West* were surprised at how little effort managers had placed in the planning and management of their careers. They found that careers were a set of improvisations based on loose assumptions about the future, rather than a coherent match between skills and goals. Managers would explain their progress as:
  - opportunistic – they happened to be in the right place at the right time, or
  - blind belief that 'things had gone well so far, therefore they will continue to do so', or
  - faith in the organisation that their talent would be spotted and rewarded, or
  - simple fatalsim that careers are determined largely by luck.[125]

Organisations need to build processes to ensure mutuality in career development by:

- informing;
- negotiating;
- monitoring;
- renegotiating and/or exiting.

***Harrison* identifies six critical success factors for career development:**

- It must embody a transparent process owned by line managers.
- It must be a process that can evolve through time and is integrated with existing HR systems.
- It must comprise a system based on full information about people's career expectations and about the needs of the organisation.
- There must be a measurement of standards to show whether the system works.
- There must be clear communication about development processes and responsibilities to all employees and provision for all employees of relevant and full information about career paths.
- There must be support for employees in planning their development.[126]

The retention of staff

The following examples are practices which have been found to help the retention of staff.

1 Career management programme

Citibank reports that intensive training placements in other countries are effective in attracting and retaining the best people. The paper reports that companies which do not have career management programmes can experience staff turnover rates in excess of 15–20 per cent. Management programmes can be passive, e.g. include regular performance reviews and setting performance goals, whereas active programmes consider overseas postings, in-house training. The most successful programmes are those which require employees to plan their own careers. The paper claims that Singaporean and Hong Kong companies are not as flexible as organisations in Australia and New Zealand in enabling individuals to design their own plans.[127]

2 Traditional processes preferred at Nestlé

Nestlé re-examined career management systems and decided the following critical success factors for their culture:

- a transparent process owned by the line manager;
- information about managers' career expectations and the needs of the organisation;
- measurement standards to determine whether it was working.

In setting up the process they concentrated on focused succession planning and introduced career management groups. These groups review the needs of the organisation and define the menu of experiences future managers will need. The system is now more focused and measurable. They decided *not* to introduce self-development, mentoring and career workshops, believing that the impact would be limited.[128]

3 Changing expectations

The starting point for SCO, a software company, was to change the expectations of the employees away from traditional ideas about career progression, to ones that were more realistic and possible. They decided on four parameters to realign individual goals and the organisation direction:

- building a learning culture through self-development and career management driven by the individual;
- improved feedback and communication;
- effective performance management system;
- increasing the ability of individuals to bring about change.

Practical interventions included:

- self-development guide – of inventories and activities;
- career management workshops;
- project teams for specific business issues;
- technical problem-solving workshops;
- lunchtime training on key issues;
- workshops on managing transition;
- review of performance management systems.[129]

4 Mentoring and networks

Used now by many organisations, benefits include developing skills in reflection and evaluation, self learning and development. Some organisations initiate formal mentoring programmes with regular one-to-one advice and guidance with an older successful role model. Aspiring managers can gain much-needed exposure and visibility. Telementoring has also been suggested as a method of developing and supporting individuals when face-to-face meetings are not possible.[130]

Women's networks can provide a communication channel enabling contact, sharing information and reducing isolation. Although there are professed benefits to be gained *McDougall and Briley* noted that in 1994 few organisations used mentoring or networking as a means of developing women and where it was used it was on an informal basis.[131]

5 Development centres

Development centres which have as their aim to provide opportunities for reflection and development have been widely commended for their benefits. The Peer Centre designed at Roffey Park has its focus on learning: how to coach, how to observe, how to give feedback constructively and how to plan development at an individual and group level. They believe it sends strong signals to employees that they are valued, they are being offered a coherent alternative to continual promotion.[132]

In short, organisations need to consider ways in which they can establish a broader de-gendered view of careers, one that takes into account the ebbs and flow of individual needs at different stages of their work cycle. A programme that allows individual to reflect, re-tool and re-energise; one that allows for greater involvement in families or communities outside work.

LEADERSHIP, MANAGEMENT AND WOMEN

Changes in the way organisations are structured and managed may be good news for a more feminine style of leadership. (*See* Chapter 10 on learning.) If the effectiveness of organisations requires a style which is facilitative and participatory, this should augur well for women who prefer the more social, less hierarchical modes of management.

Changing ideas on leadership

A pull towards a more feminine style

There is support for the view that flexible forms of organisations are encouraging a new way of constructing management and leadership in less masculine ways than has traditionally been the case. Themes such as identity, cohesion teams and social integration all suggest a non-masculine direction. 'If more participatory, non-hierarchical flexible and group-oriented style of management is viewed as increasingly appropriate and this is formulated in feminine terms then women can be marketed as carriers of suitable orientations for occupying positions as managers.'[133]

A decade ago *Judy Rosener* identified an interactive leadership style in the female managers that she studied. She found that these women 'actively work to make their interactions with subordinates positive for everyone involved'. Specifically she described four characteristics of this style:

- **Encourage participation** – by making people feel part of the organisation, instilling group identity and facilitating inclusion and participation in all aspects of work.
- **Share power and information** – willingly sharing power and information rather than guarding and coveting it. They are not preoccupied with 'the turf'.
- **Enhance the self-worth of others** – by not asserting their own superiority and giving credit, praising publicly and recognising individual efforts. Most disliked practices that set them apart from others (separate parking/dining etc.).
- **Energise others** – by being enthusiastic for the work and encouraging others to see work as challenging and fun.[134]

Research conducted by *Alimo-Metcalfe*[135] supports the view that the modern style of leadership required for organisations is one that embraces vision, individual consideration, strengthening participation and nurtures growth and self-esteem. Alimo-Metcalfe was positive that women managers were bringing with them real qualities of 'warmth, consideration for others, nurturance of self-esteem and above all, integrity'. In a later article leadership is described as not about being a wonder woman (or man) but as someone who:

- values the individuality of their staff;
- encourages individuals to challenge the status quo;
- possesses integrity and humility.

She claims that myths of leadership are dangerous because they suggest that leadership is rare, found mainly at the top of organisations and is about being superhuman.[136] This she claims distinguishes her study from those from the US which tend to focus on 'distant leaders'. The characteristics of the distant leader may be different to those valued in 'nearby leaders – the immediate line manager'. Although vision, charisma, courage are qualities that are ascribed to the distant leader subordinates seek qualities in their nearby leader such as being sociable, open and considerate. These were rated more highly in their research and it was found that women scored higher than men in 11 out of the 14 characteristics.

A push to maintaining status quo: male as leader

However, the interest in 'New Leadership' research and transformational leadership in particular has focused on 'heroes' and the nature of charisma. Many studies have focused on public figures, notably men. *Goffee and Jones* claim that inspirational leaders share four unexpected qualities:

- They selectively show their weaknesses.
- They rely heavily on intuition to gauge the appropriate timing and course of their actions.
- They manage employees with tough empathy.
- They reveal their differences; they capitalise on what is unique about them. However, Goffee and Jones suggest that gender differences can lead to stereotyping and to a double bind situation. They suggest that women may opt to 'play into' their stereotype and make themselves invisible 'by being more like the men' or deliberately play the role of nurturer or set themselves apart by campaigning for rights in the workplace. Whichever route is chosen females are playing into a negative stereotype. Goffee and Jones ask the question 'Can female leaders be true to themselves?'[137]

The extent to which women's experiences and skills offer something different to men is still in debate but there is a clear push in the literature concerning the significance of skills and qualities associated with being feminine. These dimensions resonate with the changing nature of organisations in the 21st century and support the notion of emotional intelligence. *Alvesson and Due Billing*, working in Sweden and Denmark, have summarised the differing and at times confusing approaches in the framework shown in Figure 9.8. In addition to the arguments on gender similarity (or not), they also consider the impact of differing organisational approaches. They argue that the notion of feminine leadership may not be especially valid or useful. Workplaces, which are organised without the stereotyping of gender, might evolve new and more effective models of leadership.[138]

What should organisations do to encourage women leaders?

Alvesson and Due Billing suggest that there are three agendas which require attention:

- **Short agenda** – To advocate ensuring women have same privileges as men: equal pay, access etc.
- **Long agenda** – To strengthen women's self-confidence and facilitate the integration of work and family.
- **Broad agenda** – To emphasise women's interests and female values with broader concerns. The consideration of women-focused activities in relationship to men. The social relations between men and women and the gendered nature of institutions would be of central concern. How the organisation reaffirms gender positions in its culture; its stories, rites and rituals.

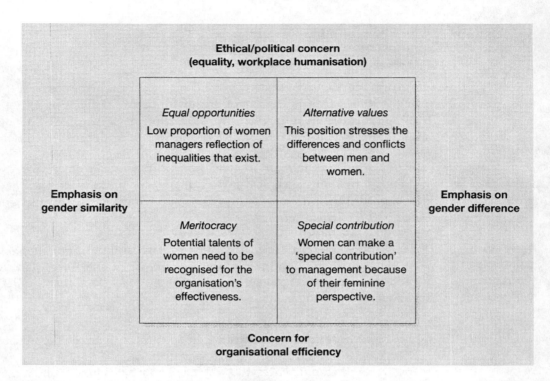

Figure 9.8 Matrix indicating differing perspectives on gender

(*Source*: Adapted from 'Approaches to the Understanding of Women and Leadership' in *Understanding Gender and Organisations* by Alvesson, M. and Due Billing, Y. Reproduced with permission from Sage Publications Ltd, 1997.)

In addition organisations could:

- help to demystify leadership and identify the competencies within the organisation to which it is to be applied;
- develop the importance of feedback and reflection – evidence suggests that successful leaders thrive on feedback and support. Provide structures to enable feedback and reflection time – 'time to think'. *Kline* advocates that organisations should become thinking environments as everything we do depends for its quality on the thinking we do first, and our thinking depends on the quality of our attention for each other. A thinking environment says 'you matter'.[139]

POSITIVE APPROACHES

Reviews and articles explaining the position and status of women typically conclude with exhortations to organisations to introduce and promote schemes which would positively help and support women. The logic of introducing such schemes is based on good business sense in that women represent an untapped human resource. There has been considerable media hype about the progress of women at work and yet this is not revealed in the latest statistics. Improving the 'lot' of women can also provoke resentment from men.

Perhaps the most positive approach to take is for an organisation to acknowledge the changing working pattern of all employees and to consider the best working practices for managing a diverse workforce. This should not be done mechanically but by analysis of the organisation and its workforce. Organisations need to analyse, consciously debate and question their unwritten assumptions and expectations in order to reveal prejudices inherent in the culture of their organisations. Analysis of the way in which culture is expressed in all its trivial detail would lead to an understanding of perceptions and attitudes. Until a full analysis is completed it remains doubtful if more egalitarian practices will develop.

Employees should go through a three-stage process of auditing existing policies, setting measurable goals and making a public commitment from top management to achieving them. A number of agencies see work/life balance (discussed in Chapter 18) as key to equality for women and men.[140] Equality Direct's appeal is to the 'bottom-line':

> *Businesses prosper if they make the best use of their most valuable resource: the ability and skills of their people. And these people, in turn, will flourish if they can strike a proper balance between work and the rest of their lives.*[141]

Why do we need a work/life balance?

The EOC claims there 'is now a mismatch between people's caring and parenting responsibilities and the demands of inflexible employment patterns' (p. 1).[142] Family patterns are more fluid and diverse requiring work environments to reflect people's changing needs. Most two-parent families are also two-earner families. There are more lone parents, more than half who work.[143] The government has made a commitment to enhancing choice and support for parents including enhancing access to good quality child care and parenting services; tailoring financial support to families' circumstances and working in partnership with business to promote the benefits of flexible working. A number of current government agencies are urging organisations to develop more flexible working practices.

They argue that if employees are given greater control and choice over where, when and how much time is in work, a more satisfied, valued, committed and less stressed workforce will result. The notion is that everybody, regardless of age, race and gender, will prefer to work to a rhythm of work that suits his or her lifestyle. The challenge of managing caring responsibilities and paid employment are too often a source of stress and anxiety. Evidence from research studies has shown the dysfunctional impact that the 'long hours' culture prevalent in Britain has on employees' home life.[144]

The push for flexibility

In a report commissioned by the CIPD entitled 'Married to the job' one in three partners of people who work more than 48 hours in a typical week said the long hours have an entirely negative effect on their personal relationship and on the relationship with chidren. The long-hours workers themselves feel they have struck the wrong work/life balance and feel guilty that they are failing to pull their weight on the domestic front. Working long hours can have a negative effect on job performance and cause accidents. CIPD reports 41 per cent of managers believe that the quality of their working life has deteriorated over the past three years. Those working in small firms are the most confident about the quality of their life.[145]

This new focus on equality has moved from one that is focusing only on women's needs to one of inclusiveness. It is a compelling idea as it avoids the difficulties of hostility and resentment potentially caused by the selective focus on women's needs. Rather than being a 'women's issue' it suggests that gender should be 'mainstreamed'; it should be a core practice of the business. The EOC identify that mainstreaming requires rethinking the traditional roles of men and women in society:

> *Simply, the gender mainstreaming approach means challenging our assumptions and stereo-types about men and women, and their roles in society and the economy. It means making evidence-based policy. This is simply good sense. Well-targeted policy which takes account of the different ways men and women may organise their time, or relate to goods and services, means better use of resources and better outcomes in terms of achieving policy objectives. In the process social and economic inequalities will be challenged.*[146]

Is work more attractive than home?

Research conducted in the US by *Hochschild* noted that attractive organisations can be 'seductive'. In her study she observed that it was possible to achieve fulfilment, satisfaction, care and confirmation at work, while home shared similarities to a 'Taylorised' environment. In such circumstance work becomes home, and home becomes work. This, she claims offers one explanation why parents choose not to take up the family-friendly (FF) schemes offered in the company as they actually prefer to be in work.[147]

Swedish experience suggests that women will initially take more advantage than men of FF policies and that many men will continue to behave as if married to a full-time housewife. However, some recent research suggests that this at last is beginning to change and that a new model of a more democratic family may be evolving in Sweden.[148]

Approaches to gender equality: a comparison

A study conducted in Australia explored the link between different EO policies and the number of women in management positions. This identified four types of approaches:

- Classical disparity – equal treatment practised but gendered roles assumed;
- Anti-discrimination – equal outcomes encouraged;
- Affirmative action – assistance for disadvantaged groups and specific actions taken (women's groups/networks/mentoring programme for women, formal mechanisms exist with women);
- Gender diversity – compensate for disadvantages through a change in culture and organisational systems – flexible systems encouraged – but specific treatment for one group discouraged, for example, job sharing, part-time work.

The study found that those organisations that took an **affirmative action** approach had significantly higher numbers of women in all management tiers. Organisations classified as gender diverse did not see such significant increases. *French* states, 'One possible explanation as to why this might be involves the fact that broad application of diversity strategies results in limited practical outcomes. That is, in trying to do everything, nothing substantive is achieved. Another explanation is that the diversity approach to substantive equity may take up to 25 years because of the slow pace of cultural and structural change without the use of direct affirmative action strategies.'[149]

There still seems to be some way to go before flexible working practices become part of our 'normal way of life'. In reality it would seem that the political and cultural nature of the organisation is a major factor in choosing working practices. It appears that there is a stigma attached to employees who choose to work part-time and people fear that if they choose to work at home they may miss out on potential promotion opportunities.

The following obstacles stand in the way of a healthy work/life balance:

- Family-friendly schemes are still perceived as concessions to women.
- Men's domestic absenteeism.
- Presenteeism (being **seen** at work) as a phenomenon linked to career success.

Only time will tell whether the exhortations will work. Will there be stigma attached to employees who choose to work part-time? Will people who choose to work at home miss out on potential promotion opportunities? Are there preferred career tracks, which exclude routes other than the traditional linear paths? So, even if the opportunities are open to all, in reality the political and cultural nature of the organisation prevents career-hungry individuals from choosing such options. (*Please see* Chapter 22 for more detail on the working of cultural processes in organisations.)

CRITICAL REFLECTIONS

'OK, so it is important to understand that managing is all about people, and every person is an individual in his or her own right. But many theories and models about behaviour appear to apply to people in general. Surely we should be more concerned with a study of differences among individuals rather than similarities among people?'

What are your own views?

Among the factors that exert pressures on our personality formation are the culture in which we are raised, our early conditioning, the norms among our family, friends, and social groups, and other influences that we experience. The environment to which we are exposed plays a substantial role in shaping our personalities.

Robbins, S. P. *Organizational Behavior*, Ninth edition, Prentice Hall International (2001), p. 93.

How would you describe the environmental factors which have helped shape your personality and how is this manifested in the work situation?

'Freud's personality theories have no practical use or value to the organisation.'

Debate.

SYNOPSIS

▓ The individual member is the first point of study and analysis in organisational behaviour. One of the essential requirements of organisations is the development and encouragement of individuality within a work atmosphere in which common goals and aims are achieved. Emphasising individual differences and valuing diversity is a recent catalyst for helping the equality agenda in business. One of the distinguishing factors of successful managers in any organisation is their ability to bring out the best in the people that work with and report to them. Managing relationships well depends on an understanding and awareness of the staff and of their talents, abilities, interests and motives. It is also dependent upon effective social skills and emotional intelligence.

▓ Encouraging and developing each member at work is essential for individual and organisational health and is a major task of management. Recognising and improving individual talent and potential is critical to ensure that the many roles and functions of an organisation are achieved effectively. However, differences between individuals can also be the source of problems and conflict. Personality clashes may occur; differences of attitudes and values may lead to polarisation and discrimination.

▓ Improved self-awareness and accelerated development are essential to the education of managers. Although psychologists do not agree in terms of the relative importance of certain factors, there is much to be gained from both nomothetic and idiographic approaches. Personality assessment techniques have been found to be helpful in terms of self-knowledge and discovery as well as adding to the rapidly enlarging repertoire of assessment centres. In mentoring an individual's development, an understanding of the causes of behaviour and past experiences can be helpful in terms of future planning.

▓ A major influencing factor affecting work performance is the ability of the employee. Ensuring that the right people are selected for work and are able to use their intelligence effectively is a critical personnel process, now helped by the appropriate use of psychological tests. However, tests are not a panacea and can, if inappropriately used, lead to a sense of false security.

■ Assessment of attitudes is vital in selecting potential employees and future managers, and yet informal measures of observation are frequently used. Given the difficulties of attitude measurement and doubts associated with predicting behaviour, such assessment is fraught with problems. Managers may hold incorrect assumptions and beliefs about their colleagues. Without a gauge to measure these attitudes, ineffective management decisions may be made. Attitudes can take on a permanency which is maintained by the culture of the organisation and thus be very resistant to change. Moreover, the power of attitudes should be recognised particularly with regard to influencing newer members of the organisation and their development.

■ Understanding the ways in which working practices may have an unintended adverse impact on women is a critical area of research to be conducted by organisations. Until practices are free of gender bias it is unlikely that women will have an equal role in organisations. The differing approaches taken by psychologists offer complementary perspectives from which to analyse individual behaviour. Practical solutions to flexible work may produce mutual benefits for employees and employers, but evaluation of these practices is a necessary outcome.

REVIEW AND DISCUSSION QUESTIONS

1 Identify the major ways in which individual differences are demonstrated at work. Discuss strengths and limitations to the employer and employee of:
   a people of the same age and/or race working together;
   b people working different hours (flexi-time, part-time).

2 You are required to interview one person from your work or study group to produce an assessment of their personality. What questions will you ask and how accurate do you feel your assessment will be? What are some of the problems of using this method?

3 What are psychometric tests and when should they not be used?

4 Why are attitudes difficult to measure and change? How would you promote awareness of the needs of students (or work colleagues) with disabilities? What would you do? What reactions might you encounter?

5 Design a simple questionnaire to administer to your work/college colleagues on attitudes towards reducing stress at work.

6 Hold a debate: 'This house believes that low intelligence cannot be improved.' Draw up evidence for and against this statement. At the end of the debate, reflect on the strength of emotional responses and consider the political arguments that have been addressed.

7 Analyse the evidence which suggests that men's and women's attitudes and motivations to work are different.

8 List recommendations you would make to young Asian women about to embark on a management career. Consider the differences you would make if you were to advise young white men. Compare your list with others in the group.

9 'Work-life balance is all about good management practice and sound business sense'. Is it? Critically evaluate this statement.

10 Men and women need to work in partnership to establish equality in the workplace. Critically discuss.

ASSIGNMENT

Role play the following situations:

SITUATION 1

Mumtaz has just completed her fast-track graduate programme and is now looking forward to a Development Centre which will determine the next promotion step. She is anticipating an international assignment.

She is already gaining a reputation for hard work and creative ideas and exudes confidence. She is acutely aware that she has been the only female Asian on the programme. The organisation's dominant culture is white and male. A letter arrives from the HR Department with the news that the Development Centre falls in the middle of Ramadan, a time when she needs to fast and partake in regular prayer. She knows that the socialising aspects of the Development Centres are important and that a formal lunch is prepared for each of the three days.

She is unsure whether she should inform her line manager of her anxieties, but she decides to arrange a meeting.

▪ Role-play the meeting in triads: playing the part of Mumtaz, the manager and the observer.

▪ Take turns playing different roles, with different outcomes.

▪ Discuss the feelings, attitudes and behaviours that were being portrayed.

SITUATION 2

Jordan is a highly successful salesman who works for an international IT organisation. As part of the rewards package for sales staff, exotic prizes are offered to the best sales teams. Jordan is part of the North West team, which has exceeded its targets over the last quarter. The team is currently in the lead to win a trip on the Orient Express and a weekend in Venice.

The announcement is made and the team has won the prize. There is great joy and celebration in the office, especially as each team member can take their partner on the trip. Jordan is gay but has not 'come out' at work. He wants to include his partner, but is uncertain of the reaction of his colleagues. At the pub that evening he broaches the subject to two of his work colleagues …

▪ Role play the meeting with one observer.

▪ Take turns playing different roles, with different outcomes.

▪ Discuss the feelings, attitudes and behaviours that were being portrayed.

PERSONAL AWARENESS AND SKILLS EXERCISE

OBJECTIVES

Completing this exercise should help you to enhance the following skills:

▶ Explore a range of issues concerned with individual differences.

▶ Reflect on the nature of motivation and satisfaction of your needs.

▶ Assess the strengths and weaknesses of using the repertory grid technique.

EXERCISE

Using Kelly's repertory grid technique and Wilson's framework (Table 9.6), **you are required to** complete your own **personal construct grid**.

1 Produce the elements and answer the following:

- the job I do now;
- an ideal job;
- a job I would not enjoy; and

- the job I used to do (where appropriate);
- a job I would enjoy;
- a job I would hate.

2 Develop the constructs

Write your answer at the top of each column. Now, select two elements (for example, 1 and 2) and compare with a third (for example, 6). State the way in which the two elements are alike, and different from the third. Write your answer in the rows. These are your constructs. For example, I am now a lecturer (element 1) and I used to be a personnel officer (element 2), and a job I would hate would be a factory operative (element 6). The ways in which I see elements 1 and 2 as alike, and different from, 6 are in the intellectual demands of the jobs. Select different triads until you have exhausted all possible constructs.

3 Score the constructs

Examine each construct in relation to the elements (jobs) you have described. Score between 7 (high) and 1 (low).

4 Now compare:

- Your pattern of scores for element 1 and element 3. What does this tell you about your current career and motivation?

- Your pattern of scores with the grid completed by an engineering craftsman as shown in the section in the text on personality. (See Table 9.7.)

- Your constructs and elements with other colleagues.

DISCUSSION

- How do you see the importance of constructs, goals and priorities in people's lives?

- What do you see as the meaning of work to the individual – central or peripheral goal?

- Explain ways in which organisations may satisfy individual needs at work.

Visit our website **www.booksites.net/mullins** for further questions, annotated weblinks, case material and Internet research material.

NOTES AND REFERENCES

1. Equality Direct can be found at *http://* www.equalitydirect.org.uk.

2. 'Littlewoods: Increasing diversity, Increasing profits' *Equal Opportunities Review,* no. 81, September/October 1998, pp. 20–7.

3. Kirton, G. and Greene, A-M. *The Dynamics of Managing Diversity*, Butterworth Heinemann (2000).

4. Liff, S. and Cameron, I. 'Changing Equality Cultures to Move Beyond Women's Problems', *Gender, Work and Organization,* vol. 4, no. 1, January 1997, pp 35–46.

5. Kandola, R. and Fullerton, J. *Managing the Mosaic Diversity in Action*, IPD (1994), p. 19.

6. Clements, P. and Jones, J. *The Diversity Training Handbook*, Kogan Page (2002), p. 45.

7. Turner, B. *Exploring the Industrial Sub-culture*, Macmillan (1977).

8. Salaman, G. 'Organisations as Constructions of Social Reality', in Salaman, G. and Thompson, K. (eds) *Control and Ideology in Organisations*, MIT Press (1983).

9. Video 'Management Revolution and Corporate Reinvention', BBC for Business (1993).

10. Eysenck, H. J. *The Structure of Human Personality*, Methuen (1960).

11. Freud, S. *New Introductory Lectures on Psychoanalysis*, Penguin (1973).

12. Kelly's theory as described by Bannister, D. and Fansella, F., in *Inquiring Mind: The Theory of Personal Constructs*, Penguin (1971).

13. Eysenck, H. J. *Eysenck on Extroversion*, Crosby, Lockwood Staples (1973).

14. Furnham, A. *Personality at Work*, Routledge, London (1992).

15. Mabey, B. 'The Majority of Large Companies Use Occupational Tests', *Guidance and Assessment Review*, vol. 5, no. 3, 1989.

16. Personality tests have been debated by: Bartram, D. 'Addressing the Abuse of Personality Tests', *Personnel Management*, April 1991, pp. 34–9; and Fletcher, C. 'Personality Tests: The Great Debate', *Personnel Management*, September 1991, pp. 38–42.

17. Cattell, R. B. and Kline, P. *The Scientific Analysis of Personality and Motivation*, Academic Press (1977).

18. Howarth, E. 'A Source of Independent Variation: Convergence and Divergence in the Work of Cattell and Eysenck', in Dreger, R. M. (ed.) *Multivariate Personality Research*, Claiton (1972).

19. McCrae, R. R. and Costa, P. T. 'More Reasons to Adopt the Five-Factor Model', *American Psychologist*, vol. 44, no. 2, 1989, pp. 451–2.

20. Bayne, R. 'The Big Five versus the Myers-Briggs', *The Psychologist*, January 1994, pp. 14–17.

21. Lord, W. and Rust, J. 'The Big Five Revisited: Where are we now? A brief review of the relevance of the Big Five for Occupational Assessment', *Selection and Development Review*, vol. 19, no. 4, August 2003, pp. 15–18.

22. Mount, M. K., Barrick, M. R. and Strauss, J. P. 'Validity of Observer Ratings of the Big Five Personality Factors', *Journal of Applied Psychology*, April 1994, p. 272.

23. Bentall, R. P. 'Personality Traits May Be Alive, They May Even Be Well, but Are They Really Useful?', *The Psychologist*, July 1993, p. 307.

24. Rogers, C. *A Way of Being*, Houghton Mifflin (1980).

25. Mead, G. H. *Mind, Self and Society*, University of Chicago Press (1934), pp. 152–64.

26. Cooley, C. 'The Social Self', in Parsons, T., Shils, E., Naegele, K. D. and Pitts, J. R. (eds) *Theories of Society*, The Free Press, New York (1965).

27. Erikson, E. H. *Identity and Life Cycle*, Norton (1980).

28. Hunt, J. W. *Managing People at Work: A Manager's Guide to Behaviour in Organisations*, Third edition, McGraw-Hill (1992).

29. Freud, S. *New Introductory Lectures on Psychoanalysis*, Penguin (1973).

30. Gross, R. D. *Psychology – The Science of Mind and Behaviour*, Arnold (1987), p. 658.

31. Andrews, B. and Brewin, C. R. 'What Did Freud Get Right?', *The Psychologist*, vol. 13, no. 12, December 2000, pp. 605–7.

32. Reason, J. 'The Freudian Slip Revisited', *The Psychologist*, vol. 13, no. 12, December 2000, pp. 610–11.

33. Morgan, G. *Images of Organization*, Second edition, Sage Publication's (1997).

34. Kets de Vries, M. F. R. 'Organizational Paradoxes', *Clinical Approaches to Management*, Second edition, Routledge (1995), p. 152.

35. Horney, K. *The Collected Works of Karen Horney*, Norton (1963).

36. Jung, C. G. *Analytical Psychology: Its Theory and Practice*, Routledge and Kegan Paul (1968). See also: Jacobi, J. *Psychology of C. G. Jung*, Seventh edition, Routledge and Kegan Paul (1968).

37. Myers, Isabel Briggs *Introduction to Type*, Sixth edition, Consulting Psychologists Press (2000) and Myers, K. D. and Kirby, L. K. *Introduction to Type Dynamics and Development*, Second edition, Consulting Psychologists Press (2000).

38. Kelly's theory as described by Bannister, D. and Fansella, F., in *Inquiring Mind: The Theory of Personal Constructs*, Penguin (1971), pp. 50–1.

39. Wilson, F. 'Deskilling of Work? The Case of Computer Numerical Control in the Engineering Industry, Case 4', in McGoldrick, J. (ed.) *Business Case File in Behavioural Science*, Van Nostrand Reinhold (1987).

40. Stone, G. 'Personality and Effective Hospitality Management', Paper presented at the International Association of Hotel Management Schools Symposium, Leeds Polytechnic, Autumn 1988; and Worsfold, P. A. 'Personality Profile of the Hotel Manager', *International Journal of Hospitality Management*, vol. 8, no. 1, 1989, pp. 55–62.

41. Bartram, D. 'Addressing the Abuse of Psychological Tests', *Personnel Management*, April 1991, pp. 34–9; Newell, S. and Shackleton, V. 'Management Selection: A Comparative Survey of Methods Used in Top British and French Companies', *Journal of Occupational Psychology*, vol. 64, 1991, p. 23.

42. Kline, P. 'The Big Five and Beyond', Conference Paper given at the British Psychological Society Occupational Psychology Conference, University of Warwick, January 1995.

43. Anastasi, A. *Psychological Testing*, Macmillan (1988), p. 560.

44. Blinkhorn, S. and Johnson, C. 'The Insignificance of Personality Testing', *Nature*, 348, 1990, pp. 671–2.

45. Goss, D. *Principles of Human Resource Management*, Routledge (1994).

46. Gibbons, P., Baron, H., Nyfield, G. and Robertson, I. 'The Managerial Performance and Competences', Conference Paper given at the British Psychological Society Occupational Psychology Conference, University of Warwick, January 1995.

47. Platt, S. with Piepe, R. and Smythe, J. *'Teams': A Game to Develop Group Skills*, Gower (1988).

48. Gray, M. J. 'Personality and Performance', *Selection and Development Review*, vol. 19, no. 1 February 2003, p. 4.

49. Rosenmann, R., Friedman, F. and Straus, R. 'A Predictive Study of CHD', *Journal of the American Medical Association*, vol. 89, 1964, pp. 15–22 and in Warr, P. and Wall, T. *Work and Well Being*, Penguin (1975).

50. Cooper, C. 'Papering over the cracks: individual strategies or organizational intervention in dealing with stress at work', Conference paper given at the British Psychological Society Occupational Psychology conference, University of Warwick, January 1995.

51. Cooper, C., Cooper, R. D. and Eaker, L. H. *Living with Stress*, Penguin (1988); Cartwright, S. and Cooper, C. L. *No Hassle! Taking the Stress out of Work*, Century (1994).

52. http://www.equalitydirect.org.uk [accessed 3.9.03].

53. Galton, Sir Francis, *Psychometric Experiments*, reprinted from Brain VI, William Clowes & Sons (1879), pp. 149–62.

54. Haynes, N. and Orrell, S. *Psychology: An Introduction*, Longman (1987).

55. Howe, M. J. A. 'Can IQ Change?', *The Psychologist*, February 1998, pp. 69–72.

56. Binet, A. and Simon, Th. 'Méthodes Nouvelles pour le Diagnostic du Niveau Intellectuel des Anormaux', *Année Psychologique* 11, 1905, pp. 191–244.

57. Terman, L. M. *The Measurement of Intelligence*, Houghton Mifflin (1916).

58. Spearman, C. *The Abilities of Man*, Macmillan (1927).

59. Vernon, P. E. 'The Hierarchy of Abilities' in Wiseman, S. (ed.) *Intelligence and Ability*, Second edition, Penguin (1973).

60. Bartram, D. and Lindley, P. A. *Psychological Testing, an Introduction*, BPS Open Learning Programme on Psychological Testing (Level A) (1994), p. 25.

61. Thurstone, L. L. 'Primary Mental Abilities', *Psychometric Monographs*, no. 1, 1938.

62. Guilford, J. P. 'Three Faces of Intellect' in Wiseman, S. (ed.) *Intelligence and Ability*, Penguin (1959).

63. Gardner, H. *Frames of Mind*, Second edition, Fontana (1993).

64. Goleman, D. *Emotional Intelligence*, Bloomsbury (1996), p. 34.

65. Goleman, D. *Working with Emotional Intelligence*, Bantam Books, New York (1998).

66. Boyatzis, R., Goleman, D and Hay/McBer, *Emotional Competence Inventory Feedback Report*, Hay Group (1999).

67. Freely, M. 'Love one another is the first lesson', *The Observer*, Sunday 31 August 2003.

68. Anastasia, A. *Psychological Testing*, Macmillan Publishing (1988), p. 23.

69. Jackson, C. *Understanding Psychological Testing*, BPS Books (1996).

70. Feltham, R., Baron, H. and Smith, P. 'Developing Fair Tests', *The Psychologist*, January 1994, pp. 23–5.

71. Inman, M. *Participants' Perceptions of Assessment Centres*, Unpublished MSc Personnel Management dissertation, University of Portsmouth (1996).

72. Ribeaux, P. and Poppleton, S. E. *Psychology and Work*, Macmillan (1978).

73. Gross, R. D. *Psychology: The Science of Mind and Behaviour*, Edward Arnold (1987).

74. Hofstede, G. *Culture's Consequences: International Differences in Work-Related Values*, Sage (1980).

75. Katz, D. 'The Functional Approach to the Study of Attitudes', *Public Opinion Quarterly*, 21, 1960, pp. 163–204.

76. La Piere, R. T. 'Attitudes versus Action', *Social Forces*, 13, 1934, pp. 230–7.

77. Gidoomal, R., Mahtani, D. and Porter, D. *The British and How to Deal With Them*, Middlesex University Press (2001).

78. Sykes, A. J. M. 'The Effect of a Supervisory Training Course in Changing Supervisors' Perceptions and Expectations of the Role of Management', *Human Relations*, 15, 1962, pp. 227–43.

79. Hofstede, G., Nevijan, B., Dhayu, D. D. and Sanders, G. 'Measuring Organisational Cultures: a qualitative and quantitative study across 20 cases', *Administrative Science Quarterly*, vol. 35, 1990, pp. 286–316.

80. Berger, P. L. and Luckmann, T. *The Social Construction of Reality*, Penguin (1966) p. 37.

81. MacPherson, Sir William *The Stephen Lawrence Inquiry* The Stationery Office, February 1999.

82. Hicks, L. *Gender and Culture: A Study of the Attitudes Displayed by Managers in the Hotel Industry*, Unpublished doctoral thesis, University of Surrey, 1991.

83. Heider, F. 'Attitudes and Cognitive Organization', *Journal of Psychology*, 21, 1946, pp. 107–12.

84. Festinger, L. A. *A Theory of Cognitive Dissonance*, Row, Peterson and Co. (1957); Reissued by Stanford University Press and Tavistock Publications (1962).

85. Alvesson, M. and due Billing, Y. *Understanding Gender and Organizations*, Sage Publications (1997), p. 7.

86. Ibid.

87. Kanter, R. M. *Men and Women of the Corporation*, Basic Books (1977).

88. Palmer, C. 'Some still more equal than others' *The Observer*, Sunday 11 February 2001.

89. Holton, V., Rabberts, J. and Scrives, S. (Ashridge Management Research Group), 'Women on the Boards of Britain's Top 200 Companies: A Progress Report', *The Occupational Psychologist*, no. 24, April 1995.

90. Higher Education Statistics Agency, Resources of Higher Education Institutions 2000/2001.

91. Purcell, K. 'Qualifications and careers equal opportunities and earnings among graduates', Working Paper Series No. 1, University of the West of England.

92. Opportunity Now awards 2003, Opportunity Now London. Can also be accessed http://www.opportunitynow.org.uk.

93. Liff, S. and Cameron, I. 'Changing Equality Cultures to Move Beyond Women's Problems', *Gender, Work and Organization*, vol. 4, no. 1, January 1997, pp. 35–46.

94. Blakemore, K. and Drake, R. *Understanding Equal Opportunity Policies*, Prentice-Hall Harvester Wheatsheaf (1996).

95. Amsden, A. (ed.) *Papers in the Economics of Women and Work*, Penguin (1980).

96. Smith, J. and Ward, M. *Women's Wages and Work in the Twentieth Century*, Rand (1984).

97. Loveridge, R. and Mok, A. 'Theoretical Approaches to Segmented Labour Markets', *International Journal of Social Economics*, no. 7, 1980.

98. Gross, R. D. *Psychology: The Science of Mind and Behaviour*, Edward Arnold (1987).

99. Maccoby, E. and Jacklin, C. *The Psychology of Sex Differences*, Stanford University Press (1974).

100. Donelson, E. *Sex Differences in Developmental Perspective*, Homewood Learning Systems (1975).

101. Condry, S. and Condry, J. C. 'Sex Differences: A Study of the Eye of the Beholder', *Annual Progress in Child Psychiatry and Child Development*, 1977, pp. 289–301.

102. Barrett, M. *Women's Oppression Today*, Verso (1980), p. 206.

103. Garbucker, M. *There's A Good Girl*, The Women's Press (1988).

104. DfES, Trends in Education and Skills chart C 3.7. http://www.dfes.gov.uk/trends [accessed 4.9.03].

105. Furnham, A. 'Thinking about Intelligence', *The Psychologist*, vol. 13, no. 10, October 2000, pp. 510–15.

106. Beloff, H. 'Mother, Father and Me: Our IQ', *The Psychologist*, vol. 5, 1992, pp. 309–11.

107. Alban-Metcalfe, B. 'Attitudes to Work: Comparison by Gender and Sector of Employment', *The Occupational Psychologist*, no. 3, December 1987, p. 8.

108. Hunt, A. *A Survey of Women's Employment*, HMSO (1968).

109. Walsh, J. 'Myths and counter-myths: an analysis of part-time female employees and their orientation to work and working hours', *Work, Employment and Society*, vol. 3, no. 2, June 1999, pp. 179–204.

110. Collinson, D. *Managing to Discriminate: A Multi-Sector Study of Recruitment Practices*, EOC Research Report (1986).

111. Webb, J. 'The Politics of Equal Opportunity: Job Requirements and the Evaluation of Women's Suitability', Paper presented at The Psychology of Women at Work International Research Conference, London, 1988.

112. Terborg, J. 'Women in Management: A Research Review', *Journal of Applied Psychology*, vol. 62, no. 6, 1977, pp. 647–64.

113. Podmore, D. and Spencer, A. 'Joining the Professionals: Gender Issues in Recruitment and Careers of Solicitors', Case 5, in McGoldrick, J. (ed.) *Business Case File in Behavioural Science*, Van Nostrand Reinhold (1987).

114. Kanter, R. M. *Men and Women of the Corporation*, Basic Books (1977).

115. Kanter, R. M. *Men and Women of the Corporation*, Basic Books (1977).

116. McLay, M. and Brown, M. 'The Under-representation of Women in Senior Management in UK Independent Secondary Schools', *International Journal of Educational Management*, vol. 14, no. 3, 2000, pp. 101–7.

117. Wren, J. 'Challenging Gender Stereotyping in Modern Apprenticeships', *Equal Opportunities Review*, no. 81, Sept/Oct 1998.

118. Crompton, R. (ed). *Restructuring Gender Relations and Employment*, Oxford University Press (1999), p. 147.

119. Lineham, M. and Walsh, J. 'Key Issues in the Senior Female International Career Move: a Qualitative Study in a European Context', *British Journal of Management*, vol. 12, 2001, pp. 85–95.

120. Mallon, M. and Cohen, L. 'Time for a Change? Women's Accounts of the Move from Organizational Career to Self-Employment', *British Journal of Management*, vol. 12, 2001, 217–30.

121. Evetts, J. 'Career and Gender: The conceptual challenge' in Evetts, J. (ed.) *Women and Career: Themes and issues in advanced industrial socieities*, Longman (1994), pp. 223–33.

122. Pieperl, M., Arthur, M., Goffee, R. and Morris, T. (eds) *Career Frontiers: New conceptions of working lives*, Oxford University Press (2000), p. 1.

123. Harrison, R. *Employment Development*, Second edition, CIPD (2000), p. 334.

124. Holbeche, Linda 'Peering into the future of careers', *People Management*, 31 May 1995, pp. 26–31.

125. Nicholson, N. and West, M. *Managerial Job Change: men and women in transition*, Cambridge University Press (1988).

126. Harrison, R. *Employee Development*, Second edition, CIPD (2000).

127. Luh Shu Shin 'In house training helps productivity' http://www.careerjournal.com/myc/management/20011015-luh.html [accessed 11.3.02].

128. Guest, D. and Mackenzie, Davey K. 'Don't Write Off the Traditional Career', *People Management*, 22 February 1996, pp. 22–5.

129. Macauley, S. and Harding, N. 'Drawing Up a New Careers Contract' *People Management*, 4 April 1996, pp. 34–5.

130. Wood, M. 'The Challenges of Telementoring', http:www.managementfirst.com/articles (2002).

131. McDougall, M. and Briley, S. *Developing Women Managers*, HMSO (1994).

132. Holbeche, Linda 'Peering into the Future of Careers', *People Management*, 31 May 1995, pp. 26–31.

133. Alvesson, Mats and Due Billing, Yvonne *Understanding Gender and Organization*, Sage Publications (1997).

134. Rosener, Judy B. 'Ways Women Lead', *Harvard Business Review* November–December 1990 pp. 119–25.

135. Alimo-Metcalfe, Beverley 'Leadership and assessment' in Susan Vinnicombe and Nina L Colwill (eds) *The Essence of Women in Management*, Prentice Hall (1995).

136. Alimo-Metcalfe, Beverley and Alban-Metcalfe, John, 'The Great and the Good,' *People Management*, 10 January 2002.

137. Goffee, R. and Jones, G. 'Why Should Anyone be Led by You?' *Harvard Business Review*, September–October 2000, pp. 62–70.

138. Alvesson, Mats and Due Billing, Yvonne *Understanding Gender and Organization*, Sage Publications (1997).

139. Kline, Nancy, *Time to Think: Listening to ignite the human mind*, Ward Lock (1999).

140. EOC (Equal Opportunities Commission) Briefing series: *The Work-Life Balance*, http://www.eoc.org.uk [accessed 4.9.03].

141. http://www.equalitydirect.org.uk [accessed 11.2.01] p. 1.

142. EOC (Equal Opportunities Commission) Briefing series: *The Work-Life Balance*, http://www.eoc.org.uk [accessed 4.9.03].

143. Department of Trade and Industry and HM Treasury *Balancing Work and Family Life: Enhancing choice and support for parents*, January 2003.

144. Glynn, C. *Enabling Balance – the Importance of Organizational Culture*, The Roffey Park Management Institute (1998).

145. CIPD *Married to the Job*, June 2001 http://www.cipd.co.uk/infosource/professionalknowledge/cipdsurvey [accessed 11.3.02].

146. EOC Examples of mainstreaming in practice, p. 1 http://www.eoc.org.uk/EOCeng/EOCcs/[accessed 5.9.03].

147. Hochschild, A.R. *The Time Bind: When work becomes home and home becomes work*, New York: Metropolitan Books (1997).

148. Bryson, V. *Feminist Debate Issues of Theory and Political Practice*, Macmillan Press (1999).

149. French, E. 'Approaches to Equity Management and their Relationship to Women in Management', *British Journal of Management*, vol. 12, 2001, pp. 267–85.

 Use the *Financial Times* to enhance your understanding of the context and practice of management and organisational behaviour. Refer to articles 10, 24 and 27 in the BUSINESS PRESS section at the end of the book for relevant reports on the issues explored in this chapter.

11 THE PROCESS OF PERCEPTION

Laurie Mullins and Linda Hicks

Perceived reality, not actual reality, is the key to understanding behaviour. How we perceive others and ourselves is at the root of our actions and intentions. Understanding the perceptual process and being aware of its complexities is essential for developing insight into managing others. The words we use and the body language we display communicates our view of the world. The power of the perceptual process in guiding our behaviour needs to be unpacked and understood for effective relationships with others.

Photo: Scott Barbour/Getty Images

LEARNING OUTCOMES

After completing this chapter you should be able to:

▶ explain the nature of the perceptual process, and selectivity in attention and perception;

▶ detail internal and external factors which provide meaning to the individual;

▶ examine the organisation and arrangement of stimuli, and perceptual illusions;

▶ identify problems, distortions and bias with particular regard to the perception of people;

▶ examine links between perception and communication, including transactional and body language;

▶ provide an understanding of women's position and status in the organisational world;

▶ review the importance to managers of the study of perception and relationships with other people.

To interact effectively (present ourselves and communicate appropriately, influence others, work with them in relationships and groups or lead them) we must have a grasp of what others are thinking and feeling, including their motives, beliefs, attitudes and intentions. In social perception, accuracy and differentiation are essential but difficult. Achieving them may be linked to the complexity of a person's system of cognitive constructs.

Maureen Guirdham

Interactive Behaviour at Work, Financial Times Prentice Hall (2002)

THE PERCEPTUAL PROCESS

The significance of individual differences is particularly apparent when focusing on the process of **perception**. We all see things in different ways. We all have our own, unique picture or image of how we see the 'real' world and this is a complex and dynamic process. We do not passively receive information from the world; we analyse and judge it. We may place significance on some information and regard other information as worthless; and we may be influenced by our expectations so that we 'see' what we expect to see or 'hear' what we expect to hear. Although general theories of perception were first proposed during the last century the importance of understanding the perceptual process is arguably even more significant today. Perception is the root of all organisational behaviour; any situation can be analysed in terms of its perceptual connotations. Consider, for instance, the following situation.

A member of the management team has sent a memorandum to section heads asking them to provide statistics of overtime worked within their section during the past six months and projections for the next six months. Mixed reactions could result:

- One section head may see it as a reasonable and welcomed request to provide information which will help lead to improved future staffing levels.
- Another section head may see it as an unreasonable demand, intended only to enable management to exercise closer supervision and control over the activities of the section.
- A third section head may have no objection to providing the information, but be suspicious that it may lead to possible intrusion into the running of the section.
- A fourth head may see it as a positive action by management to investigate ways of reducing costs and improving efficiency throughout the organisation.

Each of the section heads perceives the memorandum differently based on their own experiences. Their perceived reality and understanding of the situation provokes differing reactions.

Individuality

We are all unique; there is only one Laurie Mullins, and one Linda Hicks, and there is only one of you. We all have our own 'world', our own way of looking at and understanding our environment and the people within it. A situation may be the same but the interpretation of that situation by two individuals may be vastly different. For instance, a lively wine bar may be seen as a perfect meeting place by one person, but as a noisy uncomfortable environment by another. One person may see a product as user-friendly, but another person may feel that it is far too simplistic and basic. The physical properties may be identical, but they are perceived quite differently because each individual has imposed upon the object/environment/person their own interpretations, their own judgement and evaluation.

SELECTIVITY IN ATTENTION AND PERCEPTION

It is not possible to have an understanding of perception without taking into account its sensory basis. We are not able to attend to everything in our environment; our sensory systems have limits. The physical limits therefore insist that we are selective in our attention and perception. Early pioneer work by psychologists has resulted in an understanding of universal laws which underlie the perceptual process. It seems that we cannot help search for meaning and understanding in our environment. The way in which we categorise and organise this sensory information is based on a range of different factors including the present situation (and our emotional state), and also our past experiences of the same or similar event.

Some information may be considered highly important to us and may result in immediate action or speech; in other instances, the information may be simply 'parked' or assimilated in other ideas and thoughts. The link between perception and memory processes becomes obvious. Some of our 'parked' material may be forgotten or, indeed, changed and reconstructed over time.[1]

We should be aware of the assumptions that are made throughout the perceptual process, below our conscious threshold. We have learnt to take for granted certain constants in our environment. We assume that features of our world will stay the same and thus we do not need to spend our time and energy seeing things afresh and anew. We thus make a number of inferences throughout the entire perceptual process. Although these inferences may save time and speed up the process they may also lead to distortions and inaccuracies.

Perception as information processing

It is common to see the stages of perception described as an information processing system: (top down) information (stimuli) (Box A) is selected at one end of the process (Box B), then interpreted (Box C), and translated (Box D), resulting in action or thought patterns (Box E), as shown in Figure 11.1. However, it is important to note that such a model simplifies the process and although it makes it easy to understand (and will be used to structure this chapter) it does not give justice to the complexity and dynamics of the process. In certain circumstances, we may select information out of the environment because of the way we categorise the world. The dotted line illustrates this 'bottom up' process.

For instance, if a manager has been advised by colleagues that a particular trainee has managerial potential the manager may be specifically looking for confirmation that those views are correct. This process has been known as 'top down', because the cognitive processes are influencing the perceptual readiness of the individual to select certain information. This emphasises the active nature of the perceptual process. We do not passively digest the information from our senses, but we actively attend and indeed, at times, seek out certain information.

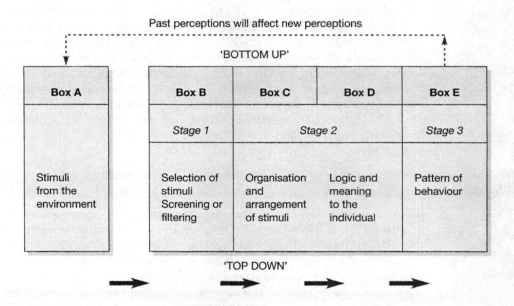

Figure 11.1 Perceptions as information processing

MEANING TO THE INDIVIDUAL

Figure 11.2

The process of perception explains the manner in which information (stimuli) from the environment around us is selected and organised, to provide meaning for the individual. Perception is the mental function of giving significance to stimuli such as shapes, colours, movement, taste, sounds, touch, smells, pain, pressures and feelings. Perception gives rise to individual behavioural responses to particular situations.

Despite the fact that a group of people may 'physically see' the same thing, they each have their own version of what is seen – their perceived view of reality. Consider, for example, the image (published by W. E. Hill in *Puck*, 6 November 1915) shown in Figure 11.2. What do you see? Do you see a young, attractive, well-dressed woman? Or do you see an older, poor woman? Or can you now see both? **And who can say with certainty that there is just the one, 'correct' answer?**

Internal and external factors

The first stage in the process of perception is selection and attention. Why do we attend to certain stimuli and not to others? There are two important factors to consider in this discussion: first, internal factors relating to the state of the individual; second, the environment and influences external to the individual. The process of perceptual selection is based, therefore, on both internal and external factors.

INTERNAL FACTORS

Our sensory systems have limits, we are not able to see for 'miles and miles' or hear very low or very high pitched sounds. All our senses have specialist nerves which respond differentially to the forms of energy which are received. For instance, our eyes receive and convert light waves into electrical signals which are transmitted to the visual cortex of the brain and translated into meaning.

Our sensory system is geared to respond to changes in the environment. This has particular implications for the way in which we perceive the world and it explains why we are able to ignore the humming of the central heating system, but notice instantly a telephone ringing. The term used to describe the way in which we disregard the familiar is 'habituation'.

Sensory limits or thresholds

As individuals we may differ in terms of our sensory limits or thresholds. Without eye glasses some people would not be able to read a car's number plate at the distance required for safety. People differ not only in their absolute thresholds, but also in their ability to discriminate between stimuli. For instance, it may not be possible for the untrained to distinguish between different grades of tea but this would be an everyday event for the trained tea taster. We are able to learn to discriminate and are able to train our senses to recognise small differences between stimuli. It is also possible for us to adapt to unnatural environments and learn to cope.[2]

We may also differ in terms of the amount of sensory information we need to reach our own comfortable equilibrium. Some individuals would find loud music at a party or gig uncomfortable and unpleasant, whereas for others the intensity of the music is part of the total enjoyment. Likewise, if we are deprived of sensory information for too long this can lead to feelings of discomfort and fatigue. Indeed, research has shown that if the brain is deprived of sensory information then it will manufacture its own and subjects will hallucinate.[3] It is possible to conclude therefore that the perceptual process is rooted to the sensory limitations of the individual.

Psychological factors

Psychological factors will also affect what is perceived. These internal factors, such as personality, learning and motives, will give rise to an inclination to perceive certain stimuli with a readiness to respond in certain ways. This has been called an individual's perceptual set. (See Figure 11.3.) Differences in the ways individuals acquire information has been used as one of four scales in the Myers–Briggs Type Indicator (discussed in Chapter 9). They distinguish individuals who 'tend to accept and work with what is given in the here-and-now, and thus become realistic and practical' (sensing types), from others who go beyond the information from the senses and look at the possible patterns, meanings and relationships. These 'intuitive types' 'grow expert at seeing new possibilities and new ways of doing things'. Myers and Briggs stress the value of both types, and emphasise the importance of complementary skills and variety in any successful enterprise or relationship.[4]

Personality and perception have also been examined in the classic experiments by *Witkin et al.* on field dependence/independence. Field dependent individuals were found to be reliant on the context of the stimuli, the cues given in the situation, whereas field independent subjects relied mainly on their own internal bodily cues and less on the environment. These experiments led Witkin to generalise to other settings outside the psychological laboratory and to suggest that individuals use, and need, different information from the environment to make sense of their world.[5]

The needs of an individual

The needs of an individual will affect their perceptions. For example, a manager deeply engrossed in preparing an urgent report may screen out ringing telephones, the sound of computers, people talking and furniture being moved in the next office, but will respond readily to the smell of coffee brewing. The most desirable and urgent needs will almost certainly affect an individual perceptual process.

The 'Pollyanna Principle' claims that pleasant stimuli will be processed more quickly and remembered more precisely than unpleasant stimuli. However, it must be noted that intense internal drives may lead to perceptual distortions of situations (or people) and an unwillingness to absorb certain painful information. This will be considered later in this chapter.

Learning from previous experiences has a critical effect throughout all the stages of the perceptual process. It will affect the stimuli perceived in the first instance, and then

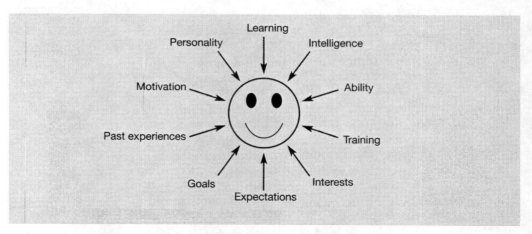

Figure 11.3 Factors affecting an individual's perceptual set

the ways in which those stimuli are understood and processed, and finally the response which is given. For example, it is likely that a maintenance engineer visiting a school for the first time will notice different things about it than a teacher attending an interview or a child arriving on the first day. The learning gained from past experiences colours what is seen and processed.

The importance of language

Our language plays an important role in the way we perceive the world. Our language not only labels and distinguishes the environment for us but also structures and guides our thinking pattern. Even if we are proficient skiers, we do not have many words we can use to describe the different texture of snow; we would be reliant on using layers of adjectives. The Inuit, however, have 13 words for snow in their language. Our language is part of the culture we experience and learn to take for granted. Culture differences are relevant because they emphasise the impact of social learning on the perception of people and their surroundings.

So, language not only reflects our experience, but also shapes whether and what we experience. It influences our relationships with others and with the environment. For instance consider a situation where a student is using a library in a UK university for the first time. The student is from South Asia where the word 'please' is incorporated in the verb and in intonation. A separate word is not used. When the student requests help, the assistant may consider the student rude because the word 'please' was not used. By causing offence the student has quite innocently affected the perceptions of the library assistant.

Much is communicated in how words are said and in the silences between words. In UK speech is suggestive and idiomatic speech is common:

'Make no bones about it' (means get straight to the point).
'Sent to Coventry' (means to be socially isolated).

And action is implied rather than always stated:

'I hope you won't mind if' (means 'I am going to').
'I'm afraid I really can't see my way to ...' (means 'no').

Cultural differences

The ways in which people interact are also subject to cultural differences and such differences may be misconstrued. Embarrassment and discomfort can occur when emotional lines are broken. This was demonstrated in an American study that researched the experience of Japanese students visiting America for the first time. The researchers felt that that the Japanese students faced considerable challenges in adapting to the new culture. Some of the surprises that the students reported related to social interaction:

Casual visits and frequent phone calls at midnight to the host room-mate were a new experience to them. The sight of opposite-sex partners holding hands or kissing in public places also surprised them ... That males do cooking and shopping in the household or by themselves, that fathers would play with children, and that there was frequent intimacy displayed between couples were all never-heard-of in their own experiences at home.[6]

The ways in which words are used and the assumptions made about shared understanding are dependent upon an individual's culture and upbringing. For example, in cultures where it is 'normal' to explain all details clearly, explicitly and directly (such as the USA) other cultures may feel the 'spelling out' of all the details unnecessary and embarrassing. In France, for instance, ambiguity and subtlety are expected and much is communicated by what is **not** said. *Hall* distinguished low context cultures (direct, explicit communication) from high context cultures (meaning assumed and non-verbal signs significant).[7]

EXTERNAL FACTORS

The knowledge of, familiarity with or expectations about, a given situation or previous experiences, will influence perception. External factors refer to the nature and characteristics of the stimuli. There is usually a tendency to give more attention to stimuli which are, for example:

- large;
- moving;
- intense;
- loud;
- contrasted;
- bright;
- novel;
- repeated; or
- stand out from the background.

Any number of these factors may be present at a given time or situation. It is therefore the **total pattern** of the stimuli together with the **context** in which they occur that influence perception. For example, it is usually a novel or unfamiliar stimulus that is more noticeable, but a person is more likely to perceive the familiar face of a friend among a group of people all dressed in the same style uniform. See for example Figure 11.4.[8] The sight of a fork-lift truck on the factory floor of a manufacturing organisation is likely to be perceived quite differently from one in the corridor of a university. The word

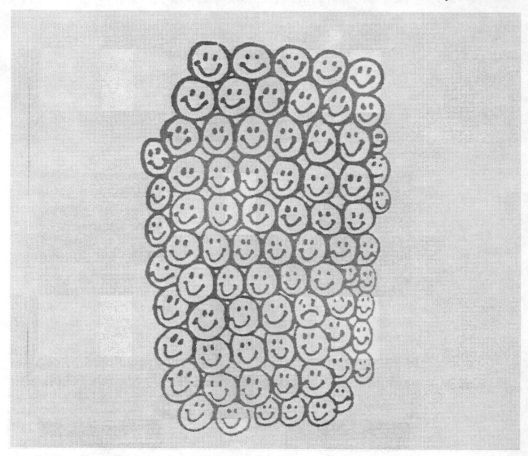

Figure 11.4 Is everybody happy?

Reproduced with permission from R. J. Block and H. E. Yuker, *Can You Believe Your Eyes?*, Robson Books (2002), p. 163.

'terminal' is likely to be perceived differently in the context of, for example: (i) a hospital, (ii) an airport or (iii) a computer firm. Consumer psychologists and marketing experts apply these perceptual principles with extraordinary success for some of their products.

ORGANISATION AND ARRANGEMENT OF STIMULI

The Gestalt School of Psychology led by Max Wertheimer claimed that the process of perception is innately organised and patterned. They described the process as one which has built-in field effects. In other words, the brain can act like a dynamic, physical field in which interaction among elements is an intrinsic part. The Gestalt School produced a series of principles, which are still readily applicable today. Some of the most significant principles include the following:

- figure and ground;
- grouping; and
- closure.

Figure and ground

The figure–ground principle states that figures are seen against a background. The figure does not have to be an object; it could be merely a geometrical pattern. Many textiles are perceived as figure–ground relationships. These relationships are often reversible as in the popular example shown in Figure 11.5.

What do you see? Do you see a white chalice (or small stand shape) in the centre of the frame? Or do you see the dark profiles of twins facing each other on the edge of the frame? Now look again. Can you see the other shape?

The figure–ground principle has applications in all occupational situations. It is important that employees know and are able to attend to the significant aspects (the figure), and treat other elements of the job as context (background). Early training sessions aim to identify and focus on the significant aspects of a task. Managerial effectiveness can also be judged in terms of chosen priorities (the figure). Stress could certainly occur for those employees who are uncertain about their priorities, and are unable to distinguish between the significant and less significant tasks. They feel overwhelmed by the 'whole' picture.

Figure 11.5

Grouping

The grouping principle refers to the tendency to organise shapes and patterns instantly into meaningful groupings or patterns on the basis of their proximity or similarity. Parts that are close in time or space tend to be perceived together. For example, in Figure 11.6(a), the workers are more likely to be perceived as nine independent people; but in Figure 11.6(b), because of the proximity principle, the workers may be perceived as three distinct groups of people.

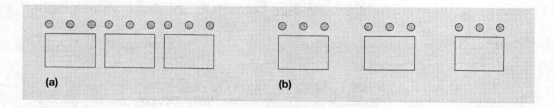

(a)   (b)

Figure 11.6

Taxi firms, for example, often use the idea of grouping to display their telephone number. In the example below which of the following numbers – (a), (b) or (c) – is most likely to be remembered easily?

347 474	347474	34 74 74
(a)	(b)	(c)

Similar parts tend to be seen together as forming a familiar group. In the following example there is a tendency to see alternate lines of characters – crosses and noughts (or circles). This is because the horizontal similarity is usually greater than the vertical similarity. However, if the page is turned sideways the figure may be perceived as alternate noughts and crosses in each line.

```
×  ×  ×  ×  ×  ×  ×  ×
o  o  o  o  o  o  o  o
×  ×  ×  ×  ×  ×  ×  ×
o  o  o  o  o  o  o  o
```

It is also interesting to note that many people when asked to describe this pattern refer to alternate lines of noughts and crosses – rather than crosses and noughts.

There is also an example here of the impact of cultural differences, mentioned earlier. One of the authors undertook a teaching exchange in the USA and gave this exercise to a class of American students. Almost without exception the students described the horizontal pattern correctly as alternate rows of crosses and noughts (or zeros). The explanation appears to be that Americans do not know the game of 'noughts and crosses' but refer to this as 'tic-tac-toe'.

Closure

There is also a tendency to complete an incomplete figure – to (mentally) fill in the gaps and to perceive the figure as a whole. This creates an overall and meaningful image, rather than an unconnected series of lines or blobs.

In the example in Figure 11.7[9] most people are likely to see the blobs as either the letter B or the number 13, possibly depending on whether at the time they had been more concerned with written material or dealing in numbers. However, for some people, the figure may remain just a series of eleven discrete blobs or be perceived as some other (to them) meaningful pattern/object. According to Gestalt theory, perceptual organisation is instant and spontaneous. We cannot stop ourselves making meaningful assumptions about our environment. The Gestaltists emphasised the ways in which the elements interact and claimed that the new pattern or structure perceived had a character of its own, hence the famous phrase: 'the whole is more than the sum of its parts'.

Figure 11.7

(Reproduced by permission of the author, Professor Richard King, University of South Carolina, from *Introduction to Psychology*, Third edition, 1996, published by the McGraw-Hill Companies Inc.)

PERCEPTUAL ILLUSIONS

Here are some examples to help you judge your own perceptive skills.
In Figure 11.8 try reading aloud the four words.

M – A – C – D – O – N – A – L – D
M – A – C – P – H – E – R – S – O – N
M – A – C – D – O – U – G – A – L – L
M – A – C – H – I – N – E – R – Y

Figure 11.8

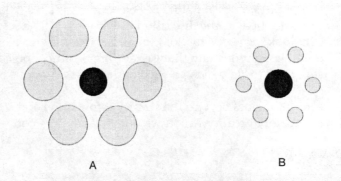

A   B

Figure 11.9

It is possible that you find yourself 'caught' in a perceptual set which means that you tend to pronounce 'machinery' as if it too were a Scottish surname.

In Figure 11.9 which of the centre, black circles is the larger – A or B?
Although you may have guessed that the two centre circles are in fact the same size, the circle on the right (B) may well **appear** larger because it is framed by smaller circles. The centre circle on the left (A) may well **appear** smaller because it is framed by larger circles.

Finally, in Figure 11.10[10] which of the three people is the tallest? Although the person on the right may appear the tallest, they are in fact all the same size.

Figure 11.10

(Reproduced with permission from Luthans, F. *Organisational Behaviour*, Seventh edition, McGraw-Hill. Reproduced with permission from the McGraw-Hill Companies Knc. (1995) p. 96.)

The physiological nature of perception has already been discussed briefly but it is of relevance here in the discussion of illusions. Why does the circle on the right in Figure 11.9 look bigger? Why does the person on the right look taller in Figure 11.10? These examples demonstrate the way our brain can be fooled. Indeed we make assumptions about our world which go beyond the pure sensations our brain receives.[11]

Beyond reality   Perception goes beyond the sensory information and converts these patterns to a three-dimensional reality which we understand. This conversion process, as we can see, is easily tricked! We may not be aware of the inferences we are making as they are part of our conditioning and learning. The Stroop experiment illustrates this perfectly.[12] (*See* Assignment 1 at the end of this chapter.) An illustration of the way in which we react automatically to stimuli is the illusion of the impossible triangle. (*See* Figure 11.11.)

Even when we know the triangle is impossible we still cannot help ourselves from completing the triangle and attempting to make it meaningful. We thus go beyond what is given and make assumptions about the world, which in certain instances are wildly incorrect. Psychologists and designers may make positive use of these assumptions to project positive images of a product or the environment. For instance, colours may be used to induce certain atmospheres in buildings; designs of wallpaper, or texture of curtains, may be used to create feelings of spaciousness or cosiness. Packaging of products may tempt us to see something as bigger or perhaps more precious.

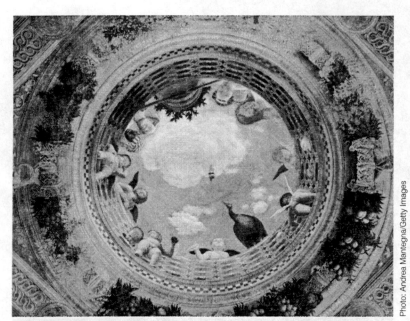

A classical illusion showing a trompe l'oeil occulus in the centre of a vaulted ceiling

Photo: Andrea Mantegna/Getty Images

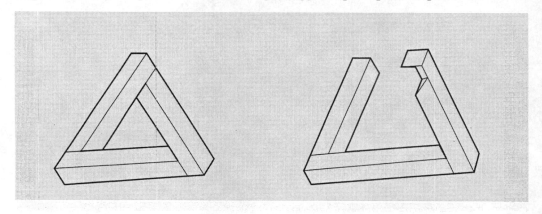

Figure 11.11

(*Source*: Gregory, R.L. *Odd Perceptions*, Methuen (1986) p. 71. Reprinted by permission of the publishers, Routledge/ITBP)

Person perception

Perceptual distortions and inaccuracies may not only affect our perception of the environment but also affect our perception of people. Although the process of perception is equally applicable in the perception of objects or people, there is more scope for subjectivity, bias, errors and distortions when we are perceiving others. The focus of the following section is to examine the perception of people, and to consider the impact this has on the management and development of people at work.

PERCEIVING OTHER PEOPLE

The principles and examples of perceptual differences discussed above reflect the way we perceive other people and are the source of many organisational problems. In the work situation the process of perception and the selection of stimuli can influence a manager's relationship with other staff. Some examples might be as follows.

- **Grouping** – the way in which a manager may think of a number of staff: for example, either working in close proximity; or with some common feature such as all clerical workers, all management trainees or all black workers; as a homogeneous group rather than a collection of individuals each with his or her own separate identity and characteristics;
- **Figure and ground** – a manager may notice a new recruit and set him/herself apart from the group because of particular characteristics such as appearance or physical features.
- **Closure** – the degree to which unanimity is perceived, and decisions made or action taken in the belief that there is full agreement with staff when, in fact, a number of staff may be opposed to the decision or action.

A manager's perception of the workforce will influence attitudes in dealing with people and the style of managerial behaviour adopted. The way in which managers approach the performance of their jobs and the behaviour they display towards subordinate staff are likely to be conditioned by predispositions about people, human nature and work. An example of this is the style of management adopted on the basis of McGregor's Theory X and Theory Y suppositions, which is discussed in Chapter 7. In making judgements about other people it is important to try and perceive their underlying intent and motivation, not *just* the resultant behaviour or actions.

The perception of people's performance can be affected by the organisation of stimuli. In employment interviews, for example, interviewers are susceptible to contrast effects and the perception of a candidate is influenced by the rating given to immediately preceding candidates. Average candidates may be rated highly if they follow people with low qualifications, but rated lower when following people with higher qualifications.[13]

The dynamics of interpersonal perception

The dynamics of person perception cannot be overestimated. Unlike the perception of an object which just exists, another individual will react to you and be affected by your behaviour. This interaction is illustrated in the following quotation:

You are a pain in the neck and to stop you giving me a pain in the neck I protect my neck by tightening my neck muscles, which gives me the pain in the neck you are.[14]

The interaction of individuals thus provides an additional layer of interpretation and complexity. The cue which we may attend to, the expectation we may have, the assumptions we may make, the response pattern that occurs, leave more scope for errors and distortions. We are not only perceiving the stimulus (that is, the other person) but we are also processing their reactions to us at the same time that they are processing our reactions to them.

Thus person perception differs from the perception of objects because:

▥ it is a continually dynamic and changing process; and
▥ the perceiver is a part of this process who will influence and be influenced by the other people in the situation.

(*See* Figure 11.12.)[15]

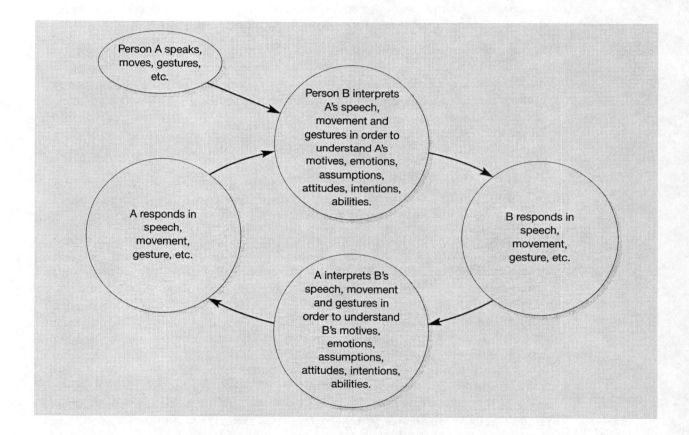

Figure 11.12 Cycle of perception and behaviour

Reproduced with permission form Maureen Guirdham, *Interactive Behaviour at Work*, Third edition, Financial Times Prentice Hall (2002), p. 162, with permission from Pearson Education Ltd.

Setting and environment

Person perception will also be affected by the setting, and the environment may play a critical part in establishing rapport. For example, next time you are involved in a formal meeting consider the following factors which will all influence the perceptual process.

For example, attending an in-house development centre:

Why?	Purpose of and motives for meeting	Likely to be an important event for the particpant, may be a catalyst for promotion and may signal new and relevant development opportunities. Chance to be visible and demonstrate skills and abilities. Opportunity to network with other managers. Thus high emotional cost to participant
Who?	Status/role/age/ gender/ethnic group/ appearance/personality/ interests/attitudes	How participant prepares for the event will be influenced by factors listed across and previous history and encounters of all parties
When?	Time, date of meeting	The timing of the event might be particularly affected by events outside of the workplace. So if the participant has dependants or responsibilities the timing of this event may become significant. If the participant is asked to attend in the middle of a religious festival than again the relevance of time is critical.
Where?	Environment/culture	Organisations will often stage development events away from the 'normal' workplace in an attempt to bring about objectivity and neutrality. How the event is staged, the amount of structure and formality, how feedback is given, the demonstration of power and control will be evidence of the culture of the organisation.
How?	Past experience Rapport	The experience of the development event will in part be influenced by the expectations of the participant. If this is the second development centre then experiences of the first will colour the perceptions, if this is the first centre then the participant may be influenced by previous experiences of similar events (selection event) or by stories from previous attendees.

Perception and communication

It is difficult to consider the process of interpersonal perception without commenting on how people communicate. Communication and perception are inextricably bound. How we communicate to our colleagues, boss, subordinates, friends and partners will depend on our perception of them, on our 'history' with them, on their emotional state, etc. We may misjudge them and regard our communication as unsuccessful, but unless we have some feedback from the other party we may never know whether what we have said, or done, was received in the way it was intended. Feedback is a vital ingredient of the communication process. The feedback may reaffirm our perceptions of the person or it may force us to review our perceptions. In our dealings with more senior staff the process of communication can be of special significance including non-verbal communication, posture and tone.[16] (The importance of body language is discussed later in this chapter.)

Neuro-linguistic programming (NLP)

John Grinder and Richard Bandler developed **neuro-linguistic programming** in the 1970s.[17] The name originates from the three disciplines which all have a part to play when people are communicating with others: neurology, language and programming.

- **Neurology** – the processes linking body and mind;
- **Linguistics** – the study of words and how these are understood and communicated;
- **Programming** – refers to behaviours and strategies used by individuals.

Originally Grinder and Bandler studied notable therapists at work with their clients. The aim was to identify 'rules' or models that could be used by other therapists to help them improve their performance. The focus was on one-to-one communication and self-management. The application of NLP shifted from therapy situations to work organisations with clear messages for communicating and managing others.

NLP emphasises the significance of the perceptual process and the way in which information is subjectively filtered and interpreted. These interpretations are influenced by others and the world in which we live. Gradually individuals learn to respond and their reactions and strategies become programmed, locked in, automatic.

At its heart NLP concerns awareness and change. Initially knowing and monitoring one's own behaviour is fundamental to the process and being able to consciously choose different reactions. Selecting from a range of verbal and non-verbal behaviours ensures control happens and changes 'automatic' reactions into consciously chosen programmes.

Many different approaches and techniques are incorporated into NLP. Some concern mirroring and matching the micro skills of communication in terms of body movements, breathing patterns or voice tempo. Others concern the positive thinking required in goal-setting 'outcome thinking' and the personal resources required in its achievement.

NLP has passionate devotees (see for instance http://www.nlpu.com) and considerable hype, for instance one practitioner claims to 'skyrocket your communication skills'. It claims NLP to be different: 'Feel what it is like; see yourself and hear yourself actually speaking, as you interact and communicate perfectly.'[18]

Some of the ideas of NLP have been incorporated in other bodies of knowledge on communication. So for example McCann bases his communication work on the findings of Grinder and Bandler to produce a technique called psychoverbal communication.[19]

TRANSACTIONAL ANALYSIS

Transactional analysis (or TA) is one of the most popular ways of explaining the dynamics of interpersonal communication. Originally developed by *Eric Berne*, it is now a theory which encompasses personality, perception and communication. Although Berne used it initially as a method of psychotherapy, it has been convincingly used by organisations as a training and development programme.[20]

TA has two basic underlying assumptions:

- All the events and feelings that we have ever experienced are stored within us and can be replayed, so we can re-experience the events and the feelings of all our past years.

- Personality is made of three ego states which are revealed in distinct ways of behaving. The ego states manifest themselves in gesture, tone of voice and action, almost as if they are different people within us.

Berne identified and labelled the ego states as follows:

- **Child ego state** – behaviour which demonstrates the feelings we remember as a child. This state may be associated with having fun, playing, impulsiveness, rebelliousness, spontaneous behaviour and emotional responses.
- **Adult ego state** – behaviour which concerns our thought processes and the processing of facts and information. In this state we may be objective, rational, reasonable – seeking information and receiving facts.
- **Parent ego state** – behaviour which concerns the attitudes, feelings and behaviour incorporated from external sources, primarily our parents. This state refers to feelings about right and wrong and how to care for other people.

He claimed that the three ego states were universal, but the content of the ego states would be unique to each person. We may be unaware which ego state we are operating in and may shift from one ego state to another. All people are said to behave in each of these states at different times. The three ego states exist simultaneously within each individual although at any particular time any one state many dominate the other two.

Preferred ego state

We all have a preferred ego state which we may revert to: some individuals may continually advise and criticise others (the constant Parents); some may analyse, live only with facts, and distrust feelings (the constant Adult); some operate with strong feelings all the time, consumed with anger, or constantly clowning (the constant Child). Berne emphasised that the states should not be judged as superior or inferior but as different. Analysis of ego states may reveal why communication breaks down or why individuals may feel manipulated or used.

Berne insists that it is possible to identify the ego state from the words, voice, gestures, and attitude of the person communicating. For example, it would be possible to discern the ego state of a manager if he/she said the following:

'Pass me the file on the latest sales figures.'
'How do you think we could improve our safety record?'
(Adult ego state)

'Let me help you with that – I can see you are struggling.'
'Look, this is the way it should be done; how many more times do I have to tell you...?'
(Parent ego state)

'Great, it's Friday. Who's coming to the pub for a quick half?'
'That's a terrific idea – let's go for it!'
(Child ego state)

A dialogue can be analysed not only in terms of the ego state but also whether the transaction produced a **complementary reaction** or a **crossed reaction**. By complementary it is meant whether the ego state was an expected and preferred response, so for instance if we look at the first statement, 'Pass me the file on the latest sales figures', the subordinate could respond: 'Certainly – I have it here' (Adult ego state), or 'Can't you look for it yourself? I only gave it to you an hour ago' (Parent ego state).

The first response was complementary whereas the second was a crossed transaction. Sometimes it may be important to 'cross' a transaction. Take the example 'Let me help you with that – I can see you are struggling' (Parent ego state). The manager may have a habit of always helping in a condescending way, making the subordinate resentful. If the subordinate meekly accepts the help with a thankful reply this will only reinforce the manager's perception and attitude, whereas if the subordinate were to respond with 'I can manage perfectly well. Why did you think I was struggling?', it might encourage the manager to respond from the Adult ego state and thus move his/her ego position.

Understanding of human behaviour

Knowledge of TA can be of benefit to employees who are dealing with potentially difficult situations.[21] In the majority of work situations the Adult–Adult transactions are likely to be the norm. Where work colleagues perceive and respond by adopting the Adult ego state, such a transaction is more likely to encourage a rational, problem-solving approach and reduce the possibility of emotional conflict.

If only the world of work was always of the rational logical kind! Communications at work as elsewhere are sometimes unclear, confused and can leave the individual with 'bad feelings' and uncertainty. Berne describes a further dysfunctional transaction, which can occur when a message is sent to two ego states at the same time. For instance an individual may say 'I passed that article to you last week, have you read it yet?' This appears to be an adult-to-adult transaction and yet the tone of voice, the facial expressions **imply** a second ego-state is involved. The underlying message says 'Haven't you even read that yet ... you know how busy I am and yet I had time to read it!' The critical parent is addressing the Child ego state. In such 'ulterior transactions' the social message is typically Adult to Adult, and the ulterior, psychological message is directed either Parent–Child or Child–Parent.

Given the incidence of stress in the workplace, analysis of communication may be one way of understanding such conflict. By focusing on the interactions occurring within the workplace, TA can aid the understanding of human behaviour. It can help to improve communication skills by assisting in interpreting a person's ego state and which form of state is likely to produce the most appropriate response. This should lead to an improvement in both customer relations and management–subordinate relations. TA can be seen therefore as a valuable tool to aid our understanding of social situations and the games that people play both in and outside work organisations.

TA emphasises the strong links between perception and communication and illustrates the way in which they affect each other. However, it does not answer how we construct our social world in the first place, what we attend to and why, or why we have positive perceptions about some people and not others. To answer these questions we can concentrate on the stages of the perceptual process – both selection and attention, and organisation and judgement – and apply these to the perception of people.

SELECTION AND ATTENTION

What information do we select and why? The social situation consists of both verbal and non-verbal signals. The non-verbal signals include:

- bodily contact;
- proximity;
- orientation;
- head nods;
- facial expression;
- gestures;
- posture;
- direction of gaze;
- dress and appearance;
- non-verbal aspects of speech.

Verbal and non-verbal signals are co-ordinated into regular sequences, often without the awareness of the parties. The mirroring of actions has been researched and is called 'postural echoing'.[22] There is considerable evidence to indicate that each person is constantly influencing the other, and being influenced.[23]

Cook has suggested that in any social encounter there are two kinds of information which can be distinguished:

- **static information** – information which will not change during the encounter: for example, colour, gender, height and age; and
- **dynamic information** – information which is subject to change: for example, mood, posture, gestures and expression.[24]

The meanings we ascribed to these non-verbal signals are rooted in our culture and early socialisation. Thus it is no surprise that there are significant differences in the way we perceive such signals. For instance dress codes differ in degrees of formality. *Schneider and Barsoux* summarise some interesting cultural differences:

> *Northern European managers tend to dress more informally than their Latin counterparts. At conferences, it is not unlikely for the Scandinavian managers to be wearing casual clothing, while their French counterparts are reluctant to remove their ties and jackets. For the Latin managers, personal style is important, while Anglo and Asian managers do not want to stand out or attract attention in their dress. French women managers are more likely to be dressed in ways that Anglo women managers might think inappropriate for the office. The French, in turn, think it strange that American businesswomen dress in 'man-like' business suits (sometimes with running shoes).[25]*

Impression management

In some situations we all attempt to project our attitudes, personality and competence by paying particular attention to our appearance, and the impact this may have on others. This has been labelled 'impression management'[26] and the selection interview is an obvious illustration. Some information is given more weight than other information when an impression is formed. It would seem that there are central traits which are more important than others in determining our perceptions.

One of these central traits is the degree of warmth or coldness shown by an individual.[27] The timing of information also seems to be critical in the impressions we form. For example, information heard first tends to be resistant to later contradictory information. In other words, the saying 'first impression counts' is supported by research and is called **'the primacy effect'**.[28] It has also been shown that a negative first impression is more resistant to change than a positive one.[29] However, if there is a break in time we are more likely to remember the most recent information – **'the recency effect'**.

Dealings with other people

There are a number of well-documented problems which arise when perceiving other people. Many of these problems occur because of our limitations in selecting and attending to information. This selectivity may occur because:

- we already know what we are looking for and are therefore 'set' to receive only the information which confirms our initial thoughts; or
- previous training and experience have led us to short-cut and only see a certain range of behaviours; or
- we may group features together and make assumptions about their similarities.

The Gestalt principles apply equally well to the perception of people as to the perception of objects. Thus we can see, for example, that if people live in the same geographical area, assumptions may be made about not only their wealth and type of accommodation but also their attitudes, their political views and even their type of personality.

ORGANISATION AND JUDGEMENT

The ways in which we organise and make judgements about what we have perceived is to a large extent based on our previous experiences and learning. It is also important at this point to be aware of the inferences and assumptions we make which go beyond the information given. We may not always be aware of our pre-set assumptions but they will guide the way in which we interpret the behaviour of others. There has been much research into the impact of implicit personality theory.[30] In the same way that we make assumptions about the world of objects, and go beyond the information provided, we also make critical inferences about people's characteristics and possible likely behaviours.

A manager might well know more about the 'type of person' A – a member of staff who has become or was already a good friend, who is seen in a variety of social situations and with whom there is a close relationship – than about B – another member of staff, in the same section as A and undertaking similar duties, but with whom there is only a formal work relationship and a limited social acquaintance. These differences in relationship, information and interaction might well influence the manager's perception if asked, for example, to evaluate the work performance of A and B.

Judgement of other people can also be influenced by perceptions of such stimuli as, for example:

■ role or status;
■ occupation;
■ physical factors and appearance; and
■ body language.

Physical characteristics and appearance

In a discussion on managing people and management style, *Green* raises the question of how managers make judgements on those for whom they are responsible including positive and negative messages.

> *In my personal research people have admitted, under pressure, that certain physical characteristics tend to convey a positive or negative message. For example, some people find red hair, earrings for men, certain scents and odours, someone too tall or too short; a disability; a member of a particular ethnic group and countless other items as negative ... Similarly there will be positive factors such as appropriate hairstyle or dress for the occasion ... which may influence in a positive way.[31]*

Related characteristics

A person may tend to organise perception of another person in terms of the 'whole' mental picture of that person. Perceptual judgement is influenced by reference to related characteristics associated with the person and the attempt to place that person in a complete environment. In one example, an unknown visitor was introduced by the course director to 110 American students, divided into five equal groups.[32] The visitor was described differently to each group as:

1 Mr England, a student from Cambridge;
2 Mr England, demonstrator in psychology from Cambridge;
3 Mr England, lecturer in psychology from Cambridge;
4 Dr England, senior lecturer from Cambridge;
5 Professor England from Cambridge.

After being introduced to each group, the visitor left. Each group of students was then asked to estimate his height to the nearest half inch. They were also asked to estimate the height of the course director after he too left the room. The mean estimated height of the course director, who had the same status for all groups, did not change signifi-

Table 11.1 Estimated height according to ascribed academic status

Group	Ascribed academic status	Average estimated height
1	Student	5' 9.9"
2	Demonstrator	5' 10.14"
3	Lecturer	5' 10.9"
4	Senior lecturer	5' 11.6"
5	Professor	6' 0.3"

(*Source*: Adapted from Wilson, P. R. 'Perceptual Distortion of Height as a Function of Ascribed Academic Status', *Journal of Social Psychology*, no. 74, 1968, pp. 97–102, published by John Wiley & Sons Limited. Reproduced with permission.)

cantly among groups. However, the estimated height of the visitor varied with perceived status: as ascribed academic status increased, so did the estimate of height. (*See* Table 11.1.)

THE IMPORTANCE OF BODY LANGUAGE

We have referred previously in this chapter to the particular significance of body language and non-verbal communication. This includes inferences drawn from posture, invasions of personal space, the extent of eye contact, tone of voice or facial expression. People are the only animals that speak, laugh and weep. Actions are more cogent than speech, and humans rely heavily on body language to convey their true feelings and meanings.[33] It is interesting to note how emotions are woven creatively into email messages. Using keyboard signs in new combinations has led to a new e-language. For example to signal pleasure :), or unhappiness :–c, or send a rose @>---> encapsulate feelings as well as words. The growth of this practice has led to an upsurge of web pages replete with examples.

According to *Mehrabian*, in our face-to-face communication with other people the message about our feelings and attitudes come only 7 per cent from the words we use, 38 per cent from our voice and 55 per cent from body language, including facial expressions. Significantly, when body language such as gestures and tone of voice conflicts with the words, greater emphasis is likely to be placed on the non-verbal message.[34]

Although actual percentages may vary, there appears to be general support for this contention. For example, according to *Pivcevic*: 'It is commonly agreed that 80 per cent of communication is non-verbal; it is carried in your posture and gestures, and in the tone, pace and energy behind what you say'.[35] And *McGuire* suggests when verbal and non-verbal messages are in conflict: 'Accepted wisdom from the experts is that the non-verbal signals should be the ones to reply on, and that what is not said is frequently louder than what is said, revealing attitudes and feelings in a way words can't express.'[36]

James suggests that in a sense, we our all experts on body language already and this is part of the survival instinct.

Even in a 'safe' environment like an office or meeting room you will feel a pull on your gaze each time someone new enters the room. And whether you want to or not, you will start to form opinions about a person in as little as three seconds. You can try to be fair and objective in your evaluation, but you will have little choice. This is an area where the subconscious mind bullies the conscious into submission. Like, dislike, trust, love or lust can all be promoted in as long as it takes to clear your throat. In fact most of these responses will be based on your perception of how the person looks.[37]

In our perceptions and judgement of others it is important therefore to watch and take careful note of their non-verbal communication. However, although body language may be a guide to personality, errors can easily arise if too much is inferred from a single message rather than a related cluster of actions. According to *Fletcher*, for example: 'you won't learn to interpret people's body language accurately, and use your own to maximum effect, without working at it. If you consciously spend half an hour a day analysing people's subconscious movements, you'll soon learn how to do it – almost unconsciously'.[38] However, as *Mann* points out, with a little knowledge about the subject it is all too easy to become body conscious. Posture and gesture can unmask deceivers but it would be dangerous to assume that everyone who avoids eye contact or rubs their nose is a fibber. Nevertheless an understanding of non-verbal communication is essential for managers and other professions where good communication skills are essential.[39]

Cultural differences

There are many cultural variations in non-verbal communications, the extent of physical contact, and differences in the way body language is perceived and interpreted.[40] For example, Italians and South Americans tend to show their feelings through intense body language, while Japanese tend to hide their feelings and have largely eliminated overt body language from interpersonal communication. When talking to another person, the British tend to look away spasmodically, but Norwegians typically look people steadily in the eyes without altering their gaze. When the Dutch point a forefinger at their temples this is likely to be a sign of congratulations for a good idea, but with other cultures the gesture has a less complimentary implication.

In many European countries it is customary to greet people with three or four kisses on the cheek and pulling the head away may be taken as a sign of impoliteness. All cultures have specific values related to personal space and 'comfort zone'. For example, Arabs tend to stand very close when speaking to another person but most Americans when introduced to a new person will, after shaking hands, move backwards a couple of steps to place a comfortable space between themselves and the person they have just met.[41]

EXHIBIT 11.1

Hospitals set to play it by ethnic book

Staff receive guide to help them tend people from different cultures, writes Tanya Johnson

Touching a patient to comfort them would be one of the most natural gestures for a nurse.

But being touched by a nurse of the opposite sex could offend an orthodox Jew because being comforted like that is not welcome in Judaism.

Similarly, touching or removing a Sikh's turban could also cause offence because it has deep spiritual and moral significance.

Now a book has been produced to help staff at Portsmouth hospitals understand the differences between ethnic minority groups and avoid unwittingly offending them.

Called the *Ethnic Minority Handbook*, it contains all the information doctors and nurses need when dealing with patients of different religious persuasions.

It was completed by Florise Elliott, Portsmouth Hospitals NHS Trust's ethnic health coordinator, who said: 'It's always important for people to be aware of other people's cultures.

'This makes staff aware of other cultures and differences in ways of living.'

The book has sections for Buddhists, Chinese people, Christians, Mormons, Hindus, Jehovah's Witnesses, Jews, Muslims, Sikhs and spiritualism and was compiled with help from representatives from each culture.

As well as guidance on diet, language, cultures, death and post-mortems, each section contains contacts hospital medical staff can ring if they need advice.

One is Jewish spokesman Julius Klein, a member of the Portsmouth and Southsea Hebrew Congregation, who welcomed the book.

He said: 'It's excellent. One of the difficulties when people go into hospital is trying to put over certain things about their culture and life that the hospital needs to know.

'Anything that helps inform the nursing staff about minorities must be a good thing.'

Each ward at Queen Alexandra Hospital, Cosham, and St Mary's Hospital, Milton, will have a copy of the book which was started by the hospital's service planning manager Petronella Mwasandube.

About 1,500 of the 37,500 annual cases the hospitals deal with are people from ethnic minority groups which does not include emergencies.

(Reproduced courtesy of *The News*, Portsmouth, 16 February 1999.)

ATTRIBUTION THEORY

It seems, therefore, that part of the process of perceiving other people is to attribute characteristics to them. We judge their behaviour and their intentions on past knowledge, and in comparison with other people we know. It is our way of making sense of their behaviour. This is known as attribution theory.

Attribution is the process by which people interpret the perceived causes of behaviour. The initiator of **attribution theory** is generally recognised as *Heider*, who suggests that behaviour is determined by a combination of **perceived** internal forces and external forces.[42]

- **Internal forces** relate to personal attributes such as ability, skill, amount of effort or fatigue.
- **External forces** relate to environmental factors such as organisational rules and policies, the manner of superiors, or the weather.

Behaviour at work may be explained by the **locus of control**, that is whether the individual perceives outcomes as controlled by themselves, or by external factors. Judgements made about other people will also be influenced strongly by whether the cause is seen as internal or external.

Basic criteria in making attributions

In making attributions and determining whether an internal or external attribution is chosen, *Kelley* suggests three basic criteria: distinctiveness, consensus and consistency.[43]

- **Distinctiveness.** How distinctive or different was the behaviour or action in this particular task or situation compared with behaviour or action in other tasks or situations?
- **Consensus.** Is the behaviour or action different from, or in keeping with, that displayed by most other people in the same situation?
- **Consistency.** Is the behaviour or action associated with an enduring personality or motivational characteristic over time, or an unusual one-off situation caused by external factors?

Kelley hypothesised that people attribute behaviour to internal forces or personal factors when they perceive **low distinctiveness**, **low consensus** and **high consistency**. Behaviour is attributed to external forces or environmental factors when people perceived **high distinctiveness**, **high consensus**, and **low consistency** (*see* Figure 11.13).

An example of these criteria related to a student who fails a mid-sessional examination in a particular subject is given in Table 11.2.[44]

An additional consideration in the evaluation of task performance within an organisational setting is whether the cause of behaviour was due to 'stable' or 'unstable' factors.

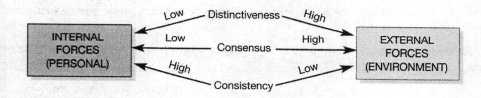

Figure 11.13 Representation of attribution theory

Table 11.2 Example of criteria in making attributions

	Distinctiveness	Consensus	Consistency
Internal attribution	Student fails all mid-sessional examinations	Student is the only one to fail	Student also fails final examination
External attribution	Student gains high marks on other mid-sessional examinations	All students in the class get low marks	Student obtains a good mark in final examination

(*Source*: Adapted from Mitchell, Terence R., *People in Organisations*, Second edition, McGraw-Hill (1982) p. 104. Reproduced with permission from The McGraw-Hill Companies Inc.)

- **Stable factors** are ability, or the ease or difficulty of the task.
- **Unstable factors** are the exertion of effort, or luck.[45]

The combination of internal and external attributions, and stable and unstable characteristics, results in four possible interpretations of a person's task performance (*see* Table 11.3).

Table 11.3 Classification of possible attributions for performance

	Internal attributions	External attributions
Stable factors	ABILITY	TASK DIFFICULTY
Unstable factors	EFFORT	LUCK

Implications of attribution theory

Employees with an internal control orientation are more likely to believe that they can influence their level of performance through their own abilities, skills or efforts. Employees with an external control orientation are more likely to believe that their level of performance is determined by external factors beyond their influence.

Studies appear to support the idea that staff with an internal control orientation are generally more satisfied with their jobs, are more likely to be in managerial positions, and are more satisfied with a participatory style of management, than staff with an external control orientation.[46] As a generalisation it might be implied that internally controlled managers are more effective than those who are externally controlled. However, this does not appear to be always the case.[47]

People with a high achievement motivation may perceive that successful performance is caused by their own internal forces, and their ability and effort, rather than by the nature of the task or by luck. If members of staff fail to perform well on their tasks they may believe that external factors are the cause, and as a result may reduce the level of future effort. On the other hand, if staff perform well but the manager perceives this as due to an easy task or to luck, the appropriate recognition and reward may not be given. If the staff perceive that good performance was due to ability and/or effort the lack of recognition and reward may well have a demotivating effect.

PERCEPTUAL DISTORTIONS AND ERRORS

We have seen that differences in perception result in different people seeing different things and attaching different meanings to the same stimuli. Every person sees things in his or her own way and as perceptions become a person's reality this can lead to misunderstandings. The accuracy of interpersonal perception and the judgements made about other people are influenced by:

- the nature of the relationship between the perceiver and the other person;
- the amount of information available to the perceiver and the order in which information is received;
- the nature and extent of interaction between the two people.[48]

There are four main features which can create particular difficulties and give rise to perceptual problems, bias or distortions, in our dealings with other people. These are:

- stereotyping;
- the halo effect;
- perceptual defence; and
- projection.

The perceptual paradox

These problems with people perception arise because of the selectivity which exists in the perceptual process. We do not enjoy living in a world where uncertainty abounds and our perceptual system works to minimise our energy consumption. We do not have to start every day afresh – we have our store of memories and experiences to guide us.

The paradox is that this process is also our downfall. Errors and bias are inherent in such a system. Although exhortations can be made for us to become more aware of our own biases and to take more time in making judgements we are working against our normal quick-fire perceptual system.

STEREOTYPING

This is the tendency to ascribe positive or negative characteristics to a person on the basis of a general categorisation and perceived similarities. The perception of that person may be based more on certain expected characteristics than on the recognition of that person as an individual. It is a form of typecasting. **Stereotyping** is a means of simplifying the process of perception and making judgements of other people, instead of dealing with a range of complex and alternative stimuli. It occurs when an individual is judged on the basis of the group to which it is perceived that person belongs. When we see all people belonging to a particular group as having the same characteristics we are stereotyping individuals. Pre-judgements are therefore made about an individual without ever really knowing whether such judgements are accurate; they may be wildly wrong.

Examples of common stereotyping may be based on:

- **nationality**, e.g., all Germans are orderly and industrious;
- **occupation**, e.g., all accountants are boring;
- **age**, e.g., all young people are unreliable, no old person wants to consider new ideas;
- **physical**, e.g., all people with red hair have a fiery temperament;
- **education**, e.g., all graduates are clever;
- **social**, e.g., all unemployed people are lazy;
- **politics**, e.g., all Labour voters are in favour of strong trade unions, all Conservative voters support privatisation.

Although stereotyping condenses the amount of information that we need to know and thus enables us to cope with a vast information flow, the consequences of attributing incorrect characteristics are extremely negative.

Social implications

Stereotyping infers that all people within a particular perceived category are assumed to share the same traits or characteristics. A significant social implication of stereotyping is therefore the perception held about particular groups of people based on, for example:

- gender;
- race;
- disability;
- religious belief;
- age.

(By way of an example, the illustrative case on pp. 459–62 focuses on the effects of stereotyping women.)

A major danger of stereotyping is that it can block out accurate perception of the individual or individual situation.[49] Stereotyping may lead to potential situations of prejudice or discrimination. An example might be the perception of people with HIV or AIDS.[50] Stereotyping may work either negatively or favourably for a particular group of people. For example, a sizeable number of employers still appear to maintain negative and inaccurate stereotypes about the capabilities and training of older workers.[51] However, B&Q, the UK's largest home-improvement chain, have claimed improved profit figures partly because of the older age profile of their employees: they have a policy of staffing certain stores with people over 50 years of age.

THE HALO EFFECT

This is the process by which the perception of a person is formulated on the basis of a single favourable or unfavourable trait or impression. The **halo effect** tends to shut out other relevant characteristics of that person. Some examples might be as follows.

- A candidate for employment who arrives punctually, is smart in appearance and friendly may well influence the perception of the selectors, who then place less emphasis on the candidate's technical ability, qualifications or experience for the job.
- A new member of staff who performs well in a first major assignment may be perceived as a likely person for promotion, even though that assignment is not typical of the usual duties the member of staff is expected to undertake.
- A single trait, such as good attendance and time-keeping, may become the main emphasis for judgement of overall competence and performance, rather than other considerations such as the quantity, quality and accuracy of work.

A particular danger with the halo effect is that, where quick judgements are made on the basis of readily available stimuli, the perceiver may become 'perceptually blind' to subsequent stimuli at variance with the original perception, and (often subconsciously) notice only those characteristics which support the original judgement.

The rusty halo effect

The process may also work in reverse: **the rusty halo effect**. This is where general judgements about a person are formulated from the perception of a negative characteristic. For example, a candidate is seen arriving late for an interview. There may be a very good reason for this and it may be completely out of character. But on the basis of that one particular event the person may be perceived as a poor time-keeper and unreliable. Another example may be a new member of staff who performs poorly in a first major assignment. This may have been due to an unusual set of circumstances and not typical behaviour, but the person may still be perceived as a bad appointment.

PERCEPTUAL DEFENCE

Perceptual defence is the tendency to avoid or screen out certain stimuli that are perceptually disturbing or threatening. People may tend to select information which is supportive of their point of view and choose not to acknowledge contrary information. For example, a manager who has decided recently to promote a member of staff against the advice of colleagues may select only favourable information which supports that decision and ignore less favourable information which questions that decision.

PROJECTION

Attributing, or projecting, one's own feelings, motives or characteristics to other people is a further distortion which can occur in the perception of other people. Judgements of other people may be more favourable when they have characteristics largely in common with, and easily recognised by, the perceiver. **Projection** may also result in people exaggerating undesirable traits in others that they fail to recognise in themselves.

Perception is distorted by feelings and emotions. For example, a manager who is concerned about possible redundancy may perceive other managers to be even more concerned. People have a tendency to perceive others less favourably by projecting certain of their own feelings or characteristics to them. As another example, supervisors may complain that their manager did not work hard enough to secure additional resources for the department, when in fact the supervisors failed to provide the manager with all the relevant information and statistics.

Discussed by *Freud* in his description of defence mechanisms, projection is a way in which we protect ourselves from acknowledging that we may possess undesirable traits and assign them in exaggerated amounts to other people. For instance, a manager who considers all subordinates as insincere may be projecting one of the manager's own characteristics. Perception of 'self' and how people see and think of themselves, and evaluate themselves, are discussed in Chapter 14.

ILLUSTRATIVE EXAMPLE – PERCEPTION OF WOMEN

The perceptual process has been outlined as selective and subjective: we perceive the world in our own terms and expect the world to 'fit' into our constructs. Throughout our development we have learned to distinguish what is important and significant (figure) from information which is additional and contextual (ground). This process is repeated when we join new organisations or have a new job within the same organisation. Fitting into the organisation involves selecting information which is necessary from that which is less significant. At times, the process can be distorted and we can also be 'tricked' into seeing the world in particular ways.

Beliefs about women and their roles

One of the most common stereotypes is to view women in terms of their biology and reproductive abilities. Unlike men, beliefs about women and their roles focus outside the workplace rather than inside. For instance, the prospect of women marrying and having children leads people to question their permanency as employees, and results in organisations viewing their engagement as high risk, with a low return on investment in their training. In middle years the additional responsibilities of having children are often assumed to be the major role of women. This leads to further beliefs regarding their assumed lack of time and ambition for senior positions. Women, for a period stretching over twenty years, could be perceived as less reliable, less promotable and less ambitious than men.

EXHIBIT 11.2

Judy Owen wins battle against Professional Golfers' Association to wear trousers

Judy Owen who has fought for her right to wear trousers to work has won her battle against the Professional Golfers' Association.

Judy told an Employment Tribunal in Birmingham how she was harassed and bullied by her manager Gerry Paton, because of her sex. She said Mr Paton had 'ordered' her to wear skirts as part of his campaign to undermine her. Eventually, as a result of this treatment she resigned.

Judy joined the PGA in April 1998 as a training manager and was shocked by the constant way in which women were undermined. Mr Paton referred to women golfers as dykes, lesbians, and described women as 'emotional and manipulating'. Ms Owen said that such disrespect for women generally was a clear demonstration of Mr Paton's inability to see professional women as equals.

On Ms Owen's second day at work she was told by Mr Paton's secretary not to wear a smart trouser suit because 'ladies don't wear trousers at the PGA'. Judy Owen had worn trousers to meetings before officially taking up her post and was not advised that this was against the PGA's policy.

She asked for clarification, but because she had not been shown any policies relating to a dress code, several weeks later she again wore a smart trouser suit to work, and was humiliated by Mr Paton sending her home to change into a skirt. Ms Owen said Mr Paton had 'bullied' and 'harassed' her. She was signed off work with stress after several incidents of bullying and harassment and eventually resigned.

The PGA denied its dress code is discriminatory and said Ms Owen had 'provoked' Mr Paton by wearing trousers. They had denied that Judy Owen was treated unfairly and confirmed that they did not have a written policy on dress code.

Ms Owen said she was 'extremely pleased' that the Employment Tribunal had found in her favour and that she hoped it would set an example to other women to stand up for their rights.

Ms Owen said:

> Trousers can be a smart, practical and sometimes more professional alternative for women at work. Out of date stereotypes of appropriate dress for women should not prevent women wearing trousers which have considerable practical advantages.
>
> Smart trousers are now a widely accepted alternative to skirts for women at work. Even conservative professions like the Bar now consider trousers to be acceptable business dress for women. Cheri Blair wears them and no-one has accused her of not being dressed appropriately. Women MPs in Parliament wear them too. The fact that the PGA thought it could inflict these kinds of prejudicial judgements on its female employees is outrageous. I'm extremely pleased that finally I have won this important judgement on behalf of women.
>
> However, I am saddened that after more than 18 months of this battle the PGA still has no written equal opportunities policy in place and that they still ban women from wearing trousers. I would have hoped that in the modern workplace, employers would accept that trousers are acceptable dress for women.

Clare Hockney, the Equal Opportunities Commission solicitor who fought the battle for Judy said:

> This is fantastic and now gives women the right to wear smart trousers to work. It has now been deemed unlawful sex discrimination to refuse to allow women to wear a smart trouser suit as an option for work. This issue had not been directly tested since 1977 and standards of what is conventional dress for men and women has moved on.

Julie Mellor, the Chair of the EOC, said:

> This is a memorable victory for Judy and for the EOC who backed her claim. We believe that women should be judged on the quality of their work, not on what they wear. Women in all walks of life now wear smart trousers to work, and it's now almost a year since David Beckham wore a sarong! It's right that the law should reflect these changes.
>
> It is no longer acceptable for employers to impose old-fashioned stereotypes about what they think it is appropriate for women or men to wear to work. Judging individuals on how they look is clearly discriminatory to women and can prevent them achieving their potential in the workplace. How can such a situation be good for business? It's a great day for Judy.

Source: www.eoc.org.uk/html/press_releases_2000_1.html.
Accessed 10 February 2001. Reproduced with permission.

Photo: David Jones/PA Photos

Sterotypes about women employees

In the workplace, there are many commonplace stereotypes about women employees. Women may be perceived as: an 'earth-mother'; a counsellor figure; a 'pet' brightening up the place; a 'seductress'; a sex object; an 'iron maiden'; a man-hater.[52] In addition, women who have made it to the top have to face other pressures concerned with their visibility and uniqueness. The token woman has to contend with additional interest because of her gender and she may be excluded from social activities and male 'chat'. Some studies have focused on the behavioural characteristics of men and women, and have noted that women may be caught in a 'double bind'. If they show typical feminine characteristics it is thought they do not have the ambition to go further; whereas if they demonstrate assertiveness and determination they can be considered to be too aggressive, pushy and masculine.

Understanding the organisational process

Although some organisations may discriminate, it is the view of the authors that perceptions of women are not always calculated: they are often made automatically and without conscious thought – in much the same way as we may be tricked by visual illusions. In fact, perceptual illusions are a very appropriate way of understanding the organisational processes affecting women. The 'Ames Room' is relevant for this purpose.[53] This is a room of an irregular size with one of the far corners at a greater distance than the other, although the room is arranged and decorated so that it gives the appearance of being rectangular. If two people of the same size stand in diagonally opposite corners, one in the furthest corner, and the other in the near corner, a visual illusion occurs whereby our perception of depth is 'tricked' to see the farthest away looking dramatically smaller. (*See* Figure 11.14.)

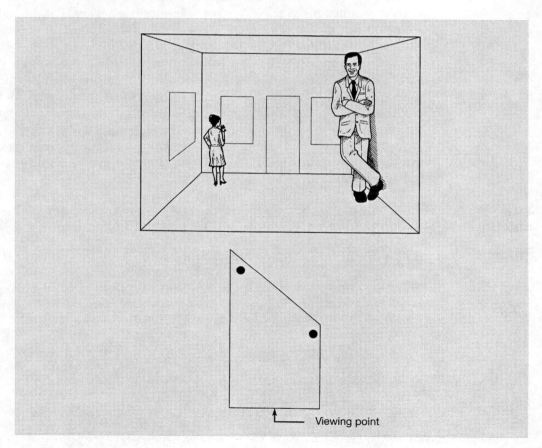

Figure 11.14 The Ames Room

(*Source*: Hicks, L. 'Gender and Culture: A Study of the Attitudes Displayed by Managers in the Hotel World'. Unpublished doctoral thesis, University of Surrey, 1991, p. 303.)

By analogy it is possible to see the room as representing the culture of the organisation surrounded by beliefs and traditions, rather like pictures on the wall. They seem reasonable, logical and appropriate. The individual standing at the farthest corner of the room could be seen as the female, the nearest the male. Both people are in the room surrounded by the culture; but one, the male, is nearest and most visible. He is perceived differently and advantageously, whereas the woman is perceived in a relatively inconsequential way. If the woman stays at the back of the room in an ancillary position, or leaves the room altogether, she is reinforcing the beliefs around the walls.

Some women, however, do become managers and these exceptional women would then join the male corner and would seem to become larger in size and more visible. However, the perceptual distortion is complete because the lone woman could legitimately be viewed as a 'trick', as an illusion. For the males, their position fits and they have only to prove their merit for a management post, and not that they are different from the norm. Their success will feed back into the system and reaffirm the beliefs that are held.

Applications to the organisational setting

This illusion can be applied to any organisational setting. *Hicks* found, for example, that even in hotels, which mirror the domestic world of women and should suit perfectly the alleged skills of women, a male ethic resides.[54] The female manager is atypical, a deviation from the norm, and women can be seen to be the disadvantaged gender group. Men and women are perceived very differently. Young, male trainees are expected and encouraged to do well, it is considered 'normal'; whereas young women and their assumed needs are less likely to fit into the demands of the industry. Young women are expected to diversify and specialise in roles considered suitable for their gender such as personnel or public relations.

For any organisation to be effective it is imperative that the staff are competent to do their work and satisfy the 'psychological contract' (discussed in Chapter 2). One part of the role of managers is to select and train those people who they predict will perform successfully on the job, and then to monitor and assess their competence for future promotion. Accordingly, it clearly seems important for managers to be aware of their own prejudices and assumptions concerning women. By opening channels and encouraging and developing all staff, trust might be fed back into the system from which equity could begin and stereotypes might end.

Britain's top businesswomen

To conclude this discussion it is of interest to note two recent comments from the *Management Today* listing of Britain's most powerful businesswomen:

> The top 50 women do not fit any pattern. They wield the kind of power and influence that defies stereotypes.[55]

> So, after 20 years of discussion and debate about how the glass ceiling is to be shattered, the proportion of women in the boardroom has grown by just 2% and Marjorie Scardino (Pearson's CEO) is still the only female chief executive of a FTSE-100 company.[56]

CRITICAL REFLECTIONS

'Managers require an understanding of perception in order to help judge the behaviour and intentions of other people.'

'Right, but remember that it is not unreasonable to argue that there is no such thing as reality – only the individual's perception or interpretation of reality.'

'But how then can managers avoid organisational problems which result from perceptual differences?'

What are your own views?

Those organizations that can create a culture that challenges unhelpful perceptual processes (stemming, say, from ignorance, prejudice or arrogance) will, in our view, be more able to absorb new information and respond intelligently to change. Broadening our mind, however, is much easier said than done. To understand why this is so, it is worth looking at influences on our perceptual processes. At the most fundamental level lie our values and beliefs. These also colour what we see and how we interpret events. Given this, it is important we reflect on how our own values influence the decisions we make.

Dainty, P. and Anderson, M. 'Mindset for Managers', in Chowdhury, S. *Management 21C*, Financial Times Prentice Hall (2000), pp. 109–10.

How would you, as a senior manager, attempt to broaden perceptions and challenge unhelpful perceptual processes among your staff?

'There is considerable truth in the commonly held perception that women's motivations and attitudes to work are different to men's.'

Debate.

SYNOPSIS

▓ The process of perception links individuals to their social world. Although we all see the world through our own 'coloured spectacles' we also have the opportunities to share our experiences with others. By learning others' perspectives and by widening our understanding of how others may see the world, depth and variety is encouraged and problems of bias and distortion become minimised. Perception is the root of all organisational behaviour and any situation can be analysed in terms of its perceptual connotations.

▓ For managers, an understanding of perception is essential to ensure that they are aware of the problems which can arise from the process of perceptual attention and selectivity. The process of perception is innately organised and patterned in order to provide meaning for the individual. The process of perception is based on both internal and external factors. The organisation and arrangement of stimuli is influenced by three important factors: figure and ground; grouping; and closure. It is important to be aware of potential perceptual illusions.

▓ Part of the process of perceiving other people is to attribute characteristics to them. We judge their behaviour and intentions on past knowledge and in comparison with other people we know. Perception gives rise to individual behavioural responses in given situations. The principles of perceptual differences reflect the way we perceive other people and are the source of many organisational problems. In the work situation, the process of perception and selection of stimuli can influence a manager's relationship with other staff.

▓   The importance of communication and the way we interact with others cannot be overestimated, as our well-being and morale can be affected by the nature of these social experiences. Communication and perception are inextricably bound. Transactional analysis (TA) is one of the most popular ways of explaining the dynamics of interpersonal communication. It is a theory which encompasses personality, perception and communication. Knowledge of TA can be of benefit to employees dealing with potentially difficult situations. Neuro-Linguistic Programming (NLP) can help when communicating with other people.

▓   The ways in which we organise and make judgements about what we have perceived is to a large extent based on previous experiences and learning. It is also important to be aware that there are inferences and assumptions which go beyond the information given. Judgements of other people can also be influenced by such stimuli as role or status; occupation; physical factors and appearance; and body language. The social situation consists of both verbal and non-verbal signals. It is necessary to be aware of cultural differences in non-verbal communications.

▓   Part of the process of perceiving other people is to attribute characteristics to them. Attribution is the process by which people interpret the perceived causes of behaviour. There are a number of difficulties which arise with interpersonal perception. Four main features which may give rise to perceptual distortions or errors are: stereotyping; the halo effect; perceptual defence; and projection. The perceptual process is selective and subjective. In the work situation perceptual differences reflect the way we perceive other people. One particularly important example is the perception of women.

REVIEW AND DISCUSSION QUESTIONS

1 Explain your understanding of the process of perception. Why is the study of perception important in the study of management and organisational behaviour?

2 Discuss those factors which affect selection and attention in the process of perception. Give examples of how perceptual selectivity is the source of organisational problems.

3 Explain the most significant principles which influence the organisation and arrangement of stimuli. Provide your own example of each of these principles.

4 What factors influence the judgements we make of other people from different cultures? Explain the main distortions or errors in interpersonal perception. Support your answer with practical examples.

5 Explain the principles of attribution theory and its importance to, and implications for, management. Apply the principles to your *own* working life.

6 Transcribe a short dialogue you have had with a colleague, friend, or boss and analyse the responses in Transactional Analysis (TA) terms.

7 Discuss the potential appeal of NLP to managers and the challenges of evaluating the value of an NLP training course.

8 Explain fully the significance and implications of stereotyping *and* the halo effect. Give practical examples from your own experience.

Stroop – illustrative experiment

a Write two vertical lists of 20 colour names in felt tip pen. For the first list use the correct colour pen for the colour word you are writing (for example, blue pen for the word blue). Repeat some of the colours but place them in random order.

b For the second list, use different colour pens for the colour word (for example, use a red pen for the word blue).

c Now ask a colleague to read out loud the colour that the word is written in (not the word itself). Compare the amount of time it takes your colleague to read out the two lists. The second list probably not only took longer, but had more mistakes and more hesitations.

William Stroop, who first conducted this experiment, noted that the task interferes with expected behaviour. It is difficult to stop yourself from reading the word (the result of our early learning) which in this case directly impairs performance.

During the period of one week carefully review all the media (television, radio, advertisements, Internet, films, newspapers and magazines) for evidence of traditional male and female stereotypes. In a small group discussion, critically evaluate the impact and power of these stereotypes. Compare your findings and evaluation with other groups. What conclusions do you draw from this assignment?

PERSONAL AWARENESS AND SKILLS EXERCISE

OBJECTIVES

Completing this exercise should help you to enhance the following skills:

▶ Distinguish between facts and assumptions or inferences.

▶ Examine the basis upon which you make judgements.

▶ Review the nature of your decision-making processes.

EXERCISE

After reading the following story **you are required to:**

1 Read the 15 statements about the story and check each to indicate whether you consider it to be true, false or ?

'T' means that the statement is definitely true on the basis of the information presented in the story.

'F' means that it is definitely false.

'?' means that it may be either true or false and that you cannot be certain of which on the basis of the information presented in the story. If any part of a statement is doubtful, mark it '?'.

Answer each statement in turn. You may refer to the story as often as needed but do not go back to change any answer later and do not re-read any statements after you have answered them.

2 After you have completed checking all 15 statements, work in small groups of three to five and discuss your individual answers. How much agreement is there among members of your group? *Do not change any of your first individual answers. However, if as a result of your group discussion you would now give a different answer to any of the statements, note this alongside your original answer.*

The story

A businessman had just turned off the lights in the store when a man appeared and demanded money. The owner opened a cash register. The contents of the cash register were scooped up, and the man sped away. A member of the police force was notified promptly.

Statements about the story

1   A man appeared after the owner had turned off his store lights.   T   F   ?

2   The robber was a man.   T   F   ?

3   The man who appeared did not demand money.   T   F   ?

4   The man who opened the cash register was the owner.   T   F   ?

5   The storeowner scooped up the contents of the cash register and ran away.   T   F   ?

6   Someone opened a cash register.   T   F   ?

7   After the man who demanded the money scooped up the contents of the cash register, he ran away.   T   F   ?

8   While the cash register contained money, the story does not state how much.   T   F   ?

9   The robber demanded money of the owner.   T   F   ?

10 A businessman had just turned off the lights when a man appeared in the store.   T   F   ?

11 It was broad daylight when the man appeared.   T   F   ?

12 The man who appeared opened the cash register.   T   F   ?

13 No one demanded money.   T   F   ?

14 The story concerns a series of events in which only three persons are referred to: the owner of the store, a man who demanded money, and a member of the police force.   T   F   ?

15 The following events occurred: someone demanded money, a cash register was opened, its contents were scooped up, and a man dashed out of the store.   T   F   ?

DISCUSSION

■ How would you explain differences in individual perceptions of the same statement?

■ On what basis did members of your group give different answers and how did their perception of the statements about the story differ?

■ To what extent can you be absolutely certain about anything?

Visit our website **www.booksites.net/mullins** for further questions, annotated weblinks, case material and Internet research material.

NOTES AND REFERENCES

1. Bartlett, F. C. *Remembering Cambridge*, Cambridge University Press (1932).
2. Kohler, I. 'The Formation and Transformation of the Visual World', *Psychological Issues*, 3, 1964, pp. 28–46, 116–33.
3. Bexton, W., Heron, W. and Scott, T. 'Effects of Decreased Variation in the Sensory Environment', *Canadian Journal of Psychology*, vol. 8, 1954, pp. 70–6.
4. Briggs-Myers, I. *Introduction to Type*, Oxford Psychologists Press (1987).
5. Witkin, H. A., Lewis, H. B., Hertzman, M., Machover, K., Meissner, P. P. and Wapner, S. S. *Personality Through Perception*, Harper & Row (1954).
6. Ling, C. and Masako, I. 'Intercultural Communication and Cultural Learning: the experience of visiting Japanese students in the US', *The Howard Journal of Communications*, vol. 14, 2003, pp. 75–96.
7. Hall E. T. 'The Silent Language of Overseas Business', *Harvard Business Review,* vol. 38, no. 3, 1960, pp. 85–7.
8. Block, J. R. and Yuker, H. E. *Can You Believe Your Eyes?*, Robson Books (2002).
9. Morgan, C. T. and King, R. A. *Introduction to Psychology*, Third edition, McGraw-Hill (1966), p. 343.
10. Luthans, F. *Organizational Behaviour*, Seventh edition, McGraw-Hill (1995), p. 96.
11. For further examples of perceptual teasers, see Tosi, H. L., Rizzo, J. R. and Carroll, S. J. *Managing Organizational Behaviour*, Third edition, Blackwell (1994).
12. Stroop, J. R. 'Studies of Interference in Serial Verbal Reactions', *Journal of Experimental Psychology*, vol. 4, no. 18, 1935, pp. 643–62; and Penrose, L. S. and Penrose, R. 'Impossible Objects: A Special Type of Illusion', *British Journal of Psychology*, part 1, February 1958.
13. Wexley, K. N., Yukl, G. A., Kovacs, S. Z. and Sanders, R. E. 'Importance of Contrast Effects in Employment Interviews', *Journal of Applied Psychology*, 56, 1972, pp. 45–8.
14. Laing, R. D. *Knots*, Penguin (1971), p. 30.
15. Guirdham, M. *Interactive Behaviour at Work*, Third edition, Financial Times Prentice Hall (2002).
16. See, for example: Pivcevic, P. 'Taming the Boss', *Management Today*, March 1999, pp. 68–72.
17. Bandler, R., Grinder, J., Dilts, R. and Delozier, J. *Neuro Linguistic Programming Volume I: The study of the structure of subject experience*, Meta Publications (1980).
18. Leading Edge Communications Ltd. *How to become an irresistible and hypnotic communicator*, p.2 http://www.nlpandhypnosis.com [accessed 1.12.03].
19. McCann, D. *How to Influence Others at Work*, Second edition, Butterworth Heinemann (1993).
20. Berne, E. *Games People Play*, Penguin (1966).
21. See, for example: Stewart, I. and Jaines, V. *TA today: A New Introduction to Transactional Analysis*, Life Space Publishing (1987).
22. Kendon, A. 'Some Functions of Gaze Direction in Social Interaction', *Acta Psychologica*, 26, 1967, pp. 22–63.
23. Mehrabian, A. *Nonverbal Communication*, Aldine Atherton (1972).
24. Cook, M. *Interpersonal Perception*, Penguin (1971).
25. Schneider, S. C. and Barsoux, J. *Managing Across Cultures*, Second edition, Financial Times Prentice Hall (2003), p. 29.
26. Goffman, E. *The Presentation of Self in Everyday Life*, Penguin (1971).
27. Asch, S. E. 'Forming Impressions on Personality', *Journal of Abnormal and Social Psychology*, 41, 1946, pp. 258–90.
28. Miller, N. and Campbell, D. T. 'Recency and Primacy in Persuasion as a Function of the Timing of Speeches and Measurements', *Journal of Abnormal and Social Psychology*, 59, 1959, pp. 1–9.
29. Hodges, B. 'Effect of Volume on Relative Weighting in Impression Formation', *Journal of Personality and Social Psychology*, 30, 1974, pp. 378–81.
30. Gahagan, J. *Interpersonal and Group Behaviour*, Methuen (1975).
31. Green, J. 'When Was Your Management Style Last Applauded?', *Chartered Secretary*, December 1998, p. 28.
32. Wilson, P. R. 'Perceptual Distortion of Height as a Function of Ascribed Academic Status', *Journal of Social Psychology*, no. 74, 1968, pp. 97–102.
33. See, for example: Torrington, D. *Face-to-Face in Management*, Prentice-Hall (1982).
34. Mehrabian, A. *Tactics of Social Influence*, Prentice-Hall (1970).
35. Pivcevic, P. 'Taming the Boss', *Management Today*, March 1999, p. 70.
36. McGuire, T. 'Don't Just Listen', *Chartered Secretary*, September 1998, p. 24.
37. James, J. *Body Talk at Work*, Judy Piatkus (2001), p. 3.
38. Fletcher, W. 'Let Your Body Do The Talking', *Management Today*, March 2000, p. 30.
39. Mann, S. 'Message in a Body', *Professional Manager*, November 2000, pp. 32–3; and Ribbens, G. and Thompson, R. *Understanding Body Language in a Week*, Institute of Management and Hodder & Stoughton (2000).
40. See, for example: Green, J. 'Can You Read Other People's Body Talk?' *Administrator*, February 1994, pp. 8–9.
41. For other examples of cultural differences, see Schneider S. C. and Barsoux, J. *Managing Across Cultures*, Second edition, Finacial Times Prentice Hall (2003).
42. Heider, F. *The Psychology of Interpersonal Relations*, John Wiley and Sons (1958).
43. Kelley, H. H. 'The Process of Causal Attribution', *American Psychologist*, February 1973, pp. 107–28.
44. Mitchell, T. R. *People in Organizations: An Introduction to Organizational Behaviour*, Third edition, McGraw-Hill (1987).
45. Bartunek, J. M. 'Why Did You Do That? Attribution Theory in Organizations', *Business Horizons*, September–October 1981, pp. 66–71.

46. Mitchell, T. R., Smyser, C. M. and Weed, S. E. 'Locus of Control: Supervision and Work Satisfaction', *Academy of Management Journal*, September 1975, pp. 623–31.

47. Durand, D. E. and Nord, W. R. 'Perceived Leader Behaviour as a Function of Personality Characteristics of Supervisors and Subordinates', *Academy of Management Journal*, September 1976, pp. 427–38.

48. For a more detailed analysis of the accuracy of interpersonal perception and problems in judgement of others, see: Krech, D., Crutchfield, R. S. and Ballachey, E. L. *Individual in Society*, McGraw-Hill (1962).

49. For a fuller discussion see, for example: McKenna, E. F. *Business Psychology and Organisational Behaviour*, Lawrence Erlbaum (1994).

50. See, for example: Atkin, A. 'Positive HIV and AIDS Policies at Work', *Personnel Management*, December 1994, pp. 34–7.

51. See also, Goss, D. and Adam-Smith, D. *Organizing Aids*, Taylor & Francis (1995).

52. Cooper, C. and Davidson, M. *High Pressure: Working Lives of Women Managers*, Fontana (1982).

53. Ames, A. 'Visual Perception and the Rotating Trapezoidal Window', *Psychological Monographs*, vol. 65, no. 7, 1951.

54. Hicks, L. 'Gender and Culture: A Study of the Attitudes Displayed by Managers in the Hotel World', Unpublished doctoral thesis, University of Surrey, 1991.

55. Hamilton, K. 'The Women Who Move Britain', *Management Today*, March 1999, pp. 39–44.

56. Wheatcroft, P. 'Britain's 50 Most Powerful Women', *Management Today*, April 2000, p. 48.

 Use the *Financial Times* to enhance your understanding of the context and practice of management and organisational behaviour. Refer to article 12 in the BUSINESS PRESS section at the end of the book for relevant reports on the issues explored in this chapter.

TOPIC SUMMARY SHEET

What are the key learning points from this topic?

TOPIC 3 – EQUAL OPPORTUNITIES

Why study this topic?

The last topic we looked at emphasised the fact that the workplace is a diverse place, where we may encounter a great variety of people and it is inevitable that prejudice and discrimination may occur.
As you will see from your reading, not all groups in society have the same opportunities to enter the workforce or advance within it. As a potential or current people manager it is essential for you to carry out your tasks with a non discriminatory approach.

The government provides us with the legislative framework which attempts to minimise levels of discrimination within the workforce. These pieces of legislation act as a protector for the potential/current employee and also for the organisation. They cover many situations in the workplace, including sex, race, disability, employment status, sexual orientation, and will soon encompass age also. Knowledge of the framework and examples of best practice will enable you to carry out your future/current duties in a fair and equitable manner, reflecting positively on yourself and your organisation.

Blackboard

E-tivity 3: Equal opportunities

MODULE MILESTONE: - SEMINARS COMMENCE

CHAPTER 24

EQUAL OPPORTUNITIES
AND DIVERSITY

THE OBJECTIVES OF THIS CHAPTER ARE TO:

1 REVIEW THE CURRENT EMPLOYMENT EXPERIENCES OF THE MEMBERS OF SOME SOCIALLY DEFINED MINORITY
   GROUPS

2 ANALYSE THE DIFFERING APPROACHES TO ACHIEVING EQUALITY FOR THOSE GROUPS, IN PARTICULAR
   CONTRASTING THE MORE TRADITIONAL EQUAL OPPORTUNITIES APPROACH WITH THE MANAGEMENT OF
   DIVERSITY APPROACH

3 EXPLORE THE IMPLICATIONS WHICH MANAGING DIVERSITY HAS FOR ORGANISATIONS

Legislation, voluntary codes of practice and equality initiatives have resulted in some progress towards equality of treatment for minority groups, but there remains inescapable evidence of continuing discrimination. More recent approaches under the banner of management of diversity include the economic and business case for equality, the valuing and managing of diversity in organisations, culture change and the mainstreaming of equality initiatives. These approaches are partly a response to the insufficient progress made so far, yet there is only limited evidence that they have made a difference. They offer some useful perspectives and practices, although the underlying concepts also raise some issues and concerns.

CURRENT EMPLOYMENT EXPERIENCES OF SOCIALLY DEFINED MINORITY GROUPS

For the purposes of this section we will consider the experiences of five socially defined minority groups: women, racial/ethnic minorities, disabled people, older people and individuals who are lesbian, gay, bisexual or transsexual. In choosing these groups we have followed, broadly, Kirton and Greene (2003), although others, such as British Telecom, have identified as many as 12 aspects of difference between employees (Liff 1999). As identified in the previous chapter there are a larger number of other minority groups for whom legal protection against discrimination is available, and we have therefore been selective in the groups we have chosen to discuss in this chapter. At the time of writing there is no legal protection against age discrimination as this will not be in place until 2006.

It should also be noted that CIPD (2003) provides a much broader definition of diversity, going beyond social category diversity, as above, to include informational diversity (differences in terms of education, tenure and functional background) and value diversity (which includes differences in personality and attitudes).

Women

If **participation** in the labour force is an indication of decreasing discrimination then recent figures are encouraging. From 1971 to 2001 the female participation rate in employment increased from 56.8 per cent to 72 per cent, compared with the male participation rate which is slowly falling, and now at 84 per cent (Equal Opportunities Review (EOR) 2002). These trends are predicted to continue. Much of this increase has been due to the replacement of full-time jobs with part-time jobs. Indeed Hakim (1993) puts forward the strong argument, based on an alternative analysis of the census and employment data, that the increasing participation of women in employment between the 1950s and the late 1980s is a myth, although a real increase does appear to have taken place since the late 1980s. Her analysis shows that 'the much trumpeted rise in women's employment in Britain consisted entirely of the substitution of part-time for full-time jobs from 1951 to the late 1980s' (p. 102). Hakim concludes from the research that only an increase in full-time employment is likely to have a wider impact on women's opportunities at work and elsewhere.

Some of the more obvious signs of discrimination, such as in recruitment advertising, may have disappeared, and there is some evidence to suggest that women are beginning to enter some previously male-dominated occupations. For example, women have now been ordained as priests in the Church of England but not without deep and continuing debate. Similarly men are beginning to enter some previously female-only occupations, such as midwifery. However, there remains a high degree of subtle, for example in access to training and support for development and promotion, and not-so-subtle discrimination, as in the continued **gender segregation** in terms of both type and level of work undertaken. There are still few women in higher levels of management and not many male secretaries. People Management (2002) reports research undertaken by Cranfield which finds a 50 per cent increase over the previous year in women is executive directors in the FTSE 100 companies. However, even after the increase the percentage of executive directors who are women is still only 15 per cent. In the same year Higginbottom and Roberts (2002) report that the EOC found only 28 per cent of elected councillors, 12 per cent of elected council leaders, and 10 per cent of local authority chiefs were women. The majority of managers and administrators are men and most women remain in three occupational groups: clerical and secretarial, personal and protective services such as catering, caring, cleaning and selling occupations (Thair and Risden 1999). These occupations are often characterised by part-time work, and poor pay, and are in a mainly narrow range of industrial sectors. Part-time workers are often described as part of the secondary labour market with pay, conditions and employment rights being vastly inferior to those of full-time permanent workers, although legislation now provides for some equalisation.

WINDOW ON PRACTICE

Gender segregation at Deloitte Touche

McCracken (2000) reports how Deloitte Touche were good at recruiting women and felt they had achieved equal opportunities, but they were finding that women were leaving at a much higher rate than men and few women were made partners. On investigating the situation they found that women were leaving, not for domestic reasons as they had anticipated, but due to the male-dominated culture. Men were assigned high-visibility assignments in manufacturing, financial services, acquisitions and mergers, whereas women were offered non-profit organisations, healthcare and retail. They also found that women were genuinely assessed on their performance levels, but that men were also assessed on their potential, which women missed out on.

Deloitte Touche made efforts to change these practical features of working life and also tried to promote work-life balance. Having identified the real problems in achieving equality they found that more women partners were coming through and that money was being saved as they were losing fewer talented women.

Summarised from: D. McCracken (2000) 'Winning the talent war for women: sometimes it takes a revolution', *Harvard Business Review*, November–December, pp. 159–65.

Pay differentials between men and women have narrowed very little except for a hike of women's pay upwards when the Equal Pay Act 1970 came into force in 1975.

Table 24.1 Barriers to the achievement of gender-based equal pay

Starting pay is frequently individually negotiated	As men usually have higher previous earnings this means they can negotiate a higher starting rate
Length of service	Men generally have longer service and fewer career breaks, and while this may result in greater experience early in a career it is less of a performance-influencing factor as general length of service increases
Broadbanding	There is a lack of transparency in such systems and there is a lack of structured progression, managers are likely to have high levels of discretion and may be unaware of biases
Lack of equal access to bonus payments	There is evidence that appraisal ratings and assessments discriminate unfairly against minority groups
Market allowances not evenly distributed	Such allowances are more likely to be given to men
Different pay structures and negotiating bodies	As some jobs are done primarily by women and some primarily by men, direct comparisons are harder to make
Job evaluation	Such schemes often perpetuate old values and may be subject to managerial manipulation

Source: Based primarily on material in IDS (2004) 'Employers move on equal pay', *IDS Report No. 897*, January, pp. 10–18.

The 2003 New Earnings Survey reports that women's full-time average weekly pay without overtime was 18 per cent less than that for full-time men (IDS 2004), having increased from around 30 per cent lower prior to the Equal Pay Act. However, if overtime is included the current gap widens as men work a greater number of hours. The same survey shows that the hourly rate of part-time women is 40 per cent less than that for full-time men, with overtime excluded. While some progress has been made towards equal pay, these factors still remain as barriers to be overcome. The abolition of the Wages Councils has not helped in this respect, but the minimum wage has provided some limited support. IDS (2004) identify a range of unintentional consequences of pay systems which prove to be a barrier to achieving equal pay, and these are shown in Table 24.1.

Racial and ethnic groups

In spite of the legislation evidence of discrimination continues to exist. The EOR (2003) reports that the level of unemployment for black and Asian communities is 12 per cent compared with that for the white population of 5 per cent. This picture of **comparative level of unemployment** has barely changed over the last 18 years, and the gap appears to be widening rather than narrowing, although there are differences between the different ethnic groups. In addition, there is continued **segregation in the labour market,** with ethnic minority male employees being employed in the hotel, catering and repairs and distribution sectors, and manufacturing industry, to a much greater extent than their white counterparts. But for construction the reverse is true. Segregation also occurs vertically. Using Labour Force Survey data, the Trades Union Congress (TUC) (2000) reports that 30.4 per cent of white people were classified as managers compared with 24.7 per cent of black people. Again the gap appears to be widening rather than narrowing. Other evidence of vertical segregation has been found by the Runnymede Trust (2000) when surveying the FTSE 100 companies. They found that 5.4 per cent of employees were from ethnic minority groups, compared with the representation of ethnic minorities in the general population of 6.4 per cent, but that this proportion fell sharply at higher grades, with 3.2 per cent of junior managers from ethnic minorities and 1 per cent of senior managers. Yet all of these companies believed that they did not unfairly discriminate. Samir Sharma OBE, Chair of the Runnymede Trust, commented that 'there is still a sea of white faces in the boardrooms of Europe' (EOR 2000). Racial discrimination may also happen less blatantly. Rana (2003) reports on a project designed to understand why ethnic minority managers are underrepresented in senior levels of local government. The researchers found that in 360-degree feedback results the line managers' assessments of ethnic minority employees were less favourable for each individual than all other assessments, which were generally similar. This discrepancy did not occur when considering the ratings of white employees. In terms of **pay**, non-white workers are also comparatively disadvantaged.

WINDOW ON PRACTICE

The *Guardian* (4 November 2000) contained the following report:

The IT industry is often considered to be one which is more open to the employment of different racial groups. But while the workforce may look more diverse the top jobs are still mostly filled by white people. The article goes on to report the experiences of two non-white IT directors. The first, Rene Carayol, is Chief Executive of an e-business consultancy, and comments that he is shocked by the racial prejudice that he encounters. For example, when Rene and the team are visiting new offices, people who have not met them before look around the team for the white faces to work out who is the boss. He comments that it takes some time for people to get used to working with him, and feels that it took him longer to rise to his present position due to his race.

The second, Sarabjit Ubhey, Head of Operational Control at BUPA, identifies the glass ceiling above which there are few senior non-white IT people. She feels that the fundamental problem is awareness, pointing out, for example, that when social/ networking events are held at a pub Muslims cannot be present. This, in addition to making them feel excluded, hinders their career progression.

Source: Adapted from R. Woolnough (2000) 'Racism reinforces the glass ceiling', *Guardian*, 4 November, p. 31.

Disabled people

Woodhams and Danieli (2000) point out that people who have a disability face common barriers to full integration into society and yet are a very varied group in that impairments can vary in severity, stability and type. There are 6.7 million people in the UK who have a current long-term health problem or disability which has a substantial adverse impact on their day-to-day activities and affects the work they can do (Bruyere 2000). People with a disability are more likely to be unemployed than their able-bodied counterparts, and once unemployed they are likely to remain so for a longer period (EOR 2003). The economic activity rate for disabled people is 53 per cent compared with 84 per cent for non-disabled people, and 49 per cent of disabled people are in employment compared with 81 per cent of non-disabled people (EOR 2003). Hammond (2002) notes that the media have a particularly poor reputation for employing disabled people. This is particularly unfortunate as this is a missed opportunity to create visible and influential role models.

Choice of job is often restricted for people with a disability, and where they do find work it is likely to be in low-paid, less attractive jobs. People with a disability are overrepresented in plant and machine operative jobs and in the personal and protective services, and are underrepresented in professional and managerial jobs (Skills and Enterprise Network 2000). Periods of high general unemployment exacerbate these problems.

Employers traditionally have had a wide range of concerns regarding the employment of disabled people, including worries about general standards of attendance and health, safety at work, eligibility for pension schemes and possible requirements for alterations to premises and equipment. The two ticks disability symbol is a government initiative and can be used by employers to demonstrate their commitment to employing disabled people. Employers who use the symbol make five commitments to action: a guaranteed job interview for disabled applicants, regular consultation with disabled employees, retaining employees if they become disabled during their employment, improving knowledge about disability for key employees, reviewing these commitments and planning ahead. However Dibben *et al.* (2001) note that the symbol appeared to have only a limited effect on support for disabled employees or potential employees.

WINDOW ON PRACTICE

The case of Val Milnes

Glover reports the experiences of Val Milnes in seeking employment after recovering from a skiing accident, which left her paralysed from the chest down. After being dismissed by her current employer six months after the accident, she began to look for work when she had been through a rehabilitation process. Her experiences of seeking employment are salutary. Little support was made in most organisations to enable her to compete on a 'level playing field', and she comments that HR professionals did not help. In terms of finding locations and carrying out interviews Val was constantly put at a disadvantage. She felt that on many occasions she was interviewed as a matter of procedure and as a way of complying with the two ticks symbol; and that there was no intention to consider her for employment. She suggests some very practical steps that employers could take to make people with a disability feel more welcome.

Source: Summarised from C. Glover (2003) 'Ticked off', *People Management*, Vol. 8, No. 2, 24 January, pp. 38–9.

Age

While advertisements are generally less obviously discriminatory in respect of age the EOR (1998) found that employers still used coded language to indicate that they were looking for a specific age group, and found phrases such as 'young', 'articulate youngsters', 'second jobber', and 'young dynamic environment'. There continue to be cultures that discriminate against older, and younger, people. There is frequently discrimination at both the shortlisting and interview stage, with line managers having negative perceptions of older workers, seeing them as less able to cope with change, training or technology and less interested in their careers. Higginbottom and Roberts (2002), reporting on a MORI poll of 2000 adults, found that they viewed age discrimination as the prime cause of discrimination at work. Philpott (2003) reports that in a survey of 600 retired people, two-fifths believe they had suffered discrimination in some way, age discrimination being the most frequent form. He goes on to argue that there are fewer older people in the workforce, not because they prefer to retire, but because they feel they have been discriminated against. Snape and Redman (2003) found partial support for this. Platman (2002) reports on National Opinion Poll (NOP) research funded by the Department for Work and Pensions which included people between the ages of 50 and 60, a quarter of whom believe that they were discriminated against when looking for a job. Nearly half the organisations in the survey had no staff aged 60 or over. Line managers said they were age friendly, although they appeared to be ignorant of the guidelines.

Given that by 2010 almost 40 per cent of the working population will be over 45 (Higginbottom 2002) and the current shortage of many skills, this presents a critical problem for organisations. Older workers are seen to be more loyal and conscientious, to have better interpersonal skills, to be more efficient in the job and their experience in the job counteracts any age-related factors lowering productivity; older workers are generally more satisfied with their jobs and have fewer accidents and a better absence record; and in any case there is considerable variation within individuals. Older workers also have lower turnover rates which saves the organisation money.

On the basis of their research Snape and Redman (2003) argue that discrimination for being too young is at least as common as that for being too old. Both forms of discrimination adversely affected commitment to the organisation, and hence, it could be argued, performance.

Sexuality

Lesbian, gay and bisexual discrimination is the most difficult to identify due to the fact that group membership is more easily concealed, usually due to the anticipation of discrimination. It is therefore difficult to quantify the extent to which these groups experience active discrimination. The protection now given to transsexuals means that they are not forced to offer historical information on their gender, but transsexuals in transition clearly cannot keep this confidential, and will need support and protection from harassment (Higginbottom 2002). Most employers have been slow to include sexual orientation in their diversity management initiatives (Ward 2003).

Wilson (2000) in an article reporting three case studies found that in two of the three organisations sexuality other than the heterosexual norm was not considered acceptable in the culture. In one engineering company, the researcher was told that you would have to be very discreet if you were gay, and that one gay person, who had not 'come out', had left the organisation. In the second, a professional partnership, the researcher was told that sexuality was 'under wraps'. Only in the third, a media organisation, were different sexual orientations considered acceptable.

In a TUC survey carried out at the end of 1998 (EOR 1999b), 44 per cent of the 440 gay, lesbian and bisexual respondents said they had experienced discrimination at work due to their sexuality. Forms of discrimination reported ranged from verbal abuse to dismissal. Even in jobs where employees feel sufficiently comfortable to disclose their sexuality, there is considerable discrimination in the terms and benefits they receive, although legislation is beginning to change this situation.

In summary

Although some of the more blatant aspects of discrimination have been significantly improved, there remain considerable discrimination and inequality in respect of minority groups in the workplace. To some extent we are only just beginning to understand the causes and nature of more subtle forms of discrimination which are the root of inequality. We now turn to the theoretical debate which underpins different organisational approaches to tackling discrimination.

DIFFERENT APPROACHES TO EQUALITY

There has been a continuing debate concerning the action that should be taken to alleviate the disadvantages that minority groups encounter. One school of thought supports legislative action, which we considered in detail in the previous chapter, and this approach is generally referred to as the equal opportunities, or liberal approach. The other argues that this will not be effective and that the only way to change fundamentally is to alter the attitudes and preconceptions that are held about these groups. This second perspective is embodied in the managing diversity approaches. The initial emphasis on legislative action was adopted in the hope that this would eventually affect attitudes. A third, more extreme, radical approach, which enjoys less support, comes from those who advocate legislation to promote positive or reverse discrimination to compensate for a history of discrimination against specified groups and to redress the balance more immediately. The arguments for and against such an approach are fully discussed by Singer (1993). In the UK legislation provides for positive action, such as special support and encouragement, for disadvantaged groups, but not positive or reverse discrimination (discriminating in their favour), although positive discrimination is legal in the USA. For a comparison of UK and US approaches to equality *see* Ford (1996).

The labels 'equal opportunities' and 'management of diversity' are used inconsistently, and to complicate this there are different perspectives on the meaning of managing diversity, so we shall draw out the key differences which typify each of these approaches, and offer some critique of their conceptual foundations and efficacy.

The equal opportunities approach

The equal opportunities approach seeks to influence behaviour through legislation so that discrimination is prevented. It has been characterised by a moral and ethical stance promoting the rights of *all* members of society. The approach, sometimes referred to as the liberal tradition (Jewson and Mason 1986), concentrates on the equality of opportunity rather than the equality of outcome found in more radical approaches. The approach is based on the understanding that some individuals are discriminated against, for example in the selection process, due to irrelevant criteria. These irrelevant criteria arise from assumptions based on the stereotypical characteristics attributed to them as members of a socially defined group, for example that women will not be prepared to work away from home due to family commitments; that a person with a disability will have more time off sick. As these assumptions are not supported by any evidence, in respect of any individual, they are regarded as irrelevant. The equal opportunities approach therefore seeks to formalise procedures so that relevant, job-based criteria are used (using job descriptions and person specifications), rather than irrelevant assumptions. The equal opportunities legislation provides a foundation for this formalisation of procedures, and hence procedural justice. As Liff (1999) points out, the use of systematic rules in employment matters which can be monitored for compliance is 'felt fair'. In line with the moral argument, and emphasis on systematic procedures, equal opportunities is often characterised as a responsibility of the HR department.

The rationale, therefore, is to provide a 'level playing field' on which all can compete on equal terms. Positive action, not positive discrimination, is allowable in order that some may reach the level at which they can compete equally. For example British Rail has given members of minority groups extra coaching and practice in a selection test for train drivers, as test taking was not part of their culture so that, when required to take a test, they were at a disadvantage.

Equal opportunities approaches stress disadvantaged groups, and the need, for example, to set targets for those groups to ensure that their representation in the workplace reflects their representation in wider society in occupations where they are underrepresented, such as the small numbers of ethnic minorities employed as firefighters and police officers, or the small numbers of women in senior management roles. These targets are not enforceable by legislation, as in the United States, but organisations have been encouraged to commit themselves voluntarily to improvement goals, and to support this by putting in place measures to support disadvantaged groups such as special training courses and flexible employment policies.

Differences between socially defined groups are glossed over, and the approach is generally regarded as one of 'sameness'. That is, members of disadvantaged groups should be treated in the same way as the traditional employee (white, male, young, able-bodied and heterosexual), and not treated differently due to their group membership, unless for the purpose of providing the 'level playing field'.

Problems with the equal opportunities approach

There is an assumption in the equal opportunities approach that equality of outcome will be achieved if fair procedures are used and monitored. In other words this will enable any minority groups to achieve a fair share of what employment has to offer. Once such minority groups become full participating members in employment, the old stereotypical attitudes on which discrimination against particular social groups is based will gradually change, as the stereotypes will be shown to be unhelpful.

The assumption that fair procedures or procedural justice will lead to fair outcomes has not been borne out in practice, as we have shown. In addition there has been criticism of the assumption that once members of minority groups have demonstrated their ability to perform in the organisation this will change attitudes and beliefs in the organisation. This is a naïve assumption, and the approach has been regarded as simplistic. Liff (1999) argues that attitudes and beliefs have been left untouched. Other criticisms point out that the legislation does not protect all minority groups (although it is gradually being extended); and there is a general lack of support within the organisation, partly because equality objectives are not linked to business objectives (Shapiro and Austin 1996). Shapiro and Austin, among others, argue that equal opportunities has often been the concern of the HR function, and Kirton and Greene (2003) argue that a weak HR function has not helped. The focus of equal opportunities is on formal processes and yet it is it not possible to formalise everything in the organisation. Recent research suggests that this approach alienated large sections of the workforce (those not identified as disadvantaged groups) who felt that there was no benefit for themselves, and indeed that their opportunities were damaged. Others felt that equal opportunities initiatives had resulted in the lowering of entry standards, as in the London Fire and Civil Defence Authority (EOR 1996). Shapiro and Austin argue that this creates divisions in the workforce. Lastly, it is the individual who is expected to adjust to the organisation, and 'traditional equal opportunities strategies encourage a view that women (and other groups) have a problem and need help' (Liff 1999, p. 70).

In summary the equal opportunities approach is considered simplistic and to be attempting to treat the symptoms rather than the causes of unfair discrimination.

The management of diversity approach

The management of diversity approach concentrates on individuals rather than groups, and includes the improvement of opportunities for *all* individuals and not just those in minority groups. Hence managing diversity involves everyone and benefits everyone, which is an attractive message to employers and employees alike. Thus separate groups are not singled out for specific treatment. Kandola and Fullerton (1994, p. 47), who are generally regarded as the main UK supporters of a managing diversity approach, express it this way:

> Managing diversity is about the realisation of the potential of all employees . . . certain group based equal opportunities policies need to be seriously questioned, in particular positive action and targets.

In the second edition of their book (1998, p. 11) they contest, in addition, that:

> if managing diversity is about an individual and their contribution . . . rather than about groups it is contradictory to provide training and other opportunities based solely on people's perceived group membership.

Further differences from an equal opportunities approach are highlighted in the following definition from the USA, where managing diversity is described as:

> the challenge of meeting the needs of a culturally diverse workforce and of sensitising workers and managers to differences associated with gender, race, age and nationality in an attempt to maximise the potential productivity of all employees.
>
> (Ellis and Sonnenfield 1994, p. 82)

Ignoring for a moment the fact that some groups are specifically excluded from this definition, we will focus, among other themes, on two key issues that this quotation raises: recognition of difference and culture. Recognition of difference is also demonstrated by the Institute of Personnel and Development (IPD, now CIPD) (1997) when they say that 'people have different abilities to contribute to organizational goals and performance' (pp. 1–2). Whereas the equal opportunities approach minimised difference, the managing diversity approach treats difference as a positive asset. Liff (1996), for example, notes that from this perspective organisations should recognise rather than dilute differences, as differences are positive rather than negative.

This brings us to a further difference between the equal opportunities approach and the managing diversity approach which is that the managing diversity approach is based on the economic and business case for recognising and valuing difference, rather than the moral case for treating people equally. Rather than being purely a cost, equal treatment offers benefits and advantages for the employer if it invests in ensuring that everyone in the organisation is valued and given the opportunities to develop their potential and make a maximum contribution. The practical arguments supporting the equalisation of employment opportunities are thus highlighted. Thompson and DiTomaso (reported by Ellis and Sonnenfield 1994) put it very well:

> [A] [m]ulticultural management perspective fosters more innovative and creative decision making, satisfying work environments, and better products because all people who have a contribution to make are encouraged to be involved in a meaningful way . . . More information, more points of view, more ideas and reservations are better than fewer.

A company that discriminates, directly or indirectly, against older or disabled people, women, ethnic minorities or people with different sexual orientations will be curtailing the potential of available talent, and employers are not well known for their complaints about the surplus of talent. The financial benefits of retaining staff who might otherwise leave due to lack of career development or due to the desire to combine a career with family are stressed, as is the image of the organisation as a 'good' employer and hence its attractiveness to all members of society as its customers. A relationship between a positive diversity climate and job satisfaction and commitment to the organisation has also been found (Hicks-Clarke and Iles 2000). Although the impact on performance is more difficult to assess, it is reasonable to assume that more satisfied and committed employees will lead to reduced absence and turnover levels. In addition, the value of different employee perspectives and different types of contribution is seen as providing added value to the organisation, particularly when organisational members increasingly reflect the diverse customer base of the organisation. This provides a way in which organisations can better understand, and therefore meet, their customer needs. The business case argument is likely to have more support from managers as it is less likely to threaten the bottom line. Policies that do pose such a threat can be unpopular with managers (Humphries and Rubery 1995).

Managing diversity highlights the importance of culture. The roots of discrimination go very deep, and in relation to women Simmons (1989) talks about challenging a system of institutional discrimination and anti-female conditioning in the prevailing culture, and the Macpherson Report (1999) identifies institutional racism as a root cause of discrimination in the police force. Culture is important in two ways in managing diversity: first, organisational culture is one determinant of the way that organisations manage diversity and treat individuals from different groups. Equal opportunity approaches tended to concentrate on behaviour and, to a small extent, attitudes, whereas management of diversity approaches recognise a need to go beneath this. So changing the culture to one which treats individuals as individuals and supports them in developing their potential is critical, although the difficulties of culture change make this a very difficult task.

Second, depending on the approach to the management of diversity, the culture of different groups within the organisation comes into play. Recognising that men and women present different cultures at work and that this diversity needs to be managed, is key to promoting a positive environment of equal opportunity, which goes beyond merely fulfilling the demands of the statutory codes. Masreliez-Steen (1989) explains how men and women have different perceptions, interpretations of reality, languages and ways of solving problems, which, if properly used, can be a benefit to the whole organisation, as they are complementary. She describes women as having a collectivist culture where they form groups, avoid the spotlight, see rank as unimportant and have few but close contacts. Alternatively, men are described as having an individualistic culture, where they form teams, 'develop a profile', enjoy competition and have many superficial contacts. The result is that men and women behave in different ways, often fail to understand each other and experience 'culture clash'. However, the difference is about how things are done and not about what is achieved. However, we must be aware that here we have another stereotypical view which simplifies reality.

The fact that women have a different culture, with different strengths and weaknesses, means that women need managing and developing in a different way, needing different forms of support and coaching. Women more often need help to understand the value of making wider contacts and how to make them. In order to manage such diversity, key management competencies for the future would be: concern with image, process awareness, interpersonal awareness/sensitivity, developing subordinates and gaining commitment. Attending to the organisation's culture suggests a move away from seeing the individual as the problem, and requiring that the individual needs to change because they do not fit the culture. Rather, it is the organisation that needs to change so that traditional assumptions of how jobs are constructed and how they should be carried out are questioned, and looked at afresh. As Liff (1999) comments, the sociology of work literature shows how structure, cultures and practices of organisations advantage those from the dominant group by adapting to their skills and lifestyles. This is the very heart of institutional discrimination, and so difficult to address as these are matters which are taken for granted and largely unconscious. The trick, as Thomas (1992) spells out, is to identify 'requirements as opposed to preferences, conveniences or traditions'. This view of organisational transformation rather than individual transformation is similar to Cockburn's

Aspect	Equal opportunities	Managing diversity
Purpose	Reduce discrimination	Utilise employee potential to maximum advantage
Case argued	Moral and ethical	Business case – improve profitability
Whose responsibility	HR/personnel department	All managers
Focuses on	Groups	Individuals
Perspective	Dealing with different needs of different groups	Integrated
Benefits for employees	Opportunities improved for disadvantaged groups, primarily through setting targets	Opportunities improved for all employees
Focus on management activity	Recruitment	Managing
Remedies	Changing systems and practices	Changing the culture

Table 24.2 Major differences between 'equal opportunities' approaches and 'management of diversity' approaches

(1989) 'long agenda' for equality, as she discusses changing cultures, systems and structures.

Finally, managing diversity is considered to be a more integrated approach to implementing equality. Whereas equal opportunities approaches were driven by the HR function, managing diversity is seen to be the responsibility of all managers. And, as there are business reasons for managing diversity it is argued that equality should not be dealt with as a separate issue, as with equal opportunities approaches, but integrated strategically into every aspect of what the organisation does; this is often called mainstreaming.

Table 24.2 summarises the key differences between equal opportunities and managing diversity.

Problems with the managing diversity approach

While the management of diversity approach was seen by many as revitalising the equal opportunities agenda, and as a strategy for making more progress on the equality front, this progress has been slow to materialise. In reality, there remains the question of the extent to which approaches have really changed in organisations. Redefining equal opportunities in the language of the enterprise culture (Miller 1996) may just be a way of making it more palatable in today's climate, and Liff (1996) suggests that retitling may be used to revitalise the equal opportunities agenda.

It has been pointed out by Kirton and Greene (2003) that only a small number of organisations are ever quoted as management of diversity exemplars, and EOR (1999b) notes that even organisations which claim to be managing diversity do not appear to have a more diverse workforce than others, and neither have they employed more minority groups over the past five years.

Apart from this there are some fundamental problems with the management of diversity approach. The first of these is its complexity, as there are differing interpretations, which we have so far ignored, and which focus on the prominence of groups or individuals. Miller (1996) highlights two different approaches to the management of diversity. The first is where individual differences are identified and celebrated, and where prejudices are exposed and challenged via training. The second, more orthodox, approach is where the organisation seeks to develop the capacity of all. This debate between group and individual identity is a fundamental issue:

> Can people's achievements be explained by their individual talents or are they better explained as an outcome of their gender, ethnicity, class and age? Can anything meaningful be said about the collective experience of all women or are any generalisations undermined by other cross-cutting ideas? (Liff 1997, p. 11)

The most common approach to the management of diversity is based on individual contribution, as we have explained above, rather than group identity, although Liff (1997) identifies different approaches with different emphases. The *individualism* approach is based on dissolving differences. In other words, differences are not seen as being distributed systematically according to membership of a social group, but rather as random differences. Groups are not highlighted, but all should be treated fairly and encouraged to develop their potential. The advantage of this approach is that it is inclusive and involves all members of the organisation. An alternative emphasis in the management of diversity is that of *valuing differences* based on the membership of different social groups. Following this approach would mean recognising and highlighting differences, and being prepared to give special training to groups who may be disadvantaged and lack self-confidence, so that all in the organisation feel comfortable. Two further emphases are *accommodating* and *utilising* differences, which she argues are most similar to equal opportunity approaches where specific initiatives are available to aid identified groups, but also where these are also genuinely open for all other members of the organisation. In these approaches talent is recognised and used in spite of social differences, and this is done, for example, by recognising different patterns of qualifications and different roles in and out of paid work. Liff's conclusion is that group differences cannot be ignored, because it is these very differences which hold people back.

There is a further argument that if concentration on the individual is the key feature, then this may reduce our awareness of social-group-based disadvantage (Liff 1999) and may also weaken the argument for affirmative action (Liff 1996). The attractive idea of business advantage and benefits for all may divert attention from disadvantaged groups and result in no change to the status quo (*see*, for example, Ouseley 1996). Young (1990) argues that if differences are not recognised, then the norms and standards of the dominant group are not questioned.

On the other hand, a management of diversity approach may reinforce group-based stereotypes, when group-based characteristics are identified and used as a source of advantage to the organisation. For example, it has been argued, in respect of women, that as these differences were treated previously as a form of disadvantage, women may be uncomfortable using them to argue the basis for equality. Others argue that a greater recognition of perceived differences will continue to provide a rationale for disadvantageous treatment.

In addition to this dilemma within managing diversity approaches, the literature provides a strong criticism of the business case argument, which has been identified as contingent and variable (Dickens 1999). Thus the business case is unreliable because it will only work in certain contexts. For example, where skills are easily available there is less pressure on the organisation to promote and encourage the employment of minority groups. Not every employee interacts with customers so if image and customer contact are part of the business case this will only apply to some jobs and not others. Also some groups may be excluded. For example, there is no systematic evidence to suggest that disabled customers are attracted by an organisation which employs disabled people. UK managers are also driven by short-term budgets and the economic benefits of equality may only be reaped in the longer term. Indeed as Kirton and Greene (2000) conclude, the business case is potentially detrimental to equality, when, for example, a cost–benefit analysis indicates that pursuing equality is not an economic benefit.

The CIPD (2003) argues that the jury is still out in respect of the business case for diversity; in other words, the evidence of performance improvements resulting from diversity is scanty. It also points to the importance of a conducive environment in gaining benefits. Furthermore it recites problems which can result from a more diverse workforce which include increased conflict, often resulting in difficulties in coming up with solutions, and poorer internal communication, with increased management costs due to these issues.

In addition there are concerns about whether diversity management, which originated in the USA, will travel effectively to the UK where the context is different, especially in terms of the demographics and the history of equality initiatives. Furthermore, there are concerns about whether diversity can be managed at all, as Lorbiecki and Jack (2000) note:

> the belief that diversity management is do-able rests on a fantasy that it is possible to imagine a clean slate on which memories of privilege and subordination leave no mark. (p. 528)

and they go on to say that the theories do not take account of existing power differentials.

Lastly, managing diversity can be seen as introspective as it deals with people already in the organisation, rather than with getting people into the organisation – managing rather than expanding diversity (Donaldson 1993). Because of this Thomas (1990) suggests that it is not possible to *manage* diversity until you actually have it.

Equal opportunities or managing diversity?

Are equal opportunities and managing diversity completely different things? If so, is one approach preferable to the other? For the sake of clarity, earlier in this chapter we characterised a distinct approach to managing diversity which suggests that it is different from equal opportunities. Miller (1996) identifies a parallel move from the collective to the individual in the changing emphasis in personnel management as opposed to HRM. However, as we have seen, managing diversity covers a range of approaches and emphases, some closer to equal opportunities, some very different.

Much of the management of diversity suggests that it is superior to and not compatible with the equal opportunities approach (see Kandola *et al.* 1996). There is, however, much support for equal opportunities and managing diversity to be viewed as mutually supportive and for this interaction to be seen as necessary for progress (*see* Ford 1996), although Newman and Williams (1995) argue that we are some way from a model which can incorporate difference and diversity in its individualised and collective sense. To see equal opportunities and management of diversity as *alternatives* threatens to sever the link between organisational strategy and the realities of internal and external labour market disadvantage.

IMPLICATIONS FOR ORGANISATIONS

Conceptual models of organisational responses to equal opportunities and managing diversity

A conceptual model of organisational responses to achieving equality, concentrating on perceived rationale and the differing contributions of equality of opportunity and managing diversity has been developed by LaFasto (1992). This is shown in Figure 24.1.

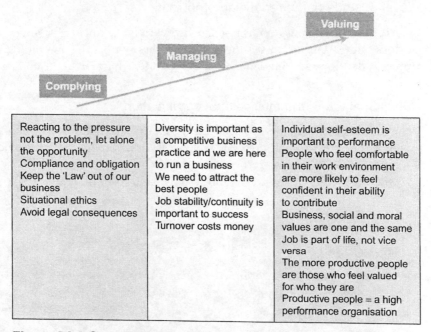

Complying	Managing	Valuing
Reacting to the pressure not the problem, let alone the opportunity Compliance and obligation Keep the 'Law' out of our business Situational ethics Avoid legal consequences	Diversity is important as a competitive business practice and we are here to run a business We need to attract the best people Job stability/continuity is important to success Turnover costs money	Individual self-esteem is important to performance People who feel comfortable in their work environment are more likely to feel confident in their ability to contribute Business, social and moral values are one and the same Job is part of life, not vice versa The more productive people are those who feel valued for who they are Productive people = a high performance organisation

Figure 24.1 Conceptual model of diversity (Source: F. LaFasto (1992) 'Baxter Healthcare Organisation', in B.W. Jackson, F. LaFasto, H.G. Schultz and D. Kelly, 'Diversity', *Human Resource Management*, Vol. 31, Nos 1 and 2, Spring/Summer, p. 28. Reproduced with permission of John Wiley and Sons, Inc. Copyright © 1992 John Wiley and Sons, Inc.)

An alternative framework is proposed by Jackson *et al.* (1992) who, concentrating on culture, identify a series of stages and levels that organisations go through in becoming a multicultural organisation:

Level 1, stage 1: the exclusionary organisation

The exclusionary organisation maintains the power of dominant groups in the organisation, and excludes others.

Level 1, stage 2: the club

The club still excludes people but in a less explicit way. Some members of minority groups are allowed to join as long as they conform to predefined norms.

Level 2, stage 3: the compliance organisation

The compliance organisation recognises that there are other perspectives, but does not want to do anything to 'rock the boat'. It may actively recruit minority groups at the bottom of the organisation and make some token appointments.

Level 2, stage 4: the affirmative action organisation

The affirmative action organisation is committed to eliminating discrimination and encourages employees to examine their attitudes and think differently. There is strong support for the development of new employees from minority groups.

Level 3, stage 5: the redefining organisation

The redefining organisation is not satisfied with being anti-racist and so examines all it does and its culture to see the impact of these on its diverse multicultural workforce. It develops and implements policies to distribute power among all groups.

Level 3, stage 6: the multicultural organisation

The multicultural organisation reflects the contribution and interests of all its diverse members in everything it does and espouses. All members are full participants of the organisation and there is recognition of a broader social responsibility – to educate others outside the organisation and to have an impact on external oppression.

ACTIVITY 24.1

Think of five organisations that you know or have read about and plot where they are on each of the two frameworks we have reviewed. Explain the evidence and examples you have used in order to support where you have located them in the frameworks.

Equal opportunities and managing diversity: strategies, policies and plans

While the use of equal opportunities policies has grown very slowly such policies are now a feature of most organisations. Our research in 1984 indicated that such policies were only produced by 60 per cent of organisations, and that on the whole they were not seen as very useful. Indeed, a large number of organisations saw their policy as irrelevant. However, in 1994, using a similar sample, we found that 89 per cent of organisations had equal opportunities policies. Itzin and Phillipson (1993) also found that three-quarters of the 221 employers which responded to their questionnaire had an equal opportunities policy. A postal survey which was sent out in July–August

1999 (EOR 1999b) showed that 95 per cent of respondent organisations had an equal opportunities policy or statement, but Cully *et al.* (1999) found that 66 per cent of organisations in the Workplace Employee Relations (WER) Survey had policies or a statement. Clearly the existence of policy or statement depends on the nature of organisations surveyed. It would also be a mistake to assume that all policies cover all potentially disadvantaged groups (*see*, for example, EOR 1999b).

It is interesting that EOR reported that organisations tended to have equal opportunities policies rather than managing diversity policies, and equal opportunities and managing diversity appeared to be viewed as complementary means of achieving equality rather than different concepts. However, some organisations appear to move from one approach to the other. Maxwell *et al.* (2001), for example, express the difficulty of transition from an equal opportunities policy to a diversity policy. They explain the need to avoid the impression that the equal opportunities approach was inadequate or that those who promoted it were ill informed or mistaken.

However, despite the prevalence of policies there is always the concern that having a policy is more about projecting the right image than about reflecting how the organisation operates. For example, Hoque and Noon (1999) found that having an equal opportunities statement made no difference to the treatment of speculative applications from individuals who were either white or from an ethnic minority group and that 'companies with ethnic minority statements were more likely to discriminate *against* the ethnic minority applicant'. The Runnymede Trust (2000) in a survey on racial equality found that the way managers explained their equal opportunities policy was different from employee views about what happened in practice. Creegan *et al.* (2003) investigated the implementation of a race equality action plan and found a stark difference between paper and practice. Line managers who were responsible for implementing the plan were operating in a devolved HR environment and so had to pay for advice, training and support from HR. The consequence of this was that in order to protect their budgets they were reluctant to seek help. Employees felt that there was no ownership of the strategy or the plan within the organisation by senior or middle managers. In respect of women there is evidence that women in senior positions are not very supportive of equal opportunities policies which help other women get on in the organisation (Ng and Chiu, 2001).

ACTIVITY 24.2

Consider the equal opportunities policy in your own organisation, or another with which you are familiar.

1 To what extent does practice match policy?

2 Explore the reasons for the achievement of a match or mismatch.

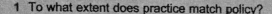

A process for managing diversity

Ross and Schneider (1992) advocate a strategic approach to managing diversity that is based on their conception of the difference between seeking equal opportunity and managing diversity. The difference, as they see it, is that diversity approaches are:

- internally driven, not externally imposed;
- focused on individuals rather than groups;
- focused on the total culture of the organisation rather than just the systems used;
- the responsibility of all in the organisation and not just the HR function.

Their process involves the following steps:

1 Diagnosis of the current situation in terms of statistics, policy and culture, and looking at both issues and causes.

2 Setting aims which involve the business case for equal opportunities, identifying the critical role of commitment from the top of the organisation, and a vision of what the organisation would look like if it successfully managed diversity.

3 Spreading the ownership. This is a critical stage in which awareness needs to be raised, via a process of encouraging people to question their attitudes and pre-conceptions. Awareness needs to be raised in all employees at all levels, especially managers, and it needs to be clear that diversity is not something owned by the personnel function.

4 Policy development comes after awareness raising as it enables a contribution to be made from all in the organisation – new systems need to be changed via involvement and not through imposition on the unwilling.

5 Managing the transition needs to involve a range of training initiatives. Positive action programmes, specifically designed for minority groups, may be used to help them understand the culture of the organisation and acquire essential skills; policy implementation programmes, particularly focusing on selection, appraisal, development and coaching; further awareness training and training to identify cultural diversity and manage different cultures and across different cultures.

6 Managing the programme to sustain momentum. This involves a champion, not necessarily from the HR function, but someone who continues in their previous organisation role in addition. Also the continued involvement of senior managers is important, together with trade unions. Harnessing initiatives that come up through departments and organising support networks for disadvantaged groups are key at this stage. Ross and Schneider also recommend measuring achievements in terms of business benefit – better relationships with customers, improvements in productivity and profitability, for example – which need to be communicated to all employees.

Ellis and Sonnenfield (1994) make the point that training for diversity needs to be far more than a one-day event. They recommend a series of workshops which allow time for individuals to think, check their assumptions and reassess between training sessions. Key issues that need tackling in arranging training are ensuring that the facilitator has the appropriate skills; carefully considering participant mix; deciding whether the training should be voluntary or mandatory; being prepared to cope with any backlash from previously advantaged groups who now feel threatened; and being prepared for the fact that the training may reinforce stereotypes. They argue that training has enormous potential benefits, but that there are risks involved.

While the ideal may be for organisations to work on all aspects of diversity in an integrated manner, the reality is often that organisations will target specific issues or groups at different times. Case 24.1 on the website is focused on improving diversity practice for people with disabilities.

WINDOW ON PRACTICE

Age equality at Derby City Council

Platman reports that in Derby City Council potential applicants would phone to find out if there was any point in applying for a particular job, expecting that their older age would rule them out. The Council felt that age discrimination restricted the pool of applicants and that they had to get rid of signals that age was not valued. They now have a code of practice which centres on dignity at work, and this applies to both councillors and employees. The aim of the code is to ensure that ageist behaviour, attitudes and language are avoided. The intention is to put across the message that the Council values the experience of older employees, and older employees are now specifically encouraged to apply for further training and promotions.

Source: Summarised from K. Platman (2002) 'Matured Assets', *People Management*, Vol. 8, No. 24, 5 December, pp. 40–2.

Changing culture is clearly a key part of any process for managing diversity. In 1995 Her Majesty's Inspectorate of Constabulory (HMIC) stressed the business case for diversity in the police force. The police force, over a number of years, has made considerable efforts to increase the recruitment and promotion of members of ethnic minorities (*see*, for example, EOR 1997). It began to tackle the issues of why individuals from different ethnic backgrounds would not even apply to the police for a career (for example, they may be seen, within some ethnic groups, as traitors for doing so). Some progress was made but the McPherson Report highlighted the issue of institutional racism, and further efforts were made to reduce discrimination. However, in 2004 there is still clear evidence of discriminatory cultures and attitudes, as evidenced by the television programme about the racist attitudes of new recruits into Manchester police. On Radio 4 on 20 January 2004 the Ali Desai case was discussed and it was argued that the metropolitan police service were racist in the way that they applied discipline to officers, picking up on smaller issues for racial minority groups than for white officers. The changes required to manage diversity effectively should not be underestimated.

Case 24.2 on the website considers the achievement of an ethnic mix on some MBA courses.

WINDOW ON PRACTICE

BT – Championing women in a man's world

BT is often used as an exemplar of an organisation which has taken significant steps to encouraging women in a male-dominated engineering environment and Equal Opportunities Review (1999a) reports on how BT has gone about this.

First, BT has top-level strategic support to increase the proportion of women at all levels in the organisation, and also has identified the need for line managers to be convinced of the economic value of such policies.

The initiatives introduced involve the appointment of a gender champion, assessing the HR director, partly on objectives relating to gender issues, and running a one-day workshop for all 5,000 managers to stress the business case and attempt to change attitudes.

In terms of access to employment BT has targeted universities with a higher proportion of women students, revised job titles and specifications and considered ways of developing eligibility criteria for jobs. BT has set improvement targets and encouraged 'take your daughters to work' days.

In respect of existing employees BT has: produced a women's development portfolio and a women's management development programme, developed strategic skills for senior women managers, a women's network and website and raised the issues of life-work balance and childcare.

Source: Summarised from EOR (1999a) 'BT: Championing women in a man's world', *Equal Opportunities Review*, No. 84, March–April, pp. 14–20.

ACTIVITY 24.3

Prepare a strategy for managing diversity which would be appropriate for your organisation, or one with which you are familiar.

SUMMARY PROPOSITIONS

24.1 The essence of much HR work is to discriminate between individuals. The essence of equality is to avoid unfair discrimination. Unfair discrimination often results from people being treated on the basis of limited and prejudiced understanding of the groups to which they belong rather than on the basis of an assessment of them as individuals. People are not always aware when they are discriminating unfairly.

24.2 Legislation can have only a limited effect in achieving equality, and does not change attitudes, beliefs and cultures and structures. Organisations and their cultures, processes and structures are founded on the needs of the majority group and individuals from other groups are expected to adapt to this norm. This explains why progress towards equality of opportunity has been very slow.

24.3 Equal opportunities approaches highlight the moral argument for equal treatment, whereas managing diversity highlights the business case.

<table>
<tr><td>24.4</td><td>Actual changes in practice relating to equalising opportunity are taking place very slowly, and only long-term organisational transformation is likely to support equality.</td></tr>
<tr><td>24.5</td><td>Equal opportunities approaches and the management of diversity are best viewed, not as alternatives, but as complementary approaches which need to be interrelated.</td></tr>
</table>

GENERAL DISCUSSION TOPICS

1 Discuss Liff's (1997) question:

'Can people's achievements be explained by their individual talents or are they better explained as an outcome of their gender, ethnicity, class and age? Can anything meaningful be said about the collective experience of all women or are any generalisations undermined by other cross-cutting ideas.' (p. 11)

2 Which is preferable – the UK approach or the US approach to equal opportunities? What are the implications of each for all members of the organisation?

FURTHER READING

Benschop, Y. (2001) 'Pride, prejudice and performance: relations between HRM, diversity and performance', *International Journal of Human Resource Management*, Vol. 12, No. 7, pp. 1166–81

This a very illuminative article which presents the experience of the impact of workforce diversity in two case study organisations. The findings indicate that an organisation's strategy for diversity influences how employees perceive and understand diversity and the impact that it has on performance.

Mattis, M. (2001) 'Advancing women in business organisations', *Journal of Management Development*, Vol. 20, No. 4, pp. 371–88

This article examines the role of key players such as middle and first line managers in supporting gender diversity initiatives. A wide range of case examples are used and the article provides a range of practical activities to support gender diversity.

REFERENCES

Bruyere, S. (2000) 'Managing disability in the workplace', *Equal Opportunities Review*, No. 92, July–August.

CIPD (2003) *Diversity: Stacking up the evidence, Executive Briefing.* London: CIPD.

Cockburn, C. (1989) 'Equal Opportunities: the long and short agenda', *Industrial Relations Journal*, Vol. 20, No. 3, pp. 213–25.

Creegan, C., Colgan, F., Charlesworth, R. and Robinson, G. (2003) 'Race equality policies at work: employee perceptions of the "implementation gap" in a UK local authority', *Work, Employment and Society*, Vol. 17, No. 4, pp. 617–40.

Cully, M., Woodland, S., O'Reilly, A. and Dix, G. (1999) *Britain at Work: As depicted by the 1998 Workplace Employee Relations Survey.* London: Routledge.

Dibben, P., James, P. and Cunningham, I. (2001) 'Senior management commitment to disability', *Personnel Review*, Vol. 30, No. 4, pp. 454–67.

Dickens, L. (1999) 'Beyond the business case: a three pronged approach to equality action', *Human Resource Management Journal*, Vol. 9, No. 1, pp. 9–19.

Donaldson, L. (1993) 'The recession: a barrier to equal opportunities?' *Equal Opportunities Review*, No. 50, July–August.

Ellis, C. and Sonnenfield, J.A. (1994) 'Diverse approaches to managing diversity', *Human Resource Management*, Vol. 33, No. 1, Spring, pp. 79–109.

Equal Opportunities Review (1996) 'Ethnic minorities in the police service', *Equal Opportunities Review*, No. 68, July–August.

Equal Opportunities Review (1997) 'Ethnic minorities in the police service', *Equal Opportunities Review*, No. 73.

Equal Opportunities Review (1998) 'Tackling Age bias: code or law?' *Equal Opportunities Review*, No. 80, July–August.

Equal Opportunities Review (1999a) 'BT: Championing women in a man's world', *Equal Opportunities Review*, No. 84, March–April, pp. 14–20.

Equal Opportunities Review (1999b) 'Equal Opportunities Policies: An EOR survey of employers', *Equal Opportunities Review*, No. 87, September–October.

Equal Opportunities Review (2000) 'Businesses urged to shape up on race', *Equal Opportunities Review*, No. 90, March–April.

Equal Opportunities Review (2002) 'Trends in female employment', *Equal Opportunities Review*, No. 112, December, pp. 19–22.

Equal Opportunities Review (2003) 'Economic activity rates of disabled people and ethnic minorities', *Equal Opportunities Review*, No. 121, September, pp. 7–8.

Ford, V. (1996) 'Partnership is the secret of success', *People Management*, 8 February, pp. 34–6.

Glover, C. (2003) 'Ticked off', *People Management*, Vol. 8, No. 2, 24 January, pp. 38–9.

Hakim, C. (1993) 'The myth of rising female employment', *Work, Employment and Society*, Vol. 7, No. 1, March, pp. 121–33.

Hammond, D. (2002) 'TV industry tackles inequality', *People Management*, Vol. 8, No. 15, 25 July, p. 9.

Hicks-Clarke, D. and Iles, P. (2000) 'Climate for diversity and its effects on career and organizational attitudes and perceptions', *Personnel Review*, Vol. 29, No. 3.

Higginbottom, K. (2002) 'The wonder years', *People Management*, Vol. 8, No. 24, 5 December, pp. 14–15.

Higginbottom, K. and Roberts, Z. (2002) 'EOC urges local authorities to confront lack of senior women', *People Management*, Vol. 8, No. 12, 13 June, p. 7.

Hoque, K. and Noon, M. (1999) 'Racial discrimination in speculative applications: new optimism six years on?' *Human Resource Management Journal*, Vol. 9, No. 3, pp. 71–82.

Humphries, J. and Rubery, J. (1995) *Research Summary of the Economics of Equal Opportunity*. Manchester: EOC.

IDS (2004) *Employers move on equal pay*, IDS Report, No. 897, January, pp. 10–18.

Institute of Personnel and Development (1997) *Managing Diversity: A Position paper*. London: IPD.

Itzin, C. and Phillipson, C. (1993) *Age Barriers at Work: Maximising the potential of mature and older people*. London: Metropolitan Authorities Recruitment Agency.

Jackson, B.W., LaFasto, F., Schultz, H.G. and Kelly, D. (1993) 'Diversity', *Human Resource Management*, Vol. 31, Nos 1 and 2, Spring/Summer, pp. 21–34.

Jewson, N. and Mason, D. (1986) 'The theory and practice of equal opportunities policies: liberal and radical approaches', *Sociological Review*, Vol. 34, No. 2, pp. 307–34.

Kandola, P. and Fullerton, J. (1994, 2nd edn 1998) *Managing the Mosaic*. London: IPD.

Kandola, R., Fullerton, J. and Mulroney, C. (1996) *1996 Pearn Kandola Survey of Diversity Practice Summary Report*. Oxford: Pearn Kandola.

Kirton, G. and Greene, A. (2003) *The dynamics of managing diversity: a critical approach*. Oxford: Butterworth Heinemann.

LaFasto, F. (1992) 'Baxter Healthcare Organisation', in B.W. Jackson, F. LaFasto, H.G. Schultz and D. Kelly, *Human Resource Management*, Vol. 31, Nos 1–2, Spring/ Summer.

Liff, S. (1996) 'Managing diversity: new opportunities for women?' *Warwick Papers in Industrial Relations* No. 57. Coventry: IRU, Warwick University.

Liff, S. (1997) 'Two routes to managing diversity: individual differences or social group characteristics?' *Employee Relations*, Vol. 19, No. 1, pp. 11–26.

Liff, S. (1999) 'Diversity and Equal Opportunities: room for a constructive compromise?' *Human Resource Management Journal*, Vol. 9, No. 1, pp. 65–75.

Lorbiecki, A. and Jack, G. (2000) 'Critical turns in the evolution of diversity management', *British Journal of Management*, Vol. 11, pp. S17–S31.

McCracken, D. (2000) 'Winning the talent war for women: sometimes it takes a revolution', *Harvard Business Review*, November–December, pp. 159–65.

Macpherson of Clung, Sir William (1999) *The Stephen Lawrence Inquiry. A Report by Sir William Macpherson of Clung*. London: HMSO.

Masreliez-Steen, G. (1989) *Male and Female Management*. Sweden: Kontura Group.

Maxwell, G., Blair, S. and McDougall, M. (2001) 'Edging towards managing diversity in practice', *Employee Relations*, Vol. 23, No. 5, pp. 458–82.

Miller, D. (1996) 'Equality management – towards a materialist approach', *Gender, Work and Organisation*, Vol. 3, No. 4, pp. 202–14.

Newman, J. and Williams, F. (1995) 'Diversity and change, gender, welfare and organisational relations', in C. Itzin and J. Newman, *Gender, Culture and Organisational Change*. London: Routledge.

Ng, C. and Chiu, W. (2001) 'Managing Equal Opportunities for women: sorting the friends from the foes', *Human Resource Management Journal*, Vol. 11, No. 1, pp. 75–88.

Ouseley, H. (1996) quoted in S. Overell, 'Ouseley in assault on diversity', *People Management*, 2 May, pp. 7–8.

People Management (2002) 'Call for women in senior roles', *People Management*, Vol. 8, No. 23, 21 November, p. 11.

Philpott, J. (2003) 'Time to tackle age-old problem', *People Management*, Vol. 9, No. 13, June, p. 22.

Platman, K. (2002) 'Matured Assets', *People Management*, Vol. 8, No. 24, 5 December, pp. 40–2.

Rana, E. (2003) 'Council appraisals discriminate', *People Management*, Vol. 9, No. 2, 23 January, p. 11.

Ross, R. and Schneider, R. (1992) *From Equality to Diversity – a business case for equal opportunities*. London: Pitman.

Runnymede Trust (2000) *Moving on up? Racial Equality and the Corporate Agenda, A Study of the FTSE 100 companies*. London: Central Books.

Shapiro, G. and Austin, S. (1996) 'Equality drives total quality', *Occasional Paper*. Brighton: Brighton Business School.

Simmons, M. (1989) 'Making equal opportunities training effective', *Journal of European Industrial Training*, Vol. 13, No. 8, pp. 19–24.

Singer, M. (1993) *Diversity-based Hiring*. Aldershot: Avebury.

Skills and Enterprise Network (2000) *Labour Market and Skills Trends*. Sheffield: DfEE.

Snape, E. and Redman, T. (2003) 'Too old or too young? The impact of perceived age discrimination', *Human Resource Management Journal*, Vol. 13, No. 1, pp. 78–89.

Thair, T. and Risden, A. (1999) 'Women in the labour market: results from the Spring 1998 Labour Force Survey', *Labour Market Trends*, March.

Thomas, R.R. (1990) 'From affirmative action to affirming diversity', *Harvard Business Review*, March–April.

Thomas, R.R. (1992) 'Managing diversity: a conceptual framework', in S. Jackson (ed.) *Diversity in the Workplace*. New York: Guildford Press.

Trades Union Congress (2000) *Qualifying for Racism*. London: TUC.

Ward, J. (2003) 'How to address sexual orientation', *People Management*, Vol. 9, No. 21, 23 October, pp. 62–3.

Wilson, E. (2000) 'Inclusion, exclusion and ambiguity – the role of organizational culture', *Personnel Review*, Vol. 29, No. 3.

Woodhams, C. and Danieli, A. (2000) 'Disability and diversity – a difference too far?' *Personnel Review*, Vol. 29, No. 3.

Woolnough, R. (2000) 'Racism reinforces the glass ceiling', *Guardian*, 4 November, p. 31.

Young, I.M. (1990) *Justice and the Politics of Difference*. Princeton, NJ: Princeton University Press.

An extensive range of additional materials, including multiple choice questions, answers to questions and links to useful websites can be found on the Human Resource Management Companion Website at **www.pearsoned.co.uk/torrington**.

TOPIC SUMMARY SHEET

What are the key learning points from this topic?

TOPIC 4 – LIFE LONG LEARNING

Why study this topic?

The key to developing a successful economy is for the workplace to have a wide range of both high and low level skills. This can attract potential organisations who know that they will be able to secure the employees they require to set up or develop the organisation.

Another important point to consider is your own marketability as an employee. The labour market of today does not support the 'job for life' concept as enjoyed by previous generations. It is therefore in an employee's best interest to have a significant range of skills available to them. This can only be achieved by investing time and often money in developing your own specific set of skills. This can either be helped or hindered by employers, governments and other external influences. This topic will enable you to evaluate the extent of the progress made and examine what lies in store for the future.

Blackboard

E-tivity 4: Life long learning

Chapter 5

Employee development

Stephen Gibb and David Megginson

Introduction

Issues and challenges in contemporary employee development (ED[1]) are considered here in relation to two sets of factors. First are learning issues about how the knowledge, skills and attitudes required for employment are formed and are linked to career, organisational and economic success. The main challenges raised are those involved in responding to the onset of the knowledge economy, the continuing interest in achieving 'skill revolutions', and the demands involved in managing employment 'cultures'. The theory and practice of contemporary ED, its strengths and weaknesses, are bound up with meeting each of these challenges.

The second set of factors concern the stakeholders involved in ED. The issues here are related to the contribution of individuals, employers and government as participants in ED. Challenges here include the dynamics of individual motivation to learn and participation in ED; the role of employers and training providers in supplying effective ED, and finally the challenge to government, in the form of policy development and implementation of initiatives in the promotion of ED.

The practice of ED needs to be analysed in the context of all these issues and challenges; managing effective learning through stakeholder interactions and partnership. Employers are certainly the 'hub' of the whole system, given employees'

---

[1] Many commentators seek to distinguish between training, education and development. While there are sometimes good reasons for this, for example when compiling survey data, the semantics of these distinctions can become unwieldy and intrusive. The essence of employees being 'trained', professionals being 'educated' and managers being 'developed' amounts to the same; support of learning for and at work. For this chapter the term 'Employee development' (ED) will be used to cover training at work and training for work, work-related vocational education and work-based on-job and off-job development, and what is generally thought of as soft 'development' in the employment context.

dependence upon them as suppliers of ED and the government's voluntarist approach in this aspect of HRM. A description of the different approaches to ED which can exist in employing organisations is provided in conclusion, as a focus for analysing and evaluating cases at an organisational level.

The context of employee development

The purpose of ED can be defined as developing human potential to assist organisations and individuals to achieve their objectives. The question of what exactly is meant by developing human potential needs to be considered more fully if the theory and practice of ED, and the challenges it faces, are to be properly defined. A common way of expanding upon this is to argue that in order to realise their potential in the context of employment people need to develop, in balance, their knowledge, skills and emotions/attitudes/values[2] (EVA). The capacity to learn and become competent, to be able to achieve the performance standards expected in employment, is fulfilled through integrated development of these three aspects of human potential. In this respect development in and for employment is the same as development in any other context.

The most evident form this takes is the standard organisation of learning experiences in and for employment into programmes which specify objectives in all these three aspects. The trinity of development in knowledge, skills and EVA is to be explicitly found in some form in many systems of human potential development, and is implicit in most others. Each aspect will be considered here in turn to explain what they involve and to raise key issues for evaluating contemporary ED.

The first types of objective in realising human potential in the context of employment are those relating to cognitive capacities: the development and extension of knowledge. The cognitive aspects of ED are concerned with the extent to which employees need to obtain and use information, models and theories to enable development and effective performance in jobs and their employing organisation. Bloom's taxonomy of cognitive categories (Bloom, 1956), given in Table 5.1, provides a continuum against which jobs can be measured.

---

[2] Conventionally, it is 'attitudes' which are defined as the third element of the learning trinity 'KSA'. Attitudes are defined as the positive or negative orientations people have with regard to themselves, others and the world – their likes and dislikes, conventionally studied within social psychology. Forming or changing people's attitudes is certainly a part of development in the context of employment. But this is too narrow to encompass the contemporary concerns of development in employment. Forming and developing values, people's core ideas on what is right and wrong, is a concern as well – often illustrated by organisations making their values explicit and requiring employee behaviour congruent with them in work. Supporting and using 'emotions', the psychology of people feeling 'mad, bad, sad or glad' also matters in developing effective performance. Indeed, emotional factors are often given the 'executive' role in controlling human behaviour; to shape and influence human behaviour in employment it is then possible – and, for some, necessary – to acknowledge and work with developing emotions and values, not just attitudes.

Table 5.1 Bloom's cognitive categories

Type	Evidence	
Knowledge	state, list, identify	*Simple*
Comprehension	explain, give examples	
Application	demonstrate, solve, use	↑
Analysis	describe, break down, select	↓
Synthesis	combine, design, create	
Evaluation	appraise, contrast, criticise	
		Complex

Different occupations will require different types and levels of cognitive development. All human potential development in the context of employment involves knowledge; the issue is the extent to which performance depends upon knowledge, and the type of knowledge involved. Occupations can be mapped against Bloom's types, to profile where the cognitive demands are. The difference which most starkly highlights this point is the distinction made between occupations where performance greatly depends on knowledge and other cognitive capacities and areas where knowledge and cognitive capacity appear to be of little relevance and concern. With the former, knowledge-intensive development for the 'professions', such as medicine, law, engineering, teaching and social work is seen as typical, requiring several years of university-level education followed by a long period of supervised practice before becoming fully licensed. As that education progresses, the cognitive capacities required become more complex. In the case of the latter, development for relatively routine forms of programmed service provision, for example serving in a fast-food outlet or administration in a call centre, is seen as requiring little cognitive complexity and that is of the more basic kind. What is required depends only upon basic education and can be supplemented by the instruction of the employer in the course of basic training within the company.

Cognitive capacities in occupational performance also vary on a continuum of certainty – from occupations where knowledge is certain and complete to jobs where knowledge is uncertain and partial. Schön (1987) makes the distinction between what he calls 'determined practice' and 'indeterminate practice'. In the former, cognition is fixed and prescribed, and used to deal with routine circumstances. In the latter, cognition is not fixed and prescribed, it comes into operation to support creative problem-solving needed to deal with unique circumstances. This distinction is not new, but it is arguably more relevant now. In a time of new sciences, new technologies, and 'new organisations' demands on the creative use of cognition rather than its prescriptive application are greater; demands in occupations are increasingly at the complex end of Bloom's categories. The cognition involved in occupations and employment is evolving and changing fast, and it is therefore more likely to be uncertain and partial even among the most 'experienced'.

This also affects the practicalities of developing human potential in employment more than the familiar distinction between cognition-intensive and low-knowledge occupations. This is because, where knowledge is felt to be certain and complete, the most appropriate form of developmental support is clearly through the instruction and 'conditioning' of those who need the knowledge by those who currently possess the knowledge. These tend to be intermediaries – whether that mediation arises in the forms of knowledge present in books, or lectures, or the Internet. Where knowledge is uncertain and fragmented the appropriate form of learning needs to be more 'experiential'. By 'experiential' is meant a process of learning that is based on direct personal experience and reflection, undertaken in a 'community' of others who have experience of synthesis and evaluation. Only cognitive skills developed in this unmediated context, rather than knowledge gained through mediated information-processing in formal education, is of any substance and value. Such knowledge cannot be effectively codified and transmitted through systems of mediated instruction. In a sense, but not entirely, the former lends itself to being learnt as a 'science'[3], a coherent package of principles, concepts and methods; while the latter lends itself to being learnt as an 'art', requiring creativity on the part of the learner while learning.

In occupations where knowledge is becoming more certain there can be an increase in both 'science'-based pedagogy and instruction-based forms of learning. The role of Information and Communications Technologies (ICT) in supporting efficiency and effectiveness in this area of learning could be central. Where knowledge is becoming more uncertain and partial then expanding forms of experiential learning, centred on long-term learning relationships in communities of practice, may become much more important. The increase in systems of mentoring (Gibb, 1999) is one indicator of this trend in many different occupational contexts.

The fundamental issue relating to knowledge in the context of employment is the question of the extent to which cognition is forming a greater or lesser part of the development of human and organisation potential in any event, regardless of how that is categorised or learned. On the one hand there are claims for the onset of the 'knowledge economy' and the 'knowledge worker' (Tapscott, 1996); this era is supposed to be characterised by the increasing importance of 'intellectual capital' (Stewart, 1997) in many occupations and organisations. 'Knowledge management' (Davenport and Prusak, 1998) is then the latest strategic aspiration and focus for reviewing organisational effectiveness. The structure, design and culture of organisation needs to be built around managing knowledge. This suggests, in essence, that cognition is more important than ever before in employment. The implication is that the possession and use of knowledge permeates all productive activity, at all levels in an organisation, and therefore the

---

[3] The distinction between science and art as paradigms for occupational development is potentially useful and stimulating. Science is characterised by organised bodies of knowledge derived from methods which enable theories to be developed and tested. Arts are characterised by organised performances derived from methods which enable symbol systems to be developed and enjoyed. Most employment and occupations can be seen to share elements of a scientific base and an artistic base in effective performance. A recent illustration of this abstract point would be the involvement of musicians in facilitating management development (Pickard, 1999). The parallels between conducting an orchestra or playing in a jazz band are investigated to illuminate the challenges facing managers and to propose some solutions for meeting those based on musicians' experiences.

development of human potential in this respect forms a greater part of ensuring organisational effectiveness than in the past. More people need to learn more knowledge than ever before. It has been commonplace to hear of skills shortages as a potential threat to economic and business development; in the future it may be that it is cognitive deficits which cause economic and business development problems.

On the other hand there are arguments that the whole knowledge economy and knowledge worker concepts have been vastly overhyped. There is less scope for knowledge work, as information technologies enable everything from the whole systems running complex plants down to interpersonal transactions between customers and the organisation's representatives to be automated. Knowledge has migrated to computer systems, leaving people in employment to tend the computers. And when the key 'knowledge'-based institutions, particularly schools, colleges and universities, are considered there is contradictory evidence about what is happening. While education is becoming a more significant and greater part of everyone's future, there is, nevertheless, pressure for these institutions to become more concerned with helping to develop basic skills and competence. This is because the absence of basic skills among the labour force is currently the greatest problem experienced by employers, not the absence of smart 'knowledge' workers. This is a finding highlighted in, for example, employer concerns about the quality of young people's and graduate recruits' employability.

The second type of objectives in human potential development are those relating to developing psychomotor skills, through practice. The more commonplace term in use now is 'competence' rather than psychomotor skills; 'competence' being defined as the ability to do things to the standards required in employment and in practice. The difference between 'knowing how' to do something and actually being able to perform effectively is the skills or competence gap. Many people 'know how' to do many things; they can appreciate the elements of cooking and follow the recipes in cookbooks, or appreciate the principles of playing certain sports. But only some are competent enough, skilled enough, to do these well enough to produce excellent meals or compete with the best on actual playing fields.

Again there is a stark distinction between areas of human development in employment which are relatively low-skilled and areas which are highly skilled. Low-skill activities require little human potential development in the form of development through practice. These are jobs where most typical mature adults would be able to achieve a successful performance without needing much practice. For example, most people could serve behind a fast-food counter, stock shelves in a supermarket, or pack mobile phones into boxes. The main performance issue in such circumstances is usually ensuring a standard performance to set guidelines and procedures; it is about managing basic competence as conformity to procedures in the occupation.

On a bigger stage the issue of skill development raises economic development and political policy questions (Crouch, Finegold and Sako, 1999). A predominance of low-skill jobs and organisations creates a low-skill economy. This is an economy in which there are few driving forces to develop human potential in this respect. A vicious cycle then arises, where that lack of interest in human potential development means that only low-skill industries and jobs can be supported and managed, and then the preponderance of low-skill jobs and industries means that there is little demand for investing in skills development. In such conditions skills shortages are unlikely to be a problem, as the development of basic 'threshold' competence is an integral part of normal human development, and needs little in the way of additional time and investment devoted to practice. The main HR problem in these circumstances is the potential shortage of people prepared to take and stay in such low-skill jobs, and the degree of problem is contingent upon prevailing labour market conditions.

High-skill activities require significant human potential development, through substantial and continuing periods of guided practice in order to create a successful performer. This initial interest in high levels of human development for employment is further reinforced by the fact that skilled performance cannot be 'stored'; it either has to be in use and therefore constantly refreshed, or it will be lost. For example, continuing the sporting theme, professional footballers may only play once a week, but they spend all week practising. Armed forces may only encounter actual active duty irregularly, but professional armies are more effective as they constantly take part in exercises to prepare for the 'real thing'. The main performance issues in such circumstances are then ensuring a quality of 'apprenticeship' prior to licensing people to practise, and maintaining sufficient practise to keep skill levels at their peak. Such an emphasis on apprenticeship and 'Continuing Professional Development' is then one necessary hallmark of a 'true' profession. The net effect is to require sophisticated and substantial support for human development related to employment.

In high-skill economies there needs to be much investment in developing human potential through skills development. In traditional professions, such as medicine and law, skills development has long been integrated with professional development as a period of supervised practice after study and before licensing. In many modern professions, of which 'HRM' and management are two relevant examples, similar systems are being developed. Without effective foresight and planning there is great potential for skills shortages to develop and become a factor constraining economic growth. The biotechnology and software development sectors provide good contemporary examples of sectors where skill shortages throughout the range of jobs involved, not just at the top professional levels, can constrain economic development. Employers' and public policy concerns are then with 'skills revolutions'; how to attain a high-skill, high-value economy and avoid the traps of being, or becoming, a low-skill economy and having skills shortages which constrain economic and business development.

The general view is that the UK has been much in need of such a skills revolution to overcome its historically low skill levels, and to avoid skills shortages in key developing industries. Yet much has been made of the absence of even the 'basic skills' of literacy and numeracy among large parts of the labour force, needed to sustain even a low-skill economy. This situation has arisen for a variety of reasons, and many commentators look at both employers and an educational system in the UK which together have failed to manage the effective development of skills over decades. Remedying this aspect of developing human potential has been the central feature of policy development in recent times, exemplified in the development of national competence frameworks defining skills in occupations and in gearing educational systems to help develop competence.

Many of the government initiatives outlined later are responses to this central issue. Whether in any event 'skills are the answer' is, as Crouch *et al.* (1999) suggest, a claim that needs to be further debated. The logic that skills are a necessary element of future economic and social development is, they argue, fair. But skills increases in themselves are not going to be sufficient to achieve the employment and economic goals seen to be associated with these policies: job creation, high levels of employment, social inclusion, increasing living standards and equal opportunities. Critics of the use of skills revolutions as the main tool argue that there are a number of reasons for this. One is that occupations requiring truly advanced skills are still a small proportion of all jobs. Many jobs just do not require high skills, and never will. Another consideration is that the skills revolution depends on the actions of firms who have no real interest in carrying the burden for 'up-skilling' on behalf of other organisations or society in general. In this situation it is actually government that is being left to deal with the problems of development for employment; in particular to deal with the problem of unemployment. This undermines the credibility of the initiatives they develop, as they are seen as solutions to unemployment, not as integral to economic and business development and useful for employers. Finally, the necessary links between firms and employers and control of skills development is still a problem. Ideally, employers should be taking the lead, as it is their interests and experience which need to be met, but in practice it is still 'detached' government departments which have the main role. Even with the best intentions public servants cannot be a substitute for employer leadership.

The final objectives involved in developing human potential in employment are those related to developing and enhancing emotions, and values and attitudes. It is arguable that the essential difference between superior performance and ordinary, or indeed incompetent, performance is linked to emotions, attitude and values. People with emotional 'intelligence' (Goleman, 1999), 'positive' attitudes and the right values will be more effective than those lacking emotional intelligence, with negative attitudes or without the right values. Certainly, different occupations call upon some common and some particular elements of emotional intelligence, attitudes and values (Johnson and Indvik, 1999). For example, when facing difficult customers staff are meant to be equable and 'professional', rather than letting their personal feelings show. More often the crucible of the workplace as a whole can provide many spurs to interpersonal and intergroup conflict in the course of normal working life between employees, and between employers and employees.

Maintaining emotional intelligence and positive attitudes in that context of performance in a job is a perpetual challenge.

Instilling, reinforcing and leveraging emotions, values and attitudes is then an integral and inescapable part of development for employment. Pinker suggests the importance of emotions is that 'the emotions are mechanisms that set the brain's highest level goals' (1997: 373). Deliberate control of emotions is a route to managing behaviour; whether that control is personal and internal or is exerted from other sources. As far as values are concerned, Rokeach (1970) points out that many organisations explicitly identify their 'core values' with the aim of encouraging employees to behave in tune with them. These may be instrumental values, relating to the appropriate modes of conduct desired from and expected of employees in the course of their work as individuals, in groups and with customers. For example, employers will seek to enhance the ethics of amity within the workforce, often through the means of team building. There may be relationship skills involved in this, but most crucial is often the development of a team spirit, co-operation and trust between the team members. Values may also be 'terminal values', relating to the types of goals and ends which organisations wish their employees to pursue; the values which will govern their behaviour in achieving a successful performance. A concern with achieving 'quality' standards, for example, is partly based on good knowledge of systems, partly on skills developed through practice, and partly on being guided by the value of achieving quality.

The argument is that where emotions, attitudes and values are not effectively developed in an employee there is a high probability that performance standards will not be attained, even though employees may have the right knowledge and appropriate skills developed through practice. Developing human potential in the context of employment invariably raises issues about emotions, values and attitudes. These may be about harnessing and reinforcing an individual's, group's or organisation's emotions, attitudes and values in the context of jobs and work. They may be about challenging and changing the emotional intelligence, attitudes and values of individuals, groups and, on occasion, entire organisations.

Another way of thinking of this aspect of development for employment is that it is about the development of the whole person, and the development of the whole organisation. Effective development requires more than the 'digestion' of knowledge and the acquisition of skills through practice to underpin effective performance; it also depends upon the effective development of the whole person in the context of the whole organisation. There needs to be a congruence of emotions, values and attitudes with the occupational role, supported by an organisational environment which nurtures and rewards those emotions, values and attitudes. For instance, the emotions, values and attitudes which underpin performance in a caring role and organisation are not the same as those underpinning an entrepreneurial role in a profit-oriented organisation.

Sometimes, then, the development issue is about broader personal or organisational concerns. From the shelves of 'transform your life' self-help books to the most recent examples of analysing organisational values (Wickens, 1999) to catalyse change, this aspect of development for employment provides a rich seam of activity. It is most evident in, and related to, the concern with 'culture' change and culture management in the workplace that has been a high-profile concern in recent years as a focus of organisational change and development. The extent to which cultures can be controlled and changed is also open to debate. There is, however, no doubt that many organisations aspire to mould individual behaviours and the overall 'culture'.

The stakeholders: individuals, employers and government

There is, then, an agenda concerning the new and changing requirements of the knowledge economy, the old and continuing need for a skills revolution and the evergreen issues of managing behaviour and cultures in occupations and the workplace. These create the environment in which ED theory and practice has been and is evolving. Responses to this environment, in the form of actual strategies for supporting human potential development for employment, depend upon the actions of a variety of stakeholders. The primary stakeholders in ED are individuals, employers and the government. Problems or successes are not due to one set of agents alone; it is how they all interact which produces either an effective outcome or a problematic situation.

Individuals

Individual factors supporting effective ED are the levels of motivation and participation which lead employees or prospective employees themselves to seek to develop their potential in employment. Options range from opting out of the world of employment altogether, and pursuing alternative lifestyles, to consistently and extensively developing oneself with the aspiration of achieving success in employment. One career survey recently classified young people in terms of those 'getting on', those getting by and those getting nowhere (ESRC, 1999). Motivators that all these will share may include seeking greater job security through enhancement of knowledge, skills and self-development and improving personal performance for its own sake, for the pleasure of competent performance. There will be differences in people's response to seeking successful career development through enhanced knowledge, skills and self-development; seeking work enrichment, through being able to do more. The net effect is to spur active and interested participation in learning or to curtail enthusiasm for and participation in development for employment.

Developing their own potential may indeed have helped many 'getting on' individual employees or prospective employees meet these objectives in the past. Now many more employers wish to encourage their employees towards self-activated and self-directed development, to planning and managing their own development. This is a natural development of more general and focused processes of performance appraisal which are concerned with development needs. It also fits with the general trend towards employees becoming active and free agents rather than being dependent upon others to be told what to do – an aspect of the whole 'empowerment' movement and the 'new deal' in employment more generally. One difficulty with this, however, is that with the declining prospect of achieving their core goals in the organisation, such as job security or career development, the natural motivators for self-directed development may be missing for everyone; whether they are 'getting on' or 'getting by'.

There are other potential problems with relying more on self-driven potential realisation. Individuals may have misconceptions of their own potential, rating themselves incorrectly as unable to achieve some objectives when they can, or as able to achieve some objectives when they cannot. And the need to be seen as competent may lead individuals to present themselves as being competent instead of accurately assessing their own learning needs. Finally, there is the influence of the course, or ontology, of human development, and the different life-styles which accompany life stages. There are varying degrees of interest in learning and different types of concern with learning at different life stages and in different lifestyles. Individuals will be more motivated to realise their potential for employment at some stages of life than at others. Some lifestyles will emphasise the importance of development for employment more than others. Conventional ideas about the normal patterns of learning and life stages and lifestyles are being challenged, with an emphasis on lifelong learning, not just learning in youth, and a need to achieve a better 'life – work' balance (Foster, 1999) across the spectrum from those socially excluded to those who may be seen as 'workaholics'.

Employers

For employers ED is a means to an end – the end being to ensure achievement of the organisation's goals and the means being basic competence in the workforce. To achieve this employers may work in partnerships with schools, colleges and universities to develop courses that relate to the needs of businesses. They will also provide development for their own employees, through the induction of new employees, basic job training and closing any 'training gaps' identified by managers or others in reviewing the performance of staff. There may also be other organisational objectives beyond ensuring competence. These include increasing competitiveness through providing more or better ED than competitors. Employers will seek to improve product and/or service quality through more investment in ED. Continuous improvement requires continuous learning. The quality of ED provided can help by attracting the best people, by using more of their potential and productivity, and by maintaining their satisfaction as employees because they are being invested in. There can also be a concern with achieving 'culture changes' through ED interventions. Finally, there is a general concern to promote the habit of learning: keeping people 'fit' to learn. The logic and provision of many Employee Development and Assistance Programmes (EDAPs) reflects this.

Developing the potential of their workforces can help organisations meet these objectives by providing more competent, adaptable and committed employees. There are typical difficulties facing employers as they do this. One is simply a lack of resources to invest in ED, with a consequent basic failure to take up the responsibility to promote human potential development even in its most rudimentary forms, such as employee induction and health and safety training. This may be due to an assumption that development for employment has been achieved elsewhere, and the employer has no interest in incurring unnecessary further expenditure. For example, why should an employer send an employee who has become an HR manager on a long and expensive course of professional development leading to a professional qualification if they already have their own set HR systems and policies in place? Another difficulty is a narrowness of concern, seeing developing human potential only in as far as it can be 'justified' by direct and explicit benefits for the employer. This normally translates into 'hard' development for the knowledge and skills required for the specific job, to the neglect of other aspects of knowledge and skill, and the whole issue of values. The problems with analysing the costs and benefits of ED are a perennial issue, and the effect can be to preclude effective development. Lastly, there are concerns with the quality of the provision of ED provided. The quality of ED, as a service, is tied to the quality of the staff providing it. Confidence in the competence of trainers or training providers must be at the heart of the system. In many organisations this is recognised, and there is confidence in trainers who are themselves well trained in their roles, or reputable providers are used. In other circumstances bad experiences with trainers or training providers can mean that confidence in investing in ED is low.

A review of companies who have invested in ED (see Table 5.2) suggests that they gain in all key business success measures. From the employers' perspective such figures appear to suggest unambiguously that effective ED is indeed a key to business success.

Table 5.2 Learning pays: the value of learning and training to employers

	Average company	IiP accredited company	Gain
Rate of return on capital (RRC)	9.21%	16.27%	77%
Pre-tax profit margins	2.54%	6.91%	172%
Average salary	£12,590	£14,195	13%
Turnover/sales per employee	£64,912	£86,625	33%
Profit per employee	£1,815	£3,198	76%

Note: The data compare average UK companies with Investor in People (IiP)-accredited companies. The IiP standard will be explained later; in essence it is awarded to organisations which can prove that they are effectively supporting ED.

Source: National Advisory Council for Education and Training Targets 1999

Organisations will evolve systems and processes of their own to manage learning and ED to at least some extent. These will range from developing induction systems for new employees, through job-specific training, to retraining and career development. Research suggests that many companies have continued to develop and retain their own in-house training function, but a number have also been cutting back in recent years. The explanations for this decrease in internally managed ED vary from it representing straightforward cost-cutting to it representing the planned outsourcing of ED. It certainly seems that many more organisations are faced with the decision of choosing an external training provider as at least a partner, if not the major provider of ED. Much ED in organisations is managed in partnerships with others. These may be private sector providers, or public sector providers, or associated with private–public initiatives such as IiP.

The main reasons for selecting an outside provider are to obtain the best training available, and because the required training cannot be supplied in-house (The Industrial Society, 1998). Other key factors influencing the choice of provider include the availability of training facilities and the quality of the training design. A dedicated training company is likely to have broad experience in designing different courses for the various needs of different clients. An in-house training department is unlikely to have this breadth of knowledge and experience. Accreditation is also gaining importance, in part due to an environment where continuing career development and the workplace as a competitive internal labour market become more important. There are also factors which make in-house training more attractive. The two factors that seem to play a crucial role in persuading companies to develop their internal ED provisions are price and the ability to tailor a course to company needs.

So organisations develop ED strategies, deliberately and in a planned way and also as events unfold in the business; this involves developing and using some in-house provisions and also using external providers. Determining exactly which approach to ED they will invest in is still an issue, given the many different options available, and these will be considered in conclusion.

The role of government

In this area of HRM there is little substantive 'legal context',[4] in a way that parallels what is found in the legal regulation of employment through employment contracts or in specific employee relations legislation in industrial relations and areas like health and safety or managing discipline. Voluntarism still provides the main philosophy in ED in the UK – in other words, it is down to the people concerned to make decisions and develop initiatives as they see fit. Rather, the role of government is to promote the supply of ED through a number of initiatives, using a number of agencies. These agencies tend to change their name, if not their nature, with bewildering frequency. At the moment the central focus is on achieving a range of National

[4] One rare example would be the 1998 Teaching and Higher Education Act which amends the Employment Rights Act 1996; 16- and 17-year-old employees who have not achieved a certain standard of education/training will be entitled to reasonable paid time off during normal working hours to pursue approved qualifications. To be able to pursue learning and get an NVQ Level 2 or equivalent at least is therefore now a right for any individual. (http:www.hmso.gov.uk/acts/acts1998)

Training Targets, through the work of *Learning and Skills Councils* (LSCs) and Learning Partnerships and the initiative *Investors in People* (IiP).

From a government perspective the problems arising are ultimately about the implementation of economic and social policy. The nuts and bolts are about raising and allocating resources for ED. The balance of responsibility for paying for ED between individuals, companies, and government remains a constant concern. It seems that everyone aspires to achieve a high knowledge-based and high-skill economy, but would like to see someone else pay for it. One important aspect of this is that for the current government the challenge of dealing with groups facing social exclusion also provides a social agenda for ED, a social aspect to learning for and at work. Social exclusion includes a wide range of concerns. In the ED context it means dealing with the problems experienced by the long-term unemployed, women returners, alienated young people, and ethnic minority groups, in achieving their human potential through work and employment. In this context schools, colleges and universities, indeed education in general at all stages of life, can help drive the development of human potential to an extent. But it is often only in the context of employment, inside organisations, that many people have the opportunity to concentrate on developing their potential in the context of job experience and working with experienced practitioners.

The government's spending on training is an integral part of its broader economic and social policy. It is hard to quantify as it is bound up with its education programmes (see Table 5.3). This has become more pronounced since the Department of Education and the Department for Employment were merged in 1995/96, to form the Department for Education and Employment (DfEE). The amount being spent on training programmes in 1998/99 was £2.36 billion, excluding £951 million being spent on the Welfare to Work programme. There is also some training included under the broad initiative of encouraging 'people to continue throughout their lives to develop their knowledge, skills and understanding and improve their employability in a changing labour market'.

Table 5.3 Expenditure by the Department for Education and Employment and OFSTED (£m), 1993/94–1998/99

	1993/ 94	1994/ 95	1995/ 96	e1997/ 98	†1998/ 99
Total expenditure	13 616	14 364	14 449	14 794	14 023
Expenditure on employment and training programmes of which‡:	2392	2394	2198	2496	3311
Welfare to Work	-	-	-	172	951
work-based training for young people	640	647	635	731	741
work-based training for adults	760	693	502	439	340
European Social Fund	96	108	181	270	308

Note: e – estimated, † – planned, ‡ – these are the largest single categories of expenditure – including the Welfare to Work programme OFSTED – Office for Standards in Education

Source: Department for Education and Employment Expenditure Plans 1998–99

There are a number of national training targets (see Table 5.4), whose achievement is meant to concentrate the minds of all those involved in the provision of ED.

Table 5.4 Training targets

Targets for 11-year-olds	80% reaching standards in literacy and 75% reaching standards in numeracy
Targets for 16-year-olds	50% getting 5 higher grade GCSEs and 95% getting at least 1 GCSE
Targets for young people	85% of 19-year-olds with a level 2 qualification and 60% of 21-year-olds with a level 3 qualification
Targets for adults	50% with a level 3 qualification, 28% with a level 4 qualification, and a learning participation target (still to be set)
Targets for organisations	45% of medium and large organisations recognised as IiP, and 10 000 small organisations recognised as IiP

Note: These are the targets for England for 2002; targets for Scotland are currently being consulted upon.

Source: DfEE, 1998c

Provisions for young people in England and Wales are being reorganised into a new 'Connexions' Service (http://www.connexions.gov.uk). This will involve a host of initiatives based on eight key principles:

- raising aspirations – setting high expectations of every individual
- meeting individual need and overcoming barriers to learning
- taking account of the views of young people, individually and collectively, as the new service is developed and as it is operated locally
- inclusion – keeping young people in mainstream education and training and preventing them from moving to the margins of their community
- partnerships – agencies collaborating to achieve more for young people, parents and communities than agencies working in isolation
- community involvement and neighbourhood renewal – through involvement of community mentors and through personal advisors brokering access to local welfare, health, arts, sport and guidance networks
- extending opportunity and equality of opportunity – raising participation and achievement levels for all young people, influencing the availability, suitability and quality of provisions and raising awareness of opportunities
- evidence-based practice – ensuring that new interventions are based on rigorous research into and evaluation of 'what works'.

The emphasis is on the evolution of a broad and integrated service to give young people 'the best start in life', not just on initiatives to train them in vocational skills.

Youth training and youth credits

The problem of developing skills in young people has attracted policy attention for some considerable time. The context is one of abiding problems with youth unemployment, general disaffection with learning and training among some youth groups, and helping people cross the bridge from school to work and careers. From the government's perspective, there are clearly both economic and social concerns wrapped up in this. Youth Training and Youth Credits were launched in 1990. Under the Youth Training scheme, the DfEE guarantees the offer of a suitable training place to all 16–17-year-olds who 'are not in full-time education, are unemployed and seeking training'. Youth Training is offered via a Youth Credits system. 16- and 17-year-old school leavers (and sometimes other special groups) can use Youth Credits to buy training to N/SVQ standard from an employer or from a specialist provider of training.

Modern Apprenticeships

The 'old' system of ED, of apprenticeships managed by companies and craft unions, has been seen to have died out over time; with a decline of the industries and often organisations in which young people were apprenticed. Modern Apprenticeships were introduced in 1995. According to the DfEE, the purpose of Modern Apprenticeships is to develop technical, supervisory and craft-level skills among 16–18-year-olds. These schemes are designed to overcome the weaknesses of other attempts to improve ED for these occupations in industry, because they are industry-specific, and have been created by industry representatives in consultation with the DfEE. At the beginning of 1998, more than 150,000 young people had begun a Modern Apprenticeship, and there are now 75 Modern Apprenticeships, covering different sectors of industry and commerce.

Of all the government schemes, the Modern Apprenticeship scheme seems to be currently the most successful, attracting a rising number of entrants. However, these figures may have been inflated by some employers who have been using the scheme to train graduates, gaining a subsidy for these training costs. The government was sufficiently concerned to formally ban graduates from Modern Apprenticeship courses.

The DfEE has been considering the possibility of introducing a separate scheme for university students, whereby company-sponsored students would be able to qualify for a new type of Modern Apprenticeship scheme, where students would leave university with both a degree and a vocational qualification.

National Traineeships

National Traineeships were introduced in 1997. They offer young people who have left compulsory education a high-quality, work-based route to qualifications at intermediate level. They operate to agreed national criteria and standards set by industry and employers. In addition to specific vocational skills National Traineeships are meant to include all the key skills and components which will help young people progress in their chosen careers. National Traineeships currently cover more than 25 sectors of industry and commerce with plans for expansion into other sectors.

Work-Based Training for Adults

In 1998/1999, a new scheme called Work-Based Training for Adults was introduced to replace existing provisions. The aim of this new scheme is to help long-term unemployed adults, particularly those at risk of exclusion from the job market, to secure and sustain employment or self-employment, through an individually tailored combination of guidance, structured work experience, training and approved qualifications. The programme has some key features. It offers a combination of pre-vocational and occupational training. It provides occupational training which significantly improves skills in demand in the labour market. It provides lifelong learning facilities following Work-Based Training for Adults.

Investors in People

The aim of Investors in People (IiP) is to encourage employers to take training more seriously and improve their levels and quality of training. Employers satisfying the criteria become IiP-accredited companies. In essence, IiP provides a national 'benchmark' standard that helps employers to look at their training needs and links investment in training to the achievement of business goals. This standard is based on four principles:

- top-level commitment to develop all employees
- a regular review of the training and development of all employees
- action to train and develop individuals on recruitment and provide training throughout their employment
- evaluation of the outcome of training and development as a basis for continuous improvement.

Companies that adopt HRM practices that satisfy these four principles will be awarded IiP accreditation by Investors in People UK. By October 1998, around 10,000 firms had achieved IiP accreditation. The government provides £1.6 million to help firms achieve this accreditation. In recent times a focus upon small firms (i.e. firms employing up to 50 people) and medium-sized firms has become evident. The IiP standard, as with many other government initiatives, is currently being reviewed. Changes in the standard and the process for achieving it are expected.

This brief empirical review of IiP would suggest that an enhancement of the positive driving forces supporting employers' activities in ED and learning at work and an elimination of the negative restraining forces in order to more effectively and efficiently promote ED is still needed. That, in most accounts, would seem to involve a range of actors, from employers and their training departments, government and quasi-governmental organisations, and training providers working with individuals, groups and organisations to improve ED. Effective and efficient ED depends upon relationships and collaboration among employers, government, and training providers.

For employers these collaborations can begin with links to education, particularly the final years of secondary education, further education and Higher Education (HE), and professional development based in HE. Arguably, most centrally it involves assuring the right quantity and quality of ED in the workplace. This involves more than doing more training; it is about ED being an integral part of major business developments and company changes. This is exemplified in the UK presently by the IiP initiative. In IiP the core issues of ED, commitment to training, the planning and actions involved in training, and the need to evaluate training are seen as central business development concerns.

Improving the training market

The DfEE has a number of programmes which are aimed at encouraging individuals' investment in learning and at improving the quality and market responsiveness of training and vocational education. Current initiatives include promoting and making more accessible the benefits of lifelong learning; promoting the use of flexible learning; establishing mechanisms to achieve greater responsiveness of the further education sector to the needs of employers and promoting continuous improvement in the performance of bodies charged with supporting and delivering employee development

Welfare to Work

Welfare to Work is based on the 'New Deal' scheme for young and long-term unemployed people. Features of the scheme include helping young people, aged 18–24, who have been unemployed for more than six months to find work. It involves offering employers who take on a young unemployed person for six months a subsidy of £60 per week, providing full-time education and training for a year, and providing work in the voluntary sector or on the Environmental Task Force for up to six months. There are also a set of initiatives aimed at helping long-term unemployed people aged over 25 to find work. These include the opportunity to study while claiming the job seeker's allowance and offering a subsidy to companies which employ the long-term unemployed for six months.

National/Scottish Vocational Qualifications

National/Scottish Vocational Qualifications (N/SVQs) were launched in 1986. There are now more than 900 N/SVQs, representing different economic sectors and industries. They are divided into five ascending levels of competence:

- Level 1 – performance of routine work activities and/or achievement of a broad foundation of work competence as a basis for progression
- Level 2 – broader range of activities involving greater responsibility
- Level 3 – skilled activities involving greater responsibility
- Level 4 – complex, technical and specialised activities, including supervision and management
- Level 5 – pursuit of a senior occupation or profession, including the ability to apply a significant range of fundamental principles and techniques.

The take-up of N/SVQs varies enormously between commerce and industry sectors. Companies that have used these qualifications consistently report an improvement in product and service quality, increased staff motivation and more targeted training. Yet estimates are that only 7 per cent of employers are using N/SVQs and that only 5 per cent of the workforce have gained an N/SVQ award.

There have been other government initiatives on education and training since the election of the Labour government in 1997 to introduce what is being called 'The Learning Age' (DfEE 1997). The four main proposals are:

- a University for Industry (UFI) based on a network of local learning centres and access points to put 'learning on the High Street'
- Individual Learning Accounts (ILAs) – study and learning vouchers, with which people can buy the education and training that they need
- childcare support for those who need to take courses during the day or evening
- Learning Direct – a helpline through which people can obtain information on courses available.

As government reform of ED continues three main issues are evident: establishing the overall costs of reforms for lifelong learning; defining how much employers should contribute; and identifying what kind of learning technologies should be supported. These issues reprise the fundamental and abiding problems with all and any policy: being able clearly to identify costs and benefits among a range of options in order to structure optimum investment in people. The issue is less 'making training pay' than 'How much will it actually cost?' and 'Who pays for it?'.

During the last decade, there have also been significant changes within the framework and institutions supporting ED. To some this amounts to a revolution in training policy since 1988; to others it smacks of reorganisation in the face of uncertainty about what to do for the best when facing the challenges of improving ED. All of the UK's ED industry's major current institutional landmarks have been developed since 1988. In particular, there is continuing uncertainty about the type of system needed to ensure there is effective liaison in the development, marketing and evaluation of supply-side and demand-side initiatives. This is a common theme in the 'revolutions' – institutional and cultural – that have been heralded several times in the last two decades. How best to get everybody working together, making optimum use of limited resources, to achieve a range of stakeholder goals is a problem that has not yet been solved. This chapter can only briefly mention the main bodies involved.

At the top stands some form of national body: in England and Wales it is the National Advisory Council for Education and Training Targets (NACETT), which monitors the progress of training in relation to national targets across the range of concerns addressed above, as well as advising the DfEE on current performance and the effect of policies designed to achieve the targets. It draws its members from the Confederation of British Industry (CBI), the Trades Union Congress (TUC), the fields of education and training, and government departments. Its equivalent in Scotland was the Advisory Scottish Committee on Training Targets

(ASCETT), though, with constitutional change and a devolved parliament taking responsibility for these matters, a new institutional system is currently being developed in Scotland. A Skills Task Force advises the DfEE on the National Skills Agenda. Its purpose is to analyse and forecast skills shortages and to propose solutions. Its recommendations do affect education and training policies.

At the next level down are National Training Organisations (NTOs). The key responsibilities of the NTOs are to identify the industry sector's training needs, establish occupational standards and qualifications for their sector, provide the sector with information on training capacity, and to ensure that the sector has relevant training capacity. NTOs are larger than previous industry bodies with a similar role, covering bigger industry sectors, and are, therefore, fewer in number. In autumn 1998, there were 55, but a total of 75 are planned. They are also required particularly to look at skills requirements in their industry. The NTO National Council has devised a programme called Skills Foresight, which the NTOs are to use in order to assess skills needs. They will make use of tools like benchmarking and scenario planning, as well as local focus groups, rather than just using the old centralised forecasting of skills demands characteristic of the old systems.

Downstream there are also geographically based bodies. Until recently these were the Training and Enterprise Companies (TECs) in England and Wales and Local Enterprise Companies (LECs) in Scotland. These were set up in 1990, to improve vocational training for young people, to raise training levels in smaller businesses, and to promote local economic growth. These are being superseded by new bodies in England from 2000, and the LECs are under review, given the devolution of government in Scotland. The principles will remain; they have been run by boards of executives, made up of members from industry, local government and the training industry. This tripartite structure is likely to remain in some form, however the actual organisations evolve. They are required to work closely with the NTOs, as their responsibilities overlap. The balance between central control and local initiative will continue to be a tension in the system whatever new forms of body emerge.

The context for the evolution of ED in this aspect in the UK is continuing institutional and policy change. All these factors increase demands for more spending on ED. Whether that is forthcoming, and whether this amounts to a government-inspired institutional and cultural revolution that is preparing the UK to face the challenges of the future is still very much open to question. Whether there is enough investment, and whether it is directed at the areas of most importance to 'UK plc' are questions different stakeholders would answer quite differently.

Employers' approaches to employee development

We conclude by briefly reviewing here the practice and the theory of ED within companies. It is at the workplace where the issues involved in managing skills, knowledge and values, and the stakeholders who are concerned with ED, interact and can be evaluated. Many employers provide much ED themselves, through having and using their own trainers and training departments. Some large organisations even aspire to create their own 'universities'. It is also employers who use the substantial and strong 'private sector' concerned with ED, in the form of companies which provide training services for organisations. And it is employers who use the substantial public sector input to the development of ED, in the form of public policies and government-backed development schemes and programmes. The hub of the whole system has to be what happens within workplaces. According to an Industrial Society survey, the most common subjects that development in employment focuses upon within companies are health and safety (68 per cent), communication (61 per cent), and customer care (53 per cent)(Industrial Society 1998). Much less common are financial (14 per cent) and leadership aspects (6 per cent).

Much training is of very short duration. Surveys of employers report that a third of all training courses last less than three days (*Employment Gazette*, 1995). Of employees who received job-related training the primary clusters of activity are around very brief courses and also around longer-term, more substantial programmes.

Table 5.5 shows that two- to three-day courses remain the most popular form of training provided by external sources, suggesting that this is the form of training most in demand when organisations seek partners to provide ED. The apparent low demand for some high-profile innovative approaches, such as mentoring and even distance learning, suggests that the short course structure is consistently appealing to organisations.

Table 5.5 Training approaches used regularly for external training (% of employers citing use of these approaches), 1998

2- to 3-day courses	82
Up to 1 day courses	79
Day release	69
Residential training	63
Evening classes	55
Distance/open learning	42
Computer-based learning	24
Outdoor training	24
Coaching/mentoring	12
Video-based learning	9
Learning resource centres	6
Action learning sets	7

Source: The Industrial Society, *Training Trends*, May/June 1998

In sum, ED typically involves organisations providing one-day courses for their own employees from a menu of options, with external private providers offering two- or three- day courses, and also with organisations providing or working in partnership with accrediting institutions to offer long programmes of study and development. These are the three primary fields of development within employment: 'short and sharp' courses, extended short courses and longer programmes.

Different approaches to ED have been identified among employers. These can be classified historically, as they have changed over time in response to new demands and priorities. An example of this (Megginson, Banfield and Joy-Matthews, 1999) is to review past 'leading ideas'.

- 1964–70 Systematic approach to diagnosis of training
- 1968–75 Standardisation of training for job categories by industry. Thorough off-job basic education for skilled occupations
- 1970–75 Systematic planning of training for all categories of employee
- 1974–80 Company contribution to training for young people and long-term unemployed to meet national needs
- 1979–90 Business-orientated training directed at improving organisational effectiveness
- 1988–present Personal development with individualised plans for which each employee and their line manager take responsibility
- 1990–present Learning company development with a focus on a conscious, systemic, whole-organisation perspective
- 1998–present Knowledge management focus with knowledge workers and their intellectual properties seen as the core significant assets of the organisation

These approaches were around for some organisations before the dates suggested above as the start, and they continue in use long after their 'heyday'. Old approaches also emerge in new forms in each era. So, for example, the standardisation of training for job categories, characteristic of the systematic approach in the late 1960s, has had a rebirth with the development of the Management Charter Initiative (MCI). MCI seeks to specify management training, as does the development of National/Scottish Vocational Qualifications (N/SVQs) for other categories of employee competence.

Survey methods to find out what is being advocated by practitioners also provide a way of categorising what is involved in ED. This methodology has the advantage of being grounded in experience, but has the disadvantage of being less neat and tidy than more conceptually elegant frameworks. A complex and detailed outline of a huge range of training ideas and their development over time in the view of 633 practitioners, is spelled out in the *Developing the Developers* report (Boydell *et al.*, 1991). A more recent example of the practitioner survey (Megginson, Banfield and Joy-Matthews, 1999) surveyed very experienced developers active in the Association of Management Education and Development (AMED) and elicited a long list of 16 possible leading ideas. The surveyors asked a wider group of human resource development (HRD) practitioners to rank this long list. They calculated the proportion of respondents listing each idea as one of their top two, and the proportion listing it as one of their bottom two. Table 5.6 shows the ideas listed according to the size of the difference between these two percentages; those at the top of the list are the ideas seen as being of highest priority in the balanced view of their respondents.

Table 5.6 Leading ideas listed in order of the size of the gap between the proportion given top two priority and the proportion given bottom two priority (N=61), listed in order of size of gap.

Leading idea	% giving top 2 ranks	% giving bottom 2 ranks	% difference between top and bottom
1. Linking development to the organisation's strategy	35	5	+30
2. Focus on company or organisation learning	21	2	+19
3. Improved communication / briefing	18	0	+18
4. Linking learning to work	22	7	+15
5. Involving and participative management	15	0	+15
6. Focus on development rather than training	19	7	+12
7. Empowerment of staff	9	2	+7
8. Learners responsible for their own development	10	5	+5
9. Building balanced lives	16	16	0
10. Learning between organisations	9	10	−1

Source: Megginson, D., Banfield, P. and Joy-Matthews, J. (1999) *Human Resource Development,* (2nd edn) Kogan Page, London (p.19).

An interesting feature of this list is that it excluded from an earlier version of the survey 'accreditation and competence'. Although quite a number of the sample rated this very highly, a much larger number rated it very low. These 'low raters' were disproportionately concentrated among the more experienced of the sample of respondents.

Reviewing the historical and the survey data the dominant approaches to ED in the UK can be classified as:

- the systematic approach
- business orientation
- competencies and accreditation
- self-development
- the learning organisation
- knowledge management.

Each of these theories and approach is briefly considered here in turn.

The systematic approach

In spite of its 'antiquity' and persistent critiques, the systematic training approach maintains a remarkable hold in the world of ED. One reason for this is that many books on training, development and HRD offer it as a core 'intellectual property', organising their text around a (usually) four-stage cycle, as shown in Figure 5.1

Another reason is its simplicity in suggesting a cycle of activity which can be managed in practice, breaking down into discrete parts. A deeper question about the persistence of this approach might be, 'Why do *authors* continue to use this framework?' One reason for the continuation of this strand of thinking about ED may be that it gives a professional identity to trainers as well as to writers on

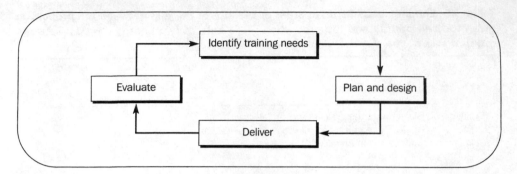

Figure 5.1

training. It provides a framework for what trainers do and enables them to describe their professional practice in a coherent way. Some of the components of this expertise are mapped in Box 5.1.

This model, however, is limited. It is a map of the 'internal content' of ED: what happens within employee development as a practical management activity; how to identify training needs, how to design and deliver training events, and how

---

BOX 5.1

The training cycle

Identify training needs
- Company and business needs
- Job and performance need
- Individual and personal need
- Self-determined needs (wants)
- Training plans and training policies
- Job analysis
- Performance appraisal
- Knowledge, skill and attitude (KSA)

Plan and design
- KSA linked to programme elements
- Learning methods linked to type of need
- Learning materials and resources
- Setting learning objectives
- On-job, at-job or off-job
- Internal or external
- Tutored or open learning resource

Deliver
- Use of range of learning methods
- Facilitation skills
- Engagement of internal providers
- Sourcing of external providers
- Instruction, coaching, mentoring
- Manage groups and teams
- A professional job role
- Being a broker of services

Evaluate
- Reactions, learning, job behaviour, organisation effects
- Feedback to learners
- Evaluating programme/strategy effectiveness

to evaluate them. The training cycle is also an essentially prescriptive model; it presents an ideal of what should be done, and does not reflect or describe what is actually done and the problems encountered.

Business orientation

The advent of the National Training Awards in Britain 1985 was the occasion when the business-oriented approach and theory were first formally advocated as a coherent framework, though of course many would have claimed prior to this that ED was integrated with business needs. The design of the awards required applicants to describe what had been done in terms of the four stages of the training cycle, outlined in the section on systematic training above, and they also required that the training must be preceded by identification of a business need and that the training outcome be shown to lead to a business outcome.

This approach was congruent with the spirit of the times, with businesses demanding 'bottom-line' contributions from all service functions if they were to survive deep cuts and downsizing. Arguably, the whole IiP approach, the central initiative in ED at the moment in the UK, is an incarnation of this approach.

The Institute of Personnel and Development (IPD) and Investors in People (IiP), arguably the two most notable proponents of ED in the UK, together launched a booklet called *Making Training Pay* (1997). This makes the business case for training and gives examples of how companies have benefited from training. The Confederation of British Industry also issued a survey-based report, which showed that, as well as putting more effort into training, two-thirds of employers were training their staff 'beyond the skills necessary for their jobs' (CBI, 1998).

Such reports are each small waves in a tide of change which has seen ED become a focus for effective business development and competitive success. Another survey claims to reveal that there is now a substantial attempt to link training with business objectives 'delivering human resource development in line with business objectives' (IPD, 1999: 11). This somewhat begs the question of what has been going on for the past several decades. The overemphasis in current times on having a business orientation may sometimes be seen as avoiding the specific challenges of evaluating exactly which approach is most effective and efficient and best provides value for money in different contexts.

Competencies and accreditation

An interesting 'mutation' of the business-oriented approach came when the UK government chose to put its authority behind approaches that advocated the identification of standardised competencies for occupations. The Management Charter Initiative (MCI) was one such initiative. This kind of set of competence statements specifying what it requires to 'do things well' in order to be effective in employment has, in fact, been a feature of training from the advent of systematic training. However, systematic training had offered the perspective that the particular needs of any specific group of managers (or any other group) needed to be identified. 'Universal' models of competence can thus seem to be a step back from this insight.

The government chose to put its weight behind the accreditation of individual competence because of a need to document progress towards the achievement of National Training Targets in the UK. The achievement of accredited qualifications gave the policy makers something to measure. From this emerged the whole panoply of N/SVQs. These qualifications were seen as having a number of advantages, discussed elsewhere in this chapter. A principal advantage was seen to be their portability – they could be related to other similar qualifications in other organisations and even in other EU countries.

The original work of Boyatzis (1982) on competencies had been based on finding out what behaviour led to superior performance by some individuals in a population. This work was therefore situated in particular contexts, and also provided a focus on what was required in order to 'do things better'. It was adopted by many large organisations in order to paint a vision of what was required in a major change project – and thus sought to encourage 'doing better things'; companies like BP and Boots developed such approaches. Many companies have now developed their own 'maps' of competence, though these are in essence, and often in detail, very similar.

Competencies were also proposed as providing a coherent framework for the integration of various HRM processes and initiatives. Some companies, including Commercial and General Union (see Case Study 5.1 at the end of this chapter) and Royal Bank of Scotland, had vigorous HR departments concerned with creating a set of initiatives bound together with a set of managerial behaviours which would lead to some future desirable state. Thus, selection, performance management, development and pay could all be tied down to some common framework. We have also identified cases, where having originally embraced competencies, senior HR people came to see that the model they imposed companywide did not capture the unique and crucial capabilities and contributions of a diversity of managerial roles and styles.

Self-development

This approach is grounded on two axioms:

- Any learning is a good thing as it leads to the embracing of the new and the extension of skills and capability.
- Learning which has the most potency to create these effects is that chosen and specified by the learners themselves.

The first axiom leads to the practice of employee development schemes, of which the most famous is the Ford's Employee Development and Assistance Programme (EDAP). Here a personal budget is provided to enable individuals to learn whatever they want in order to initiate or reawaken the habit of learning, and to offer a commitment on behalf of the employer to making this happen.

Recently some authorities (Hamblett and Holden, 2000) have been suggesting that employee-led development has a component that makes a difference – namely, the fact that overall control of the scheme is in the hands of the workforce or their representatives. This participation ensures effective development.

The second axiom leads to an approach to development where the learner is given central responsibility for and control over the process of identifying and meeting learning needs, and others have roles to support this development. Often personal development plans (see the CGU case study at the end of this chapter) are a part of the process, and line managers can have an important role in supporting and stimulating the consideration of development. Training functions are seen as enablers and can provide advice on the resources to deliver training or development opportunities. The experience of the authors in designing and supporting such programmes (in, for example, Texaco and ICL) is that competencies are sometimes used and found helpful in the first round of need-identification. However, they are often rejected in favour of a more individual expression of need once the learner gains confidence in expressing their own needs (Megginson and Whitaker, 1996).

The learning organisation

Ideas of organisational learning, which had been present in the literature for more than 20 years, became popular in the early 1990s with the publication of Senge (1990) in the USA and Pedler, Burgoyne and Boydell (1991) in the UK. Essentially, both advocated a systemic rather than a systematic approach to development. By this we mean that they saw that everything was connected to everything else. Simple cause and effect models (we sometimes call them 'boxes and arrows' approaches) do not capture the complex interactions between components of a system. Learning, if it is to generate new possibility for action, needs to recognise that most of our actions are grounded in basic assumptions of which we may not be aware. These assumptions limit our thinking and acting, and at the same time seal off from us the awareness that we are thus limited (Argyris and Schön, 1978).

Many trainers claim to be adopting this approach by following a recipe of prescriptions (such as Pedler et al.'s (1991) eleven characteristics of a learning company). Trainers do this in spite of the authors' clear advice to the contrary, and without the systemic perspective of Senge (1990). They also often lack the willingness and skill required to question basic assumptions inherent in the writing of Argyris and Schön (1978). This approach is, it would seem, much less commonly adopted than the rhetoric of its adherents would suggest.

Knowledge management

An emerging approach, which may establish itself and displace the systematic training approach, is the approach to learning via the concerns of knowledge management. Knowledge management gurus argue that knowledge held by knowledge workers creates intellectual capital which represents the intangible assets of modern organisations. These intangible assets have often far greater worth than the tangible assets of buildings and machinery. Development is therefore crucially concerned with the management and enhancement of these knowledge assets. As the field develops, there seem to be contributions from three currents of thinking. The first is the information systems (IS) perspective, which emphasises the capture, store and retrieval of knowledge. The second is the organisation learning (OL) perspective, which focuses on learning as being mediated, situated, provisional, pragmatic and contested (Easterby-Smith *et al.*, 1999). The third is a strategic perspective, which emphasises the value of intellectual capital and the worth of knowledge as embodied in patents and corporate core competencies (Davenport and Prusak, 1998). The prospect of a fusion of these perspectives is beguiling for developers, who find that conversations about learning often do not engage the attention of strategic management in the way that a hard-headed concern for tangible assets can.

Conclusion

There are a variety of approaches to achieving development in employment, with no single best way being evident in theory or practice. In a prescriptive sense, as outlined in the beginning, ED is concerned with learning for and learning at work to help individuals and organisations achieve their full potential. Individuals have development needs throughout their lives. These range from gaining basic knowledge and basic skills in education and pre-employment vocational development, through to induction and initial job-related training with an employer, and on to their lifelong performance and career development up to leaving the employer on redundancy or retirement. Employers are concerned with ensuring that their workforce is competent and that the development activities used to achieve competency are effective and efficient. This requires employers' involvement in a range of activities, from influencing and shaping government policy on education through to organising their own development activities for individuals, specific job roles and the organisation as a whole. While some issues come to more prominence in some contexts than others, there is no settled, universal and dominant prescriptive approach.

In terms of evidence for a positive evaluation of employers' activities in ED in the UK, many UK work organisations have often looked to ED as an integral part of becoming and remaining efficient and more effective. There is a long and substantial tradition of investing in ED in many UK organisations, and those which it has been quick and easy to accredit as Investors in People (IiPs) reflect that. This is simply and logically because, other things being equal, an organisation with well-developed and therefore competent employees will be more efficient and effective than an organisation with poorly developed and therefore incompetent employees.

In the light of greater challenges to be 'excellent' in order to compete successfully or to provide better-quality public services, a greater concern with ED among employers has been reinforced as a route to helping achieve these aspirations. In partnership with employers, the government has reformed the education and training system that underpins ED in the UK, to make it better fit the country's economic and social needs. The development of employees and the promotion of learning at work are now seen as a means of transforming organisations from struggling businesses or services into world-class and successful organisations. All the driving forces in the business environment push most employers towards greater levels and improved quality of ED. Evidence in the form of organisations who adopt this philosophy and succeed is plentiful; see Case Study 5.2.

However, investment in effective ED does not appear to be the norm among UK employers seeking to develop their businesses. The need for promotional initiatives like IiP, raises questions about the extent to which there is indeed a general, common-sense and logical case for transforming organisations through employers increasing their investing in ED. As exemplary employers in this respect are not the norm, either employers are ignorant of the returns to be achieved, or are led to other conclusions in reality. Perhaps the 'unambiguous' data supporting the returns on ED is discounted as unrealistic. Kellaway (2000) claims that there is

---

BOX 5.2

Chase Advanced Technologies Ltd

In 1996 Chase Advanced Technologies won a major contract to provide electronic components for fruit machines across the UK. But the contract led to problems for the company, including poor pass rates and high levels of reworking. At one point things were so bad that internal pass rates fell to 38 per cent.

An intensive training programme to tackle the immediate crisis was devised which involved 60 employees undertaking basic training in printed circuit board assembly. Quality levels began to rise, reaching 80 per cent in a few months. The company then introduced a skills training and National Vocational Qualification (NVQ) initiative and an in-house workmanship training culture, set up with support from a local college and Electronic ITEC, Bradford College's electronic training centre. A multimedia computer-based training package to support the delivery of the NVQ was also developed.

Finally the change management team began to lay the foundations for a genuine training culture. They made a commitment to the Investors in People standard and offered staff access to a nationally recognised qualification.

After 2 years of heavy losses Chase returned to profit in 1998 and the company is now a thriving organisation with a skilled and committed workforce. Managing director Eugene Martinez commented 'The training programme has led to a new spirit of enthusiasm among our staff. Having been given an opportunity to learn, many have developed a real hunger for knowledge. A working grandmother was one of the first people to gain a NVQ and has recently gained a level 3 qualification in manufacturing support. Many staff are so keen that they are even undertaking NVQ work in their own time.'

Source: DfEE Employment News, December/January 2000, p.5. Quoted in full with permission.

indeed much hype and inflation surrounding ED. As a trenchant critic of UK employers' susceptibility to management fads and fashions, she asserts that:

> Some of the dullest days I have spent in my 18 years as a wage slave have been on training courses. Training is only good if it succeeds in teaching you something useful. But most of it doesn't or doesn't do it very effectively.

> (Kellaway, 2000: 81)

It seems that many employers share her views, rather than being gulled, as she supposes, by the 'nonsense' claims that ED can transform a company. A negative evaluation of employers' activities in ED in the UK would also be supported by the fact that many work organisations have failed to make ED a priority. Investment in ED in companies in the UK is consistently lower than in other countries. Employers continue either to operate inefficiently and ineffectively, or seek to become more efficient and effective by other means – the primary strategy being through deskilling work and minimising costs by actually neglecting ED. While the high-quality development of a few professionals and managers may be achieved in some companies, the limited ED that is provided by employers, and their influence on schools, colleges and universities, is of dubious quality and value. This has resulted in systematic problems in achieving even basic competence amongst the general labour force and in specific workforces, which leaves UK employers at a disadvantage. Effects range from poor health and safety standards, through poor standards of customer service and up to ineffective strategic management of the organisation as a whole. This leads to the UK being saddled with a 'low-skill, low-wage' economy. It is also badly placed to restructure and meet the demands of the knowledge economy and society.

The apparent failure of employers to support ED is compounded by governmental failures to challenge them. Government has actively handed responsibility over to employers to lead the 'skills revolutions' they seek, but employers have been found wanting. Government has thus failed to identify and resource properly the priorities and institutions needed to break free from the 'low-skill, low-wage' economy the UK is seen to have. Skills shortages cause problems not only for immediate business and service development, the main concern of employers; they can also constrain longer-term economic growth and social restructuring, a primary concern of government. As a result, UK organisations are falling further and further behind their competitors in the rest of the world. Other nations' greater governmental emphasis on investment in ED pays general economic and social dividends, while in the UK the gaps between those who are successful and those who are 'socially excluded' widen and deepen (Hutton, 1995).

The truth would seem to lie somewhere between the simplified and exaggerated negative and positive evaluations of employers' activities in ED in the UK. One estimate (Keynote, 1998) was that the total amount spent on training by the private sector in 1998 was £13.2 billion, spent on a workforce of around 21 million where around 3 million people in the year were participants in off-job training. In

---

BOX 5.3

Skills shortages

For 42% of employers with hard-to-fill vacancies the main reason given is not enough suitable skilled people.

Areas

- Catering occupations
- Road transport
- Miscellaneous sales and services
- Engineers and technologists
- Health and related occupations
- Health associate professionals
- Miscellaneous clerks
- Receptionists and telephonists
- Computer analysts and programmers
- Telephone sales
- Specialist managers

Effects

- Increased running costs
- Loss of quality
- Restrict business developments

Changes in skill needs

68% of employers say skills needed are increasing due to changes in processes, technology and management practices.

Skills that matter

Technical and practical skills
Computer literacy
General communication skills
Customer handling skills
Management skills
Teamworking skills
Problem-solving skills
Managing own development

Source: IRS ED Bulletin 110:*Skill Needs in Great Britain and NI 1998*

---

the UK the average spend is then £62 per person if all employees are considered, or £440 per person for those who actually received off-job training.[5]

The negative evaluators would be challenged by this trend, but not the basic fact. They would still wonder whether this level of activity and the development it involves are good enough. And questions about the efficiency and effectiveness of investments in ED remain in any event. The pessimist would also question where resources invested in ED are actually going. Research (DfEE: *Labour Market Trends*, 1998) shows that there is a marked bias towards younger age groups as

---

[5] There are no available estimates for similar figures on ED in the public sector.

participants in ED. This makes sense as the early career stages are when learning needs would seem most evident. But in an era where the promotion of 'lifelong learning' is important, and where organisational and job changes are so prevalent, it seems that ED needs to be – but is not yet in practice – a lifelong activity.

There are also significant variations in the occupational characteristics of ED activity (ONS, 1996). Professional employees are the most likely to receive ED, while regular training is lowest among manual workers. Again these statistics seem to reflect a 'reality' where professional jobs require more learning, and therefore attract more resources. However, many commentators argue that the provision of ED for all is a precondition of successful performance for any organisation, and in the UK it is problems with basic and intermediate ED (or vocational education and training (VET)) which present the greatest areas of need. The concentration of resources and activity among certain occupational groups may reflect an anomaly inherited from history rather than an effective allocation of resources.

There are also sector variations. Some sectors invest more in ED than others. One survey (Industrial Society, 1998) shows, for example, that off-the-job training is more widespread in the financial sector than in manufacturing. This discrepancy may reflect greater use of on-the-job ED in manufacturing rather than the financial sector, so the balance of overall investment in ED may be more equal than it first seems. It may also be the case that there are greater ED needs in the financial sector than in manufacturing; for example, due to the introduction of legislation and the demand for improved levels of competence in the selling of financial services. The pessimists' suspicion would be that ED in manufacturing is neglected because it is a low-skill, low-wage sector, thus contributing to the overall decline of that sector within the UK economy. They may also suspect that much of the investment in ED in the financial sector is of dubious value.

So learning in and for the workplace depends upon the outcome of complex interactions between individuals, employers and government. The hope is that optimum investment by each in development brings maximum gains: individuals gain attractive and useful employment, employers gain business success in high-skill industries, and governments achieve the social and economic goals they were elected to pursue. There is then a weight of expectation hanging on ED, exerted by the dependence of all these stakeholders upon it. Whether, in principle, ED can deliver on these expectations, and whether, in practice, one approach is better than another, are questions which have exercised many in HRM in recent times and which need to be pursued further.

This chapter has described and evaluated the nature of ED, what it involves and what the issues and challenges are, particularly from an employer's perspective. Seeing employers' activities as the hub of the matter is, indeed, only one way of concluding a review of ED; but it has the merit of leading on to theoretical case study analysis of workplace and employer examples, rather than to specialist theories and matters of motivation and involvement in learning, or to the evaluation of government policies and initiatives in the broader context of evaluating social and economic goals and aspirations.

From an employer's perspective the context is one of achieving their goals through creating a competent workforce. This involves them in a range of activities, from organising their own employees' development, to influencing education and development policy and taking the lead in evolving supportive national policies and systems. In all these respects the evaluation of employers' activities in ED can be positive: education is being reformed to meet the economic and social needs of the contemporary workforce, employers are investing more in ED, with gains for all; and as a result of these activities, broader social and economic goals and aspirations can be met. Changes and restructuring in companies are bringing about changes in people's tasks and responsibilities, with a subsequent need for more ED. All sectors appear to be supporting change: companies are reviewing their internal provisions, government provides new and salient frameworks which are funded and a dynamic private sector provides a range of ED options 'for all tastes and budgets'. Changes in markets, in customer requirements, and in approaches to ED are forcing providers to review their products and services, which leads to better products and services. For the government there are continuing economic, social and political gains to be made in promoting 'supply-side' policies that involve motivating employers and individuals to increase skills and employability rather than achieving economic and social aims by 'taxing and spending'.

The evaluation can also be negative: education is becoming too vocationalised and losing its fundamental purpose; insufficient investment in development in organisations is the stubborn norm; policies and institutions which are employer-led fail to deliver on longer-term economic and social goals and aspirations. The three main stakeholders arguably continue to underfund their rhetoric. Companies are still prone to limiting ED budgets; the government does not follow through on funding for its initiatives; and individuals are reluctant to pay themselves for ED. In addition, ED standards vary considerably. Internal provisions, and those offered externally by the private and public sector, are often criticised. There appear to be a significant proportion of ED programmes that are poorly planned and structured, despite decades of established advice on how to do it properly. There are continuing critiques of the success and viability of government programmes – for example, the merits of the IiP initiative. Evaluating the worth of ED, in terms of costs and benefits, has never been easy; its higher profile further exposes this, paradoxically leading to greater criticisms of ED as it grows in popularity as a business development tool. Also, current investment in ED is concentrated among the large companies, whose share of total employees is declining, and in certain employment categories and age groups.

There is then a huge demand for ED: within companies, from competent external providers, and in the form of public sector initiatives designed to support individuals and organisations. Computer-based learning is gaining popularity and may be particularly suited to some sectors which involve jobs that are heavily dependent on using IT. School, university and personal use of ICT systems is clearly growing, and this whole aspect of the design and delivery of training will be a major concern in the future. The shift towards self-managed learning offers the prospect of better focused and greater personal and professional development. New entrants to the ED market, such as computer companies and publishers, are expanding the range of courses available and offering cheaper training. Non-profit organisations are competing strongly against the commercial training companies.

Yet in companies there is a threat to training budgets and initiatives in the face of cost reduction factors and the imperatives of production/service delivery in lean organisations concerned to maintain limits to working hours. Greater use in companies of learning resource centres may increase the demand on internal company training, but may not deliver the goods without trained trainers there to facilitate. Governments are struggling to sort out the 'Who pays?' part of the equation. Getting bogged down in this, or making decisions that prove unpopular with major stakeholders, can undo all the efforts that have hitherto been made.

In many respects there is a great deal of inertia in the system. Despite promulgating and promoting the benefits of ED, it takes time and a lot of resources to establish and co-ordinate efforts which can bring real business and social benefits. Dissatisfaction with the quantity and quality of ED provided, both by the public sector and the private sector as well as within companies, can be expected to spur the further evolution of innovative approaches to ED and further restructuring of the overall system. The potential of technologies, for example, has yet to be fully realised. All this means that further, and perhaps greater, change is likely in the future. Such changes can be expected to succeed or fail according to how well they engage individuals, employers and government in partnerships as much as they will depend upon the relevance and accuracy of the substantive knowledge, skill and values identified as priorities for future human potential development.

Where that interaction involves individuals motivated to learn, able to access learning within employment and elsewhere, supported by investing employers and guided by principled economic and social policy being effectively implemented, then a synergy is possible with all benefiting. Where that interaction involves people unwilling or unable to participate in learning, compounded by employers who fail to invest in ED and there is a lack of principle or effective implementation in economic and social policy then a vicious cycle will exist, with all paying the price. These realities of providing development for employment present human, organisational and political challenges which are at the heart of HRM.

Case study 5.1

Employee development in Commercial & General Union

Stephen Gibb and David Megginson

The context

Commercial Union, a large British general insurance company, initiated a strategic change project, called Best Place to Work (BPTW), in 1996. BPTW aimed to change beliefs about working relationships and performance towards a more competitive and customer-focused set of values. Current management styles were to be challenged, structures were to become more customer-focused, and processes would be redesigned to enable more front-line decision-making. Reward systems were to become more performance-focused and awareness of the redefined brand was to be increased. A BPTW survey showed that staff wanted 'to grow and develop', and felt that opportunities were scarce. A Personal Development Planning (PDP) process was set in train to meet this aspiration, and to reinforce other aspects of the BPTW programme.

ED in the company before this point was focused upon:

- Professional insurance industry qualifications, with relatively little attention paid to N/SVQs
- IiP, which was being pursued by various parts of the business
- A tradition of attendance on residential courses at the company's training centre – Douce's Manor, in Kent.

During 1997 a relationship was established with Cranfield Business School, which delivered residential training for senior managers. During 1998 a Certificate, Diploma and MBA programme was set up with the Open University Business School for people who self-nominated and were supported by their managers.

The aims of the PDP initiative were to enable staff to:

1. Take personal responsibility for acquiring the right technical, interpersonal and business skills to do the job now, and to gain management support for this process.
2. Think ahead about their career and future possibilities – and start to chart a way forward; to see patterns in what they had done, and rethink whether they wanted them to continue or change.
3. Tune into the changes going on around them, recognise the impact of change on them and develop coping/success skills.
4. Recognise the value of developing outside of work, and gain management support for this.

The scheme had been launched and rolled out to the 8,000 staff in CU(UK) when, in February 1998, a merger was announced with another UK insurer, General Accident (GA). This merger was realised in June 1998, to form Commercial and General Union (CGU). Thereafter, attention was diverted from the PDP scheme to more pressing concerns of creating new structures and roles, and implementing a voluntary redundancy scheme.

Processes

The company's approach to the project:

- Initial research was carried out to find out what had worked elsewhere.
- Leading outside consultants were brought in to challenge thinking and assist in development of workshop design, workbooks and video.
- There was close liaison with other HR system developments, especially an emerging competency framework, IiP and a performance management system.
- Communication with stakeholders in the business was important during the development of the process.
- Champions were sought at each of the company sites, and they were trained in PDP principles and practices, and briefed in how to train managers in supporting the PDP process.
- Champions trained the managers at their site in how to support staff in preparing PDPs.
- Managers worked with their staff in supporting the development of their PDPs.
- Staff worked on developing and implementing their own PDPs.

Workbooks were produced for the workshops, outlining the process and the format for a PDP. A video was produced describing CU staff's reactions to such a process. It showed endorsement of PDPs by senior managers.

The stages in the PDP process described in the staff's 'Guide to personal development planning' were:

- Identify your 'here and now' needs – from the performance management system and from feedback from others.
- Develop for future business needs – from the competency framework, from expected role changes within BPTW, from business changes in CU, and from personal awareness of changes in business.
- Set goals based on recognising past success, get in touch with your own dream for your development, and identify an extraordinarily realistic self-image.
- Create your own plan, with prioritised needs, development goals and development actions.
- 'Do it and review it', including logging learning and learning from experience. They were given a checklist for a personal development review.

Outcomes

All the above processes had taken place for the vast majority of CU(UK) staff before the merger with GA was confirmed. Plans had been made for embedding the scheme and ensuring its continuation over subsequent years. However, these plans were put on hold in the flurry of activity surrounding the merger.

Informal soundings of HR staff involved in supporting staff through the changes necessitated by the merger indicate that ex-CU staff may have been better equipped to make choices for themselves and for the new CGU Insurance.

It is difficult to evaluate the absolute success of the PDP programme, as it was never intended to be a discrete product, but was part of a wider (BPTW) process of change. However all three sets of workshops were very well received, and managers' workshops had an average rating of 3.25 on a scale of 1–4, where 3 = Well and 4 = Very well, in response to a range of questions asked. The staff workshops had average ratings of 3.40.

Typical comments about the workshops were:

'Interesting and well presented'

'Whilst enjoyable – a long day, lots to take in'

'Enjoyable, fun – but could have been condensed slightly'

'Facilitators assisting and guiding during activities was helpful'

'Overall a good course. Showed the importance of PDPs. Ran in a relaxed manner with plenty of activities. Plenty of motivation'

'We managers need more help in ensuring that expectations are not raised too high'

'Interesting – not as boring as I thought it would be'

'Good variety of activities and facilitator participation'

'Nice to know that CU is committed to the development of staff'

'Useful to apply in my private life'

Questions

1. Which approach to ED is this employer using ?

2. Which concern seems uppermost in this example: knowledge development, skills development or EVA development ?

3. In what ways does the example reflect a use of the three sectors: internal ED, adoption of public initiatives and use of external providers/partners ?

4. Do the evaluation findings suggest that this ED initiative achieved the objectives the company had in mind ?

5. What else might you want to evaluate to analyse the efficiency and the effectiveness of this ED initiative ?

External training providers

Stephen Gibb and David Megginson

The effectiveness of ED overall depends in large part on the effectiveness of private providers. Private training providers work in a very fragmented industry, supporting a large number of training providers, which range from sole practitioners to some very large training companies. Estimates of the number of private providers vary. There appear to be around 400 principal training organisations in the UK, with many more organisations, companies, partnerships and sole practitioners which provide training. The number of value-added tax (VAT)-based enterprises listed as training providers totals 4,475 (Keynote, 1998). In addition, there are many smaller training providers who escape VAT categorisation, either because their turnover is too low or because their main business is not in training. According to the Association for Management Education and Development (AMED), there are around 10,000 independent trainers. The majority of providers fall into the categories shown below.

- **Independent, commercially run training companies** – there seem to be around 400 of these in the UK, including some long-established firms.
- **Professional/institutional bodies** – most professional bodies offer some form of training, which often complements their role as accreditation bodies. Examples include the Institute of Personnel and Development, the Chartered Institute of Marketing, and the Institute of Directors.
- **Business schools/universities** – there are over 100 training providers in this category. Business schools and universities are now heavily promoted as centres of vocational learning and training.
- **Colleges of further education** – supplying mainly vocational training.
- **Product/service companies**; for example computer companies who provide training along with hardware and software purchases.
- **Open learning providers** – there are many examples, including, of course, the Open University. The uptake of multimedia and internet systems means many open learning providers are leading the way in technological developments.
- **Sole practitioners** – many ex-company in-house trainers set themselves up as independent trainers. They may work totally independently, in collaboration with other sole practitioners, or as subcontractors of training companies.
- **Management consultancies** – some consultancies offer training, although this tends to form only a small part of their activities.

Being able to tailor a course to a company's needs is obviously of primary importance for external training providers (The Industrial Society, 1998). Training companies are increasingly offering 'tailored' courses rather than off-the-shelf options. Quality and perceived value for money are also seen to be extremely important. For an employer it is argued that price is less important (i.e. differentials between one training company and another) than the company's image and professionalism. The need for a course to be 'locally' based is no longer a consideration for most companies; the quality and subject matter are the main determinants. Even the location of local colleges and universities as external partners is less important, in view of the availability of distance learning and internet technologies. This opens up the market for the provision of ED on a global basis; providing both a threat and opportunity to private providers of ED in the UK.

The most popular choice of external partner for employers is a private sector trainer, followed by an educational institution, a professional association/institute or a non-profit making training body (Table 5.7).

Table 5.7: External training providers – percentage of organisations using each source

Type of training provider	1997	1998
Private sector trainers/providers	73	78
University/college/other FE body	56	68
Professional association/institute	45	55
Non-profit-making training body (e.g. The Industrial Society)	51	48
Equipment supplier	32	33
Training and Enterprise Council/ Local Enterprise Council	25	24
Informal employers' network/club	10	10

Note: FE – further education

Source: The Industrial Society, Training Trends, May/June 1998

Around a third of all training still takes place at an employer's workplace or training centre. This proportion is likely to rise as employers increase the amount of in-house training that they purchase. Further education and technical colleges are also important sites of learning, as are adult education centres and universities. Educational/academic institutions are becoming more important as sources and places of training. Figure 5.2 shows the main location of face-to-face teaching for all taught learning episodes in England and Wales during 1997 (DfEE: *Labour Market Trends*, 1998).

With only a few exceptions, private suppliers and partners are wholly UK-owned and UK-staffed. Arguably, this is because the involvement of foreign companies is problematic in the context of the specific needs of the workforce skills, knowledge and values within a nation or region. Moreover, the educational and cultural framework of each country is different, and this is reflected in training approaches and

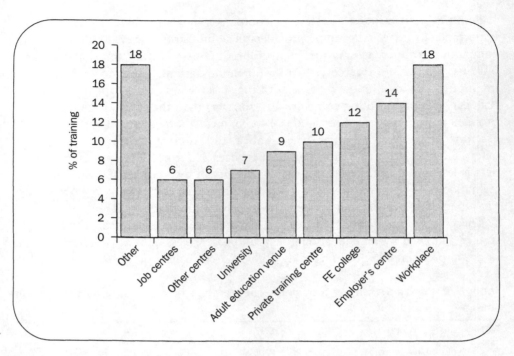

Figure 5.2 Venues for training

content. Management practice and style also vary from one country to another, as indeed does HRM practice. As a result, ED tends to be indigenous to each country. Partnerships between organisations in different parts of Europe may emerge with further Europeanisation, and harmonisation in economic and social matters.

The major exception at the moment to this national specialisation is the development of 'European managers' by some of the multinational companies. However, this type of training tends to be influenced by the corporate style emanating from the company headquarters, which, in some cases, is still culturally oriented towards one country. There is also the traditional 'North American' influence on much personal and management development. As Europe becomes more integrated, there are likely to be increased calls for some kind of mechanism by which qualifications in one country can be equated with those of another. The first step towards this is the Europass, a passport-type document which will contain details of the owner's training and the government training schemes they have been on.

Questions

1. What are the advantages and disadvantages of using external training providers?
2. What factors explain the increasing use of external training providers in the UK?
3. What factors influence an organisation's choice of external training providers?

References to Chapter 5

Argyris, C. and Schön, D. (1978) *Organizational Learning*, Reading, Mass: Addison-Wesley.
Bloom, B.S. (ed) (1956) *Taxonomy of Educational Objectives: The Classification of Educational Goals: Handbook 1, Cognitive Domain*, New York: Longman.
Boyatzis, R. (1982) *The Competent Manager*, New York: Wiley.
Boydell, T., Leary, M., Megginson, D. and Pedler, M. (1991) *Developing the Developers*, London: AMED.
Blackler, F. (1995) 'Knowledge, knowledge work and organizations', *Organization Studies*, 16(6): 1021–46.
CBI (1998) *Employment Trends*, London: CBI.
Crouch, C., Finegold, D., Sako, M. (1999) 'Are skills the answer? The political economy of skill creation in advanced industrial countries', Oxford: Oxford University Press.
Davenport, T. and Prusak, L.(1998) *Working Knowledge*, Boston, Mass: Harvard Business School.
DfEE (1995) 'Length of training courses', *Employment Gazette*, 103 (7): 37.
DfEE (1996) *Labour Force Survey*, London: DfEE.
DfEE (1998a) *The Learning Age: a New Renaissance for a New Britain*, London: DfEE.
DfEE (1998b) *Labour Market Trends*, London: DfEE.
DfEE (1998c) *National Learning Targets for England 2002*, London: DfEE.
Easterby-Smith, M., Burgoyne, J., Avaujo, L. (eds) (1999) *Organizational Learning and the Learning Organization*, London: Sage.
ESRC (1999) 'Twenty-Something in the 1990s', ESCR briefing.
Foster, J. (1999) 'Looking for balance', London: The National Work-Life Forum.
Gibb, S. (1999) 'The usefulness of theory: a case study in evaluating formal mentoring schemes', *Human Relations*, 52(8): 1055–75.
Goleman, D. (1996) *Emotional Intelligence: Why it can Matter More than IQ*, London: Bloomsbury.
Hamblett, J. and Holden, R. (2000) 'Employee-led development: another piece of left luggage?', *Personnel Review*, 29(4): 509–20.
Hutton, W. (1995) *The State We're In*, London: Jonathan Cape.
Industrial Society (1998) *Training Trends*, May/June, London: Industrial Society
IPD (1997) *Making Training Pay*, London: IPD/IiP.
IPD (1999) *Training and Development in Britain 1999*, London: IPD.
Johnson, P. and Indvik, J. (1999) 'Organizational benefits of having emotionally intelligent managers and employees', *Journal of Workplace Learning*, 11(3): 84–88
Kellaway, L. (2000) *Sense and Nonsense in the Office*, London: FT/Prentice Hall.
Keynote (1998) *Training*, Keynote marketing report.
Megginson, D., Banfield, P. and Joy-Matthews, J. (1999) *Human Resource Development*, 2nd edition, London: Kogan Page.
Megginson, D. and Whitaker, V. (1996) *Cultivating Self-development*, London: IPD.
ONS (1996) *Social Trends*, London: HMSO.
Pedler, M., Burgoyne, J. and Boydell, T. (1991) *The Learning Company*, Maidenhead: McGraw-Hill,
Pickard, J. (1999) 'Keynote speakers', *People Management*, 5(11).
Pinker, S. (1997) *How the Mind Works*, London: Penguin.
Rokeach, M. (1970) *Beliefs, Attitudes and Values: A Theory of Organisation and Change*, San Francisco: Jossey-Bass.
Schön, D. (1987) *Educating the Reflective Practitioner*, San Francisco: Jossey-Bass.
Senge, P. (1990) *The Fifth Discipline*, London: Century.
Stewart, T. (1997) *Intellectual Capital*, London: Nicholas Brealey Publishing.
Tapscott, D. (1996) *The Digital Economy: Promise and Peril in the Age of Networked Intelligence*, New York: McGraw Hill.
Wickens, P. (1999) 'Values added', *People Management*, 5(10): 33–38.

TOPIC SUMMARY SHEET

What are the key learning points from this topic?

TOPIC 5 – TEAMS

Why study this topic?

Teams are a key feature of many organisations and it is very probable that most of us have either worked in a team before or will in the future. Teams are regarded as an effective way to achieve organisational goals, therefore it is important that we examine them in more depth.

This topic will allow you to understand how teams are formed and how they are used within organisations. Additionally, you will be able to explore the different structures and compositions they can have. Another important issue for you to consider is the role of the manager in this process, as this can also have a significant effect on the success of the team.

Blackboard

E-tivity 5: Teams

13 THE NATURE OF WORK GROUPS AND TEAMS

Groups and teams are a major feature of organisational life. The work organisation and its sub-units are made up of groups of people. Most activities of the organisation require at least some degree of co-ordination through the operation of groups and teamwork. An understanding of the nature of groups is vital if the manager is to influence the behaviour of people in the work situation. The manager must be aware of the impact of groups and teams, and their effects on organisational performance.

Photo: E. J. van Koningsveld/Red Arrows

There are more myths, more stereotypes, about groups and committees than about most subjects in organizations ... Groups there must be. Individuals must be co-ordinated and their skills and abilities meshed and merged. But let us not be mesmerized. Let us realize that a proper understanding of groups will demonstrate how difficult they are to manage. Let us pay more attention to their creation and be more realistic about their outcomes

Charles Handy
Understanding Organizations, Penguin Books (1993)

LEARNING OUTCOMES

After completing this chapter you should be able to:

▶ explain the meaning and importance of work groups and teams;

▶ distinguish between groups and teams, and between formal and informal groups;

▶ explain the main reasons for the formation of groups and teams;

▶ examine factors which influence group cohesiveness and performance;

▶ review the characteristics of an effective work group and assess the impact of technology;

▶ analyse the nature of role relationships and role conflict;

▶ evaluate the importance of groups and teams for effective organisational performance.

THE MEANING AND IMPORTANCE OF GROUPS AND TEAMS

Individuals seldom work in isolation from others. **Groups** are a characteristic of all social situations and almost everyone in an organisation will be a member of one or more groups. Work is a group-based activity and if the organisation is to function effectively it requires good teamwork. The working of groups and the influence they exert over their membership is an essential feature of human behaviour and of organisational performance. The manager must use groups in order to achieve a high standard of work and improve organisational effectiveness.

Definitions of a group

There are many possible ways of defining what is meant by a group. The essential feature of a group is that its members regard themselves as belonging to the group. Although there is no single, accepted definition, most people will readily understand what constitutes a group. A popular definition defines the group in psychological terms as:

> **any number of people who (1) interact with one another; (2) are psychologically aware of one another; and (3) perceive themselves to be a group.**[1]

Another useful way of defining a work group is a collection of people who share most, if not all, of the following characteristics:

- a definable membership;
- group consciousness;
- a sense of shared purpose;
- interdependence;
- interaction; and
- ability to act in a unitary manner.[2]

Essential feature of work organisations

Groups are an essential feature of the work pattern of any organisation. Members of a group must co-operate in order for work to be carried out, and managers themselves will work within these groups. People in groups influence each other in many ways and groups may develop their own hierarchies and leaders. Group pressures can have a major influence over the behaviour of individual members and their work performance. The activities of the group are associated with the process of leadership (discussed in Chapter 8). The style of leadership adopted by the manager has an important influence on the behaviour of members of the group.

The classical approach to organisation and management tended to ignore the importance of groups and the social factors at work. The ideas of people such as *F. W. Taylor* popularised the concept of the 'rabble hypothesis' and the assumption that people carried out their work, and could be motivated, as solitary individuals unaffected by others. The human relations approach, however, gave recognition to the work organisation as a social organisation and to the importance of the group, and group values and norms, in influencing behaviour at work.

THE DIFFERENCE BETWEEN GROUPS AND TEAMS

Whereas all teams are, by definition, groups it does not necessarily follow that all groups are teams. In common usage and literature, including to some extent in this book, there is however a tendency for the terms 'groups' and 'teams' to be used interchangeably. And it is not easy to distinguish clearly between a group and a team.[3] For example, *Crainer* refers to 'teamworking' as becoming highly fashionable in recent years. It is a side effect of increasing concentration on working across functional divides and fits neatly with the trend towards empowerment. However, despite the extensive literature about teams and teamworking, the basic dynamics of teamworking often remain clouded and uncertain.

> *Teams occur when a number of people have a common goal and recognize that their personal success is dependent on the success of others. They are all interdependent. In practice, this means that in most teams people will contribute individual skills many of which will be different. It also means that the full tensions and counter-balance of human behaviour will need to be demonstrated in the team.*[4]

According to *Holpp*, while many people are still paying homage to teams, teamwork, empowerment and self-management, others have become disillusioned. Holpp poses the question: what are teams? 'It's a simple enough question, but one that's seldom asked. We all think we know intuitively what teams are. Guess again. Here are some questions to help define team configurations.'

- Are teams going to be natural work groups, or project-and-task oriented?
- Will they be self-managed or directed?
- How many people will be on the teams; who's in charge?
- How will the teams fit into the organisation's structure if it shows only boxes and not circles or other new organisational forms?

Holpp also poses the question: why do you want teams? If teams are just a convenient way to group under one manager a lot of people who used to work for several downsized supervisors, don't bother. But if teams can truly take ownership of work areas and provide the kind of up-close knowledge that's unavailable elsewhere, then full speed ahead.[5]

Cane suggests that organisations are sometimes unsure whether they have teams or simply groups of people working together.

> *It is certainly true to say that any group of people who do not know they are a team cannot be one. To become a team, a group of individuals needs to have a strong common purpose and to work towards that purpose rather than individually. They need also to believe that they will achieve more by co-operation than working individually.*[6]

Teamwork a fashionable term

Belbin points out that to the extent that teamwork was becoming a fashionable term, it began to replace the more usual reference to groups and every activity was now being described as 'teamwork'. He questions whether it matters if one is talking about groups or teams and maintains that the confusion in vocabulary should be addressed if the principles of good teamwork are to be retained. Belbin suggests there are several factors that characterise the difference between groups and teams. (*See* Figure 13.1.) The best differentiator is size: groups can comprise any number of people but teams are smaller with a membership between (ideally) four and six. The quintessential feature of a small well-balanced team is that leadership is shared or rotates whereas large groups typically throw up solo leaders.[7]

While acknowledging the work of Belbin it appears that the term 'group' is often used in a more general sense and 'team' in a more specific context. We continue to refer to 'group' or 'team' according to the particular focus of attention and the vocabulary of the quoted authors.

	Team	Group
Size	Limited	Medium or Large
Selection	Crucial	Immaterial
Leadership	Shared or rotating	Solo
Perception	Mutual knowledge understanding	Focus on leader
Style	Role spread co-ordination	Convergence conformism
Spirit	Dynamic interaction	Togetherness persecution of opponents

Figure 13.1 Differences between a team and a group

(Reproduced with permission from R. Meredith Belbin, *Beyond the Team*, Butterworth-Heinemann, Division of Reed Educational and Professional Publishing Ltd, © 2000.)

GROUP VALUES AND NORMS

The power of group membership over individual behaviour and work performance was illustrated clearly in the famous Hawthorne experiments at the Western Electric Company in America,[8] already referred to in Chapter 3. A significant feature was the attention drawn to the importance and influence of group values and norms. One experiment involved the observation of a group of 14 men working in the bank wiring room. It may be remembered that the men formed their own sub-groups or cliques, with natural leaders emerging with the consent of the members. Despite a financial incentive scheme where workers could receive more money the more work they did, the group decided on 6000 units a day as a fair level of output. This was well below the level they were capable of producing. Group pressures on individual workers were stronger than financial incentives offered by management.

Informal social relations

The group developed its own pattern of informal social relations and codes and practices ('norms') of what constituted proper group behaviour.

- **Not to be a 'rate buster'** – not to produce at too high a rate of output compared with other members or to exceed the production restriction of the group.
- **Not to be a 'chiseller'** – not to shirk production or to produce at too low a rate of output compared with other members of the group.
- **Not to be a 'squealer'** – not to say anything to the supervisor or management which might be harmful to other members of the group.
- **Not to be 'officious'** – people with authority over members of the group, for example inspectors, should not take advantage of their seniority or maintain a social distance from the group.

The group had their own system of sanctions including sarcasm, damaging completed work, hiding tools, playing tricks on the inspectors, and ostracising those members who did not conform with the **group norms**. Threats of physical violence were also made, and the group developed a system of punishing offenders by 'binging' which involved striking someone a fairly hard blow on the upper part of the arm. This process of binging also became a recognised method of controlling conflict within the group.

According to *Riches*, one way to improve team performance is to establish agreed norms or rules for how the team is to operate and rigorously stick to them. Norms could address the obligations of individual members to the team, how it will assess its performance, how it will work together, what motivation systems will be used, how it will relate to customers, and the mechanisms to facilitate an honest exchange about the team norms and behaviour.[9]

A recent study from the *Economic & Social Research Council* draws attention to the importance of social norms among employees and questions whether employees are guided not only by monetary incentives but also by peer pressure towards social efficiency for the workers as a group. 'Intuitively, social norms among workers must be important if they work in teams where bonuses are dependent on group, rather than individual effort.'[10] (You may see some similarity here with the Bank Wiring Room experiment, discussed above.)

A 'summary outline' of group norms is presented in Figure 13.2 on p. 522.

THE IMPORTANCE OF TEAMWORK

How people behave and perform as members of a group is as important as their behaviour or performance as individuals. Not only must members of a group work well as a team but each group must also work well with other groups. Harmonious working relationships and good teamwork help make for a high level of staff morale and work performance. Effective teamwork is an essential element of modern management practices such as empowerment, quality circles and total quality management, and how groups manage change. Teamwork is important in any organisation but may be especially significant in service industries, such as hospitality organisations where there is a direct effect on customer satisfaction.[11]

According to ACAS (the Arbitration, Conciliation and Advisory Service), teams have been around for as long as anyone can remember and there can be few organisations that have not used the term in one sense or another. In a general sense, people talk of teamwork when they want to emphasise the virtues of co-operation and the need to make use of the various strengths of employees. Using the term more specifically, teamworking involves a reorganisation of the way work is carried out. Teamwork can increase competitiveness by:

- improving productivity;
- improving quality and encouraging innovation;
- taking advantage of the opportunities provided by technological advances;
- improving employee motivation and commitment.[12]

An account of teamwork in a small (40-person) company is given in Management in Action 13.1.

The general movement towards flatter structures of organisation, wider spans of control and reducing layers of middle management, together with increasing empowerment of employees, all involve greater emphasis on the importance of effective teamworking. 'There's no doubt that effective teamwork is crucial to an organisation's efforts to perform better, faster and more profitably than their competitors.'[13]

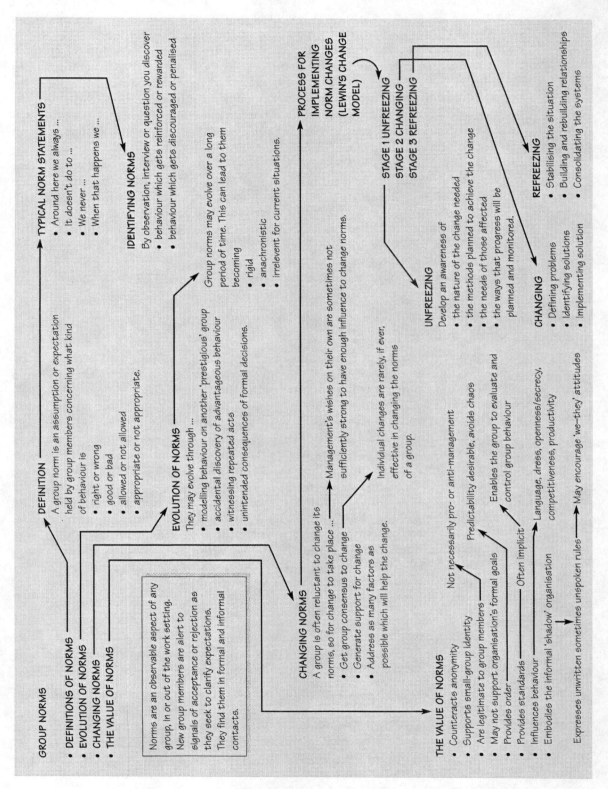

Figure 13.2 Summary outline of group norms

(Reproduced with permission of Training Learning Consultancy Ltd, Bristol.)

Skills of effective teamworking

From a recent study of Europe's top companies, *Heller* refers to the need for new managers and new methods, and includes as a key strategy for a new breed of managers in a dramatically changed environment: 'making team-working work – the new, indispensable skill'.[14] The nature and importance of teamwork is discussed further in Chapter 14.

> All of us know in our hearts that the ideal individual for a given job cannot be found ... but if no individual can combine all the necessary qualities of a good manager, a team of individuals certainly can – and often does. Moreover, the whole team is unlikely to step under a bus simultaneously. This is why it is not the individual but the team that is the instrument of sustained and enduring success in management.
>
> **Antony Jay[15]**

> A successful climbing team involves using management skills essential to any organisation ... The basic planning is the foundation on which the eventual outcome will be decided. Even if it is the concept of a single person, very quickly more and more people must become involved, and this is where teamwork and leadership begin.
>
> **Sir Chris Bonington[16]**

According to *Guirdham*, the growth of teamwork has led to the increased interest in interface skills at work.

> *More and more tasks of contemporary organisations, particularly those in high technology and service businesses, require teamwork. Taskforces, project teams and committees are key elements in the modern workplace. Teamwork depends not just on technical competence of the individuals composing the team, but on their ability to 'gel'. To work well together, the team members must have more than just team spirit. They also need collaborative skills – they must be able to support one another and to handle conflict in such a way that it becomes constructive rather than destructive.*[17]

A similar point is made by *Ashmos and Nathan*: 'The use of teams has expanded dramatically in response to competitive challenges. In fact, one of the most common skills required by new work practices is the ability to work as a team.'[18]

Happy teams at Heineken

Included in a study of top European companies and 'making teamwork work', Heller refers to the happy teams at Heineken. Part of the cultural strength of Heineken is a realisation that: 'the best culture for an organisation is a team culture'; and that 'any large organization is a team of teams – and people who have to work together as a team must also think together as a team'.[19] Heller also lists Heineken's manifesto for 'professional team-thinking' (*see* Figure 13.3) and maintains that 'Arguing with any of these eleven points is absurd'.

1   The aim is to reach the best decision, not just a hasty conclusion or an easy consensus. The team leader always has the ultimate responsibility for the quality of the decision taken – and therefore, for the quality of the team-thinking effort that has led up to the decision.

2   To produce the best professional team-thinking, the team leader must ensure that ego-trips, petty office politics and not-invented-here rigidity are explicitly avoided. There should be competition between ideas – not between individual members of the team.

3   The team-thinking effort must first ensure that the best question to be answered is clearly and completely formulated.

4   The team-thinking process is iterative – not linear. Therefore, the question may have to be altered later and the process repeated.

5   The team leader is responsible for seeing that sufficient alternatives and their predicted consequences have been developed for evaluation by the team.

6   The team leader will thus ask 'what are our alternatives?' – and not just 'what is the answer?'

7   The team leader also recognizes that it is wiser to seek and listen to the ideas of the team before expressing his or her own ideas and preferences.

8   In any professional team-thinking effort, more ideas will have to be created than used. But any idea that is rejected will be rejected with courtesy and with a clear explanation as to why it is being rejected. To behave in this way is not naive, it is just decent and smart.

9   A risk/reward equation and a probability of success calculation will be made explicitly before any important decision is taken.

10 Once a decision is made professionally, the team must implement it professionally.

11 When you think, think. When you act, act.

Figure 13.3 Manifesto for professional team-thinking at Heineken

(Reproduced with permission from Robert Heller, *In Search of European Excellence*, HarperCollins Business © 1997, p. 231.)

EXHIBIT 13.1   FT

Teamwork's own goal

There are limitations to the application of teamwork methods in the workplace writes **Victoria Griffith**.

Teamwork has become a buzzword of 1990s' management theory. By grouping employees into problem-solving taskforces, say the theorists, companies will empower workers, create cross-departmental fertilisation, and level ineffective hierarchies.

Yet executives know that, in reality, teams and taskforces do not always produce the desired results. Part of the problem may lie with the way teams are organised. Members may fail to work well together for several reasons, from lack of a sense of humour to clashing goals.

Academics in the US have been studying team dynamics to try to identify problems.

Too much emphasis on harmony
Teams probably work best when there is room for disagreement. Michael Beer, a professor at Harvard Business School, says: 'Team leaders often discourage discord

because they fear it will split the team.' He studied teams at Becton Dickinson, the medical equipment group, in the 1980s, and found that efforts to paper over differences sometimes led to bland recommendations by taskforces.

One working group at the company, for example, said the division's overall strategic objective was 'fortifying our quality, product cost, and market share strengths, while also transforming the industry through expanded customer knowledge and product/service innovation'. The group, says Beer, offered no organisation guidance as to which factor was more important and why.

Too much discord
Excessive tension can also destroy team effectiveness. A study published in the *Harvard Business Review* in June 1997 found that corporate team members disagreed less and were more productive when everyone had access to

up-to-date information. Conflict arising from misinformation tended to escalate into interpersonal resentment.

Jean Kahwajy, a management consultant with the California-based Strategic Decision Group and an author of the *HBR* study, says: 'Nasty fights mean there will be too much politicking and wasted time.' The study recommended that team members prepare for meetings by focusing on the facts. All members should have detailed knowledge of the issues at hand and work with the same information.

An emphasis on individualism

Teams failed to deliver desired results at Apple Computer in the 1980s, says Beer, because of the emphasis the company placed early in its existence on individualism. While individual creativity served the company well in its initial phase, growth heightened the need for communication between employees.

Workers were assigned to cross-functional teams to set corporate strategy. It did not work, according to Beer, and the failure of Apple's research and development, marketing and manufacturing departments to work together undermined the corporation. 'When the dominant culture stresses the value of individual achievement and accountability, rather than collective accomplishment, team structures won't be effective,' he says.

Even companies that value collective efforts may undermine teams by basing salaries and promotion more on individual than on collective accomplishments. 'Unless the team's success is important to the employees' career, they probably won't pay much attention to it,' says Kahwajy.

A feeling of powerlessness

To work well, teams must be able to influence decisions. Jay Bourgeois, a professor at the University of Virginia's business school and co-author of the recent *HBR* article, says: 'The team that has no power ends up writing a meaningless memo. You can only do that so many times before your workers decide it's not worthwhile.' Empowerment can help convince reluctant members of the importance of a project. When Unifi, a company that guarantees fax delivery, asked employees to form a team to set out Internet strategy, initial reluctance was eventually overcome when it was made clear that the group was helping to form corporate strategy.

The failure of senior management to work well together

This creates problems because team members may walk into meetings with different priorities. 'Teams can't sort out problems that have been created at a higher level,' says Beer. 'Members can be expected to be loyal to their bosses, and if their bosses have very different priorities, there will be little common ground.'

Meeting-itis

Teams should not try to do everything together. Excessive time spent in meetings not only means wasted hours, it also means the group will be exposed to less diversity of thought. 'If everyone goes in with prepared thoughts and ideas, developed on their own, discussion will be lively, and the group will have more options,' says Kahwajy. 'If everything is done together, a couple of lead people may end up running the show.' Kahwajy warns that too much homogeneity in teams can also stifle creativity.

Seeing teams as the solution for all problems

Bourgeois says he is working with a corporation that expects its country managers – who are scattered all over the world – to work as a team. 'They have very little contact and they don't share the same goal, except in the very vague sense of serving the same corporation,' says Bourgeois. 'It's silly to see them as a team.' Moreover, there are probably some tasks that are more readily accomplished by individuals, rather than groups. 'You probably don't want to have a group decision when you're landing an aircraft at Heathrow,' he says. 'Sometimes a project is best carried out by a single person.'

(Reproduced with permission from the Financial Times Limited, © *Financial Times*)

FORMAL AND INFORMAL GROUPS

Groups are deliberately planned and created by management as part of the formal organisation structure. However, groups will also arise from social processes and the informal organisation which was discussed in Chapter 4. The informal organisation arises from the interaction of people working within the organisation and the development of groups with their own relationships and norms of behaviour, irrespective of those defined within the formal structure. This leads to a major distinction between formal and informal groups.

Formal groups Groups are formed as a consequence of the pattern of organisation structure and arrangements for the division of work, for example the grouping together of common activities into sections. Groups may result from the nature of technology employed and the way in which work is carried out, for example the bringing together of a number of people to carry out a sequence of operations on an assembly line. Groups may also develop when a number of people of the same level or status within the organisation see themselves as a group, for example departmental heads of an industrial organisation, or chief officers of a local authority. **Formal groups** are created to achieve specific organisational objectives and are concerned with the **co-ordination of work activities**. People are brought together on the basis of defined roles within the structure of the organisation. The nature of the tasks to be undertaken is a predominant feature of the formal group. Goals are identified by management, and certain rules, relationships and norms of behaviour established.

Formal groups tend to be relatively permanent, although there may be changes in actual membership. However, temporary formal groups may also be created by management, for example the use of project teams in a matrix organisation. Formal work groups can be differentiated in a number of ways, for example on the basis of membership, the task to be performed, the nature of technology, or position within the organisation structure.

Informal groups

Within the formal structure of the organisation there will always be an informal structure. The formal structure of the organisation, and system of role relationships, rules and procedures, will be augmented by interpretation and development at the informal level. **Informal groups** are based more on personal relationships and agreement of group members than on defined role relationships. They serve to satisfy psychological and social needs not related necessarily to the tasks to be undertaken. Groups may devise ways of attempting to satisfy members' affiliation and other social motivations which are lacking in the work situation, especially in industrial organisations.

The membership of informal groups can cut across the formal structure. They may comprise individuals from different parts of the organisation and/or from different levels of the organisation, both vertically and diagonally, as well as from the same horizontal level. An informal group could also be the same as the formal group, or it might comprise a part only of the formal group. (*See* Figure 13.4.) The members of an informal group may appoint their own leader who exercises authority by the consent of the members themselves. The informal leader may be chosen as the person who reflects the attitudes and values of the members, helps to resolve conflict, leads the group in satisfying its goals, or liaises with management or other people outside the group. The informal leader may often change according to the particular situation facing the group. Although not usually the case, it is possible for the informal leader to be the same person as the formal leader appointed officially by management.

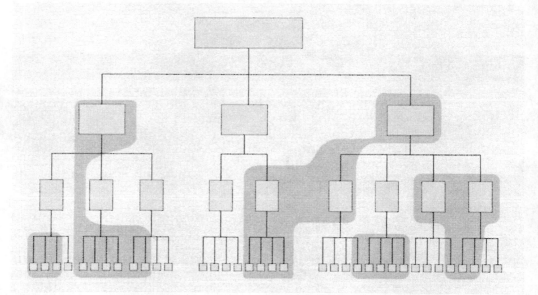

Figure 13.4 Examples of informal groups within the formal structure of an organisation

Major functions of informal groups

Lysons suggests four main reasons for informal groups.

- **The perpetuation of the informal group 'culture'**. Culture in this context means a set of values, norms and beliefs which form a guide to group acceptance and group behaviour. Unless you broadly subscribe to the group culture, you will not belong and be an 'outsider' or 'isolate'.

- **The maintenance of a communication system**. Groups want all the information that affects their welfare, either negatively or positively. If groups are not apprised of policies and motives behind actions, they will seek to tap into formal communication channels and spread information among group members.

- **The implementation of social control**. Conformity to group culture is enforced by such techniques as ridicule, ostracism and violence. This is illustrated, for example, by the enforcement of group norms in the Bank Wiring Room discussed above.

- **The provision of interest and fun in work life**. Many jobs are monotonous and fail to hold the attention of the workers. Work may also offer few future prospects. Workers may try to compensate by interpersonal relations provided by the group and in such activities as time wasting by talking, gambling, practical joking and drinking.[20]

An example of informal groups

A lack of direction and clear information flow within the formal structure can give rise to uncertainty and suspicion. In the absence of specific knowledge, the grapevine takes on an important role, rumours start and the informal part of the organisation is highlighted, often with negative results. A typical example concerned an industrial organisation which was in a highly competitive market and was experiencing a drop in sales. Two top managers had suddenly lost their jobs without any explanation to members of staff and there were board meetings seemingly every other day. Although there was no specific information or statements from top management the general feeling among the staff was that whatever was about to happen it was most unlikely to be good news.

At lunchtime three junior members of staff, one female and two male, each from different departments, were having a chat. With a half smile the female member said to the others that she could well be seeing a lot more of both or at least one of them before long. She said that she had heard, unofficially, from her manager that the department was about to be awarded a very profitable order. She surmised that the other departments, which she had also heard had lost their parts of the same contracts and not had many orders recently, would have to integrate into the successful department with the possible loss of certain jobs. The other two members both believed this and talked about it within their own departments as if it were a fact. The result? Even more uncertainty throughout the organisation, increased gloom and distraction from the task. In fact, no such integration did take place, only a minor restructuring of the organisation with no direct loss of jobs other than through voluntary early retirement. However, it proved very difficult for top management to effectively quash the rumour and restore trust and morale.

REASONS FOR FORMATION OF GROUPS OR TEAMS

Individuals will form into groups or teams, both formal and informal, for a number of different reasons relating to both work performance and social processes.

- **Certain tasks can be performed only through the combined efforts of a number of individuals working together**. The variety of experience and expertise among members provides a synergetic effect which can be applied to the increasingly complex problems of modern organisations.

- **Collusion between members** in order to modify formal working arrangements more to their liking – for example, by sharing or rotating unpopular tasks. Membership therefore provides the individual with opportunities for initiative and creativity.
- **Companionship and a source of mutual understanding and support from colleagues.** This can help in solving work problems, and also to militate against stressful or demanding working conditions.
- **Membership provides the individual with a sense of belonging.** It provides a feeling of identity, and the chance to acquire role recognition and status within the group or team.
- **Guidelines on generally acceptable behaviour.** It helps to clarify ambiguous situations such as, for example, the extent to which official rules and regulations are expected to be adhered to in practice, the rules of the game, and what is seen as the correct actual behaviour. The informal organisation may put pressure on members to resist demands from management on such matters as, for example, higher output or changes in working methods. Allegiance to the group or team can serve as a means of control over individual behaviour and discipline individuals who contravene the norms – for example, the process of 'binging' in the bank wiring room, mentioned above.
- **Protection for its membership.** Group or team members collaborate to protect their interests from outside pressures or threats.

Expectations of group membership

Individuals have varying expectations of the benefits from group membership. Groups are a potential source of motivation and of job satisfaction, and also a major determinant of effective organisational performance. However, working in groups may mean that members spend too much time talking among themselves rather than doing. Groups may also compete against each other in a non-productive manner. It is a question of balance. It is important, therefore, that the manager understands the reasons for the formation of groups and is able to recognise likely advantageous or adverse consequences for the organisation.

GROUP COHESIVENESS AND PERFORMANCE

Social interaction is a natural feature of human behaviour but ensuring harmonious working relationships and effective teamwork is not an easy task. The manager's main concern is that members of a work group co-operate in order to achieve the results expected of them. Although there are potential disadvantages of cohesive groups (discussed below) they may result in greater interaction between members, mutual help and social satisfaction, lower turnover and absenteeism, and often higher production.[21] Co-operation among members is likely to be greater in a united, cohesive group. Membership of a cohesive group can be a rewarding experience for the individual, can contribute to the promotion of morale, and aid the release of creativity and energy. Members of a high-morale group are more likely to think of themselves as a group and work together effectively. **Strong and cohesive work groups can, therefore, have beneficial effects for the organisation.**

Factors affecting cohesiveness

In order to develop the effectiveness of work groups the manager will be concerned with those factors that contribute to group cohesiveness, or that may cause frustration or disruption to the operation of the group. The manager needs to consider, therefore, both the needs of individual members of staff, and the promotion of a high level of group identity and cohesion. There are many factors which affect **group cohesiveness** and performance, which can be summarised under four broad headings, as shown in Figure 13.5.

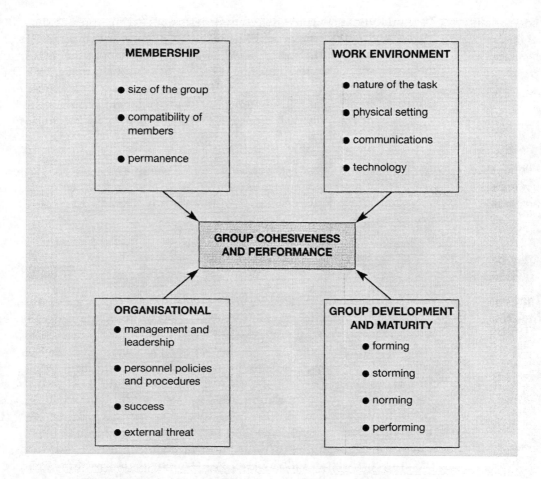

Figure 13.5 Factors contributing to group cohesiveness and performance

MEMBERSHIP

**Size of
the group**

As a group increases in size, problems arise with communications and co-ordination. Large groups are more difficult to handle and require a higher level of supervision. Absenteeism also tends to be higher in larger groups. When a group becomes too large it may split into smaller units and friction may develop between the sub-groups.

It is difficult to put a precise figure on the ideal size of a work group and there are many conflicting studies and reports. Much will depend upon other variables, but it seems to be generally accepted that cohesiveness becomes more difficult to achieve when a group exceeds 10–12 members.[22] Beyond this size the group tends to split into sub-groups. A figure of between five and seven is often quoted as an apparent optimum size for full participation within the group.[23] Many readers will be familiar with the classic 1957 movie *Twelve Angry Men* in which one juror persuades the other 11 to change their minds over a murder verdict. This drew attention to a range of intra-group conflicts and the difficulty in groups of more than 10 people reaching consensus.

Cane asks the question: how many people should be in a team?

The answers from different organizations as to what is the perfect number vary from between four and fifteen depending on a whole range of variables. Fifteen is about the maximum number of people anyone can communicate with without having to raise their voice significantly and any less than four has a restriction in the amount of creativity and variety that can be produced. It is interesting to note that these figures range between the maximum and minimum numbers of sports teams – perhaps less of a coincidence than it seems.[24]

Compatibility of the members

The more homogeneous the group in terms of such features as shared backgrounds, interests, attitudes and values of its members, the easier it is usually to promote cohesiveness. Variations in other individual differences, such as the personality or skills of members, may serve to complement each other and help make for a cohesive group. On the other hand, such differences may be the cause of disruption and conflict. Conflict can also arise in a homogeneous group where members are in competition with each other. Individual incentive payment schemes, for example, may be a source of conflict.

Permanence of group members

Group spirit and relationships take time to develop. Cohesiveness is more likely when members of a group are together for a reasonable length of time, and changes occur only slowly. A frequent turnover of members is likely to have an adverse effect on morale, and on the cohesiveness of the group.

WORK ENVIRONMENT

The nature of the task

Where workers are involved in similar work, share a common task, or face the same problems, this may assist cohesiveness. The nature of the task may serve to bring people together when it is necessary for them to communicate and interact regularly with each other in the performance of their duties – for example, members of a research and development team. Even if members of a group normally work at different locations they may still experience a feeling of cohesiveness if the nature of the task requires frequent communication and interaction – for example, security guards patrolling separate areas who need to check with each other on a regular basis. However, where the task demands a series of relatively separate operations or discrete activities – for example, on a machine-paced assembly line – it is more difficult to develop cohesiveness. Individuals may have interactions with colleagues on either side of them but little opportunity to develop a common group feeling.

Physical setting

Where members of a group work in the same location or in close physical proximity to each other this will generally help cohesiveness. However, this is not always the case. For example, in large open-plan offices staff often tend to segregate themselves from colleagues and create barriers by the strategic siting of such items as filing cabinets, bookcases or indoor plants. The size of the office and the number of staff in it are, of course, important considerations in this case. Isolation from other groups of workers will also tend to build cohesiveness. This often applies, for example, to a smaller number of workers on a night shift.

Communications

The more easily members can communicate freely with each other, the greater the likelihood of group cohesiveness. Communications are affected by the work environment, by the nature of the task, and by technology. For example, difficulties in communication can arise with production systems where workers are stationed continuously at a particular point with limited freedom of movement. Even when opportunities exist for interaction with colleagues, physical conditions may limit effective communication. For example, the technological layout and high level of noise with some assembly line work can limit contact between workers. Restrictions on opportunities for social interaction can hamper internal group unity.

Technology

We can see that the nature of technology and the manner in which work is carried out has an important effect on cohesiveness, and relates closely to the nature of the task, physical setting and communications. Where the nature of the work process involves a craft or skill-based 'technology' there is a higher likelihood of group cohesiveness.

However, as mentioned earlier, with machine-paced assembly line work it is more difficult to develop cohesiveness. Technology also has wider implications for the operation and behaviour of groups and therefore is considered in a separate section later.

ORGANISATIONAL FACTORS

Management and leadership
The activities of groups cannot be separated from management and the process of leadership. The form of management and style of leadership adopted will influence the relationship between the group and the organisation, and is a major determinant of group cohesiveness. In general terms, cohesiveness will be affected by such things as the manner in which the manager gives guidance and encouragement to the group, offers help and support, provides opportunities for participation, attempts to resolve conflicts, and gives attention to both employee relations and task problems. *McKenna and Maister* draw attention to the importance of the group leader establishing a level of trust among the group by helping them understand the behaviours that build trust. 'The job of the group leader is to encourage people to earn the trust of others in their group and then show them how it can translate into greater commitment, greater creativity, greater professional satisfaction, and better performance.'[25]

Personnel policies and procedures
Harmony and cohesiveness within the group are more likely to be achieved if personnel policies and procedures are well developed, and perceived to be equitable with fair treatment for all members. Attention should be given to the effects that appraisal systems, discipline, promotion and rewards, and opportunities for personal development have on members of the group.

Success
The more successful the group, the more cohesive it is likely to be; and cohesive groups are more likely to be successful. Success is usually a strong motivational influence on the level of work performance. Success or reward as a positive motivator can be perceived by group members in a number of ways. For example, the satisfactory completion of a task through co-operative action; praise from management; a feeling of high status; achievement in competition with other groups; benefits gained, such as high wage payments from a group bonus incentive scheme.

External threat
Cohesiveness may be enhanced by members co-operating with one another when faced with a common external threat, such as changes in their method of work, or the appointment of a new manager. Even if the threat is subsequently removed, the group may still continue to have a greater degree of cohesiveness than before the threat arose. Conflict between groups will also tend to increase the cohesiveness of each group and the boundaries of the group become drawn more clearly.

GROUP DEVELOPMENT AND MATURITY

The degree of cohesiveness is affected also by the manner in which groups progress through the various stages of development and maturity before getting down to the real tasks in hand. This process can take time and is often traumatic for the members. *Bass and Ryterband* identify four distinct stages in group development:

- mutual acceptance and membership;
- communication and decision-making;
- motivation and productivity; and
- control and organisation.[26]

An alternative, and more popular, model by *Tuckman* also identifies four main successive stages of group development and relationships: **forming**, **storming**, **norming** and **performing**.[27]

- **Stage 1 – forming**. The initial formation of the group and the bringing together of a number of individuals who identify, tentatively, the purpose of the group, its composition and terms of reference. At this stage consideration is given to hierarchical structure of the group, pattern of leadership, individual roles and responsibilities, and codes of conduct. There is likely to be considerable anxiety as members attempt to create an impression, to test each other, and to establish their personal identity within the group.
- **Stage 2 – storming**. As members of the group get to know each other better they will put forward their views more openly and forcefully. Disagreements will be expressed and challenges offered on the nature of the task and arrangements made in the earlier stage of development. This may lead to conflict and hostility. The storming stage is important because, if successful, there will be discussions on reforming arrangements for the working and operation of the group, and agreement on more meaningful structures and procedures.
- **Stage 3 – norming**. As conflict and hostility start to be controlled members of the group will establish guidelines and standards, and develop their own norms of acceptable behaviour. The norming stage is important in establishing the need for members to co-operate in order to plan, agree standards of performance and fulfil the purpose of the group. This co-operation and adherence to group norms can work against effective organisational performance. It may be remembered, for example, that, in the bank wiring room experiment of the Hawthorne studies, group norms imposed a restriction on the level of output of the workers.
- **Stage 4 – performing**. When the group has progressed successfully through the three earlier stages of development it will have created structure and cohesiveness to work effectively as a team. At this stage the group can concentrate on the attainment of its purpose and performance of the common task is likely to be at its most effective.

Another writer suggests that new groups go through the following stages:

- the polite stage;
- the why are we here, what are we doing stage?
- the power stage, which dominant will emerge?
- the constructive stage when sharing begins; and
- the unity stage – this often takes weeks, eating together, talking together.[28]

POTENTIAL DISADVANTAGES OF STRONG, COHESIVE GROUPS

If the manager is to develop effective work groups then attention should be given to those factors which influence the creation of group identity and cohesiveness. However, strong and cohesive groups also present potential disadvantages for management. Cohesive groups do not necessarily produce a higher level of output. Performance varies with the extent to which the group accepts or rejects the goals of the organisation. Furthermore, with a very high level of cohesiveness and attention to social activities, there may even be a fall in output. The level of production is likely to conform to a standard acceptable as a norm by the group and may result in maintaining either a high or a restricted level of output.[29]

Individual differences in personality mean that people make a contribution to the work of the organisation in different ways and this influences the extent to which they wish to be committed to a group or team culture. For example, as *Green* points out:

'Some people find teamwork contrary to their normal style and are embarrassed; some are probably marginalised.'[30]

People also have a greater or lesser need for personal space and their own sense of individual identity.

> Everyone had at least a handful of items they preferred to keep private: love letters, photographs, mementoes, a personal journal, whatever. Nothing shameful was likely to be hidden in the lockers ... The purpose of the lockers was merely to maintain a totally personal space as a way to preserve each person's necessary sense of identity in a claustrophobic and communal environment where, in time, it was easy to feel absorbed into a group identity and thereby become psychologically disassociated and quietly depressed.
>
> Dean Koontz[31]

Once a group has become fully developed and created cohesiveness, it is more difficult for the manager successfully to change the attitudes and behaviour of the group. It is important that the manager should attempt to influence the group during the norming stage when members are establishing guidelines and standards, and their own norms of acceptable behaviour. When a group has become fully developed and established its own culture it is more difficult to change the attitudes and behaviour of its members.

Inter-group conflict

Strong, cohesive groups may develop a critical or even hostile attitude towards people outside the group or members of other groups. This can be the case, for example, when group cohesiveness is based on common status, qualifications, technical expertise or professional standing. Group cohesiveness may result in lack of co-operation with, or opposition to, non-members. As a result, resentment and inter-group conflict may arise to the detriment of the organisation as a whole. In order to help prevent, or overcome, unconstructive inter-group conflict, the manager should attempt to stimulate a high level of communication and interaction between the groups, and to maintain harmony. Rotation of members among different groups should be encouraged.

On the other hand, inter-group rivalry may be deliberately encouraged as a means of building stronger within-group cohesiveness.[32] The idea is that a competitive element may help to promote unity within a group. However, inter-group rivalry and competition need to be carefully handled by the manager. Groups should not normally be put in a situation where they have to compete for resources, status or approval.[33]

The manager should attempt to avoid the development of 'win–lose' situations. Emphasis should be placed on overall objectives of the organisation and on superordinate goals. These are goals over and above the issues at conflict and which, if they are to be achieved, require the co-operation of the competing groups.

CHARACTERISTICS OF AN EFFECTIVE WORK GROUP

The characteristics of an effective work group are not always easy to isolate clearly. The underlying feature is a spirit of co-operation in which members work well together as a united team, and with harmonious and supportive relationships. This may be evidenced when members of a group exhibit:

- a belief in shared aims and objectives;
- a sense of commitment to the group;
- acceptance of group values and norms;
- a feeling of mutual trust and dependency;

- full participation by all members and decision-making by consensus;
- a free flow of information and communications;
- the open expression of feelings and disagreements;
- the resolution of conflict by the members themselves; and
- a lower level of staff turnover, absenteeism, accidents, errors and complaints.

However, as *Brooks* points out, as teams operate at the higher order of group dynamics this list is arguably more reflective of 'effective **work teams** rather than work groups and this is how it should be – these are teams not groups'.[34]

Understanding group behaviour

The effective management of work groups requires an understanding of the psychological and social influences on behaviour within organisations. *Allcorn* distinguishes between defensive and non-defensive work groups, and provides a typology based on four differing sets of culture.[35]

- Homogenised   **Defensive groups**. They provide collective and
- Institutionalised   individual defences against anxiety that results
- Autocratic   from group membership.

- Intentional   **Non-defensive group**. Deals with group participation in a
                     non-defensive way. The type of group that is desirable in
                     the workplace.

Changing the culture of a group

Attempting to change the culture of a defensive group into that of an intentional group in not easy. The intervention strategy is likely to be perceived as threatening to members of the group. Allcorn suggests that successful intervention involves the comparisons of perceptions and understandings in order to provide a thoughtful summary of the group's perceptions which is accepted by the members. This requires sensitivity to the anxiety of group members and the forces that militate against change. Members need to understand the actions associated with the intentional group as a basis for establishing and maintaining an intentional culture. Allcorn reminds us that 'individual and group behaviour is highly complex, difficult to understand and even more difficult to manage'. It is important to further develop group-process skills.

Working in groups and teams, and the analysis of individual behaviour are discussed in Chapter 14.

THE EFFECTS OF TECHNOLOGY ON WORK GROUPS

The nature of technology and the work flow system of the organisation is a major determinant of the operation of groups, and the attitude and behaviour of their members. Low morale and a negative attitude towards management and the job are often associated with a large number of workers undertaking similar work. A number of different early studies have drawn attention to the relationship between technology and work groups.[36] The nature of technology and the work organisation can result in a feeling of alienation, especially among manual workers. Factors which have been shown to affect alienation include the extent to which the work of the individual or the group amounts to a meaningful part of the total production process, and the satisfaction which workers gain from relationships with fellow workers and group membership. Recall the work of *Trist* and others in their study of changing technology in the coal mining industry (discussed in Chapter 3). New technological methods resulted in changes to the previous system of group working and disrupted traditional social relationships and the integration of small groups.[37]

In a study of assembly line and other factory work, *Goldthorpe* found that the technology was unfavourable for the creation of work groups.[38] However, he also found a group of workers who, although alienated, were still satisfied. Membership of a meaningful work group was not necessarily an important source of job satisfaction. The workers, all married men, aged between 21 and 46, were not interested in maintaining close relationships with fellow workers or supervisors. Their earnings were well in excess of the average manual wage at the time – they were 'affluent' workers. Goldthorpe recognised, however, that in other situations where there is the opportunity for teamwork, the workers will have greater social expectations and the membership of work groups may be very important to them.

Technology and group behaviour

TECHNOLOGY SOLUTIONS

www.booksites.net/mullins

Technology is clearly a major influence on the pattern of group operation and behaviour. The work organisation may limit the opportunities for social interaction and the extent to which individuals are able to identify themselves as members of a cohesive work group. This in turn can have possible adverse effects on attitudes to work and the level of job satisfaction. In many assembly line production systems, for example, relationships between individual workers are determined by the nature of the task, the extent to which individual jobs are specified, and the time cycle of operations.

ACAS draws attention to technological advances and how new technology enables production to be tailored quickly to customer requirements, often on an individual basis.

> *Mass production techniques, where jobs are broken down into simple tasks, are not suitable for the new customer focused manufacturing nor the expectations of an educated workforce. Organisations need workers to be more flexible, to co-operate with other workers, supervisors and managers throughout the organisation, to operate sophisticated technology and to be more adaptable. In addition, the sheer complexity of operations in industry, commerce and the services place them beyond the expertise and control of any one individual. In these circumstances some form of teamwork becomes not just desirable but essential.[39]*

Impact of information technology

You may recall from our discussion in Chapter 4 that the impact of information technology demands new patterns of work organisation, and affects the formation and structure of groups. It will influence where and how people interact. Movement away from large-scale centralised organisation to smaller working units can help create an environment in which workers may relate more easily to each other. Improvements in telecommunications mean, for example, that support staff need no longer be located within the main production unit. On the other hand, modern methods of communication mean that individuals may work more on their own, from their own homes, shared offices or hotels, or work more with machines than with other people.[40]

TECHNOLOGY SOLUTIONS

www.booksites.net/mullins

Virtual teams

Increasingly common is the idea of a **'virtual' team** where the primary interaction among members is by some electronic information and communication process.[41] This enables organisations to function away from traditional working hours and the physical availability of staff.[42]

According to *Hall*, the virtual team is a potential future compromise between fully fledged teams and well-managed groups.

> *I am watching the rise of this idea with interest but am sceptical that it will actually create a 'third way'. Real teams can only be forged in the crucible of personal interaction: videoconferences and Net communications are still poor substitute for this. Of course, once a team has formed it can use these media, as members will know each other well, but that's not the important bit. It's the forming, norming and storming that make a team.[43]*

Communication and leadership skills

However, *Parker* highlights that remote working may also have an impact on the social aspects of organisational working with an increasing feeling of isolation. 'Remote team working is not simply a matter of ensuring staff have access to a laptop and telephone line, and assuming that they will be able to continue with their work. The management and communication skills that this new working culture requires are also key to success.'[44]

An account of remote team working at the Prudential is given in Management in Action 13.2.

Symons considers one advantage of virtual teamworking using asynchronous media is the clarity and richness of contributions when respondents are removed from the urgency of immediate interaction, and this can be particularly relevant in cross-cultural groups. However, as the leader cannot influence by their physical presence, and as hierarchies fade on-line, managing dispersed teams requires a range of subtly different leadership skills. It is important to develop mutual trust, a democratic approach of shared control and decision-making, and to adopt the role and style of a coach. 'The leader has to establish and maintain "credit" with the group, as "position power" has little or no currency in virtual working.'[45]

ROLE RELATIONSHIPS

In order that the organisation can achieve its goals and objectives, the work of individual members must be linked into coherent patterns of activities and relationships. This is achieved through the 'role structure' of the organisation.

A 'role' is the expected pattern of behaviours associated with members occupying a particular position within the structure of the organisation. It also describes how a person perceives their own situation. The concept of 'role' is important to the functioning of groups and for an understanding of group processes and behaviour. It is through role differentiation that the structure of the work group and relationships among its members are established. The development of the group entails the identification of distinct roles for each of its members. Some form of structure is necessary for teamwork and co-operation. The concept of roles helps to clarify the structure and to define the pattern of complex relationships within the group.

The formal organisational relationships (line, functional, staff or lateral) – discussed later in Chapter 15 – can be seen as forms of role relationships. These individual authority relationships determine the pattern of interaction with other roles.

The role, or roles, that the individual plays within the group is influenced by a combination of:

- **situational factors**, such as the requirements of the task, the style of leadership, position in the communication network; and
- **personal factors** such as values, attitudes, motivation, ability and personality.

The role that a person plays in one work group may be quite different from the role that person plays in other work groups. However, everyone within a group is expected to behave in a particular manner and to fulfil certain role expectations.

A person's role-set

In addition to the role relationships with members of their own group – peers, superiors, subordinates – the individual will have a number of role-related relationships with outsiders – for example, members of other work groups, trade union officials, suppliers, consumers. This is a person's '**role-set**'. The role-set comprises the range of associations or contacts with whom the individual has meaningful interactions in connection with the performance of their role. (*See* Figure 13.6.)

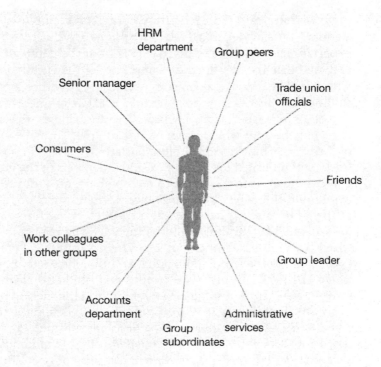

HRM department

Group peers

Senior manager

Trade union officials

Consumers

Friends

Work colleagues in other groups

Group leader

Accounts department

Administrative services

Group subordinates

Figure 13.6 Representation of a possible role-set in the work situation

Role incongruence

An important feature of role relationship is the concept of '**role incongruence**'. This arises when a member of staff is perceived as having a high and responsible position in one respect but a low standing in another respect. Difficulties with role incongruence can arise from the nature of groupings and formal relationships within the structure of the organisation. There are a number of work-related relationships, such as doctor and nurse or senior manager and personal assistant, which can give rise to a potential imbalance of authority and responsibility.

A classic account of role incongruence can be seen in *Whyte's* study of the American restaurant industry.[46] The chefs, who regarded themselves as of high status and were generally recognised as such by the staff, resented being 'told' what to do by the waiting staff who were generally regarded to be of lower status. As a result arguments broke out, disrupting performance. The conflict of status was resolved by the introduction of an ordering process by which the chefs received customers' orders without the appearance of taking instructions from the lower status waiting staff.

Difficulties with role incongruence can also arise in line-staff relationships: for instance, a relatively junior member of the personnel department informing a senior departmental manager that a certain proposed action is contrary to the policies of the organisation. Another example with staff relationships is where a person establishes him or herself in the role of 'gatekeeper' to the boss[47] – for instance, where a comparatively junior personal assistant passes on the manager's instructions to one of the manager's more senior subordinates or where the personal assistant attempts to block a more senior member of staff having access to the manager.

Problems over role incongruence can also lead to the possibility of role stress, discussed later in this chapter.

Role expectations

Many **role expectations** are **prescribed formally** and indicate what the person is expected to do and their duties and obligations. Formal role prescriptions provide guidelines for expected behaviours and may be more prevalent in a 'mechanistic' organisation. Examples are written contracts of employment, rules and regulations, standards, policy decisions, job descriptions, or directives from superiors. Formal role expectations may also be derived clearly from the nature of the task. They may, in part at least, be defined legally, for example under the Health and Safety at Work Act, or as with the obligations of a company secretary under the Companies Acts, or the responsibilities of a district auditor under the Local Government Acts.

Not all role expectations are prescribed formally, however. There will be certain patterns of behaviour which although not specified formally will nonetheless be expected of members. These informal role expectations may be imposed by the group itself or at least communicated to a person by other members of the group. Examples include general conduct, mutual support to co-members, attitudes towards superiors, means of communicating, dress and appearance. Members may not always be consciously aware of these informal expectations yet they still serve as important determinants of behaviour. Under this heading could be included the concept of a psychological contract which was discussed in Chapter 2. The psychological contract implies a variety of expectations between the individual and the organisation. These expectations cover a range of rights and privileges, duties and obligations which do not form part of a formal agreement but still have an important influence on behaviour.

Some members may have the opportunity to determine their own role expectations, where, for example, formal expectations are specified loosely or only in very general terms. Opportunities for **self-established roles** are more likely in senior positions, but also occur within certain professional, technical or scientific groups, or where there is a demand for creativity or artistic flair. Such opportunities may be greater within an 'organic' organisation and will also be influenced by the style of leadership adopted – for example, where a *laissez-faire* approach is adopted.

ROLE CONFLICT

Photo: Robbie Jack/Corbis

Matthew Bourne's critically-acclaimed version of *Swan Lake* with male dancers in the lead roles

The concept of role focuses attention on aspects of behaviour existing independently of an individual's personality. Patterns of behaviour result from both the role and the personality. **Role conflict** arises from inadequate or inappropriate role definition and needs to be distinguished from personality clashes. These arise from incompatibility between two or more people as individuals even though their roles may be defined clearly and understood fully. In practice, the manner in which a person actually behaves may not be consistent with their expected pattern of behaviours. This inconsistency may be a result of role conflict. Role conflict as a generic term can include:

- role incompatibility;
- role ambiguity;
- role overload; and
- role underload.

These are all problem areas associated with the creation of role expectations. (*See* Figure 13.7.)

- ▩ **Role incompatibility** arises when a person faces a situation in which simultaneous different or contradictory expectations create inconsistency. Compliance with one set of expectations makes it difficult or impossible to comply with other expectations. The two role expectations are in conflict. A typical example concerns the person 'in the middle', such as the supervisor or section head, who faces opposing expectations from workers and from management. Another example might be the situation of a manager who believes in a relaxed, participative style of behaviour more in keeping with a Theory Y approach, but whose superior believes in a Theory X approach and expects the manager to adopt a more formal and directive style of behaviour.

- ▩ **Role ambiguity** occurs when there is lack of clarity as to the precise requirements of the role and the person is unsure what to do. The person's own perception of their role may differ from the expectations of others. This implies that insufficient information is available for the adequate performance of the role. Role ambiguity may result from a lack of formally prescribed expectations. It is likely to arise in large, diverse groups or at times of constant change. Uncertainty often relates to such matters as the method of performing tasks, the extent of the person's authority and responsibility, standards of work, and the evaluation and appraisal of performance.

- ▩ **Role overload** is when a person faces too many separate roles or too great a variety of expectations. The person is unable to meet satisfactorily all expectations and some

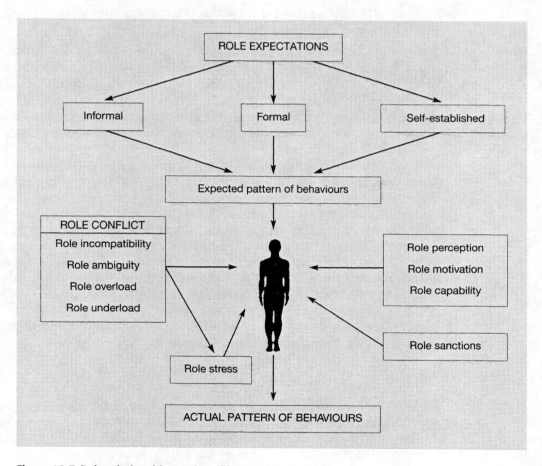

Figure 13.7 Role relationships and conflicts
(*Source*: Adapted from Miner, J. B., *Management Theory*, Macmillan (1971) p. 47.)

must be neglected in order to satisfy others. This leads to a conflict of priority. Some writers distinguish between role overload and work overload. Role overload is seen in terms of the total role-set, and implies that the person has too many separate roles to handle. Where there are too many expectations of a single role – that is, a problem of quantity – this is work overload.[48]

▪ **Role underload** can arise when the prescribed role expectations fall short of the person's own perception of their role. The person may feel their role is not demanding enough and that they have the capacity to undertake a larger or more varied role, or an increased number of roles. Role underload may arise, for example, when a new member of staff is first appointed, or from the initial effects of delegation.

Role conflict and matrix organisation

Problems of role conflict can often arise from the matrix form of organisation (which is discussed in Chapter 15) and, for example, from the use of flexible project teams. Where staff are assigned temporarily, and perhaps on a part-time basis, from other groups this creates a two-way flow of authority and responsibility.

Unless role differentiations are defined clearly this can result in conflicting expectations from the manager of the person's own functional grouping, and from the manager of the project team (role incompatibility). It can also lead to uncertainty about the exact requirements of the part the person is expected to play as a member of the project team (role ambiguity). The combinations of expectations from both managers may also result in role overload.

ROLE STRESS

Role conflict can result in role stress. An example of role stress can also be seen in *Whyte's* study of the American restaurant industry (referred to above under role incongruence). A number of waiting staff found the job very stressful and they cried often. One reason for this was the constant conflict between the demands of the customer to be served quickly and pressure from the chefs who were unable to produce the food in time. The waiting staff were caught between two incompatible expectations and were pulled both ways.

A survey conducted among subscribers of *Management Today* reported Britain's managers feeling burdened with increasing levels of pressure and disillusioned by diminishing control over their working lives. Many managers claimed the organisation's culture contributes to their stress and call for a change in working practices. Under considerable stress themselves managers admit to transmitting problems to their staff.[49]

Although a certain amount of stress may **arguably** be seen as a good thing, and especially at managerial level helps to bring out a high level of performance, it is also potentially very harmful. Stress is a source of tension, frustration and dissatisfaction. It can lead to difficulties in communication and interpersonal relationships and can affect morale, effectiveness at work and health.[50]

Role stress, then, is a major influence on job satisfaction and work performance. It will be discussed further in Chapter 18.

Reducing role conflict and role stress

Greater attention is now given to health problems that are classified as stress-related.[51] There is increasing evidence concerning illnesses, such as cardiovascular diseases, and social problems – for example, marriage breakdowns – which can have stress as a factor. Decreasing efficiency resulting from work stress is also extremely costly to organisations. It is important, therefore, that managers make every effort to minimise the causes of stress.[52]

There are a number of ways in which management might attempt to avoid or reduce role conflict, and the possibilities of role stress.

- Increase specification and clarity of prescribed role expectations, for example through written statements on objectives and policy, use of manuals and set procedures, introduction of appropriate rules, and detailed job descriptions. However, such measures may be resented by staff. They may restrict the opportunity for independent action and personal development, giving rise to even more role conflict.
- Improved recruitment and selection and the careful matching of abilities, motivation, interests and personalities to the demands of a particular role.
- Attention to induction and socialisation programmes, job training and retraining, staff development and career progression plans.
- Medical examinations and health screening to give early indications of potential stress-related problems.
- The creation of new roles or assimilation of existing roles. The reallocation or restructuring of tasks and responsibilities. The clarification of priorities, and the elimination or downgrading of minor roles.
- Giving advance notice and explanation of what is likely to happen, for example of an expected, additional heavy workload which must be completed urgently. Where possible and appropriate provide an opportunity for practice or experience.
- Attention to factors which may help improve group structure and group cohesiveness, and help overcome inter-group conflict.
- Change in management system and leadership style – for example, the move towards System 4 management (discussed in Chapter 7).
- Review of organisation structure, information flow and communication networks, for example members of staff being answerable to more than one superior. Bureaucratic interference and poor delegation are all common causes of work stress, whereas greater autonomy and the introduction of autonomous work groups can result in a marked reduction in stress.[53]

Other influences on behaviour

Even if there is an absence of role conflict and role stress, a person's actual behaviour may still be inconsistent with their expected pattern of behaviours. *Miner* gives three reasons that may account for this disparity.[54]

- The person does not perceive their job in the way the role prescriptions specify. This is a form of role ambiguity but may arise not because the role prescriptions themselves are unclear, but because the person misunderstands or distorts them.
- Motivation is lacking, and the person does not want to behave in the way prescribed.
- The person does not have the capabilities – knowledge, mental ability or physical skills – required to behave in the way the role prescriptions specify.

Application of sanctions

Organisations apply a number of both positive and negative sanctions as inducements for members to contribute and behave in accordance with their prescribed roles. Typical examples are: an increase in salary or wages; promotion; a sideways or downwards move in the organisation structure; the threat of dismissal.

There are also a number of less direct sanctions which may be adopted. These include: the size of office or work area; the allocation of unpopular tasks; giving opportunities for paid overtime work; level of supervision or empowerment; the amount of information given or the extent of consultation; granting or withholding privileges.

Role sanctions may also be applied through the operation of the informal organisation. Members of the group may impose their own sanctions and discipline individuals who contravene the norms of the group or expected standards of behaviour.

CRITICAL REFLECTIONS

'I recognise that groups are an integral part of the work organisation but I do value my individuality and own identity, and enjoy the right of self expression.'

'That shouldn't be a problem. After all the skill of management is to make full use of people's individuality for the mutual benefit of the group as a whole.'

'Oh, I see – I think.'

What are your own views?

While teamwork may be about empowering workers, devolving responsibility, and reversing repressive workplace control structures, it can also mean intensifying attention. Instead of an individual exercising a degree of influence over their own work, they can now influence the work of others in their team through suggestion, demonstration, and exhortation. Life in teams can be stressful as individuals are subject to intense peer pressure to conform to group norms.

Wilson, F. M. *Organizational Behaviour: A Critical Introduction*, Oxford University Press (1999), p. 93.

How would you attempt to overcome or reduce the potentially stressful features of teamwork?

'Personal self-interest and opportunism are natural features of human behaviour and will always take preference over the demands and best interests of the group.'

Debate.

SYNOPSIS

▧ Work is a group-based activity, and groups and teams are a major feature of human behaviour and work organisation. Members must co-operate with one another for work to be carried out. Harmonious working relationships and good teamwork help make for a high level of staff morale and organisational performance. There is a tendency for the terms 'groups' and teams' to be used interchangeably. Whereas all teams are groups, it does not necessarily follow that all groups are teams. Groups develop their own pattern of values and norms of behaviour.

▧ Groups are formed as a consequence of the pattern of organisation structure and arrangements for the division of work. There are two main types of groups at work, formal and informal. Formal groups are deliberately planned and created by management as part of the organisation structure, and to achieve specific organisational objectives. Informal groups are based on personal relationships and develop irrespective of the formal structure. Informal groups serve to satisfy members' psychological and social needs. Groups are formed, therefore, for a number of reasons relating to both work performance and social processes.

▧ Individuals will form into groups or teams, both formal and informal, for a number of different reasons relating to both work performance and social processes. The manager's main concern is that members co-operate with one another. Factors which affect group cohesiveness can be considered under the broad headings of: membership; work environment; organisational; and group development and maturity. Membership of strong and cohesive groups can be a rewarding experience for the individual and have beneficial effects for the organisation.

■ There are, however, potential disadvantages of strong, cohesive groups and the manager should attempt to prevent unconstructive inter-group conflict. On the other hand, inter-group rivalry may be deliberately encouraged as a means of building stronger within-group cohesiveness. Individuals make a contribution to the work of the organisation in different ways. The effective management of work groups requires an understanding of the psychological and social influences on behaviour within organisations.

■ The characteristics of an effective work group are not always easy to isolate. The underlying feature is a spirit of co-operation in which members work well together as a united team, and with harmonious and supportive relationships. The nature of technology and the work flow system of the organisation is a major influence on the operation of groups. The impact of information technology is likely to lead to new patterns of work organisation, and affect the formation and structure of groups.

■ The concept of 'role' is important to the functioning of groups, and for an understanding of group processes and behaviour. It is through role differentiation that the structure of work groups and relationships among members is established. Role expectations may be established formally, they may be informal or they may be self-established. Inadequate or inappropriate role definition can result in role conflict including: role incompatibility, role ambiguity, role overload and role underload. Role conflict can result in role stress. It is important that the manager makes every effort to minimise role conflict and the causes of role stress.

MANAGEMENT IN ACTION 13.1

Teamwork in a small company

Eddie Brennan

Introduction

This is the story of a small (40-person) Dublin-based multimedia company, which we started four years ago. The main activity is producing computer courseware for a large International Company. Four of us had started the company. Our mix of backgrounds is: a journalist/marketeer; a computer systems integrator; a former company director/business consultant; and an organizational consultant in banking.

The staff numbers rose from one to ten over about four months. They were young and newly qualified, just out of third level college. This was their first job. The mix of skills were systems integrator, graphic designers and technical writers.

Difficulties

Some difficulties became apparent fairly quickly. Because the quality control function was then run by the client, the normal tension between developers and quality control was complicated by trying to keep good relations with the client. The day-to-day frustrations were exacerbated by the delays in the throughput in the client's work, which had a knock-on effect on our work.

Because of the inexperience of our young staff problems were being referred back to the Managing Director who then had to discuss the matter with the client. This was time consuming and staff morale was starting to suffer. In discussions with the client's top management it was evident that

■ they were very happy with our work, and
■ they were not aware that they had problems in their own work flow.

Our cash flow was affected by the delays as payment was made on completion of specific pieces of work.

A full review with the client's top Management and Financial Controller was held on the whole work programme. They were anxious that we take on more work. When the difficulties were discussed the client agreed to pay a set amount each month, to review work progress every six months and that part of the quality control function was to be passed to us.

This immediately improved the whole relationship and helped us to concentrate on developing a longer-term strategy for the company.

Developing a strategy

When we were developing our strategy two objectives were decided early on:

■ we needed to develop the business so that we were not totally dependent on the one client, while still keeping them happy;

▶

Management in Action 13.1 continued

■ we wanted to maintain and to develop an innovative and creative atmosphere in the company.

To achieve the first objective we set a target of reducing the dependence on our one client by 20% per year over the next three years. We needed to build up staff numbers to allow enough 'slack' in the contract work so that there was the capacity to take on new work. Fortunately the client was encouraging us to take on more staff and promised that they could give us as much work as we could handle. We increased our staff to 15, to 20, and then to 25 over a period of 15 months.

To achieve the second objective depended on making early progress on the first. The routine production of course-ware was now becoming that – just routine. Our young staff were becoming bored. To retain staff in a computer/technical environment people must feel that they are continuing to learn new processes and are being kept up to date with new technology. If they are to remain interested/satisfied/fulfilled it is important that they are challenged to think.

From the work in the early days a large library of graphics and computer routines had been built up and it was possible to incorporate these in subsequent work thus shortening the development time. This increase in productivity on the 'boring stuff' freed up staff to get at the exciting new bits.

We decided to develop autonomous teams who would be responsible for specific areas. Having read several discussions on team working over the years in QWL the profile of our small company seemed an ideal environment to implement this structure. We started a series of three-hour sessions with all of the staff. These covered subjects such as organizational development; management theory; stress management; financial management. Workshops were held on team building; customer relations; and interpersonal relationships. In all six afternoon/evening meetings were held, followed usually by a drink in the pub across the road.

What was apparent very early on was the interest and willingness of the staff to understand and to support the two strategic goals we had set ourselves. They quickly appreciated that their futures were dependent on how successful the company was in achieving them and were particularly tuned into the financial needs. (This was due to the fact that the financial controller made it very clear that if the money was not there then the new equipment was not bought – unless they preferred not to be paid that month!)

The management was surprised by the maturity, responsibility and interest that the staff took (and still take) in the health and development of the company once they were given the chance.

What is today's position?

The company is still running and now has a 60/40 split on the client dependency. Staff turnover has been very low by computer industry standards roughly 10% per year. Seven or eight of the original 10 are still working there and continue to grow with the company. What's worth noting is that the staff that do leave maintain a very good relationship with the company and many have been responsible for sending us new customers.

The salaries tend to be approximately 15% lower than industry norms, but staff feel it's 'a fun place to work' and that they have opportunities to learn new skills. They stay because of this. We have even had applications from people who have heard from friends about working conditions and want to come to work for us.

Discipline and work throughput has not been a great problem. The team structure keeps it under control largely by peer pressure, if someone on the team is not pulling their weight then their workmates let them know very quickly. Not everyone has felt comfortable with the 'flat' structure of the company and when it became apparent that they did not fit in they left. Two left for this reason.

The company earned the ISO 9000 standard within 18 months of introducing the team structure. This gave a big boost to the staff's morale. They now have an independent organization giving them feedback on their systems. The discipline imposed by ISO 9000 has proved very useful internally – the actual mechanics of ISO 9000 have given a very clear framework for introducing new staff to the processes.

Clear project plans are developed with definite work objectives agreed with all staff. Teams are organized around specific projects like putting together a group in the film industry. Each project requires a different mix of skills so people regroup to the different projects requirements. Discussions take place on individual goals and achievements albeit in an informal way. Within this project plan work time and time keeping is very flexible. Nine to five are the normal hours but these vary for any individual at any specific time/work. It is not unusual to find groups of people working late into the night. This demands flexible security arrangements as well of course.

There is a high level of tolerance of individuals. One anecdote will help illustrate this. An individual who is particularly skilled in detecting hardware/system problems finds it very difficult to keep regular hours, yet seems to have an uncanny ability to appear when needed, day or night. His success rate in solving problems is so well appreciated, that everyone from the MD down will not have a word said against him!

What is important to staff is to feel that they are progressing in their skills. As new recruits come straight from third-level colleges they bring with them up-to-date thinking and pass this to the 'old boys'. The 'old boys' in turn train them in the internal skills and processes. This develops the trust needed in the team structure.

An unexpected development has been the formation of the 'social teams'. These have formed independently of the project teams and are more permanent groups. They arose around such activities as the annual 'PIX' awards. These PIX awards are internal company competitions organized to acknowledge individuals and teams for: e.g. The Most Creative Film; The Most Innovative Graphics; or The Most Original Use of Diverse Technology. Football competitions and other social activities are now organized around these teams.

What are the weaknesses?

Cash flow is still a problem. It is difficult to balance the enthusiasm to innovate with the commercial reality of 'only doing what the client is willing to pay for'.

The speed of developments in both hardware and software means that there is a constant need to invest in new processes, with the resulting training lag before they can be exploited commercially. This is a problem in such a small company as it leaves budgets very tight. There just is not sufficient spare cash to fund 'R & D' in the broadest sense.

At this stage the future will have to be amalgamation with a larger company but everyone fears that will mean a more hierarchal organization which could destroy some of the creativity and the 'fun'.

What have we learned?

- Autonomous teamwork works and saves money.
- Management needs to be self-confident, to see themselves as leaders rather than controllers.
- Teamwork saves time and allows management to concentrate on business development.
- Quality of the work improves and so does communication between different disciplines.
- It must be OK to make mistakes and OK to admit that you are in difficulties (experience is that team members willingly dig each other out – they know it could be their turn to get help next).
- Staff are very responsible and interested when treated as adults.

- It is important that staff continue to have the opportunity to learn.
- Good customer relations are developed and maintained by giving staff the ability to respond to client's requests.

It is important that the development team and the client's users get to know each other and understand each other. In many situations that we have experienced in other firms we noticed that communication between supplier and client goes through the Sales/Marketing Departments and the Head of Departments. We encourage the business analysts/developers to talk directly with the client's staff who will use the product. This has reduced misunderstanding and increased both the customer satisfaction and the developers' work. The teams have displayed a high level of creativity and innovation in their work and have developed several new processes for clients.

If we are asked 'what one thing has made the team structure a success?' the answer is that 'no one thing' works. A combination of trust, adult one-to-one relationships are vital but these must be combined with a sense of fun and achievement for everyone.

Reproduced with permission from Eddie Brennan, *QWL News and Abstracts*, ACAS, No. 144, Autumn 2000, pp. 8–10.

Eddie Brennan, Consultant, Uni-world Ltd. The company specialises in change management and team building by using and training the client's own staff. Contact email: brennanu@indigo.ie

---

MANAGEMENT IN ACTION 13.2

Remote control – a case study

Remote team working is not simply a matter of ensuring staff have access to a laptop and a telephone line, and assuming that they will be able to continue with their work. The management and communications skills that this new working culture requires are also key to success. When one of Britain's leading financial services providers. Prudential, decided to introduce extensive remote working as part of its drive to build stronger customer relationships they called on the experience and expertise of Chameleon Training & Consulting. The Prudential were keen to ensure that their employees not only had the technology, but also the skills, to maximise the individual and business benefits offered by this new way of working. **Chris Parker**, *Chameleon's Marketing Manager, explains how technology is only the starting point to developing an effective remote team.*

Technology has been a constant driver for change in British business over the last decade. The myth has been that the technological changes alone have single-handedly propelled workplace culture from the age of telephone and typewriters into the broadband world of high speed networks, email and mobile communication, mobile phones and laptops. The reality is a need to adapt management techniques, working culture and employee skill levels. Working in the training and HR industry we know that these requirements cannot be ignored. In addition, many companies have attempted to introduce

PRUDENTIAL

Courtesy Prudential

technology for the sake of it, or brought in 'new' gadgets without looking at the impact on the organisation, or individual workers, and have spent even less time looking at the role training can play in integrating the new technology into the processes and working culture of an organisation.

The pace of change

Prudential is one of the largest and most prestigious financial services organisations, with more than 150 years experience building long and successful relationships with both shareholders, customers and policyholders alike. The financial services industry has changed and continues to change at a faster pace than almost any other, and for this reason, technology, and the delivery of the skills required to integrate new ways of working into employees' daily processes and functions, is more important than in any other area of business.

Practice Head of Prudential's B2B division, and responsible for the development of the team, Martin Boniface says that this changing marketplace was one of the core reasons ▶

Management in Action 13.2 continued

Prudential decided to change their working culture, embracing technology, and ensuring that their employees have the skills to work effectively in this new environment. 'We realised that technology, and the effective utilisation of it through training, offered us a flexible, customer facing approach to our business, offering benefits for the company, its customers and Prudential employees.'

How to achieve this was going to be another matter entirely, and one which would prove to be far more wide-ranging than originally thought.

A question of image

According to Boniface, 'We wanted to develop a culture where we were able to be proactive, rather than reactive to the needs of our customers. One of the challenges that Prudential faced in this changeable market was to move away from the traditional view of the "man from the Pru" that policyholders know, towards a more modern image in keeping with the changing market's requirements, and this needed to be replicated throughout the business. Representatives were spending hours travelling to visit corporate customers, whilst still spending time at a centralised office. We realised that in order to offer a more customer focused approach to our corporate clients, we would have to fundamentally change our working culture.' Remote working was positively encouraged for staff in the B2B division at Prudential, with employees using laptops and mobile phones to allow the team to function effectively, but initially this was the exception rather than the rule.

Focus on the customer

'In the B2B division, we made some fairly radical changes', says Boniface. 'We realised that remote working was the way forward for us, and reorganised our business to focus on our customers, rather than their geographical location – as had been the way in the past. This meant that remote working now became the rule, with the exception of members of our support team who still had a centrally based office location. The ability of our employees to work remotely allowed us to spend more time concentrating on the individual requirements of our corporate customers, and offered financial and efficiency benefits for both the company, and our employees. We weren't asking our staff to travel from their homes to an office, and spend hours travelling out to customers' premises, back to the office, before heading home in the evening. This energised and invigorated the team instantly.'

Managing culture change

Having implemented this new way of working for a couple of months, it became obvious that whilst much of the culture change was benefical, there were also areas which could be improved, and some that emerged which had not been expected. 'It was at this point that Prudential looked for expert help in remote team management, in order to refine and improve the new remote team working practices, and develop solutions designed to enable staff to manage their new working environment and the change of culture', says Philippa Muress, Chameleon's Head of Consultancy Services.

'Having trialled remote working, Prudential carried out a number of focus groups to identify areas which needed refining. As a result, we were presented with a number of management challenges and objectives.'

Whilst the remote team working had been generally successful, with Prudential ensuring that staff had been supported in terms of hardware, with budgets provided for selecting computer technology, installing high speed communications access, and addressing Health and Safety issues, an overwhelming need for emotional support and remote, or virtual, team building had been identified.

The significant difference between central office-based working and remote working is that it is difficult to develop a team spirit, a sense of camaraderie, working remotely through new electronic and telecommunications methods. Morale and motivation had also been identified as areas with which Prudential's new virtual team required some assistance.

'Communication and trust are key elements of developing strong remote team working', says Philippa Muress. 'There is a difference between managing a team in a traditional office environment, and managing a remote team of workers which requires new skills and new management techniques. Some of these skills can be adapted from traditional management methodology, but there are also specific techniques and skills, which are critical in the development of an effective remote team. These are exactly the areas which we help organisations to develop through our Managing Remote Teams programmes.'

'You can't control the volume of email', adds Boniface. 'You have no way of knowing the emotional state of the recipient of an email, or how they perceive the content of the message, which means that trust has to be central to the team, and clarity is essential to avoid misunderstandings.' The ability for open discussion where things are unclear forms a central part of ensuring that the team is both effective and efficient. 'The last thing you want is for conflicts to grow from small misunderstandings because someone has not picked up the phone to say, "Do I understand this correctly?"'

The delivery of the course has taken a number of different forms, with Chameleon using a blend of input sessions, assessment tools and role-play techniques during the implementation of the first phase of Prudential's Remote Teams training. Issues of management techniques, motivation and empowerment, and developing a team spirit from remote locations have all been central in the work, ensuring that staff have received a totally bespoke solution tailored to the specific needs of the organisation. Philippa Muress says, 'One of the most important parts of developing a training programme is ensuring that the development and implementation addresses the aims and objectives of both the team and the wider organisation. When developing an effective remote team it is important that you don't isolate the remote members from the rest of the organisation.'

The programme has highlighted the development needs, not only of the managers and remote workers, but also of those who provide support back in the office, and one-day workshops have been arranged for the whole team. 'We recognise the need for a strategic and co-ordinated programme of change in order to develop long-standing effective and successful remote teams', says Boniface. 'There is a very important coaching element to the remote teams programme which Chameleon has developed for us, which offers vital support and reassurance. Working remotely can be a lonely if the necessary skill training is not a place, and we're delighted with the way that Chameleon has been there at every step. Our single point of contact has been one of their Remote Team experts, who understands our business, our aims and our specific business focus.'

Enjoying the benefits of managed change

The benefits of this new virtual team are already being experienced at 'the Pru'. Their vision of creating a more customer-faced commercial approach is generating more business with less cost, (which has occurred, in part, as a result of the reduced requirement for desk space), and has raised customer satisfaction levels in the process.

In a market which has experienced considerable change, this has generated substantial competitive advantage for the company, and boosted morale within the CRM team. Chameleon's Philippa Muress says that the benefits experienced by the Prudential are all classic traits of effective Remote Teams training, 'Technology is only the beginning of developing a remote team environment – without the necessary tools to manage the new working practices, the new approach to managing and being managed, and the new communication and emotional skills, remote team working will not bring the efficiencies and financial rewards which can be achieved with a co-ordinated, structured and expertly delivered programme.'

Further information can be found on the Chameleon website: **www.chameleon training.co.uk**

Reproduced with permission from *Manager, The British Journal of Administrative Management*, March/April 2002, pp. 30–31 and with the permission of Murray Blair, Chameleon Training and Consulting, Surrey.

REVIEW AND DISCUSSION QUESTIONS

1 What is a group? Explain the importance and influence of group values and norms, and give practical examples from within your own organisation.

2 How would you distinguish between a 'group' and a 'team'? To what extent do you believe the distinction has practical significance for managers?

3 Distinguish between formal and informal groups, and provide your own supporting examples. What functions do groups serve in an organisation?

4 Identify different stages in group development and maturity. What other factors influence the cohesiveness of work groups? Give examples by reference to a work group to which you belong.

5 Assess the impact of technology as a determinant of group behaviour and performance. What action might be taken by management to help remove some of the alienating or stressful aspects of technology?

6 What is meant by the role structure of an organisation? Construct a diagram which shows your own role-set within a work situation. Give examples of informal role expectations to which you are, or have been, a party.

7 Explain different forms of role conflict which can result in role stress. Give an account of a work situation in which you have experienced role conflict/role stress. As manager, what action would you have taken in an attempt to rectify the situation?

8 Detail fully what you believe are the essential characteristics of a successful work group or team.

9 As a manager, explain how you would attempt to develop effective group/team relationships and performance. Explain clearly the communication and leadership skills required.

ASSIGNMENT

Obtain, or prepare, a chart depicting the formal groupings within your organisation or a large department of the organisation.

a Using this chart, identify clearly the informal groups that exist within the formal structure.

b Discuss ways in which these informal groups aid, and/or conflict with, the work of the organisation/department.

c Explain the extent to which management recognise the influence of the informal groups.

d What conclusions do you draw from this assignment?

PERSONAL AWARENESS AND SKILLS EXERCISE

OBJECTIVES

Completing this exercise should help you to enhance the following skills:

▶ Observe and record the development and maturity of a small work group.

▶ Analyse the behaviour of individual members of the group.

▶ Identify those factors that most influence the cohesiveness of the group.

EXERCISE

You are required to observe a small group or project team at work; *alternatively*, recall the working of any small group of which you have recently been a member.

1 Complete the following grid by giving a tick in the appropriate box to denote each contribution by individual members.

	Names of group members (or reference numbers)				
Forming					
Storming					
Norming					
Performing					

2 Give specific examples of the group values or norms that constituted 'proper' behaviour of group members.

3 Detail sanctions applied to those members who did not conform to the group norms and the apparent effectiveness of these sanctions.

4 Comment critically on the effectiveness of the group as a whole.

DISCUSSION

■ To what extent do you believe groups develop clearly through the four main successive stages of forming, storming, norming and performing?

■ Which in your opinion is the most crucial stage?

■ Give your views, with supporting reasons, on the apparent satisfaction derived by individuals from membership of the group.

Visit our website **www.booksites.net/mullins** for further questions, annotated weblinks, case material and Internet research material.

Floating on air: the importance of teamwork at Hovertec

Background information

Hovertec plc is a large public company which has been manufacturing civilian and military helicopters for nearly 50 years. The company is very successful in its field and during 19xx/19xx achieved total sales of over £280 million. Profits before taxation exceeded £16.5 million. Hovertec plc employs over 6000 people, most of whom work in three manufacturing plants which are situated in South-West England, Scotland and Northern Ireland.

The company has developed two main types of helicopters since the Second World War. These are the 'Falcon' range of small helicopters, which are sold to civilian operators, and the 'SX/Hawk' range of small and large military helicopters which are produced for government defence projects. Some export orders of 'SX/Hawk' helicopters are manufactured for NATO countries and other friendly countries. The precise number and size of Ministry of Defence contracts is not published and is regarded as classified information by Hovertec plc.

Nevertheless, it is possible to gain some insight into the close relationship between the Ministry of Defence and the company from the details of the research and development (R&D) expenditure which is published in the Hovertec plc Annual Report and Accounts. During 19xx/19xx, the R&D expenditure exceeded £43 million, of which £13 million was 'raised from private venture expenditure', £2.5 million was 'funded in civilian helicopter sales prices' and £28 million was 'covered by classified research contracts'. All the research and development projects, as well as all the military and some civilian contracts, are undertaken at the largest plant in South-West England. The remaining civilian helicopter contracts are shared between the two smaller factories in Scotland and Northern Ireland.

The manufacture of a helicopter

Without going into technical details, the manufacture of a helicopter can be divided into five interconnected processes:

1 *The power unit*, which 'drives' the helicopter like an engine drives a motor car.
2 *The helicopter loom*, which is an inter-woven collection of between 1200 and 2000 insulated

copper wires and electrical cables, connecting the power unit with the various 'control' switches, dials, buttons and levers in the cockpit and passenger/crew compartment, and can be compared, in human terms, with the function of the spinal cord in linking the brain with the arms and legs, etc.
3 *The external rotor blades*, which are mounted over the cockpit and passenger/crew compartment, and also above the tail of the helicopter.
4 *The cockpit and passenger/crew compartment*, which has a different layout, services and accessories (viz. electronic weapon systems), depending on whether the helicopter is intended for civilian or military purposes.
5 *The superstructure or 'shell'*, which encases the helicopter in a similar manner to the 'bodywork' on a motor car.

Although the latest technology is used in these production and assembly processes, the manufacture of a complete helicopter is a relatively slow process, taking three weeks for a civilian unit and four weeks for the larger, more sophisticated military helicopter. The main 'bottleneck' in the process is the long time taken to assemble the helicopter loom and complete the 1200–2000 connections between the power unit and the numerous helicopter systems and services.

Assembling a helicopter loom

Because of the complexity of the task and the high risk of error, the assembly of each helicopter loom is normally carried out by one loom technician who takes up to two weeks (ten working days) to assemble a complete loom unit. Production output is maintained by a team of 24 loom technicians who work in two shifts of 12 technicians per shift. The loom technicians are all qualified maintenance fitters who have received extensive training from the company in loom-assembly procedures. They are the highest-paid section of the workforce after the supervisors and management, and they receive other benefits, such as membership of the company pension scheme, free BUPA medical insurance and additional holiday entitlement which is related to length of service with the company.

All of these technicians are men, aged between 36 and 50 years with between 8 and 15 years' service with the company. Many were recruited from either the Royal Navy or the Army Engineering Corps, where they received their basic training as maintenance fitters. This form of recruitment is adopted, first, because the loom technicians help to assemble both civilian and military helicopters and possible security risks have to be minimised on Ministry of Defence contracts. Second, the majority of Hovertec plc managers possess Army or Naval backgrounds and strong links are maintained with the armed services.

Perhaps the one striking difference between the working conditions at the Hovertec plc factory in South-West England and those at their previous employment in the Armed Services is that all the loom technicians belong to a trade union which is recognised by the company, although in practice the Hovertec plc management frequently circumvent the union representatives by informing the workforce directly of changes in procedures, policy, etc., using 'briefing' procedures.

An improved helicopter loom-assembly method

The 19xx company Corporate Plan concluded that: 'Because of the constricting squeeze on defence projects and on the finances of civilian helicopter operators, which appears likely to continue until the world recession ends and general demands picks up, future activity in the three factories will be at a lower level during the next two to three years than seemed likely a few years ago'.

A detailed cost-cutting exercise was introduced on the strength of this plan, with particular emphasis on the helicopter loom workshop. For example, all overtime working was withdrawn in September 19xx. Meanwhile, the Research and Development Laboratories had devised a radically new method of assembling helicopter looms which, under pilot-scheme conditions, reduced the assembly time from two weeks (ten working days) to two working days. The new method had the added advantage of allowing unskilled labour to be employed and resulted in a saving of assembly costs.

Instead of one technician assembling a single loom, by following a blueprint in a painstaking way, the new method relies upon a team of five operatives working together and following a sequence of 'instructions' provided by a computer. The 1200–2000 insulated copper wires and electrical cables are previously 'colour coded' in terms of the ten main helicopter operating systems. Each operative is given responsibility for two sets of colour-coded wires and cables and is required to thread the leads of one colour through the loom, one at a time, by following a 'map' which is set out on a personal visual display unit.

The total computerised layout, which appears on a separate large screen, resembles a coloured map of the London Underground system. For example, as one operative threads each blue electrical cable through the loom, a blue light flicks on as each correct 'station' is reached. If an error is made, the appropriate light fails to appear and a buzzing alarm sounds continuously until the mistake is corrected and the correct 'route' is re-established. At the same time, the computer-directed system can also be used for the other 'colour-coded' electrical connections and the team is therefore able to assemble the loom simultaneously, without slowing down or interfering with each other's work.

Further trials conducted by the Research and Development Laboratories indicated that small groups of five female workers achieved, on average, 40 per cent higher productivity than similar teams of male operatives. The highest productivity was consistently achieved under laboratory conditions by a team of 16- to 17-year-old female school-leavers, who were permitted to choose their working partners and were also allowed to change from one 'colour code' to another whenever they became bored with one colour or started to make errors. This team was given ten-minute 'rest pauses' every hour to change 'colour codes' and was supervised by a member of the Research and Development Laboratory team, who also collected data on the group's productivity, etc.

Proposed changes in the helicopter loom workshop

Within six months, a decision was taken by the Hovertec plc senior management to transfer the new computerised system pilot-scheme to the loom workshop on a three-months' trial basis. Management informed the workforce about the proposed trials beforehand and the loom technicians accepted the proposed change after receiving a personal assurance that no redundancies would occur as a result of the trials. The company wrote to their trade union about ten days later, during the week when the trials began, to inform them of the new situation; and also pointed out that the trials would allow full-time employment to be offered to five female school-leavers, who would otherwise be out of work.

Outcome of the trials

Within two weeks of the new computerised system being installed, three of the five girls in the work group handed in their notice because of continual abuse from and arguments with the loom technicians. Productivity fell far below the expected targets on every day after the first loom was completed (in four days). The cause of low productivity was invariably due to breakdowns of equipment (loss of VDU pictures was the most frequent fault) which, according to the Research and Development Department, was the direct result of vandalism. A serious argument broke out on one occasion between a loom technician and the Research and Development Supervisor, who had earlier asked the technician to leave the VDU area and return to his own work area, and the outcome was that disciplinary action had to be taken against the loom technician.

Three days later, the trade union representing the loom technicians advised the company that the men were unwilling to work alongside the girls on classified defence contracts in future. The reason given was that the girls were considered to be irresponsible and were more of a 'security risk' than the service-trained loom technicians. Management were swift to point out that none of the girls possessed any expertise in engineering or electronic systems and, in fact, three of the girls were close relatives of different loom technicians.

Output in the loom workshop fell during April and May and the company began to fall behind on outstanding defence contracts. A senior Ministry of Defence official visited the plant in South-West England to advise senior management of the 'Whitehall View' that the new computersed loom assembly trials should be suspended on all defence contract helicopters until further notice.

YOUR TASKS

(a) Using your knowledge of different approaches to organisation and management, comment on the Research and Development Laboratory trials carried out by Hovertec with the team of young, female workers.

(b) Discuss the conditions which contributed to the cohesiveness of the loom technicians as a work group.

(c) What factors might explain the difficulties between the group of loom technicians and the team of female workers?

(d) What action would you propose should be taken by the management of Hovertec?

NOTES AND REFERENCES

1. Schein, E. H. *Organizational Psychology*, Third edition, Prentice-Hall (1988), p. 145.
2. Adair, J. *Effective Teambuilding*, Gower (1986).
3. See, for example: Riley, M. *Human Resource Management in the Hospitality and Tourism Industry*, Second edition, Butterworth Heinemann (1996).
4. Crainer, S. *Key Management Ideas: Thinkers that changed the management world*, Third edition, Financial Times Prentice Hall (1998), p. 237.
5. Holpp, L. 'Teams: It's All in the Planning', *Training & Development*, vol. 51, no. 4, April 1997, pp. 44–7.
6. Cane, S. *Kaizen Strategies for Winning Through People*, Pitman Publishing (1996), p. 116.
7. Belbin, R. M. *Beyond the Team*, Butterworth-Heinemann (2000).
8. Roethlisberger, F. J. and Dickson, W. J. *Management and the Worker*, Harvard University Press (1939).
9. Riches, A. 'Emotionally Intelligent Teams', Organisational Change & Leadership Development, www.anneriches.com.au, accessed 11 March 2003.
10. Huck, S., Kubler, D. and Weibull, J. 'Social Norms and Economic Incentives in Firms', Economic & Social Research Council, 5 March 2003.
11. See, for example: Mullins, L. J. *Hospitality Management and Organisational Behaviour*, Fourth edition, Longman (2001).
12. *Teamwork: Success Through People*, Advisory Booklet, ACAS, April 2003.
13. Lucas, E. 'And the Winner is Everyone', *Professional Manager*, January 2001, p. 10.
14. Heller, R. *In Search of European Success*, HarperCollins Business (1997), p. xiv.
15. Jay, A. 'Nobody's Perfect – But a Team Can Be', *Observer Magazine*, 20 April 1980, pp. 26–33.
16. Bonington, Sir Chris 'Moving Mountains', *The British Journal of Administrative Management*, November/December 1996, pp. 12–14.
17. Guirdham, M. *Interactive Behaviour at Work*, Third edition, Financial Times Prentice Hall (2002), p. 12.
18. Ashmos, D. P. and Nathan, M. L. 'Team Sense-Making: A mental model for navigating uncharted territories',

Journal of Managerial Issues, vol. 14, no. 2, Summer 2002, p. 198.

19. Heller, R. *In Search of European Excellence*, HarperCollins Business (1997), p. 229.

20. Lysons, K. 'Organisational Analysis', *Supplement to The British Journal of Administrative Management*, no. 18, March/April 1997.

21. Argyle, M. *The Social Psychology of Work*, Second edition, Penguin (1989).

22. See, for example: Jay, A. *Corporation Man*, Penguin (1975). In an amusing historical account of the development of different forms of groups, Jay suggests that ten is the basic size of human grouping.

23. See, for example: Handy, C. B. *Understanding Organizations*, Fourth edition, Penguin (1993).

24. Cane, S. *Kaizen Strategies for Winning Through People*, Pitman Publishing (1996), p. 131.

25. McKenna, P. J. and Maister, D. H. 'Building Team Trust', *Consulting to Management*, vol. 13, no. 4, December 2002, pp. 51–3.

26. Bass, B. M. and Ryterband, E. C. *Organizational Psychology*, Second edition, Allyn and Bacon (1979).

27. Tuckman, B. W. 'Development Sequence in Small Groups', *Psychological Bulletin*, vol. 63, 1965, pp. 384–99.

28. Cited in Green, J. 'Are your teams and groups at work successful?', *Administrator*, December 1993, p. 12.

29. Seashore, S. E. *Group Cohesiveness in the Industrial Work Group*, Institute for Social Research, University of Michigan (1954).

30. Green, J. 'Team Building in Practice', *Chartered Secretary*, November 1997, p. 35.

31. Koontz, D. *Icebound*, BCA, by arrangement with Headline Books Ltd (1995), p. 185.

32. See, for example: Staw, B. M. 'Organizational Psychology and the Pursuit of the Happy/Productive Worker', *California Management Review*, vol. 28, no. 4, Summer 1986, pp. 40–53.

33. See, for example: Schein, E. H. *Organizational Psychology*, Third edition, Prentice-Hall (1988).

34. Brooks, I. *Organisational Behaviour: Individuals, Groups and Organisation*, Second edition, Financial Times Prentice Hall (2003) p. 98.

35. Allcorn, S. 'Understanding Groups at Work', *Personnel*, vol. 66, no. 8, August 1989, pp. 28–36.

36. See, for example: Walker, C. R. and Guest, R. H. *The Man on the Assembly Line*, Harvard University Press (1952); and Scott, W. H. *et al. Technical Change and Industrial Relations*, Liverpool University Press (1956).

37. Trist, E. L. *et al. Organizational Choice*, Tavistock Publications (1963).

38. Goldthorpe, J. H. *et al. The Affluent Worker*, Cambridge University Press (1968).

39. 'Teamwork: Success Through People', Advisory Booklet, ACAS, April 2003, p. 9.

40. See, for example: Kinsman, F. 'The Virtual Office and The Flexible Organisation', *Administrator*, April 1994, pp. 31–2; and Chowdhury, S. *Management 21c*. Financial Times Prentice Hall (2000).

41. See, for example: Johnson, P., Heimann, V. and O'Neill, K. 'The "Wonderland" of Virtual Teams', *The Journal of Workplace Learning*, vol. 13, no. 1, 2001, pp. 24–30.

42. Young, R. 'The Wide-awake Club', *People Management*, 5 February 1998, pp. 46–9.

43. Hall, P. 'Team Solutions Need Not Be the Organisational Norm', *Professional Manager*, July 2001, p. 45.

44. Parker, C. 'Remote Control – a Case Study', *Manager, The British Journal of Administrative Management*, March/April 2002, p. 30.

45. Symons, J. 'Taking Virtual Team Control', *Professional Manager*, vol. 12, no. 2, March 2003, p. 37.

46. Whyte, W. F. *Human Relations in the Restaurant Industry*, McGraw-Hill (1948).

47. See, for example: Lerner, P. M. 'Beware the Gatekeeper', *Amtrak Express*, July/August 1994, pp. 14–17.

48. See, for example: Handy, C. B. *Understanding Organizations*, Fourth edition, Penguin (1993).

49. Oliver, J. 'Losing Control', *Management Today*, June 1998, pp. 32–8.

50. See, for example: *Are Managers Under Stress? A Survey of Management Morale*, The Institute of Management (September 1996).

51. See, for example: Gwyther, M. 'Stressed for Success', *Management Today*, January 1999, pp. 22–6.

52. See, for example, Newton, T. *Managing Stress: Emotion and Power at Work*, Sage Publications (1995).

53. Hall, K. and Savery, L. K. 'Stress Management', *Management Decision*, vol. 25, no. 6, 1987, pp. 29–35.

54. Miner, J. B. *Management Theory*, Macmillan (1971).

Use the *Financial Times* to enhance your understanding of the context and practice of management and organisational behaviour. Refer to articles 14 and 15 in the BUSINESS PRESS section at the end of the book for relevant reports on the issues explored in this chapter.

14   WORKING IN GROUPS AND TEAMS

Photo: Jim Four/Lebrecht Music Collection

If the manager is to make the most effective use of staff, then it is important to have an understanding of working in groups and teams. It is necessary to recognise the nature of human relationships and the functions, roles and factors which influence team performance and effectiveness. Attention must be given to the analysis of behaviour of individuals in group situations. The manager must be aware of the interactions and operation of work groups and teams.

LEARNING OUTCOMES

After completing this chapter you should be able to:

▶ explain interactions among members of a group and membership of successful teams;

▶ detail main types of contributions or team roles;

▶ contrast patterns of communication networks within small work groups;

▶ examine methods of analysing the behaviour of individual members;

▶ distinguish different group functions and member roles, and explain the use of frameworks of behavioural analysis;

▶ evaluate the nature of individual or group or team performance;

▶ review the importance of, and influences on, effective teamworking.

Twenty people in a room doesn't make a team. Teams don't just happen. They have to be developed, facilitated and motivated.

Robert Kriegel and David Brandt
Sacred Cows Make the Best Burgers, Warner (1996)

It may sound obvious, but a team of ten people can get something done a lot faster than one person working alone. Of course, if it's obvious, why are there so many solo acts in most organisations and so few teams?

Mark McCormack
McCormack on Managing, Century (1995)

INTERACTIONS AMONG MEMBERS

In the previous chapter we mentioned that how people behave and perform as members of a group is as important as their behaviour or performance as individuals, and drew attention to the importance of effective teamwork. Our main focus of attention in this chapter is the actual roles, behaviours and performance of people working in groups or teams. Once again, however, we should be aware of the tendency for the terms 'groups' and 'teams' to be used interchangeably. 'To remain competitive organisations need to make optimum use of equipment and people if they are to thrive or even survive ... In a general sense people talk of teamwork when they want to emphasise the virtues of co-operation and the need to make use of the various strengths of employees.'[1]

In order to help improve the performance of the organisation it is necessary to understand the nature of human relationships and what goes on when groups of people meet.[2] Working in a group is likely to be both a psychologically rewarding, but also a potentially demanding, experience for the individual. Group performance and the satisfaction derived by individuals are influenced by the interactions among members of the group. As an example of this, Figure 14.1 gives an unsolicited commentary from five final-year business studies degree students after completing a group-based assignment. In order to understand the functions and processes of a group, it is necessary to understand what happens when people meet; the actions and behaviour of individual members; the parts people play; the patterns of interactions and forces within the group; and influences on individual and group performance. According to Guirdham, for example:

Many of the concepts that have helped us understand interactive behaviour in work relationships are also needed for understanding it in groups, including role behaviour, norms and co-operation, competition, conflict and conflict resolution. Most of what there is to understand about group work applies equally to both decision-making groups and teams but there are some further issues particular to the two different kinds of groups. There is, however, no suggestion that teams do not have to solve problems![3]

If groups are to be successful and perform effectively there must be a spirit of unity and co-operation. Members of a group must work well together as a team. As *Crainer* reminds us, in most teams people will contribute individual skills many of which will be different. However, referring to the work of *Obeng*,[4] Crainer points out that it is not enough to have a rag-bag collection of individual skills.

*The various behaviors of the team members must mesh together in order to achieve objectives. For people to work successfully in teams, you need people to behave in certain ways. You need some people to concentrate on the task at hand (**doers**). You need some people to provide specialist knowledge (**knowers**) and some to solve problems as they arise (**solvers**). You need some people to make sure that it is going as well as it can and that the whole team is contributing fully (**checkers**). And you need some people to make sure that the team is operating as a cohesive social unit (**carers**).*[5]

Although everyone operates fundamentally as a loner at work, *James* draws attention to the need in most jobs for the eponymous 'teamworking'.

The idea, as you probably know, is that teams achieve more than individuals. Throw people into a random group and somewhere along the line their mutual strengths will outweigh their individual weaknesses. This of course depends upon the dynamics of the team. If it works, great. If not, disaster. Any team, no matter how hand-picked and honed, can be brought down if there is an outbreak of whingeing, bitching, favouritism, office politics, laziness, negativity, stupidity, internal competition, power-posturing, back stabbing ... in fact, all and any of the usual suspects.[6]

WHAT WE FEEL WE HAVE LEARNT FROM WORKING IN A GROUP

1   'We learnt that we had to listen to everybody's points of view and take these into consideration.'

2   'We found that we had to be prepared to make certain sacrifices and adopted a democratic decision process. However, if an individual felt very strongly about a specific point and persisted with a valid argument then this had to be included.'

3   'We often felt frustrated.'

4   'It was time-consuming and difficult to schedule meetings due to differences in timetables and preferences in working hours.'

5   'We learnt that it is good to pool resources because this increased the overall standard of the piece of work. We feel this was only because we all set high personal standards and expected these from our fellow group members. We learnt that it is possible to work in other less productive groups where individual levels of achievement may decrease.'

6   'We learnt that it is better to work in a smaller and not a larger group, as there is a tendency for individual ideas to be diluted.'

7   'Groups formed on the basis of friendship alone are not as effective as groups formed with work as the major influence. The former tend to be unproductive.'

8   'We found that it was good to get positive response, encouragement and feedback from team members. Likewise, it was demotivating to receive a negative response.'

9   'We learnt a lot about our individual personalities.'

10 'We benefited from sharing personal experiences from our industrial placements.'

11 'It is important to separate work and personal relationships.'

Figure 14.1 Unsolicited commentary from students after completing a group-based assignment

BELBIN'S TEAM-ROLES

One of the most popular and widely used analyses of individual roles within a work group or team is that developed by *Meredith Belbin*. Following years of research and empirical study, Belbin concludes that groups composed entirely of clever people, or of people with similar personalities, display a number of negative results and lack creativity. The most consistently successful groups comprise a range of roles undertaken by various members. The constitution of the group itself is an important variable in its success.[7] Initially, Belbin identified eight useful types of contribution – or team-roles. A **team-role** is described as a pattern of behaviour, characteristic of the way in which one team member interacts with another whose performance serves to facilitate the progress of the team as a whole. In a follow-up publication, Belbin discusses the continual evolution of team-roles, which differ in a few respects from those originally identified and adds a ninth role.[8] Strength of contribution in any one role is commonly associated with particular weaknesses. These are called allowable weaknesses. Members are seldom strong in all nine team-roles. A description of the evolved nine team-roles is given in Table 14.1.

The types of people identified are useful team members and form a comprehensive list. These are the key team-roles and the primary characters for successful teams. Creative teams require a balance of all these roles and comprise members who have characteristics complementary to one another. 'No ones's perfect, but a team can be.' Belbin claims that good examples of each type would prove adequate for any challenge, although not all types are necessarily needed. Other members may be welcome for their personal qualities, for example a sense of humour, but experience suggests there is no other team-role that it would be useful to add.

Table 14.1 Belbin's evolved nine team-roles

Roles and descriptions – team-role contribution	Allowable weaknesses
Plant	Creative, imaginative, unorthodox. Solves difficult problems.	Ignores details. Too preoccupied to communicate effectively.
Resource investigator	Extrovert, enthusiastic, communicative. Explores opportunities. Develops contacts.	Over-optimistic. Loses interest once initial enthusiasm has passed.
Co-ordinator	Mature, confident, a good chairperson. Clarifies goals, promotes decision-making. Delegates well.	Can be seen as manipulative. Delegates personal work.
Shaper	Challenging, dynamic, thrives on pressure. Has the drive and courage to overcome obstacles.	Can provoke others. Hurts people's feelings.
Monitor-Evaluator	Sober, strategic and discerning. Sees all options. Judges accurately.	Lacks drive and ability to inspire others. Overly critical.
Team worker	Co-operative, mild, perceptive and diplomatic. Listens, builds, averts friction, calms the waters.	Indecisive in crunch situations. Can be easily influenced.
Implementer	Disciplined, reliable, conservative and efficient. Turns ideas into practical actions.	Somewhat inflexible. Slow to respond to new possibilities.
Completer	Painstaking, conscientious, anxious. Searches out errors and omissions. Delivers on time.	Inclined to worry unduly. Reluctant to delegate. Can be a nit-picker.
Specialist	Single-minded, self-sharing, dedicated. Provides knowledge and skills in rare supply.	Contributes on only a narrow front. Dwells on technicalities. Overlooks the 'big picture'.

(Reprinted with permission from Belbin, R. M., *Team Roles at Work*, The Butterworths Division of Reed Elsevier (UK) Limited/ Belbin Associates (1993) p. 23.)

Back-up team-roles and functional roles

The most consistently successful teams were 'mixed' with a balance of team-roles. The role that a person undertakes in a group is not fixed and may change according to circumstances. Individuals may have a 'back-up team-role' with which they have some affinity other than their primary team-role. If certain roles were missing members would call upon their back-up roles. Team-roles differ from what Belbin calls 'functional-roles'. These are the roles that members of a team perform in terms of the specifically technical demands placed upon them. Team members are typically chosen for functional roles on the basis of experience and not personal characteristics or aptitudes.

Belbin has developed a Self-Perception Inventory designed to provide members of a group with a simple means of assessing their best team-roles.

The value of Belbin's Team-Roles Inventory

A study undertaken by *Furnham, Steel and Pendleton* had the aim of examining the psychometric properties of the Belbin Team-Role Self Perception Inventory. They believe (admittedly from relatively small samples) that there is little psychometric support for the structure of the inventories which do not give confidence in the predictive or construct validity. In a response, Belbin argues that the Inventory was a quick and useful way of intimating to readers what their own team-roles might be; and Furnham, Steele and Pendleton acknowledge that Belbin's contribution is substantial and his measure imaginative.[9]

Despite possible doubts about the value of Belbin's Self-Perception Inventory, it remains a popular means of examining and comparing team-roles. For example, in order to explore whether local government managers were distinctively different from the model of private sector management, *Arroba and Wedgwood-Oppenheim* compared samples of the two groups of managers and Belbin's key team-roles. There were noticeable similarities between the two groups with the noticeable exception of the marked difference between private sector managers and local government officers in the score for team workers and the team-roles they preferred to adopt. The individual characteristics of managers in the two sectors differed. The data implied that local government officers were committed to organisational objectives and dedicated to task achievement but the low score for team workers suggested the high commitment to organisational tasks was not supplemented by a concern for interpersonal processes. In local government, the drive and enthusiasm and emphasis on task were exaggerated, while attention to idea generation and productive interpersonal relationships was less marked.[10]

Constructing the perfect team

Referring to the research of Belbin, *White* refers to a team in the proper sense of the word as something about the way they work as a group that adds up to a sum greater than the individual parts – a collective spirit, a managerial alchemy that makes them such a force. If business people are happy to accept that group effort is always better than individuals working in isolation, the research of Belbin may help in constructing the perfect team. White suggests that in the end it is all about trust. The chances are that the dream team is out there, sitting opposite you or just around the corner. All you have to do is to fit them into Belbin's nine defined roles.[11]

Distribution of team roles among UK managers

Using Belbin's model, *Fisher et al.* undertook a study of the distribution of team roles among managers. Over the past 15 years many layers of management have been removed and the gap in people to lead and motivate has increasingly been filled by the creation of multitudes of teams. The participants of the study were 1441 male and 355 female managers, all with some management experience. All had completed a personality questionnaire, and were candidates short-listed for a range of management positions in both the private and public sector. The study analysed data supplied by ASE/NFER Publishing Company and results were then compared with the Belbin model. The data broadly agreed with the Belbin model. The authors conclude that as much is still unknown about teams, it is reassuring that further support has been found for the popular Belbin team-role model. There are several unresolved problems with teamworking but these might lie more with practices in staff recruitment than in team theory.[12]

An account of profiling managers using the Belbin programme for leadership development in a cross-section of South African organisations is given in Management in Action 14.1 at the end of this chapter.

PATTERNS OF COMMUNICATION

The level of interaction among members of a group or team is influenced by the structuring of channels of communication. Laboratory research by *Bavelas*[13] and subsequent studies by other researchers such as *Leavitt*[14] have resulted in the design of a series of communication networks. These networks were based on groups of five members engaged in a number of problem-solving tasks. Members were permitted to communicate with each other by written notes only, and not everyone was always free to communicate with everyone else.

There are five main types of communication networks – Wheel, Circle, All-Channel, Y and Chains (*see* Figure 14.2).

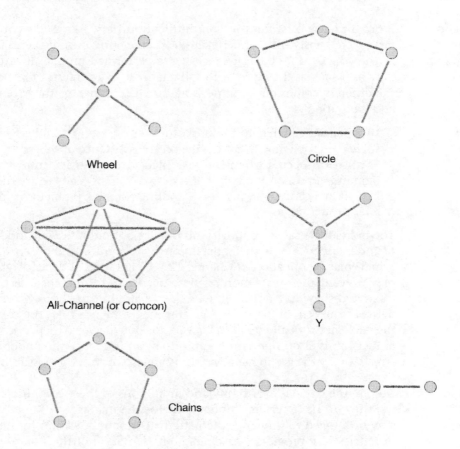

Figure 14.2 Communication networks

▪ **The wheel**, also sometimes known as the star, is the most **centralised network**. This network is most efficient for simple tasks. Problems are solved more quickly with fewer mistakes and with fewer information flows. However, as the problems become more complex and demands on the link person increase, effectiveness suffers. The link person is at the centre of the network and acts as the focus of activities and information flows, and the co-ordinator of group tasks. The central person is perceived as leader of the group and experiences a high level of satisfaction. However, for members on the periphery, the wheel is the least satisfying network.

▪ **The circle** is a more **decentralised network**. Overall it is less efficient. The group is unorganised, with low leadership predictability. Performance tends to be slow and erratic. However, the circle is quicker than the wheel in solving complex problems, and also copes with change or new tasks more efficiently. The circle network is most satisfying for all the members. Decision-making is likely to involve some degree of participation.

▪ **The all-channel (or comcon) network** is a decentralised network which involves full discussion and participation. This network appears to work best where a high level of interaction is required among all the members in order to solve complex problems. Leadership predictability is very low. There is a fairly high level of satisfaction for members. The all-channel network may not stand up well under pressure, in which case it will either disintegrate or reform into a wheel network.

▪ **A 'Y' or chain network** might be appropriate for more simple problem-solving tasks, requiring little interaction among members. These networks are more centralised, with information flows along a predetermined channel. Leadership predictability is high to moderate. There is a low to moderate level of satisfaction for members.

Satisfaction of group members

From a review of studies in communication networks, *Shaw* confirmed that simple tasks were consistently undertaken most efficiently in more centralised networks such as the wheel. More complex tasks were performed more efficiently by decentralised networks such as the circle or the all-channel.[15] (*See* Figure 14.3.) The characteristics of the different communication networks are determined by the extent of 'independence' and 'saturation'.

▪ **Independence** refers to the opportunities for group members to take action and to solve the problem without relying on the assistance of others.

▪ **Saturation** occurs when the task places an excessive information load or other demands upon a member of the network. This leads to inefficiency. The central person in a centralised network handling complex problems is more likely to experience saturation.

The individual's satisfaction with his or her position in the network relates to the degree of independence and the satisfaction of recognition and achievement needs. (See achievement motivation in Chapter 12.) A high level of dependence on other members may prevent the satisfaction of these needs, and if members of the network become frustrated they may not be so willing to share information with others. In the wheel network the central person has greater independence than the other members, but in the circle network all members have a moderate degree of dependence upon each other. Leadership is also important because this can influence the opportunity for independent action by the group members, and can also control the possibility of saturation.

Implications for the manager

Despite the obvious artificiality and limitations of these communication network studies, they do have certain implications for the manager. A knowledge of the findings may be applied to influence the patterns of communication in meetings and committees. They also provide a reasonable representation of the situations that might apply in large organisations. It will be interesting for the manager to observe the patterns of communication adopted by different groups in different situations. The manager can also note how communication networks change over time and how they relate to the

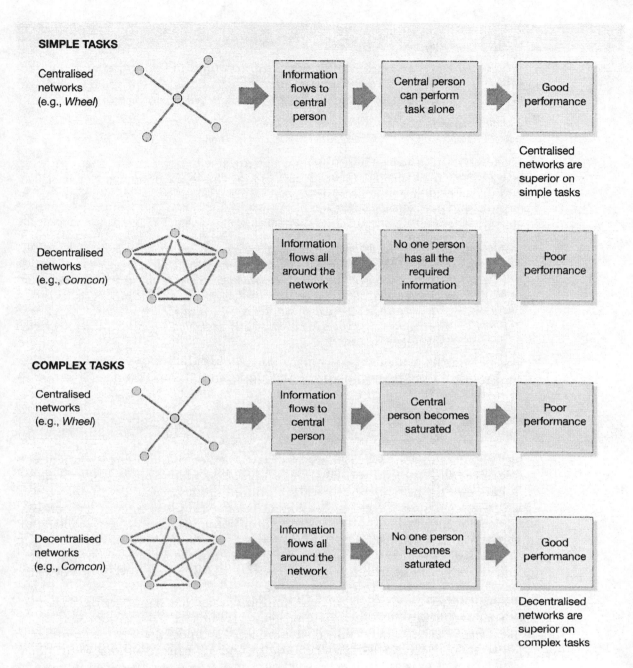

Figure 14.3 Communication networks and task complexity

(*Source*: Baron/Greenberg, *Behaviour in Organisations: Understanding Managing*, Third edition, Prentice-Hall Inc., Upper Saddle River, NJ.)

performance of the group. According to *Moreland and Levine*, patterns of communication influence the accuracy of transmission and receiving of messages, level of task performance and the satisfaction of members.[16]

No one network is likely to be effective for a range of given problems. The studies draw attention to the part of the manager's job which is to ensure the most appropriate communication network for the performance of a given task. Problems which require a high level of interaction among members of the group may not be handled efficiently if there are inadequate channels of communication or sharing of information. The choice of a particular communication network may involve trade-offs between the performance of the work group and the satisfaction of its members.

ANALYSIS OF INDIVIDUAL BEHAVIOUR

In order to understand and to influence the functioning and operation of a group or team, it is necessary to study patterns of interaction, and the parts played by individual members. For example, in a more recent publication *Belbin* acknowledges that:

> *Teamwork does not, of course, guarantee in itself good results. As in sport, there can be good teams and poor teams. And as in sport, it all depends on how the players play together.*[17]

It is necessary to balance the requirement for effective performance of the team with respect for the individuality of its members and to achieve the right mix. Not all skilled and capable individuals are necessarily good team players and it may sometimes be an advantage to have someone who will have a more sceptical attitude and be more open to change. For example, *Stanley* refers to the challenge of managing a high-performance team.

> *When assembling a high-performance team, you are gathering together energy-packed employees, who are a lot like thoroughbreds. Keep in mind, they have an innate drive to excel. Their thoughts run outside the mundane and familiar. With a flare for the unique, they are extraordinary and can generate new ideas that will keep the organisation ahead of the competition ... Along with assigning each member appropriate tasks, the manager must monitor individual performance. By encouraging members to maximise their individual effort, the team will greatly increase the probability of success.*[18]

Two of the main methods of analysing the behaviour of individuals in group situations are **sociometry** and **interaction process analysis**.

SOCIOMETRY

Originally developed by *Moreno*,[19] **sociometry** is a method of indicating the feelings of acceptance or rejection among members of a group. A sociogram is a diagrammatical illustration of the pattern of interpersonal relationships derived from sociometry. The sociogram depicts the choices, preferences, likes or dislikes, and interactions between individual members. It can also be used to display the structure of the group and to record the observed frequency and/or duration of contacts among members.

The basis of sociometry, however, is usually 'buddy rating' or 'peer rating'. Each member is asked to nominate or to rate, privately, other members in terms of some given context or characteristic – for example, with whom they communicate, or how influential or how likeable they are. Questions may relate to either work or social activities. For example: who would you most prefer or least prefer as a workmate? Who would make a good leader? With whom would you choose and not choose to go on holiday? Positive and negative choices may be recorded for each person, although sometimes positive choices only are required. The choices may be limited to a given number or they may be unlimited. Sometimes individuals may be asked to rank their choices.

Sociograms   Members' choices could be shown in tabular form. For example, Table 14.2 shows first and second choices for a group of final-year degree students. Members were asked to indicate, in confidence, those whom they would most prefer to talk to about: (i) a major work-related problem; and (ii) a difficult personal problem. Positive choices only were requested.

An advantage of the diagrammatical illustration, however, is that the sociogram provides a visual description of the sociometric structure of a group. It can indicate cliques and sub-groups, compatibility, and members who are popular, isolated or who act as links. Figure 14.4 gives a simple illustration of an actual sociogram for a group of 15 members with single, positive choices only.

1 G and M are popular (the stars) and most often chosen by members.
2 M is the link between two overlapping cliques, KML and MNO.
3 H and P are unpopular (isolated) and chosen least by members.

Table 14.2 Example of a 'tabulated' sociogram (positive choices only)

Work-related problem			Personal problem	
Second choice	First choice		First choice	Second choice
		A		///
		B	/	//
///	/	C	//	/
/		D	//	
		E	/	
	/	F	/	//
		G	//	
/////	//	H	//	
		J	/	/
	//	K		
////	///////	L		//
	/	M	/	/
		N		//
/		O	/	
14	14		14	14

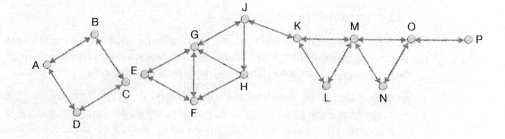

Figure 14.4 A simple illustration of a sociogram

4 JKMO is a chain.
5 ABCD is a sub-group and separated from the rest of the members.

It should be noted, however, that there are several methods of compiling and drawing sociograms, and a number of potential criticisms and limitations with the contribution of Moreno. Problems also arise over *how* to draw the sociogram and how to interpret the roles of individual members; 'the drawing of a sociogram is a highly arbitrary and time-consuming task'.[20] In the experience of the author less concern should be given to the concept of sociometry itself. It is better seen as a useful vehicle which, if handled sensitively, can serve to encourage meaningful discussions on patterns of social interactions, group behaviour and the perceptions of individual members towards one another.

INTERACTION ANALYSIS

The basic assumption behind **interaction analysis** is that behaviour in groups may be analysed from the viewpoint of its function. This approach has developed largely from the work of *Bales* on methods for the study of small groups. This aim is to provide ways of describing group process and indications of factors influencing the process.[21] In Bales's

'Interaction Process Analysis' every act of behaviour is categorised, as it occurs, under twelve headings. These differentiate between 'task' functions and 'socio-emotional' functions. The categories apply to both verbal interaction and non-verbal interaction.

A Socio-Emotional: Positive Reactions
  1 **Shows solidarity**, raises others' status, gives help, reward.
  2 **Shows tension release**, jokes, laughs, shows satisfaction.
  3 **Agrees**, shows passive acceptance, understands, concurs, complies.
B Task: Attempted Answers
  4 **Gives suggestion**, direction, implying autonomy for others.
  5 **Gives opinion**, evaluation, analysis, expresses feeling, wish.
  6 **Gives orientation**, information, repeats, clarifies, confirms.
C Task: Questions
  7 **Asks for orientation**, information, repetition, confirmation.
  8 **Asks for opinion**, evaluation, analysis, expression of feeling.
  9 **Asks for suggestion**, direction, possible ways of action.
D Socio-Emotional: Negative Reactions
  10 **Disagrees**, shows passive rejection, formality, withholds help.
  11 **Shows tension**, asks for help, withdraws out of field.
  12 **Shows antagonism**, deflates others' status, defends or asserts self

In an extension of interaction process analysis, Bales gives 27 typical group roles which are based on various combinations of these original main behavioural categories.[22]

Task and maintenance functions

If the group is to be effective, then, whatever its structure or the pattern of interrelationships among members, there are two main sets of functions or processes that must be undertaken – **task functions** and **maintenance functions**.

- **Task functions** are directed towards problem-solving, the accomplishment of the tasks of the group and the achievement of its goals. Most of the task-oriented behaviour will be concerned with 'production' activities, or the exchange and evaluation of ideas and information.
- **Maintenance functions** are concerned with the emotional life of the group and directed towards building and maintaining the group as an effective working unit. Most of the maintenance-oriented behaviour will be concerned with relationships among members, giving encouragement and support, maintaining cohesiveness and the resolution of conflict.

Task and maintenance functions may be performed either by the group leader or by members. Ultimately it is the leader's responsibility to ensure that both sets of functions are carried out and the right balance is achieved between them. The appropriate combination of task-oriented behaviour and maintenance-oriented behaviour is essential to the success and continuity of the group.

In addition to these two types of behaviour members of a group may say or do something in attempting to satisfy some personal need or goal. The display of behaviour in this way is termed **self-oriented behaviour**. This gives a classification of three main types of functional behaviour which can be exhibited by individual members of a group: **task-oriented**, **maintenance-oriented** and **self-oriented**.

Classification of member roles

A popular system for the classification of member roles in the study of group behaviour is that devised originally by *Benne and Sheats*.[23] The description of member roles performed in well-functioning groups is classified into three broad headings: **group task roles**, **group maintenance roles** and **individual roles**.

- **Group task roles**. These assume that the task of the group is to select, define and solve common problems. Any of the roles may be performed by the various members or the group leader.
- **Group building and maintenance roles**. The analysis of member functions is oriented towards activities which build group-centred attitudes, or maintain group-centred behaviour. Contributions may involve a number of roles, and members or the leader may perform each of these roles.
- **Individual roles**. These are directed towards the satisfaction of personal needs. Their purpose is not related either to group task or to the group functioning.

FRAMEWORKS OF BEHAVIOURAL ANALYSIS

Several frameworks have been designed for observers to categorise patterns of verbal and non-verbal behaviour of group or team members. Observers chart members' behaviour on specially designed forms. These forms may be used to focus on single individuals, or used to record the total interaction with no indication of individual behaviour. The system of categorisation may distinguish between different behaviours in terms of the functions they are performing. The completed observation forms can be used as a basis for discussion of individual or group performance in terms of the strengths/weaknesses of different functional behaviour. In the framework shown in Figure 14.5 there are two observation sheets, one covering six types of leader–member **task-function behaviour** and the other covering six types of leader–member **group building and maintenance function behaviour**.

Use of different frameworks

Different frameworks use a different number of categories for studying behaviour in groups. The interaction analysis method can become complex, especially if non-verbal behaviour is included. Many of the categories in different frameworks may at first sight appear to be very similar. It is important, therefore, to keep the framework simple, and easy to understand and complete. The observer's own personality, values and attitudes can influence the categorisation of behaviour. For these reasons it is preferable to use trained observers, and wherever possible and appropriate to use more than one observer for each group. The observers can then compare the level of consistency between their categorisations. Observation sheets can be designed to suit the particular requirements of the group situation and the nature of the activity involved. An example of a reasonably simple, ten-point observation sheet used by the author is given in Figure 14.6.

Completing the observation sheet

Where appropriate, it may be helpful to note the initial seating, or standing, arrangements of the group. This will help in the identification of group members. Depending on the nature of the activity involved, it might also be possible to indicate main channels of interaction among individuals – for example, to whom eye contact, hand movements, or ideas and questions are most frequently directed. A note could also be made of changes in arrangements during, and at the end of, the activity. Headings on the observation sheet are not necessarily exclusive. For example, leadership could be included under Taking Initiative, or under Performing Group Roles. Similarly, the role of humorist could be included under Performing Group Roles, but might also appropriately be included under the heading of Harmonising.

Observers will tend to use their own methods for completing the sheet: for example, a simple stroke or tick for each contribution and perhaps a thick stroke for a particularly significant contribution. Some observers might use some other distinguishing

---

TASK FUNCTIONS

1 **Initiating:** proposing tasks or goals; defining a group problem, suggesting a procedure or ideas for solving a problem.

2 **Information or opinion seeking:** requesting facts, seeking relevant information about a group concern, asking for suggestions and ideas.

3 **Information or opinion giving:** offering facts, providing relevant information about group concern; stating a belief; giving suggestions or ideas.

4 **Clarifying or elaborating:** interpreting or reflecting ideas and suggestions; clearing up confusions; indicating alternatives and issues before the group, giving examples.

5 **Summarising:** pulling together related ideas, restating suggestions after group has discussed them; offering a decision or conclusion for the group to accept or reject.

6 **Consensus testing:** sending up 'trial balloons' to see if group is nearing a conclusion; checking with group to see how much agreement has been reached.

GROUP BUILDING AND MAINTENANCE FUNCTIONS

1 **Encouraging:** being friendly, warm and responsive to others, accepting others and their contributions, regarding others by giving them an opportunity for recognition.

2 **Expressing group feelings:** sensing feeling, mood, relationships within the group, sharing one's own feelings with other members.

3 **Harmonising:** attempting to reconcile disagreements, reducing tension through 'pouring oil on troubled waters', getting people to explore their differences.

4 **Compromising:** when own idea or status is involved in a conflict, offering to compromise own position, admitting error, disciplining oneself to maintain group cohesion.

5 **Gatekeeping:** attempting to keep communication channels open, facilitating the participation of others; suggesting procedure for sharing opportunity to discuss group problems.

6 **Setting standards:** expressing standards for group to achieve, applying standards in evaluating group functioning and production.

Figure 14.5 Observation sheets for behavioural analysis
(*Source:* National Training Laboratory, Washington DC (1952).)

mark to indicate non-verbal behaviour such as body movements, smiles or eye contact. The most important point, however, is that the charting should not become too complex. The observer should feel happy with the framework and be capable of explaining the entries in a meaningful way. Where more than one observer is present there should be some degree of consistency between them.

AN ESSENTIAL FEATURE OF WORK ORGANISATIONS

Groups and teams are an essential feature in the life of the work organisation. For example, as Coghlan points out:

Membership of teams and groups shape an individual's perception and participation in organizational change ... Groups and teams play a key role in the process of planned organizational change. The change process typically involves teams in the organization's hierarchy responding to the change agenda and adapting to it in terms of its tasks and processes.[24]

Nature of group						
Nature of activity						
Date		*Name of observer(s)*				

Initial arrangement of group

```
                C  D
          B              E
   A                        F
```

Name of group members
(or reference letters)

	A	B	C	D	E	F
Taking initiative – e.g. attempted leadership, seeking suggestions, offering directions						
Brainstorming – e.g. offering ideas or suggestions, however valid						
Offering positive ideas – e.g. making helpful suggestions, attempting to problem-solve						
Drawing in others – e.g. encouraging contributions, seeking ideas and opinions						
Being responsive to others – e.g. giving encouragement and support, building on ideas						
Harmonising – e.g. acting as peacemaker, calming things down, compromising						
Challenging – e.g. seeking justification, showing disagreement in constructive way						
Being obstructive – e.g. criticising, putting others down, blocking contributions						
Clarifying/summarising – e.g. linking ideas, checking progress, clarifying objectives/proposals						
Performing group roles – e.g. spokesperson, recorder, time keeper, humorist						
Other comments						

Figure 14.6 Observation sheet for behaviour in groups

Individuals on teams interact extensively with one another, and with other teams in the organisation. Team-based management is used to improve communication, co-ordination and co-operation within the organisation.[25] For example, as *Green* maintains:

The generally perceived advantages of working in teams are the release of creativity and energy, much more interaction between people satisfying the need to belong ... Team working can improve efficiency by people planning activities together with cooperation and communication. Team members together should be able to identify many ways to improve work organisation; how information, ideas and outputs flow and how team-working can reduce costs and improve productivity.[26]

Balance between the team and the individual

We mentioned previously the need to balance effective team performance with respect for the individual members. For example, as *James* points out: 'Effective teams need equilibrium, no matter how uneasy. The perfect team will have balance, with each member aware of their role and happy to add that value to the task. The natural leaders for any given job will be in charge and their leadership will be cherished by mutual consent. Being a perfect team member means commitment to the task overrides personal ambition and glory. Unfortunately this is rarely achieved in the workplace.'[27]

Successful organizations are good at building teams and exploiting teamwork. People need to be able to work in teams; they need to subordinate their own agenda to the wellbeing of the group. Further, organizations need to foster diversity, which entails respect for the individual and makes group decision making more creative.[28]

Skills for successful teamwork

The increasing need for collaboration and teamwork together with recognition for the individual has highlighted the need for attention to social skills and effectively relationships among people. If people are not working together they are essentially a collection of individuals. For example, *Douglas* refers to the importance of helping people to master the so-called 'soft' skills.

Organisations in most sectors – and especially in ones that are particularly demanding from a scientific or technical point of view – are operating in environments where collaboration, teamwork, and an awareness of the commercial consequences and implications of technical research are as important as scientific and technical skills themselves. Personnel with scientific and technical skills significantly disproportionate to their 'people' skills – by which I primarily mean people management capabilities and the knowledge of how to work with maximum effectiveness as part of a team – are increasingly unlikely to be as much of an asset to their organisation as they ought to be.[29]

An example of teamwork in action

Photo: Peter Spurrier/Action Plus

However, Douglas points out that as we all interact with people to a greater or lesser extent in our everyday lives there is a tendency to assume that people management skills are merely an extension of our natural abilities. In fact people management skills are the more difficult and rare type of skill but to a large extent they can be learned.

Building successful teams also requires effective leadership with an emphasis on trust, clear communications, full participation and self-management. 'The influence and usefulness of team leaders comes, not from their delivery of traditional supervisory and control methods, but from their ability to lead from the front and in training, coaching and counselling their team members to high standards of performance.'[30]

INDIVIDUAL COMPARED WITH GROUP OR TEAM PERFORMANCE

It is, however, difficult to draw any firm conclusions from a comparison between individual and group or team performance. An example of this can be seen from a consideration of decision-making. Certain groups, such as committees, may be concerned more specifically with decision-making, but all groups must make some decisions. Group decision-making can be costly and time-consuming.

One particular feature of group versus individual performance is the concept of social loafing and the 'Ringelmann effect', which is the tendency for individuals to expend less effort when working as a member of a group than as an individual. A German psychologist, *Ringelmann*, compared the results of individual and group performance on a rope-pulling task. Workers were asked to pull as hard as they could on a rope, performing the task first individually, and then with others in groups of varying size. A meter measured the strength of each pull. Although the total amount of force did increase with the size of the work group, the effort expended by each individual member decreased with the result that the total group effort was less than the expected sum of the individual contributions.[31] Replications of the Ringelmann effect have generally been supportive of the original findings.[32]

According to *Hall*, there is a danger of elevating teams into a 'silver bullet' – a magic solution to all business problems. 'It is not that I don't think teams work. They clearly do and it would be difficult to run an organisation of any size if you couldn't create and manage a team ... The truth is that teams are not always the right answer to a problem. Often a well-briefed and well-managed group of individuals will do a task fine ... A further point is that some very skilled individuals are not good team players.'[33]

However, the general feeling appears to be that the collective power of a group outshines individual performance.[34] 'Even though individuals working on their own are capable of phenomenal ingenuity, working together as a team can produce astounding results and a better decision.'[35] *Guirdham* believes that: 'Compared with individuals, groups can make objectively better decisions to which people feel more commitment, while teams can perform functions and carry out projects better and more efficiently. This can only happen, however, if the people have the special skills and abilities needed.'[36]

One might expect, therefore, a higher standard of decision-making to result from group discussion. However, on the one hand, there is the danger of compromise and decisions being made in line with the 'highest common view'; and, on the other hand, there is the phenomenon of the so-called risky-shift.

THE RISKY-SHIFT PHENOMENON

This suggests that instead of the group taking fewer risks and making safer or more conservative decisions, the reverse is often the case. Pressures for conformity means there is a tendency for groups to make more risky decisions than would individual members of the group on their own. Studies suggest that people working in groups generally advocate more risky alternatives than if they were making an individual decision on the same problem.[37]

Presumably, this is because members do not feel the same sense of responsibility for group decisions or their outcomes. 'A decision which is everyone's is the responsibility of no one.' Other explanations offered for the **risky-shift** phenomenon include:

1 People inclined to take risks are more influential in group discussions than more conservative people.
2 Risk-taking is regarded as a desirable cultural characteristic which is more likely to be expressed in a social situation such as group working.[38]

However, groups do appear to work well in the evaluation of ideas and to be more effective than individuals for problem-solving tasks requiring a range of knowledge and expertise. From a review of the research Shaw suggests that evidence supports the view that groups produce more solutions and better solutions to problems than do individuals.[39]

'GROUPTHINK'

The effectiveness of group behaviour and performance can be adversely affected by the idea of '**groupthink**'. From an examination of some well-known government policy-making groups, *Janis* concluded that decisions can be characterised by groupthink which he defines as: 'a deterioration of mental efficiency, reality testing, and moral judgment that results from in-group pressures'.[40] Groupthink results in the propensity for the group to just drift along. It is a generalised feature and can be apparent in any organisational situation where groups are relied upon to make important decisions.

Janis identifies a number of specific symptoms of groupthink.

1 There is an **illusion of invulnerability** with excessive optimism and risk-taking.
2 The discounting or discrediting of negative feedback which contradicts group consensus results in **rationalisation** in order to explain away any disagreeable information.
3 An unquestioned belief in the **inherent morality of the group** which leads members to be convinced of the logical correctness of what it is doing and to ignore ethical or moral consequences of decisions.
4 The group's desire to maintain consensus can lead to **negative stereotyping** of opponents or people outside the group, or to the acceptance of change.
5 There is **pressure on individual members to conform and reach consensus** so that minority or unpopular ideas may be suppressed.
6 Each member of the group may impose **self-censorship** in order to suppress their own objectives, or personal doubts or disagreements.
7 As a result of self-censorship, there is an **illusion of unanimity** with a lack of expressed dissent and a false sense of unity.
8 In the unlikely event of dissent or contrary information, this will give rise to the **emergence of 'mind guards'** who act as filters, guarding group leaders, deflecting opposition and applying pressure on deviants.

According to *Hambrick*: 'Groupthink tends to occur when group members have very similar experiences and frame of references, particularly when they have relatively long tenures in the group. A company head who dislikes conflict or who punishes dissenters also creates the conditions for groupthink.'[41]

BRAINSTORMING

A **brainstorming** approach involves the group adopting a 'freewheeling' attitude and generating as many ideas as possible, the more wild or apparently far-fetched the better.[42] As an illustrative exercise a group may be asked to generate as many and varied possible uses as they can for, for example, a house brick or a car fan belt.

There are a number of basic procedures for brainstorming.

- It is based on maximum freedom of expression with a totally informal approach.
- The initial emphasis is on the quantity of ideas generated, not the quality of ideas.
- No individual ideas are criticised or rejected at this stage, however wild or fanciful they may appear.
- Members are encouraged to elaborate or build on ideas expressed by others, and to bounce suggestions off one another.
- There is no comment on or evaluation of any particular idea until all ideas have been generated.

Brainstorming is based on encouraging members to suspend judgement, the assumption that creative thinking is achieved best by encouraging the natural inclinations of group members, and the rapid production and free association of ideas. The quantity of ideas will lead to quality of ideas.

An interesting and popular exercise to help illustrate the suspension of initial perceived barriers and the encouragement of creative thinking is given in Figure 14.7. This exercise may also be used to compare individual and group/team-based performance. **Your tutor will provide the (or least one) answer. There may be others that the author is unaware of!**

The task is to see if it is possible to touch each of the nine spots using only four straight, interconnected lines.

Figure 14.7 An example of creative thinking

Effectiveness of brainstorming groups

One might reasonably expect that members of a brainstorming group would produce more creative problem-solving ideas than if the same members worked alone as individuals. Availability of time is an important factor. Over a longer period of time the group may produce more ideas through brainstorming than individuals could. Perhaps surprisingly, however, there appears to be doubt about the effectiveness of brainstorming groups over an individual working under the same conditions. Research findings suggest that brainstorming groups can inhibit creative thinking. The general tenor appears to be that research studies have not substantiated claims that brainstorming groups generate more and better ideas than the same number of individuals working on their own.[43] Nevertheless, brainstorming still appears to have many advocates and is a popular activity for staff development programmes.[44] (*See* Figure 14.8.) Despite the rather negative view of nominal group brainstorming, we should recognise the importance of innovation for successful organisational performance.[45] Any procedure which aids the process of creativity should be welcomed and there are a number of potential positive achievements in terms of related structural techniques for stimulating innovation. These include the Delphi technique and quality circles.

BRAINSTORMING

Brainstorming is a problem-solving/solution-finding technique which can be used by individuals, groups or teams. Its full benefit is gained by sharing ideas and possibilities with others.

The first step is to define the problem or situation to which the group or team wants solutions or ideas. Ideally one person should act as scribe, and write up ideas on a flipchart. He or she can contribute, but should not comment on others' suggestions. Every idea should be written up, however far-fetched or silly it might seem, without challenge from others.

Everyone should be encouraged to participate.

When all possibilities have been exhausted, suggestions can be examined, clarified, amended, accepted or rejected.

It may be that several options are accepted as possible ways forward. Reverse brainstorming looks at the possibilities and then brainstorms all the *problems* associated with the ideas. This helps give an objective view of ideas or solutions.

If performed correctly, brainstorming is an excellent, non-threatening way to include all members of a team in the problem-solving/decision-making process. It has the added benefit of producing many and various ideas, some of which will be of no value, but others which may be of immediate or future benefit. Creativity is contagious, and one idea will spark off another. Often, it is one of the most apparently silly ideas that points the way to a solution.

Brainstorming:

- involves everyone;
- focuses the mind;
- encourages creativity;
- meets individual needs for team inclusion;
- encourages communication – listening, information sharing;
- maximises ideas/possible solutions to problems;
- minimises risk of overlooking elements of the problem or issue under question.

Figure 14.8 Advantages of brainstorming

Source: Susan Bishop and David Taylor, *Developing Your Staff*, Pitman Publishing/Longman Training (1994). Reproduced with permission from Pearson Education Ltd.)

The **Delphi technique** is based on multiple, anonymous inputs from individual members of the group. Ideas and suggestions are recorded by a central manager and then recirculated to other members for their feedback. The central manager collates the responses and continues the circulation process again until consensus is reached. Although a time-consuming process the Delphi technique helps to overcome the limitations of face-to-face brainstorming and symptoms of groupthink.

Quality circles are discussed in Chapter 18.

EXHIBIT 14.1

Management: brainstorm in a rainstorm

Use the theatre to fire creativity writes **Arkady Ostrovsky**

Jackets come off, ties are loosened; 20 senior business people howl, whisper and run around throwing their arms about.

Their bizarre behaviour is part of an exercise to use theatre to fuel their imagination and creativity.

One participant, Richard Hardman, international exploration director at US oil group Amerada Hess, says: 'If you want to get fit physically you go to the gym, but what do you do if your imagination needs some stretching? Theatre is very good for it.'

Four weeks of visits to theatrical events and a day's seminar and workshop took place recently during the annual London International Festival of Theatre. Events were held in association with the Global Business Network, a business strategy group, and the FT.

At one, executives took a barefoot, sensual journey through a dark labyrinth inhabited by personifications of destiny and death. At another, they were deafened by music and sprinkled with water and tickertape as they stood in a darkened warehouse watching Argentinian troupe De La Guarda's crazed, swooping musician-acrobats.

Richard Wise, chief financial officer at Coutts, the bank, says: 'You are so bound up with day-to-day imperatives that you lose the creative aspect. We tend to deal in very rationalised business structures – these performances show the benefit of brainstorming unconventional solutions.'

Performers and business people had a chance to meet after events – to the benefit of both sides, says Julia Rowntree, of the festival. 'It encourages the artist to learn more about the motives that drive the business world and, in some way, to have their say in it. For business people, it is a chance to discover what is going on outside their offices and to look at their own business from an outside perspective.'

The benefits of such exercises are notoriously difficult to measure. But, says Rick Haythornthwaite, director of Premier Oil, and a participant: 'If you test the success of this venture through the quality of thinking and the open-mindedness of the people who participate in it, back in the work place over the coming months and years, it is undoubtedly working.'

(Reproduced with permission from the Financial Times Limited, © *Financial Times*.)

GROUP DYNAMICS

Interest in the study of group process and behaviour has led to the development of **group dynamics** and a range of group training methods aimed at increasing group effectiveness through improving social interaction skills.

Group dynamics is the study of interactions and forces within small face-to-face groups. It is concerned with what happens when groups of people meet.

A central feature of group dynamics is **sensitivity training**, in which members of a group direct attention to the understanding of their own behaviour and to perceiving themselves as others see them. The objectives are usually stated as:

- to increase sensitivity (the ability to perceive accurately how others react to oneself);
- diagnostic ability (the skill of assessing behavioural relationships between others and reasons for such behaviour); and
- behavioural flexibility, or action skill (the ability to relate one's behaviour to the requirements of the situation).

An account of 'problems' that have arisen with team-building exercises is given in Management in Action 14.2.

T-GROUPS

A usual method of sensitivity training (which is increasingly used as a generic term) is the **T-group** (training group), sometimes called laboratory training.

A T-group has been defined as:

an approach to human relations training which, broadly speaking, provides participants with an opportunity to learn more about themselves and their impact on others, and in particular to learn how to function more effectively in face-to-face situations.[46]

The original form of a T-group is a small, leaderless, unstructured, face-to-face grouping. The group normally numbers between 8 and 12 members who may be strangers to each other or who may come from the same organisation (a family group). A deliberate attempt is made to minimise any status differentials among members. There is no agenda or planned activities. Trainers are present to help guide the group, but do not usually take an active role or act as formal leader. The agenda becomes the group's own behaviour in attempting to cope with the lack of structure or planned activities. Training is intended to concentrate on process rather than content, that is on the feeling level of communication rather than the informational value of communication.

Faced with confusion and lack of direction, individuals will act in characteristic ways. With the guidance of the trainers these patterns of behaviour become the focus of attention for the group. Participants are encouraged to examine their own self-concepts and to be more receptive to the feelings and behaviours of others. Feedback received by individuals from other members of the group is the main mechanism for learning. This feedback creates a feeling of anxiety and tension, and the individual's own self-examination leads to consideration of new values, attitudes and behaviour. Typically, the group meets for a $1\frac{1}{2}$- to-2-hour session each day for up to a fortnight. The sessions are supported by related lectures, study groups, case studies and other exercises.

The Johari window

A simple framework for looking at self-insight, which is used frequently to help individuals in the T-group process, is the 'Johari window' (see Figure 14.9). This classifies behaviour in matrix form between what is known–unknown to self and what is known–unknown to others.[47] A central feature of the T-group is reduction of the individual's 'hidden' behaviour through self-disclosure and reduction of the 'blind' behaviour through feedback from others.

▪ **Hidden behaviour** is that which the individual wishes to conceal from, or not to communicate to, other group members. It is part of the private self. An important

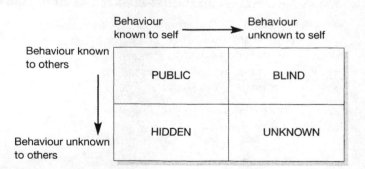

Figure 14.9 The Johari window

role of the group is to establish whether members conceal too much, or too little, about themselves from other members.

■ **The blind area** includes mannerisms, gestures, and tone of voice, and represents behaviour of the impact of which on others the individual is unaware. This is sometimes referred to as the 'bad breath' area.

Members must establish an atmosphere of openness and trust in order that hidden and blind behaviours are reduced and the public behaviour enhanced.

Value and effectiveness of T-Groups

Reactions to the value and effectiveness of T-group training are very mixed. The experience can be very disturbing and unpleasant, at least for some members. For example, participants have described it as 'a bloodbath and a psychological nudist colony in which people are stripped bare to their attitudes'.[48] Participants are required to lay bare their inner emotions and may feel an invasion of their privacy. The unstructured situation may permit trainers to impose their own perceptions and social viewpoints on members of the group.[49]

T-group training is difficult to evaluate objectively and there is still a main problem of the extent to which training is transferred 'back home' to practical work situations. However, a number of studies do suggest that participation as a member of a T-group does increase interpersonal skills, induce change, and lead to open communications and more flexible behaviour. T-groups probably do result in a change of behaviour but it is not always clear whether such change is positive or related to improved organisational performance.[50]

T-groups now take a number of different forms. Some place emphasis on the understanding of group processes, others place more emphasis on the development of the individual's self-awareness and feelings towards the behaviour of other people. They are now used frequently as a means of attempting to improve managerial development and organisational performance. The *Blake and Mouton* managerial grid seminars, discussed in Chapter 7, can be seen as an applied, and refined, form of T-group. A number of different training packages have been designed, often under the broad heading of interpersonal skills, which are less confrontational and less disturbing for participants. The training often involves an analysis of group members' relationships with one another and the resolution of conflict.[51]

EFFECTIVE TEAMWORKING

Whatever the debate about a comparison between individual and group or team performance, effective teamworking is of increasing importance in modern organisations. This demands that the manager must be aware of, and pay attention to, a number of interrelated factors, including:

■ clarification of objectives and available resources;
■ organisational processes and the clarification of roles;
■ empowerment, decision-making and channels of communication;
■ patterns of interaction, and attention to both task and maintenance functions;
■ social processes and the informal organisation;
■ management systems and style of leadership;
■ training and development.

The effectiveness of the team will also be influenced by the tasks to be undertaken, the nature of technology and the organisational environment. Ultimately, however, the performance of the team will be determined very largely by the characteristics of its members. The nature of group personality means that what works well for one team may not work well for an apparently similar team in the organisation.

As *Wilson*, points out, for example, although teamworking, like most management ideas, is very simple, nevertheless this simplicity conceals a great challenge.

> The principles of teamworking may be easily understood, but the task of installing it can be quite daunting. Introducing teamworking is not a straightforward grafting job, the simple matter of adding a new idea to those already in place. It is about making a fundamental change in the way people work. Every teamworking application is different. Each organisation, department and individual group is faced with unique problems and in some situations it is more about getting rid of old ways of doing things than injecting new ones.[52]

Ten ways to motivate your team[53]

1 Be clear about your own goals	6 Get to know individuals
2 Inform everyone of theirs	7 Incentivise everyone
3 Give the right training	8 Be tough when necessary
4 Coach and encourage	9 Give people space to grow
5 Listen to members	10 Let them get on with it

A 'summary outline' of effective work groups is presented in Figure 14.10.

Continuous process of improvement and innovation

The requirement for continual development and improvement is a necessary part of effective teamwork. However as *Riches*, for example, points out: 'Understandably, teams are pre-occupied with getting the job done. Few teams regularly take time out to reflect on how the team itself is working and what it needs to do to improve the way its modus operandi. Even fewer set measurable objectives for team functioning and/or get feedback from internal and external customers about the team's effectiveness.'[54]

The ACAS advisory booklet concludes that although self-regulation is necessary if the potential of teamworking is to be realised, teams will always need some degree of management direction. The task of management is to oversee the development of teams and provide the necessary support and training. Even when in place, teams will need constant monitoring and development. Teamworking is not a finite project but a process of continuous improvement and innovation.

> The introduction of team working is a major step for an organisation to take. It is important that management, trade unions and employees ensure they know how teamworking will contribute to their business strategy and that it is likely to involve a long-term transformation ... The early challenge and excitement of establishing teams may fade and it is easy for organisations to accept a level of performance which is short of optimum ... In order to achieve high performance, teams require regular changes and challenges. These may include: changes to team personnel; new tasks; re-examining the contribution the team makes to the overall business aims; and ensuring that the team has regular dealings with other teams.[55]

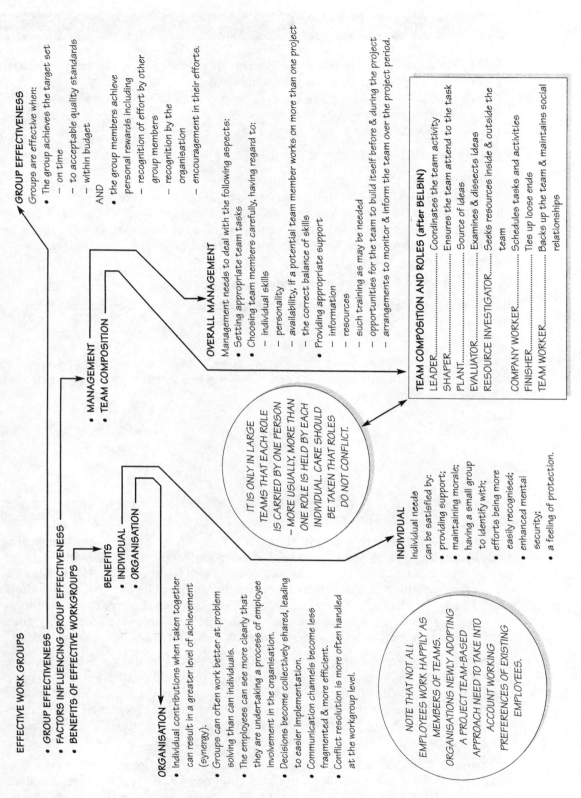

EFFECTIVE WORK GROUPS

- GROUP EFFECTIVENESS
- FACTORS INFLUENCING GROUP EFFECTIVENESS
- BENEFITS OF EFFECTIVE WORKGROUPS

BENEFITS
- INDIVIDUAL
- ORGANISATION

ORGANISATION
- Individual contributions when taken together can result in a greater level of achievement (synergy).
- Groups can often work better at problem solving than can individuals.
- The employees can see more clearly that they are undertaking a process of employee involvement in the organisation.
- Decisions become collectively shared, leading to easier implementation.
- Communication channels become less fragmented & more efficient.
- Conflict resolution is more often handled at the workgroup level.

NOTE THAT NOT ALL EMPLOYEES WORK HAPPILY AS MEMBERS OF TEAMS. ORGANISATIONS NEWLY ADOPTING A PROJECT TEAM-BASED APPROACH NEED TO TAKE INTO ACCOUNT WORKING PREFERENCES OF EXISTING EMPLOYEES.

- MANAGEMENT
- TEAM COMPOSITION

GROUP EFFECTIVENESS
Groups are effective when:
- The group achieves the target set
  - on time
  - to acceptable quality standards
  - within budget
  AND
- the group members achieve personal rewards including
  - recognition of effort by other group members
  - recognition by the organisation
  - encouragement in their efforts.

OVERALL MANAGEMENT
Management needs to deal with the following aspects:
- Setting appropriate team tasks
- Choosing team members carefully, having regard to:
  - individual skills
  - personality
  - availability, if a potential team member works on more than one project
  - the correct balance of skills
- Providing appropriate support
  - information
  - resources
  - such training as may be needed
  - opportunities for the team to build itself before & during the project
  - arrangements to monitor & inform the team over the project period.

IT IS ONLY IN LARGE TEAMS THAT EACH ROLE IS CARRIED BY ONE PERSON – MORE USUALLY, MORE THAN ONE ROLE IS HELD BY EACH INDIVIDUAL. CARE SHOULD BE TAKEN THAT ROLES DO NOT CONFLICT.

TEAM COMPOSITION AND ROLES (after BELBIN)

LEADER	Coordinates the team activity
SHAPER	Ensures the team attend to the task
PLANT	Source of ideas
EVALUATOR	Examines & dissects ideas
RESOURCE INVESTIGATOR	Seeks resources inside & outside the team
COMPANY WORKER	Schedules tasks and activities
FINISHER	Ties up loose ends
TEAM WORKER	Backs up the team & maintains social relationships

INDIVIDUAL
Individual needs can be satisfied by:
- providing support;
- maintaining morale;
- having a small group to identify with;
- efforts being more easily recognised;
- enhanced mental security;
- a feeling of protection.

Figure 14.10 Summary outline of effective work groups
(Reproduced with permission of Training Learning Consultancy Ltd., Bristol.)

CRITICAL REFLECTIONS

'I found all this discussion about group membership and building successful teams very interesting and enlightening. It certainly makes good sense to me.'

'Umm, I'm not so sure. It sounds fine in the classroom but I wonder how it works in practice for example with managing workers on a production assembly line, in a gay pub, or professionals such as doctors or lawyers?'

What are your own views?

Well-constructed and well-balanced teams have a good chance of succeeding in the modern world. But success is not ensured, however well the team functions. A common problem lies with the environment of the team. The team may be mature but the organization may not be. Hierarchies run organizations. They tolerate teams but are loath to see teams as alternatives to hierarchical decision-making.

Belbin, R. M. *Beyond the Team*, Butterworth-Heinemann (2000), p. 68.

How would you attempt to ensure the success of teams within a hierarchical organisation structure?

'Individuals will complete a task more efficiently and effectively than a group. And training in group dynamics, whilst interesting, has no practical value as a means of increasing the standard of group performance.'

Debate.

SYNOPSIS

▓ Organisational performance and the satisfaction derived by individuals are influenced by the interactions among members of the group. Members of a group must work well together as a team and there must be a spirit of unity and co-operation. *Belbin* suggests key contributions or team-roles for successful groups. The level of interaction is influenced by the channels of communication. There are five main types of communication networks – wheel, circle, all-channel, Y and chains. Despite the artificiality, they provide a reasonable representation of situations that might apply in large organisations.

▓ In order to understand and to influence the functioning and operation of a group, it is necessary to study the behaviour of individual members. Two main methods are (i) sociometry, and (ii) interaction analysis. Sociometry is usually based on 'buddy rating' or 'peer rating'. It is a method of indicating feelings of acceptance and/or rejection among members of a group. A sociogram gives a diagrammatical illustration of the pattern of interpersonal relationships derived from sociometry.

▓ Interaction analysis is based on the assumption that the behaviour of individuals may be analysed from the viewpoint of its function or process. Two essential functions necessary for the success and continuity of a group are: (i) task-oriented behaviour; and (ii) maintenance-oriented behaviour. In addition, members may display self-oriented behaviour. Several frameworks have been designed for observers to categorise patterns of verbal and non-verbal behaviour of members. It is important, however, that the frameworks do not become too complex.

▓   Groups and teams are an essential feature in the life of the work organisation but it is difficult to draw any firm comparison with individual performance. Group decision-making would appear to offer a number of advantages but can be adversely affected by the 'risky-shift' phenomenon and by 'groupthink'. There also appears to be some doubt about the effectiveness of brainstorming over an individual working under the same conditions. Interest in the study of groups and teams has lead to the development of training methods aimed at improving social interaction skills and self-insight.

▓   Viewing the effectiveness of teamworking must take into account a variety of inter-related factors, especially the characteristics and behaviour of their members. Building successful teams also requires effective leadership with an emphasis on trust, clear communications, full participation and self-management. Although self-regulation is necessary if the potential of teamworking is to be realised, teams will always need some degree of management direction. The task of management is to oversee the development of teams and provide the necessary support and training. The requirement for continual development and improvement is a necessary part of effective teamwork.

MANAGEMENT IN ACTION 14.1

Profiling of managers for leadership development in a cross-section of South African organisations

THE SITUATION

With the acceleration of 'transformation' from white manager domination in South Africa to a more legally equitable[56] distribution of management and leadership in both the private and public sector, it has become increasingly important to (a) develop both the managerial and leadership skills of aspiring black leaders and (b) find more objective, user friendly and efficient ways of profiling management and leadership behaviour, thereby providing a means of raising self-awareness and monitoring the leadership and management profiles of an organization. There must be few countries in the world where there is a greater need for assessing or profiling managers in a helpful and constructive way so as to motivate corporate and individual management development. And there must be few countries in the world where there is a greater need to bridge the gap between 'ideal' management requirements and the large number of new inexperienced managers in both the public and private sectors.

I use the terms 'management and leadership' here in the sense of an equal **partnership between management and leadership**, rather than two mutually exclusive approaches to getting the work done with and through others. The Leadership Development Project, outlined later in this paper, places equal stress on the need for sound **management thinking** and the need for sound **leadership interaction** and relationships in the workplace. [For the sake of convenience I will use the word 'management' from here onwards to capture the notion of an equal partnership between management and leadership behaviour in the workplace.]

The objectives of this paper are:

(i)   to present and explore a practical means of management profiling with the aid of the Belbin programme, and illustrate how it is used in a Leadership Development Project run in a cross-section of South African organizations,

(ii) to draw attention to the gaps between actual and 'ideal' profiles for managers, mentors or technical specialists, and the likely implications of these gaps for management development, and

(iii) to suggest possible courses of action to deal with these gaps.

When using the word 'ideal' profile or 'ideal' requirements one is automatically tempted to fall into the trap of claiming to have found this will-o'-the-wisp 'ideal' manager or 'ideal' mentor, or whatever profile one is examining. There are many instruments and many approaches to this search for the 'ideal' manager or 'ideal' manager profile. The one proposed here makes extensive use of the Belbin Team Role computer-aided package[57] for identifying a job profile, since it produces profiles which are consistent with profiles from the intuitive rankings of managers from a wide range of organizations; it is user friendly and lends itself well to providing a foundation to motivate learning and development.

THE LEADERSHIP DEVELOPMENT PROJECT (LDP)

Briefly, the Leadership Development Project is a well-tested project which has been running since 1984 and has been employed in a wide range of public service and private sector ▶

organizations. The aim of the project is to raise individual and corporate management performance through a series of one-day seminars run at two- to three-week intervals which (a) provide practical thinking and interactive tools for participants to use in the work situation, and (b) require them to apply these tools in a series of on-the-job assignments between seminars. It is referred to as a 'project' since there is a serious attempt to move away from the 'training course' paradigm to an 'organization development' paradigm where the whole organizational unit, top-down–bottom-up, is involved in finding better ways of managing for the present and the future. For more detail on this project, the reader is referred to a comprehensive text[58] which covers the thinking and interactive tools, as well as a more recent shorter text[59] on the subject. Approximately 800 managers have been through the project in some form, but it is only since 1994 that deliberate use has been made of the Belbin instrument. Clearly, as one uses it more, its application and interpretation become more refined and helpful to participants.

The following diagram, Figure 14.11, outlines the flow of the LDP process from phase 1 to phase 6. The strong link between phase 2 and phase 5 is important since the tools and skills the participants acquire on the seminars at phase 4 are applied, at phase 5, to some of the real life issues identified at phase 2.

In order to provide time for participants to apply what they have learned between seminars, seminars are run at two- to three-week intervals, during which time participants or teams of participants complete and submit formal reports on their applications assignments.

The Belbin profiles have a particular role to play at phase 1 of the project, although together with other means of feedback throughout the seminars and the assignments, constant reference is made to these profiles and their implications for the participants at all phases of the project. The Belbin profiles, together with other means of feedback, form part of a strong commitment to experiential learning[60] where feedback plays an important role in opening up the 'window' to participants on how they are seen and how they see themselves.

THE BELBIN TEAM ROLE INSTRUMENT

For about ten years the author has been testing out different approaches to using the Belbin Team Role (Interplace) programme. One of its strongest appeals is that it is user friendly. Once participants have an understanding of the following terms, they can start relating their profiles to their own orientation as managers and identify their own strengths and limitations in tackling management work. Belbin's nine team roles[61] are summarized below in the form they are used on the Leadership Development Project:

- **Plant (PL)** – Someone who 'plants' creative and innovative ideas. Imaginative. Unorthodox. Brings new ideas to difficult problems. *Limitations*: Tends to be caught up in his/her ideas and does not communicate (listen and receive) easily with others. Prone to come in with new ideas when all seems settled.
- **Resource Investigator (RI)** – Someone who keeps in touch with resources/people outside his/her immediate environment. Extrovert. Enthusiastic. Communicative. Explores opportunities. *Limitations*: Tends to lose interest once the initial ideas have been launched. Does not sustain effort in the same directon and continues to seek new 'contacts'.
- **Co-ordinator (CO)** – Someone who co-ordinates the contributions of others. Mature. Confident and trusting. Good chairman and facilitator. Clarifies goals and promotes participative decision making. *Limitations*: Not necessarily the most clever or creative member of a group. May have limited input to the team effort. Could run the risk of being seen as indecisive or not initiating ideas or action.
- **Shaper (SH)** – Someone who gets others to 'shape up' and get the job done. Dynamic, outgoing. Pushes and pressurizes and is determined to get around obstacles. *Limitations*: Prone to provocation and shortlived outbursts in his/her need to get on with the job and produce results. Tends to be predominantly task focused.

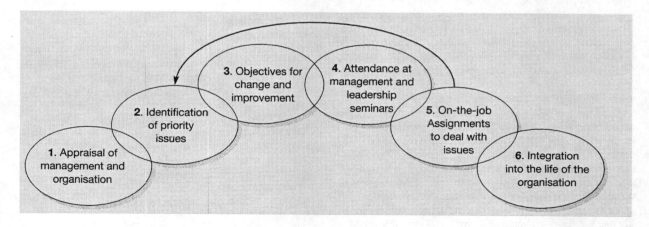

Figure 14.11 Flow of the Leadership Development Project

- **Monitor Evaluator (ME)** – Someone who monitors and evaluates clearly and analytically. Clear and rational thinker. Sober. Discerning. Considers all options. Evaluates carefully and accurately in making decisions. *Limitations*: Tends to focus too much on clarity and logic. Too analytical at times and tends to lose others in his/her search for logic, evidence and clarity. Could slow things down with too much systematic thinking and analysis.
- **Teamworker (TW)** – Someone who is sensitive towards and concerned about others and how they feel. Social, mild, perceptive and accommodating. Listens and builds on others' ideas. Smooths friction. *Limitations*: Tends to be over accommodating and indecisive in crunch situations where a decision – particularly an unpopular one – has to be made. Can become too people focused and neglect the job at hand.
- **Implementer (IMP)** – Someone who concentrates on implementation of ideas and decisions. Disciplined. Reliable and efficient in getting the job done. Turns ideas into practical action. *Limitations*: Tends to get too quickly into 'how' and once actively involved in the plan is slow to respond to changes or new possibilities.
- **Completer-Finisher (CF)** – Someone who wants to get the job completely right and strives to finish perfectly and on time. Searches out errors and mistakes. Painstaking and conscientious. *Limitations*: Tends to worry too much about accuracy and getting the job right. Reluctant to delegate for fear of errors creeping in.
- **Specialist (SP)** – Someone who brings specialist knowledge and expertise to the job or problem. Dedicated. Single-minded. Focused on his/her subject. Provides skills in rare supply. *Limitations*: Tends to contribute on a very narrow front. Does not contribute across a wide range of issues and problems. May miss the importance of other disciplines and specialities.

In summary, each participant completes a questionnaire and is also invited to find four observers who know the participant in the work context and complete an observer questionnaire of positive and negative terms in confidence and anonymously to the participant. (The observer forms are returned to the facilitator directly for analysis.) The information from the completed questionnaires is fed into a computer program and the results shared with the participants in confidence at the start of the Leadership Development seminars. A corporate picture of the leadership team roles, together with the results from a 60-item management performance questionnaire, is also shared anonymously with the top management team (who have also completed the questionnaires). The purpose of presenting these is twofold: (i) to raise awareness of the gaps between actual profiles and reasonably well researched 'ideal' profiles, and (ii) to provide a basis for identifying needs and promoting learning and improvements in performance.

BELBIN PROFILES ON THE LEADERSHIP DEVELOPMENT PROJECT

This is not the place to go into further details of the Belbin instrument itself. The above section should provide sufficient background on the Belbin programme and how it works. On the Leadership Development Project the following takes place:

1 Participants are briefed on the project with particular emphasis on the Belbin questionnaires and how to use them.
2 Self-assessment questionnaires are completed and returned to the facilitator with at least four observers questionnaires (anonymously and confidentially).
3 The data from the questionnaires are fed into a computer program and individual reports are printed.
4 In addition to the computer reports, 'ideal' profiles for a manager, a mentor and a technical specialist are provided and both individual and corporate profiles are compared with these 'ideal' profiles with the aid of graphs showing deviations from the 'ideal' profiles.
5 During the first seminar, participants spend about three to four hours discussing and exploring their own profiles and their computer-generated reports.
6 The gaps between their 'ideal' and 'actual' profiles are discussed in relation to what is offered on the seminars, and the participants invited to plan what they would like to do:
   a Accept their strengths and limitations and find ways of accommodating their limitations by finding someone else to fill in the gaps (e.g. a poor Shaper may look for help when he or she has to discipline someone).
   b Focus on practising the tools offered during the seminars which will help them to bridge some of the gaps through learning and development of new skills.
   c Give more attention to their natural orientations and not get too hung up about their limitations – build on their strengths within the context of their present jobs.
   d Find ways of restructuring or even changing their jobs so that they can accommodate their limitations and make better use of their strengths (e.g. a strong Specialist and Monitor Evaluator may decide to move out of management work into more technical troubleshooting work, or perhaps restructure his/her present job to help accommodate natural strengths and limitations).

The Belbin team role framework relates very easily to some of the **thinking** and **interactive tools** presented on the Leadership Development Project. Participants are able to examine the gaps in their own performance and, where appropriate, use the relevant tools to develop the skills which will help them to bridge these gaps. For example, Co-ordinator (CO) is clearly related to **team building**, and **organizing for action** which are offered as tools on the seminars. Similarly, Shaper (SH) is related to the **telling, selling and consultation** modes of communication, **setting clear objectives, identifying priorities** and **evaluating performance**.

Graphs of the Belbin profiles

The three graphs (Figure 14.12) show the relative fit of a cross section of 446 managers attending the LDP, with the 'deal' profiles of manager, mentor and technical specialist. Participants were from 14 different organizations (private sector, public sector and local govenument) and made up of 40% White, and 60% Black (Coloured, African and Indian) participants. 284 of the 446 were involved in either local government or the police services. The graphs tell the story of the gap between the ideal and actual average self-perception profiles for this group of 446 managers. These three profiles were chosen since all managers, although their main role is to ▶

Management in Action 14.1 continued

manage, also play a partial mentor and technical specialist role. Showing how managers compare with the mentor and technical specialist profiles provides a useful basis for comparison. For the purposes of this paper, however, only the implications of the manager profile will be discussed in any depth.

At the outset, it must be stressed that these graphs and comments on them are not the direct product of the Belbin computer printouts, but are drawn from the Belbin computer software statistics. The intention is to draw clear visual distinctions between 'good' and 'poor' management behaviours, and to reach conclusions about improving management performance. It must also be stressed that Belbin's emphasis has been on producing well-balanced teams, which are considered to be more effective than poorly balanced teams where there is not a good mix of the various team roles. Effective and well-balanced teams are, clearly, essential. We know, for example, what happens when a group of Shapers (SH) get together and try to reach consensus – they tend to fight and argue to establish who is 'boss' instead of concentrating on the problem or task at hand. In this paper, the profiles focus more on manage-

ment behaviour and how to deal with management strengths and limitations, rather than the dynamics of management teams and how to form effective ones.

How are these graphs used on the LDP?

Similar graphs are used on the LDP and provide a fruitful basis for discussion and learning. Individuals plot their own individual profiles based on what is referred to in the Belbin computer printouts as 'assessment results in rank order'. This shows their (i) self perception profiles, (ii) how each observer ranks them on the 9 team role dimensions and (iii) their overall profile which is a consolidation of self and observer assessments. They then draw their own conclusions about the discrepancies between these profiles, and explore why they see themselves differently from others and why they don't fit the ideal profiles as well as they would like to fit them. To stimulate further motivation, the average % fit for the group as a whole is calculated, and a rough group profile is plotted, so that each person can compare how well he/she shapes up against the group as a whole.

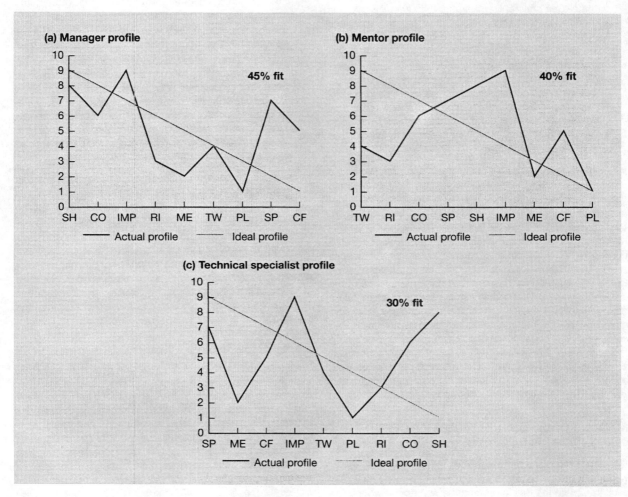

Figure 14.12 Comparing 'actual' with 'ideal' profiles in a cross-section of 446 managers

Matching the manager profile

Figure 14.12 (Management Profile) shows the comparison of a large sample of 446 managers with the ideal manager profile where there is a 45% fit for this group of 446 managers.

It is interesting to compare the overall average fit of 45% with the 60% fit of a nine-person top executive team – which was one of the 14 groups identified in the sample of 446 managers. Is it safe to assume that this top team is better than the overall average manager in this sample of 446? I suggest that it is probably a safe assumption. It is also interesting that four chief executive officers who completed Belbin ratings from this particular sample of managers all scored 50% fit or above on their self-assessments as compared with the average of 45% fit for the group as a whole. There is some evidence, therefore, that the better the % fit with the 'ideal' manager, the greater the likelihood of occupying a more senior job.

However, this is a very general statement. One can have a good overall fit as one finds in this sample of managers, but still have some serious limitations on *particular dimensions*. Even in this large sample of 446 managers, the manager profile in Figure 14.12 illustrates a tendency towards too much attention to detail (CF) and an orientation towards narrow specialization (SP), which are less desirable tendencies in management work. This profile also illustrates a general need for more attention to looking outwards and keeping in touch with events and circumstances in the environment, which is characteristic of the RI.

One particular chief executive, when comparing his *overall profile* (which included the ratings of at least four observers) with the ideal profile for a manager (see Figure 14.13), matched very well on coordinator (CO) and this was evident from his ability to listen and draw others in when tackling issues, and make best use of their abilities. However, as can be seen from the graph (Figure 14.13) he was well below on Shaper (SH) and Resource Investigator (RI), and had a bit too much Monitor Evaluator (ME) for the job of a chief executive officer. This pointed to his need to: (i) push more for results (SH); (ii) focus on what was happening in the broader market place (RI) – making good contacts with important role players in the busi-

ness; and (iii) spend less time analysing problems (ME) and focus more on broad strategic decisions. It is also interesting that this particular executive rated himself at a 50% fit with the ideal management profile based on his *self-perception*, whereas comparing his *overall profile* (which included the ratings of at least four observers) with the ideal manager profile, he had a 30% fit. Clearly, he saw himself being more effective as a chief executive than his observers saw him.

Do the Belbin profiles and the LDP make a real difference back on the job?

This is always the million-dollar question to be answered in this kind of work. Clearly, the Belbin profiles are only one aspect of the LDP and provide some of the stimulus for learning and change. The other dimensions in the LDP play a major role through the seminars and the application assignments, where particular performance issues are addressed. The final phase of the LDP strategy (phase 6, Figure 14.11) provides for participants on the project to meet after the formal seminars are over, and work out a plan for integrating what they have learned into the life of the organization. This often involves presentations to the top management team who, in general, are very supportive if they have had sufficient exposure to the LDP themselves.

Evaluation of the impact of the LDP takes place at three levels. **First**, there is a final 'test' of the concepts and understanding of the tools and their applications. This, together with the marks from the assignments, provides the final mark for success on the LDP. Our experience has been that the inclusion of a test of understanding and application adds motivation and commitment to learning, and is accepted at all levels of management if it is appropriately 'sold' as an aid to learning and better performance. The average pass mark on the last 10 projects is 67%. **Second**, participants rate their perceived shift in ability on the course objectives from the start to the finish of the course. The average at the start is 42% and, at the end, 82%, which shows a substantial perceived increase in ability on the course objectives. **Third**, wherever possible, the organization is invited to assess the extent to which their initial project objectives were achieved (see phase 3 of the project). Limited studies done so far show that, on average, 80% of the participants and their colleagues rate the LDP as having a high impact on the project objectives. The ratings of high impact on particular project objectives range from 50% to 95%, showing that the impact of the LDP on the project objectives was higher for some objectives than for other objectives.

CONCLUSIONS

The objectives of this paper were:

(i)   to present and explore a practical means of management profiling with the aid of the Belbin programme and illustrate how it is used in a Leadership Development Project run in a cross-section of South African organizations,

(ii) to draw attention to the gaps between actual and 'ideal' profiles for managers, mentors or technical specialists, and the likely implications of these gaps for management development, and

(iii) to suggest possible courses of action to deal with these gaps.

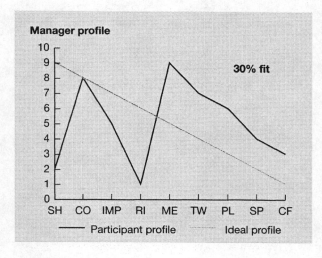

Figure 14.13 Profile for one chief executive

Management in Action 14.1 continued

Use of Belbin profiles in the Leadership Development Project

By comparing actual profiles based on the Belbin 'team role' dimensions with the 'ideal' profiles, participants on the Leadership Development Project gain insight into themselves and their organizations, and identify possible areas for change and improvement. Particular reference is made to comparisons between the actual and ideal profiles for management work, mentoring work and technical specialist work. Although this group of 446 managers fits the manager profile (45%) substantially better than the specialist profile (30%), there seems to be a tendency for managers to continue to adhere to their specialist role, to give too much attention to detail, and to give insufficient attention to looking outwards so as to keep in touch with important events and role players in the external environment. As managers and leaders move into different roles, they can use these profiles to identify and address these gaps in their own performance. The Leadership Development Project helps to bridge some of these gaps by providing relevant *thinking* and *interactive tools* which participants practise and apply in assignments back on the job.

Implications of the gaps with mentor and technical specialist profiles

When comparing managers' actual profiles with other profiles such as the mentor and technical specialist profiles, it is clear that there are gaps which need to be filled – depending on the extent to which the particular manager is required to be a 'mentor' or a 'technical trouble shooter' in his or her job. Meeting the requirements of the technical specialist is probably a less important role than being an effective mentor, since most managers are required to develop their staff and release responsibility through appropriate empowerment and delegation. Too much focus on implementation (IMP – details of how to do the job properly) and having insufficient sensitivity to others (relatively low on team worker – TW) are general areas of concern in this sample of 446 managers, most of whom have mentoring as well as management responsibilities.

Specific courses of action to deal with the gaps

While overall % fit provides a rough indication of how well individuals fit the ideal profiles, each person examines partic- ular gaps on particular dimensions, and explores how particular thinking and interactive tools provided on the seminars can help him or her to change or improve. Gaps between ideal and actual profiles can be addressed through formal training such as that provided on the LDP seminars. But it is stressed that most is achieved by applying what is learned on the job itself through carefully designed assignments and feedback. First-hand experience encourages real life experiential learning, and the best seminars in the world are unlikely to be a substitute for what we learn by doing it ourselves in the 'real world' environment. It is also suggested that not all of the gaps between what managers are and what they would like to be can be or should be overcome through training and attempts to change their own behaviour. **Restructuring the job, improving systems and procedures, finding others** to address these gaps are alterative strategies. Trying to be all things to all people in all situations is probably unrealistic. Changing job structures, providing support systems or just getting help from others are worthwhile alternatives. There is also a risk of over-emphasizing the correcting weaknesses and devoting insufficient energy to developing strengths.

WHERE FROM HERE?

This paper has dealt with the **corporate needs** of 446 managers in 14 organizations/groups rather than **individual needs** arising from the LDP and the Belbin profiles. How individual profiles, needs, assignments and learning are tackled on the LDP has not been discussed in any depth. In-depth examination and evaluation of the impact of the LDP with the aid of the Belbin questionnaires and other instruments used on the LDP would require separate research. However, this paper has shown the likely benefits from this work and avenues for further exploration.

H. J. Misselhorn
M.O.D. Consulting, South Africa

I am grateful to Hugo Misselhorn for providing this information, which is reprinted with permission.

MANAGEMENT IN ACTION 14.2

Barriers come down to build up team spirit

Corporate executives who regard 'team-building' exercises as a chance to let their hair down may well have paused for thought following news that a Railtrack session led to the suspension of a senior manager for allegedly drunken behaviour.

Yet the perception that corporate bonding events are a well-earned opportunity to pop a few corks endures – and catering for them is a booming business for hotels and management consultants, worth £600m a year.

Alcohol-fuelled antics at the Railtrack team-building exercise last week allegedly outraged clients and staff at the Balmer Lawn Hotel in Hampshire, and led to the suspension of Paul White, head of national contracts.

Photo: Jurgen Reisch/Getty Images

Earlier this month, Jim Hodkinson lost his job as chief executive of New Look, the fashion retailer, for groping the bottom of a female colleague during a corporate event.

But Roland Ayling, general manager of Dunston Hall hotel in Norwich, which regularly hosts company get-togethers, is not surprised. 'Of course, you get people becoming boisterous from drinking,' he says. 'That's part of the day.'

Although some events may get out of hand, once out of the office barriers come down as managers mingle with secretaries. That is why companies are happy to spend often large sums of money to help their employees get to know each other better, in the belief that it will help them work more efficiently.

'During team-building events, employees will develop a rapport which they have never had before,' says Jason Ludlow, of Events UK, which organised a team-building treasure-hunting trek in the New Forest for Railtrack managers last week.

However, not everyone agrees. Critics say few employees bring back the newly found complicity to the office. 'Nobody ever forgets where the hatchet is buried,' says one former Marks and Spencer manager, who is a veteran of many bonding sessions. 'The sense of common purpose developed during these exercises dissipates once it is subject to the hurlyburly of everyday life at work.'

An advertising manager adds: 'When people feel they are under pressure to bond, they stay away from these events and from one another afterwards.'

Popular team-building exercises include treasure hunting, clay pigeon shooting and sailing. Some will be tailor-made to reflect subtly a main corporate activity. For example, employees can be asked to help strangers in the street fix a tyre to test customer service skills. Some managers question the relevance of the games they have to play. 'The fact that I can build a raft to cross the river does not mean I can manage people properly,' says Edward Pickard who used to work at Aon Corporation, the insurance brokerage, before joining Tindall Riley.

(Reproduced with permission from the Financial Times Limited, © *Financial Times*.)

1 Discuss critically and with supporting practical examples the likely advantages and disadvantages of working in a small group or team.

2 Contrast different types of communication networks. Give examples of a situation in which each type of network is likely to be most appropriate.

3 Assess the practical value to the manager of the analysis of individual behaviour. Explain how you would go about constructing a sociogram.

4 Distinguish between: (a) group task roles; (b) group building and maintenance roles; and (c) individual roles. Give your own examples of each of these types of group member roles.

5 Suggest a framework for the analysis and categorisation of patterns of individual behaviour in group situations. What considerations need to be kept in mind when using such frameworks?

6 Explain what is meant by: (a) 'groupthink'; (b) the risky-shift phenomenon; and (c) brainstorming. Assess critically the likely standard of individual, compared with group or team performance.

7 Explain the meaning and purpose of sensitivity training. Give your views on the relevance and practical value of group dynamics.

8 Detail fully the main factors to be considered in a review of effective teamworking.

ASSIGNMENT 1

Attempt, *preferably*, to observe a small group or project team at work; *alternatively*, next time you are involved in a small group discussion observe the members of your group.

a (i) Explain the nature of the **content** of the group's discussion and contrast this with the **process** of the discussion.

   (ii) Complete the grid below by giving a tick in the appropriate box to denote the behaviour of individual members in terms of:
   – group task roles;
   – group building and maintenance roles;
   – individual roles.

	Names of group members (or reference numbers)							Totals
Group task roles								
Group building/maintenance roles								
Individual roles								
Totals								

b Explain the conclusions you draw concerning the conduct and apparent effectiveness of the group.

ASSIGNMENT 2

From your experience of working within a small group and/or project team at work, and as directed by your tutor, attempt to undertake **at least two** of the following tasks.

TASK 1

Consider how individual members fit best into the Belbin's revised nine team roles (Table 14.1, page 557).

Elaborate on both:

- their specific team-role contribution; and
- their allowable weaknesses.

_____

_____

_____

_____

_____

_____

Comment critically on the extent to which the people identified collectively help to form a balanced and comprehensive list of team-roles.

TASK 2

Analyse the communication network(s) adopted and level of interaction among members (Figure 14.2, page 559). Comment critically on the general level of satisfaction apparently experienced by individual group members.

_____

_____

_____

_____

_____

_____

TASK 3

Classify individual member roles in terms of the amount of emphasis placed on:

- task functions;
- maintenance functions; and
- self-oriented behaviour.

_____

_____

_____

_____

_____

_____

Comment critically on the overall structure or pattern of interrelations among members of the group/team.

Assignment 2 continued

TASK 4

Using your understanding of Sociometry, provide **in confidence** to your tutor the names of two people from your group/team with whom you would:

- most prefer to accompany you on a 'safari' type holiday;
- feel least uncomfortable in confiding to about a potentially embarrassing personal health or hygiene problem; and
- choose to discuss concern about progress on your course of study or at your place of work.

_____

_____

_____

_____

_____

TASK 5

Develop a list of critical indicators that you believe would best provide objective measures of how successfully the group/team is performing and its contribution to the overall effectiveness of the organisation.

_____

_____

_____

_____

_____

ASSIGNMENT 3

Working within a small group, and as directed by your tutor, adopt a brainstorming approach to providing as many uses as possible for:

- a 1970 edition of an American 900-page textbook on management; and
- a man or woman's leather belt

Elect a member to record **all** of your responses. At the end of the allotted time delete any **obvious** duplication, total the numbers of ideas for each separate exercise, and then be prepared to share and compare with ideas and total scores from other groups.

What conclusions do you draw from this assignment?

_____

_____

_____

_____

_____

PERSONAL AWARENESS AND SKILLS EXERCISE

OBJECTIVES

Completing this exercise should help you to enhance the following skills:

▶ Analyse the range of roles that are necessary for most teams to work effectively.

▶ Evaluate the role(s) you play within the team.

▶ Identify which roles could be developed and used more to increase effectiveness.

EXERCISE

Referring to the 12 Roles Summary Sheet below, **you are required to:**

1 Complete the Team Role – Self Assessment Sheet.

2 Refine and validate the results by asking others who know you well to complete the Team Role – Colleague Assessment Sheet for you.

3 Compare the results and instigate a discussion to understand the reasons for colleagues' perceptions of you.

4 Observe the way in which people operate who are strong in the roles in which you are weak and consider ways in which you can use your strengths to help others develop.

Roles summary Sheet

Team leader Forms the team Identifies strengths and weaknesses Determines contributions Monitors performance Calls meetings Provides structure Reviews team needs	**Challenger** Adopts unconventional approaches Looks afresh Challenges accepted order Provides the unexpected Ideas man Challenges complacency Provides stimulus Provides radical review	**Expert** Provides specialist expertise Acts as expert witness Provides professional viewpoint
Ambassador Develops external relationships Shows concern for external environment Sells the team Builds bridges	**Judge** Listens Evaluates Ponders Avoids arguments Avoids advocacy Promotes justice Avoids rushing Acts logically Acts pragmatically Provides balance Checks wild enthusiasm Seeks the truth	**Innovator** Uses imagination Proposes new methods Evaluates ideas Nurtures ideas Builds on others' ideas Visualizes opportunities Transforms ideas into strategies Deals with complex issues Provides vision Provides ingenuity Provides logic Helps understanding
Diplomat Promotes diplomatic solutions Has high influence Good negotiator Orientates the team Builds alliances Aids consensus Pragmatic Sees way ahead	**Conformer** Fills gaps Co-operative Helps relationships Jack of All Trades Avoids challenges to accepted order Observes Conservative	**Output pusher** Self motivated Preoccupation with output and results 'Drives' Imposes time scales Chases progress Shows high commitment to task Intolerant Abrasive
Quality controller Checks output orientation Preoccupation with quality Inspires higher standards Acts as team conscience Shows relationship concern	**Supporter** Builds morale Puts people at ease Ensures job satisfaction Resolves conflicts Gets to root of problem Gives advice Supports Encourages	**Reviewer** Observes Reviews performance Promotes regular review Gives feedback Acts as 'mirror' Looks for pitfalls Is process-orientated

▶

Personal awareness and skills exercise continued

Team Role – Self Assessment Sheet

Review the twelve roles outlined on the Roles Summary Sheet and rank them according to the frequency with which you play each role.

1 _____   2 _____
3 _____   4 _____
5 _____   6 _____
7 _____   8 _____
9 _____   10 _____
11 _____ 12 _____

Summary

Strong roles	Weak roles

Team Role – Colleague Assessment Sheet

Referring to the descriptions on the Roles Summary Sheet place in rank order your perception of how strongly the person plays each role.

Rank the strongest role 1 and the weakest 12.

1 _____   2 _____
3 _____   4 _____
5 _____   6 _____
7 _____   8 _____
9 _____   10 _____
11 _____ 12 _____

Make remarks which you feel would be helpful in:

(a) Developing weak roles.

(b) Enabling the person to play roles which you feel would be helpful to the team.

DISCUSSION

- To what extent do you agree with the list of 12 roles needed to make most teams effective?

- Comment honestly and critically on your colleague's team role assessment sheet. Did the ranking surprise you?

- What conclusions do you draw from this exercise?

Visit our website **www.booksites.net/mullins** for further questions, annotated weblinks, case material and Internet research material.

NOTES AND REFERENCES

1. 'Teamwork: Success Through People', Advisory Booklet, ACAS, April 2003, pp. 6–7.
2. See, for example: Allcorn, S. 'Understanding Groups at Work', *Personnel*, vol. 66, no. 8, August 1989, pp. 28–36.
3. Guirdham, M. *Interactive Behaviour at Work*, Third edition, Financial Times Prentice Hall (2002), p. 463.
4. Obeng, E. *All Change*, Pitman Publishing (1994).
5. Crainer, S. *Key Management Ideas: Thinkers that changed the management world*, Third edition, Financial Times Prentice Hall (1998), p. 238.
6. James, J. *Body Talk at Work*, Judy Piatkus (2001), p. 211.
7. Belbin, R. M. *Management Teams: Why They Succeed or Fail*, Butterworth-Heinemann (1981).
8. Belbin, R. M. *Team Roles at Work*, Butterworth-Heinemann (1993).
9. Furnham, A., Steele, H. and Pendleton, D. 'A Psychometric Assessment of the Belbin Team-Role Self-Perception Inventory', *Journal of Occupational and Organizational Psychology*, 66, 1993, pp. 245–61.
10. Arroba, T. and Wedgwood-Oppenheim, F. 'Do Senior Managers Differ in The Public and Private Sector? An Examination of Team-Role Preferences', *Journal of Managerial Psychology*, vol. 9, no. I, 1994, pp. 13–16.
11. White, J. 'Teaming with Talent', *Management Today*, September 1999, pp. 57–61.
12. Fisher, S. G., Hunter, T. A. and Macrosson, W. D. K. 'The Distribution of Belbin Team Roles among UK Managers', *Personnel Review*, vol. 29, no. 2, 2000, pp. 124–40.
13. Bavelas, A. 'A Mathematical Model for Group Structures', *Applied Anthropology*, vol. 7, 1948, pp. 19–30, and Bavelas, A. 'Communication Patterns in Task-Oriented Groups', in Lasswell, H. N. and Lerner, D. (eds) *The Policy Sciences*, Stanford University Press (1951).

14. Leavitt, H. J. 'Some Effects of Certain Communication Patterns on Group Performance', *Journal of Abnormal and Social Psychology*, vol. 46, 1951, pp. 38–50. See also: Leavitt, H. J. *Managerial Psychology*, Fourth edition, University of Chicago Press (1978).
15. Shaw, M. E. 'Communication Networks', in Berkowitz, L. (ed.) *Advances in Experimental Social Psychology*, vol. 1, Academic Press (1964).
16. Moreland, R. L. and Levine, J. M. *Understanding Small Groups*, Allyn and Bacon (1994).
17. Belbin, R. M. *Changing The Way We Work*, Butterworth-Heinemann (1997), p. 13.
18. Stanley. T. J. 'The Challenge of Managing a High-Performance Team', *SuperVision*, vol. 63, no. 7, July 2002, pp. 10–12.
19. Moreno, J. L. *Who Shall Survive?* Beacon House (1953). See also: Moreno, J. L. and Jennings, H. H. *The Sociometry Reader*, Free Press of Glencoe (1960).
20. Rogers, E. M. and Kincaid, D. L. *Communication Networks: Towards a New Paradigm for Research*, The Free Press (1981), p. 92.
21. Bales, R. F. 'A Set of Categories for the Analysis of Small Group Interaction', *American Sociological Review*, vol. 15, April 1950, pp. 257–63.
22. Bales, R. F. *Personality and Interpersonal Behaviour*, Holt, Rinehart and Winston (1970).
23. Benne, K. D. and Sheats, P. 'Functional Roles of Group Members', *Journal of Social Issues*, vol. 4, 1948, pp. 41–9.
24. Coghlan, D. 'Managing Organizational Change Through Teams and Groups', *Leadership & Organization Development Journal*, vol. 15, no. 2, 1994, pp. 18–23.
25. Whitfield, J. M., Anthony, W. P. and Kacmar, K. M. 'Evaluation of Team-Based Management: A Case Study', *Journal of Organizational Change Management*, vol. 8, no. 2, 1995, pp. 17–28.

26. Green, J. R. 'Team Building in Practice', *Chartered Secretary*, November 1997, pp. 34–5.

27. James, J. *Body Talk at Work*, Judy Piatkus (2001), p. 212.

28. Kets de Vries, M. 'Beyond Sloan: Trust Is at the Core of Corporate Values', in Pickford, J. (ed.), *Financial Times Mastering Management 2.0*, Financial Times Prentice Hall (2001), p. 268.

29. Douglas, M. 'Why Soft Skills Are an Essential Part of the Hard World of Business', *Manager, The British Journal of Administrative Management*, New Year 2003, pp. 34–5.

30. 'Teamwork: Success Through People', Advisory Booklet, ACAS, April 2003, p. 31.

31. Kravitz, D. A. and Martin, B. 'Ringelmann Rediscovered: The Original Article', *Journal of Personality and Social Psychology*, May 1986, pp. 936–41.

32. See, for example: Karau, S. J. and Williams, K. D. 'Social Loafing: A Meta-Analysis Review and Theoretical Integration', *Journal of Personality and Social Psychology*, October 1993, pp. 681–706.

33. Hall, P. 'Team Solutions Need Not Be the Organisational Norm', *Professional Manager*, July 2001, p. 45.

34. See, for example: Blanchard, K. and Bowles, S. *High Five: None of Us Is As Smart As All of Us*, HarperCollins Business (2001).

35. Stanley, T. J. 'The Challenge of Managing a High-Performance Team', *SuperVision*, vol. 63, no. 7, July 2002, pp. 10–12.

36. Guirdham, M. *Interactive Behaviour at Work*, Third edition, Financial Times Prentice Hall (2002), p. 498.

37. Kogan, N. and Wallach, M. A. 'Risk-Taking as a Function of the Situation, the Person and the Group', in Newcomb, T. M. (ed.) *New Directions in Psychology III*, Holt, Rinehart and Winston (1967).

38. For a comprehensive review of the 'risky-shift' phenomenon, see, for example: Clarke, R. D. 'Group Induced Shift Towards Risk: A Critical Appraisal', *Psychological Bulletin*, vol. 76, 1971, pp. 251–70. See also: Vecchio, R. P. *Organizational Behavior*, Third edition, Harcourt Brace and Company (1995).

39. Shaw, M. E. *Group Dynamics*, McGraw-Hill (1976).

40. Janis, J. L. *Victims of Groupthink*, Houghton Mifflin (1972) and Janis, J. L. *Groupthink*, Second edition, Houghton Mifflin (1982).

41. Hambrick, D. 'Putting the Team into Top Management', in Pickford, J. (ed.), *Financial Times Mastering Management 2.0*, Financial Times Prentice Hall (2001), p. 289.

42. Osborn, A. F. *Applied Imagination: Principles and Procedures of Creative Thinking*, Scribner's (1963).

43. Diehl, M. and Strobe, W. 'Productivity Loss in Brainstorming Groups: Towards the Solution of the Riddle', *Journal of Personality and Social Psychology*, vol. 53, 1987, pp. 497–509.

44. See, for example: Bishop, S. and Taylor, D. *Developing Your Staff*, Pitman Publishing/Longman Training, (1994).

45. See, for example: Waterman, R. *The Frontiers of Excellence*, Nicholas Brealey (1994).

46. Cooper, C. L. and Mangham, I. L. (eds) *T-Groups: A Survey of Research*, Wiley (1971), p. v.

47. Luft, J. *Group Processes: An Introduction to Group Dynamics*, Second edition, National Press (1970). (The term 'Johari Window' was derived from a combination of the first names of the original authors, Joseph Luft and Harry Ingham.)

48. Davis, K. *Human Behavior at Work*, Fifth edition, McGraw-Hill (1977), p. 183.

49. Davis, K. and Newstrom, J. W. *Human Behavior at Work: Organizational Behavior*, Eighth edition, McGraw-Hill (1989).

50. See, for example: McKenna, E. Business *Psychology and Organisational Behaviour*, Lawrence Erlbaum (1994).

51. For an overview of experimental small group methods and training needs, see, for example: Smith, P. B. *Group Processes and Personal Change*, Harper and Row (1980). See also: Brown, R. *Group Processes: Dynamics Within and Between Groups*, Basil Blackwell (1988).

52. Wilson, J. 'Building Teams – with Attitude', *Professional Manager*, September 1998, p. 13.

53. Browning, G. 'Brain Food: Matters for the Mind to Chew On', *Management Today*, April 2000, p. 20.

54. Riches, A. 'Emotionally Intelligent Teams', Organisational Change & Leadership Development, www.anneriches.com.au, accessed 11 March 2003.

55. *Teamwork: Success Through People*. Advisory Booklet, ACAS, April 2003, p. 34.

56. South African Employment Equity Act, 55, 1998.

57. Belbin, R. M. *Management Teams*, Butterworth-Heinemann (1991); supported by a computer software package used under licence from Belbin and Associates.

58. Misselhorn, H. J. *Understanding and Managing your Organization*, M.O.D. Consulting (S.A.) (1998).

59. Misselhorn, H. J. *The Head and Heart of Management*, M.O.D. Consulting (S.A.) (2003).

60. Experiential learning refers to the learning that occurs from active first-hand involvement in the subject or task to be learned, plus meaningful feedback to the learner from successful and unsuccessful understanding or performance.

61. These nine team roles were not developed from conceptual models but based on empirical observations by Belbin and his team over a number of years at Henley-on-Thames Management College. The terms used help to get away from the management jargon and find words which capture, in layman's language, something of these typical behaviour patterns.

FT Use the *Financial Times* to enhance your understanding of the context and practice of management and organisational behaviour. Refer to articles 8, 14 and 15 in the BUSINESS PRESS section at the end of the book for relevant reports on the issues explored in this chapter.

TOPIC SUMMARY SHEET

What are the key learning points from this topic?

TOPIC 6 – MOTIVATION

Why study this topic?

How an employee performs in the workplace is crucial to an organisations' success. Motivation is central to this process, and this chapter will present a description and evaluation of the most commonly discussed motivational theories. Understanding these theories allows organisations and the managers within them to take steps to ensure that any problems with low morale can be tackled and hopefully resolved.

As you will see, there are several important approaches that can be implemented, and this depends on many organisational factors which are also discussed within this topic.

Blackboard

E-tivity 6: Motivation

12 WORK MOTIVATION AND REWARDS

The relationship between the organisation and its members is influenced by what motivates them to work and the rewards and fulfilment they derive from it. The manager needs to know how best to elicit the co-operation of staff and direct their performance to achieving the goals and objectives of the organisation. The manager must understand the nature of human behaviour and how best to motivate staff so that they work willingly and effectively.

Photo: Simon Reddy/Travel Ink

LEARNING OUTCOMES

After completing this chapter you should be able to:

▶ explain the meaning and underlying concept of motivation;

▶ detail main types of needs and expectations of people at work;

▶ explain frustation-induced behaviour and possible reactions to frustration at work;

▶ contrast content and process theories of motivation;

▶ examine main theories of motivation and evaluate their relevance to particular work situations;

▶ explain the importance of the motivation of knowledge workers and a climate of creativity;

▶ review the complex nature of work motivation and rewards.

Motives do not operate in a vacuum, and the behaviour in which they do operate is affected by the processes of perception, learning and thinking. Theories of motivation ought to be related to theories of learning and perception.
Robert Woodworth
Dynamics of Behaviour, Columbia University Press (1918)

There aren't many motivating forces more potent than giving your staff an opportunity to exercise and express their idealism.
Anita Roddick
Business As Unusual, Thorsons (2000)

THE MEANING OF MOTIVATION

The study of **motivation** is concerned, basically, with why people behave in a certain way. The basic underlying question is 'why do people do what they do?'[1] In general terms, motivation can be described as the direction and persistence of action. It is concerned with why people choose a particular course of action in preference to others, and why they continue with a chosen action, often over a long period, and in the face of difficulties and problems.[2]

From a review of motivation theory, *Mitchell* identifies four common characteristics which underlie the definition of motivation.[3]

- **Motivation is typified as an individual phenomenon.** Every person is unique and all the major theories of motivation allow for this uniqueness to be demonstrated in one way or another.
- **Motivation is described, usually, as intentional.** Motivation is assumed to be under the worker's control, and behaviours that are influenced by motivation, such as effort expended, are seen as choices of action.
- **Motivation is multifaceted.** The two factors of greatest importance are: (i) what gets people activated (arousal); and (ii) the force of an individual to engage in desired behaviour (direction or choice of behaviour).
- **The purpose of motivational theories is to predict behaviour.** Motivation is not the behaviour itself, and it is not performance. Motivation concerns action, and the internal and external forces which influence a person's choice of action.

On the basis of these characteristics, Mitchell defines motivation as 'the degree to which an individual wants and chooses to engage in certain specified behaviours'.

Underlying concept of motivation

The underlying concept of motivation is some driving force within individuals by which they attempt to achieve some goal in order to fulfil some need or expectation. This concept gives rise to the basic motivational model, which is illustrated in Figure 12.1.

People's behaviour is determined by what motivates them. Their performance is a product of both ability level and motivation.

Performance = function (ability × motivation)

Kreitner et al. suggest that although motivation is a necessary contributor for job performance it is not the only one. Along with ability, motivation is also a combination of level

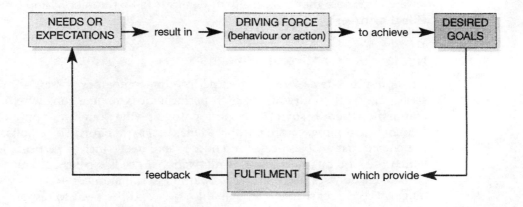

Figure 12.1 A simplified illustration of the basic motivational model

of skill; knowledge about how to complete the task; feelings and emotions; and facilitating and inhibiting conditions not under the individual's control.[4] However, what is clearly evident is that if the manager is to improve the work of the organisation, attention must be given to the level of motivation of its members. The manager must also encourage staff to direct their efforts (their driving force) towards the successful attainment of the goals and objectives of the organisation.

> Over 22 million people are currently in employment and we cannot afford to underestimate the extent to which our economy depends on maintaining the motivation and improving the ability of the workforce.
>
> **Sir Brian Wolfson, Chairman of Investors in People UK[5]**

But what is this driving force? What are people's needs and expectations, and how do they influence behaviour and performance at work? Motivation is a complex subject, it is a very personal thing, and it is influenced by many variables. Individuals have a variety of changing, and often conflicting, needs and expectations which they attempt to satisfy in a number of different ways. *Farren* reminds us of the 12 human needs that been around since the beginning of recorded history: family; health and well-being; work/career; economic; learning; home/shelter; social relationships; spirituality; community; leisure; mobility; and environment/safety. 'Work and private life in the new millennium will continue to revolve around the 12 human needs.'[6]

We can consider how the various theories of motivation at work discussed later in this chapter relate to this set of human needs.

NEEDS AND EXPECTATIONS AT WORK

The various needs and expectations at work can be categorised in a number of ways – for example the simple divisions into physiological and social motives, or into intrinsic and extrinsic motivation.

Extrinsic motivation is related to 'tangible' rewards such as salary and fringe benefits, security, promotion, contract of service, the work environment and conditions of work. Such tangible rewards are often determined at the organisational level and may be largely outside the control of individual managers.

Intrinsic motivation is related to 'psychological' rewards such as the opportunity to use one's ability, a sense of challenge and achievement, receiving appreciation, positive recognition, and being treated in a caring and considerate manner. The psychological rewards are those that can usually be determined by the actions and behaviour of individual managers.[7]

Higher set of motivational needs

According to *Kets de Vries* the best-performing companies possess a set of values that create the right conditions for high performance; he questions whether in such best companies there is something more going on that touches upon a deeper layer of human functioning, causing people to make an extra effort. The emphasis is on widening choice that enables people to choose more freely, instead of being led by forces of which they are unaware; and it is motivational needs system on which such choice is based. Kets de Vries suggests that in addition to the motivation needs system for physiological needs, sensual and enjoyment needs, and the need to respond to threatening situations, companies that get the best of their people are characterised by a higher set of motivational needs system:

■ **attachment/affiliation** – concerning the need for engagement and sharing, a feeling of community and a sense of belonging to the company; and

■ **exploration/assertion** – concerning the ability to play and work, a sense of fun and enjoyment, the need for self-assertion and the ability to choose.[8]

Broad classification for motivation to work

Given the complex and variable nature of needs and expectations, the following is a simplistic but useful, broad three-fold classification as a starting point for reviewing the motivation to work. (*See* Figure 12.2.)

■ **Economic rewards** – such as pay, fringe benefits, pension rights, material goods and security. This is an **instrumental** orientation to work and concerned with 'other things'.

■ **Intrinsic satisfaction** – derived from the nature of the work itself, interest in the job, and personal growth and development. This is a **personal** orientation to work and concerned with 'oneself'.

■ **Social relationships** – such as friendships, group working, and the desire for affiliation, status and dependency. This is a **relational** orientation to work and concerned with 'other people'.

A person's motivation, job satisfaction and work performance will be determined by the comparative strength of these sets of needs and expectations, and the extent to which they are fulfilled. For example, some people may make a deliberate choice to forgo intrinsic satisfaction and social relationships (particularly in the short term or in the earlier years of their working life) in return for high economic rewards. Other people are happy to accept comparatively lower economic rewards in favour of a job which has high intrinsic satisfaction and/or social relationships. Intrinsic satisfaction is a personal attitude which varies according to the individual and particular circumstances. It will also vary from job to job and often between different parts of the same job. Social relationships would appear to be an important feature for many people, especially, for example, for those working in the hospitality industry where interactions with other people and the importance of supportive working relationships and good teamwork can be strong motivators at work.[9]

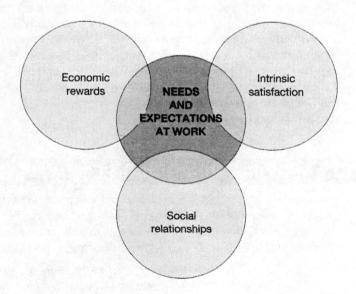

Figure 12.2 Needs and expectations of people at work

Culture and motivating factors

In previous chapters we have drawn attention to the significance of culture as an influence on organisational systems and processes.[10] According to *Cartwright*: 'A culture has the power and authority not only to determine lifestyle but also to form individual personality traits, behaviours and attitudes.' From a three-year study into the psychology of Total Quality Management, Cartwright reveals nine key motivating factors that also form the basis of cultural assessment.

- **Identification** – motivation through influencing others by what we say and do and influence by others in what we think and how we feel.
- **Equity** – a balance between expectations and rewards, inputs and outputs, perception and reality. Equity is what we think is fair.
- **Equality** – everyone should be treated with equal respect irrespective of status, and the concept of 'equal pay for equal work' should be well established.
- **Consensus** – the arrival of a mutual understanding that is much deeper and more inclusive than compromise and is dependent on shared values and social harmony.
- **Instrumentality** – a tool or device by which something is effected, the agency or means by which to achieve an objective.
- **Rationality** – introduces the idea of a scientific approach to management and problem-solving which is highly motivating.
- **Development** – the motivation for self-improvement. Development of the individual and organisation through training and education.
- **Group dynamics** – positive group motivations are created through individual loyalty to the group, consensus and a mutual understanding of and commitment towards achieving group goals.
- **Internalisation** – of cultural beliefs and values. Internalisation determines our attitudes, convictions and behaviours, and is the most powerful and permanent of the nine motivating factors.

Each of these factors represents an important psychological characteristic of motivation at work and together have developed into the nine-factor methodology for measuring the motivational aspects of organisational cultures.[11]

The psychological contract

One of the strongest influences on people's level of motivation is attitudes and expectations. In addition to the above categories, the motivation to work is also increasingly influenced by the changing nature of the work environment and the concept of the 'psychological contract', which was discussed in Chapter 2. The psychological contract involves a series of expectations between the individual member and the organisation. These expectations are not defined formally, and although the individual member and the organisation may not be consciously aware of the expectations, their relationship is still affected by these expectations.

MOTIVATION AND ORGANISATIONAL PERFORMANCE

In Chapter 6 we discussed the task of management as getting work done through other people. Organisations achieve their goals and objectives by the co-ordinated efforts of their members. Organisational success is dependent upon members being motivated to use their full talents and abilities, and directed to perform well in the right areas.

The best companies have stimulating workplaces where their staff feel motivated and valued. But they do not end up this way by accident. Without exception, the creation of an outstanding workplace has been a deliberate act by top management. So what's the secret? Benefits such as holidays and share schemes are important. But these perks are less of an influence in determining a great place to work than the overall tone of management.[12]

According to a major international study undertaken by *Proudfoot Consulting*, a major reason for productivity loss was poor working morale. Aspects of poor working morale included: people feeling undervalued and poorly rewarded; an absence of positive team spirit; low motivation; lack of attention to quality; unwillingness to see a job well done; and a poor sense of belonging.[13]

Allen and Helms suggest that different types of reward practices may more closely complement different generic strategies and are significantly related to higher levels of perceived organisational performance.

> *Our findings have important, practical implications for senior managers and others responsible for the implementation of strategies and rewards in organizations. Top managers must work closely with lower-level managers as well as human resources professionals to craft reward systems that are consistent with motivational concepts and at the same time support their chosen organizational strategy. The relationship between strategy and rewards needs to be clearly communicated to the employees so they understand the organization's strategy as well as the linkages between their rewards and strategy.[14]*

With a positive motivation philosophy and practice in place, productivity, quality and service should improve because motivation helps people towards: achieving goals; gaining a positive perspective; creating the power to change; building self-esteem and capability; and managing their development and helping others.[15]

FRUSTRATION-INDUCED BEHAVIOUR

What happens if a person's motivational driving force is blocked and they are unable to satisfy their needs and expectations, and what is the likely effect on their work performance? There are two possible sets of outcomes: constructive behaviour or frustration. (*See* Figure 12.3.)

Constructive behaviour

Constructive behaviour is a positive reaction to the blockage of a desired goal and can take two main forms: problem-solving or restructuring.

■ **Problem-solving** is the removal of the barrier – for example, repairing a damaged machine, or bypassing an unco-operative superior.

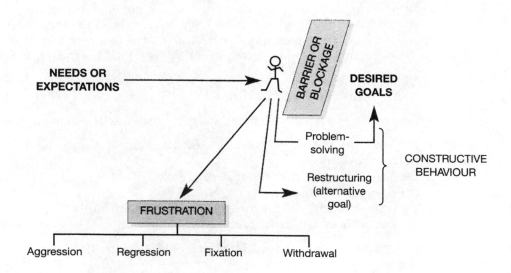

Figure 12.3 A basic model of frustration

Restructuring, or compromise, is the substitution of an alternative goal, although such a goal may be of a lower order – for example, taking an additional part-time job because of failure to be promoted to a higher grading.

Note: Even if a person engages in constructive behaviour in response to a barrier or blockage it could be said that the person was 'frustrated', if only mildly or in the short term, in an attempt to satisfy a desired goal. However, the term frustration is usually interpreted as applying to **negative responses** to a barrier or blockage which prevents satisfaction of a desired goal.

Frustration (negative responses)

Frustration is a negative response to the blockage of a desired goal and results in a defensive form of behaviour. There are many possible reactions to frustration caused by the failure to achieve a desired goal. These can be summarised under four broad headings: aggression; regression; fixation; and withdrawal.[16] However, these categories are not mutually exclusive. Most forms of frustration-induced behaviour at work are a combination of aggression, regression and fixation.

Aggression is a physical or verbal attack on some person or object; for example, striking a supervisor, rage or abusive language, destruction of equipment or documents, malicious gossip about a superior. This form of behaviour may be directed against the person or object which is perceived as the source of frustration, that is the actual barrier or blocking agent. However, where such direct attack cannot be made, because, for example, the source of frustration is not clear or not specific, or where the source is feared, such as a powerful superior, then aggression may be displaced towards some other person or object.

With **displaced aggression** the person may find an easier, safer person or object as a scapegoat for the outlet of frustration – for example, picking arguments with colleagues, being short-tempered with subordinates, shouting at the cleaners or kicking the waste-paper bin. A more constructive form of displaced aggression is working off frustrated feelings through demanding physical work or sport, or perhaps by shouting/cursing when alone or in the company of an understanding colleague.

Regression is reverting to a childish or more primitive form of behaviour – for example, sulking, crying, tantrums, or kicking a broken machine or piece of equipment.

Fixation is persisting in a form of behaviour which has no adaptive value and continuing to repeat actions which have no positive results – for example, the inability to accept change or new ideas, repeatedly trying a machine which clearly will not work, insisting on applying for promotion even though not qualified for the job.

Withdrawal is apathy, giving up or resignation – for example, arriving at work late and leaving early, sickness and absenteeism, refusal to accept responsibility, avoiding decision-making, passing work over to colleagues, or leaving the job altogether.

Factors influencing frustration

Among the factors which determine an individual's reaction to frustration are:

- the level and potency of need (*see*, for example, Maslow's theory of motivation, discussed below);
- the degree of attachment to the desired goal;
- the strength of motivation;
- the perceived nature of the barrier or blocking agent; and
- the personality characteristics of the individual.

It is important that managers attempt to reduce potential frustration through, for example:

- effective recruitment, selection and socialisation;
- training and development;

- job design and work organisation;
- equitable personnel policies;
- recognition and rewards;
- effective communications;
- participative styles of management;
- attempting to understand the individual's perception of the situation.

Proper attention to motivation, and to the needs and expectations of people at work will help overcome boredom and frustration-induced behaviour.

MONEY AS A MOTIVATOR

Earlier writers, such as *F. W. Taylor*, believed in economic needs motivation. Workers would be motivated by obtaining the highest possible wages through working in the most efficient and productive way. Performance was limited by physiological fatigue. For Taylor, motivation was a comparatively simple issue – what the workers wanted from their employers more than anything else was high wages.[17] This approach is the **rational–economic concept of motivation**. The ideas of F. W. Taylor and his 'rational–economic needs' concept of motivation (discussed in Chapter 3) and subsequent approaches to motivation at work have fuelled the continuing debate about financial rewards as a motivator and their influence on productivity.

Where there is little pleasure in the work itself or the job offers little opportunity for career advancement, personal challenge or growth, many people may appear to be motivated primarily, if not exclusively, by money. For example, Weaver suggests that for many hourly workers in the hospitality industry, such as dishwashers, waiting or housekeeping staff, their work does not change much among different companies and there is little attachment to a particular company. For such staff, Weaver proposes a 'Theory M' programme of motivation based on direct cash rewards for above average performance. A percentage base is calculated from the average performance of workers on the staff.[18]

In a survey of attitudes to work involving a random sample of 1000 workers, when asked to specify the biggest problem at work the most popular response was poor pay at 18 per cent.[19] Another survey of human resource managers responding to *Personnel Journal* found that it is often difficult to attract, retain and motivate minimum wage workers on pay alone. The survey uncovered that 62 per cent of respondents had a problem retaining minimum wage workers strictly because of pay. Many employers must provide other incentives such as bonuses or prizes – on top of pay – to keep workers in the job.[20]

On the other hand, we frequently see pronouncements from prominent business figures that motivation is about much more than money.

> I was convinced that the success of any business depended on having the right people and motivating them properly. As I thought about this, I decided that motivation was not just about money. It was about creating an environment in which people enjoyed working. When I joined Morgan Grenfell, my aim would be to get the best out of people whether they were young or old, experienced fund managers or less experienced.
>
> **Nicola Horlick, formerly Managing Director, Morgan Grenfell Investment Management**[21]

The short answer appears to be: that for the vast majority of people, money is clearly important and a motivator at work **but** to what extent and **how** important depends upon their personal circumstances and the other satisfactions they derive from work.

The bottom line is surely the extent to which money motivates people to work **well** and to the best of their abilities. Although pay may still make people tick, there are now a number of other important influences on motivation.

Motivation other than by money

The *Income Data Services (IDS)* draws attention to the challenges of motivation during economic circumstances of low inflation. 'Most of us have lived and worked through a unique period during which pay and prices rose continuously for decades.' IDS found that although the importance of large bonuses in motivating people could not be ignored, especially in high growth companies, there is a need to provide new forms of recognition for employees that do not depend on promotion or money. In the main employers agreed that they now face the prime challenges of: breaking with the habit of automatic annual increases in pay; shifting the focus of reward from individual performance to team success; moving from 'quantity' to 'quality'; and managing a more diverse workforce by policies which recognise different needs.[22]

As *Grayson and Hodges* point out, historically loyalty was bought and employers offered gradual progression up the hierarchy, a decent salary and job security in return for a hard day's work. 'Increasingly, motivation is based on values rather than purely on financial reward.'[23] And a similar point is made by *Saunders*:

> *If the 1980s were all about money, and people were only as good as their last bonus, in more recent years time has become the new money, and quality-of-life issues have come to the fore. Benefits that replenish the psychological contract are becoming the most valuable. So holiday arrangements, career breaks and potential for flexible hours and homeworking are now on the agenda.*[24]

A recent study from the Economic & Social Research Council analysed the influences on employee behaviour and productivity and raises the question of: what if employees are guided not only by monetary incentives but also social norms? Social norms interact with economic incentives and may have a large effect upon organisational performance.[25]

THEORIES OF MOTIVATION

There are many competing theories which attempt to explain the nature of motivation. These theories may all be at least partially true, and help to explain the behaviour of certain people at certain times. However, **the search for a generalised theory of motivation at work appears to be in vain**. A major determinant of behaviour is the particular situation in which individual workers find themselves. Motivation varies over time and according to circumstances. It is often most acute for younger people starting on their career, for people at mid-career positions or for those who find limited opportunities for promotion or further advancement. For employers there may be difficulties in motivating staff both in the longer term as well as in the short run.

Complexity of motivation

It is because of the complexity of motivation, and the fact that there is no ready-made solution or single answer to what motivates people to work well, that the different theories are important to the manager. They show there are many motives which influence people's behaviour and performance. Collectively, the different theories provide a framework within which to direct attention to the problem of how best to motivate staff to work willingly and effectively.

It is important to emphasise, however, that these various theories are not conclusive. They all have their critics (this is particularly true of the content theories of motivation), or have been subject to alternative findings which purport to contradict the original ideas. Many of these theories were not intended, originally, to have the significance that some writers have subsequently placed upon them. It is always easy to quote an example which appears to contradict any generalised observation on what motivates people to work. However, these different theories provide a basis for study and discussion, and for review of the most effective motivational style. (*See* Figure 12.4.)

> You don't motivate individuals. You provide them with an environment to be self-motivated. It is a personal decision, but it's management's job to provide the right environment.
>
> **Kathy Schofield, Director of Human Resources, HFC Bank**[26]

The manager, therefore, must judge the relevance of these different theories, how best to draw upon them, and how they might effectively be applied in particular work situations. The manager should be aware of at least the main theories of motivation.[27]

Content theories and process theories

The usual approach to the study of motivation is through an understanding of internal cognitive processes – that is, what people feel and how they think. This understanding should help the manager to predict likely behaviour of staff in given situations. These different cognitive theories of motivation are usually divided into two contrasting approaches: content theories and process theories.

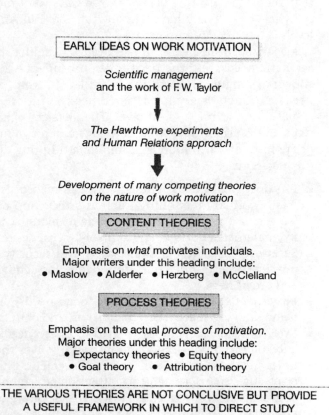

Figure 12.4 An overview of main theories of work motivation

- **Content theories** attempt to explain those specific things which actually motivate the individual at work. These theories are concerned with identifying people's needs and their relative strengths, and the goals they pursue in order to satisfy these needs. Content theories place emphasis on the nature of needs and **what motivates.**
- **Process theories** attempt to identify the relationship among the dynamic variables which make up motivation. These theories are concerned more with how behaviour is initiated, directed and sustained. Process theories place emphasis on the **actual process of motivation.** These theories are discussed later in this chapter.

CONTENT THEORIES OF MOTIVATION

Major content theories of motivation include:

- *Maslow's* hierarchy of needs model;
- *Alderfer's* modified need hierarchy model;
- *Herzberg's* two-factor theory; and
- *McClelland's* achievement motivation theory.

MASLOW'S HIERARCHY OF NEEDS THEORY

A useful starting point is the work of *Maslow*, and his theory of individual development and motivation, published originally in 1943.[28] Maslow's basic proposition is that people are wanting beings, they always want more, and what they want depends on what they already have. He suggests that human needs are arranged in a series of levels, a hierarchy of importance.

Maslow identified eight innate needs, including the need to know and understand, aesthetic needs, and the need for transcendence. However, the hierarchy is usually shown as ranging through five main levels, from, at the lowest level, physiological needs, through safety needs, love needs, and esteem needs, to the need for self-actualisation at the highest level. The **hierarchy of needs** may be shown as a series of steps, but is usually displayed in the form of a pyramid (Figure 12.5). This is an appropriate form of illustration as it implies a thinning out of needs as people progress up the hierarchy.

- **Physiological needs.** These include homeostasis (the body's automatic efforts to retain normal functioning) such as satisfaction of hunger and thirst, the need for oxygen and to maintain temperature regulation. Also sleep, sensory pleasures, activity, maternal behaviour, and arguably sexual desire.
- **Safety needs.** These include safety and security, freedom from pain or threat of physical attack, protection from danger or deprivation, the need for predictability and orderliness.
- **Love needs** (often referred to as social needs). These include affection, sense of belonging, social activities, friendships, and both the giving and receiving of love.
- **Esteem needs** (sometimes referred to as ego needs). These include both self-respect and the esteem of others. Self-respect involves the desire for confidence, strength, independence and freedom, and achievement. Esteem of others involves reputation or prestige, status, recognition, attention and appreciation.
- **Self-actualisation needs.** This is the development and realisation of one's full potential. Maslow sees this as: 'What humans can be, they must be', or 'becoming everything that one is capable of becoming'. Self-actualisation needs are not necessarily a creative urge, and may take many forms which vary widely from one individual to another.

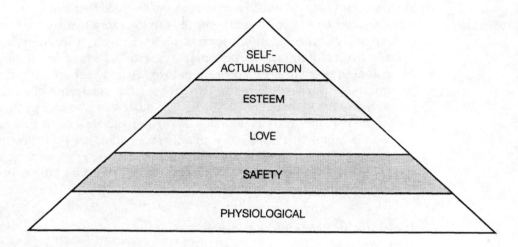

Figure 12.5 Maslow's hierarchy of needs model

Once a lower need has been satisfied, it no longer acts as a strong motivator. The needs of the next higher level in the hierarchy demand satisfaction and become the motivating influence. Only unsatisfied needs motivate a person. Thus Maslow asserts that 'a *satisfied need is no longer a motivator*'.

Not necessarily a fixed order

Although Maslow suggests that most people have these basic needs in about the order indicated, he also makes it clear that **the hierarchy is not necessarily a fixed order**. There will be a number of exceptions to the order indicated. For some people there will be a reversal of the hierarchy, for example:

- Self-esteem may seem to be more important than love to some people. This is the most common reversal of the hierarchy. It is often based on the belief that the person most loved is strong, confident or inspires respect. People seeking love try to put on a show of aggressive, confident behaviour. They are not really seeking self-esteem as an end in itself but for the sake of love needs.
- For some innately creative people the drive for creativity and self-actualisation may arise despite lack of satisfaction of more basic needs.
- Higher-level needs may be lost in some people who will continue to be satisfied at lower levels only: for example, a person who has experienced chronic unemployment.
- Some people who have been deprived of love in early childhood may experience the permanent loss of love needs.
- A need which has continued to be satisfied over a long period of time may be undervalued. For example, people who have never suffered from chronic hunger may tend to underestimate its effects, and regard food as rather an unimportant thing. Where people are dominated by a higher-level need this may assume greater importance than more basic needs.
- People with high ideals or values may become martyrs and give up everything else for the sake of their beliefs.

Maslow claims that the hierarchy is relatively universal among different cultures, but he recognises that there are differences in an individual's motivational content in a particular culture.

Degrees of satisfaction

Maslow points out that a false impression may be given that a need must be satisfied fully before a subsequent need arises. **He suggests that a more realistic description is in terms of decreasing percentages of satisfaction along levels of the hierarchy.** For example, arbitrary figures for the average person may be: satisfied 85 per cent in physiological needs; 70 per cent in safety needs; 50 per cent in love needs; 40 per cent in esteem needs; and 10 per cent in self-actualisation needs. There is a gradual emergence of a higher-level need as lower-level needs become more satisfied. The relative importance of these needs changes during the psychological development of the individual. Maslow subsequently modified his views by noting that satisfaction of self-actualisation needs by growth-motivated individuals can actually enhance these needs rather than reduce them. Furthermore, he accepted that some higher-level needs may still emerge after long deprivation of lower-level needs, rather than only after their satisfaction.

Evaluation of Maslow's theory

Based on Maslow's theory, once lower-level needs have been satisfied (say at the physiological and safety levels) giving more of the same does not provide motivation. Individuals advance up the hierarchy as each lower-level need becomes satisfied. Therefore, to provide motivation for a change in behaviour, the manager must direct attention to the next higher level of needs (in this case, love or social needs) that seek satisfaction.

Applications to the work situation

However, there are a number of problems in relating Maslow's theory to the work situation. These include the following:

- People do not necessarily satisfy their needs, especially higher-level needs, just through the work situation. They satisfy them through other areas of their life as well. Therefore the manager would need to have a complete understanding of people's private and social life, not just their behaviour at work.
- There is doubt about the time which elapses between the satisfaction of a lower-level need and the emergence of a higher-level need.
- Individual differences mean that people place different values on the same need. For example, some people prefer what they might see as the comparative safety of working in a bureaucratic organisation to a more highly paid and higher status position, but with less job security, in a different organisation.
- Some rewards or outcomes at work satisfy more than one need. Higher salary or promotion, for example, can be applied to all levels of the hierarchy.
- Even for people within the same level of the hierarchy, the motivating factors will not be the same. There are many different ways in which people may seek satisfaction of, for example, their esteem needs.
- Maslow viewed satisfaction as the main motivational outcome of behaviour. But job satisfaction does not necessarily lead to improved work performance.

A useful basis for evaluation

Although Maslow did not originally intend that the need hierarchy should necessarily be applied to the work situation, it still remains popular as a theory of motivation at work. Despite criticisms and doubts about its limitations, the theory has had a significant impact on management approaches to motivation and the design of organisations to meet individual needs. It is a convenient framework for viewing the different needs and expectations that people have, where they are in the hierarchy, and the different motivators that might be applied to people at different levels.

The work of Maslow has drawn attention to a number of different motivators and stimulated study and research. The need hierarchy model provides a useful base for the evaluation of motivation at work. For example, *Steers and Porter* suggest a list of general rewards and organisational factors used to satisfy different needs (*see* Table 12.1).[29]

Table 12.1 Applying Maslow's need hierarchy

Needs levels	General rewards	Organisational factors
1 Physiological	Food, water, sex, sleep	**a** Pay **b** Pleasant working conditions **c** Cafeteria
2 Safety	Safety, security, stability, protection	**a** Safe working conditions **b** Company benefits **c** Job security
3 Social	Love, affection, belongingness	**a** Cohesive work group **b** Friendly supervision **c** Professional associations
4 Esteem	Self-esteem, self-respect, prestige, status	**a** Social recognition **b** Job title **c** High status job **d** Feedback from the job itself
5 Self-actualisation	Growth, advancement, creativity	**a** Challenging job **b** Opportunities for creativity **c** Achievement in work **d** Advancement in the organisation

(*Source*: Steers, R. M. and Porter, L. W, *Motivation and Work Behaviour*, Fifth edition, McGraw-Hill (1991) p. 35. Reproduced with permission from The McGraw-Hill Companies Inc.)

Saunders contends that despite the time that has elapsed, Maslow's theory remains watertight.

> *When prehistoric man first took shelter in a cave and lit a fire, he was satisfying his lowest – physiological and safety needs. When a Buddhist achieves a state of nirvana, she is satisfying the fifth and highest – self-actualisation ...The cave these days might be a three-bedroom semi with garden and off-street parking, but the fact remains that once we've got enough to feed, clothe and house our families money is a low-level motivator for most people. The dash for cash is soon replaced by the desire for recognition, status and ultimately (although Maslow reckoned that a lot of us never get this far) the need to express yourself through your work.*[30]

Pyramid of employee commitment

Revisiting and developing Maslow's hierarchy, *Stum* looked at the dynamic between an individual and the organisation, and proposes a new employee/employer social contract that enables organisations to improve employee commitment and retention. The five levels of workforce needs hierarchy are shown in a 'Performance Pyramid'.

- **Safety/security** – the need to feel physically and psychologically safe in the work environment for commitment to be possible;
- **Rewards** – the need for extrinsic rewards in compensation and benefits;
- **Affiliation** – the intrinsic need for a sense of belonging to the work team or organisation;
- **Growth** – addressing the need for positive individual and organisational change to drive commitment;
- **Work/life harmony** – the drive to achieve a sense of fulfilment in balancing work and life responsibilities.[31]

ALDERFER'S MODIFIED NEED HIERARCHY MODEL

A modified need hierarchy model has been presented by *Alderfer*.[32] This model condenses Maslow's five levels of need into only three levels based on the core needs of existence, relatedness and growth (ERG theory). (*See* Table 12.2.)

- **Existence needs** are concerned with sustaining human existence and survival, and cover physiological and safety needs of a material nature.
- **Relatedness needs** are concerned with relationships to the social environment, and cover love or belonging, affiliation, and meaningful interpersonal relationships of a safety or esteem nature.
- **Growth needs** are concerned with the development of potential, and cover self-esteem and self-actualisation.

A continuum of needs

Like Maslow, Alderfer suggests that individuals progress through the hierarchy from existence needs, to relatedness needs, to growth needs, as the lower-level needs become satisfied. However, Alderfer suggests these needs are more a continuum than hierarchical levels. More than one need may be activated at the same time. Individuals may also progress down the hierarchy. There is a frustration–regression process. For example, if an individual is continually frustrated in attempting to satisfy growth needs, relatedness needs may reassume most importance. The lower-level needs become the main focus of the individual's efforts.

Alderfer proposed a number of basic propositions relating to the three need relationships. Some of these propositions followed Maslow's theory, some were the reverse of the theory. A number of studies were undertaken to test these propositions across different samples of people in different types of organisations. Results from the studies were mixed. For example, the proposition that the less existence needs are satisfied the more they will be desired received constant support from all six samples. However, the proposition that satisfaction of existence needs activates desire for relatedness needs was not supported in any of the six samples.

Satisfaction of needs

Unlike Maslow's theory, the results of Alderfer's work suggest that lower-level needs do not have to be satisfied before a higher-level need emerges as a motivating influence. The results, however, do support the idea that lower-level needs decrease in strength as they become satisfied. ERG theory states that an individual is motivated to satisfy one or more basic sets of needs. Therefore if a person's needs at a particular level are blocked then attention should be focused on the satisfaction of needs at the other levels. For example, if a subordinate's growth needs are blocked because the job does

Table 12.2 Linking Maslow's, Alderfer's and Herzberg's theories of motivation

Maslow's hierarchy of needs	Alderfer's ERG theory	Herzberg's two-factor theory
PHYSIOLOGICAL	EXISTENCE	HYGIENE FACTORS
SAFETY		
LOVE	RELATEDNESS	
ESTEEM	GROWTH	MOTIVATORS
SELF-ACTUALISATION		

not allow sufficient opportunity for personal development, then the manager should attempt to provide greater opportunities for the subordinate to satisfy existence and relatedness needs.

HERZBERG'S TWO-FACTOR THEORY

Herzberg's original study consisted of interviews with 203 accountants and engineers, chosen because of their growing importance in the business world, from different industries in the Pittsburgh area of America.[33] He used the critical incident method. Subjects were asked to relate times when they felt exceptionally good or exceptionally bad about their present job or any previous job. They were asked to give reasons and a description of the sequence of events giving rise to that feeling. Responses to the interviews were generally consistent, and revealed that there were two different sets of factors affecting motivation and work. **This led to the two-factor theory of motivation and job satisfaction.**

Hygiene and motivating factors

One set of factors are those which, if absent, cause dissatisfaction. These factors are related to job context, they are concerned with job environment and extrinsic to the job itself. These factors are the **'hygiene' or 'maintenance' factors** ('hygiene' being used as analogous to the medical term meaning preventive and environmental). They serve to prevent dissatisfaction. The other set of factors are those which, if present, serve to motivate the individual to superior effort and performance. These factors are related to job content of the work itself. They are the **'motivators' or growth factors**. The strength of these factors will affect feelings of satisfaction or no satisfaction, but not dissatisfaction (*see* Figure 12.6).

The hygiene factors can be related roughly to Maslow's lower-level needs and the motivators to Maslow's higher-level needs (Table 12.2) Proper attention to the hygiene factors will tend to prevent dissatisfaction, but does not by itself create a positive attitude or motivation to work. It brings motivation up to a zero state. **The opposite of dissatisfaction is not satisfaction but, simply, no dissatisfaction.** To motivate workers to give of their best the manager must give proper attention to the motivators or growth factors. Herzberg emphasises that hygiene factors are not a 'second class citizen system'. They are as important as the motivators, but for different reasons. Hygiene factors are necessary to avoid unpleasantness at work and to deny unfair treatment. 'Management should never deny people proper treatment at work.' The motivators relate to what people are allowed to do and the quality of human experience at work. They are the variables which actually motivate people.

Evaluation of Herzberg's work

The motivation–hygiene theory has extended *Maslow's* hierarchy of need theory and is more directly applicable to the work situation. Herzberg's theory suggests that if management is to provide positive motivation then attention must be given not only to hygiene factors, but also to the motivating factors. The work of Herzberg indicates that it is more likely good performance leads to job satisfaction rather than the reverse.

Herzberg's theory is, however, a source of frequent debate. There have been many other studies to test the theory. The conclusions have been mixed. Some studies provide support for the theory.[34] However, it has also been attacked by a number of writers. For example, *Vroom* claims that the two-factor theory was only one of many conclusions that could be drawn from the research.[35]

King suggests that there are at least five different theoretical interpretations of Herzberg's model which have been tested in different studies.[36] Each interpretation

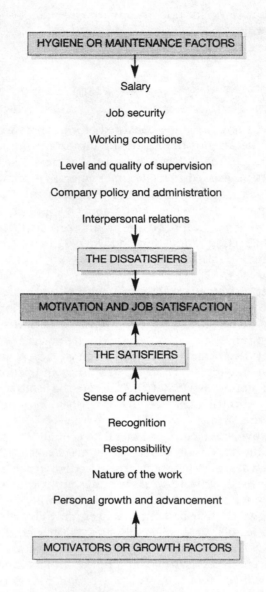

Figure 12.6 Representation of Herzberg's two-factor theory

places a different slant on the model. This suggests doubts about the clarity of statement of the theory.

Two general criticisms

There are two common general criticisms of Herzberg's theory. One criticism is that the theory has only limited application to 'manual' workers. The other criticism is that the theory is 'methodologically bound'.

It is often claimed that the theory applies least to people with largely unskilled jobs or whose work is uninteresting, repetitive and monotonous, and limited in scope. Yet these are the people who often present management with the biggest problem of motivation. Some workers do not seem greatly interested in the job content of their work, or with the motivators or growth factors.

A second, general criticism concerns methodology. It is claimed that the critical incident method, and the description of events giving rise to good or bad feelings, influences the results. People are more likely to attribute satisfying incidents at work, that is the motivators, as a favourable reflection on their own performance. The dissatisfying incidents, that is the hygiene factors, are more likely to be attributed to external influences, and the efforts of other people. Descriptions from the respondents had to be interpreted by the interviewers. This gives rise to the difficulty of distinguishing clearly between the different dimensions, and to the risk of possible interviewer bias.

Continuing relevance of the theory?

More recent studies still yield mixed conclusions about the practical relevance of the two-factor theory. For example, from an examination of the relevance to industrial salespeople, *Shipley and Kiely* generally found against Herzberg. Their results:

> seriously challenge the worth of Herzberg's theory to industrial sales managers. Its application by them would result in a less than wholly motivated and at least partially dissatisfied team of salespeople.[37]

Despite such criticisms, there is still evidence of support for the continuing relevance of the theory. For example, although based on a small sample of engineers within a single company in Canada, *Phillipchuk* attempted to replicate Herzberg's study in today's environment. He concludes that Herzberg's methods still yield useful results. Respondents did not offer any new event factors from the original study although some old factors were absent. Salary and working conditions were not mentioned as a satisfier or a dissatisfier, and advancement as a satisfier did not appear. The top demotivator was company policy and the top motivator was achievement.[38]

And according to *Crainer and Dearlove*:

> Herzberg's work has had a considerable effect on the rewards and remuneration packages offered by corporations. Increasingly, there is a trend towards 'cafeteria' benefits in which people can choose from a range of options. In effect, they can select the elements they recognise as providing their own motivation to work. Similarly, the current emphasis on self-development, career management and self-managed learning can be seen as having evolved from Herzberg's insights.[39]

Whatever the validity of the two-factor theory much of the criticism is with the value of hindsight, and *Herzberg* did at least attempt an empirical approach to the study of motivation at work. Furthermore, his work has drawn attention to the importance of job design in order to bring about job enrichment, self-development and self-managed learning. Herzberg has emphasised the importance of the 'quality of work life'. He advocates the restructuring of jobs to give greater emphasis to the motivating factors at work, to make jobs more interesting and to satisfy higher level needs. Job design and job enrichment are discussed in Chapter 18.

MCCLELLAND'S ACHIEVEMENT MOTIVATION THEORY

McClelland's work originated from investigations into the relationship between hunger needs and the extent to which imagery of food dominated thought processes. From subsequent research McClelland identified four main arousal-based, and socially developed, motives:

- the Achievement motive;
- the Power motive;
- the Affiliative motive; and
- the Avoidance motive.[40]

The first three motives correspond, roughly, to Maslow's self-actualisation, esteem and love needs. The relative intensity of these motives varies between individuals. It also tends to vary between different occupations. Managers appear to be higher in achievement motivation than in affiliation motivation. McClelland saw the achievement need (n-Ach) as the most critical for the country's economic growth and success. The need to achieve is linked to entrepreneurial spirit and the development of available resources.

Use of projective tests

Research studies by McClelland use a series of projective 'tests' – Thematic Apperception Test (TAT) to gauge an individual's motivation. For example, individuals are shown a number of pictures in which some activity is depicted. Respondents are asked to look briefly (10–15 seconds) at the pictures, and then to describe what they think is happening, what the people in the picture are thinking and what events have led to the situation depicted.[41] An example of a picture used in a projective test is given in Assignment 2 at the end of this chapter. The descriptions are used as a basis for analysing the strength of the individual's motives.

People with high achievement needs

Despite the apparent subjective nature of the judgements research studies tend to support the validity of TAT as an indicator of the need for achievement.[42] McClelland has, over years of empirical research, identified four characteristics of people with a strong achievement need (n-Ach): a preference for moderate task difficulty; personal responsibility for performance; the need for feedback; and innovativeness.

- They prefer **moderate task difficulty** and goals as an achievement incentive. This provides the best opportunity of proving they can do better. If the task is too difficult or too risky, it would reduce the chances of success and of gaining need satisfaction. If the course of action is too easy or too safe, there is little challenge in accomplishing the task and little satisfaction from success.
- They prefer **personal responsibility for performance**. They like to attain success through the focus of their own abilities and efforts rather than by teamwork or chance factors outside their control. Personal satisfaction is derived from the accomplishment of the task, and recognition need not come from other people.
- They have the need for **clear and unambiguous feedback** on how well they are performing. A knowledge of results within a reasonable time is necessary for self-evaluation. Feedback enables them to determine success or failure in the accomplishment of their goals, and to derive satisfaction from their activities.
- They are **more innovative**. As they always seek moderately challenging tasks they tend always to be moving on to something a little more challenging. In seeking short cuts they are more likely to cheat. There is a constant search for variety and for information to find new ways of doing things. They are more restless and avoid routine, and also tend to travel more.

Extent of achievement motivation

The extent of achievement motivation varies between individuals. Some people think about achievement a lot more than others. Some people rate very highly in achievement motivation. They are challenged by opportunities and work hard to achieve a goal. Other people rate very low in achievement motivation. They do not care much and have little urge to achieve. For people with a high achievement motivation, money is not an incentive but may serve as a means of giving feedback on performance. High achievers seem unlikely to remain long with an organisation that does not pay them well for good performance. Money may seem to be important to high achievers, but they value it more as symbolising successful task performance and goal achievement. For people with low achievement motivation money may serve more as a direct incentive for performance.

McClelland's research has attempted to understand the characteristics of high achievers. He suggests that n-Ach is not hereditary but results from environmental influences, and he has investigated the possibility of training people to develop a greater motivation to achieve.[43] McClelland suggests four steps in attempting to develop achievement drive:

- Striving to attain feedback on performance. Reinforcement of success serves to strengthen the desire to attain higher performance.
- Developing models of achievement by seeking to emulate people who have performed well.
- Attempting to modify their self-image and to see themselves as needing challenges and success.
- Controlling day-dreaming and thinking about themselves in more positive terms.

McClelland was concerned with economic growth in underdeveloped countries. He has designed training programmes intended to increase the achievement motivation and entrepreneurial activity of managers.

The need for power

McClelland has also suggested that as effective managers need to be successful leaders and to influence other people, they should possess a high need for power.[44] However, the effective manager also scores high on inhibition. Power is directed more towards the organisation and concern for group goals, and is exercised on behalf of other people. This is 'socialised' power. It is distinguished from 'personalised' power which is characterised by satisfaction from exercising dominance over other people, and personal aggrandisement.

PROCESS THEORIES OF MOTIVATION

Process theories, or extrinsic theories, attempt to identify the relationships among the dynamic variables which make up motivation and the actions required to influence behaviour and actions. They provide a further contribution to our understanding of the complex nature of work motivation. Many of the process theories cannot be linked to a single writer, but major approaches and leading writers under this heading include:

- Expectancy-based models – *Vroom*, and *Porter and Lawler*
- Equity theory – *Adams*
- Goal theory – *Locke*
- Attribution theory – *Heider*, and *Kelley* (this was discussed in Chapter 11).

Expectancy theories of motivation

The underlying basis of expectancy theory is that people are influenced by the expected results of their actions. Motivation is a function of the relationship between:

1 effort expended and perceived level of performance; and
2 the expectation that rewards (desired outcomes) will be related to performance.

There must also be

3 the expectation that rewards (desired outcomes) are available.

These relationships determine the strength of the 'motivational link'. (*See* Figure 12.7.)

Performance therefore depends upon the perceived expectation regarding effort expended and achieving the desired outcome. For example, the desire for promotion will result in high performance only if the person believes there is a strong expectation that this will lead to promotion. If, however, the person believes promotion to be based solely on age and length of service, there is no motivation to achieve high performance. A person's behaviour reflects a conscious choice between the comparative evaluation of alternative behaviours. **The choice of behaviour is based on the expectancy of the most favourable consequences.**

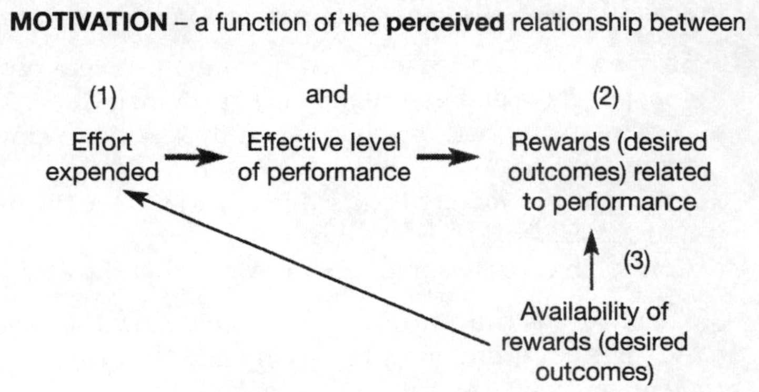

MOTIVATION – a function of the **perceived** relationship between

Figure 12.7 Expectancy theory: the motivational link

Expectancy theory is a generic theory of motivation and cannot be linked to a single individual writer. There are a number of different versions and some of the models are rather complex. More recent approaches to expectancy theory have been associated with the work of *Vroom* and of *Porter and Lawler*.

VROOM'S EXPECTANCY THEORY

Vroom was the first person to propose an expectancy theory aimed specifically at work motivation.[45] His model is based on three key variables: **valence**, **instrumentality** and **expectancy** (VIE theory or expectancy/valence theory). The theory is founded on the idea that people prefer certain outcomes from their behaviour over others. They anticipate feelings of satisfaction should the preferred outcome be achieved.

Valence

The feeling about specific outcomes is termed **valence**. **This is the attractiveness of, or preference for, a particular outcome to the individual.** *Vroom* distinguishes valence from value. A person may desire an object but then gain little satisfaction from obtaining it. Alternatively, a person may strive to avoid an object but find, subsequently, that it provides satisfaction. **Valence is the anticipated satisfaction from an outcome**. This may differ substantially from value, which is the actual satisfaction provided by an outcome.

The valence of certain outcomes may be derived in their own right, but more usually they are derived from the other outcomes to which they are expected to lead. An obvious example is money. Some people may see money as having an intrinsic worth and derive satisfaction from the actual accumulation of wealth. Most people, however, see money in terms of the many satisfying outcomes to which it can lead.

Instrumentality

The valence of outcomes derives, therefore, from their instrumentality. This leads to a distinction between first-level outcomes and second-level outcomes.

■ **The first-level outcomes are performance-related**. They refer to the quantity of output or to the comparative level of performance. Some people may seek to perform well 'for its own sake' and without thought to expected consequences of their actions. Usually, however, performance outcomes acquire valence because of the expectation that they will lead to other outcomes as an anticipated source of satisfaction – second-level outcomes.

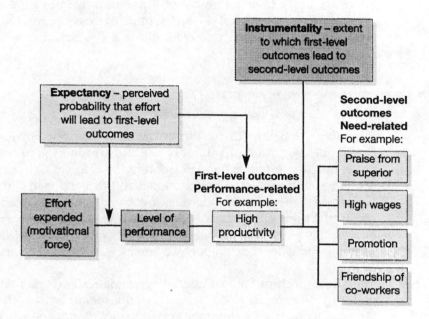

Figure 12.8 Basic model of expectancy theory

■ **The second-level outcomes are need-related.** They are derived through achievement of first-level outcomes – that is, through achieving high performance. Many need-related outcomes are dependent upon actual performance rather than effort expended. People generally receive rewards for what they have achieved, rather than for effort alone or through trying hard.

On the basis of *Vroom's* expectancy theory it is possible to depict a general model of behaviour. (*See* Figure 12.8.)

Expectancy   When a person chooses between alternative behaviours which have uncertain outcomes, the choice is affected not only by the preference for a particular outcome, but also by the probability that such an outcome will be achieved. People develop a **perception** of the degree of probability that the choice of a particular action will actually lead to the desired outcome. This is **expectancy**. It is the relationship between a chosen course of action and its predicted outcome. Expectancy relates effort expended to the achievement of first-level outcomes. Its value ranges between 0, indicating zero probability that an action will be followed by the outcome, and 1, indicating certainty that an action will result in the outcome.

Motivational force

The combination of valence and expectancy determines the person's motivation for a given form of behaviour. This is the **motivational force**. The force of an action is unaffected by outcomes which have no valence, or by outcomes that are regarded as unlikely to result from a course of action. Expressed as an equation, motivation (*M*) is the sum of the products of the valences of all outcomes (*V*), times the strength of expectancies that action will result in achieving these outcomes (*E*). Therefore, if either, or both, valence or expectancy is zero, then motivation is zero. The choice between alternative behaviours is indicated by the highest attractiveness score.

$$M = \sum^{n} E \cdot V$$

There are likely to be a number of different outcomes expected for a given action. Therefore, the measure of $E \cdot V$ is summed across the total number of possible outcomes to arrive at a single figure indicating the attractiveness for the contemplated choice of behaviour.

THE PORTER AND LAWLER EXPECTANCY MODEL

Vroom's expectancy/valence theory has been developed by *Porter and Lawler*.[46] Their model goes beyond motivational force and considers performance as a whole. They point out that effort expended (motivational force) does not lead directly to performance. It is mediated by individual abilities and traits, and by the person's role perceptions. They also introduce rewards as an intervening variable. Porter and Lawler see motivation, satisfaction and performance as separate variables, and attempt to explain the complex relationships among them. Their model recognises that job satisfaction is more dependent upon performance, than performance is upon satisfaction.

Explanation of relationships

These relationships are expressed diagrammatically (Figure 12.9) rather than mathematically. In contrast to the human relations approach which tended to assume that job satisfaction leads to improved performance, Porter and Lawler suggest that satisfaction is an effect rather than a cause of performance. It is performance that leads to job satisfaction.

- **Value of reward** (Box 1) is similar to valence in Vroom's model. People desire various outcomes (rewards) which they hope to achieve from work. The value placed on a reward depends on the strength of its desirability.
- **Perceived effort–reward probability** (Box 2) is similar to expectancy. It refers to a person's expectation that certain outcomes (rewards) are dependent upon a given amount of effort.

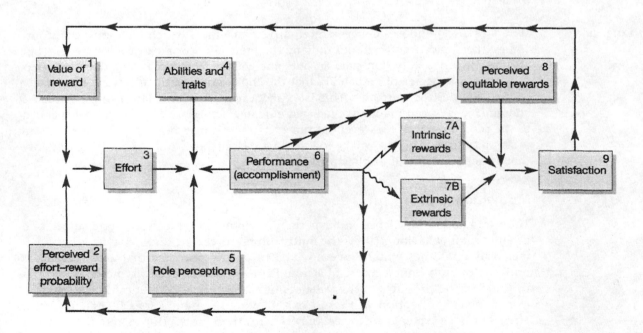

Figure 12.9 The Porter and Lawler motivation model

(*Source*: Porter, I. W. and Lawler, E. E. *Managerial Attitudes and Performance*. Copyright © Richard D. Irwin Inc. (1968) p. 165.)

- **Effort** (Box 3) is how hard the person tries, the amount of energy a person exerts on a given activity. It does not relate to how successful a person is in carrying out an activity. The amount of energy exerted is dependent upon the interaction of the input variables of value of reward, and perception of the effort–reward relationship.
- **Abilities and traits** (Box 4). Porter and Lawler suggest that effort does not lead directly to performance, but is influenced by individual characteristics. Factors such as intelligence, skills, knowledge, training and personality affect the ability to perform a given activity.
- **Role perceptions** (Box 5) refer to the way in which individuals view their work and the role they should adopt. This influences the type of effort exerted. Role perceptions will influence the direction and level of action which is believed to be necessary for effective performance.
- **Performance** (Box 6) depends not only on the amount of effort exerted but also on the intervening influences of the person's abilities and traits, and their role perceptions. If the person lacks the right ability or personality, or has an inaccurate role perception of what is required, then the exertion of a large amount of energy may still result in a low level of performance, or task accomplishment.
- **Rewards** (Boxes 7A and 7B) are desirable outcomes. Intrinsic rewards derive from the individuals themselves and include a sense of achievement, a feeling of responsibility and recognition (for example Herzberg's motivators). Extrinsic rewards derive from the organisation and the actions of others, and include salary, working conditions and supervision (for example Herzberg's hygiene factors). The relationship between performance and intrinsic rewards is shown as a jagged line. This is because the extent of the relationship depends upon the nature of the job. If the design of the job permits variety and challenge, so that people feel able to reward themselves for good performance, there is a direct relationship. Where job design does not involve variety and challenge, there is no direct relationship between good performance and intrinsic rewards. The wavy line between performance and extrinsic rewards indicates that such rewards do not often provide a direct link to performance.
- **Perceived equitable rewards** (Box 8). This is the level of rewards people feel they should fairly receive for a given standard of performance. Most people have an implicit perception about the level of rewards they should receive commensurate with the requirements and demands of the job, and the contribution expected of them. Self-rating of performance links directly with the perceived equitable reward variable. Higher levels of self-rated performance are associated with higher levels of expected equitable rewards. The heavily arrowed line indicates a relationship from the self-rated part of performance to perceived equitable rewards.
- **Satisfaction** (Box 9). This is not the same as motivation. It is an attitude, an individual's internal state. Satisfaction is determined by both actual rewards received, and perceived level of rewards from the organisation for a given standard of performance. If perceived equitable rewards are greater than actual rewards received, the person experiences dissatisfaction. The experience of satisfaction derives from actual rewards which meet or exceed the perceived equitable rewards.

Investigation of the model

Porter and Lawler conducted an investigation of their own model. This study involved 563 questionnaires from managers in seven different industrial and government organisations. The main focus of the study was on pay as an outcome. The questionnaires obtained measures from the managers for a number of variables such as value of reward, effort–reward probability, role perceptions, perceived equitable rewards, and satisfaction. Information on the managers' effort and performance was obtained from their superiors. The results indicated that where pay is concerned, value of reward and perceived effort–reward probability do combine to influence effort.

Those managers who believed pay to be closely related to performance outcome received a higher effort and performance rating from their superiors. Those managers who perceived little relationship between pay and performance had lower ratings for effort and performance. The study by Porter and Lawler also demonstrated the interaction of effort and role perceptions to produce a high level of performance. Their study suggested, also, that the relationship between performance and satisfaction with their pay held good only for those managers whose performance was related directly to their actual pay.

LAWLER'S REVISED EXPECTANCY MODEL

Following the original Porter and Lawler model, further work was undertaken by *Lawler* (*see* Figure 12.10).[47] He suggests that in deciding on the attractiveness of alternative behaviours, there are two types of expectancies to be considered: effort–performance expectancies (E → P); and performance–outcome expectancies (P → O).

The first expectancy (E → P) is the person's perception of the probability that a given amount of effort will result in achieving an intended level of performance. It is measured on a scale between 0 and 1. The closer the perceived relationship between effort and performance, the higher the E → P expectancy score.

The second expectancy (P → O) is the person's perception of the probability that a given level of performance will actually lead to particular need-related outcomes. This is measured also on a scale between 0 and 1. The closer the perceived relationship between performance and outcome, the higher the P → O expectancy score.

Motivational force to perform

The multiplicative combination of the two types of expectancies, E → P and the sum of the products P → O, determines expectancy. The motivational force to perform (effort expended) is determined by multiplying E → P and P → O by the strength of outcome valence (V).

$$E \text{ (Effort)} = (E \rightarrow P) \times \sum[(P \rightarrow O) \times V]$$

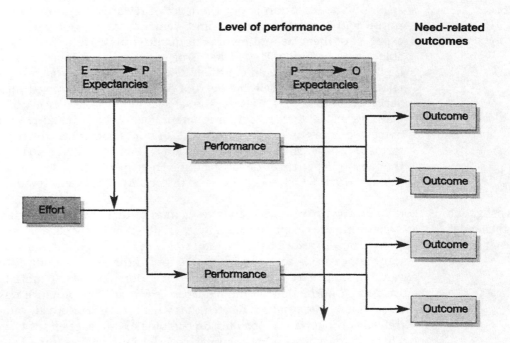

Figure 12.10 An illustration of the Lawler expectancy model

The distinction between the two types of expectancies arises because they are determined by different conditions. E → P expectancy is determined in part by the person's ability and self-confidence, past experience, and the difficulty of the task. P → O expectancy is determined by the attractiveness of the outcomes and the belief about who controls the outcomes, the person him/herself or other people.

IMPLICATIONS FOR MANAGERS OF EXPECTANCY THEORIES

There are a number of different versions of expectancy theory. The main elements tend to be very similar, however, and this suggests the development of a generally accepted approach. Numerous research studies aimed at testing expectancy models appear to suggest general support for the theory,[48] but they also highlight difficulties with some of the concepts involved and with methodology. Expectancy models are not always easy to understand, or to apply. There are many variables which affect behaviour at work. A problem can arise in attempting to include a large number of variables or in identifying those variables which are most appropriate in particular situations.

Expectancy theory does, however, draw attention to the complexities of work motivation. It provides further information in helping to explain the nature of behaviour and motivation in the work situation, and helps to identify problems in performance. Expectancy theory indicates that managers should give attention to a number of factors, including the following:

- Use rewards appropriate in terms of individual performance. Outcomes with high valence should be used as an incentive for improved performance.
- Attempt to establish clear relationships between effort–performance and rewards, as perceived by the individual.
- Establish clear procedures for the evaluation of individual levels of performance.
- Pay attention to intervening variables such as abilities and traits, role perceptions, organisational procedures, and support facilities, which, although not necessarily direct motivational factors, may still affect performance.
- Minimise undesirable outcomes which may be perceived to result from a high level of performance, such as industrial accidents or sanctions from co-workers; or to result despite a high level of performance, such as short-time working or layoffs.

Just a model   *Porter and Lawler* emphasise that the expectancy theory model applies only to behaviours which are under the voluntary control of the individual. The two general types of choices over which individuals have voluntary control of work performance in organisations are:

1 the amount of effort and energy expended; and
2 the manner in which they go about performing their work.

Porter and Lawler also emphasise that the expectancy model is just a model.

People rarely actually sit down and list their expected outcomes for a contemplated behaviour, estimate expectancies and valences, multiply, and add up the total unless, of course, they are asked to do so by a researcher. Yet people do consider the likely outcomes of their actions, do weigh and evaluate the attractiveness of various alternatives, and do use these estimates in coming to a decision about what they will do. The expectancy model provides an analytic tool for mirroring that process and for predicting its outcome, but it does not purport to reflect the actual decision-making steps taken by an individual.[49]

EQUITY THEORY OF MOTIVATION

One of the major variables of satisfaction in the Porter and Lawler expectancy model is perceived equitable rewards. This leads to consideration of another process theory of motivation – **equity theory**. Applied to the work situation, equity theory is usually associated with the work of *Adams*.[50]

Equity theory focuses on people's feelings of how fairly they have been treated in comparison with the treatment received by others. It is based on exchange theory. People evaluate their social relationships in the same way as buying or selling an item. People expect certain outcomes in exchange for certain contributions, or inputs. Social relationships involve an exchange process. For example, a person may expect promotion as an outcome of a high level of contribution (input) in helping to achieve an important organisational objective. People also compare their own position with that of others. They determine the perceived equity of their own position. Their feelings about the equity of the exchange are affected by the treatment they receive when compared with what happens to other people.

Most exchanges involve a number of inputs and outcomes. According to equity theory, people place a weighting on these various inputs and outcomes according to how they perceive their importance. When the ratio of a person's total outcomes to total inputs equals the *perceived* ratio of other people's total outcomes to total inputs there is **equity**. When there is an unequal comparison of ratios the person experiences a sense of **inequity**. The feeling of inequity might arise when an individual's ratio of outcomes to inputs is either less than, or greater than, that of other people. For example, Adams suggests that workers prefer equitable pay to overpayment. Workers on piece-rate incentive payment schemes who feel they are overpaid will reduce their level of productivity in order to restore equity.

Behaviour as a consequence of inequity

A feeling of inequity causes tension, which is an unpleasant experience. The presence of inequity therefore motivates the person to remove or to reduce the level of tension and the perceived inequity. The magnitude of perceived inequity determines the level of tension. The level of tension created determines the strength of motivation. Adams identifies six broad types of possible behaviour as consequences of inequity (*see* Figure 12.11).

- **Changes to inputs.** A person may increase or decrease the level of his or her inputs, for example through the amount or quality of work, absenteeism, or working additional hours without pay.
- **Changes to outcomes.** A person may attempt to change outcomes such as pay, working conditions, status and recognition, without changes to inputs.
- **Cognitive distortion of inputs and outcomes.** In contrast to actual changes, people may distort, cognitively, their inputs or outcomes to achieve the same results. Adams suggests that although it is difficult for people to distort facts about themselves, it is possible, within limits, to distort the utility of those facts: for example, the belief about how hard they are really working, the relevance of a particular qualification, or what they can or cannot obtain with a given level of pay.
- **Leaving the field.** A person may try to find a new situation with a more favourable balance, for example, by absenteeism, request for a transfer, resigning from a job or from the organisation altogether.
- **Acting on others.** A person may attempt to bring about changes in others, for example to lower their inputs or accept greater outcomes. Or the person may cognitively distort the inputs and outcomes of others. Alternatively, a person may try to force others to leave the field.

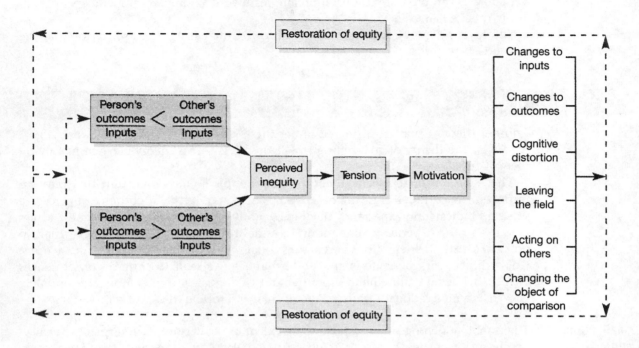

Figure 12.11 An illustration of Adams's equity theory of motivation

■ **Changing the object of comparison**. This involves changing the reference group with whom comparison is made. For example, where another person with a previously similar outcome–input ratio receives greater outcomes without any apparent increase in contribution, that other person may be perceived as now belonging to a different level in the organisation structure. The comparison need not necessarily be made with people who have the same inputs and outcomes. The important thing is a similar ratio of outcomes to inputs.

Under the control of the manager

The manager may seek to remove or reduce tension and perceived inequity among staff by influencing these types of behaviour – for example, by attempting to change a person's inputs or encouraging a different object of comparison. However, there are likely to be only two courses of action under the direct control of the manager. Outcomes can be changed by, for example, increased pay, additional perks or improved working conditions; or by instigating a person leaving the field through transfer, resignation or, as an extreme measure, dismissal.

Kreitner et al. suggest at least seven practical implications of equity theory.

■ It provides managers with another explanation of how beliefs and attitudes affect job performance.
■ It emphasises the need for managers to pay attention to employees' **perceptions** of what is fair and equitable.
■ Managers benefit by allowing employees to participate in making decisions about important work outcomes.
■ Employees should be given the opportunity to appeal against decisions that affect their welfare.
■ Employees are more likely to accept and support organisational change when they believe it is implemented fairly.

- Managers can promote co-operation and teamwork among group members by treating them equally.
- Employees denied justice at work are turning increasingly to arbitration and the courts.[51]

GOAL THEORY

Another theory usually considered under the heading of motivation to work is goal theory, or the theory of goal-setting (*see* Figure 12.12). This theory is based mainly on the work of *Locke*.[52]

The basic premise of goal theory is that people's goals or intentions play an important part in determining behaviour. Locke accepts the importance of perceived value, as indicated in expectancy theories of motivation, and suggests that these values give rise to the experience of emotions and desires. People strive to achieve goals in order to satisfy their emotions and desires. Goals guide people's responses and actions. Goals direct work behaviour and performance, and lead to certain consequences or feedback. Locke subsequently pointed out that 'goal-setting is more appropriately viewed as a motivational technique rather than as a formal theory of motivation.'[53]

Goal-setting and performance

The combination of goal difficulty and the extent of the person's commitment to achieving the goal regulates the level of effort expended. People with specific quantitative goals, such as a defined level of performance, or a given deadline for completion of a task, will perform better than people with no set goal or only a vague goal such as 'do the best you can'. People who have difficult goals will perform better than people with easier goals.

Gratton refers to 'Stretch goals' which are ambitious, highly targeted opportunities for breakthrough improvements in performance. These goals should stem from critical success indicators and come from deep discussions within the company, and from collaboration within and across task forces, and lead to development of activities and tactics to achieve the goals.[54] People lacking positive motivation at work may also help gain improved results and a better sense of achievement by setting themselves specific goals, and identifying tasks directly related to their work and measurable targets of time and performance.

Practical implications for the manager

Goal theory has a number of practical implications for the manager.

- Specific performance goals should systematically be identified and set in order to direct behaviour and maintain motivation.

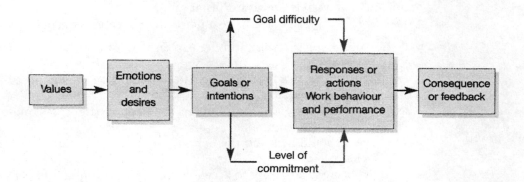

Figure 12.12 An illustration of Locke's theory of goal-setting

- Goals should be set at a challenging but realistic level. Difficult goals lead to higher performance. However, if goals are set at too high a level, or are regarded as impossible to achieve, performance will suffer, especially over a longer period.
- Complete, accurate and timely feedback and knowledge of results is usually associated with high performance. Feedback provides a means of checking progress on goal attainment and forms the basis for any revision of goals.
- Goals can be determined either by a superior or by individuals themselves. Goals set by other people are more likely to be accepted when there is participation. Employee participation in the setting of goals may lead to higher performance.[55]

Much of the theory of goal-setting can be related to the system of Management by Objectives (discussed in Chapter 7). MBO is often viewed as an application of goal-setting, although MBO was devised originally before the development of goal-setting theory.

A number of research studies have attempted to examine the relationship between goal-setting and performance. Although, almost inevitably, there are some contrary findings, the majority of evidence suggests strong support for the theory, and its effects on motivation.[56] However it is viewed, the theory of goal-setting provides a useful approach to work motivation and performance. And *Hannagan* goes so far as to suggest that: 'at present goal-setting is one of the most influential theories of work motivation applicable to all cultures'.[57]

ATTRIBUTION THEORY

A more recent approach to the study of motivation is attribution theory. Attribution is the process by which people interpret the perceived causes of behaviour. Attribution theory has been discussed in Chapter 11.

RELEVANCE OF THEORIES OF MOTIVATION

Given that most major theories of motivation date back many years it is inevitable that questions will be raised about their relevance today. For example, *Reis and Pena* question whether motivating people to work in the 21st century with theories conceived during the past 100 years is likely to be infeasible. They conclude that the core message is that managers should reconsider the outdated motivational patterns utilised to maintain role performance in organisations and adopt a fresh motivation formula for the 21st century based on friendship, work and respect.[58]

However, we have seen from the discussions above that there still appears to be general support for the theories – and, perhaps ironically, particularly for the early theories of Maslow and Herzberg and McGregor. A Chartered Management Institute checklist maintains that these theories are still valid today. 'A basic understanding of their main principles will be invaluable for building a climate of honesty, openness and trust.'[59] From a 12-year study of the use of management concepts in technical organisations, *Flores and Utley* found the work of Maslow and McGregor the most popular motivational theories and also refer to the relationship between Maslow and Herzberg and the successful implementation of quality systems.[60]

Whatever the popularity of different theories of motivation, doubts are raised about their universality on the ground that they have not adequately addressed the factor of culture.[61]

CROSS-CULTURAL DIMENSIONS OF MOTIVATION

Are theories of motivation universally applicable or are there meaningful differences in motivation at work, or in life more generally, in different societies? Many readers may feel able to recognise perceived variations in extrinsic, intrinsic and relational aspects of motivation as a result of experience of foreign cultures. Do similarities in workplace attitudes and behaviour outweigh differences? A number of writers have questioned whether motivational theories and models originating in one culture are amenable to transference to other parts of the world. *Francesco and Gold* devote a substantial proportion of a discussion of motivation to examining the extent to which American motivation theories are applicable outside the United States.

In Chapter 2 it was noted that classifications of culture often delineate societies along dimensions such as individual or group orientation or attitudes to power distance, so it would appear perfectly reasonable to identify the extent to which our own understanding of motivation is culture-specific. When discussing Maslow's contribution to this topic and, in particular, the concept of a hierarchy of needs, Francesco and Gold suggest that: 'the circumstances and values of a particular culture can influence the ordering and importance of needs. The values of individualism and collectivism can make the hierarchy more or less relevant.'[62] These authors go on to indicate that cultures which in Hofstede's framework are high on uncertainty avoidance may see individuals value safety and security needs more than the so-called higher order needs such as self-actualisation, while citizens of 'feminine' societies may place a particularly high importance on working relationships and work/life balance. See p. 49 for a summary of Hofstede's model and the clusters of countries he identifies.

In evaluating McClelland's work, Francesco and Gold question whether the meaning of an underlying concept, in this case achievement, can even be understood worldwide in the sense it was intended: 'Another concern with Learning Needs Theory is that the concept of achievement is difficult, if not impossible, to translate into languages other than English.'[63]

It has already been suggested that one criticism of content theories of motivation centres on its relative applicability in different circumstances and the suggestion that there may be variations across cultures falls within this line of reasoning. However, perhaps less obviously, process theories of motivation have also been criticised for being culture-bound. As they focus on process rather than content, such theories may appear to be more applicable in diverse cultural contexts. Nonetheless it has been suggested that process theories of motivation contain certain inbuilt assumptions that are themselves culturally derived.

Adler reminds us that expectancy models of motivation assume that individuals believe that they can, to some extent, control their environment and influence their own fate. If, as in the cases of more fatalistic cultures such as China, people do not have the same sense of internal attribution, the expectancy model may have less force and therefore applicability. When Adams's equity theory is applied across the world differences in interpretation have been recorded.[64] *Chen* suggests that while individualistic cultures place a high regard on equity, collectivist cultures value equality more than equity. Again we see here the possibility that while a theory of motivation may be essentially valid in principle, it is legitimate to think about the ways in which national culture can intervene in terms of its interpretation in different societies.[65]

THE MOTIVATION OF KNOWLEDGE WORKERS

Recent advantages in telecommunications and in scientific and technological knowledge have led to greater emphasis on the knowledge and expertise of staff, and the importance of creativity. *Tampoe* suggests that at the core of the new industrial trend are the 'knowledge workers' – those employees who apply their theoretical and practical understanding of a specific area of knowledge to produce outcomes of a commercial, social or personal value. The performance of knowledge workers should be judged on both the cleverness of ideas and the utility and commercial value of their applied knowledge. Creativity is necessary and needs to be encouraged but should be bounded by commercial realism. This presents management with a new challenge of how to motivate the knowledge workers.[66]

Tampoe suggests that the personal motivation of knowledge workers is based on the value they place on the rewards they expect to earn at work. In addition to the individual's own motivation, the performance of knowledge workers is dependent upon four key characteristics (*see* Figure 12.13).

- task competence;
- peer and management support;
- task and role clarity; and
- corporate awareness.

The challenge to management is to ensure the effectiveness of the four key variables and to recognise the need for staff to supervise and manage themselves and the wider rewards expected by knowledge workers.

Suggestions on developing reward strategies to motivate and compensate knowledge workers are given in Management in Action 12.1 at the end of this chapter.

A climate of creativity

Lucas draws attention to skills shortages as one of the biggest challenges facing employers in the new millennium. In order to attract and keep talented individuals, the so-called knowledge workers, organisations cannot rely simply on a pay rise or cash bonus but have to be more creative about the way they structure remuneration packages. Individual performance-related pay is still the most widely used reward strategy, but attention is also given to employee share ownership, competence-related pay and to team reward – and also to non-cash incentives such as gift vouchers. However, Lucas points out that employees, especially high flyers, rank challenging and interesting work and freedom higher on their motivational list than money and performance-

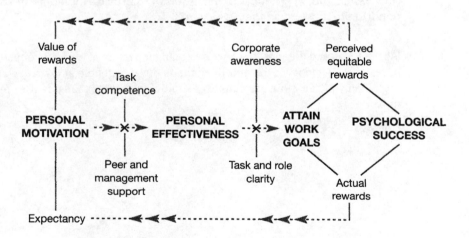

Figure 12.13 Motivating knowledge workers

(Reproduced with permission from Mahen Tampoe, 'Knowledge Workers – The New Management Challenge', *Professional Manager*, Institute of Management, November 1994, p. 13.)

related pay. 'Research suggests that most organisations haven't recognised the need to identify and tap into their employees' personal motivators.'[67]

A report from the *Chartered Institute of Personnel and Development* draws attention to the management of knowledge workers highlighting the importance of autonomy, challenging work and sharing in the creation of organisational values. With the development of new technology it is important to motivate employees to capture, share and transfer knowledge.[68]

Whitmore suggests that in order to create a climate for creativity among employees, recognition must be given to the importance of two human needs that rise above all others and exist independent of race, creed and culture – the need for self-belief and the development of emotional intelligence; and the ever-present need that every human being has for a sense of meaning and purpose in their lives. 'Self-belief and meaningful work are the fundamental bedrocks that underlie business performance. Of course, pay and conditions are important too, but we know that. It is these two others that are barely recognised ... but business leaders ignore them at their peril.'[69]

CRITICAL REFLECTIONS

'Why all this fuss about motivation? Surely, motivating people is easy – I was taught that if you are not motivated, then you are dead. And I seem to remember something about a natural hierarchy of human needs ...'

'Yes, fair enough but the real issues for management is motivating people to work to the best of their abilities and directing their efforts to the goals of the organisation – and this is certainly not always easy.'

What are your own views?

In an organisation, empowerment means that each staff member is responsible for creating that organisation's culture. There aren't many motivating forces more potent than giving your staff an opportunity to exercise and express their idealism.

Roddick, A. *Business As Unusual: the Triumph of Anita Roddick*, Thorsons (2000), p. 70.

How would you, in practical terms, attempt to provide members of your staff with the opportunity to exercise their idealism?

'All the ideas and theories that abound about motivation at work are redundant when it comes to basic issues – money is the only thing that motivates people in the real world. For example, in a recession you can motivate employees to do anything as long as they feel their job is under threat.'

Debate.

SYNOPSIS

■ The study of motivation is concerned, basically, with why people behave in a certain way. The underlying concept of motivation is some driving force within individuals by which they attempt to achieve some goal in order to fulfil some need or expectation. Individuals have a variety of changing, and often competing, needs and expectations which they attempt to satisfy in a number of different ways. One useful three-fold classification of individual needs and expectations at work is economic, intrinsic and social.

■ If a person's motivational driving force is blocked and they are unable to satisfy their needs and expectations, this may result either in constructive, problem-solving behaviour or in frustration-induced behaviour. Main reactions to frustration are aggression, regression, fixation and withdrawal. The rational–economic concept of motivation has drawn attention to the influence of money as a motivator. Although clearly a motivator for the majority of people the importance of and extent to which money influences organisational performance depends upon personal circumstances and other available rewards.

■ There are many competing theories which attempt to explain motivation at work. The different theories may be divided into two contrasting groups: content theories and process theories. Content theories place emphasis on what motivates and are concerned with identifying people's needs and their relative strengths, and the goals they pursue in order to satisfy these needs. Main content theories include: Maslow's hierarchy of needs model; Alderfer's modified need hierarchy model; Herzberg's two-factor theory; and McClelland's achievement motivation theory.

■ Process theories place emphasis on the actual process of motivation. These theories are concerned with the relationships among the dynamic variables which make up motivation, and with how behaviour is initiated, directed and sustained. Many of the process theories cannot be linked to a single writer, but major approaches under this heading include: expectancy-based models; equity theory; goal theory; and also attribution theory.

■ These different theories are not conclusive and have been subject to alternative findings, particularly the content theories. However, it is because of the complexity of motivation that these different theories are important to the manager and many writers still expound their relevance today. They help demonstrate the many motives that influence people's behaviour at work. They provide a framework within which to direct attention of how best to motivate and reward staff to work willingly and effectively. The manager must evaluate their relevance and judge how best and to what extent they might be applied with advantage in particular work situations.

■ One major doubt concerning the different theories of motivation is about their universality, on the grounds that they do not adequately address the factor of culture. A number of writers have drawn attention to cross-cultural dimensions of motivation and questioned whether theories and models originating in one culture are amenable to transference to other parts of the world. With developments in telecommunications and scientific and technological knowledge, management faces a new challenge of how best to motivate knowledge workers and create a climate of creativity.

MANAGEMENT IN ACTION 12.1

Developing reward strategies to motivate and compensate knowledge workers

Mahen Tampoe

Introduction

This is a synopsis of research-based findings on the motivation of knowledge workers and suggests that current reward strategies fail to excite the intrinsic motivational drives of this category of staff; furthermore, it suggests that in certain circumstances current reward strategies are counter-productive. It then goes on to offer a motivation and performance model which links reward strategies, organisational climates and individual competencies and to suggest actions which organisations can take to realise the promise of this model.

Knowledge workers – who are they?

Knowledge workers are those who apply their theoretical and practical understanding of an area of knowledge to produce outcomes that have commercial, social or personal value. They are likely to be drawn from a wide variety of professionally qualified and scientifically trained staff. Among them would be: doctors, scientists, computer specialists, personnel professionals, qualified accountants, managers, project managers and supervisors of knowledge workers who themselves have been promoted from being technologists to managers.

Characteristics of knowledge workers

Certain characteristics of knowledge workers differentiate them from other process dominant workers. While some of these are to do with their education and training, others are to do with the standards and expectations of their profession. Their work can also be distinguished in different ways. Namely, their work is:

- unlikely to be routine or repetitive;
- carried out to professional or quality standards and subject to these as well as the organisation's own standards of verification and approval (sometimes resulting in a conflict between work and professional standards);
- aimed at meeting operational or strategic targets derived from project objectives or established as part of a problem-solving activity;
- intrinsically motivational and provides the inner drive (as opposed to external stimulus) for creative achievement;
- continuously developing their knowledge and skill in their chosen area of expertise;
- amenable to self-management;
- not easily supervised, partly because of the specialist nature of their work and partly due to the fact that their work is not amenable to physical observation and measurement;
- less easy to procedurise and/or quantify, making it often more difficult to specify clear unambiguous performance targets;
- likely to have areas of high ambiguity, and to be susceptible to many different yet feasible solutions and outcomes.

Motivators for knowledge workers

Based on research carried out by the author, the work of other researchers and from personal experience of managing IT professionals over many years, the rewards and expectations of these knowledge workers can be summarised as a mixture of the following:

- **personal growth**, especially self-development rather than growing managerial or professional skills;
- **autonomy**, which gives them the freedom to work within the rules rather than working to rule or being allowed to define their own rules;
- **creative achievement**, where the work is of commercial value rather than meeting assigned targets or being work that is intellectually stimulating but not of commercial value;
- **financial rewards**, where salary plus bonus on personal effort is valued more than salary plus bonus on group effort or purely receiving a salary and fringe benefits.

Financial rewards played a very small part in this as most of those who supported the research study were in well paid jobs and were seeking self-actualisation rewards.

The strength of preference shown for these different motivators and the findings of other researchers in this field over the last 50 years suggest that the law of diminishing returns applies very definitely to financial incentives. However, when it comes to intrinsic incentives such as personal growth, creative achievement and autonomy, the law of escalating returns seems to apply. This is most pronounced in the area of creative achievement where the more they get the more they wish to get. The expectancy theory of motivation (*Vroom, Porter and Lawler* among others) suggests that reward strategies should be designed to optimise these inherent and intrinsic motivational drivers while allowing for *Herzberg's* theory of dissatisfiers and satisfiers.

Theoretical fit

Motivational researchers and theorists who have studied the motivation of knowledge workers agree that the Expectancy Theory of motivation is the most appropriate for this category of employee. The application of expectancy theory in reward strategies does suggest a very close and intricate link between rewards, the likelihood of earning those rewards and the realisation of those rewards, if performance is delivered. Based on my research and developing on others, it is possible to hypothesise a motivation and performance model. The model suggests that the creative energy of people needs to be applied to task achievement through the application of their personal capability and the organisation's strengths, usually made up of resources, peer support, management support and finances.

Adverse effects of current reward strategies

This conflicts with current reward strategies in organisations that seem to support and reinforce hierarchies rather than lateral co-operation. In addition, they tend to reward the job rather than the individual. Usually, career progression and bonus payments (for those whose results are not measurable using hard data) depend on patronage rather than merit and there is a tendency to reward those who sustain the status quo rather than those who are innovative and entrepreneurial. Finally, most reward strategies have unfairness built into them. For example, it is easier to reward sales staff on their personal performance than scientists in research laboratories. The sense of unfairness creeps in if staff who help sales people design and develop the 'winning' solution do not share in the bonus that accompanies a successful sale. Managers often sympathise with the scientists but do nothing to change the system on the grounds that it is 'too difficult', and has historical precedence. The more hard-nosed managers usually suggest that those scientists who want bonuses should join the salesforce or stop bellyaching about their lot. This approach just does not make sense in a world hungry for innovation and the rewards that it brings.

Reward options

Staff and managers should realise that rewards are multi-faceted and usually come in bundles that combine money, achievement, personal and professional growth and self-esteem. This means that the reward options open to management are very varied, as the examples in Table 12.3 show.

Table 12.3 Reward options for knowledge workers

Financial rewards	Non-financial rewards
Salary + bonus based on gain sharing	Personal growth
Salary + profit sharing	Knowledge or professional growth
Employee ownership	Status and public or private recognition
High salary + benefits	
	Career growth
Salary and bonus on individual or team effort	Job security

What managers should do is create reward bundles (fruit-bowls of choice) that more closely fit the needs of a group of employees rather than impose a blanket system on them all. For example, an individual or group could be offered a bundle which comprises salary plus profit sharing, status, personal growth. Another group or individual could be offered a different bundle comprising salary plus bonus on personal effort, career growth and professional growth. The reward bundles, drawn from a reward portfolio, are probably the fairest way to reward individual effort and contribution.

Performance measures

Inappropriate performance measures do more harm than good. In knowledge-based organisations, performance must be judged primarily by how the individual or group contributes to the **knowledge added value** of the organisation. This may take the form of specific creative outcomes, new knowledge generated or knowledge disseminated. Meeting targets and deadlines and solving critical problems, which contribute to **customer added value**, should also feature as measures.

Climate for optimising reward strategies proposed

Whatever scheme is used, it is imperative that those subject to these schemes can earn the promised rewards if they fulfil their part of the bargain. This means first of all that they can achieve the task they have been set. Among the necessary ingredients for this are:

- role and goal clarity;
- having the knowledge and skills or having the opportunity to acquire them;
- having sufficient autonomy and delegated authority to get the job done;
- having a wider understanding of what the organisation or department is trying to achieve and how the individual's work fits in with this;
- quality standards and defined deliverables;
- having a good knowledge of what is happening in the organisation as a whole and the threats and opportunities that it may experience.

However, where these conditions do not prevail and where there is strong hierarchical governance, reward strategies are wasted because the individual's skills and talents are not being tapped.

What should organisations do?

- Define and create a climate for success to match its business objectives.
- Widen opportunities for career growth by adopting multiple career streams, effective review systems, personal mentoring and strive to ensure equality of treatment for all employees.
- Reward managers on their ability to create and sustain the climate for success.
- Devise fruit-bowls of reward options.
- Revise the career expectations of staff so that they value professional and technical skills development and status as highly as clambering up the management ladder.
- Reward the individual rather than the post and reward each according to his or her contribution.
- Reward staff for enhancing their own knowledge value, the collective knowledge of the organisation and contributing to the organisation's core competences.
- Measure corporate climates and fine-tune them.
- Measure knowledge value added.
- Measure customer value added.

(Reproduced with permission of Professor Mahen Tampoe.)

REVIEW AND DISCUSSION QUESTIONS

1 Explain what you understand by the underlying concept of motivation. Summarise the main needs and expectations to be taken into account in considering the motivation of people at work.

2 What do you understand by frustration-induced behaviour? Give a practical example, preferably from your own work experience, of each of the main forms of this behaviour.

3 Why is the study of the different theories of motivation important to the manager? Distinguish between content and process theories of motivation.

4 Critically assess the practical value of Maslow's hierarchy of needs model to improving the motivation of people at work. Give examples of the extent to which the theory could meaningfully be applied to staff in your own organisation.

5 Discuss critically the validity of the contention that the motivation for staff to work well depends on more than a high salary and good working conditions.

6 Explain your understanding of expectancy-based theories of motivation. Use a simple diagram to help explain an expectancy theory of your choice. What implications do expectancy theories of motivation have for the manager?

7 Give practical examples of situations in which each of the following theories of motivation might be appropriate: (i) achievement motivation; (ii) equity theory; (iii) goal theory.

8 Discuss how you believe managers might best develop reward strategies to motivate and compensate knowledge workers.

9 Explain fully and with supporting reasons which one theory of motivation you believe is likely to be most appropriate in a particular work situation of your choice.

ASSIGNMENT 1

a List, as far as possible in rank order, the specific needs and expectations which are most important **to you as an individual.** (Do *not* include basic physiological needs such as to satisfy thirst or hunger, or a *minimal* standard of accommodation.)

b Explain, briefly, to what extent these needs and expectations are met currently from your present work situation; and/or to what extent you anticipate they will be met from your future career ambitions.

c Think of any work experience which you have had – even a short-term, vacation or part-time job. Briefly describe:

(i) those aspects of the job and/or experiences which motivated you to work well; and

(ii) those which had a demotivating influence on your behaviour/actions.

d Be prepared to share your feelings and comments as part of a class discussion.

ASSIGNMENT 2

a Write a brief description of what you think is happening to the people in the picture and what you think will happen to them in the future.

b After you have written your description compare your response with those of your colleagues.

PERSONAL AWARENESS AND SKILLS EXERCISE

OBJECTIVES

Completing this exercise should help you to enhance the following skills:

▶ Assess the strength of your different motivational needs.

▶ Avoid generalisations about what motivates people.

▶ Take account of individual differences and meet the needs of others.

EXERCISE

You are required to complete the Motivation Grid by taking each factor in order as follows.

1 Compare Salary (A) with Structure (B) – cell 1. Choose which factor you value more in relation to your work and write the code for that factor in the cell. For example, if you choose a good salary as being more important to you than structure and guidelines, enter A in the cell. If you prefer to have well-explained procedures and clarity in your work rather than a high salary, enter B in the cell (for structure).

2 Move to cell 2 – Salary (A) versus Social contact (C) – and enter your chosen letter code. Continue along the top line comparing Salary (A) with the other factors and entering the chosen letter code in each cell. Move to the second line and compare Structure (B) with each other factor.

3 When you have filled in all 36 cells, add up the number of entries for each letter code and enter these sub-totals into the score table.

4 If you find it very difficult to choose between two factors, you may put both letters in the cell – you will then score half a point for each: do not do this too often (it weakens your responses), say no more than five times.

Motivation Grid

The scores show a mirror reflection of what you felt as you filled in the Grid. These scores alter over time, as you develop in your career and as your domestic, social and physical

	Structure B	Social C	Recognition D	Achievement E	Influence F	Change G	Creativity H	Interest I
Salary A	1	2	3	4	5	6	7	8
	Structure 9	10	11	12	13	14	15
		Social 16	17	18	19	20	21
			Recognition 22	23	24	25	26
				Achievement 27	28	29	30
					Influence 31	32	33
						Change 34	35
							Creativity 36

needs change. The factors that tend to change most over time and circumstances are A, B and G. High scores for a factor indicate a high level of need, and low scores indicate a low level of need, relative to other factors.

The norms obtained from 1355 managers and professionals (kept on our database) will be given to you by your tutor. If you are below the norm, you have a low need for the factor, if you are above it, you have a high need.

Motivation Grid score sheet

Please fill in the score table below. Add up the number of times you have put A in any cell on the Grid and enter that total in the column 'Your score' against A. Continue for B, C and the other factors until you have totalled all nine of them. Your tutor will give you the norms later.

Factor	Your score	Norm
A – Salary		
B – Structure		
C – Social contact		
D – Recognition		
E – Achievement		
F – Influence		
G – Change		
H – Creativity		
I – Interest		
	Total = 36	

DISCUSSION

■ How surprised were you with your 'score' and to what extent did it differ from the 'norm'?

■ What factors should managers bear in mind when designing incentive and reward systems?

■ How important is an understanding of perception for the effective motivation of staff?

■ What conclusions do you draw from this exercise?

Note: Keep a record of your Motivation Scores for a subsequent exercise in Chapter 18.

The full 12-factor Motivation to Work Profile, from which this Grid is extracted, is copyright to and available from Sheila Ritchie of Elm Training and all international rights are reserved. It was created in 1989, developed and tested (with the help of Peter Martin of Arlington Associates from 1989–98). Further testing has been done in the UK and internationally, especially for its use as a team working development tool to date. Copies of the Profile may be obtained by e-mail to sritchie@elm-training.co.uk or by telephone on +44-18487-773254.

Visit our website **www.booksites.net/mullins** for further questions, annotated weblinks, case material and Internet research material.

CASE STUDY 12.1

Staff motivation: not so much a pyramid, more a slippery slope

My contact with my direct line manager is limited to irregular e-mails which are purely directional and/or informative. At no point is there any attempt to either help with my staffing problems or to acknowledge that these may be stress related. It follows then that there is no form of motivation downwards from him to me, although it is taken for granted that I will be self-motivated and able to motivate my team.

In the highly competitive world of international air passenger transport, the bottom line is everything. As such, all aspects of flight operations are subject to the rigorous cost–benefit analysis known as revenue per kilometre flown. This has led to some decisions which would deeply disturb Joe Public. When he purchases an airline ticket he is taking part in a lottery – the element of chance being the availability of the flight, seat class or flight time of his choice. Joe Public feels that buying his ticket gives him this automatic right – but he should read the small print.

Price banding restrictions linked to historical marketing statistics allow airlines to estimate the number of passengers who will present themselves for a particular flight as opposed to those who will choose to exercise their flexibility muscle. For example, if 70 per cent of the plane's capacity is made up of economy seats, a condition of which is that no changes are allowed, then it can be reasonably assumed that this group will travel on the given day or not at all. Flexibility to price ratio continues up the scale until the top notch ticket is reached. The high price tag at this level promises that the airline will strive to provide the frequent flyer with all that he requires. Further, statistics indicate that having made this investment, he will almost certainly travel since, *ceteris paribus*, he has chosen to pay an inflated price to guarantee that he will reach his destination when and how he wishes.

At this stage there remains only one small percentage of passenger statistics to be correlated and here restrictions linked to price again come into play, limiting the degree of usage of the flexibility muscle to the minority of passengers travelling 'open jaw'. These people will have paid a sufficiently large supplement in order to allow themselves the luxury of being flexible in their travel arrangements. As one would expect, this market segment has been shown to be the most likely not to travel and it is this information which the airlines use in their cal-

Photo: Nancy Wegard/Getty Images

culations. Should, as is likely, a proportion of this user group decide to change their plans, as is their right, then the airline would be faced with the economic disaster of high revenue seats flying empty and seriously reducing the company's desired margin of revenue. In order to cover this contingency proactively, the company chooses always to overbook these seats by the calculated percentage of passengers who will probably choose not to travel.

The above organisational difficulties are not new, however the systems in which they operate have changed drastically both in the attitude to acceptable levels of passenger discomfort and in the variety and number of duties which staff are now expected to carry out. As a manager in this environment Piet Andaro faces many challenges daily, the most daunting of which is to find a way to motivate his team who know with absolute certainty that during every shift they will have irate passengers. They, the passengers, will see them as the acceptable outlet for their outrage at what they perceive as unjust/unfair treatment, not to mention downright bad service. When the expected treatment fails to materialise Joe Public is not so much outraged by the failure of the actual mechanics but that his faith and trust have been misplaced.

It is then the role of Piet and his team to achieve the unachievable – to not give the customer what he wants but to send him on his way feeling that he has received outstanding service by people who genuinely care about his needs. Most importantly to the airline, he will take with him such a positive feeling that he will happily use the airline in the future and encourage others to do so.

These problems are not eventualities – most operators working in such a fast-moving environment are equipped to deal with most of these – but certainties, built into the system in order to maximise profit. Part of this drive towards even greater profits has, as with many multinationals in the 1990s, resulted in a restructuring of operations which in real terms has meant a paring down of the workforce to what senior management call optimum efficiency. In this case it also involves a flattening of the management structure to be a 'leaner fitter organisation'.

At the most extreme level, management in the organisation has been subject to great change, some enforced and some planned. Although the management structure is traditional and hierarchical, it is simultaneously attempting to achieve flatter organisation status. The motivation system therefore is roughly as follows:

1 Senior management should motivate themselves.
2 Piet should motivate himself and his team.
3 Individual members of the team should motivate themselves.
4 Sideways motivation is due to the fact that although each manager has the same title there are varying grades of responsibility and support

All those with the designation 'manager' may have the same title, but their knowledge, experience and skills levels vary dramatically. Not only do skills vary dramatically, so does motivation. To be lacking in a skill is a solvable problem, given time and the appropriate training. To be lacking in motivation is almost incurable, according to Piet. 'Although some members of management may not have perfect knowledge, built into the system is a way of finding most of what you need to know. However they would rather pick up the phone and ask me even if by doing so he is causing an already stressed customer to wait while he does so.'

A recent buzzword for organisations has been 'strategy' with each aspect of the business having its own strategy while being interdependent on all the others. Particularly highlighted and linked have been the communications minefields of customer service and human resource management. Practitioners tell us that the only way for a human resource initiative to be effective is that it must be integrated and strategic. There are arguments as to whether the human resource element should be considered first and operations based around it, or whether the operations should be put in place and then the appropriate human resource found. It is generally agreed that all human resource functions should be integrated to each other and that 'best fit' should be obtained. Often, though, this is sold to the company at all levels not as best fit but as best practice; however, once in place, as in our case study, these systems and operations are looked on as success panaceas and are never examined for their functionality. The rationale is that as they have been designed by experts at great cost then they should be left alone.

On paper the system should work, with the less able learning from the proficient, however in the real world of the service industries, people dealing with people, management demands consistency. Failure to provide this results in frustrated staff and aggrieved passengers, leaving those at the sharp end to constantly bear the brunt of the results of this revenue versus service conundrum.

Stress-related illness has been well documented and Piet is unfortunately acquainted with this phenomenon, faced as he is with a daily stress-related absenteeism of around 25 per cent. This non-existence of one-to-one or even regular verbal contact is further exacerbated by the fact that although appraisals are built into the system, in reality they are never carried out. This means that senior management has no feedback on the operational problems and difficulties which Piet encounters and as there is no procedure in place they are never communicated. Also the question is raised of how he will be able to face the daily aggression and stress without support.

Sometimes I just feel like not going to work but the act of putting on the uniform brings about a kind of metamorphosis – I begin to look forward to the day. Each shift brings a new set of problems and with it I find new capabilities and competencies within myself. I like to be proactive wherever possible, for example if I know a flight is going to be seriously overbooked then myself and my team will have a contingency plan or plans ready for when the crisis hits. I think the secret is to treat every event as completely new; it would be very easy to become cynical as it could be said that one overbooked flight is much like another in terms of problem solving.

That is simply not the case, each flight carries a set of passengers who as individuals have unique needs and expectations. I guess you could say that my motivation comes from the satisfaction of being able to make a difference. I may not be able to materialise a seat on an aircraft which does not exist but I can try to make the situation easier by means of finding the best alternative and to compensate them any way I can.

The contrast between two managers could not be greater. Piet as a self-motivator needs no praise in order to give 120 per cent effort. He never contacts his supervisor with problems and never complains, he is seen as a reliable but uninteresting plodder. Robert, on the other hand, is only motivated by extrinsic gain. What upsets Piet and his staff is that management are starting to look on Robert as a 'high flyer', the change in attitude being so great that it is apparent to everyone: 'once he heard about the promotion on offer he became a new man'.

Case study 12.1 continued

Everyone knows that Piet is far too conscientious, but the plus-side of this is that when his team leave for other posts then they also will be fully trained and have the same attitude to customer service as Piet, whom they all admire greatly. However when Robert moves on he will leave behind a team as demotivated as himself who will continue with the lazy could-not-care-less attitude simply because they have become used to not caring.

The summary of this dire motivational situation can be divided into four parts.

- The individual who has the correct attitude to customer service in any form, that is, someone who has a natural desire to help people, needs no outside motivation.
- The person who only sees the job as a way of getting a salary and who sees customers as numbers will constantly need outside stimulus to maintain even a mediocre performance and is in fact in the wrong job with the wrong attitude.
- Senior management who buy a 'cure all' package and then fail to check on its effects will soon discover customers leaving in droves.
- Unfortunately managers of the calibre of Piet will eventually burn out either physically or emotionally as they finally realise that no matter how hard they try they will never solve the built-in problems as well as they would like to.

I am grateful to Linda Fleming for providing this case study.

YOUR TASKS

1 Consider the probable outcomes both short and long term should the present situation continue for:
   - Piet Andaro
   - the airline
   - the customer

2 Is the failure to recognise the high percentage of stress-related absenteeism deliberate on the part of the airline, i.e. would it be more costly and therefore less cost-effective to attempt to find a remedy, given that airlines traditionally have a particularly high staff turnover?

3 A new CS0 is appointed after a spate of public relations disasters. The CSO investigates and decides that poor motivation is at the root of the problem. Compare the main process and content theories of motivation and discuss their suitability.

4 Many of today's fast-moving industries have a very public policy that they '... don't motivate individuals ... we provide an environment for them to be self-motivated'. To what extent has the airline created this type of environment? Do you see a problem simply of poor recruitment?

5 What behavioural factors are important when attempting to find a method of motivation suitable to both Piet and Robert? Discuss whether it is possible to find one which will suit both.

NOTES AND REFERENCES

1. See, for example: Pate, L. E. 'Understanding Human Behaviour', *Management Decisions*, vol. 26, no. 1, 1998, pp. 58–64.
2. Krech, D., Crutchfield, R. S. and Ballachey, E. L. *Individual in Society*, McGraw-Hill (1962).
3. Mitchell, T. R. 'Motivation: New Directions for Theory, Research, and Practice', *Academy of Management Review*, vol. 7, no. 1, January 1982, pp. 80–8.
4. Kreitner, R., Kinicki, A. and Buelens, M. *Organizational Behaviour*, First European edition, McGraw-Hill (1999).
5. Wolfson, Sir Brian 'Train, Retain and Motivate Staff', *Management Today*, March 1998, p. 5.
6. Farren, C. 'Mastery: The Critical Advantage' in Chowdhury, S. *Management 21C*, Financial Times Prentice Hall (2000), p. 95.
7. See, for example: Rudolph, P. A. and Kleiner, B. H. 'The Art of Motivating Employees', *Journal of Managerial Psychology*, 4 (5), 1989, pp. i–iv.
8. Kets de Vries, M. 'Beyond Sloan: trust is at the core of corporate values' in Pickford, J. (ed.) *Financial Times Mastering Management 2.0*, Financial Times Prentice Hall (2001), pp. 267–70.
9. For a fuller discussion, see: Mullins, L. J. *Hospitality Management and Organisational Behaviour*, Fourth edition, Longman (2001).
10. See for example: Schneider, S. C. and Barsoux, J. *Managing Across Cultures*, Second edition, Financial Times Prentice Hall (2003).
11. Cartwright, J. *Cultural Transformation*, Financial Times Prentice Hall (1999).
12. Caseby, R. '100 Best Companies to Work For', *Sunday Times*, 24 March 2002.
13. 'Untapped Potential: The barriers to optimum corporate productivity', Proudfoot Consulting, October 2002.
14. Allen, R. S. and Helms, M. M. 'Employee Perceptions of the Relationship between Strategy, Rewards and

Organizational Performance', *Journal of Business Strategies*, vol. 19, no. 2, Fall 2002, pp. 115–39.

15. 'Motivating Your Staff in a Time of Change', *Management Checklist 068*, Chartered Management Institute, 2001.

16. See, for example: Brown, J. A. C. *The Social Psychology of Industry*, Penguin (1954 and 1986).

17. Taylor, F. W. *Scientific Management*, Harper and Row (1947).

18. Weaver, T. 'Theory M: Motivating with Money', *Cornell HRA Quarterly*, vol. 29, no. 3, November 1988, pp. 40–5.

19. Hudson, A., Hayes, D. and Andrew, T. *Working Lives in the 1990s*, Global Futures (1996).

20. 'What You Thought: Motivating Minimum-Wage Workers', *Personnel Journal*, vol. 75, no. 3, March 1996, p. 16.

21. Vine, P. 'Women in Business', *The British Journal of Administrative Management*, November/December 1997, p. 14.

22. 'IDS Focus', *Incomes Data Services Ltd*, No. 92, Winter 1999.

23. Grayson, D. and Hodges, A. *Everybody's Business: Managing risks and opportunities in today's global society*, Financial Times (2001), p. 76.

24. Saunders, A. 'Keep Staff Sweet', *Management Today*, June 2003, p. 73.

25. Huck, S., Kubler, D. and Weibull, J. 'Social Norms and Economic Incentives in Firms', Economic & Social Research Council, 5 March 2003.

26. Cited in Crainer, S. 'Re-engineering the Carrot', *Management Today*, December 1995, p. 66.

27. For a discussion on the relevance of different theories for managers, see for example: Ritchie, S. and Martin, P. *Motivation Management*, Gower (1999).

28. Maslow, A. H. 'A Theory of Human Motivation', *Psychological Review*, 50, July 1943, pp. 370–96 and Maslow, A. H. *Motivation and Personality*, Third edition, Harper and Row (1987).

29. Steers, R. M. and Porter, L. W. *Motivation and Work Behaviour*, Fifth edition, McGraw-Hill (1991).

30. Saunders A, 'Keep Staff Sweet', *Management Today*, June 2003, p. 75.

31. Stum, D. L. 'Maslow revisited: building the employee commitment pyramid', *Strategy and Leadership*, vol. 29, no. 4, 2001, pp. 4–9.

32. Alderfer, C. P. *Existence, Relatedness and Growth*, Collier Macmillan (1972).

33. Herzberg, F., Mausner, B. and Snyderman, B. B. *The Motivation to Work*, Second edition, Chapman and Hall (1959).

34. For examples, see: (i) Bockman, V. M. 'The Herzberg Controversy', *Personnel Psychology*, vol. 24, Summer 1971, pp. 155–89, which analyses existing evidence from a wide variety of studies; (ii) Filley, A. C., House, R. J. and Kerr, S. *Managerial Process and Organizational Behavior*, Second edition, Scott Foresman (1976). A number of different sets of interviews found a high level of validity for the theoretical prediction.

35. Vroom, V. H. *Work and Motivation*, Wiley (1964). (Also published by Krieger (1982).)

36. King, N. 'A Clarification and Evaluation of the Two-Factor Theory of Job Satisfaction', *Psychological Bulletin*, vol. 74, July 1970, pp. 18–31.

37. Shipley, D. and Kiely, J. 'Motivation and Dissatisfaction of Industrial Salespeople – How Relevant is Herzberg's Theory?', *European Journal of Marketing*, vol. 22, no. 1, March 1988, pp. 17–28.

38. Phillipchuck, J. 'An Inquiry Into the Continuing Relevance of Herzberg's Motivation Theory', *Engineering Management Journal*, vol. 8, no. 1, March 1996, pp. 15–20.

39. Crainer, S. and Dearlove, D. (eds) *Financial Times Handbook of Management*, Second edition, Financial Times Prentice Hall (2001), p. 361.

40. McClelland, D. C. *Human Motivation*, Cambridge University Press (1988).

41. For examples of pictures, see: Osland, J. S., Kolb, D. A. and Rubin, I. M. *Organizational Behaviour: An Experimental Apporach*, Seventh edition, Prentice Hall (2001).

42. See, for example: Spangler, W. D. 'Validity of Questionnaire and TAT Measures of Weed for Achievement Two Meta-Analyses', *Psychological Bulletin*, July 1992, pp. 140–54.

43. McClelland, D. C. 'Business Drive and National Achievement', *Harvard Business Review*, vol. 40, July–August 1962, pp. 99–112.

44. McClelland, D. C. and Burnham, D. H. 'Power is the Great Motivation', *Harvard Business Review*, vol. 54, March–April 1976, pp. 100–10.

45. Vroom, V. H. *Work and Motivation*, Wiley (1964). (Also published by Krieger (1982).)

46. Porter, L. W. and Lawler, E. E. *Managerial Attitudes and Performance*, Irwin (1968).

47. Lawler, E. E. *Motivation in Work Organizations*, Brooks/Cole (1973).

48. See, for example: Eerde, van W. and Thierry, H. 'Vroom's Expectancy Models and Work-Related Criteria: A Meta-Analysis', *Journal of Applied Psychology*, October 1996, pp. 575–86.

49. Porter, L. W., Lawler, E. E. and Hackman, J. R. *Behavior in Organizations*, McGraw-Hill (1975), pp. 57–8.

50. Adams, J. S. 'Injustice in Social Exchange', in Berkowitz, L. (ed.) *Advances in Experimental Social Psychology*, Academic Press (1965). Abridged in Steers, R. M. and Porter, L. W. *Motivation and Work Behavior*, Second edition, McGraw-Hill (1979), pp. 107–24.

51. Kreitner, R., Knicki, A. and Buelens, M. *Organisational Behaviour*, First European edition, McGraw-Hill, (1999).

52. Locke, E. A. 'Towards a Theory of Task Motivation and Incentives', *Organizational Behavior and Human Performance*, vol. 3, 1968, pp. 157–89.

53. Locke, E. A. 'Personal Attitudes and Motivation', *Annual Review of Psychology*, vol. 26, 1975, pp. 457–80.

54. Gratton, L. *Living Strategy: Putting people at the heart of corporate purpose*, Financial Times Prentice Hall (2000), p. 193.

55. For a summary of research supporting these conclusions, see: Miner, J. B. *Theories of Organizational Behavior*, Holt, Rinehart and Winston (1980).

56. For examples, see: Pinder, C. C. *Work Motivation*, Scott Foresman (1984); and Locke, E. A. and Latham, G. P. *A Theory of Goal-setting and Task Performance*, Prentice Hall (1990).

57. Hannagan, T. *Management*, Third edition, Financial Times Prentice Hall (2002), p. 328.

58. Reis, D. and Pena, L. 'Reengineering the Motivation to Work', *Management Decision*, vol. 39, no. 8, (2001), pp. 666–75.

59. 'Motivating Your Staff in a Time of Change', *Management Checklist 068*, Chartered Management Institute, 2001.

60. Flores, G. N. and Utley, R. 'Management Concepts in Use – a 12-year perspective', *Engineering Management Journal*, vol. 12, no. 3, September 2000, pp. 11–17.

61. See, for example: Cheng, T., Sculli, D. and Chan, F. S. 'Relationship Dominance – Rethinking management theories from the perspective of methodological relationalism', *Journal of Managerial Psychology*, vol. 16, no. 2, 2001, pp. 97–105.

62. Francesco, A. M. and Gold, B. A. *International Organizational Behavior: Test, Readings, Cases and Skills*, Prentice Hall (1998), p. 89.

63. Ibid., p. 92.

64. Adler, N. J. *International Aspects of Organizational Behaviour*, Third edition, South Western College Publishing (1997).

65. Chen, C. C. 'New Trends in Reward Allocation Preferences: A Sino-US Comparison', *The Academy of Management Journal*, vol. 38, no. 2, 1995, pp. 402–28.

66. Tampoe, M. 'Knowledge Workers – The New Management Challenge', *Professional Manager*, November 1994, pp. 12–13.

67. Lucas, E. 'Turning on the Knowledge Workers', *Professional Manager*, May 1999, pp. 10–12.

68. 'Managing Knowledge Workers: the HR dimension', Chartered Institute of Personnel and Development, January 2002.

69. Whitmore, Sir John 'Breaking Down the Barriers to Management Creativity', *Manager, The British Journal of Administrative Management*, May/June 2002, pp. 24–6.

 Use the *Financial Times* to enhance your understanding of the context and practice of management and organisational behaviour. Refer to articles 3, 12, 13, 19 and 21 in the BUSINESS PRESS section at the end of the book for relevant reports on the issues explored in this chapter.

TOPIC SUMMARY SHEET

What are the key learning points from this topic?

TOPIC 7A – WORK DESIGN

Why study these topics?

The previous topic was concerned with how we motivate staff so that organisational success can be achieved. The implementation of work design techniques have an important part to play in the motivational process, and it is these techniques we will focus on here. It is a relatively straightforward process, but one that many organisations often don't get right or attempt to implement. It's key concern is the nature of the tasks which combine to form the overall job.

This chapter will explain the different techniques used in the job design process. Also introduced will be the job design model, which is another key concept of this topic. This chapter will also make you think about your own employment experiences, and how your tasks could have been better designed or improved.

Topic 7b – Employee Resourcing

Employing the right person for the job is essential if an organisation is to perform effectively. This process can be a lengthy and involved one, as there can be many techniques that can be used.

This chapter introduces you to a large variety of these techniques, and their strengths and weaknesses. As we all either have been or will be involved in a selection process, this chapter will increase your understanding of the activities that take place.

Blackboard

E-tivity 7: Work design/ Employee resourcing

18 JOB SATISFACTION AND WORK PERFORMANCE

To make the best use of people as a valuable resource of the organisation, attention must be given to the relationship between staff, and the nature and content of their jobs. The work organisation and the design of jobs can have a significant effect on staff and their levels of performance and productivity. Attention needs to be given to the quality of working life. The manager needs to understand how best to make work more satisfying for staff and to overcome obstacles to effective performance.

Photo: with permission from Microsoft Corporation

LEARNING OUTCOMES

After completing this chapter you should be able to:

► explain the meaning, nature and main dimensions of job satisfaction;

► detail a framework of study;

► explore the nature of stress at work;

► detail main approaches to improving work organisation and job design;

► examine broader organisational approaches to improved job design;

► evaluate main influences on job satisfaction;

► review the relationships between job satisfaction and improved work performance.

There is always a choice about the way you do your work, even if there is not a choice about the work itself. We can choose the attitude we bring to our work.

Stephen Lundin, Harry Paul and John Christensen

Fish: A Remarkable Way to Boost Morale and Improve Results, Hyperion Press (2001). The story of the world famous Pike Place Fish Market, Seattle

I like work: it fascinates me. I can sit and look at it for hours. I love to keep it by me: the idea of getting rid of it nearly breaks my heart.

Jerome K. Jerome

Three Men in a Boat, Arrowsmith (1889)

THE MEANING AND NATURE OF JOB SATISFACTION

Attempting to understand the nature of job satisfaction and its effects on work performance is not easy. **Job satisfaction** is a complex and multifaceted concept, which can mean different things to different people. Job satisfaction is usually linked with motivation, but the nature of this relationship is not clear. Satisfaction is not the same as motivation. **Job satisfaction is more of an attitude, an internal state. It could, for example, be associated with a personal feeling of achievement, either quantitative or qualitative.**

One view is that job satisfaction is necessary in order to achieve a high level of motivation and performance. However, although the level of job satisfaction may well affect strength of motivation, this is not always the case. The content theories of motivation (discussed in Chapter 12) tend to assume a direct relationship between job satisfaction and improved performance. For example, *Herzberg's* two-factor theory is essentially a theory of job satisfaction.[1] However, the process theories of motivation recognise the greater complexity of work motivation and consider in more detail the wider relationships involving motivation, satisfaction and performance.

In recent years attention to job satisfaction has become more closely associated with broader approaches to improved job design and work organisation, and the quality of working life movement, and with stress and the work/life balance.

Job satisfaction and performance

The relationship between job satisfaction and performance is an issue of continuing debate and controversy. One view, associated with the early human relations approach, is that satisfaction leads to performance. An alternative view is that performance leads to satisfaction. *Luthans*, however, suggests that:

> Although most people assume a positive relationship, the preponderance of research evidence indicates that there is no strong linkage between satisfaction and productivity.[2]

Bassett also suggests that research studies have found only a limited relationship between satisfaction and work output and offer scant comfort to those seeking to confirm that a satisfied worker is a productive worker. Staff turnover and absenteeism are commonly associated with dissatisfaction but although there may be some correlation there are many other possible factors. There appear to be no universal generalisations about worker satisfaction or dissatisfaction that offer easy management solutions to problems of turnover and absenteeism. Bassett suggests that it is primarily in the realm of job design that opportunity for constructive improvement of worker satisfaction appears to be high.[3] (Job design is discussed later in this chapter.)

You may recall that Herzberg identified a sense of achievement as affecting feelings of job satisfaction. *Reeves* draws attention to the relationship between accomplishment at work and the need to 'work harder'.

> All this busy-ness and stress is creating more heat than light. It is a sign not of work being too hard but too shallow. Human nature is driven by a desire to accomplish things, and so the fewer opportunities for accomplishment a job contains, the more likely we are to fill the void by tearing around in a frenzy in an effort to persuade ourselves and others that our work has a purpose, that it is important.[4]

DIMENSIONS OF JOB SATISFACTION

There is some doubt whether job satisfaction consists of a single dimension or a number of separate dimensions. Some workers may be satisfied with certain aspects of their work and dissatisfied with other aspects. There does, however, appear to be a positive correlation between satisfaction in different areas of work. This suggests a single overall factor of job satisfaction. However, it seems that there is no one, general, comprehensive theory which explains job satisfaction.[5]

Job satisfaction is itself a complex concept and difficult to measure objectively. The level of job satisfaction is affected by a wide range of variables relating to individual, social, cultural, organisational and environmental factors.

- **Individual factors** include personality, education and qualifications, intelligence and abilities, age, marital status, orientation to work.
- **Social factors** include relationships with co-workers, group working and norms, opportunities for interaction, informal organisation.
- **Cultural factors** include underlying attitudes, beliefs and values.
- **Organisational factors** include nature and size, formal structure, personnel policies and procedures, employee relations, nature of the work, technology and work organisation, supervision and styles of leadership, management systems, working conditions.
- **Environmental factors** include economic, social, technical and governmental influences.

These different factors all affect the job satisfaction of certain individuals in a given set of circumstances but not necessarily in others. The various studies of job satisfaction all have some validity. For example, in previous chapters we have drawn attention to the increasing emphasis placed on teamwork. According to *Cane*: 'When teams are well set up and clearly focused, they have been proven to lead to high productivity, more new ideas, greater employee satisfaction and motivation, and higher and more consistent performance.'[6] Note, however, that there is also some doubt today about the value and effectiveness of teamwork, and the effects on the quality of working life.[7]

The work environment

An increasingly important issue affecting job satisfaction and efficiency is the nature of the work environment and workplace facilities. *Handy*, for example, argues that an inspired workplace will result in inspired workers and draws attention to the importance of the atmosphere, quality and style of buildings and offices for work performance.[8]

A recent study by the Chartered Management Institute reports on UK managers' attitudes to and experiences of their physical working environment. The study was undertaken among a random sample of 4000 managers across all levels, and sectors and size of organisation. Topics addressed include hours worked, commuting and travel, flexible working, the existing and preferred layout of offices and the use of new technologies. Concerns were expressed about the need for more quiet areas, underequipped meeting rooms, lack of adequate meeting space, and their offices not making a good impression on clients and visitors. Nearly half of those surveyed would relinquish one week's annual leave for a better office and sizeable numbers would forgo £1000 in salary or private medical insurance for a significantly upgraded workspace. And even if the role, salary and benefits were no better, 45 per cent would contemplate changing companies in return for an improved work environment. [9, 10]

Differences between industries

There may also be significant differences in terms of what employees want from their work in different industries. For example, in a study by *Simons and Enz*, responses from hospitality workers showed a marked difference from those described in earlier studies of workers in manufacturing industries. Overall, for industrial workers, the three things most wanted were interesting work, appreciation and the feeling of being in on things; for the hospitality workers, the three things most wanted were good wages, job security and opportunities for advancement and development.[11]

Five contractual areas

Mumford examines job satisfaction in two ways:

1 in terms of the fit between what the organisation requires and what the employee is seeking; and
2 in terms of the fit between what the employee is seeking and what he/she is actually receiving.

On the basis of various schools of thought on job satisfaction, Mumford identifies five contractual areas by which this organisational/employee relationship can be examined: the knowledge contract; the psychological contract; the efficiency/reward contract; the ethical contract; and the task structure contract.[12] (*See* Table 18.1.)

An account of the fit between Mumford's five contractual areas and experiences at a branch of one of the UK's largest supermarket chains is given in Management in Action 18.1 at the end of this chapter.

Alienation at work

One main approach to job satisfaction is in terms of frustration and **alienation** at work. Job satisfaction can be seen as the obverse of frustration at work (discussed in Chapter 12). Alienation refers to the detachment of the person from his or her work role. The concept of alienation at work is associated originally with the views of *Marx*.[13] He saw the division of labour in pursuit of profit, and exploitation by employers, as a denial of the workers' need for self-expression. Workers become estranged from the product of their work. Work no longer provided a satisfying experience in itself, but represented a means of satisfying other external demands. The concept of alienation has been extended by *Blauner*.[14] He describes alienation in terms of four dimensions: powerlessness, meaninglessness, isolation and self-estrangement.

Table 18.1 Five contractual areas relating to job satisfaction

	The firm	The employee
The knowledge contract	Needs a certain level of skill and knowledge in its employees if it is to function efficiently	Wishes the skills and knowledge he/she brings with him/her to be used and developed
The psychological contract	Needs employees who are motivated to look after its interests	Seeks to further interests private to self, e.g. to secure: achievement, recognition, responsibility, status
The efficiency/rewards contract	Needs to implement generalised output, quality standards and reward systems	Seeks a personal, equitable effort–reward bargain and controls, including supervisory ones, which are perceived as acceptable
The ethical (social value) contract	Needs employees who will accept the firm's ethos and values	Seeks to work for an employer whose values do not contravene his/her own
The task structure contract	Needs employees who will accept technical and other constraints which produce task specificity or task differentiation	Seeks a set of tasks which meets his/her requirements for task differentiation, e.g. which incorporate variety, interests, targets, feedback, task identity and autonomy

(Reproduced with permission from Mumford, E. 'Job Satisfaction: A Method of Analysis', *Personnel Review*, vol. 20, no. 3, 1991, p. 14.)

- **Powerlessness** denotes the workers' lack of control over management policy, immediate work processes, or conditions of employment.
- **Meaninglessness** stems from standardisation and division of labour. It denotes the inability to see the purpose of work done, or to identify with the total production process or finished product.
- **Isolation** is not belonging to an integrated work group or to the social work organisation, and not being guided by group norms of behaviour.
- **Self-estrangement** is the failure to see work as an end in itself or as a central life issue. Workers experience a depersonalised detachment, and work is seen solely as a means to an end.

In recent years greater attention has been given to issues of employee involvement and empowerment (referred to later in this chapter) as important determinants of improved job satisfaction.

FRAMEWORK OF STUDY

We have seen that there are many possible approaches from which to view the subject of job satisfaction. One possible framework of analysis is given in Figure 18.1.

Some of the major factors which have a particular influence on job satisfaction include:

- information communications technology;
- stress at work;
- work organisation and individual job design;
- comprehensive model of job enrichment;
- broader organisational approaches;
- quality of working life;
- work/life balance;
- involvement, empowerment and groups;
- flexible working arrangements;
- quality circles.

A 'summary outline', setting out some of the main features of job satisfaction is presented in Figure 18.2.

INFORMATION COMMUNICATIONS TECHNOLOGY

TECHNOLOGY
SOLUTIONS

www.booksites.net/mullins

The work of *Blauner* has drawn attention to the nature of technology as a major influence on job satisfaction. Technology relates to both the physical aspects of machines, equipment, processes and work layout, and the actual methods, systems and procedures involved in the carrying out of work. Technology is therefore a major influence on the general climate of the organisation and the behaviour of people at work.[15] The impact of information technology can also have a significant influence on job satisfaction. Information technology will demand new patterns of work organisation. It will affect the nature and content of individual jobs; the function and structure of work groups; changes in the nature of supervision; the hierarchical structure of jobs and responsibilities; the employment conditions of staff; and the management task.

Advances in sophisticated systems of information communications technology and greater opportunities for more and more people to work from home are helping to create and support the virtual office. However, in Chapter 4 we drew attention to developments in the technical systems of communications generating a working

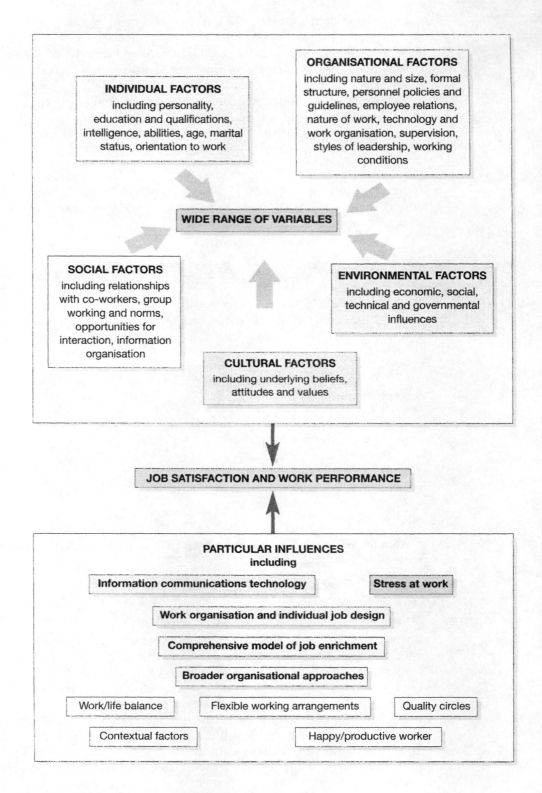

Figure 18.1 A framework for the study of job satisfaction

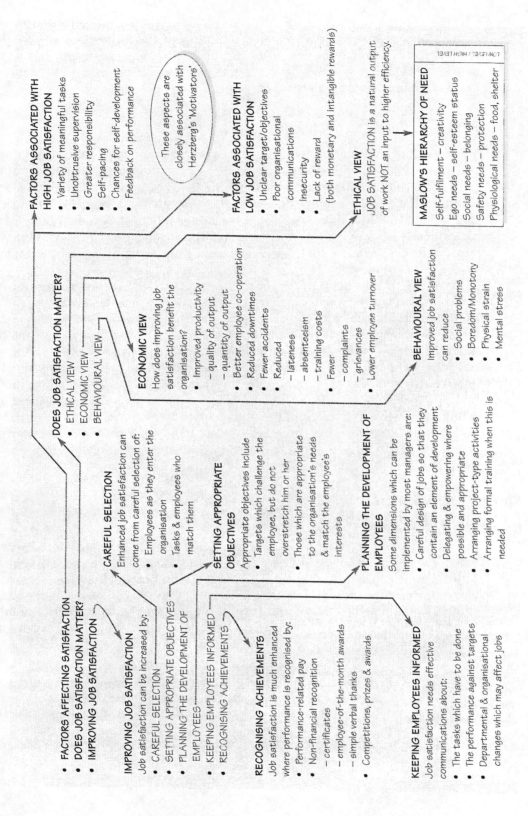

Figure 18.2 Summary outline of job satisfaction
(Reproduced with permission of Training Learning Consultancy Ltd. Bristol.)

climate in which there is a greater expectation of the immediacy of receipt and response; and adding to the dangers of information overload. For example, a report by management company Pitney Bowes claims that the ever-increasing use of email is a cause of rising stress levels in the workplace.[16]

Potential benefits and disadvantages

The growth of information technology means that many individuals can undertake their work at any time and anywhere, and provides for greater mobility. *Lucas* maintains that 'the benefits to organizations, in terms of improved productivity, staff retention and employee motivation are well documented'.[17] However, *Thomas* suggests that it is impossible at this stage to draw conclusions about the impact of mobile working, which is a hugely varied experience. Whilst for some people it is good news and may be clearly liberating, for others doing extra work and long hours of uninteresting work is less appealing.[18]

According to *Law*, managers of the future, especially in larger organisations, will be someone who is a 'personal area network' wherever they may be, always connected to the Internet. Managers will be using personal digital assistants (PDAs) – handheld mobile devices that can access the Internet and act as a basic personal organiser by setting up a diary. However, if too many people are working remotely too often there is a risk of alienation and there is also the potential problem of pressures on staff who are permanently contactable.[19] *Reeves* maintains that IT is potentially the most progressive force for change in the workplace. It could free millions of workers from the drudgery of the nine-to-five and the absurdity of presenteeism. However, far from being liberating, IT feels enslaving. Email becomes a daily tyranny, the mobile phone a corporate electronic tagging device. Companies still expect their staff to work set hours even when IT makes this unnecessary.[20]

STRESS AT WORK

According to a report cited in *Financial Times*: 'Stress at work is the biggest problem problem in European companies.'[21] There appears little doubt that one of the major adverse influences on job satisfaction, work performance and productivity, and absenteeism and turnover is the incidence of **stress** at work.[22] Stress is a complex and dynamic concept. It is a source of tension and frustration, and can arise through a number of interrelated influences on behaviour, including the individual, group, organisational and environmental factors discussed in Chapter 2.

According to *McKenna*, for example:

> In human terms any situation that is seen as burdensome, threatening, ambiguous or boring is likely to induce stress. This is the type of situation that would normally strike the individual as deserving immediate attention or concern and is viewed as unfortunate or annoying. There tends to be the feeling that the situation should not exist, but because of it the person feels disappointed or annoyed and eventually is prone to anxiety, depression, anger, hostility, inadequacy, and low frustration tolerance.[23]

The nature of stress

Figures from the Heath and Safety Executive (HSE) suggest that work-related stress is the main cause of work sickness absence. 'It's an issue that employers are clearly going to have to take more seriously in the future. The HSE is introducing tough new stress standards – and organisations that don't come up to scratch could face fines. Experts advise that if companies want to ease the pressure, they should start by putting their working culture and management style under the microscope.'[24] There appears to be a similar situation in the US where a survey of 333 US companies found that more workers are calling in absent because of family issues, stress and personal needs.[25]

Broad draws attention to the level of absenteeism in large public-sector organisations in this country, which is nearly a third higher than staff absence in the private sector. In the public sector, absenteeism caused by stress is preventing the delivery of quality services. There are heavy costs associated with stress. It lowers productivity and increases staff sickness. Pressure on the public sector to deliver is set to increase, with the funding being tied to reform and results.[26]

York contends that despite all the business-speak people get seriously vague when it comes to definitions and raises the question: What is stress? Is it a new name for an old-fashioned condition such as unhappiness or overwork: or is it peculiar to our uniquely pressured times? York suggests there is something in the idea that stress isn't just about hard work or unhappiness, but about conflict, confusion and frustration. It's about the anxiety generated by multi-tasking and balancing priorities, meeting contradictory demands, about knowing where to start and papering over the cracks when you want to do too much.[27]

Pressure and stress

Stress, however, is a very personal experience, as is the response of each individual to it and their beliefs about how best to cope with the causes and effects of stress. For example, *Orpen* questions the prevalent view among managers in Britain which seems to be that stress at work is something to be avoided at all costs. Just as there are circumstances when individuals may have too much stress, there are also circumstances when individuals may have too little stress for effective performance.[28] This view also appears to be supported by *Gwyther*, who points out that although stress appears to have become public health enemy number one and is viewed as the culprit of a myriad of complaints, the term is bandied about far too readily and there is a need to stand back and attempt to get things into some sort of perspective. A measure of stress is natural. A degree of stress at work is no unhealthy thing and without it nothing would ever get done.[29]

A certain amount of stress may **arguably** not necessarily be seen as a bad thing and may even help promote a higher level of performance. But what is the distinction between pressure and stress? 'Pressure' can be seen as a positive factor which may be harnessed to help people respond to a challenge and function more effectively. On the other hand, 'stress' may be regarded a continuous negative response arising from extreme pressure or other demands and the individual's inability to cope.

> *Personal performance may improve with pressure, up to a certain point. Beyond that point, continuous pressure leads to a fall in performance as the person is no longer able to cope. Signs of this are fatigue, poor judgement and bad decision making. In turn, this can lead to serious business problems.*[30]

However, it is important to bear in mind that stress can potentially be very harmful.

The results of unrelieved stress on the individual and on business are worrying. The result may be higher accident rates, sickness absence, inefficiency, damaged relationships with clients and colleagues, high staff turnover, early retirement on medical grounds, and even premature death ... The cost of stress is huge. It is devastating to the individual and damaging to the business at a time when the need to control business costs and ensure an effective and healthy workforce is greater than ever. It is in everyone's interest to tackle the taboo on talking about emotional problems because it is this which inhibits individuals from seeking help.

Simon Armson, Chief Executive, The Samaritans[31]

Lack of delegation and autonomy

Research into managers in various types of organisation in Western Australia showed that delegation of responsibility to middle managers required great skill, which was too seldom present. Replies from 532 managers in 36 organisations indicated a clear correlation between lack of autonomy and stress at work. Stress was often caused by the hierarchical structure of the organisation not permitting sufficient autonomy. As a result, projects were frequently delayed and also managers' authority within their own departments was undermined.[32]

Are managers under stress?

The Institute of Management has undertaken research into stress management issues. The research involved the view of nearly 1100 managers in order to explore the impact of job-related stress among managers. A key finding was that organisational changes such as redundancies, introduction of new technology and loss of key personnel place extra demands on managers and increase stress. One conclusion was that the major causes of stress in the workplace are unreasonable deadlines and office politics. Flatter management structures do not lead to the anticipated advances in communications, efficiency, decision-making and employee involvement. The research confirms that stress affects all levels and types of manager. Almost 90 per cent of respondents believe that stress is having an adverse effect on morale, health, work effectiveness and relationships.[33]

ROLE RELATIONSHIPS AND CONFLICT

One potential major source of work stress arises from role incongruence and role conflict (discussed in Chapter 13). Role stress can lead to difficulties in communication and interpersonal relationships and can have an adverse affect on morale, performance and effectiveness at work, and health. Demands for improved business competitiveness and lower operating costs have frequently led to restructuring of organisations and reductions in staffing levels. This has placed greater pressures on remaining staff and resulted in a growing number of work-related health problems, work stress and a less efficient workforce.[34] In the case of customer service, *Jamison* suggests that if there is a conflict between the requirements of a customer and the requirements of the organisation this will induce unhelpful behaviour as a result of stress.[35]

Handy suggests five organisational situations that are likely to create role problems and therefore stress for the individual:

- **Responsibility for the work of others** – reconciling overlapping or conflicting objectives of groups and organisations, of groups and individuals, of self and superiors.
- **Innovative functions** – conflicting priorities and different psychological demands between the routine and administrative aspects of the job and the creative side.
- **Integrative or boundary functions** – the particularly stressful role to the co-ordinator, link person or outside contact, perhaps due to the lack of control over their demands or resources.
- **Relationship problems** – difficulties with a boss, subordinates or colleagues. For some people, particularly those with a technical orientation, the need to work with other people is a worrying complication.
- **Career uncertainty** – if future career prospects become doubtful the uncertainty can quickly become stressful and spread to affect the whole of a person's work.[36]

A summary of sources of role stress at work is given in Figure 18.3.

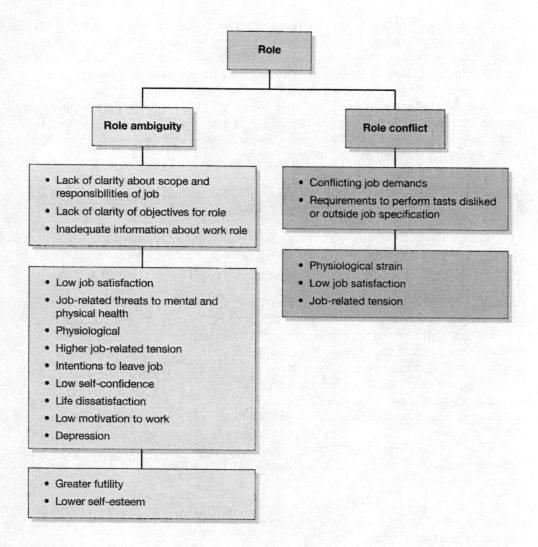

Figure 18.3 Source of role stress at work

(Source: Arnold, J., Cooper, C. L. and Robertson, I. T. *Work Psychology: Understanding Human Behaviour in the Workplace*, Third edition, Financial Times Prentice Hall (1998) p. 434, with permission from Pearson Education Ltd.)

LEVELS OF STRESS

An increasing number of surveys report, perceived or actual, increases in levels of stress. There have also been a number of highly publicised reports of successful legal claims against the effects of stress. Understandably, however, there is also a level of scepticism about the amount of emphasis placed on stress, and a number of press and other articles feature the 'myth' of work stress.

An interesting report from the *Institute for Social and Economic Research* suggests that claims of workplace pressure may be misplaced. Levels of job satisfaction and mental distress vary systematically according to the day of the week on which respondents are interviewed. Stress appears to disappear on Friday and Saturday. When genuine dissatisfaction was found, it tended to be because employees were working too few or too many hours. However, the main cause of stress was money difficulties, caused by unemployment or debt. The research casts a question mark over the generous compensation regularly handed out by the courts to employees claiming they suffer from stress.[37] *Randall* also makes the point that: 'Whichever lawyer first hit on the idea of promoting stress as either a reason for not going to work or a way to make others cough up could hardly have done more damage to Britain's work ethic than if he or she had arranged a quintupling of dole payments.'[38]

COPING WITH STRESS

There are a number of measures by which individuals and organisations can attempt to reduce the causes and effects of stress. The Health and Safety Executive (HSE) define stress as: 'The adverse reaction people have to excess pressure. It isn't a disease. But if stress is intense and goes on for some time, it can lead to a mental and physical ill health (e.g. depression, nervous breakdown, heart disease).'[39] HSE has set out problems that can lead to work-related stress under the headings of: culture, demands of the job, control, relationships, change, role, support and the individual; together with what management can do. (*See* Figure 18.4.) There are also many suggested techniques to help individuals bring stress under control – for example, changing your viewpoint; identifying causes of distress; laughing and telling jokes; working on stress reduction; and appreciating some stress can be useful.[40] Organisations also need to give greater attention to training, support and counselling; and to the work organisation and job design (discussed below).

The Engineering Employers' Federation set out a checklist of strategies relating to building corporate awareness and managerial understanding, and avoiding and minimising stress by attention to:

- job design;
- structure of the organisation and resources;
- management style; and
- helping the individual to cope.

Effective management of stress can reduce absence; increase work quality and performance; reduce resistance to change; improve relationships with customers, colleagues and suppliers; and reduce staff turnover.[41]

The importance of conversations

Effective communications at all levels of the organisation are clearly important in helping to reduce or overcome the level of stress. However, in addition to good communications, *Reeves* also refers to the importance of conversation for maintaining relationships and suggests a case for a conversation culture. The ability to hold good-quality conversations is becoming a core organisational and individual skill. Unlike communication, conversations are intrinsically creative and roam freely across personal issues, corporate gossip and work projects. 'Conversations are a defence against stress and other mental health problems. People with good social relationships at work are much less likely to be stressed or anxious.'[42]

A 'summary outline' of the meaning, causes and avoidance of stress is given in Figure 18.5.

CULTURE

Problems that can lead to stress
- lack of communication and consultation
- a culture of blame when things go wrong, denial of potential problems
- an expectation that people will regularly work excessively long hours or take work home with them

What management can do
- provide opportunities for staff to contribute ideas, especially in planning and organising their own jobs
- introduce clear business objectives, good communication, and close employee involvement, particularly during periods of change
- be honest with yourself, set a good example, and listen to and respect others
- be approachable – create an atmosphere where people feel it is OK to talk to you about any problems they are having
- avoid encouraging people to work excessively long hours

CONTROL

Problems that can lead to stress
- lack of control over work activities

What management can do
- give more control to staff by enabling them to plan their own work, make decisions about how that work should be completed and how problems should be tackled

RELATIONSHIPS

Problems that can lead to stress
- poor relationships with others
- bullying, racial or sexual harassment

What management can do
- provide training in interpersonal skills
- set up effective systems to prevent bullying and harassment (ie, a policy, agreed grievance procedure and proper investigation of complaints)

CHANGE

Problems that can lead to stress
- uncertainty about what is happening
- fears about job security

What management can do
- ensure good communication with staff
- provide effective support for staff throughout the process

DEMANDS OF THE JOB

Problems that can lead to stress
- too much to do, too little time
- too little/too much training for the job
- boring or repetitive work, or too little to do
- the working environment

What management can do
- prioritise tasks, cut out unnecessary work, try to give warning of urgent or important jobs
- make sure individuals are matched to jobs, provide training for those who need more, increase the scope of jobs for those who are over-trained
- change the way jobs are done by moving people between jobs, giving individuals more responsibility, increasing the scope of the job, increasing the variety of tasks, giving a group of workers greater responsibility for effective performance of the group
- make sure other workplace hazards, such as noise, harmful substances and the threat of violence, are properly controlled

ROLE

Problems that can lead to stress
- staff feeling that the job requires them to behave in conflicting ways at the same time
- confusion about how everyone fits in

What management can do
- talk to people regularly to make sure that everyone is clear about what their job requires them to do
- make sure that everyone has clearly defined objectives and responsibilities linked to business objectives, and training on how everyone fits in

SUPPORT AND THE INDIVIDUAL

Problems that can lead to stress
- lack of support from managers and co-workers
- not being able to balance the demands of work and life outside work

What management can do
- support and encourage staff, even when things go wrong
- encourage a healthy work-life balance
- see if there is scope for flexible work schedules (eg flexible working hours, working from home)
- take into account that everyone is different, and try to allocate work so that everyone is working in the way that helps them work best

Figure 18.4 Work-related stressors

Extract takes from INDG281Rev1. Crown Copyright 2003. Reproduced with permission of the Controller of Her Majesty's Stationery Office.

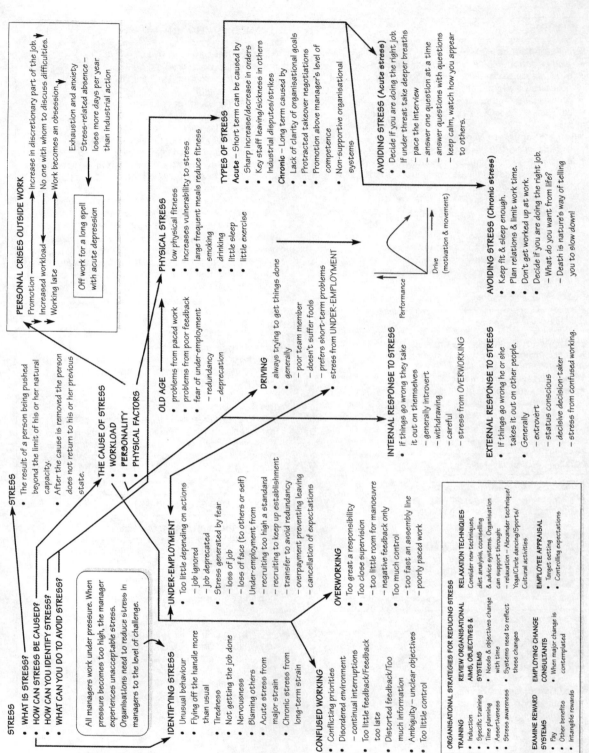

Figure 18.5 Summary outline of stress
(Reproduced with permission of Training Learning Consultancy Ltd, Bristol).

No easy remedies

However, there are not always easy remedies for stress and much depends upon the personality of the individual. Techniques such as relaxation therapy may help some people, although not others, but still tend to address the symptoms rather than the cause. For example, as *Vine and Williamson* point out, stress-inducing hazards are hard to pin down, much less eliminate. It is important to know how people feel about the things which cause them stress as well as which 'stressors' are most common in a particular industry and occupation. Human resource policy should include several stress management building blocks within the organisation structure including management education, employee education, counselling and support, critical incident briefing, and good sound management.[43]

A study by *van ZylKobus Lazenby* found that South African managers in affirmative action positions are functioning in a stressful environment which can give rise to unethical acts. Results indicated that high stress correlates substantially with: claiming credit for a subordinate's work; failing to report a co-worker's violation of company policy; offering potential clients fully paid holidays; and purchasing shares upon hearing privileged company information.[44]

Stress and counselling

Hayes and Hudson advance an argument that stress has been divorced from the working environment in which it develops and become an autonomous beast – a beast that can be tamed by counselling rather than by more pay and a shorter working day or by clear job control and security. The phenomenon of stress is on the one hand an individualistic response to the traditional experience of work in more onerous times. This is an element of continuity. This accounts for the response to the TUC 'bad boss' hotline set up in December 1997. The TUC reported 2400 calls in the first two days. On the other hand stress is also the phenomenon of a newer more responsible and deferential worker who has internalised the needs of the company but is not sure whether he or she has done so correctly and in the right degree. This is an element of change in workplace relations which even though it is more individualised is the contemporary form of social mediation.

Far from being a positive development this is harmful for two reasons. The first reason is that for the individual who appeals to 'stress' as a pragmatic palliative the outlook encourages a sense of victimhood rather than one of problem-solving. The second reason is that the new relationship between employer and employee very often represents a form of regulation in workplace behaviour which is highly intrusive. The very concept of stress becomes an instrument of self-regulation. Stress is not resolved by higher pay, reduced hours or a better working environment, which have a collective aspect to them, but by a trip to the counsellor in which the individualised experience of the workplace is reinforced. The employee is at risk not from exploitation or intensification but from failure to adjust to a new working environment. The employee can be protected not through collective action but through a series of regulations and codes of behaviour. If this is the case there then exists an attempt to solve the perceived problem of an absence of social links and networks through the codification of atomisation.[45]

An account of the elusive but expensive concept of stress is given in Management in Action 18.2.

WORK ORGANISATION AND JOB DESIGN

The application of motivational theories, and greater understanding of dimensions of job satisfaction and work performance, have led to increasing interest in **job design**. The nature of the work organisation and the design of jobs can have a significant effect on the job satisfaction of staff and on the level of organisational performance. Job design is associated with the ideas of the neo-human relations approach (discussed in Chapter 3) and the work of writers such as Herzberg. According to *Burns*: 'Job Design is a direct attack on the precepts of the Classical approach. Whereas Taylorist tradition seeks to fit people to rigidly defined and controlled jobs, Job Design theorists argue that jobs can and should be fitted to human needs.'[46]

Job design is concerned with the relationship between workers and the nature and content of jobs, and their task functions. It attempts to meet people's personal and social needs at work through reorganisation or restructuring of work. There are two major reasons for attention to job design:

- to enhance the personal satisfaction that people derive from their work; and
- to make the best use of people as a valuable resource of the organisation and to help overcome obstacles to their effective performance.

INDIVIDUAL JOB REDESIGN

Earlier approaches to job design concentrated on the restructuring of individual jobs and the application of three main methods: (i) job rotation; (ii) job enlargement; and (iii) job enrichment.

- **Job rotation** is the most basic form of individual **job redesign**. Job rotation involves moving a person from one job or task to another. It attempts to add some variety and to help remove boredom, at least in the short term. However, if the tasks involved are all very similar and routine, then once the person is familiar with the new task the work may quickly prove boring again. Job rotation may lead to the acquisition of additional skills but does not necessarily develop the level of skills. Strictly, job rotation is not really job design because neither the nature of the task nor the method of working is restructured. However, job rotation may help the person identify more with the completed product or service. It can also be used as a form of training and a means of establishing connections.
- **Job enlargement** involves increasing the scope of the job and the range of tasks that the person carries out. It is usually achieved by combining a number of related operations at the same level. **Job enlargement is horizontal job design; it makes a job structurally bigger.** It lengthens the time cycle of operations and may give the person greater variety. Job enlargement, however, is not always very popular and may often be resisted by workers. Although it may give the person more to do, it does little to improve intrinsic satisfaction or a sense of achievement. Workers may see job enlargement as simply increasing the number of routine, boring tasks they have to perform. Some workers seem to prefer simple, routine tasks which they can undertake almost automatically, and with little thought or concentration. This enables them to day-dream and to socialise with colleagues without affecting their performance.
- **Job enrichment** is an extension of the more basic job rotation and job enlargement methods of job design. Job enrichment arose out of *Herzberg's* two-factor theory. It attempts to enrich the job by incorporating motivating or growth factors such as increased responsibility and involvement, opportunities for advancement and the sense of achievement. **Job enrichment involves vertical job enlargement.** It aims to give the person greater autonomy and authority over the planning, execution and control of their own work. It focuses attention on intrinsic satisfaction. Job enrichment increases the complexity of the work and should provide the person with a more meaningful and challenging job. It provides greater opportunities for psychological growth.

Main methods of achieving job enrichment include the following:

- permitting workers greater freedom and control over the scheduling and pacing of their work as opposed to machine pacing;
- allowing workers to undertake a full task cycle, build or assemble a complete product or component, or deliver a complete service;
- providing workers with tasks or jobs which challenge their abilities and make fuller use of their training, expertise and skills;
- giving workers greater freedom to work in self-managing teams with greater responsibility for monitoring their own performance and the minimum of direct supervision; and
- providing workers with the opportunity to have greater direct contact with clients, consumers or users of the product or service.

A COMPREHENSIVE MODEL OF JOB ENRICHMENT

Attempts to improve intrinsic motivation must not only include considerations of job characteristics but also take account of individual differences and attributes, and people's orientation to work. A popular and comprehensive model of job enrichment has been developed by *Hackman and Oldham* (*see* Figure18.6).[47] The model views job enrichment in terms of increasing five core job dimensions: skill variety, task identity, task significance, autonomy and feedback. These core job characteristics create three psychological states:

- experienced meaningfulness of the work;
- experienced responsibility for the outcomes of the work; and
- knowledge of the actual results of the work activities.

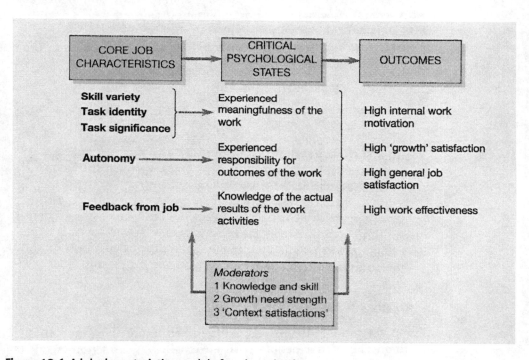

Figure 18.6 A job characteristics model of work motivation

(Source: Hackman, J. R. and Oldham, G. R. *Work Redesign*, Figure 4.6, p. 90. © 1980 by Addison-Wesley Publishing Company, Inc.)

Five core dimensions

The five core job dimensions can be summarised as follows:

- **skill variety** – the extent to which a job entails different activities and involves a range of different skills and talents;
- **task identity** – the extent to which a job involves completion of a whole piece of work with a visible outcome;
- **task significance** – the extent to which a job has a meaningful impact on other people, either inside or outside the organisation;
- **autonomy** – the extent to which a job provides freedom, independence and discretion in planning the work and determining how to undertake it;
- **feedback** – the extent to which work activities result in direct and clear information on the effectiveness of job performance.

An example of a job with little enrichment could be that of a production assembly line worker, or a kitchen porter, where all five core characteristics are likely to score low. An example of an enriched job could be that of a parish priest who draws upon a wide range of social skills and talents, who can usually identify with the whole task, and whose job has clear and important meaning and significance. There is a very high level of autonomy, and likely to be direct and clear feedback.

Motivating potential score

From these five core job dimensions, Hackman and Oldham have developed an equation which gives a single index of a person's job profile. By answering a questionnaire – the Job Diagnostic Survey (JDS) – and by giving a score (between 1 and 7) to each job dimension, the person can calculate an overall measure of job enrichment, called the motivating potential score (MPS).

Examples of questions from the JDS are:

- How much variety is there in your job?
- To what extent does your job involve doing a whole and identifiable piece of work?
- In general, how significant or important is your job?
- How much autonomy is there in your job?
- To what extent does doing the job itself provide you with information about your work performance?

$$MPS = \frac{\left\{ \begin{array}{c} Skill \\ variety \end{array} + \begin{array}{c} Task \\ identity \end{array} + \begin{array}{c} Task \\ significance \end{array} \right\}}{3} \times Autonomy \times Feedback$$

The first three job dimensions of skill variety, task identity and task significance are averaged, since it is the combination of these dimensions which contributes to experienced meaningfulness of work. The remaining two job dimensions, autonomy and feedback, stand on their own. Since scores for skill variety, task identity and task significance are additive, this means that the absence of one dimension can be partially offset by the presence of the other dimensions. However, if either autonomy or feedback is absent then, because of the multiplicative relationship, the MPS would be zero. The job would offer no potential to motivate the person.

Empirical support for the model

Empirical support for the model is mixed. From their own studies, Hackman and Oldham claim that people with enriched jobs, and high score levels on the Job Diagnostic Survey, experienced more satisfaction and internal motivation. The core job dimensions of skill variety, task identity and task significance combined to predict the level of experienced meaningfulness of the work. The core dimensions of autonomy and feedback did not relate so clearly to experienced responsibility and knowledge of results. Some of the other dimensions were as good, or better, in predicting these psychological conditions. In general, however, the results of their studies showed that jobs which scored high on the core dimensions were associated with high levels of personal and work outcomes.

In a study of a sample of six hotels (with between 35 and 65 bedrooms) in Great Yarmouth, *Lee-Ross* undertook an examination of the reliability of the job diagnostic survey among seasonal workers. From an analysis of 163 questionnaires, Lee-Ross concludes that in general reliability scores were compatible with those of Hackman and Oldham. The job diagnostic survey appears to hold just as well for hotel workers as for workers in other industries.[48]

Based on integrating Hackman and Oldham's job characteristics model with Maslow's hierarchy of needs, *Roe et al.* propose a general model of work motivation, tested with Bulgarian, Hungarian and Dutch workers. The model indicates that situational characteristics lead to critical psychological factors, inducing two main motivational factors – **job involvement** and **organisational commitment** – which in turn lead to two proximal outcomes of work motivation – **effort** and **job satisfaction**, which affect **performance**, **stress** and **tendency to leave the organisation**. Although there were some differences there was also a large degree of similarity in results across the three countries. [49]

BROADER ORGANISATIONAL APPROACHES TO IMPROVED JOB DESIGN

Approaches to improved job design now take on a broader perspective. For example, in the context of technological change the focus of attention has spread from manipulating the tasks of individual jobs to the wider organisational context. Attention needs to be given to improving the effectiveness of the organisation in achieving its goals and objectives; and helping the development of skills and resources to manage successfully changes in the way the organisation functions. (*See* Figure 18.7.)

The quality of working life

Increased interest in job design has been associated with the development of a broader social concern for the quality of working life (QWL). The concept of QWL is not new but an approach to the organisation of work and managing people that has evolved over a long period of time. In 1973 a Department of Employment report, *On the Quality of Working Life*, summarised case studies of people's experiences of work and descriptions of experiments in improving work systems in four countries, including the UK.[50] It made recommendations for future government initiatives. The report dealt with five main themes:

- efficiency at work;
- satisfaction at work;
- the link between satisfaction and efficiency;
- the influence of environmental factors and particularly work technology; and
- developments of thought in social science and people's expectations from work.

It is not always easy to determine the extent to which attention to QWL is based on the exercise of a genuine social responsibility (discussed in Chapter 5) or based on the pursuit of increased economic efficiency. In practice, the distinction is blurred and attention to QWL is likely to be motivated by a combination of concern with two related issues:

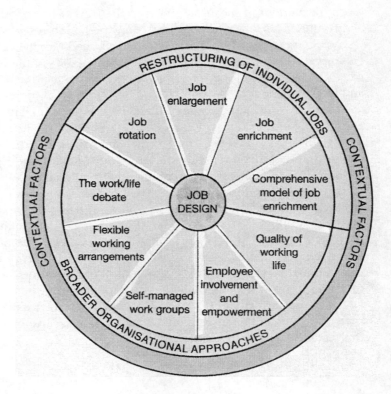

Figure 18.7 Main approaches to job design

■ a moral or ethical motivation based on the recognition of broader educational standards, changing social values and wider expectations of the quality of working life, including the satisfaction that people derive from their work, and the functioning and management of organisations; and

■ motivation through good business practice and enlightened self-interest, the need for cost competitiveness, and attempts to overcome high levels of absenteeism, staff turnover and dissatisfaction, and other obstacles to the search for improved organisational performance.

The essential culture of QWL

Since the publication of the Department of Employment report increasing emphasis is being given to the importance of a QWL culture. Such a culture can be seen as a necessary foundation for a successful strategy of Total Quality Management. In order to translate the concept of QWL into practice it is best understood if it is seen as a goal, as a process for achieving that goal and as a philosophy setting out the way people should be managed.

■ **QWL as a goal** – improving organisational effectiveness through the creation of more challenging, satisfying and effective jobs and work environments.

■ **QWL as a process** – calling for efforts to realise this goal through the active involvement of people throughout the organisation. It is about organisational change usually from a 'control' to an 'involvement' organisation.

■ **QWL as a philosophy** – viewing people as 'assets' capable of contributing skills, knowledge, experience and commitment, rather than as 'costs' that are merely extensions of the production process. It argues that encouraging involvement and providing the environment in which it can flourish produces tangible rewards for both individuals and organisations.

The QWL approach is therefore a broad and flexible strategy rooted in the involvement and participation of people at all levels in the organisation.[51]

Quality of working life study

A major study into the quality of working life carried out by the Institute of Management and University of Manchester Institute of Science and Technology tracked 5000 managers over a five-year period. The survey revealed a serious mismatch between the values and expectations of individuals and company behaviour. Almost 60 per cent say they value their work and home life equally, yet only 15 per cent report that their organisation makes any attempt to help them balance their work and home commitments. The majority of professionals feel under constant time pressure with tight deadlines as the main reason for working long hours and over half suffer from information overload. Since the study began, 85 per cent of the managers taking part in the study report that the biggest change in the workplace is the sheer volume of information they have to deal with.[52]

According to a survey carried out by Robert Half International on behalf of *Management Today*, 67 per cent of respondents dismissed the job-for-life as a key demand for their working lives. 'People are no longer relying on their companies to provide career development or even satisfaction – they want a more maverick lifestyle.' A further trend, especially among younger managers, was the attraction of flexibility and working from home.[53]

EXHIBIT 18.1

If you want people to do a good job, give them a good job to do

Institutionalising change

Today's business climate is increasingly characterised by fierce global competition and rapid change with ever rising standards of reliability, performance and quality. Success in such a competitive environment requires continuous improvement in methods of production and service delivery and an ability to spot opportunities and respond to them. Organisations must adapt to this environment and keep on adapting it is not a once and for all task. It is not enough for example to identify successful practices of competitors and copy them, because by the time the changes have been implemented the competition may well have moved on. What organisations must do is come to terms with change and build it into the culture of their organisations. Change, in other words, must be institutionalised.

How does an organisation become responsive to change? There is no simple answer to this question and factors such as sufficient investment and up to date technology play an important part but it is generally the people who work in organisations who make the biggest difference. The 1997 European Commission's Green Paper 'Partnership for a new organisation at work' identified people as the key resource in the way work should be organised in future if Europe is to be competitive. In the words of the Green Paper 'Organisations are valued not only on the basis of their products or machines but primarily on the knowledge creating capacity of the workforce,

the people who work for them, how they work, what work means to them. The rate of innovation and change in products and technologies is so rapid that the competitive advantages of companies and countries will be the capacity of the workforce to create knowledge.'

Improving the quality of working life

ACAS's own experience accords with many of the messages of the European Green Paper, particularly the importance of organising work to get the best from people. ACAS has produced two advisory booklets 'Effective organisations: the people factor' and 'Teamwork: success through people'. These booklets describe an approach to improving organisational effectiveness by enhancing the quality of working life through more challenging, satisfying jobs coupled with the involvement and commitment of employees and their representatives. This way of working promotes understanding and responsibility which combined with open communication can help an organisation become more responsive. If people understand what they are doing and why they are doing it they are more likely to understand when and why change is needed. Inherent in this approach are a number of general principles and I intend to use the rest of this article to look at some of these in more detail.

First of all managers must believe in people as 'assets' capable of contributing skills, knowledge, experience and

▶

Exhibit 18.1 continued

commitment, rather than as 'costs' that are merely extensions of the production process. Douglas McGregor's well-known polarisation of managers into Theory 'X' or Theory 'Y' types illustrates the two extremes that managers might assume about what motivates human behaviour. Theory 'X' managers believe that people inherently dislike work and will avoid it if they can and must therefore be directed bribed or coerced and controlled. Theory 'Y' managers on the other hand assume that people find work as natural as play or rest and will exercise self-direction and self-control to achieve objectives to which they are committed and have more potential than is generally used. Flexible workers willing to contribute ideas are more likely to be developed by managers of the theory 'Y' persuasion.

Well-designed jobs

Second, in the words of Herzberg used as the title of this article 'If you want people to do a good job, give them a good job to do'. Work that is broken down into small simple processes is likely to provide little in the way of job satisfaction, understanding or commitment. If jobs are to provide these rewards they must intrinsically interesting and worthwhile. Jobs in other words must be well designed and although it is never possible to incorporate all desirable characteristics they should ideally:

■ form a coherent whole, either independently or with related jobs. Performance of the job (or jobs) should make a significant contribution to the completion of the product or service, a contribution which is visible to the job holder;
■ provide some variety of pace, method, location and skill;
■ provide feedback of performance, both directly and through other people;
■ allow for some discretion and control in the timing, sequence and pace of work efforts;
■ include some responsibility for outcome;
■ provide some opportunity for learning and problem solving (within the individual's competence);
■ be seen as leading towards some sort of desirable future;

■ provide opportunity for development in ways that the individual finds relevant.

Third, the management style must complement the way work is organised. Authoritarian management is inappropriate where people are being developed to take responsibility for their own area of work. The manager's role should be that of initiator, counsellor and facilitator with particular tasks to:

■ provide a vision and communicate it;
■ encourage effective teamwork and co-operation;
■ encourage the free flow of ideas and initiative;
■ develop subordinates rather than rigidly controlling them;
■ oversee more flexible less authoritarian work structures and ensure objectives are met.

The need to initiate and manage change will place increasing emphasis on leadership skills with a manager's authority coming not from his or her status but earned through competence. Managers will need to be able to motivate and inspire those around them. The skills required will include the ability to build trust and openness, support self motivation and delegate decision making to the relevant locations and people. Managers should also be able to accept questioning and debate as part of the organisation's search for the best answer and understand and manage the interactions of people individually and in groups. In addition managers will need to help employees develop appropriate skills to enable them to adopt joint problemsolving and continuous improvement techniques.

The two ACAS booklets provide more detail on the principles involved in this way of working and contain practical advice on such matters as introducing teamwork and choosing and developing teams. In addition an ACAS Occasional Paper 'Teamwork: key issues and developments' discusses the development of teamwork and the implications for industrial relations.

(Reprinted with permission from Brian Chaney, Senior Adviser ACAS, *QWL News and Abstracts*, No. 142, Spring 2000, pp. 12–14.)

THE WORK/LIFE BALANCE

Arising from the QWL approach, increasing attention is focused today on the debate of the work/life balance. In 1998, *Management Today* conducted their first 'Worklife Survey'. Results of the survey found that although for many, work remained a high source of satisfaction, it wasn't going too well for Britain's managers. The price of a satisfying career can be high with 84 per cent admitting to making important personal sacrifices in pursuit of their career.[54]

Using the original 1998 survey as a benchmark, *Management Today* undertook a second survey in 2001.

> *Things have changed since we brought managers into the thick of the work/life debate with our first survey into staff attitudes in 1998. Today, achieving a proper balance is seen as an entitlement by almost all those who work ... And that in turn is a reflection of the changing contract between organisations and individuals.[55]*

Achieving a work/life balance isn't always easy

Results of the survey showed evidence that the long-hours culture is levelling off and even improving, but that cutting back on office hours and even introducing flexible working schedules is not having the expected effect on relieving pressure and improving the sense of balance. Three-quarters of respondents report that their workload pressure has increased over the past three years and the number of managers who feel they have been forced to put work before family life is slightly up. A recent study from the Department of Trade and Industry (DTI) draws attention to the fact that the workplace has altered dramatically over the last decade and old methods are no longer appropriate as employers accept that their most valuable asset is their workforce.

Employers worldwide are recognising of their own accord that it makes good business sense to provide opportunities for their workforce to achieve a better work-life balance – with a pay back of increased morale, better effectiveness and productivity, and the ability to embrace change.[56]

The results also show there is no one standard work/life balance policy that will suit every business. Arguably there is no such thing as work/life balance but different work/life balances with different parts of the jigsaw taking on greater importance at different times in our working lives.[57] *Summers and Nowicki* suggest that the more secure the organisation and the less competitive the environment, the more latitude the manager has to encourage employees to lead balanced lives.[58]

Attitude to work

An interesting point of view is put forward by *Reeves* who contends that our attitude to work needs a radical overhaul and that it is nonsense that 'wicked work' gets the blame for most of our ills. Work is our community, how we identify ourselves and it is becoming more central to our lives. It is a provider of friends, gossip, networks, fun, creativity, purpose, comfort, belonging, identity – and even love. Work is where life is. People doing work they enjoy are happy – not only at work but generally in the other areas of their lives too. Happiness lies in meaningful work for us all. The line between 'work' and 'life' is rapidly being rubbed out. Few people want to put their work in a box labelled 'nine to five'.[59]

In contrast, however, *Armitage* maintains that the image presented by the media is one where work is made so attractive to the extent it surpasses the Protestant ethic of being good for the soul and becomes something we must all do for the good of our well-being. Armitage questions whether it is time to re-assess what we do and whether we get satisfaction from it. Although we may not have unlimited control over what we do, we have to make greater effort to balance the amount of time and effort we put into our work and our personal lives. 'Once work begins to take over one's life to the exclusion of all other interests, that is the time to call a halt. If not, then we run the very real risk of not only becoming a workaholic, but also of endangering personal relationships and friendships and maybe even suffering the longer-term effects of ill health.'[60]

Case study examples of the work/life balance are given in Management in Action 18.3.

A central feature of the work/life balance is flexible working arrangements – discussed below.

EMPLOYEE INVOLVEMENT

The general movement away from mass production and towards customer-driven niche markets, the downsizing of organisations, and advances in scientific and technological knowledge have emphasised the demand for a highly skilled, trained and motivated workforce. Recognition of the efficient use of human resources for business success together with advances in social democracy have highlighted the increasing importance of employee involvement and industrial partnership including the role played by trade unions.[61]

ACAS draws attention to the importance of exchanging information, pooling ideas and sharing concerns with employees and their representatives and developing mutual trust. Hazards of not sharing information, ideas and concerns lead to: suspicion and distrust; rumours and gossip; wasting of employees' time, knowledge, skills and ideas; inefficiency; and dissatisfied customers. There is a checklist indicating priority for action to see if there is a need to take action to improve the way you:

- provide employees with written statements of the main terms and conditions of employment together with grievance and disciplinary procedures;
- give employees up-to-date information about the organisation and listen to what they have to say;
- use a variety of ways for sharing ideas and information – for example, briefings, staff meetings, newsletters, email, notice boards;
- communicate with all employees including part-timers, shift workers and those away from the workplace;
- make information available to employees and job candidates who have language difficulties, impaired vision or other disabilities;
- consult with trade unions and other employee representatives and individuals;
- work together with employees and their representatives.[62]

Is participation really working?

Despite many people believing that participation leads to higher productivity and is necessary for survival in an increasingly competitive world, *Heller* questions whether organisation participation is really working. Taking a panoramic view of the evidence, the result is not very reassuring and Heller reports on a chequered history. On average, employees at the lowest level of organisation have very little influence even over their own immediate tasks. There are a number of *ad hoc* schemes of participation, some of which are successful at least in the short term, but others are inauthentic or fail to achieve promises. In order to overcome problems with organisational participation, Heller maintains that it is necessary for clarity about what participation is meant to achieve, it must be recognised as an essential antecedent to the full utilisation of an organisation's skill and experience, and the design of influence sharing has to be seen as a systematic and integrated feature of organisational governance.[63]

> Boredom and frustration at work is often the result of an employee's lack of involvement with the company's goals and a feeling that their ideas are not wanted or listened to. For the employer, staff turnover increases as employees walk out of the door for more interesting jobs. There is also an impact on levels of customer service and quality – both key areas of success in today's competitive environment.
>
> **Sir Brian Wolfson, Chairman of Investors in People UK**[64]

EMPOWERMENT AND JOB SATISFACTION

Increasing business competitiveness demands that organisations have to offer the best quality products or services for the best price. This requires that organisations develop and harness the talents and commitment of all their employees. Getting the best out of people and attempting to improve job satisfaction demand a spirit of teamwork and co-operation, and allowing people a greater say in decisions that affect them at work. In order to improve business performance, managers will need to relinquish close control in favour of greater **empowerment** of employees (discussed in Chapter 21).

Although there is a continuing debate about the real benefits of empowerment there appears to be a general assumption that: 'empowerment programmes will result in motivated staff, quality customer service and improved profits'.[65] From a discussion of the benefits and problems of empowerment and a review of its operation in a number of companies, *Pickard* concludes that empowerment does appear to be having a radical effect on the way people work. As an example, Pickard describes improved job satisfaction and the changing attitude of staff arising from the introduction of empowerment at Harvester restaurants. Within a framework handed down from head office, staff work in teams which are responsible for making decisions on the running of individual restaurants.[66]

In a review of issues and debates about empowerment, *Wilkinson* reports that:

> All these theories share a common assumption that workers are an untapped resource with knowledge and experience and an interest in becoming involved, and employers need to provide opportunities and structures for their involvement. It is also assumed that participative decision making is likely to lead to job satisfaction and better quality decisions and that gains are available both to employers (increased efficiency) and workers (job satisfaction), in short an everyone-wins scenario.[67]

SELF-MANAGED WORK GROUPS

An important development in work redesign and job enrichment is a form of work organisation based on self-managed work groups, and teamworking (discussed in Chapter 14). This involves a socio-technical approach with technological processes, production methods and the way in which work is carried out integrated with the social system of the organisation, including the informal group structure. Although the effectiveness of self-managed groups does not appear to be all positive, individual members of the group do have higher levels of job satisfaction.[68]

The group assumes greater autonomy and responsibility for the effective performance of the work. Key features of the self-managed work group include the following:

- specific goals are set for the group but members decide the best means by which these goals are to be achieved;
- group members have greater freedom and choice, and wider discretion over the planning, execution and control of their own work;
- collectively members of the group have the necessary variety of expertise and skills to successfully undertake the tasks of the group;
- the level of external supervision is reduced and the role of supervisor becomes more one of giving advice and support to the group;
- feedback and evaluation is related to the performance of the group as a whole.

Popularity and applications

In the USA, self-managed teams are widespread and increasing in popularity.[69] Pressures to demonstrate cost competitiveness may result in autonomous work groups being incorporated into a package of changes associated with the requirements for high-performance work design. It also seems likely that greater concern for the quality of working life, current trends in restructuring and increasing demands for work flexibility are likely to promote a greater interest in self-managed teams.

Wilson points out that self-directed teams feature high in the list of most popular management tools in a study by the Institute of Management with Bain & Company. 'Once people are fully committed to team working and enthusiastic about getting on with it, training can be a rewarding experience for everyone involved and also great fun.'[70] However, despite the apparent potential advantages, to date self-managed teams appear to have only limited applications. For example, *Torrington* suggests that the twenty-first century has brought a much more sceptical attitude to autonomous working groups and teamwork as a way of improving the quality of working life and empowering employees. 'While there remain many strong supporters and many organisations are committed to this approach, it is in the achievement of improved performance where teamwork has often fallen short.'[71]

Autonomy and control

A strong supporter of the idea of the autonomous work group is *Waterman*. In order to build spirit, morale and commitment in any organisation Waterman believes that people should be in control of at least some part of their lives and that they should be given some influence over things that affect them. The quintessence of this belief is the self-managing team – groups of three to ten people who work without any direct supervision. Employees should be organised into teams that cut across old boundaries, trained and placed in jobs that challenge their abilities, given the information they need, informed of what they need to accomplish, and then turned loose.[72]

ACAS also strongly supports autonomous work groups for both increased competitiveness and for the quality of working life.

> *The concept of autonomous teams may be misleading as teams will always be answerable to management and rely on the provision of resources and other support. Nevertheless, one of the best ways to ensure that teams continue to develop is to move towards self-regulation – an important way of monitoring the progress of teams is to assess the level of dependence on management. It is for management to encourage progress by helping the teams develop greater independence.*
>
> *Reorganising the workforce into teams is not easy but when successfully developed, teamworking has been shown to be a way of improving competitiveness and at the same time enhancing the quality of working life for employees.*[73]

FLEXIBLE WORKING ARRANGEMENTS

In Chapter 16, we discussed the demand for greater flexibility in patterns of work organisation and the workforce, including the flexible firm and core and peripheral workers and new legal rights for parents. Moves towards greater flexibility may have noticeable effects on the job satisfaction and performance of staff. For example, a survey by the Institute of Management and Manpower plc indicates that **flexible working** has become a permanent feature of the UK employment scene. Employers seek competitive advantage by reducing the number of core staff, using methods of more flexible employment and alternative ways of working.[74]

A joint management/union publication points out that flexible employment is now a vital element of both corporate and UK competitiveness.

> *Although part-time employees are more likely to be working in lower grades, their presence is increasingly at more senior levels ... For some employees, part-time work is seen as a 'half-way house' offering a chance to progress towards full-time employment. However for many, part-time employment is their preferred choice enabling them to balance work and home life ... While an individual may be regarded by an organisation as a part-time employee, that individual might*

work for three or four different organisations during the course of any week, month, or year, and regard him/herself as working full time – the so-called portfolio worker.[75]

Rawcliffe suggests that the introduction of an equitable system of performance-related pay could be highly successful for a flexible workforce:

it seems that for many small businesses, it will be a major way to attract employees away from larger enterprises. With a part-time, multi-skilled workforce holding several jobs at a given moment, many of the problems faced by small firms in developing flexible staffing levels could be obsolete.[76]

Control over working arrangements

Demands for greater flexibility may afford opportunities for employers to have more freedom and control over their working arrangements. Flexible working arrangements are a range of options designed to help employees balance work and home life. The Department of Trade and Industry (DTI) refer to employers developing a wide range of work/life balance options that cover flexible working arrangements, and which in many instances can be used in a wide variety of workplaces:

- flexi-time;
- staggered hours;
- time off in lieu;
- compressed working hours;
- shift swapping;
- self rostering;
- annual hours;
- job sharing;
- term-time working;
- work at or from home;
- teleworking;
- breaks from work.

The DTI also provide illustrations of how innovative companies have used policies to reduce absenteeism, boost productivity and reduce long hours.[77] Case study examples of flexible working practices are also provided by the Equal Opportunities Commission.[78]

An account of flexible working at IBM, 'Beyond the nine-to-five' is given in Management in Action 18.4.

EXHIBIT 18.2

Have a life and keep your job

The right balance between home and work improves both, but it's not so easy to find writes **Lucy Kellaway**.

Every day at 6 pm Louisa stuffed a wad of papers into her briefcase and dashed for the door of her City solicitors' office. Every day her colleagues exchanged glances, passed comment, or gave her extra work as she flew by.

A year earlier she had been told that when she returned to work after the birth of her baby it would be fine to leave work promptly to relieve the childminder. But it was not fine, and after 18 months she quit.

When I related this everyday tale of mismanagement to Rhona Rapoport, a look of weary recognition crossed her face. She has been writing about the issues of home and work for more than three decades and has devoted much of her working life to finding a solution to problems similar to Louisa's.

'That woman should not have had to fight for her right to leave on time', she says. 'The answer is for work to finish at that time for everybody.' A utopian solution, you might think. Yet Rapoport has just finished a five-year research project with the Ford Foundation and the findings suggest she may have a point.

▶

Exhibit 18.2 continued

The research, *Relinking Life and Work*, set about redesigning the way employees work, irrespective of their sex or family circumstances. It tore up assumptions about home and work being separate and started again.

This may sound like every company's nightmare: anything that sets out to redress the balance between work and home must be bad news for shareholders. Cutting up the cake in a different way surely means home gets more and work gets less.

Rapoport argues otherwise. She and her fellow researchers worked with three US corporations – Xerox, Corning and Tandem Computers – helping each to redraw its boundaries between home and work. In each case they found productivity did not fall – in fact, it went up.

The experience indicates that by linking work and family issues, workers tend to become more efficient and less stressed. Barriers and demarcations disappear, innovation flourishes. Armed with these findings, she is off to New York in September to spread the word. She will address a seminar of 200 chief executives in an attempt to convince them that their methods of work are outdated and everyone could benefit from a bit of experimentation.

But Rapoport is no evangelist. She is a realist, well aware of the troubles that lie ahead.

'It's all very difficult. You have to be so careful,' she says. From her study in Hampstead, North London, she seems far from optimistic about her chances of success.

'When we started the project in 1991, companies realised that they had a problem in losing their women, but they did not recognise the reason was the way they organised their work.' Many companies have since installed family-friendly policies, designed to tackle the problem by encouraging flexible working, but these are not being taken up. Women are either leaving or working just as before.

One explanation doing the rounds in the US is that women actually prefer being at work to being at home – office life being adult and civilised, home life being chaotic and stressful. This view, expressed in a new book, *The Time Bind* by Arlie Hochschild, a US academic, incenses Rapoport. 'It distorts reality, and may only be true of a minority of women,' she says.

By contrast, she claims that the reason women are not taking up flexible working policies is that they do not want to be labelled 'mommy trackers' and shunted into the slow lane. If you suggest that the problem is one of rigid male attitudes, she winces. The problem, she argues, goes much deeper. She thinks there are entrenched assumptions about work which date from the Industrial Revolution and which are unsympathetic to achieving a balance between home and work.

The first assumption is that an employee's time is an infinite resource. The second is a celebration of the individual: to be a work hero you must do everything for yourself. The third is the emphasis placed on solving problems rather than on preventing them arising in the first place. All three result in a way of working that is macho and inefficient.

The researchers talked to workers singly and in groups about their problems combining work and home. The groups then came up with new ways of arranging workloads across whole departments.

In one department at Xerox in which everyone had felt over-worked and over-stressed, it turned out workers were being hindered by too much bureaucracy, too many meetings and too many interruptions. The solution was to designate some parts of each day as uninterrupted time, when people could get on with their work quietly. As a result, everyone got their work done faster, and stress levels fell.

Rapoport is quick to admit that creating this sort of effect is one thing. Sustaining it is another.

We found at first that we were stimulating a new level of energy. Everyone was so pleased to get these issues out in the open. But how do you retain that? Cultural change takes eight to ten years and there are very few people who are interested in funding a project that takes that long.

A second problem is that there is no simple formula for redesigning work. It is not a matter of taking the results from the three companies and extending them more generally.

When we had success at Xerox, other companies said: 'We'll introduce quiet time too.' But we said that might not work. First of all a company has to look at what its own business problems are. And then try to relate those to its employees' personal work-life problems.

Surely there are some businesses where changing work patterns could involve costs rather than savings? In most cases productivity will improve. There may be exceptions in which this sort of thing could hit profits. But does it help to focus on this now? If a company asked me, I would say, 'Start and see what happens'.

(Reproduced with permission from the Financial Times Limited, © *Financial Times*.)

One popular example of giving people greater freedom and control over the scheduling of their work is **flexible working hours** or **flexitime**. Within certain limits ('core' times) staff are free to vary arrival, lunch and departure times at work to suit their own individual needs and preferences. Developments in information technology have also provided greater opportunities for 'home-based' teleworking which appears to offer a number of distinct advantages to both employers and employees.[79]

Although there are potential problems with flexible working such as teleworking, *Philpott* maintains that, if implemented properly, flexible working style can make good sense and it can motivate staff, leading to an increase in productivity.[80] However, the Chartered Management Institute workplace survey found that despite UK workplaces becoming more flexible in recent years, 33 per cent of managers confirm their employer has made no provision for employees to work remotely.[81]

QUALITY CIRCLES

One particular feature associated as a part of the quality of working life movement is the concept of **quality circles**. **A quality circle is a group of people within an organisation who meet together on a regular basis to identify, analyse and solve problems relating to quality, productivity or other aspects of day-to-day working arrangements using problem-solving techniques.** Quality circles are broadly compatible with the quality of working life in that they provide an opportunity for people at work to become more involved in matters which have a bearing on the jobs that they do.[82]

Although quality circles actually originated in America they were exported to Japan and are more usually associated with their wide applications (since 1962) in Japanese manufacturing industries, as well as in some white-collar operations. Since the refinement of the quality circle process in Japan there has been increasing interest in their use in America and Britain as well as in many other countries. In America, quality circles appear to have been first implemented in 1974.[83]

The essential features of a quality circle group include the following:

- membership is voluntary;
- the group usually numbers between five and ten members;
- membership is normally drawn from people undertaking similar work or from the same work station;
- the group selects the problems to be tackled and the methods of operation;
- a leader can be chosen from within the group but is usually the immediate supervisor;
- the group members receive training in communication and problem-solving skills, quality control techniques and group processes;
- the group recommends solutions to management and, where possible, have authority to implement agreed solutions.

Potential limitations

There are a number of potential limitations on the effectiveness of quality circles.

- Any attempt at solving organisational problems cannot be considered as a single dimension. The promotion of quality circles needs to be approached in terms of possible effects on related sub-systems of the organisation, for example human resource management and industrial relations procedures.
- Quality circles can rely too heavily on intrinsic motivation and the assumption that involvement and recognition are sufficient rewards in themselves. This reflects a major difference between the operation of quality circles in the west and in Japan. Workers in Japan appear, for example, to accept that financial gains will go to the organisation.
- The greater involvement of members in problem-solving and decision-making may be resented by some groups, for example quality control departments, or by managers or trade union officials who may be suspicious of possible challenges to their traditional authority.

Applications of quality circles

The application of quality circles does appear simple and straightforward, but early experience must be viewed in the context of Japanese culture and management systems. However, quality circles offer a number of potential benefits. They provide problem-solving at a more local level and the participation of employees in work-related decisions which concern them. Quality circles do work and have been used successfully by a number of British organisations.

There are some doubts, however, as to the extent to which the hopes for, or potential benefits of, quality circles are realised fully in organisations.[84] In appropriate applications, quality circles can be part of a broad, long-term strategy for organisational change aimed both at improved economic performance and the quality of working life. Quality circles are now seen to be part of a broader total quality management (TQM) approach, discussed in Chapter 23.

MANAGEMENT STYLE AND CULTURE

The potential benefits of improved job design are unlikely to be realised if attention is focused on the content of jobs alone. Of equal, if not more, importance is the process by which redesign is carried out. This has led to recognition of the importance of management style and, increasingly, of organisation culture.[85] Central to improving the quality of working life is a participative, open style of management involving employees in decisions that affect them, including the design or choice of the technology itself. Personnel policies, including, for example, those relating to pay and benefits, should facilitate and help new concepts of improved job design. Management should attempt to develop a relationship of trust among all members and sections of the organisation, and a confident partnership approach to trade unions.

Supervision involves technical knowledge, human relations skills and co-ordination of work activities. Effective supervision is necessary for job satisfaction and high levels of work performance.[86] Kindly and thoughtful leader behaviour is likely to generate high worker satisfaction. Supervisors who adopt a considerate manner towards workers tend to have the more highly satisfied work groups.[87] Lack of job satisfaction and unhappiness at work may also arise from problems connected with managers.[88]

Crow and Hartman suggest that:

Instead of trying to improve employee satisfaction, it may be time to consider new leadership approaches and management programmes that reduce employee dissatisfaction.[89]

The increasing pace of technological and structural change has made it imperative to address the issues of managing change in ways that would ensure the best outcomes for organisations and for the people in them. An important issue is still the jobs which people are asked to do. When change is being planned, particularly if new technology is to be introduced, a 'window of opportunity' exists to think about the work that people will do and the design of their jobs. The aim is to ensure that the quality of working life is enhanced rather than undermined.

CONTEXTUAL FACTORS IN JOB DESIGN

The different methods of job design are not necessarily separate approaches. They are interrelated and there is some overlapping among them. For example, goal-setting, which was discussed in Chapter 12, is sometimes viewed as another approach to job design. Goal-setting involves building goals, feedback and incentives into the structure of the job. In addition, there are many other associated (contextual) factors which affect job design, including, for example: organisational culture; organisation structure; the system of management and style of leadership; trade unions; personnel policies and procedures; communications; group norms; ergonomics; and the working environment.

Concern for the quality of working life has also been supported by government legislation, for example in the areas of employment protection, employee involvement, health and safety at work and flexible working. Such legislation directs management attention to the importance of the work environment and the context in which work is carried out, which in turn can have a direct effect on job satisfaction.

Job satisfaction and HRM

Theories of work motivation and job satisfaction have influenced management systems and styles of leadership, and developments in personnel policies and procedures. The human resource management function is centred on people's needs while working in an organisation, and ways in which their work promotes or frustrates the fulfilment of these needs.[90] The practice of modern human resource management is directed towards providing conditions under which people work willingly and effectively, and contribute to the success of the organisation. This involves concern for employee motivation and job satisfaction.

THE HAPPY/PRODUCTIVE WORKER

Despite many theories and studies of the relationship between job satisfaction and work performance, there are still doubts as to how to manage an organisation so that staff have both high job satisfaction and productivity. *Staw* suggests that it is difficult to bring about changes in both satisfaction and performance and that it is necessary to lower expectations in the pursuit of the 'happy/productive worker'.[91]

Instead of the alternating practice of fanfare and despair, Staw puts forward three approaches that may make for sustained slow progress in overcoming forces for stability in both job attitudes and performance.

- **The individually-oriented system.** This is based on traditional good management and would emphasise, for example: extrinsic rewards linked to performance; realistic and challenging goals; accurate employee performance; equitable promotions policy; training and skills development; job enlargement and job enrichment. The major principle underlying such features is to structure work and/or reward systems so that high performance is either intrinsically or extrinsically rewarding to the individual, and to create a situation in which high performance contributes to job satisfaction. However, to be effective the individually-oriented system needs to be implemented correctly, and into a well-run organisation with an efficient structure and motivational system.
- **The group-oriented system.** This is where satisfaction and performance are derived from group participation. This would include methods such as: work organised around intact groups; resources distributed on a group basis; greater group autonomy for selection, training and reward systems; the use of the group to enforce norms of behaviour; and encouraging inter-group rivalry to build within-group solidarity. Group-oriented systems may be difficult to control but they can be very powerful. Because individuals will work to achieve group praise and loyalty, an effectively managed group-oriented system can make a potential contribution to high job satisfaction and performance.
- **The organisationally-oriented system.** This is where working conditions are organised so that individuals gain satisfaction from contribution to the welfare of the organisation as a whole, for example, through applying the principles of Theory Z organisation. If individuals can identify closely with the organisation as a whole, then organisational performance will be intrinsically rewarding to the individual. This system would include common features such as: effective socialisation into the organisation; job rotation in different units; long training periods with the development of skills specific to the organisation; long-term or protected employment; decentralised operations; few status distinctions; education and sharing of information about the organisation; linking individual rewards to organisational performance through profit sharing, bonuses and share options.

Job satisfaction and work performance

We should note the words of Bassett who draws attention to the complex relationship between job satisfaction and work performance:

> *It is primarily in the realm of job design that opportunity for constructive improvement of worker satisfaction appears high ... [However,] the long-presumed link between satisfaction and work output will never be supported by the evidence of human relations research alone ... Worker satisfaction is a complex matter that deserves careful thought and consideration in any management systems design decision. But it cannot and should not be the touchstone of efforts to invent high-performance systems. The satisfied worker is a productive worker paradigm doesn't work. It is much more complicated than that.*[92]

In conclusion, we should note the work of *Frank Heller* of the Tavistock Institute who draws a distinction between the Human Relations Model and the Human Resource Model. With the Human Relations Model there is an assumed causal relationship through which job satisfaction is thought to cause higher productivity, although available research is unreliable. By comparison, the Human Resources Model is more fact-based and refers to a relationship between participation, a better use of competence leading to superior performance and as a consequence, improved job satisfaction.[93]

CRITICAL REFLECTIONS

'I read recently a major study that says, although people may not wish to admit to it openly, the greatest influence on job satisfaction is how much they are paid and how this compares with other people.'

'Well, I read recently quotes from celebrity CEOs that what is most important to people and their performance at work is not money but genuine recognition and praise.'

What are your own views?

More than any other element, fun is the secret of Virgin's success. I am aware that the idea of business being fun and creative goes right against the grain of convention, and it's certainly not how they teach it at some of those business schools, where business means hard grind and lots of 'discounted cash flows' and 'net present values' ... For us, our employees matter most. It just seems common sense to me that, if you start off with a happy, well motivated workforce, you're much more likely to have happy customers. And in due course the resulting profits will make your shareholders happy.

Branson, R. *Losing My Virginity*, Virgin Publishing (1998), pp. 431, 444.

How would you attempt to make business 'fun and creative' while still satisfying the demands of customers and shareholders?

'The extent to which any organisation has happy, helpful and efficient members of staff is a direct result of the manner in which they are treated by top management.'

Debate.

SYNOPSIS

■ Attempting to understand the nature of job satisfaction and links with work performance is not easy. Although the level of job satisfaction may well affect the strength of motivation this is not always the case. Job satisfaction is more of an internal state and could be associated, for example, with a feeling of personal achievement. The relationship between job satisfaction and effective work performance is an issue of continuing debate and controversy.

■ Job satisfaction is a complex concept and difficult to measure objectively. The level of job satisfaction is affected by a wide range of individual, social, organisational and cultural variables. There is also a wide range of specific factors which influence job satisfaction. Major dimensions of job satisfaction include consideration of: alienation; information communications technology; employee involvement and empowerment. The application of motivational theories and a greater understanding of dimensions of job satisfaction has led to increasing interest in improving job design.

■ Earlier approaches to job design concentrated on the restructuring of individual jobs and application of job rotation, job enlargement and job enrichment. Attention has also been given to a comprehensive model of job enrichment. Approaches to improving job design now take a wider perspective, and in the context of technological change, for example, focus attention on broader organisational approaches including the quality of working life (QWL).

■ There appears little doubt that one of the major adverse influences on job satisfaction, performance, work sickness absence and productivity is stress at work. However, a certain amount of pressure or stress may **arguably** not be a bad thing but help promote a higher level of performance. Arising from the QWL approach, increasing attention is focused on the debate of the work/life balance and changing attitudes to work. A central feature of the work/life debate is flexible working arrangements. Moves towards greater flexibility provide a range of options to help balance work and home life, and may have noticeable effects on job satisfaction and performance of staff.

■ Increasing business competitiveness and recognition of the need for the effective use of human resources have highlighted the importance of employee involvement and empowerment. An important development in work redesign and job satisfaction is self-managed work groups and team working. One particular feature associated with the quality of working life movement is the concept of quality circles. Recognition must also be given to the importance of management style and culture.

■ Despite many theories and studies there are still doubts as to how to manage an organisation so that staff have both high job satisfaction and productivity. Account must also be taken of contextual factors. It may be necessary to lower expectations in the pursuit of the 'happy/productive worker' and to make for sustained, slow progress in overcoming forces for stability in both job attitudes and performance. Three possible approaches are: the individually-oriented system, the group-oriented system and the organisationally-oriented system. There is a complex relationship between job satisfaction and work performance.

MANAGEMENT IN ACTION 18.1

Job satisfaction: the fit between expectations and experiences

One of the UK's largest supermarket chains decided in the mid-1990s to undertake a company-wide review of staff attitudes. While this survey acknowledged strengths in downward communication, atmosphere and customer service philosophy, it also acknowledged certain shortcomings with respect and support, satisfaction and how valued staff felt. These results prompted the author to research the concept of job satisfaction in the autumn of 1996. The study focuses on one of the largest stores in the company, located in the south of England.

BUT WHAT IS JOB SATISFACTION?

Job satisfaction is an emotion, a feeling, an attitude and a matter of perception. It results from an appraisal of an employee's experiences at work. Job satisfaction involves likes, dislikes, extrinsic and intrinsic needs. It is within an employee's control and yet also beyond his or her control. *Enid Mumford* provides a useful framework for analysing job satisfaction and it was this framework that was applied to the study. Mumford sees job satisfaction as a fit between what the organisation requires, what the employee is seeking and what the employee is receiving. The degree of fit will determine the extent to which the employee is satisfied. The fit can also be divided into five 'contractual areas': knowledge, psychology, efficiency, ethics and task structure.

METHODOLOGY

In order to develop a picture of job satisfaction at the branch, staff attitudes in each of the five areas were assessed via a survey distributed to a random selection of staff who called into the personnel office during a three-week period. Supplementary information was also gathered through a series of informal discussions.

A wide variety of staff participated in the research with all age groups, shift patterns and grades being represented. The gender split in the research also closely reflected the company-wide gender representation.

JOB SATISFACTION – THE SITUATION AT THE BRANCH

Given the link between customer satisfaction and employee satisfaction and the company's need to develop stronger sales and profit growth, the issue of job satisfaction was and is vital to every branch of the supermarket chain. A thorough analysis of the survey responses, revealed the following.

The knowledge contract

- **Staff skills were not properly utilised**. While most employees wanted their existing knowledge and skills to be utilised and developed, many felt that their real skills and capabilities were not put to use.

- **Staff were inadequately informed about careers**. While staff wanted to develop and advance with the company, many believed that they were not encouraged by their managers nor were they advised or informed of the career options available.
- **Some categories of staff were not interested in pursuing careers**. Most women and students did not wish to pursue a career with the company and some did not wish to stay with the company.
- **Staff responsibilities needed to be clarified**. Many employees claimed to be unclear about their job descriptions.
- **Training should be individualised**. Some employees felt they had not received correct or adequate training for their job.

The psychological contract

- **Financial rewards did not concern staff**. Lower order needs were well satisfied with pay and benefits being perceived as above average for the nature of the work undertaken.
- **Attention needed to be paid to the higher order needs**. Many employees wanted responsibility and advancement, but few seemed happy with their ability to satisfy this need.
- **The social needs of employees were being satisfied**. Many staff felt that social and belonging needs play a key role in the psychological contract, and believed that friendly teamwork atmosphere among staff satisfied this need.
- **Job security needed to be improved**. This was of particular importance to managers, since three-quarters of the managers felt insecure in their jobs.
- **Recognition was seen as very important**. While many staff understood the satisfaction that recognition of effort brings, just over half of the staff confirmed that thanks were always given.
- **Employees had, in general, a high need for achievement**. While most staff wanted more responsibility for performance and opportunities for checking and controlling their own work, staff believed that they were not receiving it.

The efficiency contract

- **Financial incentives would improve performance**. While all employees saw the work–wage exchange as equitable, many staff felt that special wage increases should be given to staff who perform well.
- **Work controls should not be restrictive**. Over one-quarter of the respondents agreed that company rules and regulations affected their ability to perform their jobs well.
- **Supervisors and managers needed to be accessible**. Not only did many staff believe that a significant management/staff divide existed, but three-quarters of the respondents saw senior management as being out of touch with the average worker.

- **Employees needed to understand the branch structure and reporting system.** One- third of respondents were unsure who reported to whom.

The ethical contract

- **Employees needed to be treated fairly.** While most staff believed that the company's values do not contradict with their own values, there were issues of concern about how the company treated and cared about employees (this was particularly a concern to female employees).
- **Staff wanted to be able to express opinions and views.** The survey revealed that staff felt they could not express their ideas and suggestions on important store issues and even when they did give their ideas, not all believed feedback would be received.
- **Communications needed to be improved in the branch.** Many employees did not agree that communications were open and honest.

The task structure contract

- **Jobs needed to promote variety, identity and autonomy.** Some jobs were perceived to be too easy or too monotonous and staff felt that more experience of other departments would aid job satisfaction.
- **Jobs needed to be designed so employees were challenged.** Employees seemed to have a high need for challenging work and not everyone felt that they had the opportunity to satisfy this need.
- **Feedback and recognition of performance were essential.** Employees identified the need for more feedback on the work they did.

Evidently, there were difficulties with the degree of fit between the employees' needs and actual experience in each of the five contractual areas. However, on the positive side, the employees were considerably satisfied with the financial and social rewards of working for the company. Taking the holistic picture, it could be suggested that there is a group of competent, capable employees who are upset and confused over what the company says it offers and what the employees actually receive. These employees felt that they wanted to develop themselves and go further but were struggling through a lack of information, a lack of communication and the inability to freely express their opinions.

(I am grateful to Amanda Stevens for providing this information.)

MANAGEMENT IN ACTION 18.2

An elusive but expensive concept: stress

Claims against companies are increasing, so ensuring a less stressful working environment could save money, writes Adrian Preston.

More than two-thirds of workers in the City of London believe they suffer from stress. According to a survey conducted by recruitment consultants Jonathan Wren and published at the beginning of May 2000, 68 per cent of surveyed employees in the banking, financial, pensions, law, insurance and IT sectors felt themselves to be under stress. More than half of those polled felt that the City had become an increasingly stressful place to work in recent years, blaming a variety of pressures from too much work to unrealistic deadlines or the introduction of new technology.

But stress, despite thousands of column inches devoted to explaining it and the ministrations of a wide variety of so-called 'stress-consultants' remains an elusive concept.

The medical profession is unable to reach unanimity on a workable definition of stress and whether or not it is harmful.

However, the cost associated with the results of stress are not theoretical and in recent years the UK courts have taken a far less ambiguous approach to stress. In 1995 John Walker, a social worker employed by Northumberland District Council, successfully sued his employer for its failure to prevent his exposure to levels of stress that precipitated a nervous breakdown.

Several other cases have followed and UK employers have been put on notice that the duty of care that they owe towards the physical well-being of their employees extends to their employees' mental health.

Howard Watson, a solicitor with City firm Herbert Smith, who specialises in defending companies against personal injury claims, says that 'since Walker, claims for stress have increased over the past three years' and though the courts have taken what he describes as a 'reasonably measured approach' the size of damages awarded to successful plaintiffs tends to be at the upper end of the personal injury scale'. These can reach into six figures and with costs added represent a sizeable expense. The record payout in the English courts came in January of this year when a council worker was awarded £203,342 compensation for job-related stress.

Reforms to the process of litigation have also helped make it easier for employees to sue their employers. The drift towards 'no-win, no-fee' actions means that the personal risks of pursuing litigation are minimised. Several claims companies and some lawyers have taken advantage of the change in the regulations governing litigation and have ▶

Management in Action 18.2 continued

A long commute: one more factor leading to stress in the workplace?

started to promote their services quite heavily to employees who feel that they have been the victims of work-related stress complaints and illnesses.

The Association of British Insurers estimates that only 2 per cent of claims ever get to court, so any attempt to count the cost of stress-related litigation must largely be a matter of guesswork. However, the costs arising from successful claims against employers, whether settled in or out of court, are minuscule in comparison with other considerations. The Confederation of British Industry estimates the cost of stress-related illness resulting in absenteeism and low productivity to be upwards of £7bn each year.

High rates of staff turnover attributable to a mismanaged, stressful environment adds another, hidden, layer of cost. Ed Radakiewicz, chief executive of Businesshealth, which specialises in assisting management to identify the costs, causes and cures for the health of employees, claims that 'if someone leaves after training and the associated investment in them it can cost the employer up to three times their salary to replace them.'

If successfully sued, directors who get dragged into court will emerge with lighter pockets but, perhaps more importantly, the reputation of the offending firm will be tainted. The solution is clearly one of prevention: i.e. identify the risks before employees take action which may damage the company's finances or its reputation.

However, this course of action brings the manager back to the quest for a workable definition of what stress is. It may be the workplace epidemic of the early 21st century, but what is it? How do you measure it? And how do you manage it?

Christine Owen is an occupation health specialist with consultants William M Mercer. Ms Owen believes that looking for 'stress' within an organisation is at best a self-fulfilling prophecy and at worst can lead management into believing it has successfully addressed a problem when in fact it has only looked at one small set of symptoms of a much deeper and potentially costlier set of maladies.

'Stress audits fail to look into the general health status of the organisation, and the prevalent attitudes and behaviour exhibited within the organisation,' she says. They also fail to identify the acceptable levels of pressure for a job.

Stress results when an individual perceives that he or she cannot cope with the levels of pressure to which they feel subject. 'It is important not to "medicise" stress,' says Christine Owen. 'There are serious mental disorders that stress might precipitate, but they should be distinguished from "stress". There is no such thing as a "stress-free environment" but employers should make sure that they have identified what any role's acceptable level of stress is.'

Ms Owen says that, unsurprisingly perhaps, 'few companies are equipped to recognise and deal with psychological illnesses'. But, she argues, companies should be looking to identify two distinct sets of issues that may contribute to high levels of stress within an organisation. She divides these into hard and soft issues. Hard issues include high rates of staff turnover and high levels of absence due to ill-health.

Soft issues relate to the character of the organisation, whether the culture could be said to be 'aggressive or collaborative'. Companies should not look for simple explanations she says.

Long working hours are a good example of a phenomenon said to contribute to stress. But, argues Ms Owen 'they are more likely to be indicative of a culture of blame or onerous management practices'.

Ed Radakiewicz says that finding the 'cure' for stress does not necessarily have to involve an expensive or disruptive change in behaviour. Quite often it is achieved simply through the application of good management practice – for example, communication. He recalls one instance where a chief executive was astonished to learn that the single biggest reason for the high level of stress within his company was a recent programme of redundancies. Remaining staff were quite naturally fearful that they faced the same fate as their erstwhile colleagues.

'But that's ridiculous,' said the chief executive, 'our downsizing programme finished months ago'. However, the staff had not been told and were still under the impression that their jobs could go at any minute. Mr Radakiewicz believes that other managers could learn from the chief executive's failure to communicate: 'Sometimes "stress management" can be as straightforward as just doing the simple things well, and keeping people informed,' he says.

MANAGEMENT IN ACTION 18.3

Work-Life Balance case studies

NATIONWIDE BUILDING SOCIETY

Nationwide Building Society is one of the founder members of the Employers for Work-Life Balance alliance and has for some considerable time acknowledged the business benefits of providing employee choice, to enable employees to balance home and work lives.

Nationwide has introduced a wide range of policies, practices and procedures to support this, including a range of flexible working options (part-time, job share, term-time, homeworking, annualised hours, compressed working week) and leave policies that benefit men and women who may have different responsibilities at different life stages. These include enhanced maternity leave, parental leave, paternity leave, employment break, domestic and family leave and an extended holiday scheme.

Nationwide is fully committed to equal opportunities for both its customers and employees and lists a number of business benefits:

■ Greater access to a wider recruitment pool from which to recruit the best person for the job.
■ Ability to attract, recruit and retain employees, which has resulted in reduced turnover, recruitment and training costs, and has identified that:
　– a multi-skilled and diverse workforce that reflects the customer base has helped the business to understand customer needs and develop appropriate business solutions; and
　– good work-life practices demonstrate that Nationwide values the contribution of all its employees, which has in turn improved 'commitment, motivation, morale and productivity' and 'reduced stress and absenteeism'.

Satisfied employees = satisfied members

Nationwide's external statisticians tell them that for every 3% increase in employee satisfaction, there is a 1% increase in member satisfaction:

■ Flexible working practices were introduced in 1995. Since 1996, there has been a 14% increase in employee satisfaction.
■ In the latest annual employee satisfaction survey, 77% of Nationwide's employees agreed with the statement 'I am satisfied Nationwide provides me with the opportunities to balance working arrangements with my personal life'. This is an increase of 5% on the previous year.

Maternity return rate

■ Nationwide's current maternity return rate is 91.5% – a 30% increase over the last 10 years, resulting in a saving of over £3 million.

■ During the last year the company has seen an increase of nearly 8% of employees returning on a part-time or flexible working arrangement following maternity leave.

Costs of turnover

■ Employee turnover is one of the lowest in the industry at 9.8%, compared with the financial services sector average of 24%. Nationwide has estimated that to move to the average, they would need to have recruited an additional 2000 employees last year at a cost of £10 million in recruitment and training.

Workforce profile

■ Nationwide's workforce is made up of 76% women and 24% men.
■ Ethnic minority employees make up 6.51% of the total workforce, in the upper quartile in the Financial Sector.
■ Employees over 50 represent 10% of the workforce and employees under 25 represent nearly 18% of the total workforce.
■ Women in senior management account for 17.27% of the workforce.

BT

British Telecommunications PLC is one of the founder members of the Employers for Work-Life Balance alliance. It has 118,000 employees in the UK and now offers 'Lifestyle Working'.

Lifestyle Working started as a one-year pilot in Cardiff and Swindon Software Engineering centres due to retention issues among women. This is now also an issue for men as more men than women in BT have childcare responsibilities. BT offers a number of benefits and entitlements to meet the needs of families in order for them to balance their professional and personal fives.

The successes and benefits of the pilot to all concerned were so great that the practices have been expanded to other teams and units within BT; and it is being used as a case study and model for the entire BT Group:

■ More than 50% of participants and line managers felt it had improved their perception of BT as employer of first choice.
■ More than 50% felt more fulfilled at work since commencing 'Lifestyle Working'.
■ 50% felt they had maintained or improved their individual efficiency.

Other findings include:

■ Project management skills were enhanced due to the need to organise work.

▶

- Team members became skilled in covering for the participant if they were out of the office, leading to a good transfer of knowledge and better succession planning.
- Team performance increased due to better succession planning and cover.
- Productivity increased, since participants could work in a quieter office environment out of hours, with fewer interruptions and improved concentration.
- The working day could be extended to meet deadlines without the need for overtime.
- Great benefits for teams working with customers and colleagues across time zones, since people were allowed to work later or start earlier, providing the team with increased cover and a saving of the cost of overtime.
- People who were able to work at home on specific tasks were more efficient due to reduced levels of interruption.

- People want to transfer into areas where there is 'Lifestyle Working'.
- Change in working patterns have meant that people are more focussed, alert and concentrated.
- Line managers said participants' performance 'dramatically improved since being on the trial'.
- Participants felt 'loyalty to BT as an employer of choice' – one person turned down a better paid job as a result of the flexibility offered by the trial. Three people returned to full-time working from part-time because of the increased flexibility on offer. Lifestyle Working means they don't have to attend the office five days a week.
- Employees 'are happier and less stressed'.
- There's 'greater personal satisfaction and therefore greater motivation'.

MANAGEMENT IN ACTION 18.4

Beyond the nine-to-five

Flexible working is becoming an increasingly significant issue. For employees this reflects the growing importance of work-life balance. For companies it is part of the war for talent, as they look at ways of improving retention, increasing productivity and becoming the employer of choice.

Misconceptions exist about flexible working. Most people would not think of it as the first choice for someone aspiring to a senior job in the company. People wonder how it is possible to work part-time and still meet customer needs or manage a team, let alone keep an eye on career progression. The 2003 Global Pulse Survey showed that two thirds of IBMers still believe colleagues would question their commitment to IBM if they were to work flexibly.

Evidence shows that flexible working can benefit all concerned. An external survey* showed that 70% of those who work flexible hours scored higher than their full-time colleagues on resilience, leadership and commitment – and also produced more work. IBM's part-time employees include men and women with roles as senior managers in strategy and solutions; Client Services Manager; senior consultants; distinguished engineers; cluster leaders; business development and as Partners. At IBM there is no reason why people in part-time roles should not enjoy fulfilling jobs and strong career prospects.

'As part of making IBM the employer of choice and encouraging the right people to stay in IBM, working flexibly – which usually means part time – should be available as a positive option for IBMers' says Larry Hirst, CGM. 'I want people who are 100% commited to IBM, whether full time or part time – the success of flexible working depends on the attitude of everyone involved.'

Many IBMers are finding that flexible hours work for them and for their part of the business. Intralink spoke to two of

them (see below). But others still come up against barriers. That's why HR will be working with managers to explain benefits of flexible working and have introduced practical changes to make it easier. And flexible working can also work to IBM's advantage. People working non-standard hours can help us cope with busier and quieter times for our customers. And as an employer, enabling people to find the work life balance that suits them is yet another way we are making IBM a great place to work.

'It is partly about removing disincentives to managers to accommodate flexible working – so for example a part-time employee no longer counts against 70% of headcount, unless they are actually working a 70% week,' explains HR Director, Paul Rodgers. 'But also it is about changing the culture. At the moment we see a dropping off in the proportion of employees who work flexibly as you go up the bands. But there is no reason at all why people who work outside the standard Monday-Friday pattern should not aspire to senior positions in this company.'

So what is flexible working? As well as the more established patterns of part-time working (shorter or fewer days in the week) IBM can offer unusual alternatives, such as working eight day fortnights, or working full time on a project then taking a few weeks off when the bid is won or the customer installation completed. IBM's strength in mobile working makes it easier to be truly flexible if an urgent customer need suddenly comes to light. 'In this industry none of us can fully plan our work so that we never work outside our regular hours', says Paul. 'There are very few roles that demand full-time, conventional working. Part-time team members are just as skilled as full-timers in juggling their work and outside priorities, from time to time, to take care of the occasional crisis.'

While flexibility is an important element in IBM's diversity policies, it is not just a women's issue. Work life balance is now the most important issue for UK employees in a range of industries. At IBM one of our most senior part-time employees in the UK is the IGS Business Development Director, Tim Shercliff – and he is enthusiastic about the benefits working part time can bring to individuals and to the company. Tim experienced some scepticism from colleagues when he first went part time two and a half years ago, but now people have seen that the arrangement can work and are generally supportive.

Focus

'Working shorter hours has encouraged me to stand back from the day-to-day issues and think about what is important, helping the whole IGS organisation remain focused. That's what my current job is all about,' says Tim.

Tim's career manager, Gary Kyle, is adamant that with the right management climate part-time IBMers can maintain their careers. 'The key is to be flexible, organised and able to delegate,' says Gary. 'Flexible working is an important issue for IBM. We must become more supportive of people who do not fit the standard five day week profile, or we will lose talented individuals.'

Tim has found a growing network of part-time employees in IBM, who can learn a lot from each other. People have different reasons for wanting to work flexibly. Part-time managers in IBM include a ballroom dancing instructor (see opposite) and people running separate businesses, as well as the larger group – men and women – who choose to keep some hours of the week to spend with family

Paul's advice to anyone thinking about working flexibly is to ask – your manager, or ask HR for advice. 'The reality is that for most people in IBM a full time job is the option that suits them best, and our mobile working technology and management structures make it easier for people to juggle full-time work with their home lives. But if you are thinking about changing the way you work don't be put off by worries about your career, IBM wants to keep good people, and we will help you.'

* Knell, J. and Savage, C. 'Desperately Seeking Flexibility', 2001.

IBM UK'S FLEXIBLE WORKING PROGRAMME

(Including changes resulting from UK Family Friendly legislation effective 6 April 2003)

The right to apply for flexible working is open to parents who meet the following criteria:

- He or she is an IBM employee, and:
- Has a child under the age of six, or under eighteen where the child is disabled.
- Has responsibilty for the upbringing of the child and is making the application to enable them to care for the child.
- Is the mother, father, adopter, guardian or foster parent of the child **or** is married to, or the partner of the child's mother, father, adopter, guardian or foster parent.
- Has worked continually for IBM for 26 weeks.

- Has not made another application for flexible working under the right during the last 12 months.

FLEXIBLE WORKING IN ACTION: JOHN FOSKETT

From Monday to Wednesday John Foskett works as a Consultant IT Architect on the Cable & Wireless account. In the evenings and on Thursdays and Fridays he teaches classes and works on accounts and marketing for the Ballroom and Latin American dancing school established by his wife in Dorking, Surrey.

Until 1992 when they turned professional John and his wife Linda were international amateur ballroom dancing competitors and part of the British amateur ballroom dancing team. Linda set up the dancing school after they turned professional, and four years ago gave up outside work to concentrate on the school and on family commitments. Demand for the classes grew, and by last summer John was finding it difficult to fit in five long days at IBM with evenings and weekends teaching dance classes, and sharing in the care of the couple's young son.

'I discussed the demands on my time with my then manager last summer. We looked at a number of options. There was a successful precedent for reduced hours working in the department, and I moved to a 25½ hour week in August 2002', says John. To date everything has gone smoothly. John's customer and team members know that he works part time. 'The one area where I have made changes is in attending meetings, many of which take place on Thursdays' explains John. 'Now I look at the agenda and input any comments by email or via a colleague. and catch up on the minutes afterwards'.

John is clear on the benefits of working part time. 'I have far more energy, and am more organised about prioritising my work.' When asked if he would return to full time working, John hesitates. 'That's a difficult question. I love working for IBM and want to stay here. The current arrangement works with my current team and customer, and suits my life outside work. Whether I stay part time in the future depends on my role in the company.'

FLEXIBLE WORKING IN ACTION: MARGARET IMMINK

Margaret Immink works a 60 per cent schedule as a Partner in Business Consulting Services. She says that flexibility is the key.

Margaret's clients are currently based in Europe and in Asia. 'As far as possible I try to restrict travelling to the early part of the week, and have Thursday and Friday to spend time with my daughter. But if I end up taking calls or spending extensive time checking email at the end of the week, I can usually trade an hour with my family on a Monday or Tuesday, or another time when I'm in the UK.'

The fact that Margaret works part time has not been an issue for her clients, 'I am dealing with senior-level people with busy diaries, we schedule discussions at times that suit both of us. For the most part my clients do not know that I work part time, the point for them is that I am around when they need me and they probably think I am working with other clients on my time off.'

▶

Management in Action 18.4 continued

Margaret was in the process of becoming a partner in PwC in the US when she first suggested that in the future she would like to move to a part-time schedule. At that time in 1999 the Idea, of operating as a part-time partner, was almost unknown. After her daughter was born she gained agreement to trail a 60 per cent schedule, and to meet quarterly with the Business Unit leader to discuss how this was working. When she moved to the UK two years ago she remained on a 60 per cent schedule.

Overall the arrangement works well, although Margaret does need to prioritise her time to concentrate on client engagements. 'I am often not around for internal meetings or activities such as presentations on new offerings, and can sometimes feel I am missing out', she admits. 'But as a Partner I can control my own time and it is relatively straight-forward to be flexible when needed. The next big challenge going forward will be to work with customers to adapt to dealing with part time consultants and managers, and for IBM BCS to open up new opportunities for flexible working for the next generation who are coming through.'

Reproduced with permission from Paul Rodgers, HR Director, Intr@linkUK, IBM, Spring 2003, pp. 32–3.

REVIEW AND DISCUSSION QUESTIONS

1 What exactly do you understand by job satisfaction? What are the main dimensions of job satisfaction? Give specific examples of causes of job dissatisfaction that you have experienced.

2 Debate critically the extent to which you believe that stress is an inevitable feature of modern work organisations.

3 What factors are likely to influence job design and what factors might affect its potential success? Contrast different approaches to job design and give examples of situations in which these approaches might be appropriate, and acceptable, to the staff concerned.

4 Discuss critically the extent to which you believe theories of job enrichment lead to improved job satisfaction. Where possible, give practical examples in support of your answer.

5 Outline the core dimensions of a job. Estimate the approximate Motivating Potential Score (MPS) for any job that you have held and/or attempt to establish the likely MPS for a job that you hope to have in the future.

6 Why do you think that increasing attention is being given to the work/life debate? As a manager, detail the main areas in which you could take action in order to improve the quality of working life of staff.

7 Debate the potential benefits and limitations of employee involvement and empowerment. Where possible, support your answer with practical examples.

8 Explain fully the essential features of (i) self-managed work groups (ii) teleworking; and (iii) a quality circle group.

9 Evaluate critically the relationship between job satisfaction and effective work performance. Give reasons in support of your views.

ASSIGNMENT 1

The following is a question, reproduced with permission, from the Institute of Chartered Secretaries and Administrators Examination paper.

'Downsizing' of personnel numbers often leads to job enlargement and job rotation so should create job enrichment and motivation. Discuss this proposition.

Working in small self-selecting groups, set out your response as fully as possible and give practical examples in support of your answer. How much agreement is there among members of your group?

ASSIGNMENT 2

a Undertake a detailed review of the extent to which flexible working arrangements have been introduced in a range of different organisations (for example by questioning your colleagues about their work experiences, and those of their families and friends).

b Detail critically the apparent effectiveness of these arrangements and their influence on job satisfaction and perceived work performance.

c As part of your investigation explain why, despite the many apparent potential advantages, working from home has not been adopted by organisations or staff to the extent that might be expected.

PERSONAL AWARENESS AND SKILLS EXERCISE

OBJECTIVES

Completing this exercise should help you to enhance the following skills:

▶ Identify the scale to which different things cause you stress.

▶ Examine relationships between causes of stress and motivation at work.

▶ Recognise that topics studied in organisational behaviour are not freestanding.

EXERCISE

You are required to:

1   Write down in 10 minutes as many things as you can that cause you stress:

_____

_____

_____

_____

_____

_____

_____

_____

_____

_____

2   Put your list in order by writing 1, 2 and 3 against the top stressors.

3   Choose a partner, according to the tutor's guidelines.

4   Exchange your Motivation scores (**from the Exercise in Chapter 12**) with your partner, but **not** your list of stressors. Keep this to yourself for now.

5   Look at your partner's Motivation scores and note what you think would be their top three causes of stress. They will do the same for you.

6   Discuss your findings with each other. How close did you get?

DISCUSSION

■ How would you explain to a sceptical listener the interrelationships between stress and motivation?

■ In addition to motivation what other topic(s) studied in organisational behaviour do you think has a **significant** relationship with stress at work?

Visit our website **www.booksites.net/mullins** for further questions, annotated weblinks, case material and Internet research material.

The wide open spaces: linking job satisfaction and work performance

RIO COSMETICS LTD

Rio Cosmetics has chosen to concentrate its effort on what it regards as the most lucrative section of the market. As its marketing manager says, 'We've gone for short-term profit maximisation – rather than for diversification.' Its production is therefore concentrated on a single tube of deodorant marketed under the brand name 'Freche'. The product is heavily advertised on TV and Rio has made considerable profits over the past 5 years. However, a substantial competitor has now entered the market, and Rio's share of the market has dropped to 18 per cent, its lowest level in three years.

The board is now looking for explanations. They have asked for reports from the Sales and Production Departments. They have also asked the Personnel Department to report on some disturbing statistics regarding the workforce. In particular:

1 There has been a dramatic increase in absenteeism over the last year.
2 Although the number of line workers has remained fairly stable (at around 2115 during the last four or five years), weekly average output has fallen from 312 000 to 287 000 units.
3 During the last year 21 per cent of the line workers have been late at least once a week, in spite of the fact that they lose a quarter of an hour's pay when this happens. (Before this year the figure was fairly constant at around 10 per cent.)

In addition, within the past four months, the number of consumers complaining direct to the company has doubled according to the information supplied by the Quality Control Department, who keep a record of the number of letters received each week. They advise that the majority of these complaints have been traced back to what they describe as 'human errors' on the production line. Furthermore, three serious cases of pilfering have been notified by the Security Section within the past week.

Other information available

The rate of pay is approximately 10 per cent higher than could be obtained by the line workers elsewhere.

Older workers are not discouraged, but the average age of the workforce is only 19 years. It is increasingly difficult to find acceptable line supervisors.

Production starts at 8 am and finishes at 5 pm – 5 days a week – with an hour lunch break and two 20-minute tea breaks.

The graphs shown have been prepared covering labour turnover and absenteeism over the past five years.

YOUR TASK

What explanations and recommendations would you offer the Board of Directors?

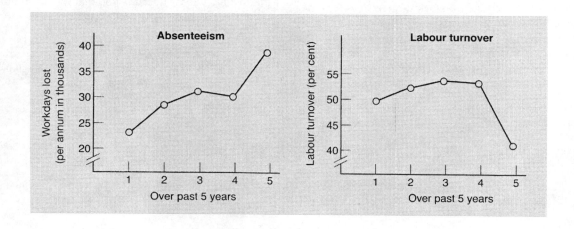

CASE STUDY 18.2

The changing role of supervisors: demonstrating the effect of communication and training on morale

You are a management consultant called in to advise an organisation which has undergone significant change, involving both voluntary and compulsory redundancies, in the last two years. Employee members have reduced by 60 per cent while the workload has remained unchanged for the organisation as a whole. Employees, including managers and supervisors, now work under significantly increased work pressure. Senior management are concerned about the low morale and commitment to the organisation which they now perceive among the remaining workforce. Six months ago the senior management team decided to introduce a major exercise to improve communication within the organisation. They wanted employees at all levels to understand better the problems of the organisation, the management strategy adopted to deal with these problems, and the senior management team's growing confidence that the situation was now improving significantly. Productivity and cost effectiveness had improved substantially. Moreover, major programmes of technical improvement and investment were now under way.

One important element of this programme was a training course in interactive skills for first-line supervisors. The personnel manager has told you that this programme has failed.

Personnel Manager: 'We wanted to build up the supervisors' role with their own people. Therefore we wanted the supervisors to talk with their people about our plans and to get their ideas and views. We put them through a one-week course in interactive skills and human relations skills. But it failed. They enjoyed the course. They all said they gained a lot from it. But when we asked them to communicate to their people about plans for this year, they said they did not feel confident enough.'

Consultant: 'Do they understand the plans? Do you feel that the plans have been presented to them in a clear enough way? Are their own managers communicating effectively with the supervisors? Do their managers provide support and encouragement to the supervisors?'

Personnel Manager: 'I'm not sure, possibly not. We give them copies of our detailed plans. They see everything. In any case I think they are afraid of being criticised by their staff. They don't want arguments with them and they don't feel sure enough about the plans. They wonder about job losses in the future.'

The role of first-line supervisors had been changed with the introduction of a professional Personnel Function. Supervisors no longer fully understood the terms and conditions of employment, bonus schemes, job evaluation systems and employment legislation relevant to the organisation. Moreover the staffing reductions had meant that supervisors were increasingly taking on tasks once carried out by their subordinates. Thus the role of the supervisor had come to be solely a technical, and no longer a managerial role.

YOUR TASKS

(a) Assess the effectiveness of the training programme, identifying the problems experienced.

(b) Identify the main issues you feel will need attention if communications within this organisation are to be improved.

(c) State what advice you will offer to the organisation about how to proceed from the current situation.

CASE STUDY 18.3

Flying like the wind: motivation, job design and culture at Falcon Car Company

The Falcon Car Company, based in Sweden, was for many years experiencing labour dissatisfaction with its traditional moving assembly lines of production. This was reflected in high levels of absenteeism and personnel turnover, as well as recruiting difficulties at its plants.

To make the jobs more interesting, the plants were designed so that the workers could operate in teams. Instead of repeating a single short task, each operator was trained to do all the jobs in their team's area. Each team has its own entrance, changing room, coffee room and sauna. The factory has been built as six distinct product workshops, each fully equipped to build a whole car, rather than mere sub-assembly. Falcon allows its workers time off for further education and lengthy paternity or maternity leave. Wages are comparatively good at Falcon and are supplemented by bonuses for high quality work. Production workers have the opportunity to be promoted from the shop floor to more senior positions. Mr Karlberg, the Production Manager, was once himself a production line worker at Falcon cars.

Cars are rigorously checked throughout the assembly process. Each team tests its own work before the car passes to the next team. If faults are identified, they are traced to the operator responsible and noted on a board in their area. If faufts are frequent or serious, their supervisor will take the operator to see the car and point out the problems.

'We let people know their mistakes in a positive manner. We don't go round with a whip,' says Mr Karlberg. The human lessons that Falcon has learned have eased the difficulties the company initially experienced with high absenteeism, high turnover of staff and recruitment.

'The factory is the closest car assembly has come to building on the spot, with operators standing still and components coming to them. People are getting more and more educated, so industry has to become more and more interesting,' says Mr Karlberg.

The consequences of the changes implemented by Falcon Cars are that morale and motivation have visibly increased. The evidence that staff turnover and absenteeism levels have significantly dropped confirm this.

YOUR TASKS

In the role of Mr Karlberg, the Production Manager of Falcon cars, write a report for the attention of the Managing Director of Falcon Cars, that answers the following questions.

(a) Suggest reasons why Falcon Cars was experiencing high staff turnover, high absenteeism and general dissatisfaction with its traditional moving assembly line.

(b) Why has the Falcon Car Company provided the teams of workers with their own entrance, changing room, coffee room and sauna?

(c) By applying appropriate theory, explain why the workers' motivation has improved.

(d) Using Falcon Cars as an example, what factors need to be addressed and means used in order to change a company's culture?

NOTES AND REFERENCES

1. Herzberg. F. 'One More Time: How do you Motivate Employees?', *Harvard Business Review*, vol. 46, 1968, pp. 53–62.

2. Luthans, F. *Organizational Behaviour*, Seventh edition, McGraw-Hill (1995), p. 129.

3. Bassett, G. 'The Case Against Job Satisfaction', *Business Horizons*, vol. 37, no. 3, May–June 1994, pp. 61–8.

4. Reeves, R. 'Reality Bites', *Management Today*, May 2003, p. 37.

5. Grunberg, M. M. *Understanding Job Satisfaction*, Macmillan (1979).

6. Cane, S. *Kaizen Strategies for Winning Through People*, Pitman Publishing (1996), p. 114.

7. See, for example: Torrington, D., Hall, L. and Taylor, S. *Human Resource Management*, Fifth edition, Financial Times Prentice Hall (2002).

8. Handy, C. 'Boring Workplace, Boring Worker', *Management Today*, November 1997, p. 29.

9. 'The Workplace Survey', Chartered Management Institute, March 2003.

10. Myerson, J. 'Workspace Heaven?', *Management Today*, June 2003, pp. 53–61.

11. Simons, T. and Enz, C. A. 'Motivating Hotel Employees: Beyond the Carrot and the Stick', *Cornell HRA Quarterly*, February 1995, pp. 20–7.

12. Mumford, E. 'Job Satisfaction: A Method of Analysis', *Personal Review*, vol. 20, no. 3, 1991, pp. 11–19.

13. Marx, K. 'The Notion of Alienation', in Coser, L. A. and Rosenburg, B. *Sociological Theory*, Collier Macmillan (1969), pp. 505–10.

14. Blauner, R. *Alienation and Freedom*, University of Chicago Press (1964).

15. See, for example: Huczynski, A. and Buchanan, D. *Organisational Behaviour: An Introductory Text*, Fourth edition, Financial Times Prentice Hall (2000).

16. *Daily Mail*, Friday, 23 June 2000

17. Lucas, E. 'Keep It Formal for Maximum Flexibility', *Professional Manager*, March 2000, p. 10.

18. Thomas, R. 'The World Is Your Office', *Management Today*, July 1999, pp. 78–84.

19. Law, S. 'Future Networking', *Professional Manager*, March 2003, p. 21.

20. Reeves, R. 'Reality Bites', *Management Today*, December 2002, p. 35.

21. *Financial Times*, 8 May 2000.

22. For a fuller discussion see, for example: Arnold, J. Cooper, C. L. and Robertson, I. T. *Work Psychology: Understanding Human Behaviour in the Workplace*, Third edition, Financial Times Pitman Publishing (1998).

23. McKenna, E. *Business Psychology and Organisational Behavior*, Lawrence Erlbaum (1994), p. 585.

24. Lucas, E. 'Work and Sickness', *Professional Manager*, vol. 12, no. 4, July 2003, pp. 32–3.

25. 'Business', *The Herald*, 17 October, 2002, p. C7.

26. Broad, M. 'Rising Stress at Work Costs £4bn a Year', *The Sunday Times*, 1 September 2002.

27. York, P. 'Getting a Grip on Stress', *Management Today*, October 2001, p. 105.

28. Orpen, C. 'Want The Best? Get Stressed!' *Chartered Secretary*, August 1996, pp. 18–20.

29. Gwyther, M. 'Stressed for Success', *Management Today*, January 1999, pp. 22–6.

30. 'Managing Stress at Work', Engineering Employers' Federation, 2001.

31. Armson, S. 'Putting Stress on the Bottom Line', *Management Today*, September 1997, p. 5.

32. Hall, K. and Savery, L. K. 'Stress Management', *Management Decision*, vol. 25, no. 6, 1987, pp. 29–35.

33. *Are Managers Under Stress?: A Survey of Management Morale*, The Institute of Management, September 1996.

34. See, for example: Ridd, J. 'Hidden Costs of Work Stress', *The British Journal of Administrative Management*, October/November 1994, pp. 14–15.

35. Jamison, C. 'Top 10 Myths of Customer Service', *The British Journal of Administrative Management*, July/August 1999, pp. 19–21.

36. Handy, C. B. *Understanding Organizations*, Fourth edition, Penguin (1993).

37. Taylor, M. 'Tell Me Why I Don't Like Mondays', Working Paper of the Institute for Social and Economic Research, October 2002.

38. Randall, J. 'Home Truths', *Management Today*, June 2001, p. 31.

39. 'Work-related stress: A short guide', Health and Safety Executive, November 2001. See also: 'Organisational Interventions for Work Stress: A risk management approach', Health and Safety Executive, 2000.

40. Black, O. 'Making Stress Work for You', *Management Today*, December 2001, p. 19.

41. 'Managing Stress at Work', Engineering Employers' Federation, 2001.

42. Reeves, R. 'Reality Bites', *Management Today*, March 2003, p. 35.

43. Vine, P. and Williamson, J. 'Run Down, Stressed Out', *The British Journal of Administrative Management*, January/February 1998, pp. 14–17.

44. Van ZylKobus Lazenby, E. 'The relation between ethical behaviour and workstress amongst a group of managers working in affirmative action positions', *Journal of Business Ethics*, vol. 40, no. 2, October 2002, pp. 111–19.

45. Hayes, D. and Hudson, A. *Attitudes to Work*, Education and Work Research Group (2000), reprinted with permission.

46. Burns, B. *Managing Change: A Strategic Approach to Organisational Dynamics*, Third edition, Financial Times Prentice Hall (2000), p. 69.

47. Hackman, J. R. and Oldham, G. R. *Work Redesign*, Addison-Wesley (1980).

48. Lee-Ross, D. 'The Reliability and Rationale of Hackman and Oldham's Job Diagnostic Survey and Job Characteristics Model among Seasonal Hotel Workers', *International Journal of Hospitality Management*, 17, 1998, pp. 391–406.

49. Roe, R. A., Zinovieva, I. L., Dienes, E. and Ten Horn, L. A., 'A Comparison of Work Motivation in Bulgaria, Hungary and the Netherlands: Test of a model', *Applied Psychology: An International Review*, vol. 49, 2000, pp. 658–87.

50. Wilson, N. A. B. *On the Quality of Working Life*: report prepared for the Department of Employment, Manpower Paper no. 7, HMSO (1973).

51. 'Effective Organisations; The People Factor', Advisory Booklet, ACAS, November 2001.

52. Cooper, C. and Worrall, L. *The Quality of Working Life, 1999 Survey of Managers' Changing Experiences*, The Institute of Management and UMIST. For a summary, *see: Professional Manager*, January 2000 and March 2001.

53. Rigby, R. 'Promiscuous Managers', *Management Today*, May 2000, pp. 60–1.

54. Oliver, J. 'Losing Control', *Management Today*, June 1998, pp. 32–38.

55. Rice, M. 'Greater Expectations', *Management Today*, June 2001, pp. 76–85.

56. 'Work-Life Balance: The Business Case', Department of Trade and Industry, September 2001, p. 3.

57. Rice, M. 'Balancing Acts', *Management Today*, September 2002, pp. 52–9.

58. Summers, J. and Nowicki, M. 'Achievement and Balance: What do Managers Really Want?', *Healthcare Financial Management*, vol. 56, no. 3, March 2003, pp. 80–4.

59. Reeves, R. 'The Joy of Work', *Management Today*, May 2001, pp. 60–3.

60. Armitage, K. 'Can We Really Achieve a Life/Work Balance?' *The British Journal of Administrative Management*, July/August 2001, pp. 14–15.

61. See, for example: Coupar, W. 'Employee Involvement and Performance: UK Experience', *European Participation Monitor*, no. 9, 1994, pp. 45–50.

62. 'Working Together: the ACAS standard', ACAS, January 2003

63. Heller, F. 'Is Participation Really Working?' QWL News and Abstracts, *ACAS*, No. 138, Spring 1999, pp. 6–11.

64. Wolfson, Sir Brian 'Train Retain and Motivate staff', *Management Today*, March 1998, p. 5.

65. Jamison, C. 'Top 10 Myths of Customer Service', *The British Journal of Administrative Management*, July/August 1999, p. 20.

66. Pickard, J. 'The Real Meaning of Empowerment', *Personnel Management*, vol. 25, no. 11, November 1993, pp. 28–33.

67. Wilkinson, A. 'Empowerment: Issues and Debates', QWL News and Abstracts, *ACAS*, no. 137, Winter 1999, p. 5.

68. Cordery, J. L., Mueller, W. S. and Smith, L. M. 'Attitundinal and Behavioral Effects of Autononmous Group Working', *Academy of Management Journal*, June 1991, pp. 464–76.

69. See, for example: Robbins, S. P. *Organizational Behaviour*, Eighth edition, Prentice-Hall (1998).

70. Wilson, J. 'Building Teams – with Attitude', *Professional Manager*, September 1998, pp. 12–13.

71. Torrington D, Hall L and Taylor S, *Human Resource Management*, Fifth edition, Financial Times Prentice Hall, (2002), p. 316

72. Waterman, R. *The Frontiers of Excellence*, Nicholas Brealey (1994).

73. *Teamwork: Success Through People*, Advisory Booklet, ACAS, April 2003, p. 34.

74. *The Survey of Long Term Employment Strategies*, The Institute of Management and Manpower plc, September 1996.

75. *Flexibility and Fairness*, Institute of Management and TUC, September 1996 reported in 'Flexible Employment's Here to Stay', *Professional Manager*, November 1996, p. 31.

76. Rawcliffe, S. 'Flexible Rewards', *Chartered Secretary*, November 1997, p. 27.

77. 'Work-Life Balance: The Business Case', Department of Trade and Industry, September 2001.

78. 'Flexible Working – Case studies', Equal Opportunities Commission, www.eoc.org.uk, 24 June 2003.

79. See, for example: Barnes, P. 'Teleworking – The Cat's Whiskers?', *Chartered Secretary*, May 1997, pp. 20–1.

80. Philpott, S. 'Making the Right Connections?' *The British Journal of Administrative Management*, July/August 1999, pp. 8–10.

81. 'The Workplace Survey', Chartered Management Institute, March 2003.

82. Russell, S. *Quality Circles in Perspective*, ACAS Work Research Unit, Occasional Paper, no. 24 (February 1983).

83. Meyer, G. W. and Scott, R. G. 'Quality Circles: Panacea or Pandora's Box', *Organizational Dynamics*, Spring 1985, pp. 34–50.

84. See, for example: Hill, S. 'Why Quality Circles Failed But Total Quality Management Might Succeed', *British Journal of Industrial Relations*, vol. 29, no. 4, 1991, pp. 541–68.

85. See, for example: Cartwright, J. *Cultural Transformation*, Financial Times Prentice Hall (1999).

86. Scarpello, V. and Vandenberg, R. J. 'The Satisfaction with My Supervisor Scale: Its Utility for Research and Practical Applications', *Journal of Management*, vol. 13, no. 3, 1987, pp. 447–66.

87. Bassett, G. 'The Case Against Job Satisfaction', *Business Horizons*, vol. 37, no. 3, May–June 1994, pp. 61–8.

88. See, for example: Green, J. R. 'Just Whistle While You Work', *Chartered Secretary*, March 1997, pp. 20–1.

89. Crow, S. M. and Hartman, S. J. 'Can't Get No Satisfaction', *Leadership & Organization Development Journal*, vol. 16, no. 4, 1995, p. 34.

90. See, for example: Torrington, D., Hall, L. and Taylor, S. *Human Resource Management*, Fifth edition, Financial Times Prentice Hall (2002).

91. Staw, B. M. 'Organizational Psychology and the Pursuit of the Happy/Productive Worker', *California Management Review*, vol. 28, no. 4, Summer 1986, pp. 40–53.

92. Bassett, G. 'The Case Against Job Satisfaction', *Business Horizons*, vol. 7, no. 3, May–June 1994, p. 67.

93. Heller, F. 'Is Participation Really Working?' QWL News and Abstracts, *ACAS*, No. 138, Spring 1999, pp. 6–11.

 Use the *Financial Times* to enhance your understanding of the context and practice of management and organisational behaviour. Refer to articles 5, 10, 13, 19, 20 and 26 in the BUSINESS PRESS section at the end of the book for relevant reports on the issues explored in this chapter.

TOPIC SUMMARY SHEET

What are the key learning points from this topic?

TOPIC 8 – THE EMPLOYMENT RELATIONSHIP

Why study this topic?

This chapter will help you to understand the often complex and difficult relationship between employer and employee. You will be provided with an insight as to what your responsibilities are as an employee, and your employer's responsibilities toward you. As part of this, you will explore the legal and contractual implications, again, information which will be of significant use as you progress through employment.

Also discussed are the various approaches which can be taken towards employee relations within an organisation. Take time to consider what you think is the approach taken in your own organisation. This can often explain why organisations implement and carry out certain policies, and this chapter should provide you with the necessary background knowledge to aid your understanding.

Blackboard

E-tivity 8: The employment relationship

MODULE MILESTONE: - ASSIGNMENT SUBMISSION

Chapter 7

Employee relations

Nick Bacon

Introduction

The terms 'employee relations' and, more traditionally, 'industrial relations' are used to indicate those areas of the employment relationship in which managers deal with the representatives of employees rather than managing employees directly as individuals (Edwards, 1995). Where employees seek collective representation they generally join trade unions and the reaction of managers to this potential challenge to management authority provides valuable insights into the nature of employment. As the membership of trade unions has declined over the past two decades a critical debate has developed around the nature of employment relations in non-union workplaces. The purpose of this chapter is to chart the changes in the collective regulation of labour and consider the implications of the increasing number of workers who are not represented by trade unions.

Management frames of reference and management style

The suggestion that employees may need some form of collective protection from employers provokes a strong response in many managers. Behind this response is a set of assumptions about the right to manage (frequently termed the management prerogative) and the correct power balance in the employment relationship. These assumptions held by managers are the mixture of a complex blend of experiences, predispositions, learned behaviour and prejudice. They combine to create management frames of reference (Fox, 1966, 1974) that capture the often deeply held assumptions of managers towards a labour force. Three separate frames of reference can be identified: unitarist, pluralist and radical. Each of these differ in their beliefs about the nature of organisations, the role of conflict and the task of managing employees. Managers holding a unitarist frame of reference believe the natural state of organisations is one of harmony and co-operation. All employees are thought to be in the same team, pulling together for the common goal of organisational success. The employee relations task of management is to prevent conflict arising from misunderstandings that result if they fail adequately to communicate organisational goals to employees. Any remaining conflicts are attributed to mischief created by troublemakers. A pluralist frame of reference recognises that organisations contain a variety of sectional groups who legitimately seek to express divergent interests. The resulting conflict is inevitable and the task of managers is to establish a system of structures and procedures in which conflict is institutionalised and a negotiated order is established. The radical critique of pluralism is not, strictly speaking, a frame of reference for understanding management views of the employment relationship. It draws upon Marxism and explains workplace conflict within a broader historical and social context and places a stress upon the unequal power struggle of opposing social classes.

There are no simple methods to assess the frame of reference held by managers – indeed, they usually hold a complex set of ideas rather than falling neatly into a single and possibly oversimplistic frame of reference. However, insights into management attitudes can be gained through their responses to questions about trade unions. From comparable questions posed to managers at the start of the 1980s and 1990s, Poole and Mansfield (1993) suggested the underlying pluralistic preferences of British managers were remarkably consistent. Another question posed more recently indicated that a majority of workplace managers do not have a single frame of reference. In the 1998 Workplace Employee Relations Survey (WERS 98) most managers (54 per cent) were 'neutral' about union membership, whereas 29 per cent were 'in favour' with 17 per cent 'not in favour' (Cully et al., 1999: 87). However, when managers are asked more directly whether they prefer to manage employees directly or through unions then unitarist preferences emerge. For example, 72 per cent of managers agreed with the statement 'we would rather consult directly with employees than with unions', whereas only 13 per cent disagreed (ibid.: 88). Consequently, management approaches to industrial relations are often characterised as a mixing and matching between unitarism and pluralism in the 'time-honoured' British fashion (Edwards et al., 1998). Many managers accept such a view on the grounds that it merely reflects the reality of managing employees who may at times need representation. The evidence suggests, however, that managers can deter or encourage employees from joining trade unions. In the 1998 Workplace Employee Relations Survey pro-union management attitudes were significantly associated with union presence in the workplace (Cully et al., 1998: 19).

Frames of reference are also important because they underlie the management style adopted in organisations towards the workforce. Many authors have attempted to classify management styles (Fox, 1974; Purcell and Sisson, 1983; Purcell and Ahlstrand, 1994; Storey and Bacon, 1993) and as the resulting models have become increasingly complex some now doubt the usefulness of producing yet more typologies (Kitay and Marchington, 1996). The most recent typologies attempt to highlight the interaction between HRM and industrial relations. The central question raised is the extent to which HRM and industrial relations are alternative or complementary systems for managing employees. Whether managers recognise trade unions indicates the extent to which a 'collective' approach to managing employees is preferred and it does capture a key factor in distinguishing between management approaches. In addition, the extent to which managers invest in and develop employees indicates the extent to which they stress 'individualism'. In Figure 7.1 Purcell and Ahlstrand (1994) use the dimensions of 'collectivism' and 'individualism' to identify six different management styles of employee relations.

Individualism and collectivism have recently become popular terms in employee relations. In comparison with the traditional management frames of reference – unitarism and pluralism – these concepts have 'common-sense' meanings and appear grounded in everyday management vocabularies and thinking about employee relations. Individualism in employment relations is traditionally used to denote non-unionism and/or a HRM-style investment approach to employees (Marchington and Parker, 1990; Purcell, 1987; Storey and Sisson, 1993). Correspondingly, collectivism in industrial relations in the 1970s is counterpoised

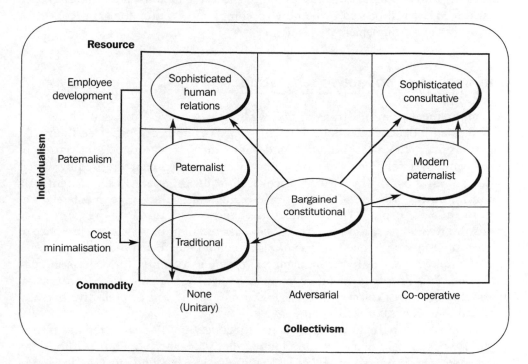

Figure 7.1 Movements in management style in employee relations

Source: Storey and Sisson, 1993, adapted from Purcell and Ahlstrand, 1994

with individualism and HRM in the 1990s (Storey and Sisson, 1993). The 'collectivism' dimension includes a unitarist position where trade unions are not recognised, an adversarial position of conflict with unions and a co-operative position of partnership with unions. The 'individualism' dimension includes a cost minimisation approach to employees, a 'paternalist' position of care for employee welfare and an employee development scenario.

Initial studies of the adoption of HRM policies in unionised workplaces (Storey, 1992) suggested little fit between HRM and industrial relations as managers attempted to bypass industrial relations processes and deal directly with employees. This comes as no great surprise as personnel management in the UK is commonly described as pragmatic and largely opportunistic (Sisson and Marginson, 1995). In seeking the appropriate recipe for managing employees during the 1980s many managers saw an opportunity to reduce the influence of unions. This involved a secular (if disputed) shift towards unitarism as managers reasserted their prerogative over employees at work. Initially, in the 1980s this appeared in an aggressive form of 'macho-management' as senior executives, often in state-owned industries, attacked unions and the customs and practices entrenched in many workplaces (Purcell, 1982). However, most companies did not derecognise unions and commentators noted that 'the lack of clarity about how industrial relations fits with the new initiatives will sooner or later have to be addressed' (Storey and Sisson, 1993: 27). In short, the main issue on the employee relations agenda appeared to be how to combine the individual and collective approaches in a complementary fashion.

The decline of collective regulation

As employment relations transformed we appear to have witnessed 'the end of institutional industrial relations' (Purcell, 1993). The third Workplace Industrial Relations Survey (WIRS 3) in 1990 underlined the extent to which the nature of British employee relations had changed and was no longer characterised by adversarial collective bargaining at workplace level (Millward *et al.*, 1992). Recent data confirm a further decline in the collective regulation of the employment relationship in the UK. Table 7.1 illustrates this change as captured by the Workplace Industrial Relations Surveys in terms of changes to union presence (the presence of one or more union members in a workplace), union membership density (percentage of employees who are union members), union recognition for negotiating pay and conditions of employment, coverage of collective bargaining (the proportion of employees in workplaces with recognised unions covered by collective bargaining) and joint consultative committees.

As almost one half of workplaces are effectively union-free a 'representation gap' (Towers, 1997) may have developed where managers operate without any independent employee voice. Three in five workplaces have no worker representatives at all (either union or non-union representatives), and this increases to nine out of ten workplaces where unions are not present (Cully *et al.*, 1999: 95).

Table 7.1 The decline of collective regulation in the Workplace Industrial Relations Surveys (figures related to percentages of workplaces)

	1980	1984	1990	1998
Union presence	73	73	64	54
Union membership density	65	58	47	36
Union recognition	65	65	53	42
Coverage of collective bargaining	–	70	54	41
Joint consultative committees	34	34	29	29

Source: Workplace Industrial Relations Surveys, see Cully *et al.*, 1999.

The decline in union recognition during the 1980s was in part due to changes in industrial relations law. However, the number of companies which have actively sought to derecognise existing trade unions in established workplaces has remained relatively small (Claydon, 1996). Although trade unions were out of favour with the UK government there was little evidence that union members wanted trade unions to abandon their traditional roles. In a survey of almost 11,000 union members conducted by Waddington and Whitston (1997) employees revealed they continued to join unions for collective protection and to improve terms and conditions (Table 7.2).

Table 7.2 What reasons do employees give for joining unions?

Reason	%
Support if I had a problem at work	72
Improved pay and conditions	36
Because I believe in trade unions	16
Free legal advice	15
Most people at work are members	14

Source: Waddington and Whitston, 1997: 521.

A more convincing explanation for union decline during the 1980s was the changing nature of the economy, with an increase in the service sector and reductions in the number of large manufacturing plants, manual work and the public sector. The traditional habitat for the UK's system of industrial relations based on adversarial collective bargaining was disappearing (Millward *et al.*, 1992). Although the decline in trade union representation continued throughout the 1990s there is evidence that the explanation has changed as 'almost all of the change arose because workplaces that joined the WIRS population between 1990 and 1998, even controlling for their sector and employment of part-time workers, were less likely to recognise unions than similar workplaces that had dropped out of the population' (Cully *et al.*, 1999: 241).

However, when we consider the scope and depth of joint consultation and bargaining trade union influence appears lower than current levels of union recognition indicate. It is difficult to assess the extent to which managers rely upon collective agreements with trade unions in workplaces. One study comparing collective agreements at the start and end of the 1980s outlined a relative stability in procedural agreements covering how issues are handled between management and labour (Dunn and Wright, 1994). A rather different picture emerged from case studies at plant level, indicating that managers were increasingly exercising their prerogative to make important changes, particularly in working methods (Geary, 1995). The latest data from the 1998 Workplace Employee Relations Surveys indicates a deeper 'hollowing out' of collective agreements. In workplaces where union representatives are present only a 'modest' level of joint regulation occurs. No negotiations occurred over any issues in one half of the workplaces with worker representatives present (Cully et al., 1999: 110). In a further 13 per cent of workplaces negotiations only occurred on non-pay issues, in 17 per cent negotiations only covered pay and in 22 per cent negotiations occurred over pay and one other issue. Managers in many workplaces appear to regard certain HR issues as 'off limits' to union representatives and do not even involve unions in providing information. In 53 per cent of workplaces with union representatives, representatives played no role at all in performance appraisals, in 52 per cent no role in recruitment, in 46 per cent no role in payment systems and in 43 per cent no role in training. This evidence suggests that in many cases trade union influence has 'withered on the vine' and where union representatives remain in place this resembles a unionised approach to industrial relations which in fact is little more than a 'hollow shell' (Hyman, 1997). Given these findings traditional debates on the most appropriate levels for collective bargaining (at the workplace, corporate or industry levels) and the balance between collective bargaining and joint consultation are giving way to the broader question of whether and on what terms trade unions are involved in any degree of joint workplace governance. The central role played by collective industrial relations has certainly declined but what types of non-union workplaces have emerged?

Non-union workplaces

According to one estimate the majority of UK workplaces had become non-union by 1995 (Cully and Woodland, 1996). In the classic account by Fox (1974) it was necessary for managers to enforce management prerogative by coercive power to justify a unitarist ideology and non-union status. Managers have often used a wide-ranging web of defences against unionisation that in their more extreme variants in the United States could combine 'sweet stuff' to make management policies more acceptable to employees, 'fear stuff' to discourage union joining and 'evil stuff' to demonise unions (Roy, 1980). A unitarist ideology can therefore include a variety of different management techniques. Returning to Figure 7.1 we can see that Purcell and Ahlstrand (1994) classify three non-union management styles in terms of whether an organisation recognises and develops individual employees. Companies adopting a 'sophisticated human relations' approach invest in staff development and use a wide range of human resource management policies to substitute for the services unions provide for members (a union substitution approach). Other non-union companies adopt a 'paternalist' approach and seek the loyalty and commitment of staff through consideration for employee welfare. Finally, some organisations maintain a 'Bleak House' strategy of cost minimisation and avoid union recruitment.

Several key commentators in the late 1980s identified the non-union sector as the most likely location for the development of HRM in the UK, foreseeing a growth in the 'sophisticated human relations' approach (Sisson, 1989). As some HRM models, but not all, are fundamentally unitarist, a non-union environment appeared well suited to the demands of developing committed and flexible employees as demonstrated by several large non-union US multinationals such as IBM, Hewlett Packard and Mars (Foulkes, 1980; Kochan et al., 1986). For example, IBM had combined corporate success, a positive employee relations climate of low conflict, low labour turnover and long service, with good pay and conditions. In addition, the company provided procedures to fulfil many of the functions met by unions, including a complex array of alternative procedures (a no redundancy policy, single status, equal opportunities policies, merit pay and performance assessments), a strong emphasis on internal communications and a grievance system.

Empirical support for the apparent link between sophisticated HRM and non-unionism was also provided by several case studies in the UK outlining a union substitution approach. In the case of 'Comco' explored by Cressey et al. (1985) employees identified strongly with the company and enjoyed 'greater benefits' and 'less disciplinary pressure'. Most employees working at an IBM plant in the UK studied by Dickson et al. (1988) were positively attached to the individualistic ethos of the company and perceived little need for union protection. Scott (1994) outlined a 'golden handcuffs' approach whereby employees in a chocolate works received good terms and conditions in return for accepting a high rate of effort and strict rules. Despite this evidence, initial studies indicated that non-union companies with a sophisticated approach to managing employees may remain the exception. A study of high-tech companies in the Southeast of England where we might expect companies to reproduce the IBM non-union model uncovered little evidence of sophisticated HRM, with companies either opportunistically avoiding unions or adopting the style of 'benevolent autocracies' (McLoughlin and Gourlay, 1994). Furthermore, the assumed benefits of a 'sophisticated human relations' approach have more recently come under closer scrutiny. Blyton and Turnbull (1994) suggest that Marks and Spencer, so often held up as an exemplar non-union company, simultaneously pursued a 'union substitution' strategy in retail outlets while forcing suppliers into a cost minimisation approach. In another case study, a steel plant had widely publicised the introduction of a HRM approach and subsequently derecognised trade unions. However, employee gains proved illusory, with managerial strategy geared towards attitudinal compliance, work intensification and the suppression of any counterbalancing trade union activity (Bacon, 1999).

HRM: a union or non-union phenomenon?

The evidence from the latest UK workplace survey (WERS98) confirms the finding of the 1990 survey (WIRS3, see Sisson, 1993: 206) that sophisticated HRM practices are to be found alongside union recognition mainly in larger workplaces and those in the public sector. In short, these surveys indicate that 'an active and strong union presence is compatible with the broad suite of high commitment management practices' (Cully *et al.*, 1999: 111). Furthermore, higher union density (the proportion of employees who are trade union members) is also associated with greater joint regulation and more high commitment management (HCM) practices. Figure 7.2 indicates that of the workplaces with no recognised unions, 41 per cent had none to three HCM practices, 54 per cent four to seven HCM practices, and 5 per cent eight or more. This compares unfavourably with 25 per cent of workplaces with recognised unions reporting eight or more high commitment management practices.

However, only 4 per cent of workplaces in the workplace survey combine a majority of the workforce in unions, collective negotiations over issues and at least one half of the measured list of high commitment work practices in place. There

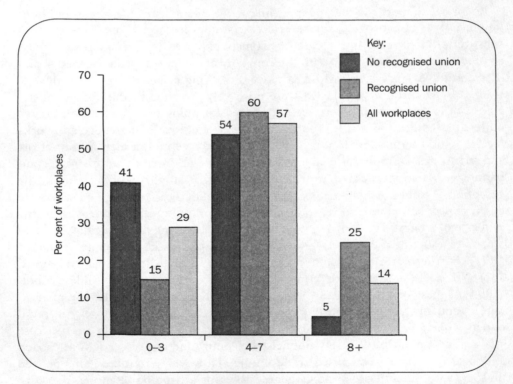

Figure 7.2 Number of high commitment management practices, by trade union recognition

Source: Cully et al., 1999

is, nevertheless, evidence from WERS98 that the combination of union recognition and HCM practices has a powerful effect on workplace performance. In the words of the WERS98 team 'workplaces with a recognised union and a majority of the HCM practices . . . did better than the average, and better than workplaces without recognition and a minority of these practices' (Cully *et al.*, 1999: 135). Sceptics of the impact of trade unions may still like to believe that adopting a wide range of HCM practices in a non-union environment may lead to even higher performance, but the fact that WERS98 could find so few such organisations casts some doubt upon this belief. In organisations where managers continue to recognise unions and are seeking to develop staff new approaches to industrial relations are developing involving 'partnership agreements'.

Partnership and the 'new unionism'

The election of 'New Labour' in 1997 has resulted in a new public policy environment. The government's Employment Relations Act 1999 and '*Fairness at Work*' programme have introduced new rights for trade unions and individual employees (Undy, 1999; Wood and Godard, 1999). In sum, this legislative programme involves a statutory route for union recognition, an extension of rights for individual employees, a national minimum wage and closer engagement with the social policies of the European Union. A central aim of this legislative programme is to 'replace the notion of conflict between employers and employees with the promotion of partnership in the longer term' (HMSO, 1998). The influence of a European approach was already felt as legislation obliged companies to establish a European works council if they employed over 1,000 employees in Europe and a minimum of 150 employees in at least two different member states. In sum, it is now commonplace to call for less destructive conflict and more co-operation to improve organisational productivity.

The issue of the balance between co-operation and conflict in union–management relations is a long-standing tension in employee relations. As the employment relationship encapsulates both shared and contrary interests the relationship between management and unions will contain elements of conflict and co-operation. As management and unions have begun to use the word 'partnership' it has become a contested term that appears inherently ambiguous and at times has no agreed meaning (Undy, 1999; Ackers and Payne, 1998). As Undy (1999: 318) has pointed out, 'What one party, or commentator, means by "partnership" is not necessarily shared by others.' As with so many terms in the area of employment relations, key pressure groups such as the TUC, the CBI and the Institute of Directors (IoDs) have sought to provide widely 'differing interpretations' of partnership (Undy, 1999: 318), defining the term for their own ends. The Institute of Personnel and Development, for example, explains that partnership 'has more to do with an approach to the relationship between employers and employees, individually and in groups, than it has to do with trade unions' (IPD, 1997: 8). Partnership can therefore be defined in both unitarist and pluralist terms. Rather unsurprisingly, the definition favoured by the TUC is pluralistic, with the stress placed on respecting union influence, whereas the IoD prefers a unitarist definition, whereby employees identify with the employer and trade unions are compliant to the wishes of management.

The Involvement and Participation Association, an independent pressure group, developed an influential definition of 'partnership' with leading companies and trade union leaders. This approach was endorsed by leading figures, including representatives from J. Sainsbury plc, the Boddington Group, the Post Office and the leaders of several trade unions (Involvement and Participation Association, 1992). This definition requires managers to declare security of employment as a key corporate objective; 'gainsharing' the results of success, and recognise the legitimacy of the employees' right to be informed, consulted and represented. In return, trade unions are required to renounce rigid job demarcations and commit to flexible working; give sympathetic consideration to the Continental model of representation of the whole workforce by means of election of representatives to new works councils, and recognise and then co-promote employee involvement methods. Case 7.2 invites you to consider the extent to which you feel companies and unions are able to sign up to a partnership agenda.

Given the lack of a general consensus on the meaning of industrial relations partnerships, it may be surprising that the term has acquired such a topical currency. A principal reason why the concept has taken hold is that it offers an industrial relations solution to the low competitiveness of much of UK industry. In this respect, partnership is no different from previous legislative changes that have sought to improve organisational performance through changes in industrial relations. Influential US literature suggests that in some companies managers may be able to forge a strategic linkage between industrial relations and HRM initiatives to create 'mutual gains enterprises' (Kochan and Osterman, 1994; Appelbaum and Batt, 1994). In such enterprises important changes are introduced in the organisation of work to enhance productivity, to the mutual benefit of employees, unions and management acting in coalition.

The signing of partnership agreements is of potential importance (IRS, 1997) although to date there is little evidence that they have become spread beyond around 40 companies. If partnerships are to become further established in UK industrial relations then managers and unions must find a workable balance between a number of key tensions beyond the above-mentioned disputes as to the meaning of the concept. The first tension is that workable partnership agreements appear to require a strategic and long-term commitment by managers to working closely with unions in the tradition of companies labelled 'sophisticated moderns' by Fox (1974). If managers are simply behaving in a short-term, contradictory or opportunistic manner then genuine industrial relations partnerships are unlikely to endure. For example, at the Royal Mail several partnership initiatives have struggled, primarily because some managers in the company are not firmly behind the partnership approach (see Bacon and Storey, 2000; Bacon and Storey, 1996).

The second tension, not unconnected to the first, is to what extent management and unions are able to commit fully to a single strategy of co-operative industrial relations. If partnerships do not secure the types of compliant trade unionism required in the CBI's definition of partnership then management commitment to such agreements may prove half-hearted. Similarly, at the same time as the TUC is supporting partnership agreements it is also pursuing an organising and campaigning approach to membership growth (Heery, 1998). It may prove difficult for unions to convince a company to sign a meaningful partnership agreement in one plant while actively recruiting union members against the wishes of the same or a similar company in another plant.

The third tension is whether partnership agreements form part of a longer-term strategy to marginalise trade unions rather than an alternative. Many observers critical of the co-operative relationships between managers and unions that are central to partnership agreements have highlighted continued employer attacks on unions (Claydon, 1989, 1996; Gall and McKay, 1994; Kelly, 1996; Smith and Morton, 1993). Although partnerships are frequently presented as a step away from attempts to derecognise trade unions this may not be the case. Evidence on this matter is not yet conclusive. Whereas one recent review of partnership agreements in six organisations reported that 'none gave serious consideration to ending recognition' (IDS, 1998: 4), a study of management attempts to restructure industrial relations in ten organisations (Bacon and Storey, 2000) revealed that derecognition had been more seriously explored. In the latter study, the new agreements signed with trade unions did not appear to reflect long-term commitments to working with trade unions nor sophisticated moves towards derecognition. Managers appeared to display unitarist preferences. However, for pragmatic reasons – for instance, the desire to maintain the trust of employees – they were willing to involve unions in joint regulation albeit within parameters managers attempted to control. In many workplaces union representatives feel they have no option but to accept management terms and union support for partnership resembles a resigned compliance. For example, in the case of United Distillers trade unions either signed the partnership agreement on offer or faced 'de facto derecognition' (Marks *et al.*, 1998: 222).

Finally, it is not yet clear whether partnership agreements will deliver greater returns for managers and trade unions. If returns are not forthcoming for either party then enthusiasm for the partnership approach may wane. Kelly (1996) has argued that, a priori, a union strategy of moderation is inferior in many respects to a militant stance. Union moderation is associated by Kelly with: eroding the willingness and capacity of union members to resist employers; inhibiting the growth of workplace union organisation; generating apathy among union members; involving union 'give' and management 'take'; resulting in attempts to drive down terms and conditions of employment and failing to genuinely represent member grievances. The key differences between militant and moderate union positions are highlighted in Case 7.3.

The extent to which Kelly is correct and neither unions nor employees will benefit from partnership agreements is an interesting question. Certainly, the number of partnership agreements signed between unions and management has increased, but remains low overall. There is little evidence that employers are able to offer the job security guarantees that unions seek or that trade unions are able to prevent managers unilaterally imposing changes in work organisation in order to bring managers to sign partnership agreements.

Conclusions

In this chapter we have argued that managers in the majority of workplaces no longer appear to support or utilise collective industrial relations in their employee management strategies. Sisson and Storey (2000: x) have recently restated that 'managing the employment relationship will demand both an individual and a collective perspective' in forthcoming years. However, recent evidence suggests that managers in few workplaces have sought to balance an individual and collective approach to employee management. Figure 7.3 presents a summary drawing upon the findings from WERS98 of the current pattern of employee relations. The predominant employee relations style in the British workplace is not to manage both individualism and collectivism, it is to manage neither. Considering all the

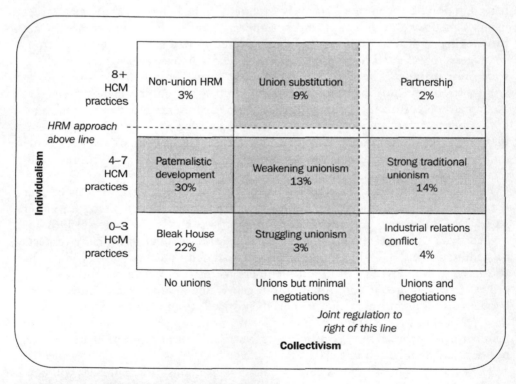

Figure 7.3 New patterns of employee relations.

workplaces which fall into the bottom left-hand quadrant of the dotted lines, approximately seven in ten (68 per cent) operate fewer than one-half of 15 high-commitment management practices and do not involve trade unions in negotiations on matters other than pay. Fifty-two per cent of workplaces in this quadrant do not recognise trade unions.

Approximately 14 per cent of workplaces could be described as pursuing a HRM approach but only 5 per cent appeared to combine individualism with either a union exclusion or partnership approach. The majority of workplaces appear to be marginalising unions, and although they remain present significant negotiations do not occur. It is tempting to classify organisations falling into the four corner boxes as having an apparently settled employee relations strategy that is unlikely to change in the near future. The numerous workplaces which fall into the 'Bleak House' classification (approximately 22 per cent) are focused upon cost reduction and will resist any attempts at unionisation. They are likely to be smaller workplaces in such sectors as wholesale and retail, hotels and restaurants. The small number of organisations which negotiate with unions but eschew developing employees ('industrial relations traditional') may be resigned to dealing with unions in the absence of a more sophisticated approach to managing employees. A few genuine examples of partnership may flourish in the current political climate but the overall number of such workplaces remains small. Companies adopting non-union HRM are likely to feel they have permanently resolved the union issue.

This leaves approximately 69 per cent of organisations (in the shaded areas of Figure 7.3) which currently operate with an opportunistic mixture of labour management policies. Organisations currently occupying these different positions face somewhat different dilemmas. Those currently using HRM policies to substitute for negotiating with unions but still recognising unions ('union substitution') may at some point in the future sign partnership deals with trade unions to share more decision-making and/or further erode union influence. Companies with 'strong traditional unionism' may further develop HR policies either to substitute for unions or develop a partnership approach. From an industrial relations perspective the most significant developments may occur within the 'weakening unionism' category. Although trade unions in these workplaces are involved in fewer negotiations managers have not developed high-commitment management practices to replace the services unions provide for members in terms of voicing collective grievances and seeking to improve terms and conditions. It would appear to be in this category of workplaces that trade unions may target recruitment to increase union density and exert greater influence. The Employment Relations Act 1999 encourages union recruitment and organising efforts as it provides a statutory recognition procedure. As so few organisations appear to have resolved the issue of managing employees through individual or collective means they are likely to face continued pressure from individual employees for increased training and more satisfying work and from employee representatives for a greater say in workplace governance.

The UK's largest private sector employers

Nick Bacon

Below is a list of the largest private sector employers in the UK taken from *Labour Research*. Which do you think:

(a) Do not recognise trade unions;
(b) Recognise and negotiate with trade unions;
(c) Recognise trade unions but only for the purposes of consultation or to represent individual employees?

Explain your decisions.

Table 7.3

Tesco	153,800	Retail – supermarkets
J Sainsbury	150,700	Retail – supermarkets
BT	125,800	Telecommunications
Lloyds-TSB	82,000	Banking and finance
Whitbread	80,000	Food and drink
Boots Co.	75,000	Retail and pharmaceuticals
Asda Group	73,700	Retail – supermarkets
Safeway Group	70,400	Retail – supermarkets
Kingfisher	69,600	Retail
Bass	67,500	Brewing and leisure
National Westminster	66,000	Banking and finance
Rentokil Initial	65,000	Business services
Barclays	60,800	Banking and finance
Granada Group	58,000	Leisure
Marks and Spencer	54,900	Retail
General Electric Co.	52,300	Electronics
HSBC Holding (Midland Bank)	50,000	Banking and finance
British Airways	47,700	Banking and finance
Allied Domecq	46,500	Food and drink
Somerfield	45,700	Retail – supermarket
Burton Group	43,700	Retail
British Steel	43,400	Steel Manufacturers
Ladbroke Group	42,000	Leisure
John Lewis Partnership	41,100	Retail – department stores
BMW – Rover Group	39,000	Motor manufacture
Scottish and Newcastle	39,000	Brewing and leisure
British Aerospace	38,500	Aerospace and engineering
MacDonald's Restaurants	36,700	Food retail
Halifax	36,000	Banking and finance
Ford	35,900	Motor manufacturing
Compass Group	35,700	Catering
Co-operative Wholesale Society	35,000	Banking, insurance, retail
OCS Group	35,000	Cleaning
Sears	32,600	Retail
Rolls Royce	31,200	Aerospace and engineering
Rank Organisation	30,300	Leisure and films
Greenhalls Group	30,100	Brewing, food, hotels
WH Smith	30,000	Retail
Royal & Sun Alliance	27,800	Insurance
Securicor Group	27,500	Security services
Wm Morrison Supermarkets	27,000	Retail – supermarkets
Unigate	27,000	Food manufacture
Lucas Varity	26,800	Engineering
BTR	26,600	Industrial conglomerate
Kwik Save Group	26,000	Retail

The principles and practices of partnership with trade unions

Nick Bacon

As explained in Chapter 6, one option for managers and trade unions is to establish a partnership agreement. However, successful agreements depend upon a serious commitment to the principles and practices of partnership. Thinking of the last organisation you worked for, an organisation you know well or your own personal 'frame of reference', to what extent do you agree or disagree with the following statements? Your answers indicate whether organisations could be committed to a partnership agreement. *(Circle one number for each statement)*

	Agree	Neutral	Disagree
Personnel managers worry about trade unions, most other senior managers would rather they disappear.	1	2	3
Trade unions don't have a useful function in organisations.	1	2	3
All managers should share all information, however sensitive, with unions.	1	2	3
Managers can get employees to work hard without making concessions to unions.	1	2	3
Job security is a myth in today's world.	1	2	3
To attract top managers organisations have to offer extra incentives such as private health insurance that are too expensive to give to all employees.	1	2	3
Companies should train all employees to a high level even though some will leave.	1	2	3

What should trade unions do?

Nick Bacon

In Chapter 7 we outlined Kelly's (1996) argument that trade unions would benefit from a militant rather than a moderate stance. Reading through the following statements, indicate the extent to which you believe trade unions should adopt a moderate or militant stance. Explain your choices.

Trade unions should:

Union militancy		Union moderation
Make ambitious demands	or	Make moderate demands
Offer few concessions	or	Offer many concessions
Rely on members' activity	or	Rely on managers' good will
Rely on collective bargaining	or	Rely on consultation
Frequently threaten industrial action	or	Rarely threaten industrial action
Believe in a basic conflict of interests	or	Believe in a basic common interest

Employee relations at North Fire Brigade

Tom Redman and Ed Snape

Background

North Fire Brigade has a current establishment of 700 whole-time operational fire-fighters located in twelve fire stations across the region with a non-uniformed support staff of 100. In addition there are 72 part-time retained firefighters located in a further six stations. Firefighting in the UK is still virtually an exclusively male occupation when compared to the slow but steady inroads of women firefighters in some other countries. North Brigade is no different in this respect, not employing a single woman firefighter. The number of firefighters per station varies from around 30 in the smallest to over 100 in the largest. Each firefighter is a member of one of four watches (red, white, blue, and green), with each watch working for two day and two night shifts on a 42-hour week duty system. Despite the introduction of new managerial practices in the 1990s the organisation of fire fighting remains hierarchical and bureaucratised, with ten levels separating the chief officer and qualified firefighter posts.

The nature of the firefighters' job makes heavy demands in terms of personal discipline and commitment to teamwork and results in a strongly collectivist work ethic. In the words of a previous general secretary of the FBU:

> When all is said and done, at the end of it firefighting comes to this: that a small number of people will go into a darkened smoke-logged building not knowing what they are going to meet, having faith in each other, in the long run prepared to risk their lives to save the lives of other people. In the long run, no matter what transformation we effect in the Fire Service, firefighting in its final stages remains just that. And we do not forget it.

This collectivist work ethic imparts high levels of loyalty and discipline to the union. North Brigade has a union density rate of nearly 100 per cent amongst uniformed staff. The TUC-affiliated FBU is the dominant trade union for fire-fighters, particularly for lower grades, with the NAFO (and CACFOA) having very limited representation amongst higher-grade employees at station officer and above. Non-uniformed staff are represented by Unison. The FBU has ambitions to be an industrial union for firefighting, with its first object being 'to organise all uniformed employees'. There has been a recent history of competition between the fire service unions, with some acrimonious disputes arising over representation rights.

Collective bargaining is organised through a National Joint Council composed on the employer's side of representatives made up of various local authority bodies. However, the national bargaining system was under pressure from management initiatives to increase the range of local bargaining, in particular to reduce the scope of the National Scheme of Conditions of Service or 'Grey Book'. Here a critical report from the Audit Commission in 1995 added momentum to a move to more local bargaining. The report suggested the national framework was constraining brigade effectiveness by preventing some possible improvements in efficiency. However, the FBU see this less as a need for local flexibility and more as a simple prelude to a concerted attack on the levels of terms and conditions provided by national bargaining arrangements. Local bargaining currently occurs between four key union representatives (from a brigade committee of some 12 representatives) and the Deputy Chief Fire Officer and Assistant Chief Officers. Typical bargaining issues include changes to 'detached' duties (terms for redeploying staff between stations), the duty mix of whole-time and retained firefighters, and meal arrangements.

Cost containment

Although the fire service has probably not been on the receiving end of some of the more drastic cutbacks in public spending over the last decade, there is now considerable pressure for cost containment and 'efficiency' within the sector. According to one senior and long-serving manager:

> In the past people accepted we put out fires and that somehow was enough. Now with the general closer scrutiny we have from auditing and performance indicators and the like, it is not sufficient. We have to be much more efficient and service-minded nowadays.

Such pressures are occurring at a time of increasing demand for fire services. The FBU estimates an increase of 87 per cent in calls to the fire service between 1979 and 1998. The funding for fire services in England is calculated by the Standard Spending Assessment (SSA) formula. The majority of English County Councils, particularly rural ones, exceed their SSA allocation. North Brigade is no exception, with 1998 seeing a budget shortfall of over £2 million needed to support the current establishment and existing levels of service provision. In particular, the physical characteristics of North Brigade's geographical location, with a large concentration of heavy chemical industries, are felt to necessitate a higher level of spending than the SSA allocation.

More recently, the cost and efficiency pressures generated by 'Best Value' were occupying managerial attention. Here the brigade had set up task teams to investigate the cost reduction potential of greater collaboration with other regional brigades in areas such as the purchasing of uniforms and equipment, training, the provision of payroll services and, more controversially, the use of joint control centres. Task teams had also been set up to examine the potential for generating income by providing training courses for industry and other fire services where

North Brigade had particular expertise, for example, in relation to dealing with hazardous materials. Increasingly, the mounting pressure for cost containment and efficiency was impacting on the industrial relations climate of the industry as management attempted to reduce costs but at the same time improve service quality levels.

Industrial relations

Industrial relations in the brigade were perceived as being typical for the industry with fewer disputes occurring in North Brigade than some other more 'militant' brigades, recent protracted disputes over terms and conditions and establishment level having occurred in Merseyside, Derbyshire and, most recently, Essex. The latter three and a half-month dispute involved over 20 strikes. Following the resolution of the dispute, the Essex MP Teresa Gorman, in an open letter to Essex Fire Brigade committee, accused the FBU of 'blackmailing' and 'shroud-waving' to protect outdated practices and overgenerous terms and conditions:

> All Britain's fire services are far too overstaffed. It is one of the last of the dinosaur industries clinging to feather bedding, using shroud-waving and blackmail to prevent the modernisation of the service. The Algarve is stuffed with healthy young British males, living comfortably, their incomes supplemented by disabled pensions from the fire service. In Arizona, when the fire service was privatised, it became obvious that 80 per cent of all 'calls' could be dealt with by two men in a fast car. And the cost of the service was halved. Who will be the first council to have an open debate on privatising its fire services and let some fresh air in to the argument?

Managers at North Brigade felt the relatively dispute-free recent past could be explained by an open relationship with the union and more 'responsible' union leaders.

> We accommodate them (the union) with whatever information they want with regard to budgets. There is a standing instruction that the union can have whatever information the Brigade has. If they want information on, say, the capital or revenue budgets they can go and get it with my authority. There are no secrets here. It comes from us being able to say to the union 'We have not got the money to do this or that. There are the figures. If you can find X thousand pounds, you can have it'.

Senior management emphasised the importance of good communication with their employees, and the need for it, given a generally better-educated workforce. Employee involvement mechanisms include a brigade Intranet, newsletters, senior management visits and informal talks 'with the troops in the stations'. The latter was seen to be particularly important to counter the perceived gulf between headquarters and the stations. According to one manager, North Brigade now had 'thinking union officers rather than the table bangers of the past'. Trade union interviewees also reported that the current senior management was, to a large extent, more willing to listen to their concerns, particularly when compared to some previous senior managers, who were reluctant even to speak to other managers below a certain rank, let alone union representatives. Union–management co-operation had extended in the recent past to a joint delegation to lobby Parliament on SSA levels.

An index of the generally positive industrial relations climate of the 1990s in North Brigade was the low level of formal grievances, with few grievances reaching the 'failure to agree' stage. This was seen as a considerable achievement when set against a backcloth of cost containment, the level of organisational change and the high potential for conflict in the character of firefighting disputes. Here the nature of an emergency led to 'life or death' service results in many disputes, according to both union representatives and managers, involving some very emotional and moral arguments being thrown around. Thus, the brigade had successfully managed to reduce its establishment levels by about 10 per cent over the last eight years without any industrial action occurring. Most recently in 1998 the brigade had removed two fireboats from service and this had resulted in the loss of 15 jobs through natural wastage. Here the union officers felt they had provided 'realistic opposition' to the cuts – the original management proposal had been to lose 43 jobs through compulsory redundancy.

However, several developments were underway which had high potential for straining future management–union relationships. In particular, a number of industry-wide issues, such as the 1998 review of the national pension scheme and the move to local bargaining, were causing concern for local relationships between management and unions. The new pension proposals contained a recommendation for a two-tier scheme with considerably reduced benefits for new starters and a diminution of terms for existing staff. Equally, increasing attempts by various brigades to renegotiate and in some cases 'buy-out' 'Grey Book' conditions was a major source of instability which was seen as eventually posing considerable problems for industrial relations in North Brigade. Local issues included managerial attempts to introduce performance appraisal; appraisal-related pay, revised duty systems and a capability procedure, all of which the union had strongly resisted. Union representatives also reported increasing interest by management in the performance of individual firefighters and increased pressure on sickness levels via the introduction of formal interview panels. A key union concern here was that such pressure resulted in some employees coming to work in an unfit state and thus becoming a danger to themselves and their colleagues. Firefighters in North Brigade had also traditionally had two days' extra annual leave above the national minimum and management was being subjected to increasing pressure from the district Audit Office to reduce this.

As a result there had been a recent increase in grievance activity in disputes, with several of these reaching the 'failure to agree' stage. Here disputes varied from the cutback of hot meals on weekend shifts; a demarcation dispute (with the ambulance service) over the use of defibrillators and basic trauma life support and management's attempt to obtain a 'seamless ambulance and fire fighting service'; management attempts to get full-time staff to undertake duties traditionally carried out by retained firemen, and more flexible rostering. Union representatives reported that they were currently working very hard to hold back the members and a senior manager lamented that, given the current IR climate, a capability procedure he had been working on for two years was 'not worth the hassle of getting it out of the drawer'. According to one union representative:

> We may have been guilty of crying wolf with the members in the past. You know, always telling them that this year the management are coming for us. But now it looks like it is probably going to happen.

Thus, the industrial relations climate was generally perceived as deteriorating somewhat under the wider pressures on the industry. For example, the union representatives reported that they were becoming increasingly more sceptical of management's espoused rhetoric of seeking a 'partnership' with the union. One union representative described management's claim of having an open door policy as being 'just words' as union concerns were now more often met by 'shoulder shrugging' and 'There is no alternative' statements. Union interviewees also reported the organisational culture of the brigade changing under the creeping use of business language and new managerial 'speak'. Here the language of 'customer service' was seen as a veil for management pushing through desired organisational changes in the search for efficiency and cost cutting. Thus:

> We used to have the feel of being a big family doing a key public service. Now it very much feels like we are working for a business. (union representative)

The 'us and them' divide in the brigade was thus perceived by union representatives as increasing. For example, in relation to the meal dispute one union representative commented that 'It now seems we cannot get a meal but they can have big cars'.

Note: The amount of funding allocated to run fire services in England is calculated using a formula know as the Standard Spending Assessment. In Scotland it is the Grant Aided Expenditure, in Wales the Revenue Support Grant and in Northern Ireland a block grant for the funding of all services.

Questions

1. Management at North Brigade is very concerned that a worsening national IR environment will undermine their relatively good local IR climate. What would you advise them to do in order to protect local relationships in such conditions?

2. Many commentators have suggested that the right to strike should be removed from essential public services, such as firefighting. Do you agree with this view? What issues would be raised by such a development?

3. Fire brigades are currently under considerable pressure to increase the number of women firefighters in the service. What IR issues would be raised by the increased recruitment of women firefighters?

References to Chapter 7

Ackers, P. and Payne, J. (1998) 'British trade unions and social partnership: rhetoric, reality and strategy', *International Journal of Human Resource Management*, 9: 529–50.

Appelbaum, R. and Batt, R. (1994) *The New American Workplace*. Ithaca: ILR Press.

Bacon, N. (1999) 'Union derecognition and the new human relations: a steel industry case study', *Work, Employment and Society*, 13(1): 1–17.

Bacon, N. and Storey, J. (1996) 'Individualism and collectivism and the changing role of trade unions' in Ackers, P., Smith, C. and Smith, P. (eds) *The New Workplace and Trade Unionism*, London, Routledge, 1–40.

Bacon, N. and Storey, J. (2000) 'New employee relations strategies: towards individualism or partnership', *British Journal of Industrial Relations*, forthcoming.

Blyton, P. and Turnbull, P. (1994) *The Dynamics of Employee Relations*, London: Macmillan.

Claydon, T. (1989) 'Union de-recognition in Britain in the 1980s', *British Journal of Industrial Relations*, 27: 214–23.

Claydon, T. (1996) 'Union recognition: a re-examination', in Beardwell, I. (ed) *Contemporary Industrial Relations*, Oxford: Oxford University Press.

Cressey, P., Eldridge, J. and MacInnes, J. (1985) *Just Managing: Authority and Democracy in Industry*, Milton Keynes: Open University Press.

Cully, M. and Woodland, S. (1996) 'Trade union membership and recognition: an analysis of data from the 1995 Labour Force Survey', *Labour Market Trends*, May: 215–25 (Norwich: HMSO).

Cully, M., Woodland, S., O'Reilly, A., Dix, G., Millward, N., Bryson, A., and Forth, J. (1998) *The 1998 Workplaces Employee Relations Survey: First Findings*, London: Department of Trade and Industry.

Cully, M., Woodland, S., O'Reilly, A. and Dix, G. (1999) *Britain at Work*, London: Routledge.

Dickson, T., McLachlan, M.V., Prior, P. and Swales, K. (1988) 'Big blue and the union: IBM, individualism and trade union strategy', *Work, Employment and Society*, 2: 506–20.

Dunn, S., and Wright, M. (1994) 'Maintaining the "status quo": An analysis of the contents of British collective agreements 1979–1990', *British Journal of Industrial Relations*, 32: 23–46.

Edwards, P. (1990) 'The politics of conflict and consent', *Journal of Economic Behaviour and Organization*, 13: 41–61.

Edwards, P. (1995) 'The employment relationship', in P. Edwards (ed) *Industrial Relations*, Oxford: Blackwell, 3–26.

Edwards, P. *et al.* (1998) 'Great Britain: from partial collectivism to neo-liberalism to where?', in Ferner, A., and Hyman, R. (eds) *Changing Industrial Relations in Europe*, Oxford: Blackwell, 1–54.

Flanders, A. (1970) *Management and Unions: The Theory and Reform of Industrial Relations*, London: Faber.

Foulkes, F. K. (1980) *Personnel Policies in Large Non-union Companies*, Englewood Cliffs, NJ: Prentice Hall.

Fox, A. (1966) 'Industrial sociology and industrial relations', *Royal Commission Research Paper* No. 3, London: HMSO.

Fox, A. (1974) *Beyond Contract: Work, Power and Trust Relations*, London: Faber and Faber.

Freeman, R.B. and Medoff, J.L. (1984) *What Do Unions Do?*, New York: Basic Books.

Gall, G. and McKay, S. (1994) 'Trade union de-recognition in Britain 1988-94', *British Journal of Industrial Relations*, 32: 433–48.

Geary, J. (1995) 'Work practices: the structure of work', in P. Edwards (ed) *Industrial Relations*, Oxford: Blackwell, 368–96.

Guest, D. (1987). 'Human resource management and industrial relations', *Journal of Management Studies*, 24(5): 503–21.

Guest, D. (1989) 'Human resource management: its implications for industrial relations and trade unions', in J. Storey, (ed) *New Perspectives in Human Resource Management*, London: Routledge, 41–55.

Guest, D. (1990). 'Human resource management and the American Dream', *Journal of Management Studies*, 27(4): 378–97.

Guest, D. (1995). 'Human resource management, trade unions and industrial relations', in Storey, J. (ed) *Human Resource Management: A Critical Text*, London: Routledge, 110–41.

Guest, D. and Hoque, K. (1994) 'The good, the bad and the ugly: Employment relations in new non-union workplaces', *Human Resource Management Journal*, 5: 1–14.

Heery, E. (1996) 'The new new unionism', in Beardwell, I. (ed) *Contemporary Industrial Relations*, Oxford: Oxford University Press, 175–202.

Heery, E. (1998) 'The re-launch of the Trades Union Congress', *British Journal of Industrial Relations*, 36: 339–60.

HMSO (1998) *Fairness at Work*, White Paper.

Hyman, R. (1987) 'Strategy or structure? Capital, Labour and Control', *Work, Employment and Society*, 1(1): 25–55.

Hyman, R. (1997) 'The future of employee representation', *British Journal of Industrial Relations*, 35(3): 309–36.

IDS (1998) 'Partnership agreements', *IDS Study 656*, October.

Institute of Directors (1994) Evidence presented to the Employment Committee Enquiry, *The Future of Trade Unions*, HC 676-II, London: HMSO.

Involvement and Participation Association (1992) *Towards Industrial Partnership: A New Approach to Management Union Relations*, London: IPA.

IPD (1997) *Employment Relations into the 21st Century*, London: Institute of Personnel and Development.

IRS (1997) Partnership at work: a survey. *Employment Trends*, 645, December: 3–24.

Kelly, J. (1996) 'Union militancy and social partnership', in Ackers, P., Smith, C. and Smith, P. (eds) *The New Workplace and Trade Unionism*, London: Routledge, 41–76.

Kitay, J. and Marchington, M. (1996) 'A review and critique of workplace industrial relations typologies', *Human Relations*, 49(10): 1263–90.

Kochan, T. and Osterman, P. (1994) *The Mutual Gains Enterprise*, Cambridge, Mass: Harvard Business School Press.

Kochan, T., Katz, H. and McKersie, B. (1986) *The Transformation of American Industrial Relations*, New York: Basic Books.

Marchington, M. and Parker, P. (1990) *Changing Patterns of Employee Relations*, Hemel Hempstead: Harvester Wheatsheaf.

Marks, A., Findlay, P., Hine, J., McKinlay, A. and Thompson, P. (1998) 'The politics of partnership? Innovation in employment relations in the Scottish spirits industry', *British Journal of Industrial Relations*, 36(2): 209–26.

McLoughlin, I. and Gourlay, S. (1994) *Enterprise Without Unions: Industrial Relations in the Non-Union Firm*, Milton Keynes: Open University Press.

Millward, N., Stevens, M., Smart, D. and Hawes, W.R. (1992) *Workplace Industrial Relations in Transition*, Dartmouth: Aldershot.

Monks, J. (1998) 'Trade unions, enterprise and the future', in Sparrow, P. and Marchington, M. (eds) *Human Resource Management: The New Agenda*, London: Pitman, 171–9.

Poole, M., and Mansfield, R. (1993) 'Patterns of continuity and change in managerial attitudes and behaviour in industrial relations 1980–90', *British Journal of Industrial Relations*, 31(1): 11–36.

Purcell, J. (1982) 'Macho managers and the new industrial relations', *Employee Relations*, 4(1): 3–5.

Purcell, J. (1987) 'Mapping management styles in employee relations', *Journal of Management Studies*, 24(5): 533–48.

Purcell, J. (1991) 'The rediscovery of management prerogative: the management of labour relations in the 1980s', *Oxford Review of Economic Policy*, 7(1): 33–43.

Purcell, J. (1993) 'The end of institutional industrial relations', *Political Quarterly*, 64(1): 6–23.

Purcell, J. and Ahlstrand, B. (1994) *Human Resource Management in the Multi-Divisional Company*, Oxford: Oxford University Press.

Purcell, J. and Sisson, K. (1983) 'Strategies and practice in the management of industrial relations', in G. Bain (ed) *Industrial Relations in Britain*, Oxford: Blackwell.

Roy, D. (1980) 'Fear stuff, sweet stuff and evil stuff: management's defences against unionization in the South', in T. Nichols (ed) *Capital and Labour: A Marxist Primer*, Glasgow: Fontana, 395–415.

Scott, A. (1994) *Willing Slaves?*, Cambridge: Cambridge University Press.

Sisson, K. (1989) 'Personnel management in transition?', in Sisson, K. (ed) *Personnel Management in Britain*, Oxford: Blackwell.

Sisson, K. (1993) 'In Search of HRM', *British Journal of Industrial Relations*, 31(2): 201–10.

Sisson, K. (ed) (1994) *Personnel Management*, Oxford: Blackwell.

Sisson, K. (1995) 'Human resource management and the personnel function', in Storey, J. (ed) *Human Resource Management: A Critical Test*, London: Routledge, 87–109.

Sisson, K., and Marginson, P. (1995) 'Management: systems, structures and strategy', in Edwards, P. (ed) *Industrial Relations*, Oxford: Blackwell, 89–122.

Sisson, K., and Storey, J. (2000) *The Realities of Human Resource Management*, Buckingham: Open University Press.

Smith, P. and Morton, G. (1993) 'Union exclusion and decollectivization of industrial relations in contemporary Britain', *British Journal of Industrial Relations*, 31(1): 97–114.

Storey, J. (1992) *Developments in the Management of Human Resources*, Oxford: Blackwell.

Storey, J., and Bacon, N. (1993) 'Individualism and collectivism: into the 1990s', *International Journal of Human Resource Management*, 4(3): 665–84.

Storey, J., Bacon, N., Edmonds, J. and Wyatt, P. (1993) 'The new agenda and human resource management: a roundtable discussion with John Edmonds', *Human Resource Management Journal*, 4(1): 63–70.

Storey, J. and Sisson, K. (1993) *Managing Human Resources and Industrial Relations*, Milton Keynes: Open University Press.

Towers, B. (1997) *The Representation Gap*, Oxford: Oxford University Press.

TUC (1993) Evidence presented to the Employment Committee Enquiry, *The Future of Trade Unions*, HC 676-II, 18 October, London: HMSO.

Undy, R. (1999) 'Annual review article: New Labour's "Industrial Relations Settlement": The Third Way?', *British Journal of Industrial Relations*, 37(2): 315–36.

Waddington, J. and Whitston, C. (1997) 'Why do people join unions in a period of membership decline', *British Journal of Industrial Relations*, 35(4): 515–46.

Wood, S. (1997) *Statutory Union Recognition*, Institute of Personnel and Development, London.

Wood, S. and Godard, J. (1999) 'The statutory union recognition procedure in the Employment Relations Bill: A comparative analysis', *British Journal of Industrial Relations*, 37: 203–44.

TOPIC SUMMARY SHEET

What are the key learning points from this topic?

TOPIC 9 – GRIEVANCE AND DISCIPLINE

Why study this topic?

It is unrealistic to expect that organisations will be free from conflict. This conflict can arise from employee behaviour or from actions taken by the organisation which have a direct impact on the workforce.

This chapter examines the role of the grievance procedure in organisations. It also discusses how the grievance procedure should be devised and implemented to ensure that it acts as an effective process to protect both employee and employer alike.

The discipline process is also an area which employees and organisations should have significant knowledge of. In the future you may be involved in administering organisational discipline, (hopefully not receiving it!) so it is important to familiarise yourself with the procedures as well as what is considered best practice. Incorrectly followed organisational disciplinary procedures can often result in employment tribunals, therefore it is important to know how to conduct this process fairly and effectively.

Blackboard

E-tivity 9: Grievance and discipline

CHAPTER 25

GRIEVANCE AND DISCIPLINE

THE OBJECTIVES OF THIS CHAPTER ARE TO:

1 EXAMINE THE NATURE AND EXPLAIN THE PLACE OF GRIEVANCE AND DISCIPLINE IN THE EMPLOYMENT CONTRACT

2 REVIEW THE MILGRAM EXPERIMENTS WITH OBEDIENCE AND USE THEM TO EXPLAIN OUR RESPONSE TO AUTHORITY

3 EXPLAIN THE FRAMEWORK OF ORGANISATIONAL JUSTICE IN THE BUSINESS

4 EXPLAIN GRIEVANCE AND DISCIPLINE PROCEDURES

Grievance and discipline are awkward words nowadays. They sound rather solemn and forbidding, more suitable for a nineteenth-century workhouse than a twenty-first-century business. They certainly have no place in the thinking of Britain's favourite entrepreneur, Sir Richard Branson:

> If you have the right people in place, treat them well and trust them, they will produce happy customers and the necessary profits to carry on and expand the work. (quoted in Handy 1999, p. 86)

We use the words as technical terms to describe the breakdown of mutual confidence between employer and employee, or between managers and managed. When someone starts work at an organisation there are mutual expectations that form the basis of the forthcoming working relationship. We explained in the opening chapter of this book how the maintenance of those mutual expectations is the central purpose of human resource management. Apart from what is written in the contract of employment, both parties will have expectations of what is to come. Employees are likely to expect, for instance, a congenial working situation with like-minded colleagues, opportunities to use existing skills and to acquire others, work that does not offend their personal value system, acceptable leadership and management from those more senior and opportunities to grow and mature. Employers will have expectations such as willing participation in the team, conscientious and imaginative use of existing skills and an ability to acquire others, compliance with reasonable instructions without quibbles, acceptance of the authority of those placed in authority and a willingness to be flexible and accept change.

That working relationship is sometimes going to go wrong. If the employee is dissatisfied, then there is potentially a grievance. If the employer is dissatisfied, there is the potential for a disciplinary situation. The two complementary processes are intended to find ways of avoiding the ultimate sanction of the employee quitting or being dismissed, but at the same time preparing the ground for those sanctions if all else fails.

Usually, the authority to be exercised in a business is impersonalised by the use of roles in order to make it more effective. If a colleague mentions to you that you have overspent your budget, your reaction might be proud bravado unless you knew that the colleague had a role such as company accountant, internal auditor or financial director. Everyone in a business has a role. Most people have several roles and each confers some authority. The canteen assistant who tells you that the steak and kidney pudding is off is more believable than the managing director conveying the same message. Normally in hospitals people wearing white coats and a stethoscope are seen as being more authoritative than people in white coats without a stethoscope.

Dependence on role is not always welcome to those in managerial positions, who are fond of using phrases like, 'I know how to get the best out of people' or 'I have a loyal staff'. This may partly be due to their perception of their role being to persuade the reluctant and command the respect of the unwilling by the use of personal leadership qualities, and it is indisputable that some managers are more effective with some groups of staff than with others, but there is more to it than personal skill: we are predisposed to obey those who outrank us in any hierarchy.

THE MILGRAM EXPERIMENTS WITH OBEDIENCE

Obedience is the reaction expected of people by those in authority positions, who prescribe actions which, but for that authority, might not necessarily have been carried out. Stanley Milgram (1974) conducted a series of experiments to investigate obedience to authority and highlighted the significance of obedience and the power of authority in our everyday lives.

Subjects were led to believe that a study of memory and learning was being carried out which involved giving progressively more severe electric shocks to a learner who gave incorrect answers to factual questions. If the learner gave the correct answer the reward was a further question; if the answer was incorrect there was the punishment of a mild electric shock. Each shock was more severe than the previous one. The 'learner' was not actually receiving shocks, but was a member of the experimental team simulating progressively greater distress, as the shocks were supposedly made stronger. Eighteen different experiments were conducted with over 1,000 subjects, with the circumstances between experiments varying. No matter how the variables were altered the subjects showed an astonishing compliance with authority even when delivering 'shocks' of 450 volts. Up to 65 per cent of subjects continued to obey throughout the experiment in the presence of a clear authority figure and as many as 20 per cent continued to obey when the authority figure was absent.

Milgram was dismayed by his results:

> With numbing regularity good people were seen to knuckle under to the demands of authority and perform actions that were callous and severe. Men who are in everyday life responsible and decent were seduced by the trappings of authority, by the control of their perceptions, and by the uncritical acceptance of the experimenter's definition of the situation into performing harsh acts. (1974, p. 123)

Our interest in Milgram's work is simply to demonstrate that we all have a predilection to obey instructions from authority figures, even if we do not want to. He points out that the act of entering a hierarchical system (such as any employing organisation) makes people see themselves acting as agents for carrying out the wishes of someone else, and this results in these people being in a different state, described as the agentic state. This is the opposite to the state of autonomy when individuals see themselves as acting on their own. Milgram then sets out the factors that lay the groundwork for obedience to authority.

1 **Family.** Parental regulation inculcates a respect for adult authority. Parental injunctions form the basis for moral imperatives, as commands to children have a dual function. 'Don't tell lies' is a moral injunction carrying a further implicit instruction: 'And obey me!' It is the implicit demand for obedience that remains the only consistent element across a range of explicit instructions.

2 **Institutional setting.** Children emerge from the family into an institutional system of authority: the school. Here they learn how to function in an organisation. They are regulated by teachers, but can see that the head teacher, the school governors and central government regulate the teachers themselves. Throughout this period they are in a subordinate position. When, as adults, they go to work it may be found that a certain level of dissent is allowable, but the overall situation is one in which they are to do a job prescribed by someone else.

3 Rewards. Compliance with authority is generally rewarded, while disobedience is frequently punished. Most significantly, promotion within the hierarchy not only rewards the individual but also ensures the continuity of the hierarchy.

4 Perception of authority. Authority is normatively supported: there is a shared expectation among people that certain institutions do, ordinarily, have a socially controlling figure. Also, the authority of the controlling figure is limited to the situation. The usher in a cinema wields authority, which vanishes on leaving the premises. As authority is expected it does not have to be asserted, merely presented.

5 Entry into the authority system. Having perceived an authority figure, an individual must then define that figure as relevant to the subject. The individual not only takes the voluntary step of deciding which authority system to join (at least in most of employment), but also defines which authority is relevant to which event. The firefighter may expect instant obedience when calling for everybody to evacuate the building, but not if asking employees to use a different accounting system.

6 The overarching ideology. The legitimacy of the social situation relates to a justifying ideology. Science and education formed the background to the experiments Milgram conducted and therefore provided a justification for actions carried out in their name. Most employment is in realms of activity regarded as legitimate, justified by the values and needs of society. This is vital if individuals are to provide willing obedience, as it enables them to see their behaviour as serving a desirable end.

Managers are positioned in an organisational hierarchy in such a way that others will be predisposed, as Milgram demonstrates, to follow their instructions. Managers put in place a series of frameworks to explain how they will exact obedience: they use *discipline*. Because individual employees feel their relative weakness, they seek complementary frameworks to challenge the otherwise unfettered use of managerial disciplinary power: they may join trade unions, but they will always need channels to present their *grievances*.

In later work Milgram (1992) made an important distinction between obedience and conformity, which had been studied by several experimental psychologists, most notably Asch (1951) and Abrams *et al.* (1990). Conformity and obedience both involve abandoning personal judgement as a result of external pressure. The external pressure to conform is the need to be accepted by one's peers and the resultant behaviour is to wear similar clothes, to adopt similar attitudes and adopt similar behaviour. The external pressure to obey comes from a hierarchy of which one is a member, but in which certain others have more status and power than oneself.

> There are at least three important differences . . . First, in conformity there is no *explicit* requirement to act in a certain way, whereas in obedience we are *ordered* or *instructed* to do something. Second, those who influence us when we conform are our *peers* (or equals) and people's behaviours become more alike because they are affected by *example*. In obedience, there is . . . somebody in *higher authority* influencing behaviour. Third, conformity has to do with the psychological need for acceptance by others. Obedience, by contrast, has to do with the social power and status of an authority figure in a hierarchical situation. (Gross and McIlveen 1998, p. 508)

In this chapter we are concerned only with discipline and grievance within business organisations, but it is worth pointing out that managers are the focal points for the grievances of people outside the business as well, but those grievances are called complaints. You may complain *about* poor service, shoddy workmanship or rudeness from an employee, but you complain *to* a manager.

HR managers make one of their most significant contributions to business effectiveness by the way they facilitate and administer grievance and disciplinary issues. First, they devise and negotiate the procedural framework of organisational justice on which both discipline and grievance depend. Second, they are much involved in the interviews and problem-solving discussions that eventually produce solutions to the difficulties that have been encountered. Third, they maintain the viability of the whole process which forms an integral part of their work: they monitor to make sure that grievances are not overlooked and so that any general trend can be perceived, and they oversee the disciplinary machinery to ensure that it is not being bypassed or unfairly manipulated.

Grievance and discipline handling is one of the roles in HRM that few other people want to take over. Ambitious line managers may want to select their own staff without HR intervention or by using the services of consultants. They may try to brush their HR colleagues aside and deal directly with trade union officials or organise their own management development, but grievance and discipline is too hot a potato.

The requirements of the law regarding explanation of grievance handling and the legal framework to avoid unfair dismissal combine to make this an area where HR people must be both knowledgeable and effective. That combination provides a valuable platform for influencing other aspects of management. The HR manager who is not skilled in grievance and discipline is seldom in a strong organisational position.

Everything we have said so far presupposes both hierarchy and the use of procedures. You may say that we have already demonstrated that hierarchy is in decline and that there is a preference for more flexible, personal ways of working than procedure offers. Why rely on Milgram's research, which is now thirty years old? Surely we have moved on since then? Our response is simply that hierarchical relationships continue, although *deference* is in decline. We still seek out the person 'in authority' when we have a grievance and managers readily refer problems they cannot resolve to someone else with a more appropriate role. Procedures may be rigid and mechanical, but they are reliable and we use them even if we do not like them.

WINDOW ON PRACTICE

At the end of the twentieth century schoolteaching in Britain saw the widespread introduction of procedures to deal with teacher capability. Research (Torrington *et al.* 2003) showed that these procedures were generally ineffective in restoring capability and effectiveness for teachers who had lost their way, because of the general reluctance by head teachers to use procedures rather than personal leadership in finding solutions. The result was that heads used an inordinate amount of time in dealing with situations and 'incapable' teachers were extremely distressed and frequently ill because matters were never properly dealt with.

WHAT DO WE MEAN BY DISCIPLINE?

Discipline is regulation of human activity to produce a controlled performance. It ranges from the guard's control of a rabble to the accomplishment of lone individuals producing spectacular performance through self-discipline in the control of their own talents and resources.

The Advisory, Conciliation and Arbitration Service (ACAS) has produced a code of practice relating to disciplinary procedures which makes precisely this point:

> Disciplinary procedures should not be viewed primarily as a means of imposing sanctions (but) . . . as a way of helping and encouraging improvement amongst employees whose conduct or standard of work is unsatisfactory. (ACAS 2000, p. 6)

First, there is managerial discipline in which everything depends on the leader from start to finish. There is a group of people who are answerable to someone who directs what they should all do. Only through individual direction can that group of people produce a worthwhile performance, like the person leading the community singing in the pantomime or the conductor of an orchestra. Everything depends on the leader.

Second, there is team discipline, where the perfection of the performance derives from the mutual dependence of all, and that mutual dependence derives from a commitment by each member to the total enterprise: the failure of one would be the downfall of all. This is usually found in relatively small working groups, like a dance troupe or an autonomous working group in a factory.

Third, there is self-discipline, like that of the juggler or the skilled artisan, where a solo performer is absolutely dependent on training, expertise and self-control. One of the few noted UK researchers working in the field of discipline concludes that self-discipline has recently become much more significant, as demonstrated in the title of his work, 'Discipline: towards trust and self-discipline' (Edwards 2000).

Discipline is, therefore, not only negative, producing punishment or prevention. It can also be a valuable quality for the individual who is subject to it, although the form of discipline depends not only on the individual employee but also on the task and the way it is organised. The development of self-discipline is easier in some jobs than others and many of the job redesign initiatives of recent years have been directed at providing scope for job holders to exercise self-discipline and find a degree of autonomy from managerial discipline. Figure 25.1 shows how the three forms are connected in a sequence or hierarchy, with employees finding one of three ways to achieve their contribution to organisational effectiveness. However, even the most accomplished solo performer has at some time been dependent on others for training and advice, and every team has its coach.

ACTIVITY 25.1

Note three examples of managerial discipline, team discipline and self-discipline from your own experience.

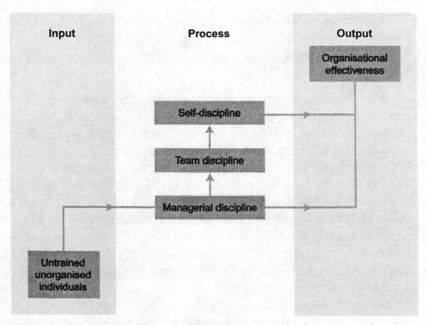

Figure 25.1 Three forms of discipline

Managers are not dealing with discipline only when they are rebuking latecomers or threatening to dismiss saboteurs. As well as dealing with the unruly and reluctant, they are developing the coordinated discipline of the working team, engendering that *esprit de corps* which makes the whole greater than the sum of the parts. They are training the new recruit who must not let down the rest of the team, puzzling over the reasons why A is fitting in well while B is still struggling. Managers are also providing people with the equipment to develop the self-discipline that will give them autonomy, responsibility and the capacity to maximise their powers. The independence and autonomy that self-discipline produces also brings the greatest degree of personal satisfaction, and often the largest pay packet. Furthermore the movement between the three forms represents a declining degree of managerial involvement. If you are a leader of community singing, nothing can happen without your being present and the quality of the singing depends on your performance each time. If you train jugglers, the time and effort you invest pays off a thousand times, while you sit back and watch the show.

WHAT DO WE MEAN BY GRIEVANCE?

Contemporary British texts virtually ignore grievance handling, but the Americans maintain sound coverage. Mathis and Jackson (1994) have a particularly helpful review. Some years ago Pigors and Myers (1977, p. 229) provided a helpful approach to the topic by drawing a distinction between the terms dissatisfaction, complaint and grievance as follows:

- **Dissatisfaction.** Anything that disturbs an employee, whether or not the unrest is expressed in words.

- **Complaint.** A spoken or written dissatisfaction brought to the attention of the supervisor and/or shop steward.
- **Grievance.** A complaint that has been formally presented to a management representative or to a union official.

This provides us with a useful categorisation by separating out grievance as a formal, relatively drastic step, compared with simply complaining. It is much more important for management to know about dissatisfaction. Although nothing is being expressed, the feeling of hurt following failure to get a pay rise or the frustration about shortage of materials can quickly influence performance.

Much dissatisfaction never turns into complaint, as something happens to make it unnecessary. Dissatisfaction evaporates with a night's sleep, after a cup of coffee with a colleague, or when the cause of the dissatisfaction is in some other way removed. The few dissatisfactions that do produce complaint are also most likely to resolve themselves at that stage. The person hearing the complaint explains things in a way that the dissatisfied employee had not previously appreciated, or takes action to get at the root of the problem.

Grievances are rare since few employees will openly question their superior's judgement whatever their private opinion may be and fewer still will risk being stigmatised as a troublemaker. Also, many people do not initiate grievances because they believe that nothing will be done as a result of their attempt.

HR managers have to encourage the proper use of procedures to discover sources of dissatisfaction. Managers in the middle may not reveal the complaints they are hearing, for fear of showing themselves in a poor light. Employees who feel insecure, for any reason, are not likely to risk going into procedure, yet the dissatisfaction lying beneath a repressed grievance can produce all manner of unsatisfactory work behaviours from apathy to arson. Individual dissatisfaction can lead to the loss of a potentially valuable employee; collective dissatisfaction can lead to industrial action.

There are three types of complaint that get progressively harder to handle. The first kind is factual and can be readily tested:

- 'The machine is out of order.'
- 'The stock we're getting now is not up to standard.'
- 'This adhesive won't stick.'

The second type is complaints that are based partly on subjective reactions:

- 'The work is messy.'
- 'It's too hot in here.'
- 'This job is too stressful.'

These statements include terms where the meaning is biologically or socially determined and can therefore not be understood unless the background of the complainant is known; seldom can their accuracy be objectively determined. A temperature of 18 degrees Celsius may be too hot for one person but equable for another.

The third, and most difficult, type of complaint is that involving the hopes and fears of employees:

- 'The supervisor has favourites, who get the best jobs.'
- 'The pay is not very good.'
- 'Seniority doesn't count as much as it should.'

These show the importance of determining not only what employees feel, but also why they feel as they do; not only verifying the facts, which are the *manifest* content of the complaint, but also determining the feelings behind the facts: the *latent* content. An employee who complains of the supervisor being a bully may actually be expressing something rather different, such as the employee's attitude to any authority figure, not simply the supervisor who was the subject of the complaint.

Each type of dissatisfaction is important to uncover and act upon, if action is possible. Action is usually prompt on complaints of the first type, as they are neutral: blame is placed on an inanimate object so individual culpability is not an issue. Action may be quick on complaints of the second type if the required action is straightforward, such as opening a window if it is too hot, but the problem of accuracy can produce a tendency to smooth over an issue or leave it 'to sort itself out' in time. The third type of complaint is the most difficult, and action is often avoided. Supervisors will often take complaints to be a personal criticism of their own competence, and employees will often translate the complaint into a grievance only by attaching it to a third party such as a shop steward, so that the relationship between employee and supervisor is not jeopardised.

ACTIVITY 25.2

Think of an example from your own experience of dissatisfaction causing inefficiency that was not remedied because there was no complaint. Why was there no complaint?

THE FRAMEWORK OF ORGANISATIONAL JUSTICE

The organisation requires a framework of justice to surround the employment relationship so that managers and supervisors, as well as other employees, know where they stand when dissatisfaction develops. An illustration of this is in Figure 25.2.

Organisation culture and management style

The culture of an organisation affects the behaviour of people within it and develops norms that are hard to alter and which provide a pattern of conformity. If, for instance, everyone is in the habit of arriving ten minutes late, a 'new broom' manager will have a struggle to change the habit. Equally, if everyone is in the habit of arriving punctually, then a new recruit who often arrives late will come under strong social pressure to conform, without need for recourse to management action. Culture also affects the freedom and candour with which people discuss dissatisfactions with their managers without allowing them to fester.

The style of managers in handling grievances and discipline reflects their beliefs. The manager who sees discipline as being punishment, and who regards grievances as examples of subordinates getting above themselves, will behave in a relatively autocratic way, being curt in disciplinary situations and dismissive of complaints. The manager who sees disciplinary problems as obstacles to achievement that do not necessarily imply incompetence or ill will by the employee will seek out the cause of

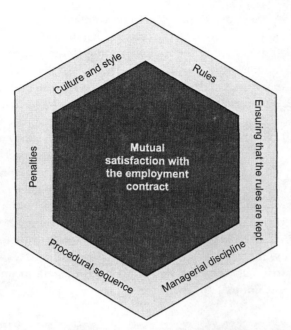

Figure 25.2 The framework of organisational justice

the problem. That problem may then be revealed as one requiring firm, punitive action by the manager, or it may be revealed as a matter requiring management remedy of a different kind. The manager who listens out for complaints and grievances, gets to the bottom of the problems and finds solutions will run little risk of rumbling discontent from people obsessed by trivial problems.

Rules

Every workplace has rules; the difficulty is to have rules that people will honour. Some rules come from legislation, such as the tachograph requirement for HGV drivers, but most are tailored to meet the particular requirements of the organisation in which they apply. For example, rules about personal cleanliness are essential in a food factory but less stringent in a garage.

Rules should be clear and readily understood; the number should be sufficient to cover all obvious and usual disciplinary matters. To ensure general compliance it is helpful if rules are jointly determined, but it is more common for management to formulate the rules and for employee representatives eventually to concur with them. Employees should have ready access to the rules through the employee handbook and noticeboard, and the HR manager will always try to ensure that the rules are known as well as published.

Rules can be roughly grouped into various types:

1   **Negligence** is failure to do the job properly and is different from incompetence because of the assumption that the employee can do the job properly, but has not.

2   **Unreliability** is failure to attend work as required, such as being late or absent.

3   **Insubordination** is refusal to obey an instruction, or deliberate disrespect to someone in a position of authority. It is not to be confused with the use of bad

language. Some of the most entertaining cases in industrial tribunals have involved weighty consideration of whether or not colourful language was intended to be insubordinate.

4 Interfering with the rights of others covers a range of behaviours that are socially unacceptable. Fighting is clearly identifiable, but harassment or intimidation may be more difficult to establish.

5 Theft is another clear-cut aspect of behaviour that is unacceptable when it is from another employee. Theft from the organisation should be supported by very explicit rules, as stealing company property is regarded by many offenders as one of the perks of the job. How often have you taken home a box of paper clips or a felt tip pen without any thought that you were stealing from the employer?

6 Safety offences are those aspects of behaviour that can cause a hazard.

The value of rules is to provide guidelines on what people should do, as the majority will comply. It is extremely difficult to apply rules that do not command general acceptance.

WINDOW ON PRACTICE

In a recent discussion with a group of senior managers, employees identified the following as legitimately taken at will:

paper clips, pencils, disposable pens, spiral pads, local telephone calls, plain paper, computer disks, adhesive tape, overalls and simple uniform.

Among the more problematic were:

- Redundant or shop-soiled stock. One DIY store insisted that the store manager should personally supervise the scrapping of items that were slightly damaged, to ensure that other items were not slightly damaged on purpose.

- Surplus materials. One electricity supplier had some difficulty in eradicating the practice of surplus cable and pipe being regarded as a legitimate perquisite of fitters at the end of installation jobs, as they suspected their engineers were using the surplus for private work. Twelve months later the level of material requisition had declined by 14 per cent.

Ensuring that the rules are kept

It is not sufficient just to have rules; they are only effective if they are observed. How do we make sure that employees stick to the rules?

1 Information is needed so that everyone knows what the rules are and why they should be obeyed. Written particulars may suffice in an employment tribunal hearing, but most people conform to the behaviour of their colleagues, so informal methods of communication are just as important as formal statements.

2 Induction can make the rules coherent and reinforce their understanding. Rules can be explained, perhaps with examples, so that people not only know the rules but also understand why they should be obeyed.

3 Placement or relocation can avoid the risk of rules being broken, by placing a new recruit with a working team that has high standards of compliance. If there are the signs of disciplinary problems in the offing, then a quick relocation can put the problem employee in a new situation where offences are less likely.

4 Training increases awareness of the rules, improving self-confidence and self-discipline. There will be new working procedures or new equipment from time to time, and again training will reduce the risk of safety offences, negligence or unreliability.

5 Reviewing the rules periodically ensures that they are up to date, and also ensures that their observance is a live issue. If, for instance, there is a monthly staff council meeting, it could be appropriate to have a rules review every 12 months. The simple fact of the rules being discussed keeps up the general level of awareness of what they are.

6 Penalties make the framework of organisational justice firmer if there is an understanding of what penalties can be imposed, by whom and for what. It is not feasible to have a fixed scale, but neither is it wise for penalties to depend on individual managerial whim. This area has been partially codified by the legislation on dismissal, but the following are some typical forms of penalty:

a Rebuke. The simple 'Don't do that' or 'Smoking is not allowed in here' or 'If you're late again, you will be in trouble' is all that is needed in most situations, as someone has forgotten one of the rules, had not realised it was to be taken seriously, or was perhaps testing the resolution of the management. Too frequently, managers are reluctant to risk defiance and tend to wait until they have a good case for more serious action rather than deploy their own, there-and-then authority.

b Caution. Slightly more serious and formal is the caution, which is then recorded. This is not triggering the procedure for dismissal, it is just making a note of a rule being broken and an offence being pointed out.

c Warnings. When the management begins to issue warnings, great care is required. This is because the development of unfair dismissal legislation has made the system of warnings an integral part of disciplinary practice, and this has to be followed if the employer is to succeed in defending a possible claim of unfair dismissal at tribunal. For the employer to show procedural fairness there should normally be a formal oral warning, or a written warning, specifying the nature of the offence and the likely outcome if the offence is repeated. It should also be made clear that this is the first, formal stage in the procedure. Further misconduct could then warrant a final written warning containing a statement that further repetition would lead to a penalty such as suspension or dismissal. All written warnings should be dated, signed and kept on record for an agreed period. The means of appeal against the disciplinary action should also be pointed out.

d Disciplinary transfer or demotion. This is moving the employee to less attractive work, possibly carrying a lower salary. The seriousness of this is that it is public, as the employee's colleagues know the reason. A form of disciplinary transfer is found on assembly lines, where there are some jobs that are more attractive and carry higher status than others. Rule breakers may be 'pushed down the line' until their contempt is purged and they are able to move back up.

e   **Suspension.** This is a tactic that has the benefit of being serious and avoids the disadvantage of being long lasting, as demotion is. The employer has a contractual obligation to provide pay, but not to provide work, so it is easy to suspend someone from duty with pay either as a punishment or while an alleged offence is being investigated. If the contract of employment permits, it may also be possible to suspend the employee for a short period without pay.

The important general comment about penalties is that they should be appropriate in the circumstances. Where someone is, for instance, persistently late or absent, suspension would be a strange penalty. Also penalties must be within the law. An employee cannot be demoted or transferred at managerial whim, and unpaid suspension can only be imposed if the contract of employment allows it.

Procedural sequence

This is the clear, unvarying logic of procedure, which should be well known and trusted. Procedure makes clear, for example, who does and who does not have the power to dismiss. The dissatisfied employee, who is wondering whether or not to turn a complaint into a formal grievance, knows who will hear the grievance and where an appeal could be lodged. This security of procedure, where step B always follows step A, is needed by managers as well as by employees, as it provides them with their authority as well as limiting the scope of their actions.

Managerial discipline

This preserves general respect for the justice framework by managers exercising self-discipline in how they work within it. With very good intentions some senior managers maintain an 'open door' policy with the message: 'My door is always open . . . call in any time you feel I can help you'. This has many advantages and is often necessary, but it has danger for matters of discipline and grievance if it encourages people to bypass middle managers. There is also the danger that employees come to see the settlement of their grievances as being dependent on the personal goodwill of an individual rather than on the business logic or their human and employment rights.

Managers must be consistent in handling discipline and grievance issues. Whatever the rules are, they will be generally supported only as long as they deserve support. If they are enforced inconsistently they will soon lose any moral authority, and will be obeyed only because of employees' fear of penalties. Equally, the manager who handles grievances quickly and consistently will enjoy the support of a committed group of employees.

The other need for managerial discipline is to test the validity of the discipline assumption. Is it a case for disciplinary action or for some other remedy? There is little purpose in suspending someone for negligence when the real problem is lack of training. Many disciplinary problems disappear under analysis, and it is sensible to carry out the analysis before making a possibly unjustified allegation of indiscipline.

GRIEVANCE PROCEDURE

Managers who believe that it introduces unnecessary rigidity into the working relationship often resent the formality of the grievance procedure: 'I see my people all the time. We work side by side and they can raise with me any issue they want, at any time they want . . .' The problem is that many people will not raise issues with the immediate superior that could be regarded as contentious, in just the same way that managers frequently shirk the rebuke as a form of disciplinary penalty. Formality in procedure provides a structure within which individuals can reasonably air their grievances and avoids the likelihood of managers dodging the issue when it is difficult. It avoids the risk of inconsistent ad hoc decisions, and the employee knows at the outset that the matter will be heard and where it will be heard. The key features of grievance procedure are fairness, facilities for representation, procedural steps and promptness.

1   Fairness is needed, to be just, but also to keep the procedure viable. If employees develop the belief that the procedure is only a sham, then its value will be lost and other means will be sought to deal with grievances. Fairness is best supported by the obvious even-handedness of the ways in which grievances are handled, but it will be greatly enhanced if the appeal stage is either to a joint body or to independent arbitration, as the management is relinquishing the chance to be judge of its own cause.

2   Representation can help the individual employee who lacks the confidence or experience to take on the management singlehandedly. A representative, such as a union official, has the advantage of having dealt with a range of employee problems and may be able to advise the aggrieved person whether the claim is worth pursuing. There is always the risk that the presence of the representative produces a defensive management attitude affected by a number of other issues on which the manager and union official may be at loggerheads, so the managers involved in hearing the grievance have to cast the representative in the correct role for the occasion.

3   Procedural steps should be limited to three. There is no value in having more just because there are more levels in the management hierarchy. This will only lengthen the time taken to deal with matters and will soon bring the procedure into disrepute. The reason for advocating three steps is that three types of management activity are involved in settling grievances. Nevertheless, it is quite common for there to be more than three steps where there is a steep hierarchy, within which there may be further, more senior, people to whom the matter could be referred. The reason for there being more steps has nothing to do with how to process grievances but is purely a function of the organisation structure.

The first step is the *preliminary*, when the grievance is lodged with the immediate superior of the person with the complaint. In the normal working week most managers will have a variety of queries from members of their departments, some of which could become grievances, depending on the manager's reaction. Mostly the manager will either satisfy the employee or the employee will decide not to pursue the matter. Sometimes, however, a person will want to take the issue further. This is the preliminary step in procedure, but it is a tangible step as the manager has the opportunity to review any decisions made that have caused the dissatisfaction, possibly enabling the dissatisfied employee to withdraw the grievance. In our experience it is rare for matters to be taken any further unless the subject of the grievance is something on which company policy is being tested.

The *hearing* gives the complainant the opportunity to state the grievance to a more senior manager, who is able to take a broader view of the matter than the immediate superior and who may be able both to see the issue more dispassionately and to perceive solutions that the more limited perspective of the immediate superior obscured. It is important for the management that the hearing should finalise the matter whenever possible, so that recourse to appeal is not automatic. The hearing should not be seen by the employees as no more than an irritating milestone on the way to the real decision makers. This is why procedural steps should be limited to three.

If there is an *appeal*, this will usually be to a designated more senior manager, and the outcome will be either a confirmation or a modification of the decision at the hearing.

4 Promptness avoids the bitterness and frustration that comes from delay. When an employee 'goes into procedure', it is like pulling the communication cord in a train. The action is not taken lightly and is in anticipation of a swift resolution. Furthermore, the manager whose decision is being questioned will have a difficult time until the matter is resolved. The most familiar device to speed things up is to incorporate time limits between the steps, specifying that the hearing should take place no later than, say, four working days after the preliminary notice and that the appeal should be no more than five working days after the hearing. This gives time for reflection and initiative by the manager or the complainant between the stages, but does not leave time for the matter to be forgotten.

Where the organisation has a collective disputes procedure as well as one for individual grievances, there needs to be an explicit link between the two so that individual matters can be pursued with collective support if there is not a satisfactory outcome. An outline grievance procedure is in Figure 25.3.

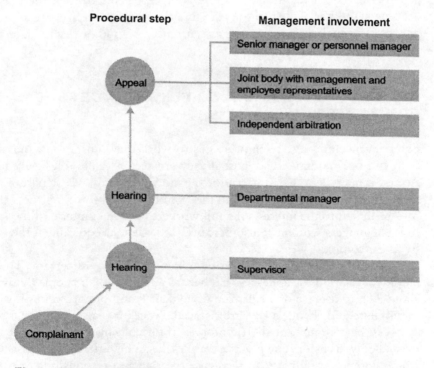

Figure 25.3 Outline grievance procedure

DISCIPLINARY PROCEDURE

Procedures for discipline are very similar to those for grievance and depend equally on fairness, promptness and representation. There are some additional features.

Authorisation of penalties

The law requires that managers should not normally have the power to dismiss their immediate subordinates without reference to more senior managers. Whatever penalties are to be imposed, they should only be imposed by people who have that specific authority delegated to them. Usually this means that the more serious penalties can only be imposed by more senior people, but there are many organisations where such decisions are delegated to the HR department.

Investigation

The procedure should also ensure that disciplinary action is not taken until it has been established that there is a problem that justifies the action. The possibility of suspension on full pay is one way of allowing time for the investigation of dubious allegations, but the stigma attached to such suspensions should not be forgotten.

Information and explanation

If disciplinary action is possible, the person to be disciplined should be told of the complaint, so that an explanation can be made, or the matter denied, before any penalties are decided. If an employee is to be penalised, then the reasons for the decision should be explained to make sure that cause and effect are appreciated. The purpose of penalties is to prevent a recurrence. An outline disciplinary procedure is in Figure 25.4.

ARE GRIEVANCE AND DISCIPLINE PROCESSES EQUITABLE?

For grievance and discipline processes to work they must command support, and they will only command support if they are seen as equitable, truly just and fair. At first it may seem that concern for the individual employee is paramount, but the individual cannot be isolated from the rest of the workforce. Fairness should therefore be linked to the interests that all workers have in common in the business, and to the managers who must also perceive the system as equitable if they are to abide by its outcomes.

Procedures have a potential to be fair in that they are certain. The conduct of employee relations becomes less haphazard and irrational: people 'know where they stand'. The existence of a rule cannot be denied and opportunities for one party to manipulate and change a rule are reduced. Procedures also have the advantage that they can be communicated. The process of formalising a procedure that previously existed only in custom and practice clarifies the ambiguities and inconsistencies within it and compels each party to recognise the role and responsibility of the other. By providing pre-established avenues for responses to various contingencies, procedures

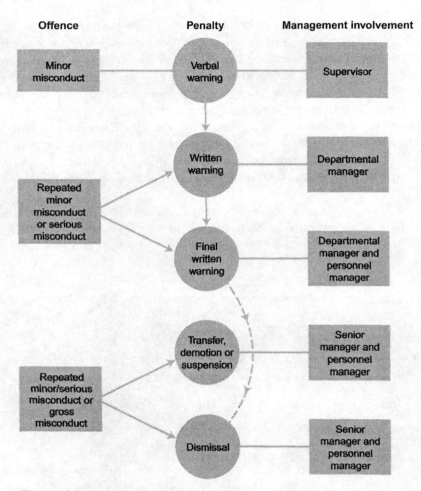

Figure 25.4 Outline disciplinary procedure

make it possible for the response to be less random and so more fair. The impersonal nature of procedures offers the possibility of removing hostility from the workplace, since an artificial social situation is created in which the ritual displays of aggression towards management are not seen as personal attacks on managers.

The achievement of equity may not match the potential. Procedures cannot, for instance, impart equity to situations that are basically unfair. Thus attempting to cope with an anomalous pay system through a grievance procedure may be alleviating symptoms rather than treating causes. It is also impossible through a grievance procedure to overcome accepted norms of inequity in a company, such as greater punctuality being required of manual employees than of white-collar employees.

A further feature of procedural equity is its degree of similarity to the judicial process. All procedures adopt certain legalistic mechanisms, such as the right of individuals to be represented and to hear the case against them, but some aspects of legalism, such as burdens of proof and strict adherence to precedent, may cause the application of standard remedies rather than the consideration of individual circumstances.

There is a nice irony in the fact that equity is best achieved when procedures are not used. Procedure is there in the background and expresses principles for fair and effective management of situations. All the while the **principles** are followed and the framework for organisational justice is observed, procedure is not invoked. The advantage of this is that individuals, whether employees or managers, are not named and shamed so that matters are much easier to deal with. Only when the matter is dealt with badly does the procedural step come closer.

The existence of the procedure becomes the incentive rather than the means for action to be taken: it is not an excuse for inaction. There have recently been several high-profile cases of medical negligence resulting in doctors being struck off the medical register and therefore being no longer able to practise. In each case it appeared that lapses had been allowed to continue for too long before remedial action was taken.

It is accepted that some employment situations require naming and shaming first, with possible remedial action following. In most sports there is on-the-spot penalising of players for breaking the rules.

WINDOW ON PRACTICE

The 'red-hot stove' rule of discipline offers the touching of a red hot stove as an analogy for effective disciplinary action:

1 The burn is immediate. There is no question of cause and effect.

2 You had warning. If the stove was red-hot, you knew what would happen if you touched it.

3 The discipline is consistent. Everyone who touches the stove is burned.

4 The discipline is impersonal. People are burned not because of who they are, but because they touch the stove.

ACTIVITY 25.3

Think of an attempt at disciplinary action that went wrong. Which of the features of the red-hot stove rule were missing?

Notions of fairness are not 'givens' of the situation; they are socially constructed and there will never be more than a degree of consensus on what constitutes fairness. Despite this, the procedural approach can exploit standards of certainty and consistency, which are widely accepted as elements of justice. The extent to which a procedure can do this will depend on the suitability of its structure to local circumstances, the commitment of those who operate it and the way that it reconciles legalistic and bargaining elements.

SUMMARY PROPOSITIONS

25.1 The authority of managers to exercise discipline in relation to others in the organisation is underpinned by a general predilection of people to obey commands from those holding higher rank in the hierarchy of which they are members.

25.2 The exercise of that discipline is limited by the procedural structures for grievance and discipline.

25.3 Grievance and discipline handling are two areas of human resource management that few other people want to take over, and provide HR managers with some of their most significant contributions to business effectiveness.

25.4 Discipline can be understood as being managerial, team or self-discipline, and the three types are connected hierarchically.

25.5 Dissatisfaction, complaint and grievance form another hierarchy. Unresolved employee dissatisfaction can lead to the loss of potentially valuable employees. In extreme cases it can lead to industrial action.

25.6 Grievance and disciplinary processes both require a framework of organisational justice.

25.7 The procedural framework of disciplinary and grievance processes is one of the keys to their being equitable.

25.8 Effective management of both discipline and grievance is achieved by following the principles of the procedures without invoking them in practice.

GENERAL DISCUSSION TOPICS

1 Do you think Milgram's experiments would have had a different outcome if the subjects had included women as well as men?

2 What examples can individual members of the group cite of self-discipline, team discipline and managerial discipline?

3 'The trouble with grievance procedures is that they encourage people to waste a lot of time with petty grumbles. Life at work is rarely straightforward and people should just accept the rough with the smooth.'

What do you think of that opinion?

FURTHER READING

Torrington, D.P., Earnshaw, J.M., Marchington, L. and Ritchie, M.D. (2003) *Tackling Underperformance in Teaching*. London: Routledge

This is a report on research regarding teachers' alleged lack of capability. The results, including a number of case studies, are really an object lesson in how *not* to deal with a problem. The reader will easily work out how the matters *should* have been dealt with. Whether they would actually have done any better is debatable. Handling misconduct is easy; handling lack of capability is much more difficult.

REFERENCES

Abrams, D., Wetherell, M., Cochrane, S., Hogg, M.A. and Turner, J.C. (1990) 'Knowing what to think by knowing who you are: Self categorization and norm formation', *British Journal of Social Psychology*, Vol. 29, pp. 97–119.

Advisory, Conciliation and Arbitration Service (2000) *Code of Practice on Disciplinary Practice and Grievance Procedures at Work*. London: HMSO.

Asch, S.E. (1951) 'Effect of group pressure upon the modification and distortion of judgements', in H. Guetzkow (ed.) *Groups, Leadership and Men*. Pittsburgh, Penn.: Carnegie Press.

Edwards, P. (2000) 'Discipline: towards trust and self-discipline', in S. Bach and K. Sisson (eds) *Personnel Management*, 3rd edn. Oxford: Blackwell.

Gross, R. and McIlveen, R. (1998) *Psychology: A New Introduction*. London: Hodder & Stoughton.

Handy, C.B. (1999) *The New Alchemists*. London: Hutchinson.

Mathis, R.L. and Jackson, J.H. (1994) *Human Resource Management*, 7th edn. Minneapolis/St Paul, Minn.: West Publishing.

Milgram, S. (1974) *Obedience to Authority*. London: Tavistock.

Milgram, S. (1992) *The Individual in a Social World*, 2nd edn. New York: Harper & Row.

Pigors, P. and Myers, C. (1977) *Personnel Administration*, 8th edn. Maidenhead: McGraw-Hill.

Torrington, D.P., Earnshaw, J.M., Marchington, L. and Ritchie, M.D. (2003) *Tackling Underperformance in Teachers*. London: Routledge.

An extensive range of additional materials, including multiple choice questions, answers to questions and links to useful websites can be found on the Human Resource Management Companion Website at **www.pearsoned.co.uk/torrington**.

TOPIC SUMMARY SHEET

What are the key learning points from this topic?

TOPIC 10 – MANAGING PERFORMANCE

 Why study this topic?

All employees expect to be rewarded for their input in the organisation. Wages and rewards are central to the morale and motivation of the work force. It is crucial for the organisation to achieve the most appropriate balance of workers' expectations and organisational resources
This chapter will discuss the various techniques available to organisations today, and will provide an evaluation of their effectiveness. You may have already experienced some of these techniques already, and this topic will help you to understand the underlying purpose behind organisational reward policies.

E-tivity 10: Managing performance

CHAPTER 10

STRATEGIC ASPECTS OF PERFORMANCE

THE OBJECTIVES OF THIS CHAPTER ARE TO:

1   IDENTIFY A CHANGING PERSPECTIVE ON PERFORMANCE

2   REVIEW SOME MAJOR INFLUENCES ON OUR CURRENT THINKING ABOUT PERFORMANCE

3   EXAMINE THE RESEARCH WHICH LINKS HUMAN RESOURCE POLICIES AND PRACTICES WITH INTERNAL AND EXTERNAL MEASURES OF COMPANY PERFORMANCE

4   EXPLORE THE MECHANISMS WHICH LINK HR POLICIES AND PRACTICES AND PERFORMANCE

5   REVIEW, BRIEFLY, A RANGE OF PERFORMANCE INITIATIVES

6   IDENTIFY SOME OF THE PROBLEMS WITH PERFORMANCE INITIATIVES

In our opening chapters we described the shift in emphasis away from the contract of employment towards the contract for performance. Even before the development of Taylor's scientific management methods a century ago, getting the most out of the workforce has always been a predominant management preoccupation, and the management literature is full of studies on the topic. Psychologists have studied motivation and leadership, ergonomists have dismantled and reconstructed every aspect of the physical environment in which people work, industrial relations specialists have pondered power relationships and reward, while sociologists discussed the design of organisations and their social structure, and operations experts have looked for ways to engineer process improvements. In 2001, Caulkin asserts:

> more than 30 studies in the US and UK leave no room for doubt; how organizations manage and develop people has a powerful – perhaps the most powerful – effect on overall performance, including the **bottom line**. (Caulkin 2001, p. 32)

A CHANGE IN PERSPECTIVE: FROM EMPLOYMENT TO PERFORMANCE

The traditional HRM approach to enhancing individual performance has centred on the assessment of past performance and the allocation of reward – rewards were provided in exchange for performance. This has been powerfully influenced by the industrial relations history, as trade unions have developed the process of collective bargaining and negotiation.

The prime purpose of trade unions has always been to improve the terms and working conditions of their members; the union has only one thing to offer in exchange for improvements in terms and conditions, that is, some opportunity for improvement in productivity or performance. With the steadily increasing influence of unions in most industrial countries through most of the twentieth century, it was inevitable that performance improvement was something of direct interest only to management. Performance therefore became stereotyped as something of no intrinsic interest to the person doing the work.

The influence of trade unions has altered and collective bargaining does not dominate the management agenda as much as it used to. This is the most significant feature in the general change in attitudes about what we go to work for. Managements are gradually waking up to this fact and realising that there is now scope for integration in a way that was previously unrealistic. Not only is it possible to say, 'Performance is rewarded', one can now begin to say, 'Performance *is* a reward.' The long-standing motivational ideas of job enlargement, job enrichment, and so forth, become more cogent when those at work are able to look for the satisfaction of their needs not only in the job, but also in their performance at the job.

Although it may seem like playing with words, this subtle shift of emphasis is fundamental to understanding the strategic approach to performance.

WINDOW ON PRACTICE

Mavis has worked in a retail store for 18 years and has recently attended a training course in customer care. She says:

> I always regarded the customer as some sort of enemy; we all did. In our coffee breaks we chatted away about the customer from hell, who was never satisfied, or who always put you down. Also I used to feel that I had to grin and bear it in trying to be nice to these enemies in order to earn commission.
>
> Since the course I feel much more in control and have more self-respect. I really feel that most customers will respond positively if I approach them in the right way. It is my performance that largely affects how they behave. I actually enjoy what I am doing most of the time (and I never thought I'd say that!), because I can see myself doing a bit of good as well as selling more than I used to.

INFLUENCES ON OUR UNDERSTANDING OF PERFORMANCE

The Japanese influence

In the 1980s the success of Japanese companies and the decline of Western organisations encouraged an exploration and adoption of Japanese management ideas and practices in order to improve performance. Thurley (1982) described the objectives of personnel policies in Japan as performance, motivation, flexibility and mobility. Delbridge and Turnbull (1992) described type 'J' organisations (based on Japanese thinking) as characterised by commitment, effort and company loyalty. A key theme in Japanese thinking appears to be people development and continuous improvement, or 'kaizen'.

Much of this thinking and the specific management techniques used in Japan, such as JIT (just in time), have been adopted into UK organisations, often in an uncritical way and without due regard for the cultural differences between the two nations. It is only where the initiatives are developed *and modified* for their location that they appear to succeed.

The American literature

Key writers from the American 'excellence' school, Peters and Waterman (1982), identified eight characteristics that they found to be associated with excellent companies – all American. These companies were chosen as excellent on the basis of their innovativeness and on a set of financial indicators, compared on an industry-wide basis. The characteristics they identified were:

- a bias for action – rather than an emphasis on bureaucracy or analysis;
- close to the customer – concern for customer wishes;
- autonomy and entrepreneurship – the company is split into small operational units where innovation and initiative are encouraged;

- productivity through people – employees are seen as the key resource, and the value of the employees' contribution is reinforced;
- hands on, value driven – strong corporate culture promoted from the top;
- stick to the knitting – pursuing the core business rather than becoming conglomerates;
- simple form, lean staff – simple organisation structure and small HQ staffing;
- simultaneous loose and tight properties – company values strongly emphasised, but within these considerable freedom and errors tolerated.

Peters and Waterman identified a shift from the importance of strategy and structural factors to style, systems, staff and skills (from the hard 's's to the soft 's's). In a follow-on book Peters and Austin (1985) identify four key factors related to excellence as concern for customers, innovation, attention to people and leadership.

However, there are problems with the research methodology used; for example, no comparison was made with companies not considered to be excellent. We do not, therefore, know whether these principles were applied to a greater extent in excellent organisations. In addition, a number of the companies quoted have experienced severe problems since the research was carried out, and there remains the problem of the extent to which we can apply the results to UK organisations.

Whatever the reservations, the influence of this work on strategic thinking about performance remains profound. Even the use of the term 'excellence' means that there is a change of emphasis away from deadpan, objective terms such as profitability, effectiveness, value added and competitive advantage towards an idea that may trigger a feeling of enthusiasm and achievement. 'Try your best' becomes 'Go for it'.

More recently there has been considerable quantitative research in the USA that aims to identify HR practices which lead to high organisational performance, for example Huselid (1995) and Pfeffer (1998). The HR practices identified are termed 'high performance work practices' and have encouraged similar investigations in the UK to determine 'high commitment work practices'.

HRM and the strategy literature

The HRM strategy literature provides different ways to understand the contribution of HR policies and practices to organisational performance. We noted in Chapter 2 that three distinct approaches to HR strategy can be identified. The universalist or best practice approach presupposes that certain HR policies and practices will always result in high performance, and the question is to identify exactly what these are. The contingency or fit approach suggests that different HR policies and practices will be needed to produce high performance in different firms depending on their business strategy and environment. Finally the resource-based view of the firm suggests that neither of these approaches is sufficient, but that every organisation and its employees should be considered as unique and that the set of HR policies and practices that will result in high performance will also be unique to that firm. From this perspective no formula can be applied, and the way that people processes contribute to organisational performance can only be understood within the context of the particular firm. These three perspectives have resulted in different investigational approaches to understanding the impact of people management on organisational performance, as will become clear in the following section.

DO PEOPLE-MANAGEMENT PROCESSES CONTRIBUTE TO HIGH PERFORMANCE?

The investigations to date have had a dual purpose, the first being to seek to establish a link between people-management practices and organisational performance. In other words, does the way that people are managed affect the bottom line? The second one follows logically from this, and is: If the answer to the first question is yes, then which particular policies and practices result in high performance? Both these questions are usually investigated in parallel. A variety of different definitions of performance have been used in these studies. These range from bottom line financial performance (profitability), through productivity measures, to measurement of outcomes such as wastage, quality and labour turnover (which are sometimes referred to as internal performance outcomes). Sometimes the respondent's view of performance is used, on the basis that bottom line figures can be influenced by management accounting procedures. The studies have generally used large datasets and complex statistical analysis to determine relationships.

Some researchers argue that the performance effects of HR policies and practices are multiplicative rather than additive, and this is often termed the 'bundles' approach (see, for example, MacDuffie 1995), and this highlights an emphasis on internal rather than external fit. In other words, a particular set of mutually reinforcing practices is likely to have more impact on performance than applying one or just some of these in isolation. Pfeffer (1998), for example, identifies seven critical people-management policies: emphasising employment security; recruiting the 'right' people; extensive use of self-managed teams and decentralisation; high wages solidly linked to organisational performance; high spending on training; reducing status differentials; and sharing information; and he suggests that these policies will benefit *every* organisation. In the UK the Sheffield Enterprise Programme (Patterson *et al.* 1997) has studied 100 manufacturing organisations over 10 years (1991–2001) and used statistical techniques to identify which factors affect profitability and productivity. It has been reported that aspects of culture, supervisory support, concern for employee welfare, employee responsibility, and training were all important variables in relation to organisational performance. Also in the UK, Wood and de Menezes (1998) identify a bundle of HR practices which they term high-commitment management, and these comprise recruitment and selection processes geared to selecting flexible and highly committed individuals; processes which reward commitment and training by promotion and job security; and the use of direct communication and teamwork.

This avenue of work has a very optimistic flavour, suggesting that not only are people-management practices related to high organisational performance, but that we can identify the innovative and sophisticated practices that will work best in combination. On a practical level there are problems because different researchers identify different practices or 'bundles' associated with high performance (see, for example, Becker and Gerhard 1996).

There have been many criticisms of this approach, partly based on the methods used – which involve, for example, the view of a single respondent as to which practices are in place, with no account taken of how the practices are implemented. A further confusion is that some studies are at establishment level, some at corporate level, some are sector based and some are cross-sector. Each of these approaches has inbuilt problems and creates extreme difficulties for any meta-analysis of the studies so far. A further problem is causality. It could be that profitable firms use best practice people-management methods, because they can afford to since they are profitable, rather than that such methods lead to profitability. A further issue concerns the conflict between different aspects of the bundle. Such contradictions are, for example, between individualism and teamwork and between a strong culture and adaptability. Lastly, this approach ignores the business strategy of the organisation.

The work we have described so far comes from a universalist/best practice perspective and an alternative way forward is to use the contingency or fit point of view (*see*, for example, the work of Wright and Snell 1998), asking the question, 'Which people-management policies create high performance in which different organisational circumstances?' This approach does bring the integration with business strategy to the fore, and draws attention to sectoral differences; for example Guest (2001) has suggested that 'high performance work practices' may be effective in producing high performance in manufacturing rather than services. However, it fails to provide a more useful way forward. Attempting to model all the different factors that influence the appropriate set of HR policies and practices that lead to high performance is an extremely complex, if not impossible, task. In addition to this Purcell *et al.* (2000) argue that the speed of change poses a real problem for the fit approach.

In summary, the extent to which all the statistical work that has been done proves the relationship between people-management practices and organisational performance continues to be hotly contested. Reviewing the academic literature Richardson and Thompson (1999) come to the conclusion that the evidence indicates a positive relationship between innovative and sophisticated people-management practices and better business performance. Guest *et al.* (2003), however, recognise that although the statistical work so far provides some associations between people management and organisational performance there is a lack of convincing evidence. Guest (2000), Hall (2002) and particularly Purcell (1999) all provide detailed expositions of the problems with the above approaches.

Purcell (1999) suggests that a more useful approach is to focus on the resource-based view of the firm, which is the third perspective on HR strategy that we considered in Chapter 2. From this perspective each organisation is a unique and complex whole, so we need to look beyond lists of HR policies and practices to explain organisational performance. We also need to consider long-term performance capability and not just short-term performance improvements. From this perspective Paauwe and Richardson (2001) argue that the move to longitudinal studies and case study work is useful, and suggest that organisational context and institutional arrangements need greater attention; Becker and Gerhart (1996) suggest that it is more likely to be the architecture of the system, not just a group of HR practices, that results in high performance, and Purcell suggests that it is how practices are implemented and change is managed that makes the difference. Hutchinson *et al.* (2000) term this 'idiosyncratic fit'. The work of Purcell and his colleagues from Bath University, which forms part of the CIPD's research in this area, attempts to address some of the deficits in large sample statistical work. They have investigated 12 case study organisations on a longitudinal basis, collecting the employees' view and concentrating on the line manager's role in implementation.

They collected data on 11 HR policy/practice areas identified from previous research as being linked to high organisational performance. In testing the link between people management and performance this study differs from others in that the measures taken were ones that were the most meaningful to each organisation.

Also the organisations were each visited twice over a two-and-a-half-year period so comparisons could be made over time. Their results are not clear-cut, but a major conclusion is that it is the way policies are implemented and the role of line mangers which are critical. They also acknowledge that it is difficult to disentangle the performance impact of HR policies from the performance impact of changing environmental circumstances and other changes such as technology. They do argue, however, that those organisations with a 'big idea', which expresses what the organisation stands for and what it is trying to achieve, were more able to sustain their performance over the longer term. For example the big idea in Jaguar is quality and in Nationwide it is mutuality. They also found that such big ideas have five characteristics in high-performing organisations:

- **Embedded** – in policies and practices
- **Connected** – connects relationships with customers, values, culture and the way people are managed
- **Enduring** – stable, longlasting values which survive even in difficult times
- **Collective** – acts as corporate glue
- **Measured and managed** – often through the use of balanced scorecard type approaches

HOW DO HR POLICIES AND PRACTICES AFFECT PERFORMANCE?

We have sufficient evidence to claim that HR policies and practices do affect company performance, although some studies (for example Lahteenmaki and Storey 1998) do not support this. We then need to understand better the processes which link these HR practices to business performance. As Purcell *et al.* (2000) point out, 'what remains unclear is what is actually happening in successful organisations to make this connection' (p. 30). Currently the focus is on commitment in mediating the impact of HR policies and practices on business performance, and we shall consider this in more detail.

Commitment

Commitment has been described as:

- **Attitudinal commitment** – that is, loyalty and support for the organisation, strength of identification with the organisation (Porter 1985), a belief in its values and goals and a readiness to put in effort for the organisation.
- **Behavioural commitment** – actually remaining with the company and continuing to pursue its objectives.

Walton (1985) notes that commitment is *thought* to result in better quality, lower turnover, a greater capacity for innovation and more flexible employees. In turn these are seen to enhance the ability of the organisation to achieve competitive advantage. Iles, Mabey and Robertson (1990) add that some of the outcomes of commitment have been identified as the industrial relations climate, absence levels, turnover levels and individual performance. Pfeffer (1998) and Wood and Albanese

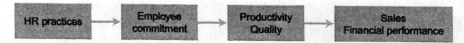

Figure 10.1 A simple model of HRM and performance (Source: D. Guest (2000) 'Human resource management, employee well-being and organizational performance'. Paper presented to the CIPD Professional Standards Conference, 11 July. Reproduced with the permission of the author.)

(1995) argue that commitment is a core variable, and Guest (1998, p. 42) suggests that:

> The concept of organizational commitment lies at the heart of any analysis of HRM. Indeed the whole rationale for introducing HRM policies is to increase levels of commitment so that other positive outcomes can ensue.

Hence we see the adoption of the terms 'high commitment work practices' and 'high commitment management' and their linkage with high performance. Meyer and Allen (1997) argue that there is not a great deal of *evidence* to link high commitment and high levels of organisational performance. Guest (2000) reports analyses of the Workplace Employment Relations Survey (WERS) data and the Future of Work Survey data to show some support for the model that HR practices have an impact on employee attitudes and satisfaction, which in turn have an impact on internal performance outcomes. He is, however, cautious about identifying causal links. In this context Guest uses commitment as shorthand for employee attitudes and values, as shown in his model in Figure 10.1.

Some authors, however, have argued that high commitment could indeed reduce organisational performance. Cooper and Hartley (1991) suggest that commitment might decrease flexibility and inhibit creative problem solving. If commitment reduces staff turnover, this may result in fewer new ideas coming into the organisation. Staff who would like to leave the organisation but who are committed to it in other ways, for example through high pay and benefits, may stay, but may not produce high levels of performance.

As well as the debate on the value of commitment to organisational performance, there is also the debate on the extent to which commitment can be managed, and how it can be managed. Guest (1992) suggests that commitment is affected by: personal characteristics; experiences in job role; work experiences; structural factors; and personnel policies.

WINDOW ON PRACTICE

Rebecca Johnson (1999) reports on performance initiatives at the Holiday Inn, Mayfair. Through a 'back to the floor' experience senior managers realised that front line staff did not have sufficient authority and autonomy to solve routine customer problems and that this was having an adverse impact on customer perceptions. A range of initiatives were thus implemented:

- training to equip front line staff to take greater responsibility in solving customer problems;

- new recruitment and selection strategies to help identify potential employees who are 'focused on going the extra mile', rather than those who have technical skills, which can be learned on appointment. Processes include 'auditions' to identify favourable attitudes;

- demonstrating a genuine commitment to employees. Initiatives included attitude surveys, continued IIP recognition, a training resource centre and a network of mentors and 'buddies';

- encouraging a sense of fun and openness;

- a performance appraisal system which is also geared towards career development, and internal promotions where possible;

- measuring customer feedback through a 'guest tracking system'.

Johnson reports that all these policies are paying off as profits have been increasing steadily for the last five years. She also reports the views of a recently appointed corporate sales executive who claims to have joined the organisation partly because of the training programme, and who noted that 'the commitment is very strong'.

Source: Adapted from a case study by R. Johnson (1999) 'Case 2: Holiday Inn Mayfair', in A. Baron and R. Collard 'Realising our assets', *People Management*, 14 October.

Lastly, it is important to consider whether using commitment as a shorthand for attitudes and satisfaction is sufficient, and whether there are other important dimensions which may be lost, by focusing on commitment alone. Patterson *et al.* (1997) found that in addition to commitment, employee satisfaction was related to organisational performance. Purcell and his colleagues (2003) give equal prominence to job satisfaction and motivation. In their model HR policies and practices are seen to impact on employee ability/skills, motivation and incentive (in that people can be motivated to use their ability productively via intrinsic and extrinsic rewards) and opportunity. In turn these three factors have an impact on commitment, individual motivation and job satisfaction, all of which have an impact on employee discretionary behaviour which in turn impacts on performance. In relation to HR practices they found that:

- job influence, career opportunities, job challenge, involvement in management decisions, training and line manager respect all influence employee motivation;

- job influence, career opportunities, job challenge and teamworking all influence job satisfaction;

- training, career opportunities, job challenge, management leadership, performance appraisal, work-life balance and communication on organisational performance all influence commitment.

MAJOR PERFORMANCE INITIATIVES

We have previously considered some HR policies and practices that have been identified as related to high performance, and have noted the idea of using practices in bundles. Many of the popular performance initiatives that companies have adopted represent similar (but not the same) bundles of HR policies and practices, and we now turn to these. There are many small initiatives every day that help to improve performance, but we are concentrating here on major strategic initiatives although the labels may, of course, mean different things in practice in different organisations. Interestingly, Guest and King (2001) found that many senior managers were not aware of the research on performance, and it is therefore unclear what is informing senior managers' choice of performance initiatives.

This brings us to the concern that too many initiatives in the same organisation will give conflicting messages to employees, particularly when they are introduced by different parts of the business. There may, for example, be contradictions between the messages of total quality management ('right first time') and those of the learning organisation type of approach ('it's OK to make mistakes as long as you learn from them').

The performance research to date focuses very much on the individual, but we agree with Caulkin (2001) who suggests that organisations also need to develop the capability of the organisation as a whole, and to this end we include in Table 10.1 three levels of initiative depending on the primary focus: organisational, team or individual. Some of them partly cover the same ground, and it would be surprising to find them in the same business at the same time.

Table 10.1 Some major performance initiatives

Organisational focus	Learning organisation
	Knowledge management
	Organisational development
	Investors in people
	Total quality management (TQM)
	Performance culture
	Lean production
	Business process re-engineering
	Just in time (JIT)
	Standards: e.g. ISO9000
	Customer care/orientation
Individual focus	Performance management
	Performance-related pay
	Self-development/continuous development
	Empowerment
Team focus	High-performance teams
	Cross-functional teams
	Self-regulating teams

ACTIVITY 10.1

1 Identify the main performance initiatives in your organisation.

2 What/who is the source of each initiative?

3 In what ways do they mutually support each other, and in what ways do they conflict?

THINGS THAT GO WRONG

The level of satisfaction with performance initiatives is typically low (Antonioni 1994), so we close this chapter with a summary of the problems most often reported.

The process/people balance

Schemes rarely strike the right balance between a people emphasis and a process emphasis. Concentrating on being brilliant at talking to the people, getting them going and talking them down gently if they don't quite make it will not suffice if there is not a clear, disciplined process that brings in the essential features of consistency and defining sensible goals. Getting the goals and measures right is a waste of time if there is not the necessary input to changing attitudes, developing skills and winning consent.

Getting the measures right

On the basis of what gets measured gets done, it is critical that the organisation selects the most useful measure of performance for the organisaton as a whole and for the individuals within it. Single measures are unlikely to be sufficiently robust. Kaplan and Norton (1992) argue convincingly that the mix of measures which an organisation should use to assess its performance should be based around four different perspectives:

- **Financial measures** – such as sales growth, profits, cash flow and increased market share.
- **Customer measures** – that is, the customer perspective, which looks at, for example, delivery time, service quality, product quality.
- **Internal business measures** – cycle time, productivity, employee skills, labour turnover.
- **Innovation and learning perspective** – including such elements as ability to innovate and improve.

The focus must be on what is achieved: results are what count. At an individual level a focus on behaviour rather than results achieved can be unhelpful, leading to personality clashes, and misleading. Doing things in the right way is no substitute for doing the right things. For a further exploration of the difficulties with performance measures see case 10.1 on the website.

Management losing interest

A constant axiom with any initiative is the need for endorsement from senior management. With a performance initiative there is the need to go a great deal further. First, senior managers have to accept that the initiative is something in which they have to participate continuously and thoroughly. They cannot introduce it, say how important it is and then go off to find other games to play:

> studies have shown that in organisations that utilise performance management, 90 per cent of senior managers have not received performance reviews in the last two years. Clearly the problem here is that PM is not used, modelled and visibly supported at the top of the organisation. Sooner or later people at lower levels catch on and no longer feel compelled to take the time to make PM work. (Sparrow and Hiltrop 1994, p. 565)

The second aspect is indicated in that quotation. Performance initiatives will not work unless people at all levels either believe in them or are prepared to give them a try with the hope that they will be convinced by the practice.

The team/individual balance

Individuals can rarely perform entirely on their own merits; they are part of a department or team of people whose activities interact in innumerable ways. Trevor Macdonald may read the television news with a clarity and sureness that is outstanding, but it would be of little value if the lights did not work or the script contained errors. Most working people, no matter how eminent, are not solo performers to that extent. Somehow the performance initiative has to stimulate both individual and team performance, working together within the envelope of organisational objectives.

ACTIVITY 10.2

Think of situations in your own experience outside working life, where there has been a potential clash between individual performance and team performance. Examples might be:

(a) the opening batsman more concerned with his batting average than with the team winning the match;

(b) the person playing the lead in the amateur operatic society's production of *The Merry Widow* who ignores the chorus; or

(c) the local councillor more concerned with doing what is needed to earn an MBE than with supporting the collective view of the council.

How was the potential clash avoided, or not? How could it have been managed more effectively to harmonise individual and team performance?

Leaving out the development part

A key feature of managing performance is developing people so that they *can* perform. This is the feature that is most often not delivered. It is often the lack of follow-up on development needs that is the least satisfactory aspect of performance management systems.

Implementing and managing the change

If, as Purcell (1999) identifies, 'our concern should be less about the precise policy mix in the "bundle" and more about how and when organisations manage the HR side of change', then the way that large and small performance initiatives are implemented and managed is critical. While this is well-trodden ground, there is considerable evidence of attempted changes which have failed for a wide range of reasons including: trust is low; change is seen as a management fad which will go away; change has been poorly communicated and understood; change is just a way to get us to work harder for the same money. Changing employee behaviour is also influenced by the culture of the organisation, and for a further exploration of the link between culture and performance initiatives see case 10.2 on the website.

GETTING IT RIGHT

Here are four suggestions for running a successful performance initiative:

1 Develop and promulgate a clear vision for the business as a framework for individual/team goals and targets.

2 In consultation, develop and agree individual goals and targets with three characteristics: (a) what to do to achieve the target; (b) how to satisfy the customer rather than pleasing the boss; (c) targets that are precise, difficult and challenging, but attainable, *with feedback*.

3 Do not begin until you are sure of: (a) unwavering commitment from the top; (b) an approach that is driven by the line and bought into and owned by middle and first-line managers; (c) a system that is run, monitored and updated by HR specialists; (d) an agreement that every development commitment or pay commitment is honoured, or a swift, full explanation is given of why not.

4 Train all participants.

SUMMARY PROPOSITIONS

10.1 Central to understanding management interest in performance is understanding the subtle change in attitudes: not only is performance rewarded, performance is also a reward.

10.2 In the UK our views of performance improvement have been influenced by the US literature, the Japanese experience and the HRM strategy literature.

10.3 There has been considerable research effort devoted to investigating the link between a bundle of people-management practices and organisational performance, and some would argue that the link has been successfully demonstrated.

10.4 Much less clear are the processes by which the link is made, for example how, why and in what context? Commitment as the moderating variable between HR practices and organisational performance is insufficient.

10.5 Things that typically go wrong with performance initiatives are getting the people/process balance wrong, not selecting the right performance measures, management losing interest and getting the team/individual balance wrong.

10.6 Factors likely to produce success relate to a clear, understood vision, effective target setting, full management commitment, training and honouring commitments.

GENERAL DISCUSSION TOPICS

1 To what extent can the American excellence literature be applied in a UK setting?

2 Can commitment, empowerment and job flexibility be pursued together? If yes, how can this be achieved? If no, why not – what are the alternatives?

FURTHER READING

Purcell, J., Kinnie, N. and Hutchinson, S. (2003) 'Open minded', *People Management*, Vol. 9, No. 10, 15 May, pp. 30–3
A useful summary of the Bath research to date, if you can't afford or haven't time to read the full report – provided in the reference list below (Purcell *et al.* 2003). Displays the whole people and performance model and discuses the importance of implementation of policies. Provides some detail on the importance of the 'big picture' and the five key attributes of this.

Truss, C. (2003) 'Complexities and controversies in linking HRM with organizational outcomes', *Journal of Management Studies*, Vol. 38, No. 8, pp. 1121–48
An excellent critique of the quantitative approach to establishing the link between people policies and organisational performance. Useful case study of Hewlett-Packard which demonstrates that even high-performing companies do not necessarily follow best practice in all areas of people management. The approach taken in this research is different in that it tracks back from high performance and looks at the people management processes which contribute to this.

REFERENCES

Antonioni, D. (1994) 'Improve the performance management process before discontinuing performance appraisals', *Compensation and Benefits Review*, Vol. 26, No. 2, pp. 29–37.
Becker, B. and Gerhard, B. (1996) 'The impact of human resource management on organizational progress and prospects', *Academy of Management Journal*, Vol. 39, No. 4, pp. 779–801.
Caulkin, S. (2001) 'The time is now', *People Management*, Vol. 7, No. 17, 30 August, pp. 32–4.

Cooper, J. and Hartley, J. (1991) 'Reconsidering the case for organisational commitment', *Human Resource Management Journal*, Vol. 3, Spring, pp. 18–32.

Delbridge, R. and Turnbull, P. (1992) 'Human resource maximisation: The management of labour under just-in-time manufacturing systems', in P. Blyton and P. Turnbull (eds) *Reassessing Human Resource Management*. Beverly Hills: Sage.

Guest, D. (1992) 'Right enough to be dangerously wrong; an analysis of the "In search of excellence" phenomenon', in G. Salaman *et al.* (eds) *Human Resource Strategies*. London: Sage.

Guest, D. (1998) 'Beyond HRM: Commitment and the contract culture', in P. Sparrow and M. Marchington (eds) *Human Resource Management: The New Agenda*. London: Financial Times Pitman Publishing.

Guest, D. (2000) 'Human Resource Management, employee well-being and organizational performance'. Paper presented at the CIPD Professional Standards Conference, 11 July.

Guest, D. (2001) 'Human resource management: when research confronts theory', *International Journal of Human Resource Management*, Vol. 12, No. 7, pp. 1092–1106.

Guest, D. and King, Z. (2001) 'Personnel's Paradox', *People Management*, Vol. 17, No. 19, 27 September, pp. 24–9.

Guest, D., Michie, J, Conway, N. and Sheehan, M. (2003) 'Human Resource management and corporate performance in the UK', *British Journal of Industrial Relations*, Vol. 41, No. 2, pp. 291–314.

Hall, L. (2002) 'HRM practices and employee and organisational performance: a critique of the research and Guest's model'. Paper presented to Manchester Metropolitan University Business School *Performance and Reward* conference, 11 April 2002.

Huselid, M. (1995) 'The impact of human resource management practices on turnover, productivity and corporate financial performance', *Academy of Management Journal*, Vol. 38, No. 3, pp. 635–73.

Hutchinson, S., Purcell, J. and Kinnie, N. (2000) 'Evolving high commitment management and the experience of the RAC call center', *Human Resource Management Journal*, Vol. 10, No. 1, pp. 63–78.

Iles, P., Mabey, C. and Robertson, I. (1990) 'Human resource management practices and employee commitment. Possibilities, pitfalls and paradoxes', *British Journal of Management*, Vol. 1, pp. 147–57.

Johnson, R. (1999) 'Case 2: Holiday Inn Mayfair', in A. Baron and R. Collard, 'Realising our assets', *People Management*, 14 October.

Kaplan, R. and Norton, D. (1992) 'The balanced scorecard – measures that drive performance', *Harvard Business Review*, Jan.–Feb., pp. 71–9.

Lahteenmaki, S. and Storey, J. (1998) 'HRM and company performance: the use of measurement and the influence of economic cycles', *Human Resource Management Journal*, Vol. 8, No. 2, pp. 51–65.

MacDuffie, J. (1995) 'Human resource bundles and manufacturing performance: organizational logic and flexible production systems in the world auto industry', *Industrial and Labor Relations Review*, Vol. 48, No. 2, pp. 197–221.

Meyer, J. and Allen, N. (1997) *Commitment in the workplace: theory, research and application*. London: Sage.

Paauwe, J. and Richardson, R. (2001) 'Editorial introduction: HRM and performance: confronting theory and reality', *International Journal of Human Resource Management*, Vol. 12, No. 7, pp. 1085–91.

Patterson, J., West, M., Lawthom, R. and Nickell, S. (1997) *The Impact of People Management Practices on Business Performance*. London: IPD.

Peters, T. and Austin, N. (1985) *A Passion for Excellence*. New York: Harper and Row.

Peters, T. and Waterman, R. (1982) *In Search of Excellence*. New York: Harper and Row.

Pfeffer, J. (1998) *The Human Equation*. Boston: Harvard Business School Press.

Porter, M. (1985) *Competitive Advantage*. New York: Free Press.

Purcell, J. (1999) 'Best practice and best fit: chimera or cul-de-sac?' *Human Resource Management Journal*, Vol. 9, No. 3, pp. 26–41.

Purcell, J., Kinnie, N., Hutchinson, S. and Rayton, B. (2000) 'Inside the box', *People Management*, 26 October.

Purcell, J., Kinnie, N., Hutchinson, S., Rayton, B. and Swart, J. (2003) *Understanding the People Performance Link: Unlocking the black box*, Research report. London: CIPD.

Richardson, R. and Thompson, M. (1999) *The Impact of People Management Practices – A Review of the Literature*. London: IPD.

Sparrow, P. and Hiltrop, J.-M. (1994) *European Human Resource Management in Transition*. London: Prentice Hall.

Thurley, K. (1982) 'The Japanese model: practical reservations and surprising opportunities', *Personnel Management*, February.

Walton, R.E. (1985) 'From control to commitment in the workplace', *Harvard Business Review*, March–April, pp. 77–84.

Wood, S. and Albanese, M. (1995) 'Can we speak of high commitment management on the shop floor?' *Journal of Management Studies*, Vol. 32, No. 2, pp. 215–47.

Wood, S. and de Menezes, L. (1998) 'High commitment management in the UK: evidence from the Workplace Industrial Relations Survey and employers' manpower and skills practices survey', *Human Relations*, Vol. 51, No. 4, pp. 485–515.

Wright, P. and Snell, S. (1998) 'Towards a unifying framework for exploring fit and flexibility in strategic human resource management', *Academy of Management Review*, Vol. 23, No. 4, pp. 756–72.

CHAPTER 12

INDIVIDUAL PERFORMANCE MANAGEMENT

THE OBJECTIVES OF THIS CHAPTER ARE TO:

1   CLARIFY THE NATURE AND PURPOSE OF PERFORMANCE MANAGEMENT AND PERFORMANCE APPRAISAL

2   EXAMINE THE STAGES OF A TYPICAL PERFORMANCE MANAGEMENT SYSTEM

3   REVIEW THE IMPLEMENTATION OF PERFORMANCE MANAGEMENT SYSTEMS

4   EXPLORE THE CONTRIBUTION OF 360-DEGREE/ MULTI-RATER FEEDBACK

The treatment of individual performance in organisations has traditionally centred on the assessment of performance and the allocation of reward. Performance was typically seen as the result of the interaction between individual ability and motivation.

Increasingly, organisations recognise that planning and enabling performance have a critical effect on individual performance. So, for example, clarity of performance goals and standards, appropriate resources, guidance and support from the individual's manager all become central.

PERFORMANCE MANAGEMENT AND PERFORMANCE APPRAISAL

Appraisal systems

Traditionally performance appraisal systems have provided a formalised process to review the performance of employees. They are typically designed on a central basis, usually by the HR function, and require each line manager to appraise the performance of their staff, usually on an annual basis. This normally requires the manager and employee to take part in a performance review meeting. Elaborate forms are often completed as a record of the process, but these are not living documents, they are generally stored in the archives of the HR department, and the issue of performance is often neglected until the next round of performance review meetings.

The nature of what is being appraised varies between organisations and might cover personality, behaviour or job performance. These areas might be measured either quantitively or qualitatively. Qualitative appraisal often involves the writing of an unstructured narrative on the general performance of the appraisee. Alternatively, some guidance might be given as to the areas on which the appraiser should comment. The problem with qualitative appraisals is that they may leave important areas unappraised, and that they are not suitable for comparison purposes.

Coates (1994) argues that what is actually measured in performance appraisal is the extent to which the individual conforms to the organisation. Some traditional appraisal was based on measures of personality traits that were felt to be important to the job. These included traits such as resourcefulness, enthusiasm, drive, application and other traits such as intelligence. One difficulty with these is that everyone defines them differently. Raters, therefore, are often unsure of what they are rating, leaving more scope for bias and prejudice. Another problem is that since the same scales are often used for many different jobs, traits that are irrelevant to an appraisee's job may still be measured.

Other approaches concentrate on linking ratings to behaviour and performance on the job. So performance may be reviewed against key aspects of the job or major headings on the job description. Specific methods of linking ratings with behaviour at work have been developed such as behaviourally anchored rating scales (BARS) and behavioural observation scales (BOS) although evidence suggests that these are not widely used (Williams 2002).

Another method of making appraisal more objective is to use the process to set job objectives over the coming year and, a year later, to measure the extent to which these objectives have been met. The extent to which the appraisee is involved in setting these objectives varies considerably. When a competency profile has been identified for a particular job, it is then possible to use this in the appraisal of performance. Many appraisal systems combine competency assessment with assessment against objectives or job accountabilities.

Lastly, performance may be appraised by collecting primary data via various forms of electronic surveillance system. There are increasing examples of how activity rates of computer operators can be recorded and analysed, and how the calls made by telephone sales staff can be overheard and analysed. Sewell and Wilkinson (1992) describe a Japanese electronics plant where the final electronic test on a piece of equipment can indicate not only faults but the individual operator responsible for them. On another level some companies test the performance of their sales staff by sending in assessors acting in the role of customer (Newton and Findlay 1996), often termed 'mystery shoppers'.

In a recent survey (IRS 2003) 79 out of 96 very large employers appraised all employees. But while performance appraisal has gradually been applied to wider groups of employees, beyond managers and professionals, there are also concerns that appraisal systems are treated as an administrative exercise, are ineffective, and do little to improve performance of employees in the future. A further problem with such systems is the lack of clarity of purpose. The Employment Studies Institute (IRS 2001) suggests that appraisal is a victim of its own expectations, in that it is expected to deliver in too many areas. Systems may focus on development, identifying future potential, reward, identifying poor performers, or motivation. In systems where appraisal results were linked to reward the manager was placed in the position of an assessor or judge. Alternatively some systems focused on support or development, particularly in the public sector. These provided a better opportunity for managers to give constructive feedback, for employees to be open about difficulties, and for planning to improve future performance. Many systems try to encompass both approaches; for example the IRS survey (IRS 2003) found that 40 per cent of the private sector companies used appraisal for both development and pay. However, as these approaches conflict, the results are typically unsatisfactory.

The effectiveness of appraisal systems hinges on a range of different factors. Research by Longenecker (1997) in the USA sheds some light on this. In a large-scale survey and focus groups he found that the three most common reasons for failure of an appraisal system were: unclear performance criteria or an ineffective rating instrument (83 per cent); poor working relationships with the boss (79 per cent); and that the appraiser lacked information on the manager's actual performance (75 per cent). Other problems were a lack of ongoing performance feedback (67 per cent) and a lack of focus on management development/improvement (50 per cent). Smaller numbers identified problems with the process, such as lack of appraisal skills (33 per cent) and the review process lacking structure or substance (29 per cent).

We would add that ownership of the system is also important. If it is designed and imposed by the HR function there may be little ownership of the system by line managers. Similarly, if paperwork has to be returned to the HR function it may well be seen as a form-filling exercise for someone else's benefit and with no practical value to performance within the job. More fundamentally Egan (1995) argues that the problem with appraisal not only relates to poor design or implementation, but is rooted deeply in the basic reaction of organisational members to such a concept. There is an increasing body of critical literature addressing the role and theory of appraisal. These debates centre on the underlying reasons for appraisal (*see*, for example, Barlow 1989; Townley 1989, 1993; Newton and Findlay 1996) and the social construction of appraisal (*see*, for example, Grint 1993). This literature throws some light on the use and effectiveness of performance appraisal in organisations.

Performance management systems

While many appraisal systems are still in existence and continue to be updated, performance management systems are increasingly seen as the way to manage employee performance, and have incorporated the appraisal/review process into this. In the Focus on skills at the end of Part III we consider the performance appraisal interview in the context of either an appraisal or a performance management system. Mabey and Salaman (1995) provide a useful definition when they state that the essence of performance management is:

> Establishing a framework in which performance by individuals can be directed, monitored, motivated and rewarded, and whereby the links in the cycle can be audited.
> (p. 189)

Bevan and Thompson (1992) found that 20 per cent of the organisations they surveyed had introduced a performance management system. Armstrong and Baron (1998a) report that 69 per cent of the organisations they surveyed in 1997 operated a formal process to measure manager performance. Such systems offer the advantage of being tied closely into the objectives of the organisation, and therefore the resulting performance is more likely to meet organisational needs. The systems also represent a more holistic view of performance. Performance appraisal or review is almost always a key part of the system, but is integrated with *performance planning* (linking an individual's objectives to business objectives) to ensure that employee effort is directed towards organisational priorities: support for *performance delivery* (via development plans, coaching and ongoing review) to enable employee effort to be successful, and that performance is *assessed* and successful performance *rewarded and reinforced*.

The conceptual foundation of performance management relies on a view that performance is more than ability and motivation. It is argued that clarity of goals is key in enabling the employee to understand what is expected and the order of priorities. In addition goals themselves are seen to provide motivation, and this is based on goal setting theory originally developed by Locke in 1968 and further developed with practical applicability (Latham and Locke 1990). Research to date suggests that for goals to be motivating they must be sufficiently specific, challenging but not impossible and set participatively. Also the person appraised needs feedback on future progress.

The other theoretical base of performance management is expectancy theory, which states that individuals will be motivated to act provided they expect to be able to achieve the goals set, believe that achieving the goals will lead to other rewards and believe that the rewards on offer are valued. We look at expectancy theory in greater depth in Chapter 14 on leadership and motivation.

Given such an emphasis on a link into the organisation's objectives it is somewhat disappointing that Bevan and Thompson found no correlation between the existence of a performance management system and organisational performance in the private sector. Similarly, Armstrong and Baron (1998a) report from their survey that no such correlation was found. They do report, however, that 77 per cent of organisations surveyed regarded their systems as effective to some degree and Houldsworth (2003), using the Henley and Hay Group survey of top FTSE companies and public sector respondents, reports that 68 per cent of organisations rated their performance management effectiveness as excellent. So performance management, such as HR systems and processes, still remains an act of faith.

As with appraisal systems, some performance management systems are development driven and some are reward driven. Whereas in the 1992 IPD survey 85 per cent of organisations claimed to link performance management to pay (Bevan and Thompson 1992), Armstrong and Baron found that only 43 per cent of survey respondents reported such a link. However, 82 per cent of the organisations visited had some form of performance-related pay (PRP) or competency-based pay, so the picture is a little confusing. They suggest that a view is emerging of performance management which centres on 'dialogue', 'shared understanding', 'agreement' and 'mutual commitment', rather than rating for pay purposes. While they may feature in more sophisticated systems, Houldsworth (2003) reports a figure of 77 per cent link with pay, and it appears that many organisations are trying to achieve both development and reward outcomes. She also contrasts systems driven by either performance development or performance measurement, finding that the real experience of developmental performance management is that it is motivational, encourages time spent with the line manager, encourages two-way communication and is an opportunity to align roles and training with business needs. Alternatively, where there is a measurement focus, performance management is seen as judgemental, a chance to assess and get rid of employees, emphasises control and getting more out of staff, raises false expectations and is a way to manage the salaries bill.

ACTIVITY 12.1

Think of the performance appraisal or performance management system at your place of work.

- To what extent does it focus on development and to what extent does it focus on reward?

- How, and how well, are each of these purposes achieved? Explain why this is.

- What would you do to improve the system, and what impacts would these actions have?

There are many different definitions of performance management and some have identified it as 'management by objectives' under another name. There are, however, some key differences. Management by objectives was primarily an off-the-peg system which was bought in and generally involved objectives being imposed on managers from above. Performance management tends to be tailor-made and produced in-house (which is why there are so many different versions), with an emphasis on mutual objective setting and on ongoing performance support and review. The term,

Table 12.1 Characteristics of performance management systems

- Top-down link between business objectives and individual objectives (compared with performance appraisal where there may be no objectives, or objectives not explicitly linked to business objectives)
- Line manager driven and owned (rather than being owned by the HR function, as typically with performance appraisal)
- A living document where performance plans, support and ongoing review are documented as work progresses, and prior to annual review (rather than an archived document retrieved at appraisal time to compare achievement with intentions)
- Performance is rewarded and reinforced

therefore, remains beyond precise definition, and rightly so, as it is critical that the system adopted fits with the culture and context of the organisation (*see*, for example, Audit Commission 2000; Hendry *et al.* 2000). As well as the right sort of culture, the right sort of leadership is needed together with a focus on the right priorities. Interestingly, though, Williams (2002) notes that performance management can be used as a tool of culture change. (*See* Table 12.1.)

STAGES IN A PERFORMANCE MANAGEMENT SYSTEM

Figure 12.1 shows a typical system, including both development and reward aspects, the main stages of which are discussed below.

Business mission, values, objectives and competencies

There is an assumption that before it is able to plan and manage individual performance the organisation will have made significant steps in identifying the performance required of the organisation as a whole. In most cases this will involve a mission statement so that performance is seen within the context of an overriding theme. Bevan and Thompson (1992) found that performance management organisations were more likely than others to have an organisational mission statement and to communicate this to employees. In addition many organisations will identify the strategic business objectives that are required within the current business context to be competitive and that align with the organisation's mission statement.

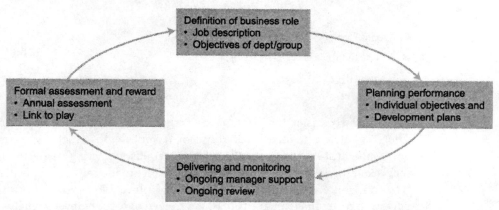

Figure 12.1 Stages of a typical performance management system

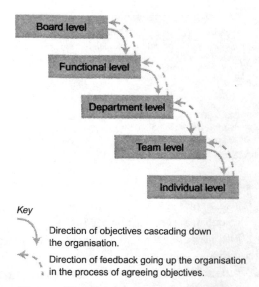

Key

Direction of objectives cascading down
the organisation.

Direction of feedback going up the organisation
in the process of agreeing objectives.

Figure 12.2 An objective-setting cascade

Many organisations will also identify core values of the business and the key competencies required. Each of these has a potential role in managing individual performance. Organisational objectives are particularly important, as it is common for such objectives to be cascaded down the organisation in order to ensure that individual objectives contribute to their achievement (for an example of an objective-setting cascade, *see* Figure 12.2).

Planning performance: a shared view of expected performance

Individual objectives derived from team objectives and an agreed job description can be jointly devised by manager and employee. These objectives are outcome/results oriented rather than task oriented, are tightly defined and include measures to be assessed. The objectives are designed to stretch the individual, and offer potential development as well as meeting business needs. It is helpful to both the organisation and the individual if objectives are prioritised. Many organisations use the 'SMART' acronym for describing individual objectives or targets:

- Specific
- Measurable
- Appropriate
- Relevant
- Timed

It is clearly easier for some parts of the organisation than others to set targets. There is often a tendency for those in technical jobs, such as computer systems development, to identify purely technical targets, reflecting the heavy task emphasis they see in their jobs. Moving staff to a different view of how their personal objectives contribute to team and organisational objectives is an important part of the performance management process. An objective for a team leader in systems development could be:

To complete development interviews with all team members by end July 2005. (written March 2005)

Clearly, the timescale for each objective will need to reflect the content of the object-ive and not timescales set into the performance management system. As objectives are met, managers and their staff need to have a brief review meeting to look at progress in all objectives and decide what other objectives should be added, changed or deleted. Five or six ongoing objectives are generally sufficient for one individual to work on at any time.

The critical point about a *shared* view of performance suggests that handing out a job description or list of objectives to the employee is not adequate. Performance expectations need to be understood and, where possible, to involve a contribution from the employee. For example, although key accountabilities may be fixed by the manager, they will need to be discussed. Specific objectives allow for and benefit from a greater degree of employee input as employees will have a valid view of barriers to overcome, the effort involved and feasibility. Expressing objectives as a 'what' statement rather than a 'how' statement gives employees the power to decide the appropriate approach once they begin to work on the issue. Incorporating employee input and using 'what' statements are likely to generate a higher degree of employee ownership and commitment. However, difficulties have been experienced with purely 'what' objectives as there may be appropriate and inappropriate ways of achieving an objective. For example, a manager with an objective to ensure that another department agrees to a plan of action could achieve this in different ways. The manager may pressure susceptible members of the other department and force agreement through without listening to the other department's perspective. This may alienate the other department and damage future good relations. Alternatively the manager could adopt a collaborative approach so that the needs of both departments are met, providing a sound basis for future cooperation between the departments. More sophisticated systems now incorporate the 'how' as well (*see* IDS 2003).

Planning the support, development and resources necessary for employees to achieve their objectives is imperative. Without this support it is unlikely that even the most determined employees will achieve the performance required.

Concerns have been expressed over restricting the objectives to those which specify output targets, and there is now evidence of increasing use of input targets, such as developing a critical competency which is valued by the organisation and relevant to the achievement of objectives. Williams (2000) argues that as individuals cannot always control their results it is important to have behavioural targets as well as output targets. It is also recommended that there is a personal development plan which would again underpin the achievement of objectives.

Delivering and monitoring performance

While the employee is working to achieve the performance agreed, the manager retains a key enabling role. Organising the resources and off-job training is clearly essential. So too is being accessible. There may well be unforeseen barriers to the agreed performance which the manager needs to deal with, and sometimes the situ-ation will demand that the expected performance needs to be revised. The employee may want to sound out possible courses of action with the manager before proceeding, or may require further information. Sharing 'inside' information that will affect the employee's performance is often a key need, although it is also something that managers find difficult, especially with sensitive information. Managers can identify information sources and other people who may be helpful.

Ongoing **coaching** during the task is especially important. Managers can guide employees through discussion and by giving constructive feedback. They are in a position to provide practical job experiences to develop the critical skills and competencies that the employee needs, and can provide job-related opportunities for practice. Managers can identify potential role models to employees, and help to explain how high achievers perform so well.

Although it is the employee's responsibility to achieve the performance agreed, the manager has a continuous role in providing support and guidance, and in oiling the organisational wheels.

ACTIVITY 12.2

Do managers actively support employee performance in your organisation? If they do, by what means do they do this and how effective is it? If they do not, why not, and what is the impact of this?

or

Think of any organisation in which you have had some involvement:

* How has individual performance been supported?

* How effective was/is this?

* How would you improve the way in which performance was/is supported?

Ongoing review is an important activity for employees to carry out in order to plan their work and priorities and also to highlight to the manager well in advance if the agreed performance will not be delivered by the agreed dates. Joint employee/ manager review is essential so that information is shared. For example, a manager needs to be kept up to date on employee progress, while the employee needs to be kept up to date on organisational changes that have an impact on the agreed objectives. Both need to share perceptions of how the other is doing in their role, and what they could do that would be more helpful.

These reviews are normally informal, although a few notes may be taken of progress made and actions agreed. They need not be part of any formal system and therefore can take place when the job or the individuals involved demand, and not according to a pre-set schedule. The purpose of the review is to facilitate future employee performance, and provide an opportunity for the manager to confirm that the employee is 'on the right track', or redirect him or her if necessary. They thus provide a forum for employee reward in terms of recognition of progress. A 'well done' or an objective signed off as completed can enhance the motivation to perform well in the future. During this period evidence collection is also important. In the Scottish Prison Service (IDS 2003) line managers maintain a performance monitoring log of their team members' positive and negative behaviours in order to provide regular feedback and to embed the practice on ingoing assessment. Employees are expected to build up a portfolio of evidence of their performance over the period to increase the objectivity of reviews and to provide an audit trail to back up any assessment ratings. It is also during this part of the cycle that employees in many organisations can collect 360-degree feedback to be used developmentally and as part of an evidence base.

Formal performance review/assessment

Regular formal reviews are needed to concentrate on developmental issues and to motivate the employee. Also, an annual review and assessment is needed, of the extent to which objectives have been met which may well affect pay received. In many organisations employees are now invited to prepare an initial draft of achievement against objectives, for example Microsoft and AstraZeneca (IDS 2003). Some organisations continue to have overall assessment ratings which have to conform to a forced distribution. So if there were a five-point rating scale percentages would be set requiring each team/department to have, say, 10 per cent of employees on the top point, 20 per cent on the next point, and so on. AstraZeneca does not encourage its managers to give an overall rating to staff as its research suggested that this was demotivating (IDS 2003). Research by the Institute for Employment Studies (IRS 2001) found that review was only seen as fair if the targets set were seen as reasonable, managers were seen to be objective and judgements were consistent across the organisation.

Some organisations encourage employees to give upward feedback to their managers at this point in the cycle. For further details of this stage in the process *see* the Focus on skills at the end of Part III.

Reward

Many systems still include a link with pay, but Fletcher and Williams (1992) point to some difficulties experienced. Some public and private organisations found that the merit element of pay was too small to motivate staff, and sometimes seen as insulting. Although performance management organisations were more likely than others to have merit or performance-related pay (Bevan and Thompson 1992), some organisations have regretted its inclusion. Armstrong and Baron (1998a) report that staff almost universally disliked the link with pay, and a manager in one of their case study companies reported that 'the whole process is an absolute nightmare' (p. 172). Mabey and Salaman (1995) provide a good discussion of the problems with the pay link and we include a detailed discussion of performance related pay in Chapter 28.

There are other forms of reward than monetary and the Institute of Employment Studies (IRS 2001) found that there was more satisfaction with the system where promotion and development, rather than money, was used as a reward for good performance.

AstraZeneca performance management principles

AstraZeneca had in place several different approaches to performance management from the time that Astra and Zeneca merged in 1999, and from that time these approaches have been developed on an ongoing basis. The company is now working to define a globally consistent approach which will apply to its 60,000+ employees.

Performance management is defined as the process by which objectives are agreed, progress towards objectives is reviewed, individuals are supported and developed through the year, *and performance (which includes 'what' and 'how') is reviewed at the year end.*

There are four principles that will govern the structures, processes and systems and behaviours for performance management, and the following is a selective summary of these:

1 **Aligned Objectives** – individual, department/function and team objectives are cascaded and aligned with current business objectives so that everyone is working towards the same overall objectives in the most effective manner.

This enables everyone in AstraZeneca to know what is expected of them and how this helps to deliver overall business objectives. Individual, departmental/functional and team objectives are regularly reviewed and updated as business need or individual circumstances change. Managers are accountable for ensuring that individual and team objectives are clear, relevant, measurable, and documented. The way in which delivery against objectives will be reviewed throughout the year will also be agreed. Managers will encourage and support managed risk-taking, creativity, innovation and challenge when agreeing an individual's objectives.

2 **Joint Responsibility** – individuals, managers, and project leaders are jointly responsible for the effectiveness of the performance management process.

Managers are accountable for creating a challenging and supportive environment in which all individuals are able to give *of their best performance, and for ensuring a reasonable total workload for individuals.* Individuals, managers and project leaders must have an equal commitment to the objectives set, including agreeing the means by which to achieve them. In addition to meeting their own objectives, individuals are expected to support others in delivering outstanding team performance.

3 **Constructive Conversations** – there is open and honest dialogue between individuals, managers and project leaders.

Individuals, managers and project leaders need to have frequent, clear, open and fair conversations with each other about the level of performance they are achieving and also how they work together. There should be clear, open and honest conversations about learning and development needs, and about aspirations and opportunities for growth and development, and plans agreed to meet these needs. Where an individual's performance and/or behaviour are not to the required standards, the manager will discuss this promptly with the individual and will work with him/her to address this.

4 **Reviewing and Rewarding Performance** – everyone in AstraZeneca is given the opportunity to understand the link between their performance and their reward and recognition.

Managers will communicate openly Performance Management and Global Remuneration principles. Managers and project leaders will demonstrate capability to carry out their performance management and reward responsibilities. There will be a demonstrable link between an individual's performance and the level of reward and recognition they achieve. AstraZeneca will deliver higher rewards to higher-performing *individuals, and also reward contribution to team performance.*

Source: Summarised from AstraZeneca (2004) *AstraZeneca Performance Management Principles*, AstraZeneca.

Implementation and critique of performance management

Performance management needs to be line driven rather than HR driven, and therefore mechanisms need to be found to make this happen. The incorporation of line managers alongside HR managers in a working party to develop the system is clearly important as it not only takes account of the needs of the line in the system design, it also demonstrates that the system is line led. Training in the introduction and use of the system is also ideally line led, and Fletcher and Williams (1992) give us an excellent example of an organisation where line managers were trained as 'performance management coaches' who were involved in departmental training and support for the new system. However, some researchers have found that line managers are the weak link in the system (*see*, for example, Hendry *et al.* 1997). The Department of Trade and Industry (DTI) (*see* IRS 2001) notes that any system is only as good as the people who operationalise it. See case 12.1 on the website which deals with the introduction of a performance management system.

WINDOW ON PRACTICE

Fletcher and Williams (1992) report on a scheme that was introduced by training a series of nominated line manager coaches from each department of an organisation. They had then to take the message back to their colleagues and train them, tailoring the material to their department (Personnel/Training providing the back-up documentation). These were serving line managers who had to give up their time to do the job. Many of them were high-flyers, and they have been important opinion leaders and influencers – though they themselves had to be convinced first. Their bosses could refuse to nominate high-quality staff for this role if they wished, but they would subsequently be answerable to the Chief Executive. This approach was taken because it fits with the philosophy of performance management (i.e. high line-management participation), and because it was probably the only way to train all the departmental managers in the timescale envisaged.

Source: Summarised from C. Fletcher and R. Williams (1992b)
Performance Management in the UK: Organisational Experience. London: IPM, p. 133.

Bevan and Thompson (1992) found incomplete take-up of performance management, with some aspects being adopted and not others. They noted that there was a general lack of integration of activities. This is rather unfortunate as one of the key advantages of performance management is the capacity for integration of activities concerned with the management of individual performance. This problem is still apparent. Hendry *et al.* (1997) reported the comments of Phil Wills from GrandMet, that there is still little understanding of what an integrated approach to performance management means. While alignment is critical, some organisations do not understand whether their HR processes are aligned or pulling in different directions. Williams (2002) suggests that there is still confusion over the nature of performance management.

Performance management seems to suffer from the same problems as traditional appraisal systems. Armstrong and Baron (1998a) report, for example, that over half the respondents to their survey feel that managers give their best ratings to people that they like (p. 202), and over half the managers surveyed felt that they had not received sufficient training in performance management processes (p. 203). They also report (1998b) that the use of ratings was consistently derided by staff and seen as subjective and inconsistent. Performance ratings can be seen as demotivating, and forced distributions are felt to be particularly unfair. Yet Houldsworth (2003) found 44 per cent of the Henley and Hay Group survey sample did this.

In terms of individual objective setting linked to organisational performance objectives, there are problems when strategy is unclear and when it evolves. Rose (2000) also reports a range of problems, particularly the fact that SMART targets can be problematic if they are not constantly reviewed and updated, although this is a time-consuming process. Pre-set objectives can be a constraining factor in such a rapidly changing business context, and they remind us of the trap of setting measurable targets, precisely because they are measurable and satisfy the system, rather than because they are most important to the organisation. He argues that a broader approach which assesses the employee's accomplishments as a whole and their contribution to the organisation is more helpful than concentrating on pre-set objectives. Williams (2002) also notes that there is more to performance than task performance, such as volunteering and helping others. He refers to this as contextual performance; it is sometimes referred to as collegiate behaviour.

A further concern with SMART targets is that they inevitably have a short-term focus, yet what is most important to the organisation is developments which are complex and longer term, which are very difficult to pin down to short-term targets (*see*, for example, Hendry *et al.* 1997). In this context systems which also focus on the development of competencies will add greater value in the longer term. Armstrong and Baron (1998b) do note that a more rounded view of performance is gradually being adopted, which involves the 'how' as well as the 'what', and inputs such as the development of competencies. There is, however, a long way to go adequately to describe performance and define what is really required for organisational success.

For an in-depth example of performance management in the Scottish Prison Service *see* case 12.2 on the website.

360-DEGREE FEEDBACK

360-degree feedback, which is a very specific term used to refer to multi-rater feedback, is increasingly being used within performance management systems and as a separate development activity.

The nature of 360-degree feedback

This approach to feedback refers to the use of the whole range of sources from which feedback can be collected about any individual. Thus feedback is collected from every angle on the way that the individual carries out their job: from immediate line manager; peers; subordinates; more senior managers; internal customers; external customers; and from individuals themselves. It is argued that this breadth of feedback provides superior feedback to feedback from the line manager's perspective only, since the latter will only be able to observe the individual in a limited range of situations, and Atwater and his colleagues (2002) suggest that 360-degree feedback provides a better way to capture the complexities of performance. Hogetts *et al.* (1999) report that more than 70 per cent of United Parcels Service employees found that feedback from multiple sources was more useful in developing self-insight than feedback from a single source. Individuals, it is argued, will find feedback from peers and subordinates compelling and more valid (*see*, for example, Borman 1998 and Atwater *et al.* 2001), and Edwards and Ewen (1996, p. 4) maintain that:

> No organizational action has more power for motivating employee behaviour change than feedback from credible work associates.

Such all-round feedback enables the individual to understand how they may be seen differently (or similarly) by different organisational groups, and how this may contrast with their own views of their strengths and weaknesses. This provides powerful information for the development of self-awareness. While 360-degree feedback may be collected using informal methods, as shown in the Window on practice box on Humberside Tec, the term itself is a registered trade mark, and refers to a very specific method of feedback collection and analysis which was devised in the United States (*see* Edwards and Ewen 1996, p. 19), and they suggest that 'simplistic, informal approaches to multi-source assessment are likely to multiply rather than reduce error'. However, informal approaches to 360-degree feedback are sometimes used quite successfully as an alternative to a survey questionnaire and statistical analysis.

WINDOW ON PRACTICE

Using an informal approach to 360-degree feedback at Humberside Tec

Storr (2000) reports on a 360-degree feedback process which is quite different from the survey approach. It is a process which has gradually been built up from upward appraisal for team leaders, has been piloted, and has gradually become standard. The process is owned by the appraisees, and is different because it is carried out face to face rather than using a paper system, and by all raters at the same time in a group-based approach for 90 per cent of individuals. It is a dialogue rather than a survey, and the only rule is that every individual must carry out at least one per year. The purpose of the system is to 'improve performance and enable people to learn and grow' (p. 38). Each group has a trained facilitator who supports both appraisers and appraisees. Different individuals have reacted differently to the approach, as might be expected: one individual said that they see it as empowerment, and many found that there was a great advantage in seeing the world from other people's point of view. Storr reports on one individual who received similar feedback from the group to that which she had received previously, from her manager, but hearing it from the six members of the group had a much stronger effect on her. Individuals often used their first experience of the process in a general way to ask the group what they should start doing, stop doing, continue doing or do differently. Over time, however, individuals began to ask more specific questions.

Source: Summarised from F. Storr (2000) 'This is not a circular', *People Management*, 11 May, pp. 38–40.

ACTIVITY 12.3

Think of your current or previous role, in paid employment or any other capacity, and:

1 Identify one or two critical incidents (such as making a presentation or attending an important meeting for the first time).

2 Identify a longer-term activity you have been involved in (such as a project group or working party).

For both of these identify who could have provided you with constructive feedback, and why, and what specific questions you would have asked of them.

Now think ahead. What plans can you make to incorporate feedback into an up-coming one-off or longer-term activity?

The formal process is a survey approach which involves the use of a carefully constructed questionnaire that is used with all the contributors of feedback. This questionnaire may be bought off the peg, providing a well-tested tool, or may be developed internally, providing a tool which is more precisely matched to the needs of the organisation. Whichever form is used, the essence is that it is based on behavioural competencies (for a more detailed explanation of these *see* Chapter 17), and their associated behaviours. Contributors will be asked to score, on a given scale, the extent to which the individual displays these behaviours. Using a well-designed questionnaire, distributed to a sufficient number of contributors and employing appropriate sophisticated analysis, for example specifically designed computer packages which are set up to detect and moderate collusion and bias on behalf of the contributors, should provide reliable and valid data for the individual. The feedback is usually presented to the individual in the form of graphs or bar charts showing comparative scores from different feedback groups, such as peers, subordinates, customers, where the average will be provided for each group, and single scores from line manager and self. In most cases the individual will have been able to choose the composition of the contributors in each group, for example which seven subordinates, out of a team of 10, will be asked to complete the feedback questionnaire. But beyond this the feedback will be anonymous as only averages for each group of contributors will be reported back, except for the line manager's score. The feedback will need to be interpreted by an internal or external facilitator, and done via a face-to-face meeting. It is generally recommended that the individual will need some training in the nature of the system and how to receive feedback, and the contributors will need some training on how to provide feedback. The principle behind the idea of feedback is that individuals can then use this information to change their behaviours and to improve performance, by setting and meeting development goals and an action plan.

Reported benefits include a stronger ownership of development goals, a climate of constructive feedback, improved communication over time and an organisation which is more capable of change as continuous feedback and improvement have become part of the way people work (Cook and Macauley 1997). Useful texts on designing and implementing a system include Edwards and Ewen (1996) from the US perspective and Ward (1998) from the UK perspective. A brief 'how to do it guide' is Goodge and Watts (2000).

Difficulties and dilemmas

As with all processes and systems there needs to be clarity about the purpose. Most authors distinguish between developmental uses, which they identify as fairly safe and a good way of introducing such a system, and other uses such as to determine pay awards. There seems to be an almost universal view that using these data for pay purposes is not advisable, and in the literature from the United States there is clearly a concern about the legal ramifications of doing this. Ward (1998) provides a useful framework for considering the different applications of this type of feedback, and reviews in some detail other applications such as using 360-degree feedback as part of a training course to focus attention for each individual on what they need to get out of the course. Other applications he suggests include using 360-degree feedback as an approach to team building, as a method of performance appraisal/management, for organisation development purposes and to evaluate training and development. Edwards and Ewen (1996) suggest that it can be used for nearly all HR systems, using selection, training and development, recognition and the allocation of job assignments as examples.

As well as clarity of purpose, confidentiality of raters is very important with most approaches to 360-degree feedback, and this can be difficult to maintain with a small team, as Hurley (1998) suggests. Thus raters may feel uncomfortable about being open and honest. The dangers of collusion and bias need to be eliminated, and it is suggested that the appropriate software systems can achieve this, but they are of course expensive, as are well-validated off-the-peg systems. Follow-up is critical and if the experience of 360-degree feedback is not built on via the construction of development goals and the support and resources to fulfil these, the process may be viewed negatively and may be demotivating.

London et al. (1997) report concerns about the way systems are implemented, and that nearly one-third of respondents they surveyed experienced negative effects. Atwater and his colleagues (2002) found some negative reactions such as reduced effort, dissatisfaction with peers who provided the feedback and a lower commitment to colleagues. Fletcher and Baldry (2001) note that there are contradictions in the results from 360-degree feedback so far, and they suggest that further research is needed on how feedback affects self-esteem, motivation, satisfaction and commitment. The DTI (2001) suggests that sufficient resources need to be devoted to planning a system and that it should be piloted before general use. Clearly, 360-degree feedback needs to be handled carefully and sensitively and in the context of an appropriate organisational climate so that it is not experienced as a threat. The DTI (2001) suggests that there needs to be a climate of openness and trust for 360-degree feedback to work. Atwater et al. (2002) suggest that to counteract any negative effects it is important to prepare people for making their own ratings and on how they can provide honest and constructive feedback to others, ensure confidentiality and anonymity of raters, make sure the feedback is used developmentally and owned by the person being rated (for example they may be the only person to receive the report), provide post-feedback coaching and encouragement and encourage people to follow up the feedback they have received.

WINDOW ON PRACTICE

Johnson (2001) reports on the merger between two pharmaceuticals companies – UniChem from the UK and Alliance Sante from France to form Alliance UniChem. In an attempt to focus managers from diverse cultures on a single vision the HR department concentrated on all aspects of performance management, in particular 360-degree feedback which was felt to be a pragmatic and practical tool. Four key values were identified, excellence, service, innovation and partnership, and competencies were drawn up to reflect these. The process had to be introduced very sensitively as 360-degree feedback was virtually unheard of in three countries covered by the company – Italy, Spain and Portugal, and in France it was seen very much as an American tool and regarded with considerable suspicion.

The most senior managers went through the process first, and it was then piloted in different countries. The tool was developed to be used in five different languages, and the customised package adopted came with development activities for each competency, and coaching sessions to ensure that feedback was not interpreted without analysis and support. The whole process formed part of a self-development programme.

Source: Summarised from R. Johnson (2001) 'Doubled entente', People Management, Vo. 7, No. 9, 3 May, pp. 38–9.

SUMMARY PROPOSITIONS

12.1 Performance management systems incorporate appraisal activity, but include other aspects such as a link to organisational objectives, an emphasis on ongoing review, motivation, coaching and support, and reinforcement/reward for performance achieved.

12.2 There is a conflict in many appraisal and performance management systems as managers frequently have a dual role as assessor and developer.

12.3 Current trends in sophisticated appraisal systems include greater employee ownership, emphasis on the how as well as the what, emphasis on evidence collection from both manager and employee, upward feedback to the line manager as well as downward feedback to the employee.

12.4 360-degree feedback is increasingly being used to provide individuals with a basis for changing behaviour and improving performance. It is important to use this process developmentally rather than linking it directly to pay awards.

GENERAL DISCUSSION TOPICS

1 In what ways is the concept of performance management different from the way in which management has been traditionally practised? What are the advantages and disadvantages for employees and employers?

2 360-degree feedback may have many advantages, but there is the argument that it can never really work because of the built-in biases, such as marking a boss well because you're due for a pay rise; marking yourself low so that you can be happily surprised by others' evaluations; marking peers down to make oneself look better. Discuss as many built-in biases as you can think of, and suggest how they might be tackled and whether substantive improvements could be made.

FURTHER READING

Neary, D. (2002) 'Creating a company-wide on-line performance management system: A case study at TRW Inc', *Human Resource Management*, Vol. 41, No. 4, Winter, pp. 491–8
An interesting example of an IT-based system across 100,000 employees based in 36 countries. Explains the design and implementation of the system.

Swinburne, P. (2001) 'How to use feedback to improve performance', *People Management*, Vol. 7, No. 11, 31 May, pp. 46–7
Short but extremely helpful and full of practical detail. Excellent guidelines on the dos and don'ts of giving feedback and some very useful tips for receiving feedback.

REFERENCES

Armstrong, M. and Baron, A. (1998a) *Performance Management – The New Realities*. London: IPD.

Armstrong, M. and Baron, A. (1998b) 'Out of the Tick Box', *People Management*, 23 July, pp. 38–41.

AstraZeneca (2000) *Management of Team and Individual Performance*. London: AstraZeneca plc.

Atwater, L., Waldman, D. and Brett, J. (2002) 'Understanding and optimising multi-source feedback', *Human Resource Management*, Vol. 41, No. 2, summer, pp. 193–208.

Audit Commission (2002) *Performance Breakthrough: improving performance in public sector organizations*. London: The Audit Commission.

Barlow, G. (1989) 'Deficiencies and the perpetuation of power: latent functions in management appraisal', *Journal of Management Studies*, Vol. 26, No. 5, pp. 499–518.

Bevan, S. and Thompson, M. (1992) 'An overview of policy and practice', in *Personnel Management in the UK: an anaylsis of the issues*. London: IPM.

Borman, W. (1998) '360 ratings: an analysis of assumptions and a research agenda for evaluating their validity', *Human Resource Management Review*, Vol. 7, pp. 299–315.

Coates, G. (1994) 'Performance appraisal as icon: Oscar winning performance or dressing to impress?' *International Journal of Human Resource Management*, No. 1, February.

Cook, S. and Macauley, S. (1997) 'How colleagues and customers can help improve team performance', *Team Performance Management*, Vol. 3, No. 1.

DTI (2001) *360 degree feedback: Best practice guidelines* (Prof C. Farrell). dti.gov.uk/mbp/360feedback.

Edwards, M.R. and Ewen, A.J. (1996) *360 Degree Feedback*. New York: Amacom, American Management Association.

Egan, G. (1995) 'A clear path of peak performance', *People Management*, 18 May, pp. 34–7.

Fletcher, C. and Baldry, C. (2001) 'Multi-source feedback systems: a research perspective', in I. Robertson and C. Cooper (eds) *Personnel Psychology and HRM*. Chichester: John Wiley and Sons Ltd.

Fletcher, C. and Williams, R. (1992) *Performance Management in the UK: Organisational experience*. London: IPM.

Goodge, P. and Watts, P. (2000) 'How to manage 360° feedback', *People Management*, 17 February, pp. 50–2.

Grint, K. (1993) 'What's wrong with performance appraisals? – a critique and a suggestion', *Human Resource Management Journal*, Vol. 3, No. 3, pp. 61–77.

Hendry, C., Bradley, P. and Perkins, S. (1997) 'Missed a motivator?' *People Management*, 15 May, pp. 20–5.

Hendry, C., Woodward, S., Bradley, P. and Perkins, S. (2000) 'Performance and rewards: cleaning out the stables', *Human Resource Management Journal*, Vol. 10, No. 3, pp. 46–62.

Hogetts, R., Luthans, F. and Slocum, J. (1999) 'Strategy and HRM initiatives for the '00s: environment redefining roles and boundaries, linking competencies and resources', *Organizational Dynamics*, Autumn, p. 7.

Houldsworth, E. (2003) 'Managing Individual performance', paper presented to the CIPD National Conference, Harrogate 22–24 November 2003.

Hurley, S. (1998) 'Application of team-based 360° feedback systems', *Team Performance Management*, Vol. 4, No. 5.

IDS (2003) *IDS Studies: Performance Management*, No. 748, April, London: IDS.

IRS (2001) 'Performance appraisal must try harder', *IRS Employment Trends*, No. 724, March, pp. 2–3.

IRS (2003) 'Time to talk – how and why employers conduct appraisals', *IRS Employment Trends*, No. 769, 7 February, pp. 7–14.

Johnson, R. (2001) 'Doubled entente', *People Management*, Vol. 7, No. 9, 3 May, pp. 38–9.

Locke, E. and Latham, G. (1990) *A Theory of Goal Setting and Task Performance*. Englewood Cliffs, NJ: Prentice-Hall.

Locke, E. (1968) 'Towards a theory of task performance and incentives', *Organisational Behaviour and Human Performance*, Vol. 3, No. 2, pp. 157–89.

London, M., Smither, J. and Adsit, D. (1997) 'Accountability: the achilles heel of multi-source feedback', *Group and Organizational Dynamics*, Vol. 22, No. 2, pp. 162–84.

Longenecker, C. (1997) 'Why managerial performance appraisals are ineffective: causes and lessons', *Career Development International*, Vol. 2, No. 5.

Mabey, C. and Salaman, G. (1995) *Strategic Human Resource Management*. Oxford: Blackwell.

Newton, T. and Findlay, P. (1996) 'Playing God? – the performance of appraisal', *Human Resource Management Journal*, Vol. 6, No. 3, pp. 42–58.

Rose, M. (2000) 'Target Practice', *People Management*, 23 November, pp. 44–5.

Sewell, G. and Wilkinson, B. (1992) 'Someone to watch over me: surveillance, discipline and the just-in-time process', *Sociology*, Vol. 26, pp. 271–89.

Storr, F. (2000) 'This is not a circular', *People Management*, 11 May, pp. 38–40.

Townley, B. (1989) 'Selection and appraisal: reconstituting social relations', in J. Storey (ed.) *New Perspectives on Human Resource Management*. London: Routledge.

Townley, B. (1993) 'Performance appraisal and the emergence of management', *Journal of Management Studies*, Vol. 30, No. 2, pp. 27–44.

Ward, P. (1995) 'A 360 degree turn for the better', *People Management*, 9 February.

Williams, R. (2002) *Managing Employee Performance*. London: Thompson Learning.

An extensive range of additional materials, including multiple choice questions, answers to questions and links to useful websites can be found on the Human Resource Management Companion Website at **www.pearsoned.co.uk/torrington**.

TOPIC SUMMARY SHEET

What are the key learning points from this topic?

TOPIC 11 – PEOPLE AND BUSINESS STRATEGY

Why study this topic?

In order for an organisation to achieve its objectives, it has to have a strategy. The strategy used will determine how the organisation will use its resources. In other words the strategy provides the organisation with a sense of direction which will determine their policies and procedures.

The organisation also has to decide how it will use its available resources. These can take the form of financial, physical and people resources. The ideal position for any organisation is that they make best use of these, especially the human resources. As we have learned so far, how human resources are used are central to an organisation's success or failure.

This chapter will help you to understand and examine the strong link between organisational strategy and people management. Additionally, you will discover how both elements of strategy and people can complement each other for the benefit of the organisation.

Blackboard

E-tivity 11: People and business strategy

LINKING HUMAN RESOURCE MANAGEMENT TO ORGANISATIONAL STRATEGY
G.A. Maxwell

11.1   INTRODUCTION

The previous chapter explores elements of human resource management (HRM) that combine to effect reward management systems. Such systems are designed and managed with the intention of contributing to the performance of employees. This chapter explains HRM from the perspective of the organisation or business as a whole, identifying the connections between HRM and organisational strategies. Its purpose is to *link the management of people at work to broader organisational strategy*. Understanding this relationship is important as an organisation's strategy provides a focus for its activities and resources. Strategies shape how organisations work and develop. Firstly, the chapter outlines strategic aspects of organisations. Secondly it links organisational strategies to HRM.

Holbeche (2002; 92) alludes to the focus that strategy provides, with reference to an extract from Lewis Carroll's Alice in Wonderland, which points to the effects of not having a guiding strategy.

Alice: "Would you tell me please which way I should go from here?"
Cat: "That depends a good deal on where you want to get to."
Alice: "I don't much care where."
Cat: "Then it doesn't much matter which way you go."

11.2   STRATEGIC ASPECTS OF ORGANISATIONS

11.2.1   Defining Strategy

Understanding what strategy means is the foundation of this chapter. Pinpointing the meaning of strategy in precise terms in an organisational context presents something of a challenge as a range of definitions exist. For example, Marginson (1988), an HRM commentator, defines strategy as 'the directions an organisation takes to plan for and secure its long term goals.' Like many definitions of strategy, this definition is quite open-ended, even vague. Johnson and Scholes (1999), widely known management commentators, define the term strategy with more description. They highlight the principal elements of strategy as: the *direction* and *scope* of organisational activity in the *long term* aimed at gaining an *advantage* for an organisation to meet its *markets'* needs and *stakeholder* expectations. This definition offers a more concrete explanation of strategy in the modern business environment. Much of the literature on organisational strategy refers implicitly to commercial, money making activities in a competitive business environment. However, as public and voluntary sector organisations increasingly adopt competitive measures to reduce costs, the general literature on **business strategy** may be relevant to them. Business strategy can also be known as **corporate strategy**, especially in large organisations.

The term strategy comes from planning for the campaigns of armies in ancient Greece.

'Strategy is the *direction* and *scope* of an organisation over the *long term* which achieves *advantage* for the organisation through its configuration of resources within a changing environment, to meet the needs of *markets* and fulfil *stakeholder* expectations'
(Johnson and Scholes, 1999; 10).

Generally, strategy can be seen to refer to:
- a longterm, holistic perspective and purpose of organisations; and/or
- the directions in which the organisation's efforts are expended.

Long termism is often taken to be a five year period. However, it can vary depending on the organisation's type and circumstances. For example, the long term for a pharmaceutical company developing an antidote to the severe acute respiratory syndrome virus (SARS) may be well over five years, while for a small, seasonal business such as a tourist attraction, one year may be considered long term. A holistic point of view encapsulates the organisation as whole, from the organisational position (as opposed to employee position, for example). The purpose of the organisation is the very reason for its existence, for example, in the case of public limited companies, to make profits for financial returns to shareholder investors by paying out dividends. Public sector organisations, like hospitals and schools, function to provide important public services with minimum costs. The directions in which the organisation's efforts are expended concern the goals for development. Examples of organisational drives in direction include product or service differentiation, centralisation or decentralisation of control, and international expansion.

> What internal and organisational external factors do you think influence an organisation's strategic direction?

11.2.2   Expressions of Strategy

Organisational strategies are usually expressed in short statements which constitute **mission statements** or statements of **strategic intent**. All organisational activity focuses on these, either directly or indirectly. Strategic missions or intentions indicate in short what the organisation seeks to achieve with reference to a range of internal and external factors. Profit margins, cash flow and quality of service are all examples of internal factors. Market share, consumer confidence, economic conditions such as interest rates, and labour markets are examples of external factors.

> There is an apocryphal story that, when asked what his job was by a visiting VIP, a cleaner at the American space agency NASA replied "Putting men on the moon."

Organisations' specific expressions of strategy can indicate the business (or market) position, priorities and management approach or style in particular organisations. They can also make for interesting reading in stylistic terms and form part of advertising or public relations statements. Here are four examples.

Peebles Hydro, Scotland (commercial leisure and hospitality):
'to persistently delight all external and internal customers, ensuring a prosperous future for the company, shareholders and staff.'

> What business priority in terms of service is suggested here?

Lothian and Borders Police, Scotland (public sector):
'to prevent crime, keep the peace, protect and reassure the community, uphold the law firmly and fairly, and pursue and identify those who break the law.'

> What is the primary organisational priority declared here?

W.L. Gore and Associates Inc., USA owned (innovative manufacturing):
'to make money and have fun ..in fostering the creativity and initiative
that contribute to technical development and innovation.'

> What management style is implied in this example?

IKEA, Swedish owned (global household retailer):
'to create a better everyday life for the many people.'

> Is a mass or elite market targeted by this company?

Whereas statements of strategy indicate <u>what</u> the organisation seeks to achieve, declared **organisational values** indicate <u>how</u> the organisation strives to achieve its strategy. Common organisational values include fairness, openness and service orientation, not least to influence customer perceptions of businesses in a positive way. Some companies go further and include values that relate to consumer concerns. For example the GAP clothes retailer and NIKE sports retailers both have codes of ethics covering child labour in their manufacturing suppliers in the far east, in an attempt to address a practically challenging issue. Just as these values may be important to market perception, so too might they be to an organisation's employees and labour market.

> The Hilton international hotel chain has individual guest experiences of quality service - Hilton moments – as its competitive strategy. The HR strategy supporting this is based on the values of respect, reward and recognition.

> What business values are important to you as a consumer and as an employee?

11.2.3   Strategy and Structure

As explained, an organisation's declared strategy is at the centre of organisational activity and understanding organisations. Chandler's (1962) famous dictum that organisational structure follows strategy reflects the centrality of organisational strategy. According to Chandler's study of the growth of 70 large US businesses, all expanding businesses go through three stages of development.

The first stage of development is the **unit firm**. As an organisation grows from a single location, with a single product or service, with a single decision maker into a unit firm, more people are employed. Consequently reporting lines are established and economies of scale are usually attempted. At this stage, strategy making is often highly centralised, especially by entrepreneurs, and a particular strength in small organisations.

> The Body Shop international retail chain expanded from one shop.

The second stage of development is into a **functional organisation** where size means specialisation by function or department is necessary. At this stage strategy making typically becomes more formalised at board or director level.

> Human Resources Department is one example of functional specialisation.

If the organisation expands still further and diversifies into different industries and products or services, the third stage is transformation into a **multi-divisional firm**. Strategy making is often a complex process in organisations of this size.

> The now collapsed company Enron is a notable example of a multi-divisional firm with complex strategies (and financing).

Miles and Snow (1984) develop Chandler's view on the basis of their extensive research. They assert that organisations need structures that support and management processes – arguably including HRM – that support their strategy in order to avoid the strategy failing. They dub the match between strategy, structure and management processes **strategic fit**.

In capitalist business systems (as explained in Part 1 Chapter 5) size is often considered a measure of organisational success. Hence organisations often try to expand and mergers and take-overs become features of big business. Organisational strategies and structures then have to be adapted so are not necessarily fixed or permanent.

→ Contextual events, such as the September 11 2001 catastrophe, can precipitate rapid changes to strategy.

11.2.4   Stages of Strategy Development

Identifying stages in the process of developing strategy provides a framework for both devising and revising strategy. Thompson and Strickland (1998) advocate five phases of strategy development.

1. Defining the business and establishing a strategic mission.
2. Setting strategic objectives and performance targets.
3. Formulating of a strategy to achieve the target objectives and performance.
4. Implementing and executing the plan.
5. Evaluating performance and reformulating the strategic plan and/ or its implementation.

As can be seen, the phases start at the basic point of defining the business itself, then defining a relevant strategic mission. At this point in the process of strategy development, the **espoused strategy** is formally declared. When the organisational performance is reviewed and compared to the espoused strategy, the end result can be called the **realised strategy**.

Peter Drucker, a widely known management commentator, famously raised the vital reflective question for businesses *'What business are we in?'*

Generally, HRM can fit into Thompson and Strickland's (1998) process of strategy development in two ways. HRM can be part of the strategic mission, for example the mission statement for Peebles Hydro (section 6.2.2) indicates an explicit role for HRM, while the mission statement for W.L. Gore (section 6.2.2) indicates an implicit role for HRM in the company. Here HRM can be considered **mainstream** to the organisation. Alternatively, HRM can fit into strategy development in the setting of objectives and performance targets which include aspects of HRM such as training and development (as discussed in Part 2, Chapter 2). Here HRM is likely to be **downstream** in the organisational priorities.

11.2.5   Organisation as Process

Another important strategic aspect of organisations is understanding that organisations can be considered as processes of decision-making rather than as just as inanimate entities. Key elements of the organisation as a process include the generic management activities of planning ahead and decision-making. HR may be an element of wider organisational planning and decisions are ultimately made by people. More importantly, and often neglected in general management literature, many of the processes within organisations, including planning and communication, are conducted by people – employees – with all their variations in perceptions, attitudes, personality, ability, skills, competence and motivation (as discussed in Part 1, Chapter 2). Thus considering organisations as a process inevitably, but often subtly, involves not only human resources but also their management. In short, HRM is in an integral element of organisations as processes.

What other generic management activities do you think involve an HR element?

One explanation for the difference between espoused and realised organisation strategy (as outlined in 6.2.4) may be the potentially powerful people factor of **organisational culture**. Crudely, organisational culture may be described as:

'the way things are done around here [in the organisation]. It is what is typical of the organisation, the habits, the prevailing attitudes, the grown up pattern of accepted and expected behaviour' (Drennan, 1992; 3).

Think of a job you have had. What were the main features of 'accepted and expected behaviour' in the group you worked in?

Just as structure and management processes should support strategy, (section 6.2.3), so too should the dominant organisational culture. Where there is a wide gap between the espoused strategy and prevalent organisational culture, there is also the distinct possibility of challenges in achieving the strategy. For instance, in an organisation like W.L. Gore which encourages and needs innovation, an organisational culture that has a high degree of control and authority at its centre is counterproductive.

11.2.6   The People Factor in Strategy Formulation

Watson (2002) underlines the point about the people factor inherent in the strategy formulation. In his model (below), strategic exchange represents the crux where the strategy is formulated. Strategy arises from those making the strategy, with their different identities, values and motivations, in conjunction with organisational factors such as organisational culture. In this way the objective, organisation perspective of strategy can be affected by individuals' perspectives. Moreover, those senior managers contributing to strategy formulation may among themselves have points to make or settle, possibly leading to political manoeuvres, rivalry and personal competition. Tensions between the most senior executives in the Ford Motor Company, for instance, have been the subject of newspaper articles.

There are some well known examples of Chief Executive Officers (CEOs) and Managing Directors (MDs) taking the lead in strategy. Bill Gates of Microsoft and Richard Branson of Virgin are two. Can you identify others?

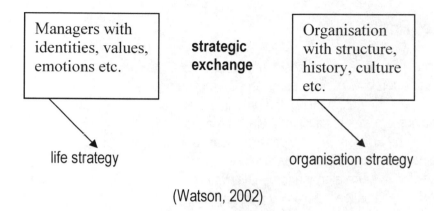

(Watson, 2002)

11.3   LINKING ORGANISATIONAL STRATEGY TO HRM

11.3.1   The People Factor in Implementing Strategy

Having the right strategy, structure, management processes and
organisational culture, important as they are, is not enough to
ensure effective organisational performance. For strategy has to be implemented -
operationalised. Pfeffer (1995; *) underlines this point:

'the key is not just having the right strategy, but being able to implement
the strategy – having, in other words, effective operational capabilities.'

Strategy implementation calls for resources, including the most dynamic
resource of all – human resources! In a sense then, organisational or
corporate capability is achieved through employees and how they are
managed. This raises the question of the nature and role of HRM in
organisations. According to Boxall and Purcell (2003; 45), furthermore:

> In customer facing,
> labour intensive and
> knowledge organisations,
> the role of HRM is arguably
> of heightened importance.
> Can you identify examples
> of these types of businesses?

'without certain kinds of human capability, firms [organisations]
 are simply not viable.'

In considering how organisational strategy may be linked directly to
HRM, the perspective must broaden from the holistic organisation to
that of individuals working within the organisation. Effective HRM is
based on an appreciation of how people behave and interact at work,
as discussed in Part 1.

11.3.2   Strategic HRM

HRM emerged as a distinctive approach to managing employees
in the 1980s. More a gradually emergent concept than a radically
new notion, one of the defining features of HRM is often levelled to be
its strategic trajectory of the HR function, although this is an area of contention
in the debate that surrounds HRM. Some commentators, for example
Armstrong (1999) contends that what sets HRM apart is its very strategic nature.
Whereas previous approaches to the management of employees were often
operational in their focus, HRM adopts a strategic perspective – that is a

> The traditional approach to
> managing people -
> personnel management -
> was typically a marginalised
> organisational function.

long term, holistic and organisationally purposive perspective.
Definitions of HRM vary. For example, Armstrong (1999; 3) defines HRM as:
'a strategic and coherent approach to the management of an organisation's most valued assets – the people working there who individually and collectively contribute to the achievement of its goals.'

While Guest (1979) argues that HRM revolves around four goals, namely **integration** (with organisational plans), employee **commitment**, flexibility/ **adaptability** (in organisational structures and employee jobs), and **quality** (of employees, performance, work standards and public image).

These definitions seemed to have developed little since the 1980s and are still not universally agreed, as Mabey *et al.* (1999) point out. Consequently, it may be useful to focus on explaining rather defining the term. McKenna and Beech (2002; 1) offer a succinct explanation that captures the basic scope of HRM:

'HRM seeks to maximise organisational performance through adoption of best practice in the management of people....HRM can be viewed as an approach to personnel management that considers people as the key resource. It subscribes to the notion that it is important to communicate well with employees, to involve them in what is going on and to foster commitment to and identification with the organisation.'

> Organisations refer to their employees in different ways: human resources, people, colleagues, associates, partners, co-workers e.g.

Leopold (2002) extends this explanation in citing Watson's (1999;20) summary of the contemporary uses of the term HRM:

° 'as a more fashionable name for personnel management.
° to refer to all managerial activity... that involves relationships between the organisation and its employees.
° to describe an area of academic study, integrating the 'subjects' of personnel management, industrial relations and elements of organisational behaviour.
° an an umbrella term for 'new management' practices, involving higher commitment from employees and giving them greater task discretion, which have been given increased emphasis in the US and UK in the latter decades of the twentieth century.'

Strategic integration (see 6.3.3), achievement of business goals and employee commitment are possibly the main hallmarks of HRM. Other characteristics include employee flexibility, employee development, unitarist employee relations, and teamwork, all of which are discussed in this text. Not only are these features of HRM, but they also constitute **HRM ideals**, implying HRM may be more idealist than realistic as a concept or theory. Significantly, HRM is not the exclusive preserve of HR specialists in providing **HR services** such as recruitment and training within organisations. Instead, HRM embraces the involvement of line managers in HR activities like coaching and appraisals.

> IBM and Hewlett Packard are examples of companies which adopted HRM early.

> What other services might an HR department provide?
> List the advantages and disadvantages of line managers being involved in HRM.

As a result, HRM has implications for management styles within organisations. Beer *et al.* (1984; p*) reinforce this point:
' HRM involves all the management decisions and actions that affect the nature of the relationship between the organisation and its employees – its human resources.'

Above all, viewing employees as an organisational asset or investment lies at the core of HRM. HRM does not centre on employees for altruistic purposes but for the instrumental purpose of achieving organisational strategy. According to Armstrong (1988; 72) there are four fundamental principles of HRM starting with and stemming from the centrality of employees in business performance:

> How significant do you think the actions, behaviours and attitudes of employees in contact with customers are to realising strategy?

'1. Human resources are the most important assets an organisation has and their effective management is the key to its success;
2. Organisational success is most likely to be achieved in the [HR] policies and procedures of the enterprise are closely linked with, and make a major contribution to, the achievement of corporate objectives and strategic plans;
3. The corporate culture and the values, organisational climate and managerial behaviour that emanate from that culture will exert a major influence of the achievement of excellence. This culture must be managed, which means that continuous effort, starting from the top, will be required to get the values accepted and acted upon.
4. Continuous effort is required to achieve integration – getting all members of the organisation involved and working together with a sense of common purpose.'

Much of the contemporary literature on HRM incorporates and even advocates these principles. This is not to say, however, that HRM is without its critics. HRM has attracted criticism on a number of fronts including its lack of definitional specificity, obscure jargon and limited application in practice. One of the most enduring criticisms is the sometimes stark difference between its potential and its implementation in organisations. Despite controversy and criticism, HRM has not proved to be a management fad but a topic of sustained and developing academic and business interest.

> Can you think of any other criticisms of HRM? Who might make these criticisms?

11.3.3   Models of HRM

HRM can be conceptually framed and practically implemented in a number of ways, versions or models of HRM. McKenna and Beech (2002) for instance identify three models of HRM: the *matching model*, the *resource-based model* and the *processual approach*. The *matching model* focuses on very close **strategic integration** of HRM and organisational strategy. For example if the business strategy is to achieve low costs with high output volumes in a manufacturing plant, then there is a need to deploy the workforce to minimise employment costs. Flexible working may support such a strategy. The *resource-based model* concentrates on analysing employees' capabilities,

> Models of HRM can help frame understanding and expectations of the role of HR function in organisations.

knowledge and skills within the organisation in order to sustain competitive advantage. Thus the main focus of this model is maintaining alignment of employee competencies to respond to opportunities in the external operating environment, like the opening up of new markets. This dynamic process emphasises the role of employee development. The *processual approach* recognises that strategy is the outcome of planned and unplanned activities. It links espoused HR policies to realised practices so that the policies remain meaningful. Employee involvement may be important in this model of strategic HRM.

One of the most often cited models of HRM is Beer *et al.'s* (1985) so-called Harvard model. (* to be added below) This model sets HRM in the broad context of the operating environment.

> Guest (1989) recognised two types of HRM: the 'hard model' where employees managed positively but in a collective, rational-economic sense; and the 'soft model' where employees are treated more individually.

11.3.4   Objectives of HR Responsibility

Another way of examining the direct links between organisational strategy and HRM is consideration of the overall role and objectives of HRM in the organisation. Holbeche (2001; 94) identifies four such **organisational roles** for HRM contribution (below) which she calls objectives of HR responsibility.

❖ *Maximum strategic impact*

- Align HR practices with business objectives.
- Conduct development programmes to support strategic changes.
- Carry out job analyses for long term objectives.
- Improve HR adaptability in changing environments.
- Enhance workforce capability and motivation.

> Where these are the HR responsibilities, HRM is highly valued in the organisation at senior levels. It is very likely that there is an HR Director.

❖ *Co-ordination*

- Improve co-ordination between various functions in the organisation.
- Improve team effectiveness.
- Improve HR project management.
- Develop pay and reward systems.
- Co-ordinate any potential HR problems.
- Integrate diverse HR functions and operations.

> A co-ordination role for HR implies a more limited contribution of HRM that centres largely on specialist HR performance. There may be an HR Manager and specialist HR department.

❖ *Communication*

- Communicate HR policies inside the organisation.
- Improve management acceptance of current HR policies.
- Improve employee involvement and understanding of HRM.
- Conduct job analyses for long term objectives.
- Communicate HRM policies outside the company.

> The communication HR responsibility implies a narrow and functionally limited role for HRM in the organisation.

❖ *Control*

- Clarify budget and resource availability.
- Manage personnel related costs.
- Improve HR budget control.
- Improve HR resource procedures and control.
- Review HRM operational procedures.

> The lowest level of all organisational roles, control suggests a procedural, administrative contribution for HRM.

(adapted from Hobeche (2002; 94))

All four of these roles indicate a downstream contribution of HRM, where HRM is secondary to the organisational strategy, not integral to it. Therefore, in all of Holbeche's roles the level of strategic integration is implicitly relatively low. The positional authority of HRM is, to varying degrees, not as high as other functional specialisms such as finance or marketing, for argument's sake. However, the personal authority of the HR specialists, where it is high, can act to improve the organisational status of HRM. The performance and credibility of HRM specialists is therefore important to the organisational responsibility roles.

> What core skills and competencies should HR specialists demonstrate in your opinion?

11.3.5   Bundles of HRM Policies

HRM can also be linked to organisational strategy through its own **functional strategies**. Examples of HRM functional strategies include organisational development, empowerment, quality management, learning organisation and work-life balance. All of these broad HRM strategies involve aspects of managing people at work explored earlier in the text. For example, organisational development covers individual perception, leadership and motivating people, and team processes, together with training and development and employment relations. Therefore broad HRM strategies typically involve integrated bundles of HR policies which complement, not contradict each other. The Royal Bank of Scotland is an example of an organisation that is adopting a work-life balance HRM strategy for its 114 000 plus employees in the UK, Europe, the USA, Hong Kong and Australia. A range of factors have led to this: rapid deregulation and increased competition in the financial sector, company buy-outs, tight labour markets, changes in

> Can you identify any HR policy areas that complement each other?

attitudes towards work and in employment law for example. The work-life balance strategy encapsulates a number of related policies, including: managing diversity, compressed working hours, job share, part time working, variable hours and term time working. Together, these policies are packaged in an HR strategy called "Your time", clearly focusing on individuals, the very essence of HRM as discussed in 6.3.2.

HRM policies, in turn, should be translated into procedures for consistent implementation by HR specialists and line managers with an HR responsibility alike. HR polices and procedures are often included in employee handbooks. Policies and procedures are, however, not always formally expressed and communicated. HR specialists would probably argue that espoused strategy is most likely to result in realised strategy if the connected HRM policies and procedures are formalised and observed by all managers as appropriate. Experiences of implementing HRM policies and procedures can inform amendments to the policies and procedures themselves and subsequent HRM strategy over time. For instance, experience of an organisational development strategy may result in the formulation of a learning organisation strategy. The connections between HRM strategy, policy and procedures is illustrated below.

> Remember Pfeffer's (1995) caution on following strategy through with operational capability.

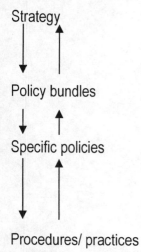

Strategy

Policy bundles

Specific policies

Procedures/ practices

> What organisational factors might interfere with this model in practice?

Bundling and applying HRM policies that represent **best practice**, that is highly developed aspects of organisational practice, will arguably help attract, develop and retain a quality workforce. Investing in employees in this way means a **resource-based** approach to HR strategy, whereby 'managers seek to gain competitive advantage through the quality of the people employed' (Tyson and York, 2000; p323).

11.4   SUMMARY PROPOSITIONS

∇   Strategy generally refers to a long term, holistic perspective and purpose of organisations; and/ or the directions in which business efforts are expended.

∇   Strategy is often expressed in mission statements or statements of strategic intent. Organisational values indicate the way in which organisations seek to achieve their strategy.

∇   Strategy is fundamental to organisations and is more important than structure. Organisational structures should support strategy.

∇   The stages of strategy development can incorporate HRM as mainstream or downstream in espoused organisational strategy.

∇   Organisational processes involve a people element. Organisational culture influences processes and therefore strategy.

∇   The senior managers who are responsible for formulating strategy bring with them individual identities, values and motivations which may influence their role in strategy formulation.

∇   HRM involves a strategic perspective of the HR function as a whole HRM services.

∇   Different models of HRM have different implications for the extent of integration of HRM with organisational strategy.

∇   The objectives of HRM in organisations vary in relation to the views of its overall role in, and responsibility for, organisational performance.

∇   Approaches to HRM in organisations are reflected in sets of HR polices and procedures which are derived from business and HR strategy.

11.5   CONCLUDING CONTENTIONS

This chapter explains the links between human resource management and organisational strategy. Much of the literature on organisational or business strategy implicitly adopts an organisational perspective, that is a general and disinterested view of organisations. In so doing it neglects to highlight that employees are an integral and inevitable part of a number of strategic aspects of strategic aspects of organisations. Therefore, organisational strategy can be considered from the perspective of human resources and their management – HRM.

In addition, HRM is reflected in organisational strategy in terms of the long term, broad view of HR activities and services that can help organisations secure their strategic mission. In different models and with varying degrees of responsibility and integration,

HRM supports organisational strategy through operationalising bundles of policies. In sum, HRM can be seen to have close links with organisational strategy. The next chapter discusses how the organisational contribution and effectiveness of HRM may be assessed in organisational performance.

11.6   REFERENCES

Armstrong M. (1999) *A Handbook of Human Resource Management Practice*, 7th ed., London: Kogan Page Ltd.

Beer *et al.* (1984) quoted in *The Reality of Strategic HRM*, Armstrong M. and Long P. (1996), p23, London: Institute of Personnel and Development.

Beer et al. (1985) cited in *Essentials of HRM* by Tyson S. and York A., London: Butterworth-Heinemann.

Beech E. and McKenna N. (2002) *Human Resource Analysis: a concise analysis*, London: Financial Times/ Prentice Hall.

Boxall P. and Purcell J. (2003) *Strategy and Human Resource Management*, London: Palgrave MacMillan.

Chandler A. (1962) cited in *Human Resource Management* (5th ed) by Torrington D., Hall L. and Taylor S., London: Financial Times/ Prentice Hall.

Guest D. (1989a) "Personnel and HRM: can you tell the difference?" *Personnel Management*, vol. 21, no.1, 48-51.

Drennan D. (1992) quoted in *Organisational Culture* (2nd ed.) by Brown A., London: Financial Times/ Prentice Hall.

Holbeche L. (2001) *Aligning Human Resources and Business Strategy*, Oxford: Butterworth-Heinemann.

Johnson G. and Scholes K. (1999) *Exploring Corporate Strategy* (5th ed.), London: Prentice Hall.

Leopold J. (2002) *Human Resources in Organisations*, London: Financial Times/ Prentice Hall.

Mabey C., Salaman G. and Storey J. (1999) *Human Resource Management: A Strategic Introduction* (2nd ed.), Oxford: Blackwell.

Marginson P. (1988) *Beyond the Workplace*, London: Blackwell Publishing.

Miles R.E. and Snow C.E. (1984) "Fit, failure and Hall of Fame", *California Management Review*, vol. 26, no. 3, 10-28, cited in *Human Resource Management* (5th ed.) by Torrington D., Hall L., and Taylor S., London: Financial Times/ Prentice Hall.

Thompson A.A. and Strickland A.J. (1998) *Strategic Management Concepts and Cases*, New York: Irwin/ McGraw-Hill.

Tyson S. and York A. (2001) *Essentials of HRM*, London: Butterworth-Heinnemann.

Watson T. (1995) quoted in Leopold, *op cit*.

11.7   SELF-ASSESSMENT QUESTIONS (EXAMPLES)

1.   What do each of the following terms mean?

   business strategy; mission statements; organisational values;
   strategic fit; espoused and realised strategy; organisational culture;
   strategic exchange; corporate capability, HRM ideals; HR services;
   strategic integration; objectives of HR responsibility; organisational
   roles; functional strategies; best practice.

2.   Identify points that support the case for strategic HRM in
   organisations.

CHAPTER 2

STRATEGIC HUMAN RESOURCE MANAGEMENT

THE OBJECTIVES OF THIS CHAPTER ARE TO:

1 CLARIFY THE USE OF THE TERMS STRATEGIC HUMAN RESOURCE MANAGEMENT AND HUMAN RESOURCE STRATEGY, AND ARRIVE AT WORKABLE DEFINITIONS OF EACH

2 EXPLAIN THE FEASIBILITY AND NATURE OF THE LINK BETWEEN BUSINESS STRATEGY AND HR STRATEGY

3 EVALUATE THREE THEORETICAL PERSPECTIVES ON THE NATURE OF HR STRATEGY AND SHOW HOW EACH EXPRESSES A DIFFERENT VIEW ON HOW THE CONTRIBUTION OF PEOPLE TO THE ORGANISATION MIGHT BE UNDERSTOOD AND ENHANCED

4 EXPLORE THE EXTENT TO WHICH THE HR FUNCTION OPERATES STRATEGICALLY

There is a strong lobby propounding the view that human resources are *the* source of competitive advantage for the business, rather than, say, access to capital or use of technology. It is therefore logical to suggest that attention needs to be paid to the nature of this resource and its management as this will impact on human resource behaviour and performance and consequently the performance of the organisation. Indeed Boxall and Steeneveld (1999) argue that there is no need to prove the relationship between firm performance and labour management as it is self-evident that the quality of human resource management is a critical influence on the performance of the firm. It is not, therefore, surprising that the rhetoric of strategic human resource management has been readily adopted, especially as a strategic approach is considered to be one of the characteristics of HRM as opposed to personnel management, which is seen as operational. If, as Boxall and Purcell (2003) suggest, HR is strategic to business success, then HR needs to be a strategic player and the role of business strategist will be a key role for HR specialists in the future (Cleland *et al.* 2000).

STRATEGIC HUMAN RESOURCE MANAGEMENT AND HUMAN RESOURCE STRATEGY

Our understanding of HR strategy has changed considerably since strategy first became the subject of great attention. We have moved from viewing strategy as a physical document to seeing it as an incremental process, affected by political influences and generating learning. Tyson's (1995) definition of human resource strategy is a useful starting point, although somewhat limited, as will be seen from our later discussion:

> the intentions of the corporation both explicit and covert, toward the management of its employees, expressed through philosophies, policies and practices. (Tyson 1995)

This definition is helpful because research on human resource strategy in the early 1980s tended to focus on seeking an HR strategy document in order to determine whether there was a strategic approach to HR and what that approach was. This was rather like searching for the Holy Grail. Not surprisingly few complete HR strategies were found and HR specialists berated themselves for having failed in this critical area. Gradually the thinking changed to encompass a view that HR strategy need not be written on a piece of paper or need not, indeed, be explicit, as the Tyson quotation illustrates. Further developments in thinking began to accept the idea that strategies are neither finished, nor complete, but rather incremental and piecemeal. There is compelling evidence to suggest that strategic HR tends to be issue based rather than the formulation of a complete and integrated strategy (for example, Grundy 1998; Hall and Torrington 1998). Strategic thinking, strategic decision making and a strategic orientation (for example, Hunt and Boxall 1998) were gradually understood as much more realistic expectations.

In parallel with this thinking there were developments in the general strategy literature which viewed strategy as a process which was not necessarily rational and top down, but a political and evolutionary process (*see*, for example, Mintzberg 1994). Mintzberg argues that strategy is 'formed' rather than 'formulated' and that any intended strategy is changed by events, opportunities, the actions of employees and so on – so that the realised strategy is different from the initial vision. Strategy, Mintzberg argues, can only be identified in retrospect and, as Boxall and Purcell suggest, is best seen in the ultimate behaviour of the organisation. Wrapped up in this view is also the idea that strategy is not necessarily determined by top management alone but can be influenced 'bottom up', as ideas are tried and tested in one part of the organisation and gradually adopted in a wholesale manner if they are seen to be applicable and successful. This is not to say that producing a strategy is an unhelpful act, and indeed research carried out by PriceWaterhouseCoopers indicated that those organisations with a written HR strategy generated 35 per cent greater revenues per employee than those without (Higginbottom 2002).

This leads on to the concept of strategy as learning both in content and in process (*see*, for example, Senge 1990; Pedler *et al.* 1991), which is supported by the notion of strategy as a process of change (*see*, for example, Hendry and Pettigrew 1992). Literature draws out the need to sense changes in the environment, develop a result-ant strategy and turn this strategy into action. While the HR function has often found itself excluded from the strategy formation process, HR strategy has more often been seen in terms of the implementation of organisational strategies. However, implementation of HR strategy has been weak, at best. Among the qualities of the most successful organisations is the ability to turn strategy into action quickly (Ulrich 1998), in other words to implement the chosen strategy (Grensing-Pophel 1999), and Guest (1987) maintained that the capability to implement strategic plans is an important feature of successful HRM. However, a lack of attention to the implementation of HR strategy has been identified (Beaumont 1992; Lundy and Cowling 1996; Skinner and Mabey 1997), and the information that does exist suggests that this is a problematic area. Legge (1995) maintained that the evidence of implementation of HR strategies was patchy and sometimes contradictory, and Skinner and Mabey (1997) found that responsibility for implementation was unclear, with only 54 per cent of respondents, in organisations with an HR director, perceiving that the HR function played a major part in implementation. In their research Kane and Palmer (1995) found that the existence of an HR strategy was only a minor influence on the HR policies and procedures that were used. Frameworks such as the HR scorecard (Becker *et al.* 2001) are aimed, at least in part, at facilitating the management and implementation of HR architecture ('the sum of the HR function, the broader HR system, and the resulting employee behaviors' p. 1) as a strategic asset.

THE LINK BETWEEN BUSINESS AND HR STRATEGY

The nature, desirability and feasibility of the link between business strategy and HR strategy is a consistent theme which runs through the strategy literature, although, as we shall discuss later, some theories suggest that implementing 'best practice' in HRM is even more important than this. Figure 2.1 is a simple model that is useful in visualising different ways in which this relationship may be played out and has relevance for the newer conceptions of strategy based on the resource-based view of the firm, as well as earlier conceptions.

In the *separation model* (A) there is no relationship at all, if indeed organisational and human resource strategy *does* exist in an explicit form in the organisation. This

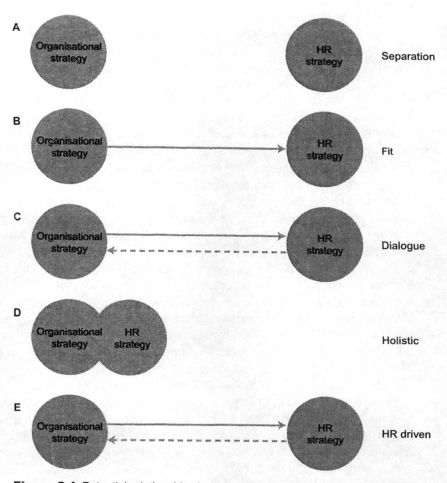

Figure 2.1 Potential relationships between organisational strategy and HR strategy

is a typical picture of twenty years ago, but it still exists today, particularly in smaller organisations.

The *fit model* (B) represents a growing recognition of the importance of people in the achievement of organisational strategy. Employees are seen as key in the implementation of the declared organisational strategy, and human resource strategy is designed to fit with this. Some of the early formal models of human resource strategy, particularly that proposed by Fombrun *et al.* (1984), concentrate on how the human resource strategy can be designed to ensure a close fit, and the same approach is used in the Schuler and Jackson example in Table 2.1.

This whole approach depends on a view of strategy formulation as a logical rational process, which remains a widely held view. The relationship in the fit model is exemplified by organisations which cascade their business objectives down from the senior management team through functions, through departments, through teams and so on. Functions, for example, have to propose a functional strategy which enables the organisational strategy to be achieved. Departments have to propose a strategy which enables the functional strategy to be achieved, and so on. In this way the HR function (as with any other) is required to respond to organisational strategy by defining a strategy which meets organisational demands.

The *dialogue model* (C) takes the relationship one step further, as it recognises the need for two-way communication and some debate. What is demanded in the organisation's strategy may not be viewed as feasible and alternative possibilities need to be reviewed. The debate, however, is often limited, as shown in the example in the Window on practice which follows.

WINDOW ON PRACTICE

In one large multinational organisation an objectives-setting cascade was put in place. This cascade allowed for a dialogue between the planned organisation strategy and the response of each function. In the organisation strategy there was some emphasis on people growth and development and job fulfilment. The HR Department's response included among other things an emphasis on line management involvement in these areas, which would be supported by consultancy help from the HR Department.

The top management team replied to this by asking the HR Department to add a strategic objective about employee welfare and support. The HR Department strongly argued that this was a line management responsibility, along with coaching, development and so on. The HR Function saw its customers as the managers of the organisation, not the employees. The result of the debate was that the HR function added the strategic objective about employee welfare.

Although the approach in this case appeared two-way, the stronger of the parties was the management team, and they were determined that their vision was the one that would be implemented!

The holistic model and the HR-driven model (D and E) show a much closer involvement between organisational and human resource strategy.

The *holistic model* (D) represents the people of the organisation being recognised as the key to competitive advantage rather than just the way of implementing organisational strategy. In other words HR strategy is not just the means for achieving business strategy (the ends), but an end in itself. Human resource strategy therefore becomes critical and, as Baird *et al.* (1983) argued, there can be no strategy without human resource strategy. Boxall (1996) develops this idea in relation to the resource-based firm, and argues convincingly that business strategy can usefully be interpreted as more broad than a competitive strategy (or positioning in the marketplace). In this case business strategy can encompass a variety of other strategies including HRM, and he describes these strategies as the pieces of a jigsaw. This suggests mutual development and some form of integration, rather than a slavish response to a predetermined business strategy.

The *HR-driven model* (E) offers a more extreme form, which places human resource strategy in prime position. The argument here is that if people are the key to competitive advantage, then we need to build on our people strengths. Logically, then, as the potential of our employees will undoubtedly affect the achievement of any planned strategy, it would be sensible to take account of this in developing our strategic direction. Butler (1988/89) identifies this model as a shift from human resources as the implementors of strategy to human resources as a driving force in the formulation of the strategy. Again this model is a reflection of a resource-based strategic HRM perspective, and sits well with the increasing attention being given to the notion of 'human capital' where it is the collective nature and quality of the people in the organisation which provide the potential for future competitive advantage (see, for example, Lengnick-Hall and Lengnick-Hall 2003).

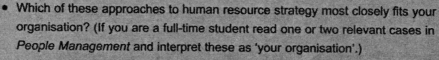

ACTIVITY 2.1

- Which of these approaches to human resource strategy most closely fits your organisation? (If you are a full-time student read one or two relevant cases in *People Management* and interpret these as 'your organisation'.)
- Why did you come to this conclusion?
- What are the advantages and disadvantages of the approach used?

THEORETICAL PERSPECTIVES OF STRATEGIC HUMAN RESOURCE MANAGEMENT

Three theoretical approaches to strategic HRM can be identified. The first is founded on the concept that there is 'one best way' of managing human resources in order to improve business performance. The second focuses on the need to align employment policies and practice with the requirements of business strategy in order that the latter will be achieved and the business will be successful. This second approach is based on the assumption that different types of HR strategies will be suitable for different types of business strategies. Thirdly, a more recent approach to strategic HRM is derived from the resource-based view of the firm, and the perceived value of human capital. This view focuses on the quality of the human resources available to the organisation and their ability to learn and adapt more quickly than their competitors. Supporters of this perspective challenge the need to secure a mechanistic fit with business strategy and focus instead on long-term sustainability and survival of the organisation via the pool of human capital.

Universalist approach

The perspective of the universalist approach is derived from the conception of human resource management as 'best practice', as we discussed in Chapter 1. In other words it is based on the premise that one model of labour management – a high-commitment model – is related to high organisational performance in all contexts, irrespective of the particular competitive strategy of the organisation. An expression of this approach can be seen in Guest's theory of HRM, which is a prescriptive model based on four HR policy goals: strategic integration, commitment, flexibility and quality. These policy goals are related to HRM policies which are expected to produce desirable organisational outcomes.

Guest (1989) describes the four policy goals as follows:

- **Strategic integration** – ensuring that HRM is fully integrated into strategic planning, that HRM policies are coherent, that line managers use HRM practices as part of their everyday work.
- **Commitment** – ensuring that employees feel bound to the organisation and are committed to high performance via their behaviour.
- **Flexibility** – ensuring an adaptable organisation structure, and functional flexibility based on multiskilling.
- **Quality** – ensuring a high quality of goods and services through high-quality, flexible employees.

Guest sees these goals as a package – all need to be achieved to create the desired organisational outcomes which are high job performance, problem solving, change, innovation and cost effectiveness; and low employee turnover, absence and grievances.

Clarity of goals gives a certain attractiveness to this model – but this is where the problems also lie. Whipp (1992) questions the extent to which such a shift is possible, and Purcell (1991) sees the goals as unattainable. The goals are also an expression of human resource management, as opposed to personnel management, and as such bring us back to the debate about what human resource management really is and the inherent contradictions in the approach (Legge 1991, 1995). Ogbonna and Whipp (1999) argue that internal consistency within such a model is extremely difficult to achieve because of such contradictions (for example the tension between flexibility and commitment). Because the prescriptive approach brings with it a set of values, it suggests that there is only one best way and this is it. Although Guest (1987) has argued that there is no best practice, he also encourages the use of the above approach as the route to survival of UK businesses.

Pfeffer (1994) and Becker and Gerhart (1996) are well-known exponents of this view. While there is some support for this perspective, there remains some debate as to which particular human resource practices will stimulate high commitment. We consider this perspective in more depth in Chapter 10 on Strategic aspects of performance. The following Window on practice gives an example of one interpretation of a high-commitment, high-performance approach to human resource management strategy.

WINDOW ON PRACTICE

High performance teams at Digital, Ayr

In an extremely competitive market the Ayr plant had to demonstrate that they could manufacture specified computer systems at a 'landed cost' competitive with other Digital plants, especially those in the Far East. To do this management had to rapidly introduce a package of changes. They had a strategic focus and a clear vision of the changes (both technical and organisational) required to promote success and they 'sold' this to the employees and corporate management. The high-performance team concept they sold had two great advantages – inbuilt quality and flexibility.

Supportive policies were put in place – such as a new skills-based pay system.

Employment policies in terms of career planning, training and development and other reward policies were also designed to be consistent with and reinforce the initiative. Management introduced unsupervised autonomous groups called 'high performance teams' with around a dozen members with full 'back to front' responsibility for product assembly, testing, fault finding, and problem solving, as well as some equipment maintenance. They used flexitime without time clocks and organised their own team discipline. Individuals were encouraged to develop a range of skills and help others in developing their capability. The ten key characteristics of the teams were as follows:

- self-managing, self-organising, self-regulating;

- front-to-back responsibility for core process;

- negotiated production targets;

- multiskilling – no job titles;

- share skills, knowledge, experience and problems;

- skills-based payment system;

- peer selection, peer review;

- open layout, open communications;

- support staff on the spot;

- commitment to high standards and performance.

Management had to learn to stand back and let the groups reach their own decisions – an approach that eventually released considerable management time. A great deal of attention was given to how the transition was managed and this was seen as critical to the success of the approach. Time was taken to ensure maximum formal and informal communication and consultation, and there was a critical mass of key individuals prepared to devote themselves to ensure success. Employees were involved to the fullest extent so they eventually felt they owned the concepts and techniques that they used. Training covered job skills, problem-solving techniques and 'attitude training' in the concepts of high-performance organisational design.

Source: Adapted from D.A. Buchanan (1992) 'High performance: new boundaries of acceptability in worker control', in G. Salaman *et al.* (eds), *Human Resource Strategies*. California: Sage.

Falling somewhere between the universalist approach and the fit approach is the Harvard model of HRM. This model, produced by Beer *et al.* (1984), is analytical rather than prescriptive. The model, shown in Figure 2.2, recognises the different stakeholder interests that impact on employee behaviour and performance, and also gives greater emphasis to factors in the environment that will help to shape human resource strategic choices – identified in the **Situational factors** box. Poole (1990) also notes that the model has potential for international or other comparative analysis, as it takes into account different sets of philosophies and assumptions which may be operating.

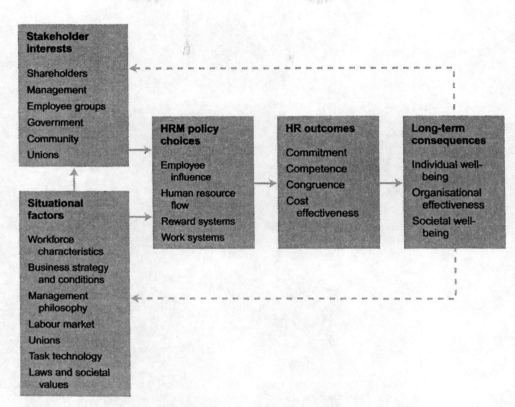

Figure 2.2 The Harvard framework for human resource management (Source: Adapted with permission of The Free Press, a Division of Simon & Schuster, Inc., from *Managing Human Assets* by Michael Beer, Bert Spector, Paul R. Lawrence, D. Quinn Mills, Richard E. Walton. New York: The Free Press. Copyright © 1984 by The Free Press.)

Although Beer *et al.*'s model is primarily analytical, there are prescriptive elements leading to some potential confusion. The prescription in Beer *et al.*'s model is found in the **HR outcomes** box, where specific outcomes are identified as universally desirable.

Fit or contingency approach

The fit or contingency approach is based on two critical forms of fit. The first is external fit (sometimes referred to as vertical integration) – that HR strategy fits with the demands of business strategy; the second is internal fit (sometimes referred to as horizontal integration) – that all HR policies and activities fit together so that they make a coherent whole, are mutually reinforcing and are applied consistently. One of the foundations of this approach is found in Fombrun *et al.* (1984), who proposed a basic framework for strategic human resource management, shown in Figures 2.3 and 2.4. Figure 2.3 represents the location of human resource management in relation to organisational strategy, and you should be able to note how the Fit model (B) is used (*see* Figure 2.1). Figure 2.4 shows how activities within human resource management can be unified and designed in order to support the organisation's strategy.

The strength of this model is that it provides a simple framework to show how selection, appraisal, development and reward can be mutually geared to produce the required type of employee performance. For example, if an organisation required

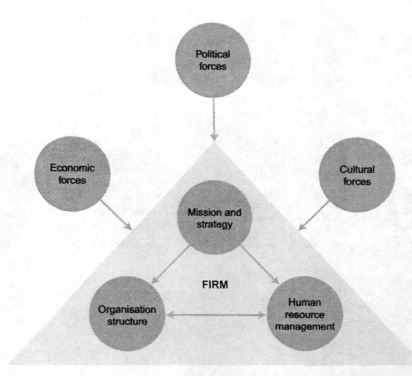

Figure 2.3 Strategic management and environmental pressures (Source: C. Fombrun, N.M. Tichy and M.A. Devanna (1984) *Strategic Human Resource Management*, p. 35. New York: John Wiley and Sons, Inc. © John Wiley and Sons Inc., 1984. Reprinted by permission of John Wiley and Sons, Inc.)

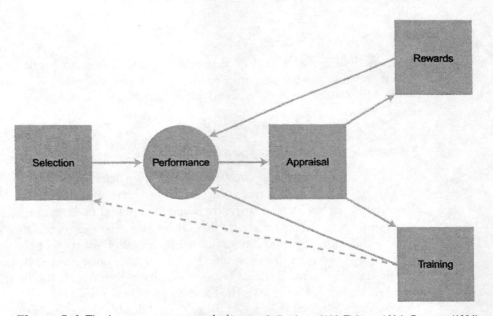

Figure 2.4 The human resource cycle (Source: C. Fombrun, N.M. Tichy and M.A. Devanna (1984) *Strategic Human Resource Management*, p. 41. New York: John Wiley and Sons, Inc. © John Wiley and Sons Inc., 1984. Reprinted by permission of John Wiley and Sons, Inc.)

cooperative team behaviour with mutual sharing of information and support, the broad implications would be:

- **Selection**: successful experience of teamwork and sociable, cooperative personality; rather than an independent thinker who likes working alone.

- **Appraisal**: based on contribution to the team, and support of others; rather than individual outstanding performance.

- **Reward**: based on team performance and contribution; rather than individual performance and individual effort.

There is little doubt that this type of internal fit is valuable. However, questions have been raised over the model's simplistic response to organisation strategy. The question 'what if it is not possible to produce a human resource response that enables the required employee behaviour and performance?' is never addressed. So, for example, the distance between now and future performance requirements, the strengths, weaknesses and potential of the workforce, the motivation of the workforce and employee relations issues are not considered.

This model has been criticised because of its dependence on a rational strategy formulation rather than on an emergent strategy formation approach; and because of the nature of the one-way relationship with organisational strategy. It has also been criticised owing to its unitarist assumptions, as no recognition is made for employee interests and their choice of whether or not to change their behaviour.

Taking this model and the notion of fit one step further, human resource strategy has been conceived in terms of generating specific employee behaviours. In the ideal form of this there would be analysis of the types of employee behaviour required to fulfil a predetermined business strategy, and then an identification of human resource policies and practices which would bring about and reinforce this behaviour. A very good example of this is found in Schuler and Jackson (1987). They used the three generic business strategies defined by Porter (1980) and for each identified employee role behaviour and HRM policies required. Their conclusions are shown in Table 2.1.

Similar analyses can be found for other approaches to business strategy, for example in relation to the **Boston matrix** (Purcell 1992) and the developmental stage of the organisation (Kochan and Barocci 1985). Some human resource strategies describe the behaviour of all employees, but others have concentrated on the behaviour of Chief Executives and senior managers; Miles and Snow (1984), for example, align appropriate managerial characteristics to three generic strategies of prospector, defender and analyser. The rationale behind this matching process is that if managerial attributes and skills are aligned to the organisational strategy, then a higher level of organisational performance will result. There is little empirical evidence to validate this link, but work by Thomas and Ramaswamy (1996) does provide some support. They used statistical analysis to investigate if there was a match between manager attributes and skills in organisations with either a defender or a prospector strategy in 269 of the Fortune 500 companies in the United States. They found an overall statistical relationship between manager attributes and strategy. Taking the analysis a step further they then compared 30 organisations which were misaligned with 30 which were aligned and found that performance in the aligned companies (whether prospector or defender) was statistically superior. While this work can be criticised, it does provide an indication of further research which can be developed to aid our understanding of the issues. Sanz-Valle *et al.* (1999) found some partial

Strategy	Employee role behaviour	HRM policies
1 Innovation	A high degree of creative behaviour	Jobs that require close interaction and coordination among groups of individuals
	Longer-term focus	Performance appraisals that are more likely to reflect longer-term and group-based achievements
	A relatively high level of co-operative, interdependent behaviour	Jobs that allow employees to develop skills that can be used in other positions in the firm
		Compensation systems that emphasise internal equity rather than external or market-based equity
	A moderate degree of concern for quality	Pay rates that tend to be low, but that allow employees to be stockholders and have more freedom to choose the mix of components that make up their pay package
	A moderate concern for quantity; an equal degree of concern for process and results	Broad career paths to reinforce the development of a broad range of skills
	A greater degree of risk taking; a higher tolerance of ambiguity and unpredictability	
2 Quality enhancement	Relatively repetitive and predictable behaviours	Relatively fixed and explicit job descriptions
	A more long-term or intermediate focus	High levels of employee participation in decisions relevant to immediate work conditions and the job itself
	A moderate amount of co-operative, interdependent behaviour	A mix of individual and group criteria for performance appraisal that is mostly short term and results orientated
	A high concern for quality	A relatively egalitarian treatment of employees and some guarantees of employment security
	A modest concern for quantity of output	Extensive and continuous training and development of employees
	High concern for process: low risk-taking activity; commitment to the goals of the organisation	
3 Cost reduction	Relatively repetitive and predictable behaviour	Relatively fixed and explicit job descriptions that allow little room for ambiguity
	A rather short-term focus	Narrowly designed jobs and narrowly defined career paths that encourage specialisation, expertise and efficiency
	Primarily autonomous or individual activity	Short-term results-orientated performance appraisals
	Moderate concern for quality	Close monitoring of market pay levels for use in making compensation decisions
	High concern for quantity of output	Minimal levels of employee training and development
	Primary concern for results; low risk-taking activity; relatively high degree of comfort with stability	

Table 2.1
Business strategies, and associated employee role behaviour and HRM policies

Source R.S. Schuler and S.E. Jackson (1987) 'Linking competitive strategies with human resource management practices', *Academy of Management Executive*, No. 3, August. Reproduced with permission of the Academy of Management.

support for the Schuler and Jackson model in terms of the link between business strategy and HR practices, but they did not investigate the implications of this link for organisational performance. The types of strategies described above are generic, and there is more concentration in some organisations on tailoring the approach to the particular needs of the specific organisation.

Many human resource strategies aim not just to target behaviour, but through behaviour change to effect a movement in the culture of the organisation. The target is, therefore, to change the common view of 'the way we do things around here' and to attempt to manipulate the beliefs and values of employees. There is much debate as to whether this is achievable.

We have previously recounted some of the concerns expressed about Fombrun et al.'s specific model; however, there is further criticism of the fit or matching perspective as a whole. Grundy (1998) claims that the idea of fit seems naive and simplistic. Ogbonna and Whipp (1999) argue that much literature assumes that fit can be targeted, observed and measured and there is an underlying assumption of stability. Given that most companies may have to change radically in response to the environment, any degree of fit previously achieved will be disturbed. Thus, they contend that fit is a theoretical ideal which can rarely be achieved in practice. Boxall (1996) criticises: the typologies of competitive advantage that are used, arguing that there is evidence that high-performing firms are good 'all rounders'; the fact that strategy is a given and no account is made of how it is formed or by whom; the assumption that employees will behave as requested; and the aim for consistency, as it has been shown that firms use different strategies for different sections of their workforce.

However, in spite of the criticisms of this perspective, it is still employed in both the academic and practitioner literature – see, for example, Holbeche's (1999) book entitled *Aligning Human Resources and Business Strategy*.

Resource-based approach

The resource-based view of the firm (Barney 1991) has stimulated attempts to create a resource-based model of strategic HRM (Boxall 1996). The resource-based view of the firm is concerned with the relationships between internal resources (of which human resources are one), strategy and firm performance. It focuses on the promotion of sustained competitive advantage through the development of human capital rather than merely aligning human resources to current strategic goals. Human resources can provide competitive advantage for the business, as long as they are unique and cannot be copied or substituted for by competing organisations. The focus is not just on the behaviour of the human resources (as with the fit approach), but on the skills, knowledge, attitudes and competencies which underpin this, and which have a more sustained impact on long-term survival than current behaviour (although this is still regarded as important). Briggs and Keogh (1999) maintain that business excellence is not just about 'best practice' or 'leapfrogging the competition', but about the intellectual capital and business intelligence to anticipate the future, today.

Barney states that in order for a resource to result in sustained competitive advantage it must meet four criteria, and Wright et al. (1994) demonstrate how human resources meet these. First, the resource must be *valuable*. Wright and his colleagues argue that this is the case where demand for labour is heterogeneous, and where the supply of labour is also heterogeneous – in other words where different firms require different competencies from each other and for different roles in the organisation, and where the supply of potential labour comprises individuals with different competencies. On this basis value is created by matching an individual's competencies with the requirements of the firm and/or the job, as individuals will make a variable contribution, and one cannot be substituted easily for another.

The second criterion, *rarity*, is related to the first. An assumption is made that the most important competence for employees is cognitive ability due to future needs for adaptability and flexibility. On the basis that cognitive ability is normally distributed in the population, those with high levels of this ability will be rare. The talent pool is not unlimited and many employers are currently experiencing difficulties in finding the talent that they require.

Third, resources need to be *inimitable*. Wright *et al.* argue that this quality applies to the human resource as competitors will find it difficult to identify the exact source of competitive advantage from within the firm's human resource pool. Also competitors will not be able to duplicate exactly the resource in question, as they will be unable to copy the unique historical conditions of the first firm. This history is important as it will affect the behaviour of the human resource pool via the development of unique norms and cultures. Thus even if a competing firm recruited a group of individuals from a competitor they would still not be able to produce the same outcomes in the new firm as the context would be different. Two factors make this unique history difficult to copy. The first is causal ambiguity – in other words it is impossible to separate out the exact causes of performance, as the sum is always more than the parts; and, second, social complexity – that the complex of relationships and networks developed over time which have an impact on performance is difficult to dissect.

Finally resources need to be *non-substitutable*. Wright and his co-authors argue that although in the short term it may be possible to substitute human resources with others, for example technological ones, in the long term the human resource is different as it does not become obsolete (like technology) and can be transferred across other products, markets and technologies.

Wright *et al.* noted that attention has often been devoted to leaders and top management in the context of a resource-based approach, and indeed Boxall (1996) contends that this approach provides the theoretical base on which to concentrate in the renewal and development of the critical resource of leaders in the organisation. However, Wright and his co-authors view all human resources in the organisation as the pool of capital. This sits well with the view of strategy as evolutionary and strategy being influenced from the bottom up as well as from the top down. Also it is likely that top managers are more easily identified for their contribution to the organisation and hence are more likely to be mobile, therefore, than other employees who may not be so easily identified. However, different segments of the human resource are viewed differently by organisations in terms of their contribution to competitive advantage, so for some organisations the relevant pool of human capital may not be the total pool of employees.

Whereas fit models focus on the means of competitive advantage (HR practices) the resource-based view focuses on the source (the human capital). Wright *et al.* argue that while the practices are important they are not the source of competitive advantage as they can be replicated elsewhere, and they will produce different results in different places because of the differential human capital in different places. The

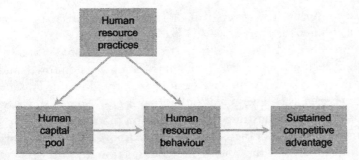

Figure 2.5 A model of human resources as a source of sustained competitive advantage
Source: P. Wright, G. McMahon and A. McWilliams (1994) 'Human resources and sustained competitive advantage: a resource-based perspective', *International Journal of Human Resource Management*, Vol. 5, No. 2, p. 318. Reproduced with the permission of Taylor and Francis Ltd. *See* www.tandf.co.uk/journals.

relationship between human capital, human resource practices and competitive advantage is shown in Figure 2.5.

Boxall (1996) argues that this theoretical perspective provides a conceptual base for asserting that human resources are a source of competitive advantage, and as such valued as generating strategic capability. Thus there is a case for viewing HR strategy as something more than a reactive matching process. Indeed Wright *et al.* argue that it provides the case for HR to be involved in the formulation of strategy rather than just its implementation. They suggest that it provides a grounding for asserting that not every strategy is universally implementable, and that alternatives may have to be sought or the human capital pool developed further, via human resource practices, where this is possible.

The importance of this perspective is underlined by the current emphasis on a firm's intangible assets. Numerous studies have shown that a firm's market value (the sum of the value of the shares) is not fully explained by its current financial results (*see*, for example, Ulrich and Smallwood 2002) or its tangible assets and the focus has moved to a firm's intangible assets such as intellectual capital and customer relationships – all of which are derived from human capital (*see*, for example, Schmidt and Lines 2002). This emphasis has resulted in a great deal of attention being paid to the evaluation of human capital through measuring, reporting and managing it. Human capital can be reported both internally and externally (as in the annual financial report, or similar), and Angela Baron from the CIPD has been reported as commenting that 'investors are demanding information on human capital' (Roberts 2002).

But human capital is loaned: 'human capital is not owned by the organization, but secured through the employment relationship' (Scarborough 2003a, p. 2) and because this is so, the strategy for the management of people is also critical. The government's White Paper, *Modernising Company Law*, suggests that the largest 1,000 companies should publish an annual operating review. Experts believe this will need to include a review about the ways that employees are managed (*People Management* 2002). In addition the Accounting Standards Board recommend that people management measures should be included in annual reports (Brown 2002).

The perceived importance of people as an intangible asset is demonstrated in the action of Barclays Group who on their Investor's Day were keen to demonstrate not only their financial results but people strategies and improvements in staff satisfaction which they believe have contributed to the results (Arkin and Allen 2002).

The Barclays approach is covered in more detail in a case study on the website **www.booksites.net/torrington**.

This approach has great advantages from an HR point of view. People in the organisation become the focus, their contribution is monitored and made more explicit, the way people are managed can be seen to add value and money spent on people can be seen as an investment rather than a cost. Some firms are using the balanced scorecard to demonstrate the contribution that human capital makes to firm performance, such as Norwich Union, and Scarborough (2003b) argues that this builds a bridge between the role of the HR function and the strategy of the firm. However, there are in-built barriers in the language of the resource-based view. One is the reference to people as 'human capital' which some consider to be unnecessarily instrumental. Another is the focus on 'firms' and 'competitive advantage' which makes it harder to see the relevance of this perspective for organisations in the public sector. There is also the issue of what is being measured and who decides this. The risk is that too much time is spent measuring and that not everything that is measured is of critical value to the organisation. So far, such measures appear very varied, although different firms will, of course, need to measure different things. Measures often appear to be taken without a coherent framework, as appears to be the case in the results documented by Scarborough and Elias (2002) for their 10 case study organisations. The balanced scorecard and the HR scorecard, however, appear to be a useful mechanism in this respect. The evaluation of human capital is considered in greater depth in Chapter 33.

Why does the theory matter?

It is tempting to think of these theories of strategic HRM as competing with each other. In other words one is right and the others are wrong. If this were the case HR managers/directors and board members would need only to work out which is the 'right' theory and apply that. This is, of course, a gross oversimplification, as each theory can be interpreted and applied in different ways, and each has advantages and disadvantages. It could be argued that different theories apply in different sectors or competitive contexts. For example Guest (2001) suggests that there is the possibility that a 'high performance/high commitment' approach might always be most appropriate in manufacturing, whereas strategic choice (which could be interpreted as choice to fit with business strategy) might be more realistic in the services sector. This could be taken one step further to suggest that different theories apply to different groups in the workforce.

Consequently, these three theories do not necessarily represent simple alternatives. It is also likely that some board directors and even HR managers are not familiar with any of these theories (*see*, for example, Guest and King 2001). In spite of that, organisations, through their culture, and individuals within organisations operate on the basis of a set of assumptions, and these assumptions are often implicit. Assumptions about the nature and role of human resource strategy, whether explicit or implicit, will have an influence on what organisations actually do. Assumptions will limit what are seen as legitimate choices.

Understanding these theories enables HR managers, board members, consultants and the like to interpret the current position of HR strategy in the organisation, confront current assumptions and challenge current thinking and potentially open up a new range of possibilities.

THE ROLE OF THE HR FUNCTION IN STRATEGY

The extent to which the HR function is involved in both organisational and human resource strategy development is dependent on a range of factors, the most often quoted being whether the most senior HR person is a member of the board of directors. Sparkes (2001) identifies a key role for the HR director as promoting the connection between organisational strategy, culture and people strategy. He maintains that being an HR director means that 'we can almost guarantee that a human element is built into everything strategic from the start' (p. 45).

There is evidence to suggest that over the past 20 years HR board membership has increased and surveys suggest that around three-fifths of larger organisations have an HR director (*see*, for example, Hall and Torrington 1998), although some surveys indicate lower percentages. However, we found, as did Kelly and Gennard (1996), that board membership, while generally identified as desirable, does not guarantee the involvement of specialists in strategy, and it was not necessarily seen as essential to strategic involvement, and this is perhaps why currently very little attention is given to assessing the percentage of organisations with an HR director:

> Thus whilst board membership is often treated as a proxy for strategic involvement, the reality of the situation is far more complex. Even looking at the most favourable evidence from the research, a picture emerges of limited involvement in strategic matters. The good news is that the IPM's survey found that representation on the top management team was predicted to increase, although there is contradictory evidence. (Tyson 1995)

While a seat on the board is undoubtably an advantage and, as Sparkes suggests, improves HR's understanding of the business context in which HR strategies need to be developed and implemented, this is not essential. Other factors influencing the role of the HR function in strategic concerns include the overall philosophy of the organisation towards the value of its people, the mindset of the Chief Executive, and the working relationship between the Chief Executive and the most senior HR person.

These influences are not particularly easy to manipulate, but what the HR function *can* do is look for opportunities in these areas, and *use* them. Building a good working relationship with the Chief Executive is critical, and doubly so, as Stiles (2001) confirms the power of the Chief Executive in selecting who should be appointed to the board. There is evidence that HR managers have to prove themselves before being given a seat on the board (*see*, for example, Hall and Torrington 1998) so building key competencies is essential. Barney and Wright (1998) suggest that one of the real reasons why HR are not involved in strategic planning is that they are not displaying the required competencies. In 2001 IRS (2001) found that only 72 per cent of HR managers in their survey reported the HR function as having a strategic/business focus. The website case study, 'People issues are central to the success of any organisation', focuses on these issues.

It is suggested that HR managers need to use business and financial language; describe the rationale for HR activities in terms of added value; act as a business manager first and an HR manager second; appoint line managers into the HR function; concentrate on priorities as defined by the business; understand the business they work in, and offer well-developed change-management skills that can be used immediately. Guest and King (2001) argue that, as senior managers and board members appear to have limited knowledge of research linking people management and performance, there is an opportunity for enthusiastic HR managers/directors to feed new ideas to Chief Executives. Increasingly, HR managers need to become closer to their accounting colleagues. In addition, the function needs to prepare itself by thinking strategically, identifying a functional mission and strategy and involving line management in the development and implementation of human resource strategy.

SUMMARY PROPOSITIONS

2.1 It is more helpful to focus on the concept of strategic HRM than on HRM strategy as the former directs us to consider strategic thinking and a strategic orientation, rather than a 'strategy' which is written down and exists as a physical entity.

2.2 The nature of the link between business strategy and HR strategy is critical and can be played out in a variety of ways.

2.3 Three theoretical perspectives on strategic HR management can be identified: universalist/best practice; contingency/fit; and the resource-based/human capital view.

2.4 The extent to which HR specialists are involved in HR strategy is influenced by the environment of the business, its culture, the perspective of the Chief Executive, HR board membership and the qualities, characteristics and working relationships of the most senior HR specialist.

GENERAL DISCUSSION TOPICS

1 Is it feasible to link business strategy with the management of people in organisations?

2 Does it really matter whether the most senior HR person is on the board of directors, or are personal work relationships, political alliances and personal track records more important?

3 Human resource strategies can be stimulating to produce and satisfying to display, but how can we make sure that they are implemented?

FURTHER READING

Khatri, N. and Budhwar, P. (2001) 'A study of strategic HR issues in an Asian context', *Personnel Review*, Vol. 31, No. 2, pp. 166–87
This article investigates strategic HR issues which are often neglected. Rather than focusing on strategic content issues, the research reported here concentrates on the structure of the HR function and its strategic relationships; HR competencies; the nature of HR strategy (for example formal or informal); and HR outsourcing. Although the study is located in a very specific context – the electronics and components sector and the machinery and equipment sector in Singapore – the literature review and results are both very useful and informative and straightforward reading.

Mayo, A. (2001) *The Human Value of the Enterprise*. London: Nicholas Brealey
Mayo provides one approach to the measurement of human capital – the human capital monitor, which is based on people as assets, people's motivation and commitment and people's contribution to added value. There is advice on maximising human capital, motivation and commitment, innovation and learning and the challenges of mergers, acquisitions and alliances.

REFERENCES

Arkin, A. and Allen, R. (2002) 'Satisfaction guaranteed', *People Management*, Vol. 8, No. 21, October, pp. 40–2.

Baird, L., Meshoulam, I. and DeGive, G. (1983) 'Meshing human resources planning with strategic business planning: a model approach', *Personnel*, Vol. 60, Part 5 (Sept./Oct.), pp. 14–25.

Barney, J. (1991) 'Firm resources and sustained competitive advantage', *Journal of Management*, Vol. 17, No. 1, pp. 99–120.

Barney, J. and Wright, P. (1998) 'On becoming a strategic partner: the role of human resources in gaining competitive advantage', *Human Resource Management*, Vol. 37, No. 1, pp. 31–46.

Beaumont, P. (1992) 'The US human resource management literature: a review', in G. Salaman (ed.) *Human Resource Strategies*. London: Sage in association with OUP.

Becker, B. and Gerhart, B. (1996) 'The impact of Human Resource Management on Organisational Performance: Progress and Prospects', *Academy of Management Journal*, Vol. 39, pp. 779–801.

Becker, B., Huselid, M. and Ulrich, D. (2001) *The HR Scorecard: Linking People, Strategy and Performance*. Boston: Harvard Business School Press.

Beer, M., Spector, B., Lawrence, P.R., Quinn Mills, D. and Walton, R.E. (1984) *Managing Human Assets*. New York: Free Press.

Boxall, P.F. (1992) 'Strategic human resource management: beginnings of a new theoretical sophistication?' *Human Resource Management Journal*, Vol. 2, No. 3.

Boxall, P.F. (1996) 'The strategic HRM debate and the resource-based view of the firm', *Human Resource Management Journal*, Vol. 6, No. 3, pp. 59–75.

Boxall, P. and Purcell J. (2003) *Strategy and Human Resource Management*. Basingstoke: Palgrave, Macmillan.

Boxall, P. and Steeneveld, M. (1999) 'Human Resource Strategy and competitive advantage: A longitudinal study of engineering consultancies', *Journal of Management Studies*, Vol. 36, No. 4, pp. 443–63.

Briggs, S. and Keogh, W. (1999) 'Integrating human resource strategy and strategic planning to achieve business excellence', *Total Quality Management*, July, p. 447.

Brown, D. (2002) 'Top-down and bottom-up', *People Management*, Vol. 8, No. 17, 29 August, p. 18.

Buchanan, D.A. (1992) 'High performance: new boundaries of acceptability in worker control', in G. Salaman *et al.* (eds) *Human Resource Strategies*. California: Sage Publications.

Butler, J. (1988/89) 'Human resource management as a driving force in business strategy', *Journal of General Management*, Vol. 13, No. 4.

Cleland, J., Pajo, K. and Toulson, P. (2000) 'Move it or lose it: an examination of the evolving role of the human resources professional in New Zealand', *International Journal of Human Resource Management*, Vol. 11, No. 1, pp. 143–60.

Fombrun, C., Tichy, N.M. and Devanna, M.A. (1984) *Strategic Human Resource Management*. New York: John Wiley and Sons.

Grensing-Pophel, L. (1999) 'Taking your "seat at the table" (the role of Human Resource Managers in companies)', *HRMagazine*, March, Vol. 44, No. 3, pp. 90–4.

Grundy, T. (1998) 'How are corporate strategy and human resources strategy linked?' *Journal of General Management*, Vol. 23, No. 3, Spring, pp. 49–72.

Guest, D. (1987) 'Human resource management and industrial relations' *Journal of Management Studies*, Vol. 24, No. 5.

Guest, D. (1989) 'Personnel and HRM: Can you tell the difference?' *Personnel Management* (January).

Guest, D. (2001) 'Human resource management: when research confronts theory', *International Journal of Human Resource Management*, Vol. 12, No. 7, pp. 1092–1106.

Guest, D. and King, Z. (2001) 'Personnel's Paradox', *People Management*, Vol. 17, No. 19, 27 September, pp. 24–9.

Hall, L. and Torrington, D. (1998) *The Human Resource Function: The Dynamics of change and development*. London: Financial Times Pitman Publishing.

Hendry, C. and Pettigrew, A. (1992) 'Patterns of strategic change in the development of Human Resource Management', *British Journal of Management*, Vol. 3, No. 3, pp. 137–56.

Higginbottom, K. (2002) 'Profits rise with a written HR strategy', *People Management*, Vol. 8, No. 25, 26 December, p. 9.

Holbeche, L. (1999) *Aligning Human Resources and Business Strategy*. Oxford: Butterworth-Heinemann. © Roffey Park Management Institute.

Hunt, J. and Boxall, P. (1998) 'Are top Human Resource Specialists strategic partners? Self-perceptions of a corporate elite', *International Journal of Human Resource Management*, Vol. 9, pp. 767–81.

IRS (2001) 'HR in 2001: the HR audit', *IRS Employment Trends*, No. 728, May, pp. 4–10.

Kane, B. and Palmer, I. (1995) 'Strategic HRM or managing the employment relationship?' *International Journal of Manpower*, Vol. 15, No. 5, pp. 6–16.

Kelly, J. and Gennard, J. (1996) 'The role of personnel directors in the Board of Directors', *Personnel Review*, Vol. 25, No. 1, pp. 7–24.

Kochan, T.A. and Barocci, T.A. (1985) *Human Resource Management and Industrial Relations: Text, Readings and Cases*. Boston: Little Brown.

Legge, K. (1991) 'Human resource management: a critical analysis', in J. Storey (ed.) *New Perspectives on Human Resource Management*. London: Routledge.

Legge, K. (1995) *Human Resource Management: Rhetorics and realities*. Basingstoke: Macmillan.

Lengnick-Hall, M. and Lengnick-Hall, C. (2003) *Human Resource Management in the Knowledge Economy*. San Francisco: Berrett-Koehler Inc.

Lundy, O. and Cowling, A. (1996) *Strategic Human Resource Management*. London: Routledge.

Miles, R.E. and Snow, C.C. (1984) 'Organisation strategy, structure and process', *Academy of Management Review*, Vol. 2, pp. 546–62.

Mintzberg, H. (1994) 'The fall and rise of strategic planning', *Harvard Business Review* (February).

Ogbonna, E. and Whipp, R. (1999) 'Strategy, culture and HRM: evidence from the UK food retailing sector', *Human Resource Management Journal*, Vol. 9, No. 4, pp. 75–90.

Pedler, M., Burgoyne, J. and Boydell, T. (1991) *The Learning Company*. Maidenhead: McGraw-Hill.

People Management (2002) 'Human Capital Review', *People Management*, Vol. 8, No. 15, 25 July, p. 9.

Pfeffer, J. (1994) *Competitive Advantage through People*. Boston: Harvard Business School Press.

Poole, M. (1990) 'Editorial: HRM in an international perspective', *International Journal of Human Resource Management*, Vol. 1, No. 1.

Porter, M. (1980) *Competitive Strategy*. New York: Free Press.

Purcell, J. (1991) 'The impact of corporate strategy on human resource management', in J. Storey (ed.) *New Perspectives on Personnel Management*. London: Routledge.

Purcell, J. (1992) 'The impact of corporate strategy on human resource management', in G. Salaman *et al.* (eds) *Human Resource Strategies*. London: Sage Publications.

Roberts, Z. (2002) 'CIPD task force to create new framework for external reporting of human capital' *People Management*, Vol. 8, No. 23, 21 November, p. 7.

Sanz-Valle, R., Sabater-Sánchez, R. and Aragón-Sánchez, A. (1999) 'Human Resource management and business strategy links: an empirical study', *International Journal of Human Resource Management*, Vol. 10, No. 4, pp. 655–71.

Scarborough, H. (2003a) *Human Capital – External Reporting Framework*. London: CIPD.

Scarborough, H. (2003b) 'Recipe for success', *People Management*, Vol. 9, No. 2, 23 January, pp. 32–5.

Scarborough, H. and Elias, J. (2002) *Evaluating Human Capital – Research Report*. London: CIPD.

Schmidt, J. and Lines, S. (2002) 'A measure of success', *People Management*, Vol. 8, No. 9, May, pp. 32–4.

Schuler, R.S. and Jackson, S.E. (1987) 'Linking competitive strategies with human resource management practices', *Academy of Management Executive*, No. 3 (August).

Senge, P. (1990) *The Fifth Discipline: The Art and Practice of the Learning Organization*. London: Century Business, Random House.

Skinner, D. and Mabey, C. (1997) 'Managers' perceptions of strategic HR change', *Personnel Review*, Vol. 26, No. 6, pp. 467–84.

Sparkes, J. (2001) 'Job's a good un', *People Management*, Vol. 7, No. 20, 11 October, pp. 44–7.

Stiles, P. (2001) 'The impact of the board on strategy: an empirical examination', *Journal of Management Studies*, Vol. 38, No. 5, pp. 627–650.

Thomas, A. and Ramaswamy, K. (1996) 'Matching managers to strategy: further tests of the Miles and Snow typology', *British Journal of Management*, Vol. 7, pp. 247–61.

Tyson, S. (1995) *Human Resource Strategy*. London: Pitman.

Ulrich, D. (1998) 'A new mandate for human resources', *Harvard Business Review*, Jan.–Feb., pp. 125–34.

Ulrich, D. and Smallwood, N. (2002) 'Seven Up', *People Management*, Vol. 8, No. 10, May, pp. 42–4.

Whipp, R. (1992) 'Human resource management, competition and strategy: some productive tensions', in P. Blyton and P. Turnbull (eds) *Reassessing Human Resource Management*. California: Sage Publications.

Wright, P., McMahon, G. and McWilliams, A. (1994) 'Human Resources and sustained competitive advantage: a resource-based perspective', *International Journal of Human Resource Management*, Vol. 5, No. 2, May, pp. 301–26.

An extensive range of additional materials, including multiple choice questions, answers to questions and links to useful websites can be found on the Human Resource Management Companion Website at **www.pearsoned.co.uk/torrington**.

TOPIC SUMMARY SHEET

What are the key learning points from this topic?

INDEX

Notes

Notes

Notes

Notes